PAUL D. SANSONE, O.F.M.

NOTES ON THE GREEK TEXT OF DEUTERONOMY

SOCIETY OF BIBLICAL LITERATURE
SEPTUAGINT AND COGNATE STUDIES SERIES

Series Editor
Bernard A. Taylor

Number 39

NOTES ON THE GREEK TEXT OF DEUTERONOMY

by

John William Wevers

NOTES ON THE GREEK TEXT OF DEUTERONOMY

by
John William Wevers

Scholars Press
Atlanta, Georgia

NOTES ON THE GREEK TEXT OF DEUTERONOMY

by
John William Wevers

Library of Congress Cataloging-in-Publication Data
Wevers, John William.
Notes on the Greek text of Deuteronomy / by John William Wevers.
p. cm. — (Septuagint and cognate studies series ; no. 39)
Includes bibliographical references and index.
ISBN 0-7885-0120-8. — ISBN 0-7885-0126-7 (pbk.)
1. Bible. O.T. Deuteronomy. Greek—Versions—Septuagint.
2. Bible. O.T. Deuteronomy—Translating. I. Title. II. Series.
BS1274.G7W48 1995
222'.15048—dc20 95-10993
CIP

Printed in the United States of America
on acid-free paper

Table of Contents

INTRODUCTORY STATEMENT

I had always felt that commentaries on the Greek text of the Old Testament would be useful tools, especially for serious students of the OT who were not expert in the use of the Greek text, but who wanted to make use of the LXX for understanding the Hebrew text. As a graduate student I had worked in the Sam-Kings complex, and I often dreamed of writing a textual commentary on these books. What deterred me was the absence of a reliable critical text. After all, only the original translation — or at least an approximation of it — would be germane as an explication of the Hebrew.

Much of my scholarly career, however, has revolved about the Pentateuch. When I had finally finished work on the editions of the Greek Pentateuch for the Göttingen Septuaginta,[1] as well as on the relevant Text Histories,[2] my old interest in commentaries on the Greek text was revived; after all, now such commentaries were possible. Accordingly my Notes on the Greek Text of Exodus was prepared and published.[3] Its reception encouraged me to continue with a companion volume on the Greek Text of Genesis.[4]

In restudying the text of Deut I found that, as in the case of the Genesis Notes, I had also gained new insights into the nature of the Deut text. In a number of cases improvements in the text suggested themselves to me, and I

1. SEPTUAGINTA Vetus Testamentum Graecum Auctoritate Acad. Scient. Gottingensis editum. I.Genesis; II,1. Exodus; II,2. Leviticus; III,1. Numeri, and III,2. Deuteronomium (Göttingen 1974, 1991, 1986, 1982, 1977).
2. Text History of the Greek Genesis; ... Exodus; ... Leviticus; ... Numbers; Deuteronomy (=MSU XI [1974]; XXI [1992]; XIX [1986]; XVI [1982], and XIII [1978] resp.
3. Society of Biblical Literature: Septuagint and Cognate Studies No.30. Atlanta, 1990
4. ibid, No.35, Altanta, 1993

have proposed such in the Notes; these have been listed in Appendix A (pp.563°564).

A second appendix, Appendix B, constitutes a study of Codex Alexandrinus in Deuteronomy. Normally one would expect such a study to be dealt with in the Text History of the book, as had been the case for the other books of the Pentateuch, but for Deut there was a wealth of papyri much earlier than Cod A, and priority was accorded these. The essay in Appendix B examines the possibility of recensional activity in its text as well as its place in the textual history of the book. The essay is somewhat more technical in nature than the Notes; it is included in order to round out the textual information germane to the LXX critic's interest.

As in the case of the Genesis and the Exodus Notes, an index of Greek words and phrases is included. Colleagues have suggested to me that an index of Hebrew words and phrases might add to the usefulness of the Notes, and I offer such an index in this volume as well. Also suggested was a topical index. This will be found as a third index (pp.651°665). The topical index is somewhat impressionistic in nature, including both grammatical and material topics. Markers were inserted into the text electronically chapter by chapter, and the inclusion of a topic means no more than that it is referred to on a particular page; in other words there was no attempt at completeness. I can only hope that it will serve a useful purpose.

1.0. The Notes presented in this volume constitute a companion volume to those on Genesis and Exodus in the same series. These Notes deal with the Greek text of Deuteronomy.

1.1. Some might well query why I should have chosen to continue my series of Notes with Deut rather than with Lev (or Num). Actually it was the challenge of the involved syntax of the Deuteronomic language, unique to this book, which particularly fascinated me. In 1851 Zacharias Frankel had judged the translator of the book to have been a gifted individual who, however, was often led astray by his precipitate course of action (Uebereilung).[5]

In my opinion this judgment is overly severe. At times the translator does not follow the syntactic cuts which the Masoretic accentuation presupposes, but of course the translator was faced with an unpointed text. What changes in syntactic patterns in Deut do suggest is that the translator read his text differently. That the Deut translator at times presupposed a different vocalization is true, but that was the case with the translators of the other books of the Pentateuch as well; it would be unreasonable to assume that he would have had exactly the same reading tradition as the Masoretes of a much later age, particularly in view of the at times quite complex syntactic patterns of the book.

1.2. Also characteristic of the book is the formulaic character of the Deuteronomic style. Such sonorous patterns as "the place which the Lord your God has chosen to invoke his name," "which I/he swore to your fathers to give," "which I am commanding you today," "that your days may be long," or "ordinances and judgments and commandments" occur again and again.

In THGD[6] I have given a list of 56 such formulae listing all their occurrences in the book. When such a formula occurred it was analyzed, and reference to its occurrence in the lists in THGD was given in a footnote; subsequent occurrences of the formula are simply referred to its occurrence where the footnote reference is given.

---

5. Ueber den Einfluss der palästinischen Exegese auf die alexandrinische Hermeneneutik (Leipzig, 1851). On pp. 228—229 he says "Deuteronom hatte einen mit ziemlicher Kenntniss begabten Mann zum Vertenten, der sich mitunter seinem eigenen Weg zu bahnen weiss, aber auch zu mancher Uebereilung sich hinreissen lässt."
6. Pp. 86—99.

1.3. Reference was made by Aejmelaeus[7] to the infrequent use of *δέ*. In Gen and Exod *δέ* occurs frequently and can only seldom be lexically distinguished from *καί*, but in Deut its usage is almost limited either to accompanying the conditional particle *ἐάν* (63 times, and once each with *εἰ* and *ὅταν*), or as a contrastive particle (32 times).

Also characteristic of the Deut translator's language, particularly over against Num, is the tendency to decline relative pronouns in oblique cases by case, gender and number through attraction to their antecedents, rather than by their grammatical relations within the clause. Randomly chosen examples illustrating this tendency are 5:16 *γης*, *ἧς κύριος ... δίδωσίν σοι*; 11:28 *θεοῖς ἑτέροις*, *οἷς οὐκ οἴδατε*; 12:18 *τόπῳ*, *ᾧ ἂν ἐκλέξηται κύριος*. Many of these are pointed out in the Notes as grammatical deviations from standard Greek.

2.0. In the companion Genesis and Exodus volumes I spoke of at least four presuppositions, ones that had evolved in the course of my many years of working in LXX, more particularly with the text of the Pentateuch. These presuppositions also serve as a basis for the present volume, and what follows is essentially a repetition of what obtained in the Genesis volume under sections 2.1. through 2.4. I trust that readers who are acquainted with the earlier volume will forgive me for my repeating much of what was said there, but in my view these are so basic to the understanding of Deut as a translation of the Hebrew Deuteronomy, that they should be restated here as well.

2.1. The first presupposition of this work is that the translators were consciously at work on a canonical text. This was clearly the case for Genesis

7. Aejmelaeus 34—47; see especially p.36.

and Exodus,[8] and it is equally so for Deuteronomy. Theirs was a sacred task, which they did not take lightly. They were, after all, interpreting God's word, written in a language imperfectly understood by many Jews of the Alexandrian community, and they rendered it into their vernacular, the Hellenistic Greek spoken and understood in Alexandria. This implied that their translation was not just a casual bit of work, something tossed off in passing, but was a studied procedure.[9] It meant that the translators considered their task thoughtfully, did not simply render Hebrew words into equivalent Greek lexemes, but tried to put into Greek dress what they believed God intended to say to his people.

The translators of the Torah realized that their product was itself God's word; it was declared canonical,[10] and presumably served as the synagogal Scriptures in Alexandria.

2.2. These Notes are also based on the presupposition that the parent text being translated was in the main much like the consonantal text of MT; in other words, the extant textual tradition must be taken seriously. The age of rampant retroversion and wild emendations has past. This is not meant to show disrespect for the great scholars of the nineteenth and earlier decades of the twentieth centuries, but rather to be distrustful of proposed readings which were extant only in the minds of scholars, eminent though they were.

---

8. A thesis which I illustrated for Exodus in my Translation and Canonicity: A Study in the Narrative Portions of the Greek Exodus, in Scripta signa vocis: Studies about Scripts, Scriptures, Scribes and Languages in the Near East, offered to J.H. Hospers by his pupils, colleagues and friends (Groningen, 1986), 295-302.
9. As opposed to the statement by Z. Frankel in footnote 5 above.
10. According to Aristeas 308—311 the priests, elders and leaders of the Jewish community, when they had heard the Greek Pentateuch read to them, stated that it had been translated both *καλῶς καὶ ὁσίως* as well as throughout accurately (*ἠκριβωμένως*). Then they ordered accursed *εἴ τις διασκευάσει προστιθεὶς ἢ μεταφέρων τι τὸ σύνολον τῶν γεγραμμένων ἢ ποιούμενος ἀφαίρεσιν*, with which statement one might well compare the NT affirmation in Apoc 22:18—19.

This statement does not, however, presuppose that the parent text of Deut was in every respect the consonantal text of BHS, but rather it suggests that Hebrew text criticism should be more responsible, more solidly based on real evidence. We do have Qumran fragments of Deuteronomy, as well as other ancient witnesses such as the Samaritan Hebrew text and the Targums; these must be carefully compared throughout, and there will indeed be passages where the translator either must have had a different reading or misread his Hebrew text; in fact, throughout the Notes that follow it is at times stated that the Deut text was based on the Samaritan rather than the BHS text; it is, however, strongly urged on the reader that he/she begin with a prejudice towards the text which we actually have. The occasions when it is clear that a reconstructed text was the basis for Deut are only rarely evident, and one should at all times be wary even of these. For an example of a Qumran text in part parent to Deut see the Notes at 32:43.

Furthermore, it makes sense to conclude that the Hebrew text which the Jewish community of Alexandria had in the third century B.C. could not have been as wildly different from MT as earlier scholars of Deuteronomy sometimes maintained. After all, it was a canonical text; it was divine law, God's instruction; it was special, and it had to be approached with reverence. Admittedly, the concept of canon had not yet taken on its later rigidity in which the form as well as the contents were thought to be inviolable, but it seems only right to begin with the consonantal text of MT, and to accept change only after all other avenues of understanding have been explored.

2.3. My third presupposition is that the product of the Alexandrian translators of the Torah was throughout sensible. Their translation may not have been perfect, but it made sense to them; they did not create nonsense, and when the modern reader is puzzled, the fault must lie with him or her, not with the translator. It means that the student of LXX must try to understand what the translators meant rather than stand in arrogant judgment over their product. This means that one must at least try to explain difficulties, seeming contradictions and problems of language from their point of view rather than from our own rationalist sense of logic and consistency.

I do not mean that the translator always understood his parent text correctly. He may well have made mistakes, and sometimes the Hebrew text is considerably clearer than the Greek. At times he was faced with a difficult passage, which he may not have fully understood. Then he would do what any good translator does: he studied the context, and produced something that fitted it, but he did not create gibberish; he made sense, something that his readers would understand.

This is essentially what the modern reader of any ancient writing faces; in our case we must bridge more than two millenia of time, transporting ourselves to the Jewish community of the third B.C. century in Alexandria, i.e. to people who spoke Hellenistic Greek, a language which they knew much better than we do, to a culture quite foreign to our twentieth century western world. They shared our humanity, but not our culture, our way of thinking, or even our demand for logical consistency. On the other hand, they feared God above all else, though they were Jews of the diaspora, and so removed from the immediacy of temple worship and priesthood as well as from the volatile politics of Palestine.

And so the Notes try to explain Deut from the point of view of the translator rather than of ours; this brings me to my fourth and last presupposition.

2.4. The Greek Pentateuch is a humanistic document of great value for its own sake; this means that Deut is of real interest by itself even without reference to a parent text. It represents what Alexandrian Jewry of the third B.C. century thought their Hebrew Bible meant.

This Greek text, and not the Targums nor the Mishnah, is the earliest exegetical source that we have for understanding the Pentateuch. As such it surely must be the first document to which one turns when trying to understand the Torah. The LXX may interpret its text incorrectly; it is not a perfect document, but it is far and away the earliest, the closest in time to the original authors, that we have.

A new appreciation of the LXX is long overdue. For far too long scholars have treated the LXX as a grabbag for emendations. Unfortunately only too many have treated the note *lege cum Graece* found again and again in the various editions of "the Kittel Bible," and by no means wholly absent from BHS, as sacred lore, almost as a divine injunction to emend the text, as superior to the text itself. It is time to stop this nonsense, to go back to the LXX and read it for what it is, a humanistic document which should be pondered both for its own sake and for understanding the Hebrew text.

I make no apology for these my prejudices. I believe them to be fundamental to the study of the Septuagint, and they underlie the Notes throughout. And I might add that my comparative review of the Greek and Hebrew texts of Deuteronomy have simply confirmed the presuppositions made for Gen and Exod as well. They are clearly applicable throughout the entire Pentateuch.

3.0. The text commented on is not that of Rahlfs (Ra), but that of the Göttingen LXX. The Ra text was not a critical text; it was a student edition, a *Handausgabe*, based mainly on the text of Codex B (Vaticanus) with its obvious errors corrected. A few readings from Codex A as well as occasional *O* (hexaplaric) readings and some *L* (Lucianic or pseudo-Lucianic) readings for certain books are given as apparatus. Rahlfs never intended this text to be anything more than an interim text, one that would eventually be replaced by the critical texts of the Göttingen Septuaginta.

It is the volumes of the Göttingen LXX that represent the state of the art; these are based on new collations of all the relevant texts available, including all the papyri remains as well as the texts of the sub-versions. What the Göttingen texts provide is as close an approximation to the original LXX as possible, limited only by the inadequacies of the editor.

It is this text which is analyzed. No attempt is made to review scholarly opinions, since it was thought to be much more appropriate to read the LXX text itself than to read about it. The text is far more important that what scholars say about it, and this is equally true of the author of these Notes as well.

The professional Greek scholar will probably find my Notes overly elementary and repetitive, but they are not intended for the professional. I have written these Notes to help serious students of the Pentateuch who want to use the LXX text with some confidence, but who are neither specialists in LXX studies nor in Hellenistic Greek. Such students might well need help in understanding the LXX text over against the Hebrew, and it is hoped that such students might find these Notes a useful guide.

4.0. The point of departure for these Notes is that of Deut, i.e. of the Greek text of Deuteronomy in the Göttingen Septuagint. The problem faced by the translator was how to render the intent of the Hebrew parent text into a Greek form which his synagogal audience and readers would understand. To do this well presupposes an artist who fully understood both the limitations and the possibilities of the two linguistic codes involved, viz. Hebrew and Hellenistic Greek.[11] Stress is intentionally placed on how well the translator carried out his work, thus on how he constructed his Greek text, on how and whether he avoided transfering the characteristics of the source language to the target language. Accordingly the Notes concentrate throughout on the morphological, syntactic and semantic levels of language.

4.1. Since Deut is by nature a translation text, a careful comparison at all levels between the presumed parent Hebrew and the resultant Greek texts is basic to the Notes. For the presumed parent text as the consonantal text of MT see the statement in 2.2. above.

Other ancient texts which were compared throughout as well were the Samaritan Hebrew (Sam), the Onkelos Targum as representing the Babylonian tradition, and the Pseudo-Jonathan and Neophyti Targums as representing the Jerusalem form of the Targums. Also compared were published Qumran fragments as well as the Peshitta (Syriac) and the Vulgate (Latin) translations. These as a group constitute the ancient witnesses.

4.2. The Notes deal principally with the work of the translator, i.e. they are concerned with how the translator, the original LXX, interpreted the text; they have disregarded how later users of the LXX interpreted the text. To have reviewed how Josephus, Philo and the Church Fathers of the early centuries understood the LXX would simply have duplicated the fine work on Deuteronomy of C.Dogniez and M.Harl.[12] Needless to say I have consulted their work at every juncture, and have profited immeasurably from this careful

11. For a comparison of these two codes see my Notes on the Greek Text of Exodus, pp.vii—xiv, as well as my "The Use of Versions for Text Criticism: the Septuagint" in La Septuaginta en la Investigacion Contemporanea (V Congreso de la IOSCS), editado por Natalio Fernández Marcos (Madrid, 1894), pp.15—24.

12. La Bible d'Alexandrie. 5. Le Deuteronome, par Cécile Dogniez et Marguerite Harl. Paris, 1992.

piece of work, but my point of departure is quite different from their volume, and the two works are to a great extent in complementary distribution. Dogniez-Harl have also given a full translation of Deut, whereas I have not done so. I have limited translations to difficult passages, wherever such might facilitate one's understanding of how the translator understood the Hebrew text.[13]

4.3. I have used the term "tradition" throughout to represent the development of the original LXX text, the autographon, from its original form as reconstructed for the critical text up to its form (or forms) in the fifteenth century, when the invention of movable type made possible the production of multiple identical copies of a text, thereby revolutionizing textual development. The tradition in its multiple forms is summarized in the first apparatus of the Göttingen edition(s).

4.3.1. But those for whom the LXX was sacred scripture did not have the original text as it left the hands of the translator, nor did they have the Göttingen text as its approximation. The countless users of the LXX throughout the centuries only had copies, in fact, copies of copies. Such readers had manuscripts which represented later forms of the LXX text. These manuscripts are all eclectic in nature, i.e. they are based on a complicated and often untraceable textual genealogy.

4.3.2. I have not recorded all the evidence for such variant readings in painstaking detail, but rather made generalizations concerning patterns of support, which are explained under 4.4.1—4 below.[14] The interested reader will

13. The IOSCS is actively engaged in planning and preparing a translation of the Greek O.T. into English.
14. I have explained some of these larger generalizations in my "The Göttingen Pentateuch: Some Post-partem Reflections," in VII Congress of the International Organization for Septuagint and Cognate Studies, edited by Claude Cox (Atlanta, 1991), pp.51—60.

find details of support in the first apparatus of the Göttingen edition. I have also simplified the evidence and largely disregarded scattered support by concentrating on support by textual families.

The first apparatus of the Göttingen editions constitutes a digest of this textual history of the LXX. That text underwent a most complicated history of revisions, which is reflected in the texts of the text families. The first apparatus is then a summary of a living text. What the synagogue, and later the church, used was that living and developing tradition. When the ancient writers quoted and commented on the scriptures, these scriptures were part of that living tradition.

4.4. The following table details these families with their members; the numbers follow those of the Rahlfs catalogue.[15]

O = G-82-376-426 Arab Syh

oI = 15-64-381-618

oII = 29-58-72-707 Arm

O′ = *O* + *oI*; *O*ʾ = *O* + *oII*; *O′*ʾ = *O* + *oI* + *oII*; *oI*ʾ =
oI + *oII*

C = 16-77-131-500-529-616-739

cI = 57-73-320-413-528-550-552-761

cII = 46-52-313-414-417-422-551-615

C′ = *C* + *cI*; *C*ʾ = *C* + *cII*; *C′*ʾ = *C* + *cI* + *cII*; *cI*ʾ = *cI* + *cII*

---

15. A. Rahlfs, Verzeichnis der griechishen Handschriften des Alten Testaments, für das Septuaginta-Unternehmen aufgestellt. MSU 2. Berlin, 1915. The Unternehmen has been keeping the Verzeichnis up-to-date, and Detlef Fraenkel has been assigned the task of preparing a revised edition by the Committee directing the affairs of the Unternehmen.

b = 18-108-118-314-537

d = 44-106-107-125-610

f = 53-56-129-246-664

n = W^{I}- 54-75-127-458-767

s = 30-85-130-321-343-344-346-730

t = 74-76-134-370-602-799

y = 71-121-318-392-527-619

z = 18-68-83-120-122-128-630-669

Uncials: A B F K(fragmentary) M V

Papyri: 847 848 916 920 957 958 963 970

Unclassified Codices = 28 55 59 319 407 416 424 508 509 646

Versions = Arab(ic), Arm(enian), Eth(iopic), Co(ptic) which includes Bo(hairic) and Sa(hidic), La (= Vetus Latina), Pal(estinian-syriac), and Syh (= Syrohexaplar)

4.4.1. A variant may be identified as a one, two or three family variant. Thus a *b f s* reading means that the reading is supported by all or a majority of the manuscripts of the *b f* and *s* families; it may also have scattered support from other manuscripts or from the versions, but that is disregarded. When such readings are identified as e.g. a *b* reading, what is meant is that the reading has been judged to be a *b* family reading. But should more than three families support a reading it is simply called a popular reading, whereas if the support includes over half of all witnesses, i.e. of manuscripts and versions, it is called a majority reading.

4.4.2. Since the uncial texts, A B F K M V, and the papyri, constitute on the whole the oldest Greek manuscript witnesses I have often listed them as well, e.g. A F *b f s*. Except for the later F^a and F^b readings uncial support is only listed if it is unclouded; thus "corrector" readings of uncial manuscripts are usually not cited.

Occasionally the + sign is used to signal manuscript support; it is to be understood as "along with scattered support." Thus the designation F+ means that a reading is found in codex F as well as in scattered manuscript(s) not identifiable as constituting a textual family or families.

4.4.3. From the table in 4.4. it appears that a large number of manuscripts constitute the Catena text. The edition has subdivided these witnesses into a main group, *C*, and two subordinate groups, *cI* and *cII*. Since most readers will probably not be interested in Catena criticism these have usually all been subsumed under the siglum *C* throughout the Notes.[16]

16. But not in Appendix B.

4.4.4. Frequent reference is also made to a Byzantine text.[17] The term applies to the family readings which characterize the text of the Byzantine lectionaries. A Byzantine textual reading means a reading supported by all or at least two of *d n t*.

5.0. Certain information has been almost routinely relegated to footnotes, not because it is unimportant, but rather since it is not central to the Notes.

5.1. The Notes do not detail reasons for choosing the readings of Deut in favor of variant readings, except where I now consider the Deut reading as secondary. Such arguments concerning the originality of the text are fully discussed in THGD Chapters 5 (Papyrus 963), 6 (The Text Character of 848), and 7 (The Critical Text [Deut]), and such matters are all referred to in footnotes where the relevant page of THGD is given. The user who is not interested in such matters can simply disregard these references.

5.2. Materials gleaned from the second apparatus of the Göttingen edition are also routinely placed in footnotes. Readings from The Three, Aq, Sym and Theod, are given, mainly without comment. In the edition the materials are presented precisely as the manuscripts have the reading, even when they are clearly faultily transmitted. I have seen fit to make judgments on these readings, and to make corrections in the footnotes in order to help the reader to understand them.

The relegation of readings to the footnotes does not constitute a judgment on the value of their evidence, but is due to the fact that the Notes deal with the LXX text, whereas the readings of the second apparatus are in essence

17. Ms 106 was assigned in the critical edition to the *d* group, but would have been accurately placed in the *t* family. For most readers this is purely an academic matter, since *d* and *t* are very similar in nature, and both belong to the Byzantine text.

extra-Septuagintal materials, usually gleaned from the margins of LXX texts or of Syh. Such readings have in the long course of LXX tradition history often influenced that tradition, sometimes actively invading it, especially through Origen's hexapla. Their origins lie in the Hebrew rather than the LXX tradition, and their interests were revisional. They are thus of importance in understanding the text history rather than the text of LXX, and so should be carefully distinguished from LXX itself.

6.0. It should be emphasized that the Notes are not simply another commentary in the usual sense of the term. Rather they examine in detail how the Greek translator interpreted his parent Hebrew text. In other words, Deut is essentially an exegetical document, and this exegesis can only be grasped by a close attention to the linguistic mode which Deut exploits. In fact, the LXX text is the first document we have in the long history of the exegesis of the O.T. What one must look for in particular are fine points of clarification made where the Hebrew is not fully clear or matters where the Greek text appears to deviate from the apparent meaning of the source text. Whenever Deut strays from the obvious intent of the Hebrew it has been noted, and I have often suggested a possible reason for such deviation.

One should not automatically presuppose a different parent text when differences between the Greek and the Hebrew obtain; rather one should first seek for and pursue other explanations. It is only through such details that a picture of the attitudes, the theological prejudices, as well as of the cultural environment of these Jewish translators can emerge. It is in the confidence that readers will learn to discover something about what these Alexandrian translators thought their Hebrew Torah meant, or ought to mean, that these Notes are presented.

7.0. As in the case of the earlier volumes no bibliography (except for the Sigla which follows this introductory statement) is included in this volume. It was never the author's intention to present a picture of the state of the art, but rather to provide the serious student some help in his/her comparison of MT and LXX. For readers who must have a detailed bibliography the Brock, Fritsch, Jellicoe Bibliography which was published some years ago may be consulted.[18]

The sigla table which follows contains references to works which I found especially useful in preparing the Notes. Occasional studies not given in the Sigla, but referred to in the Notes are given with full bibliographical details in the footnotes.

8.0. It would be remiss of me were I not to acknowledge gratefully the debt I owe to my colleagues in Near Eastern Studies, who have sustained me with their friendship and support for more than forty years, and in whose midst I have continued to work in spite of official retirement from the University. In particular I owe much to my colleague, Albert Pietersma, whom I often consulted on difficult matters of Greek syntax and other grammatical matters, and who was always ready with wise and learned counsel. And I am equally grateful to Bernard Taylor, the editor of IOSCS, who generously offered to proofread my finished manuscript, and who saved me from many embarrassing errors. Neither of these men is, however, responsible for what I have written; for that I assume full and sole responsibility.

9.0. As in the case of the parallel volumes on Genesis and Exodus which appeared in this series, the author prepared camera ready copy. The software

18. A Classified Bibliography of the Septuagint, compiled by S.P.Brock, C.T.Fritsch and S.Jellicoe. Leiden, 1973. This fullsome bibliography is now being supplemented and updated by Mdme Cécile Dogniez of Paris, and should be appearing presently.

used was Nota Bene 4.1 plus Lingua, and was printed on an HP Laser Jet IV. I owe Paul J. Bodin of Berkeley, CA, formerly of Union Theol. Seminary, NYC, a particular debt of gratitude for his help in overcoming difficulties with the software used in the extraction of the three indices; his expertise was freely shared, and I appreciate his friendly advice at a time when I was rather desperately in need of it.

Sigla

- AASF = Annales Academiae Scientiarum Fennicae
- Aejmelaeus = Aejmelaeus, A., Parataxis in the Septuagint: A Study of the Renderings of the Hebrew Coordinate Clauses in the Greek Pentateuch. AASF: Dissertationes Humanarum Litterarum 31. Helsinki, 1982.
- Aq = Aquila
- Appositives = Wevers, J.W., Yahweh and its Appositives in LXX Deuteronomium, Festschrift C.J.Labuschagne, Suppl. V.T. LIII, (1994), 259—270.
- Aristeas = Aristeas to Philcrates (Letter of Aristeas), edited and translated by M. Hadas. New York, 1973
- Bauer = Arndt, W.P. and Gingrich, F.W., A Greek-English Lexicon of the New Testament and Other Early Christian Literature, transl. and adapt. from W. Bauer, Griechisch-Deutsches Wörterbuch zu den Schriften des Neuen Testaments und der übrigen urchristlichen Literatur, 4te Aufl., 1952. Chicago, 1957; 2nd ed. revised and augmented by F.W.Gingrich and F.W.Danker from the 5te Aufl.
- BDB = Brown, F., Driver, S.R. and Briggs, C.A., A Hebrew and English Lexicon of the Old Testament, with an Appendix containing the Biblical Aramaic. Boston and New York, 1907
- BHS = Biblia Hebraica Stuttgartensia, ed. K.Elliger et W.Rudolph. Stuttgart, 1977; librum Deuteronomium ed. J.Hempel, 1992
- Bl-Debr = Blass, F., Debrunner, A. u. Rehkopf, Fr., Grammatik des neutestamentlichen Griechisch, 14te völlig neubearb. Aufl. Göttingen, 1975

- Boisacq = Boisacq, E., Dictionaire étymologique de la langue Grecque. Paris, 1938

- Cox, Hex = Cox, Claude E., Hexaplaric Materials Preserved in the Armenian Version, SCS 21, Atlanta, 1986

- idem, VI Congress = Cox, Claude, ed., VI Congress of the International Organization for Septuagint and Cognate Studies: Jerusalem 1986, SBL: Septuagint and Cognate Studies Series 23, Altanta, 1986

- idem, VII Congress =Cox, Claude, ed., VII Congress of the International Organization for Septuagint and Cognate Studies: Leuven 1989, SBL: Septuagint and Cognate Studies Series 31, Atlanta, 1991

- Crönert = Crönert, W., Memoria Graeca Herculanensis, Lipsiae, 1903

- Daniel = Daniel, S., Recherches sur le vocabulaire de culte dans le Septante. Études et Commentaires 61. Paris, 1966

- De Septuuginta = Pietersma A. and Cox, C., edd., De Septuaginta: Studies in honour of John William Wevers on his sixty-fifth birthday. Mississauga, Ont, 1974

- Deut = The text of SEPTUAGINTA Vetus Testamentum Auctoritate Academiae Scientiarum Gottingensis editum. III,2. Deuteronomium edidit John William Wevers. Göttingen, 1977. Also used to indicate Deuteronomy.

- Dogniez-Harl = Dogniez, C. et Harl, M., Le Deutéronome: Traduction du texte grec de la Septante, Introduction et Notes. La Bible d'Alexandrie 5. Paris, 1992

- Dos Santos = Elmar Camilo Dos Santos, An Expanded Hebrew Index for the Hatch-Redpath Concordance to the Septuagint, Jerusalem, n.d.

- Driver = Driver, S.R., A Critical and Exegetical Commentary on Deuteronomy. The International Critical Commentary. New York: 1895

- Field = Field, Fr., Origenis Hexaplorum quae supersunt. Oxonii, 1867-1875

- GK = Gesenius' Hebrew Grammar as edited and enlarged by the late E.Kautzsch. Second English edition revised by A.E.Cowley. Oxford, 1910
- Helbing = Helbing, R., Die Kasussyntax der Verba bei den Septuaginta. Göttingen, 1928
- Helbing, Gramm. = Helbing, R., Grammatik der LXX: Laut- und Wortlehre. Göttingen, 1907
- HR = Hatch, E. & Redpath, H.A., A Concordance to the Septuagint and the other Greek Versions of the O.T. I-II, Suppl. Oxford, 1897-1906
- Jer B = Jerusalem Bible
- Johannessohn, Gebrauch = Johannessohn, M., Der Gebrauch der Präpositionen in der Septuaginta. MSU 3,3. Berlin, 1926
- KB = Koehler, L. and Baumgartner, W., Lexicon in Veteris Testamenti Libros. Leiden, 1953.
- König, E., Das Deuteronomium . Leipzig, 1917
- Lampe = Lampe, G.W.H., A Patristic Greek Lexicon, Oxford, 1961
- Later Revisers = *οἱ λοιποί* or *οἱ λ´*
- Lee = Lee, J.A.L., A Lexical Study of the Septuagint Version of the Pentateuch. Chico, 1983
- LS = Liddell, H.G., Scott, R., & Jones, H.S., A Greek-English Lexicon, 9th ed., Oxford, 1940
- Mayser = Mayser, E., Grammatik der griechischen Papyri aus der Ptolemäerzeit. I., Leipzig, 1906. II 1, Berlin, 1926. II 2, 1933/34. II 3, 1934. 2 Aufl. I 1, 1970. I 2, 1938. I 3, 1936
- Mayes, A.D.H., Deuteronomy (New Century Bible Commentary). Grand Rapids/London, 1979
- MSU = Mitteilungen des Septuaginta-Unternehmens
- MT = Masoretic Text as found in BHS

- NIV New International Version
- NJPS = TANAKH The Holy Scriptures; The New JPS Translation According to the Traditional Hebrew Text
- NRSV = New Revised Standard Version
- Note at Exod = Wevers, J.W., Notes on the Greek Text of Exodus. Altanta, 1990
- Note at Gen = idem, Notes on the Greek Text of Genesis. Atlanta, 1993
- Pesh = Peshiṭta. The O.T. in Syriac according to the Peshiṭta Version. Part I, fasc 2. Deuteronomy by W.M.Van Vliet. Leiden, 1991
- Porter = Porter, S.E. Verbal Aspect in the Greek of the New Testament with Reference to Tense and Mood. Studies in Biblial Greek, Vol.I. New York, 1989
- Prijs = Prijs, L., Jüdische Tradition in der Septuaginta. Leiden, 1948
- Ra = Rahlfs, A., Septuaginta, Stuttgart,1935
- Reider-Turner = An Index to Aquila by the late J.Reider, completed and revised by N.Turner. Supplements to VT, Vol.XII, Leiden, 1966
- Sam = Samaritan Pentateuch. Der hebräische Pentateuch der Samaritaner, herausg. von A. von Gall. Giessen, 1918
- Schl = Schleuser, J.F.,Novus Thesaurus philologico-criticus, sive Lexicon in LXX et reliquos interpretes Graecos ac Scriptores Apocryphos V.T. Lipsiae, 1820-1821
- SCS = SBL: Septuagint and Cognate Studies Series (Scholars Press)
- Sollamo = Sollamo, R., Renderings of Hebrew Semiprepositions in the Septuagint, AASF: Dissertationes Humanarum Litterarum 19. Helsinki, 1979
- SS = Soisalon-Soininen, I., Studien zur Septuaginta-Syntax, AASF 237. Helsinki, 1987

- SS Inf = idem, Die Infinitive in der Septuaginta. AASF 132, 1. Helsinki, 1965

- Suidas = (Suda). Suidae Lexicon, Graece & Latine ... Aemilii Porti. Cantabrigiae, 1705

- Suppl.V.T. = Supplements to Vetus Testamentum

- Syh = The Syrohexaplar

- Sym = Symmachus

- Targ = The Targums Jonathan, Neophiti, and Onkelos

- Tar^{J} = Targum Pseudo-Jonathan of the Pentateuch: Text and Concordance. E.G.Clarke. Hoboken, NJ, 1984

- Tar^{O} = Targum Onkelos. Sperber, A., The Bible in Aramaic based on Old Manuscripts and Printed Texts. Vol.I. The Pentateuch according to Targum Onkelos. Leiden, 1959

- Tar^{P} = The Palestinian Targum. A. Díez Macho, NEOPHYTI 1: Targum Palestinense ms de la Biblioteca Vaticana. Tomo V Deut. Madrid, 1978

- Thack = Thackeray, H.St.J., A Grammar of the Old Testament in Greek according to the Septuagint: I. Introduction, Orthography and Accidence. Cambridge, 1909

- The Others = *οἱ λοιποί* or *οἱ λ´*

- The Three = *οἱ γ´*

- Theod = Theodotion

- THGD = Wevers, J.W. Text History of the Greek Deuteronomy, MSU 13, Göttingen, 1978

- THGE = idem, Text History of the Greek Exodus, MSU 21, Göttingen, 1992

- THGG = idem, Text History of the Greek Genesis, MSU 11. Göttingen, 1974

- THGL = idem, Text History of the Greek Leviticus, MSU 19. Göttingen, 1986
- THGN = idem, Text History of the Greek Numbers, MSU 16. Göttingen, 1982
- Tov = Tov, E., The Text-Critical Use of the Septuagint in Biblical Research, Jerusalem Biblical Studies 3. Jerusalem, 1981
- VT = Vetus Testamentum
- Vulg = The Vulgate. Biblia Sacra: Vulgatae Editionis Sixti V Pont. Max. iussu recognita et Clementis VIII auctoritate edita. Romae, 1965
- Walters = Walters, P., The Text of the Septuagint, edited by D.W.Gooding. Cambridge, 1973
- ZürB = Die Zürcher Bibel

NOTES

1:1 The initial words are the superscription for the book, which parallels the subscription to Num: "these are the ἐντολαὶ καὶ τὰ δικαιώματα καὶ τὰ κρίματα which the Lord commanded by the hand of Moses on the western part of Moab besides the Jordan over against Jericho." Here the book is called οἱ λόγοι, which is defined by a relative clause as those which Moses spoke to all Israel. The term is meant as an inclusive one comprising all the three terms used in the Num's subscription. But this superscription also designates what follows as a new document, thereby justifying the term τὸ δευτερονόμιον (τούτο) of 17:18, which was taken over by the LXX as the name of the book. The geographic modifiers in the verse are puzzling. The term πέραν τοῦ Ἰορδάνου locates the delivery of the words as being on the east bank of the Jordan, but the rest of the verse betrays the translator's lack of understanding. This is clear from the rendering of בערבה as πρὸς δυσμαῖς "towards the west"; this term occurs seven times in Deut MT, and only at 11:30, where the text refers to the place where the Canaanite was dwelling, does LXX translate the term as from the root signifying "sunset," hence "evening," but also "west." Elsewhere (v.7 2:8 3:17 twice and 4:49), it is taken as a place name and is transliterated.[1] In the tradition the accusative is quite popular, but this is not surprising since πρός plus accusative is far more frequent throughout the OT than the dative. The translator also understood סוף as referring to the ים סוף which was regularly rendered by ἐρυθρὰν θάλασσαν; מול סוף "in front of Suph" is thus mistranslated by πλησίον τῆς ἐρυθρᾶς "near the Red (Sea)."[2] This is followed in MT by "between Paran and between Tophel and Laban and Haseroth and Dizahab." None of these place names has been identified with any confidence, but one presumes that places in Moab are intended. The LXX text is no more lucid than MT is; in fact, by omitting the second "between" it creates even more confusion; at least in MT the location is between Paran and the other four places, but this is not clear in LXX, though by omitting a καί before Tophol this may have been intended to represent MT. This interpretation is fostered by the critical text which has a comma after Φαράν.

---

1. Aq rendered the phrase by ἐν ὁμαλεῖ taking the noun to refer to a plateau or plain (presumably of Moab).
2. So too Tar^{O} and Vulg, but not Pesh.

Furthermore, the Greek translates the last two places: חצרת becomes Αὐλῶν "courts, enclosures"[3] and די זהב as Καταχρύσεα "according to gold," i.e. a place concerned with gold.[4]

In the tradition, ἐρυθρᾶς is identified as *θαλασσης* by *O* Byz+, which is not surprising since ἐρυθρᾶς as a place name is always "Red Sea" elsewhere in LXX. Τόφολ has *και* before it in the *b* text, and hex added a full *και ανα μεσον* before it under the asterisk. The name was unknown to copyists who changed the vowels in various ways. The *oI* text has *φολον*; other misspellings include *τοφελ*, *τοφοα*, *τοφαλ*, *τοφαν*, *τοφων*, *τοφορ*, *γοφολ*. The name Λοβόν was also changed; homophonic spellings changed *ο* to *ω*, but *λαβων* also appears as well as *λαβαν*, *λοβ* and *δοβον* (by uncial confusion). The last name appeared in the genitive as *καταχρυσεων* in *C*, and as a phrase *κατα τα χρυσεα* in a number of witnesses as well.

1:2 The genitive ἕνδεκα ἡμερῶν interprets the verse as the time within which the journey ἐκ Χωρήβ ... ἕως Καδῆς Βαρνή takes place. It constitutes the predicate, i.e. the road ... is eleven days in duration. The term Χωρήβ is regularly used in place of Sinai throughout Deut, which occurs in MT only at 33:2 where LXX has Σινά. The popular B variant *εν* for ἐκ is palaeographically inspired, and is barely sensible; in fact, it is not clear what an *εν* phrase would here modify.[5]

The particular ὁδός travelled is described as ἐπ' ὄρος Σηίρ, i.e. along Mt. Seir, the mountainous area of ancient Edom. The preposition has no counterpart in MT which simply has "(the way of) Mt. Seir," but ἐπ' defines more precisely the relation of ὁδός and ὄρος. As might be expected, Σηίρ, with its two itacistic vowels is mishandled in the tradition as: *σηηρ*, *σιηρ*, *σιειρ*, *σειειρ*, *σηηιρ*, *σηειρ*, all representing /siir/, as well as the reduction to *σηρ*. The names Καδῆς and Βαρνή are quite stable; dittography resulted in a *καδδης* spelling in a few scattered mss, and the only non-itacistic variant for Βαρνή is *βαρνως* in a pair of *f* mss.

---

3. Aq Sym rightly transcribe the term by Ἀσηρώθ.
4. Aq translates די by ἱκανόν "sufficiency (of gold)"; comp his rendering of באל שדי at Exod 6:3 by ἐν θεῷ ἱκανῷ.
5. See THGD 117.

1:3 ויהי introducing a time designation is rarely used in Deut, occurring only here and at 2:16 5:23 9:11 and 31:24. Only here and 9:11 is the apodosis not introduced by the conjunction *waw*/*καί*. Only here and at 2:16 is it rendered by the passive *ἐγενήθη*, also twice (5:23 9:11) by the middle *ἐγένετο* and once, 31:24, ויהי כ is translated by *ἡνίκα δέ*. The verb is otiose in Greek.

The addressee is the בני ישראל, a phrase which occurs 13 times in Deut, whereas the כל ישראל of 1:1 occurs 10 times. LXX witnesses to *πάντας υἱοὺς* Ἰσραήλ.[6] Some mss do attest to כל בני ישראל and a few to כל ישראל as at v.1, so that there is some certainty as to the parent text.[7] The *ὅσα* clause is a literal rendering of MT, including the awkward *πρὸς αὐτούς* at the end, which can either be taken as a parallel recapitulating "to call the Israelites" modifying *ἐλάλησεν* or as a synecdoche for "speak to them," a solution which some versions (La Eth Co) prefer (i.e. prefixing *loqui* to *πρὸς αὐτούς*). A popular M text has transposed *κύριος αὐτῷ*, thereby conforming to the urge to place a pronominal modifier immediately after the verb.

1:4 V.4 is to be construed as a new beginning, as belonging syntactically with v.5, rather than with v.3 which would also be theoretically possible; the *μετά* construction then modifies *ἤρξατο* of v.5. For the conquest narratives concerning the Amorrite kings Seon and Og, see Num 21:21—35. The subject of the infinitive is, however, Μωυσῆς of v.3. Hex, by adding *αυτον* after *πατάξαι* under the asterisk to equal MT, makes this explicit. As at Num 21:21 the first mention of "king of the Amorrites" has Ἀμορραίων unarticulated even though MT has the article; in all later references to "kings of the Amorrites" it is always articulated (3:2,8 4:46,47 31:4 over against Num 21:26,29,34). Furthermore the gentilic noun האמרי is correctly understood as a collective, and accordingly realized by the plural in LXX. In the tradition a popular A F variant did articulate the word, but this must be adjudged to be ex par.

For Heshbon as Seon's capital city see Bible Dictionaries. Northern Moab historically remained a contested area between Israelites and Moabites at least until the time of Ahab. The name was misspelled as *εσσεβων* by dittography in a number of scattered witnesses, as well as through aphaeresis as

---

6. The Three articulated *υἱούς*. This is unexpected in the case of Aq who normally did not do so in the case of a bound element in a bound phrase.
7. Kenn 15,232* add כל before בני, whereas Kenn 17,18,232[c] substitute כל for בני.

σεβων, but Ἐσεβών is original. The name also occurs at 2:24,26,30 3:2,6 4:46 and 29:7 always with the same spelling.

The other king is Ὢγ king of Bashan and is often coordinated with Seon; cf Num 21:33 and Deut 3:1,3,11 4:47 29:7 31:4. Both kings are introduced by את in MT, and the tradition popularly supports the article τον for both, but this is almost certainly recensional. According to LXX, Og had two royal cities, Asteroth and Edrain. MT lacks the conjunction;[8] thus באדרעי modifies the infinitive הכתו in v.4, i.e. it is the place where the Israelites smote Og. Both Pesh and Vulg support the interpretation of LXX. The name Ἀσταρώθ occurs only here in Deut; its spelling is quite stable, only ασθαρωθ (by dental confusion), ασαρωθ by syncopation, σταρωθ by aphaeresis and (εν) νασταρωθ by dittography being attested as variants. The name Ἐδράιν also occurs at 3:1,10. but created much confusion in the tradition. The Hebrew name is אדרעי, and εδραει, the reading of ms 426, probably reflects a hex correction; cf also the *O* ms 72 with αγραι, the reading in *y* mss εσδραι and in *z* mss: αδραι and εδραι. An infixed *sigma* produced both εδρασιν and εσδραειν, vowel attraction created αδραιν, and nasal confusion led to εδραειμ. The origin of the final *nu* in LXX is uncertain.

1:5 The term πέραν τοῦ Ἰορδάνου refers to the east side of the Jordan; so "beyond the Jordan" presupposes a narrator on the west side. The location is assured by the phrase ἐν γῇ Μωάβ.

The main clause for vv.4 and 5 is ἤρξατο Μωυσῆς διασαφῆσαι τὸν νόμον τοῦτον "Moses began to clarify this law," which is modified by the temporal μετά clause of v.4 and the two locative phrases introducing v.5. The term "this law" recurs at 31:11, is modified by πάντα at 4:8 27:8, and occurs in the genitive modifying ῥήματα at 28:58 29:29 31:9, as λόγους/λόγοις at 27:3,26 31:12,24, and at 28:61 as τῷ βιβλίῳ. These references make clear that what is referred to is internal; in fact, it begins immediately after the direct speech marker λέγων which follows. The direct speech which begins with v.6 continues through 29:1 as the repetition of ἐν γῇ Μωάβ there makes clear: "these are the words of the covenant which the Lord commanded Moses to set up for the Israelites in the land of Moab." In other words it constitutes

8. Though Kenn 191 does read ובאדרעי.

the explicated instruction *διασαφῆσαι τὸν νόμον*, which at 17:18 is called *τὸ δευτερονόμιον*.

1:6 In the opening words of Moses' explication he identifies himself as part of the people by calling the Lord *ὁ θεὸς ἡμῶν*. The designation "our God" occurs 27 times in the book; far more frequent is the second person, either singular or plural,[9] but the first person plural is peculiarly appropriate in the opening clause of the Moses address to the people with its reference to the Lord having spoken "to us at Choreb," which, in contrast to the time of Moses' address "in the fortieth year" (in v.3), occurred at the beginning of the desert wanderings; cf the time indication at Exod 19:1.

The idiom רב לכם is well rendered by *ἱκανούσθω ὑμῖν* "let it be sufficient for you" with its subject *κατοικεῖν*, i.e. "let the dwelling in this mountainous area (at Choreb) be enough for you."[10]

1:7 The opening imperatives constitute orders to move: "turn about and leave, (even you,) and go to," each in turn regular equivalents in the Pentateuch for the Hebrew וסעו, פנו and באו resp. The use of *ὑμεῖς* is LXX's way of rendering לכם modifying the imperative סעו. This is better left untranslated, since English has no such usage. I suppose one could say "depart (I mean you)," but this puts far too much stress on "you."[11] All it does is direct the audience explicitly to the addressee already implicit in the imperative form.

That to which the Israelites were directed was that of the ideal land of promise, comprising the "hill country of the Amorrites (for which term see comment at v.4), and to all the inhabitants of the Araba (even) to hill and plain, both to the south and to the seashore (i.e. the west), (both) the land of the Canaanites and the (region of) Antilebanon as far as the great river Euphrates." LXX has idiomatically rendered "and to all his (i.e. the Amorite) neighbours in the Arabah" of MT by "to all *τοὺς περιοίκους* 'Αραβά." Here in contrast to v.1 בערבה is properly taken as referring to the low lying area

9. See my article Appositives 259—270.
10. The anonymous reading *πολὺ ὑμῖν* is the usual rendering for the idiom by The Three.
11. Such terms as *dativus commodi* or *dativus ethicus* at GK 119s may sound learned, but they explain nothing, and merely confuse the reader.

south of the Dead Sea, simply transcribed as *Araba*.[12] The terms *ὄρος* and *πεδίον* are intended to describe the hill country and the plain area, whereas the directional terms *λίβα* and *παραλίαν* refer to the Negeb or south land and the Mediterranean seacoast resp. MT uses the same preposition to govern "hill country, plain, southern area and seacoast," but LXX distinguishes among them; *ὄρος καὶ πεδίον* are governed by *εἰς* since the Israelites are to go in to these areas. *λίβα καὶ παραλίαν* are directional, and the ב is rendered by *πρός*.

How the "land of the Canaanites" was distinguished from "the hill country of the Amorrites" is not immediately clear, but since this is coordinated with the Antilebanon, i.e. the eastern Lebanon range, the term may have referred to the northern part of Canaan, just as the eastern limits were the Antilebanon. The term הלבנון occurs only three times in the book (also at 3:25 11:24), and is used only as defining the borders of the Promised Land. The translator throughout thinks of the eastern range, i.e. the Antilebanon; see also Jos 1:4 9:1 which contrast with *τοῦ Λιβάνου*/*τὸν Λίβανον* at 11:17 12:7 13:5,6. The extent northward (and eastward) was up to the great river Euphrates. MT repeats נהר before "Euphrates," and a substantially supported FM text (possibly hex) is represented by *ποταμου*, thus "the great river, the river Euphrates."

In the tradition a popular variant has added *ουν* after the opening imperative, showing the logical connection between the orders given and the statement of v.6 that the Israelites had been in the neighbourhood of Choreb long enough. The transcription Ἀραβά becomes *αρραβα* or (*τοὺς*) *σαραβα* by dittography, appears as *αρουβα* by change of middle vowel (dissimilation?), and as *αρα* by apocopation. The Byz text makes explicit that the seashore is *θαλασσης*, and *oI*+ read *χαναaν* for "Canaanites."

1:8 The verse continues with what the Lord our God said. The opening MT clause modifier ראה is rendered by the plural following the text of Sam, and is in turn supported by Tar and Pesh. The verb *παραδέδωκα* "I have transmitted, handed over" is modified by a prepositional phrase, *ἐνώπιον ὑμῶν*. The verb

12. For Ἀραβά Aq has *ἐν ὁμαλῇ*, for which see f.n. no.1 at v.1; Sym has a doublet *ἐν τῇ πεδιάδι* and Theod, *ἐν δυσμαῖς* for which see comment at v.1; see also the discussion at Salvesen 141.

chosen represents נתתי, which with לפני must mean "I have set before," and LXX must be understood as a calque of the Hebrew sense.[13]

The land which the Israelites are ordered to enter and possess is described by a relative clause as ἣν ὤμοσα to your fathers. Since this is still part of the orders given by the Lord this is more appropriate than MT's אשר נשבע יהוה.[14] The relative clause is a formulaic one in Deut.[15] The verb in first person also occurs at v.35 10:11 31:20,21 34:4, where in each case MT has נשבעתי. Here Sam does as well, and it is also supported by Tar and Pesh. MT has the main verbs of the clause as two imperatives, באו ורשו; LXX idiomatically subordinates the first one as a participle, εἰσελθόντες. In the tradition this appears as εισπορευθεντες in B *b f*+ or as πορευθεντες in *n*+; only the text tradition can decide which is original.[16]

In apposition to πατράσιν ὑμῶν are the names of the three patriarchs, "Abraam and Isaak and Jacob," with only the first one articulated as τῷ Ἀβραάμ, thereby determining the case for all three.[17] In MT each name is governed by the preposition ל in accordance with good Hebrew usage. Majority variant traditions also articulate the other two, but this is unnecessary in Greek. In MT the middle name ליצחק has no conjunction prefixed, but LXX always has a καί before Ἰσαάκ in this context; cf also 6:10 9:5,27 29:13 30:20 34:4. The divine oath is not only to these patriarchs, however, but also to "their seed after them"; God's promise thus extends to the Israelites in the desert as well.

1:9 The reference in ἐν τῷ καιρῷ is not clear, since the event described in vv.9—18 and referred to in Exod 18 preceded the giving of the law at Sinai/Choreb in Exod 20ff., but comp the appointment of the 70 elders at Num 11:14—17,24—30. Moses' complaint is rather oddly put into the future δυνήσομαι, which does accord with LXX's usual practice of rendering the Hebrew prefix inflection by the future, and it may well be based on LXX of Num 11:14. Moses' difficulty is not future, but a present reality as the reading

13. For the use of this verb in Deut see list no.11, THGD 89.
14. The Others all read ὤμοσεν κύριος.
15. See THGD 86—87, list 1 for a list of occurrences.
16. See THGD 133 as well as Lee 86—87.
17. See THGD 105.

of ms V: δυναμαι also suggests. The collocation *φέρειν ὑμᾶς* literally renders שאת אתכם, but is figurative for running your affairs as Exod 18 makes clear.[18]

1:10 This verse substantiates the complaint of v.9, and becomes the basis for the request of v.13. The Lord has increased the Israelites to such an extent that "behold you are today as the stars of heaven in abundance." This simile, along with that of the sand on the seashore, is a common one for an uncountable amount; cf e.g. Hebr 11:12 and in the Pentateuch 10:22 Gen 15:5 22:17 32:12 and Exod 32:13. In the tradition *ὑμῶν* appears in cir. a third of the Greek witnesses as *ημων*; the variant may be sensible, but it is a homophone in Hellenistic Greek, i.e. it is simply a misspelling of *ὑμῶν* as the Hebrew אלהיכם makes clear.

1:11 LXX uses two optatives to express the potential intended by the Hi short form יסף and the coordinate יברך.[19] Thus "may the Lord ... add a thousand fold ... and may he bless you." The use of the adverb *χιλιοπλασίως* nicely yields the intent of אלף פעמים. The *καθότι* clause refers to the covenantal promises and often recurs in Deut.[20] The Lord is described as *ὁ θεὸς τῶν πατέρων ὑμῶν*, which ties this verse to the fathers to whom God had sworn an oath in v.8.[21]

1:12 Moses elaborates on his statement of v.9, but in a *πῶς* question form, therein defining specifically what he was unable to bear,[22] viz. *τὸν κόπον ὑμῶν καὶ τὴν ὑπόστασιν ὑμῶν καὶ τὰς ἀντιλογίας ὑμῶν*. The first term translates טרח which occurs only once elsewhere in LXX, Isa 1:14, where it refers to the burden borne of which God has grown weary. This is adequately rendered by *κόπον* toil, burden."[23] The second word *ὑπόστασιν* is much more difficult; it has a wide range of usage, but it usually means "basis, foundation," hence "plan, undertaking" on the one hand, or "substance, reality, essential nature"

18. Aq has *αἴρειν* which along with the compound *ἐπαίρειν* is regularly used by Aq for נשא.
19. See THGD 87—88 (no.7).
20. See THGD 88 (no.8).
21. For the phrase in Deut see list no.5, THGD 87.
22. For the rendering of אשא by *δυνήσομαι φέρειν* see SS Inf 136.
23. Aq uses *ὄχλησιν* "disturbance, distress."

on the other. MT has משא "burden, load."[24] LXX here probably contrasts with *κόπον* "actual toil or burden" and with *ἀντιλογίας* "trial, legal controversy" in understanding משא in a psychological sense; the burden consists of Israel's rebellious nature as typified in their murmurings in the desert; cf Num 11.[25] The third term translates ריב "a legal strife," i.e. a case brought forward for a legal decision.[26]

1:13 That *δίδωμι* is often used hebraistically in LXX is clear from *δότε* (*ἑαυτοῖς*) where it can not possible mean "give," but must take on the meaning of הבו לכם "take, provide (for yourselves)." What is intended is that the Israelites are to choose men חכמים ונבנים וידעים "wise and understanding and knowledgeable," which LXX renders literally by *σοφοὺς καὶ ἐπιστήμονας καὶ συνετούς*. These are to be "according to your tribes," for which LXX uses a distributive *εἰς* "by your tribes."

MT reads "and I will set them as your chieftains, בראשיכם." Though LXX usually renders ב phrases by *ἐν*, here the clause is idiomatically translated by *καταστήσει* plus two accusative modifiers *αὐτοὺς ἡγουμένους ὑμῶν* "them as your leaders."[27]

1:14 The relative clause modifying *ῥῆμα* is somewhat ambiguous in that the subject of the infinitive is unstated. It could mean "what you said you should do," i.e. what you proposed to do, thereby understanding the subject of the infinitive to be the same as that of *ἐλάλησας*, or it could be translated as "what you said that we should do." The ambiguity is taken over from MT.

1:15 MT refers to the ראשים twice, first as את ראשי שבטיכם modifying "I took" and again as ראשים as a second modifier of אתן "I set (them) as chieftains." LXX simplfiies this by omitting the first reference entirely. In place of the lacuna LXX adds *ἐξ ὑμῶν*, i.e. "I took from you." LXX then takes the accusative modifiers for *ἔλαβον* directly from v.13 rather than fol-

24. Aq renders this by *ἄρμα* formed from *αἴρω*, Aq's usual rendering for נשא. Sym has *βάρος*, something weighty, and so a burden.
25. See especially L.Perlitt, MSU XX, 299—311. Dogniez-Harl render the term well by "état d'esprit."
26. Aq translates by *δικασία* "lawsuit."
27. For the originality of *αὐτούς* see THGD 124.

lowing MT which omits the middle term ונבנים. Moses then set them *ἡγεῖσθαι* (*ἐφ' ὑμῶν*), i.e. LXX avoids the noun ראשים in favor of an infinitive, thereby limiting a literal rendering of the noun to v.13.

Moses then established them either as שרים "captains" or as שטרים "officials," with the former in four ranks: captains of thousands, of hundreds, of fifties, and of tens, which also occurred at Exod 18:21; see Note ad loc. These terms, *χιλιάρχους*, *ἑκατοντάρχους*, *κ.τ.λ.* are quasi-military terms, but their role was that of judicial decisions in all but the most difficult cases (vv.16—17). The term שטרים is rendered by the neologism *γραμματοεισαγωγεῖς*, by which some kind of interpreters of the law is probably meant.[28] The term was borrowed from here at Exod 18:21, where it had no equivalent in MT. In the Hebrew these five associates to Moses were distributed לשבטיכם "for your (individual) tribes"; what is meant is that they were to function within their own tribes. LXX, however, has *τοῖς κριταῖς ὑμῶν* "for your judges," which in view of their designation as שפטיכם in the next verse is a reasonable improvement.[29]

1:16 *διακούετε* is a present imperative, since the command "hear (cases)" is intended to extend indefinitely; it correctly renders the Hebrew free infinitive שמע, which is imperatival when used in isolation; its use is identical to the isolate form of the verb in English, e.g. "hear," or "speak." LXX interprets the noun צדק quite properly by the adverb *δικαίως*. The verb *κρίνετε* is modified by three *ἀνὰ μέσον* phrases, with the last one governing *προσηλύτου αὐτοῦ*. Since the middle phrase, *ἀνὰ μέσον ἀδελφοῦ*, lacks an *αυτου* (over against MT's בין אחיו) the antecedent of *αὐτοῦ* is uncertain. In MT the suffix of גרו must refer to איש. A majority A F M reading (hex?) does add *αυτου* after *ἀδελφοῦ*, thereby clarifying the antecedent of *αὐτοῦ* as *ἀνδρός* in the last phrase. The verb continues the present tense of *διακούετε* rather than changing to the aorist *κρινατε* with the B *b*+ text.[30]

28. Aq has *ἐκβιβαστάς* "those who carry out the law" (retroverted from Syh), and Sym probably had *παιδευτάς* "instructors," (cod: *ἐκβιβαστὰς ἢ παιδευτάς*; the first one is clearly Aq and only the second can be Sym.)
29. Aq and Sym corrected to *ταῖς φυλαῖς ὑμῶν*.
30. See THGD 140.

1:17 Over against MT, LXX has v.17a in the singular, only following MT's consistent plural in v.17b (*ἀφ' ὑμῶν ἀνοίσετε*) and in v.18. The first clause forbids *ἐπιγνώσῃ πρόσωπον ἐν κρίσει*; to "recognize a face" means to show partiality; comp its context at 16:19. In NT comp the extended discourse on partiality at James 2:1—9.

This is then explicated in the next two clauses. The use of two coordinate *κατά* phrases in the sense of "the one like the other" is a Hebraism for כ ... כ. For a correct rendering of this usage see Gen 18:25: *ἔσται ὁ δίκαιος ὡς ὁ ἀσεβής*. What is meant here is: you shall judge both small and great alike. LXX does not use *διακούω* to render תשמעון as in v.16, but *κρίνεις*, probably a stylistic adjustment under the influence of *κρίσει* in the preceding clause and of *κρίσις* in the *ὅτι* clause. The next clause restates the principle of the need for impartiality negatively: *οὐ μὴ ὑποστείλῃ πρόσωπον ἀνθρώπου* "not shall you draw back a man's face," i.e. you shall not be afraid of anyone or be overly awed by someone.[31] The Hebrew has לא תגורו "not shall you be in dread of."[32]

The reason for the demand for evenhandedness in justice lies in the fact that *ἡ κρίσις τοῦ θεοῦ ἐστιν*. That *κρίσις* must be just is rooted in its divine source; it belongs to and thus comes from God. LXX translates the comparative מן in the clause "which is too hard for you" by *ἀπό*, which is not normal Greek (comp also 17:8),[33] and is probably due to LXX's usual equation of *ἀπό* and מן. MT has no equivalent for *αὐτό* modifying *ἀνοίσετε*. It is obviously unnecessary, since the object of תקרבון is הדבר; LXX added it since the referent is rather distant from the verb.

1:18 For *πάντας τοὺς* (*λόγους*) the majority A F M V reading has *τους παντας*, which probably originated in a hex correction in word order to reflect את כל. The future verb in the relative clause is hardly prospective in nature; it is deliberative.[34]

---

31. Rashi approximates *ὑποστείλῃ* by his secondary explanation: לא תכנים דבריך מפני איש.
32. Aq has *κρύφῃς* "hide," and Sym uses *δολιεύῃ* "deal treacherously." I suspect that the attested singular is due to a scribal adjustment to the LXX text rather than to Aq and Sym.
33. SS 151 bluntly states that "it is impossible to explain *ἀπό* as comparative." I would rather say that it is a Hebraism.
34. See Porter 424—425.

1:19 The verse is in first person plural, and introduces a long narrative recalling the desert experiences of the people (vv.19—46). Moses recalls that נסע מחרב ונלך which LXX puts into a single clause as *ἀπάραντες ἐκ Χωρὴβ ἐπορεύθημεν*. The main verb is unusually modified by an accusative, *πᾶσαν τὴν ἔρημον*, probably to represent the את construction of MT, thus "travelled all the desert." The accusative *ὁδόν* limits the earlier accusative *ἔρημον*; we travelled not all that great and terrible desert, but only the *ὁδὸν ὄρους τοῦ Ἀμορραίου*. The genitive of *Ἀμορραῖος* is, except for vv.19,20, always in the plural in Deut in spite of the consistent singular of MT; for *ὄρους τοῦ Ἀμορραίου* see comment at v.7. Kades Barnea was according to v.2 an eleven day journey from Choreb; it lies on the northern edge of the Sinai desert, almost straight north (and slightly east) of Mt. Choreb.

In the tradition Cod A has the baffling *σοχωθ* instead of *Χωρήβ*; comp Num 33:5 (variant reading). The A copyist must have been dreaming! The articulation of *ὄρους* by Byz is a stylistic change, but the unarticulated noun is original here as well as in v.20.[35]

1:20—21 Moses addresses the Israelites directly. In v.20 reference is again made to their arrival at the hill country of the Amorrite, which is described by the relative clause *ὃ κύριος ὁ θεὸς ἡμῶν δίδωσιν ὑμῖν*,[36] using the present tense as the standard equivalent for the Hebrew participle, i.e. the Lord is in the process of giving you the hill country of the Amorrite. Somewhat problematic is the second person pronoun *ὑμῖν*, since MT has לנו. Only A and four scattered cursives read *ημιν* here, which agrees with MT; this reading is either an itacism or original text. I would with some hesitation defend *ὑμῖν* as original here, i.e. as marking a transition to second plural for all of v.21. After all, Moses is speaking to the people directly, and this makes the popular *υμων* for *ἡμῶν* immediately before *ὑμῖν* part of the same problem. The text tradition here illustrates how careful one must be in assessing variants in pronouns involving first and second person. Since they are in all their cases homophonic in the plural as well as for the oblique cases in the singular, the choice

35. See THGD 104.
36. The clause is extremely common in Deut; for a list of occurrences see no.10 in THGD 88—89. For the text see *idem* 107.

between ὑμῶν and ἡμῶν is not determined by the nature or quality of ms support but only by the Hebrew, because confusion is hardly possible between נו– and כם– or between אותנו and אתכם or אנחנו vs אתם. Only rarely should this be disregarded.

The tense of the verb in the relative clause contrasts with v.21 where Moses says *παραδέδωκεν ὑμῖν κύριος ... τὴν γῆν*, i.e. a perfect tense. MT uses the same root נתן, but LXX uses the compound *παραδίδωμι* for the second, thereby specifying a transferal, a handing over; God has bestowed the land; now all that remains is for the Israelites actually to take possession. In MT the text of v.21 is inexplicably in the singular within a plural context that continues through v.30. LXX, however, levels the text by a consistent plural. It has also added an ad sensum *ὑμῖν* to modify *παραδέδωκεν*, which a popular A F M V variant text omits. This omission might well represent a prehexaplaric omission on the basis of the Hebrew.

The central notion of v.21 is the order *ἀναβάντες κληρονομήσατε* for עלה רש. The aorist imperative is likely original LXX, though the majority A F M present imperative *κληρονομειτε* merits some consideration. The question is whether the translator wanted to stress the process of taking possession of the land. Since the participle is also aorist the choice of the aorist imperative must be preferred. The *ὃν τρόπον* clause is another formulaic piece of text which occurs, usually though not always, with some verb denoting speech.[37] The verse ends with the formulaic negative calls to confidence: *μὴ φοβεῖσθε μηδὲ δειλιάσητε*. This pair also occurs at 31:6,8 though in the singular; comp also 20:8. The formula with *φοβέω* is common, occurring within the Pentateuch eight times in Gen, three times in Num and eight times in Deut, whereas that with *δειλιάω* is limited to the three occurrences coordinated with *φοβέω* noted above. In fact, the *δειλιάω* formula only occurs elsewhere in LXX in Jos, and each time it is coordinate with the *φοβέω* formula (1:9 8:1 10:25). For the meaning of the formula, 31:6 is particularly instructive (as are the three cases in Jos), since the negative commands contrast with their positive counterparts: *ἀνδρίζου καὶ ἴσχυε* "be manly and strong."

1:22 A majority M reading has the second aorist *προσηλθετε* instead of the Hellenistic form of LXX. Of more interest is the addition of *υμεις* after

37. See list 9 in THGD 88 for *ὃν τρόπον* clauses.

πάντες which is clearly of hex origin so as to represent MT's כלכם more exactly.

What the people propose is "let us send men ... *καὶ ἐφοδευσάτωσαν* for us the land." The verb means to go on a tour of inspection, to explore, and occurs only here and in the deuterocanonical books. MT has יחפרו "search out."[38] Coordinate with this clause in MT is וישבו אתנו הדבר את הדרך ... ואת הערים. The construction is unusual in that the verb (Hi of שוב) is triply modified: by "us," "the word" and "the way ... and the cities." LXX has dealt with this by the dative *ἡμῖν* and the accusatives *ἀπόκρισιν τὴν ὁδόν* ... *καὶ τὰς πόλεις* all in modification of another third plural imperative *ἀναγγειλάτωσαν*, thus "let them give us a report as to the way ... and the cities," with the coordinate accusatives intended to specify what the *ἀπόκρισιν* was all about. The unusual idiom *ἀναγγειλάτωσαν ἀπόκρισιν* probably means "to make a public report" (literally "announce a reply"), and neatly capsules the intent of the Hebrew ישבו הדבר.

Each of the coordinate accusative modifiers is in turn modified by a relative clause with a future verb, which inflection implies a desiderative use of the future, thus "through which we should go up" and "which we might enter."[39] Both clauses contain the recapitulated prepositional phrases of the Hebrew within the clauses, thus *δι' ἧς* ... *ἐν αὐτῇ* and *εἰς ἅς* ... *εἰς αὐτάς*, which are much better Hebrew than Greek constructions, and represent the rather literalistic approach which our translator took to his work.

1:23 *ἤρεσεν ἐνώπιόν μου* represents ייטב בעיני; the verb normally takes a dative of person, though the modification by an *ἐνώπιον* phrase does occur in the NT as well,[40] but that usage was probably inspired by LXX. בעיני is normally rendered in the Pentateuch by one of the semiprepositions *ἐναντίον*, *ἐνώπιον* or *ἔναντι*, and occasionally by the dative. בעיני occurs 15 times in Deut. Twice (3:27 34:4) it is rendered by a dative of means, *τοῖς ὀφθαλμοῖς*. Nine times it occurs in the construction בעיני יהוה which is always translated by *ἔναντι κυρίου*. There are three cases (12:8 15:18 24:1) of *ἐναντίον*, and

38. Sym has *ἵνα κατασκέψονται* "that they may spy out."
39. Instead of *εἰσπορευσόμεθα* Theod witnesses to the simplex form though in the present tense *πορευόμεθα*, whereas Aq Sym testify to *εἰσελευσόμεθα*. The future *εἰσπορευσόμεθα* of LXX occurs only here in the Pentateuch; see Lee 87.
40. See Bl-Debr 214.6. note 9.

only here is it rendered by ἐνώπιον.[41] For the twelve men by tribes see Num 13:1—16 where they are all named as well. The collocation ἕνα κατὰ φυλήν simply means "one man per tribe."

1:24 The term τὸ ὄρος hardly means "hill," but is shorthand for the southern part of Palestine; cf comment on ὄρος 'Αμορραίων at v.7. Wadi Eshkol is not transcribed but translated as Φάραγγος βότρυος "the wadi of the grape cluster" as at Num 13:24.[42] In contrast to v.22 they κατεσκόπευσαν αὐτήν, "they spied (it) out," a good translation for ירגלו. A Cat variant reading has the verb κατεσκοπησαν which means the same as the LXX verb.

1:25 MT has "and they took בידם" which LXX sensibly rendered by the plural ἐν ταῖς χερσὶν αὐτῶν.[43] What they took was ἀπὸ τοῦ καρποῦ τῆς γῆς; the ἀπό represents the partitive מן of MT;[44] "they took some of the fruit...."

MT refers to their report as וישבו אתנו דבר ויאמר for which LXX simply has καὶ ἔλεγον; the shorter text is also supported by Vulg. Hex supplied και επεστρεψαν ημιν ρημα under the asterisk to fill the lacuna. For the relative clause modifying γῆ see comment at vv.20—21.

1:26 The verb ἠπειθήσατε is modified by τῷ ῥήματι, i.e. "you disobeyed the word (of the Lord your God)." The Hebrew word rendered is תמרו "be rebellious, defiant," translated similarly at 9:7,23,24. Here it refers to the defiant attitude and actions of the people in vv.26—45. The dative noun interprets the Hebrew metaphor פי "mouth" correctly.[45]

1:27 The verb תרגנו, Ni of רגן, occurs only here in the Pentateuch, but is correctly translated by διεγογγύσατε "you murmured, grumbled."[46] This was,

41. Comp Table 13 in Sollamo 124. Her statistics need revision, however, since they are based on Rahlfs' text.
42. Aq normally reserved φάραγξ for גיא, and has χειμάρρου here for נחל, which again is his usual equation.
43. See SS 136.
44. See SS 162.
45. Aq translates תמרו by προσηρίσατε "strive against, be rebellious," whereas Sym follows LXX. Theod understood the verb as derived from מרר "be bitter" becoming causative in Hi, thus translating the collocation παρεπικράνατε τὸ στόμα κυρίου.
46. Aq translated by ἐτονθρύσατε "mumbled"; Sym Theod retained the LXX text.

however, not a public protest but ἐν ταῖς σκηναῖς ὑμῶν, i.e. among yourselves. The grumbling was against the Lord. The marked infinitive τὸ μισεῖν is modified by two accusatives: κύριον ἡμᾶς. That the first one is the subject and the second the object is clear from the main construction ἐξήγαγεν ἡμᾶς (ἐκ γῆς Αἰγύπτου).[47]

The second infinitive is purposive. The people interpret the Lord's redemptive act of deliverance from Egypt as due to his hatred, i.e. the act is not redemptive but destructive; the Lord wanted to deliver them into the power of the enemy. The verb παραδίδωμι is often modified by εἰς τὰς χεῖρας, always in the sense of "into the grasp, power of";[48] cf 2:24,30,36 3:2,3 7:2,23,24.

The final infinitive is popular in Deut. The verb שמד (Hi or Ni) is usually rendered as here by the verb ἐξολεθρεύω (19 times; both mean "to exterminate"), whereas ἐκτρίβω is used by the translator only five times. The infinitive modifies παραδοῦναι, i.e. the Lord delivered us ... in order to exterminate us. The people thereby accuse their God of acting contrary to his own covenant promise, in fact, of wanting to exterminate his own people.

In the tradition the B F M *oI z*+ text articulated both χεῖρας and Ἀμορραίων so as to improve the style. The Byz text did not take the final infinitive as the purpose underlying παραδοῦναι, but coordinated the two by means of a και.

1:28 The opening query ποῦ ἡμεῖς ἀναβαίνομεν represents a Hebrew interrogative nominal clause with a participial predicate. The interrogative is best understood in the context of the people's grumbling, as asking "into what kind of situation are we being invited to go," and it presupposes the bad report returned by ten of the spies given in Num 13:29—34.

MT states "our brother המסו our hearts." The verb means "caused to melt," and the metaphor means "they scared us." LXX uniquely translates the verb by ἀπέστησεν, so "caused our hearts to revolt."[49] This report by our

47. For the common Deut collocation "brought us out of the land of Egypt" see THGD 87, list 3.
48. See SS 136.
49. Sym translated by ἐξέλυσαν, so set free, relaxed." Schl translated the collocation by *timidos fecerunt* and then adds as explanation "*Liquescere* enim haud raro de hominibus usurpatur ad *metum*, *consternationem* et *anxietatem* indicandam."

brothers is then quoted: "(There is) a nation great and numerous and stronger than us and cities great and walled up into the sky." The rendering *πολύ* is hardly a rendering for רם, but rather of רב, as at 2:10, and especially at 2:21 which has the same text as here. In both of these רב ורם occur; Sam has רב instead of רם here. The comparative is relatively rare in Deut.[50] The notion of cities being walled up *ἕως τοῦ οὐρανοῦ* translates בשמים (also at 9:1); one might have expected *εἰς* plus an accusative, but *ἕως* does emphasize the height of the cities' walls. After all, what the report intended to convey was that of impenetrable cities.

The last clause is introduced by וגם, and LXX tried to reproduce it by *ἀλλὰ καί* plus a preposed modifier *υἱοὺς γιγάντων*; I would render the clause by "But we also saw the offspring of giants." The *ἀλλὰ καί* is unusual, and apparently LXX wanted to translate the two morphemes separately, though וגם is hardly an adversative particle. In MT the preposed modifier is בני ענקים. The term ענקים or its singular ענק occurs six times in Deut, and it is always transcribed as Ἀνακίμ or (υἱοὶ) Ἐνάκ except here.[51] In fact, the use of *γίγας* for ענק(ים) is to be found only here in LXX, and is almost certainly based on Num 13:34 where MT has ושם ראינו את הנפילים בני ענק מן הנפילים, for which LXX only has *καὶ ἐκεῖ ἑωράκαμεν τοὺς γίγαντας*.

In the tradition, hex has transposed *ἡμῶν/τὴν καρδίαν* to agree with MT. Also to be noted is the majority A F M V text which adds *δε* after *οἱ* to mark a transition from the question form to the following statement, but this is a stylistic variant which would misinterpret MT. The lack of contrast in MT is intentional, and LXX has correctly understood this by its asyndetic structure.

1:29 In the next five verses Moses tries to convince the people that with God on their side they are invincible. As in v.21 he encourages them not to cower nor to be afraid of the inhabitants. *πτήξητε* is used intransitively, and *φοβηθῆτε* is modified by an *ἀπό* phrase which imitates the Hebrew מהם, a construction unusual (though attested) in Classical Greek.[52]

---

50. According to SS 150 in only four cases out of 17 does Deut use the comparative with the genitive to render the Hebrew adjective plus מן.
51. The Others also transcribe it with Ἐνακείμ.
52. See Bl-Debr 149, note 2.

1:30 The initial *κύριος — προσώπου ὑμῶν* is a pendant nominative construction with the pronoun *αὐτός* serving as the actual subject of the verb *συνεκπολεμήσει*, thus "As for the Lord your God who is going ahead before you,[53] he (will fight them alongside you)." The verb modified by a *μετά* phrase gives a somewhat different stress from MT which reads ילחם לכם; in MT Yahweh will fight for you, but in LXX the Lord will fight them along with you. The *αὐτούς*, though without an MT equivalent, is normal for this verb.

The relative clause also differs somewhat from MT.[54] Instead of במצרים LXX has added "land," i.e. *ἐν γῇ Αἰγύπτῳ*, but then MT goes on with another locative phrase לעיניכם, which LXX has disregarded. Hex has added under an asterisk the equivalent phrase *κατα οφθαλμων υμων*. A number of *O* witnesses have also omitted *γῇ*, which does equal MT and may represent an early omission under the influence of the Hebrew. Also in the tradition a popular F M 963 reading *ημων* for (*ὁ θεὸς*) *ὑμῶν* obtains, which is rooted in homophony, and is not a genuine variant text. Of more consequence is the addition in the *C s* text of *και* before *αὐτός*. This variant is probably due to a misunderstanding of the pendant construction, and is clearly inferior to LXX. I would translate the variant *και αυτος* by "even he."

1:31 The opening "and in this desert" is joined to the preceding clause, i.e. "in Egypt land and in this desert"; this is in turn modified by *ἣν εἴδετε*, which verb in turn is explicated by what follows in the verse, thus "how the Lord your God nourished you as if a man would nourish his son."[55]

The verb *τροφοφορέω* "nourish, sustain" is a neologism created by LXX for this context, and contextually interprets נשא "carry, bear." The translator probably had the divine provision of manna in the wilderness in mind as evidence of God's bearing up the people. The first instance is simply in the aorist indicative as a reminder of what the Lord did for his people. The second case, *τροφοφορῆσαι*, is an aorist optative inflection, since it is introduced by the

53. Variants on this contruction may be seen in THGD 87, list 6.
54. The construction *πάντα ὅσα ἐποίησεν* occurs in various forms as THGD 89—90, list 12 shows.
55. Aq has *ἦρεν ... ὡσεὶ ἄραι τροφὸς τὸν υἱόν*. The use of *τροφός* "nurse" for איש is, one suspects, not really Aq, but represents a bit of rationalisic speculation of the (Cat) commentator. Sym rendered the verbal forms by *ἐβάστησεν* and *βαστάσαι*.

conditional particle εἰ, showing a potential condition. This is certainly preferable to the future inflection in B V+.[56]

The second ὡς construction is interruptive, and the next prepositional phrase modifies ἐτροφοφόρησεν, i.e. "the Lord ... nourished you ... along the way which you travelled." In MT the verb הלכתם is modified by עד plus a bound infinitive which in turn is modified by an עד plus a nominal. LXX smoothes out the construction by interpreting the infinitive as an aorist verb ἕως ἤλθετε, and the final construction as a prepositional εἰς phrase, thus "until you came to this place."[57] Somewhat problematic is the presence of τις in the second ὡς clause, since it seems to render איש twice, i.e. as τις before the verb (without MT support) and as ἄνθρωπος after the verb. It could be interpreted as an early gloss though its odd placement as well as its support by B 963, the two oldest witnesses, do in my opinion tip the scales in favor of its originality.

In the tradition the 963 readings of ετροποφορησεν ... τροποφορησαι receive considerable support. The variant text does make fine sense in the context; it means "bear with one's moods," thus it emphasizes the patience of God with his people, and that of a father with his son, but it is secondary, created by confusion of the labial stops φ — π. A V Cat+ variant changes the Classical ἤλθετε to the Hellenistic ηλθατε.

1:32 The phrase ἐν τῷ λόγῳ τούτῳ must be understood in the sense of its parent בדבר הזה, i.e. "in this matter," referring to what Moses has just been saying in vv.29—31. The compound verb ἐνεπιστεύσατε is unexpected as a translation of מאמינם; to represent a participle one would have expected an imperfect rather than an aorist inflection, since the Hebrew participial predicate is normally rendered either by a present or an imperfect verb. Presumably the translator wanted to avoid the imperfect, i.e. did not want to stress the ongoing character of the Israelites' lack of faith; after all, the reference is to their reaction on a specific occasion. Furthermore, the verb האמין is usually translated by the simplex; the compound occurs here for the first time, and is only rarely used in LXX, except for Sir. For the popular B V 963 misspelling of ὑμῶν as ημων see comment at v.10.

---

56. See THGD 141.
57. See SS Inf 113.

1:33 The verse is a relative clause which modifies *κύριος ὁ θεός* of v.31. Its verb is *προπορεύεται* "goes ahead" which is then modified by *πρότερος ὑμῶν* "who goes ahead before you," for which see comment at v.30. The verb is modified by a purposive infinitive *ἐκλέγεσθαι* "to be choosing, selecting."[58] The lexeme is unique as a rendering for לתור "to spy out"; in fact, it is almost exclusively used as an equivalent for בחר, though it is not inappropriate here. In fact, it avoids any pejorative sense which לטור might imply, but it retains the notion of selection common to both words.

In MT the modifier of the infinitive is מקום לחנתכם "a place for you to pitch the tents." This is then followed by באש לילה לראתכם "by fire at night for you to see."[59] It should be noted that the Masoretes made the first cut between the two collocations, i.e. placed לחנתכם under an *ethnach*. LXX did not cut here, and was puzzled by the notion of the action involved by fire at night. By transposing two consonants in the first infinitive as לנחתכם "to lead you" it translated as *τόπον ὁδηγῶν ὑμᾶς ἐν πυρὶ νυκτός*, i.e. a place, leading (i.e. the Lord) you by fire at night.[60] The next infinitive was then taken as though Hi, thus *δεικνύων ὑμῖν* "pointing out to you (the road)," which is also how the Masoretes understood it. The road is identified as *καθ' ἣν πορεύεσθε ἐν αὐτῇ* with the Hebraic recapitulating prepositional phrase reflecting the parent אשר תלכו בה.[61] The closing *καὶ ἐν νεφέλῃ ἡμέρας* is coordinate with the earlier *ἐν πυρὶ νυκτός* and so modifies *ὁδηγῶν*. This is much clearer than MT.

1:34 The basis for the divine anger is *τὴν φωνὴν τῶν λόγων ὑμῶν* in vv.27—28. The people had profaned the Lord's redemption; cf comment at v.27. In the tradition the *C*'' *s* text changed *τὴν φωνήν* to the genitive, but *ἀκούω* normally takes an accusative for what is heard, and the genitive for the person heard.

---

58. Aq translates literally by *κατασκοπῆσαι* "to spy out."
59. Apparently Aq rendered לחנתכם באש לילה by *κυκλοῦν ὑμᾶς πυρὶ ἐν νυκτί* (retroverted from Syh). I suspect, however, that *α´* is an error for *σ´* in the Syh tradition.
60. For a present participle rendering a marked infinitive see SS Inf 59.
61. That *ἐν αὐτῇ* is original rather than the popular B variant *επ αυτης* is demonstrated in THGD 118.

1:35 The divine oath is quoted directly and is introduced by the conditional particle *εἰ* followed by a future inflection. This imitates the parent text's אם plus a verb in the prefix inflection, which is a strong negative in Hebrew, and LXX's literalistic rendering must be taken as a hebraistic calque;[62] its presence in NT, as e.g. at Mk 8:12, shows the influence of LXX translation Greek on the NT writers.

What God swears is that no one *τῶν ἀνδρῶν τούτων* will see this good land. In MT באנשים האלה is followed by the appositive הדור הרע הזה which LXX does not recognize. Its omission certainly improves the text. Hex has added under the asterisk its equivalent *η γενεα η πονηρα αυτη*, which is then in apposition to *τις*. What is not immediately clear is the reference to "these" men, though in view of the second plural context in which this occurs it must be the people in general, and not just the spies who brought in their report. The fuller statement at Num 14:22—23 limits the application to the men "who saw my glory and the signs which I did in Egypt and in this desert," whereas those who would inherit the land are *τὰ τέκνα αὐτῶν*. The land of promise is called *τὴν γῆν τὴν ἀγαθὴν* (*ταύτην*), a favored term in Deut (comp also 3:25 6:18 8:7,10 9:4,6 11:17 31:20,21). The relative clause modifying *γῆν* is formulaic.[63] The לתת of MT is omitted, and hex has added *δουναι* after *ὤμοσα* to equal MT.[64]

1:36 זולתי is a conjunction meaning "only, except," occurring only twice in the Pentateuch (also at 4:12 where it is rendered by *ἀλλ' ἤ*); here it is rendered by *πλήν* in LXX.[65] Chaleb the son of Iephonne is the named exception to the ban; cf also Num 14:24. *Χαλέβ* was quite stable in the tradition with only one or two witnesses supporting the following misspellings: *χαλεφ*, *χαλευ*, *χαλβ*, *χαλεμ*. His father's name received much rougher treatment. Aside from homophonic misspellings the following occur in the tradition: *ιεφονη*, *ιεφονι*, *ιεφεννι*, *ιεφωνη*, *ιεφωνει*, *ιεφθονη*, *ιεφθοννη* and *ιφοννη*.

---

62. Cf-Debr 454.5 calls it an "eindeutiger Hebraismus."
63. For this Deut collocation see THGD 86, list 1.
64. SS Inf 42 believes this to be a textual matter; cf the omission of לתת in Kenn 152.
65. Aq uses *παρεκτός* which also means "except."

The initial "except Chaleb the son of Iephonne" is a pendant construction, and οὗτος is the pronominal subject of ὄψεται, with its antecedent being Χαλέβ. The land which he and his sons will be given is characterized as ἐφ' ἣν ἐπέβη. The aorist verb is appropriate, since as one of the 12 spies he had actually walked on it.

The reason for Chaleb's special treatment is given as due to *τὸ προσκεῖσθαι αὐτὸν τὰ πρὸς κύριον* "his adherence to matters concerning the Lord,"[66] which is a free but accurate rendering of MT which has מלא אחרי יהוה "had fully followed Yahweh."[67]

1:37 This is the only reference in the book to God's anger with Moses on the people's account. The preposed ἐμοί centers the attention on Moses, sandwiched in between Chaleb and Joshua who alone of the adults were to enter the Promised Land. Just why Moses should have been included in the divine wrath against the people is not said, though it was δι' ὑμᾶς.

1:38 The name יהושוע/יהושע is always spelled as Ἰησοῦς (-οῦ, -οῦ, οῦν); this reflects a later pronunciation as Yeshua, either with a *sere* or a *shwa* in the first syllable. This development is unusual for theophoric names with יהו prefix, which are commonly transcribed with ιω- e.g. Ἰωαδά, Ἰωακίμ, Ἰωανάν, Ἰωαχάζ, Ἰωναθάν, Ἰωράμ, etc. It might be noted that in Chr Esr and Neh the name does appear as ישוע for which the Masoretes pointed the first syllable with a *sere*.[68] Equally unusual, though consistent throughout LXX, is the transcription of the father's name as Ναυή for נון. Ναυή could be understood as an early error by uncial confusion of H - N from *Ναυν, but there is no textual evidence of any kind for it.[69] Iesous is identified as ὁ *παρεστηκώς σοι*, for which comp Note at Exod 24:13; here, however, the participle renders העמד rather than משרת. The σοι is a free rendering for לפניך.[70] Syntactically the initial "Iesous the son of Naue the one attending you" is a pendant construction; comp comment at v.36 for a similar structure.

---

66. Tar^{O} interprets this as אשלים בתר דחלתא דיי.
67. Aq insists on a literal translation for מלא with his πληρῶσαι.
68. As might be expected Aq transcribes the name here as'Ἰωσοῦα.
69. The Hebrew name occurs 30 times and it always occurs in LXX as Ναυή.
70. See SS 102.

The preposed modifier *αὐτόν* is in imitation of the Hebrew. The verb is *κατίσχυσον* which is here used for the first time in LXX for חזק Pi in the sense of "strengthen, encourage"; cf also 3:28. The basis for such an order is that he will *κατακληρονομήσει αὐτὴν τῷ Ἰσραήλ*. Unusual is the use of both an accusative of thing plus a dative of person, thus "assign it (i.e. the land) as a possession to Israel." A popular A F M V reading has *κατακληροδοτησει* with no real difference in meaning.

It might also be noted that הוא occurs twice in this verse; the first time it is translated by *οὗτος* and the second time by *αὐτός*. This shows that the translator did not distinguish between the two as subject pronouns.

1:39 MT begins with וטפכם אשר אמרתם לבז יהיה, and then continues with ובניכם; LXX simply has *καὶ πᾶν παιδίον νέον*.[71] This free rendering does rid the text of a troublesome doublet. The Hebrew text distinguishes between "your little ones who you said would become booty" and "your children who now know neither good nor evil." By adding *πᾶν* the translator included בניכם as well as טפכם under the umbrella term "and every young child who now knows neither good nor evil." Hex has added under the asterisk *και τα παιδια υμων α ειπατε εν διαρπαγη εσεσθαι* at the beginning,[72] though *τα παιδια υμων* is more suitable for טפכם than for בניכם. I suspect that the reading is really that of Theod. The lack of gender concord for *ὅστις* is ad sensum. The point being made is that all children at the time referred to were still innocent, and so were not subject to the ban imposed on their sinful elders. The verb *οἶδεν* modified by *σήμερον* emphasizes the present condition, i.e. "do not now know (good or evil)."

The translator neatly distinguishes between a transitive (Hi of נחל) in v.38 and the intransitive (Qal of ירש) by changing from the compound *κατακληρονομέω* to the simplex; these children will inherit the land in contrast to Iesous' making Israel inherit the land in v.38.

1:40 LXX wisely does not translate לכם as at v.7; cf comment ad loc. Odd is the use of *στρατοπεδεύσατε εἰς τὴν ἔρημον*. The verb means "to encamp,

71. Which is at best a free rendering; cf SS Inf 129,150.
72. Which reading is attributed to Aq in the tradition, though usually Aq retains *παιδίον* for ילד, and uses *νήπιον* for טף, but see SS Inf 200.

bivouac," but here it translates סעו המדברה "travel into the desert."[73] Elsewhere (as at Gen 12:9) when it renders סעו it is modified by a locative phrase (ἐν at Gen 12:9; ὀπίσω at Exod 14:10); obviously εἰς is used in a locative sense.[74] Here the verb is also modified by an accusative showing extent of space: "the road towards the Red Sea." The intent then is: "bivouac in the desert on the way towards the Red Sea;" comp Num 14:25. LXX transposed ים סוף as ἐρυθρᾶς θαλάσσης over against 2:1 11:4. Usage in the Pentateuch varies. ים סוף occurs five times in Exod; four times the order is ἐρ. θαλ. (10:19 13:18 15:4 23:31), and once (15:22) as θαλ. ἐρ. The phrase occurs four times in Num and LXX always follows the Hebrew order. In Deut (three cases) only here does the order ἐρ. θαλ. occur.

In the tradition the majority text read the aorist indicative *εστρατοπεδευσατε* instead of the imperative. The variant text voids the intent of both MT and LXX in which God orders the Israelites to turn and go in a direction opposite to the land of promise, changing it to a statement of what Israel did. In view of the following verses this cannot be correct.[75]

1:41 For vv.41—45 comp Num 14:40—45. The Hebrew חטאנו ל means "we have sinned against," which LXX renders by ἡμάρτομεν ἔναντι, i.e. "sinned before, in the presence of," which would more accurately have rendered "we have sinned לפני." LXX also follows Sam rather than MT in its κυρίου τοῦ θεοῦ ἡμῶν for יהוה. The collocation יהוה אלהינו also occurs in the relative clause which LXX rendered by (κατὰ πάντα) ὅσα ἐνετείλατο κύριος ὁ θεὸς ἡμῶν ἡμῖν. The dative modifier represents the suffix of צונו, which hex did not recognize because of the intervention of the subject, and wrongly placed under the obelus. Textually uncertain is LXX's use of the hortatory subjunctive πολεμήσωμεν for נלחמנו. Moses is quoting what the Israelites in a rebellious mood had said. The indicative inflection is a well-supported one including B F V 963, but the age of the mss is unfortunately irrelevant since the subjunctive

73. Aq has καὶ ὑμεῖς νεύσατε αὐτοῖς καὶ ἐπάρατε τὴν ἔρημον. Sym has ἀναστρέψαντες ἐπάρατε εἰς τὴν ἔρημον. For Theod only ἐπιστραφέντες and ἐπάρατε are attested. The reading ἐπάρατε is not certain for Aq; ms 344 attests to ἀπάρατε, and since this is the more usual Aq equivalent, it may well be the better reading.
74. See Bauer sub voce 9.
75. See also THGD 140.

and the indicative were homophonic at the time these witnesses were copied, and thus only exegetical considerations are valid for determining the text of LXX. Since it is immediately followed by precipitate action the notion of hortation is probably superior.[76] That precipitate action consisted first of all of *ἀναλάβοντες ἕκαστος τὰ σκεύη τὰ πολεμικὰ αὐτοῦ*. The participle is used uniquely for תחגרו; it is certainly a free rendering "taking up (your warlike weapons)" instead of "you strapped on."[77]

This was followed by *καὶ συναθροισθέντες ἀνεβαίνετε εἰς τὸ ὄρος*. MT has a verb תהינו modified by a marked infinitive לעלת plus "to the mountainous area." The Hebrew verb is a hapax legomenon, and its meaning was unknown to the ancients, who in various ways invoked the context.[78] LXX simply used a neutral word "coming together, assembling" as something that was fitting before actually going up to battle.[79] Note the intelligent use of the imperfect in *ἀνεβαίνετε εἰς τὸ ὄρος*.[80]

1:42 For this verse see Num 14:42. Moses in response to the Lord's instructions[81] forbids the contemplated action in God's name "because I am not with you," a good rendering for the nominal כי אינני בקרבכם.

The final clause is given as a clause coordinate to the nominal one: "and not shall you be smitten before your enemies." What is clearly meant is "lest you be ...."[82] LXX renders the syntactical pattern literally with a negative plus finite verb (*συντριβῆτε* aorist passive subjunctive), "and not should you be crushed before your enemies."[83] The Greek text is somewhat ambiguous since

---

76. See also THGD 141—142.
77. The Three rendered more literally, Aq by *ἐζώσασθε*, and Sym Theod by *περιζωσάμενοι*.
78. See the textual note on ותהינו in Driver ad loc.
79. Aq similarly used a word agreeable to the context *ὁμονοήσαντες* "being in concord, agreeing." I suspect that Aq would not actually have used a participle but rather an aorist verb *ομονοησαν* (plus an infinitive) in view of MT. Tar guessed with שריתון "you began (to go up)." Rashi played with הננו citing Num 14:40 הננו ועלינו אל המקום. SS Inf 46 in referring to the rendering of the infinitive says "nicht korrekt wiedergegeben."
80. For the use of *εἰς* see Johannessohn 297—298.
81. Εἰπόν is incorrectly accented according to Walters 99—100; it should be changed to *εἶπον*.
82. Aq has a colorful rendering: *καὶ οὐκ μαστιχθήσεσθε* "and not shall you be flogged" (retroverted from Syh).
83. For *οὐ ... εἰμι* translating אינני see SS 77.

it could also be read as a prediction, but this would be incongruous in the context, and the potential nature of the subjunctive must be insisted on.

1:43 Comp Num 14:44. MT uses שמעתם absolutely, but LXX adds *μου* ad sensum, which hex has placed under the obelus to indicate its absence in MT. This unwillingness to listen to Moses is then explicated by three coordinate verbs in MT: "תמרו (the mouth of Yahweh) and תזדו and תעלו to the hill country." LXX divides into two syntactic units "*παρέβητε* (*τὸ ῥῆμα κυρίου*) and *παραβιασάμενοι ἀνέβητε* ...." The verb מרה is translated by *παραβαίνω* only twice in LXX, once for the Qal at Num 27:14 and once here for the Hi, both with *τὸ ῥῆμα* as modifier. The state of rebelliousness is explained as being a turning aside of the divine word. *ῥῆμα* realizes the metaphor involved in פי, i.e. "mouth" means "word."

The participle used means "doing a thing by force, constraining by violence," thus "by force (you went up)." Only here is *παραβιάζομαι* used to render the verb זיד "to be or do a thing arrogantly, presumptuously." The Greek verb was first used of the Sodomites constraining, violently pressing Lot outside the door of his house at Gen 19:9, where MT had the root פצר; cf comment ad loc.

In the tradition the Byz text has a variant reading for *καὶ παρέβητε τὸ ῥῆμα* viz. *ουδε εποιησετε* (or *-σατε*) *κατα το ρημα* "you did not act according to the word of the Lord," a free variation which tones down the LXX text by means of a negative statement. The *f* text has a doublet for *καὶ παραβιασάμενοι*, viz. *και υπερηφανησατε*, which is a literal rendering of MT and may well be Aq in origin; cf 17:13 18:20.

1:44 Comp Num 14:45. The phrase *εἰς συνάντησιν* is used in LXX regularly to translate לקראת, both the Hebrew and the Greek modifying a verb of movement. It only occurs four times in Deut (first used at Gen 14:17), and always modifies *ἐξῆλθεν*. That האמרי/*ὁ Ἀμορραῖος* was understood as a collective is obvious from the coordinated verb which is in the plural (in both LXX and MT).

The apt comparison of swarming bees is put into a conditional structure of *εἰ* plus an optative, thus "as bees might do." The area of the rout is defined as *ἀπὸ Σηὶρ ἕως Ἑρμά*. Neither location is certainly identified, but both appear to be situated in the southern part of Palestine, i.e. in the general area of the Negeb. The name Σηίρ is often misspelled in the tradition due to itacism. Other misspellings include *σηρ*, *ασιειρ*, *ασηειρ*, *ειρ*, *σηειρρ* as well as *αροερ/αρωερ* in the *n* tradition. Over against this name that of Ἑρμά was quite stable, only *ερμαν* and *σερμα* (by dittography) being attested variants.

1:45 The Masoretes vocalized תשבו as from the root שוב, but LXX followed the Sam tradition as from ישב, i.e. *καθίσαντες* "sitting down (you were weeping)." LXX properly used the imperfect ἐκλαίετε for תבכו, since a process of weeping before the Lord as a means of placating deity was involved. A popular gloss adding *του θεου υμων*, identifying *κυρίου* as "your God" is not inappropriate in this context, though it is hardly original LXX.

The Lord's negative reaction is not introduced by an adversative particle, but rather by *καί* in imitation of MT. The contrast is, however, clear from the change of subject: you were weeping ... and the Lord did not listen to your voice." The Lord's reaction is doubly told: The Lord did not listen to your voice *οὐδὲ προσέσχεν ὑμῖν* "nor did he pay attention to you." The Hebrew verb is a denominative one from the word אזן "ear," thus "give ear."

1:46 MT here vocalizes ותשבו as derived from ישב. LXX, however, distinguishes this one from that presupposed in v.45. Here the Greek has the compound *ἐνεκάθησθε* "you settled down." The name Καδής is given in its fuller form in v.19 as Καδὴς Βαρνή, for which see comment ad loc.

The accusative showing extent of time is oddly expressed by *ἡμέρας πολλὰς ὅσας ποτὲ ἡμέρας ἐνεκάθησθε* "(the) many days whichever days you did settle down." This imitates the Hebrew ימים רבים כיום אשר ישבתם; what is meant is that they settled down a long time, which time constituted the entire time in which they were not on the move. To make this clear LXX added the indefinite particle *ποτέ*, which hex placed under the obelus since it has no specific equivalent in MT.

Chapter 2

2:1 The text in MT reading נסע המדברה דרך ים סוף is the same as in 1:40 except that there the verb is in the imperative, סעו; LXX, however, renders it quite differently. The verb chosen is the more usual one used to render נסע, *ἀπήραμεν*, and the locative is completely in the accusative, *ὁδὸν θάλασσαν ἐρυθράν*; at 1:40 ים סוף became *τὴν ἐπὶ τῆς ἐρυθρᾶς θαλάσσης*. The locative accusative simply means "along the Red Sea road."

The collocation *ὃν τρόπον* is the usual rendering for כאשר (as at 1:21); in fact, it is used to translate כאשר 23 times in Deut, and only once does it occur for אשר. כאשר is translated twice by a *ὡς* construction (1:31 12:22), and once by *ὡς εἰ* (1:44). Odd is the use of *ἐκυκλώσαμεν* "we went around (Mt. Seir)," but it accurately renders MT's נסב; going around or encircling the area may simply be understood as "going about it." Apparently they stayed outside the hill country of Seir, i.e. did not enter the area forbidden them, viz. the southern part of Palestine. Unusual is the articulation of Σηίρ in the book. It occurs only twice (also at v.5) and that in apposition to *τὸ ὄρος*. It occurs unarticulated eight times.

2:2 LXX did not include the direct speech marker, and so hex added *λεγων* under the asterisk at the end of the verse to represent MT.

2:3 Reference made to the encircling of the hill country of Seir reflects v.1b; this wandering about (*κυκλοῦν τὸ ὄρος τοῦτο*) is now to come to an end (*ἱκανούσθω ὑμῖν*; see 1:6). It is presupposed that the Israelites are still on the southern border of the Negeb. The order to turn south is tied to v.3a by the logical particle *οὖν*. What is meant is that since they have wandered about sufficiently they are now to change direction. An A plus Cat group text has *προς* instead of *ἐπί*, making clear thereby that north is the direction towards which they are to move, i.e. *ἐπιστράφητε* "be turned."[1] For לכם 2° see comment at 1:40.

---

1. See THGD 61.

2:4 The preposed modifier *τῷ λαῷ* is in imitation of MT. MT continues with a nominal clause אתם עברים. A participial predicate is commonly rendered in LXX by a present tense, which being inflected for person would make a rendering of אתם unnecessary, but it is usually translated by *ὑμεῖς* to reflect its separate status in the parent text. The present tense is one of incipient action, thus "as for you, you are about to cross (the borders of your brothers)." This is a statement of fact, not a reference to the *ἔντειλαι*, which is to appear only in vv.5—6. The word translated by *τῶν ὁρίων* is גבול, rightly understood as a collective; actually, a plural inflection is rare, occuring only eight times in MT.[2] The "brothers" are identified as *υἱῶν Ἠσαὺ οἱ κατοικοῦσιν ἐν Σηίρ*. The offspring of Esau were the "Edomites in the hill country of Seir" according to Gen 36:9, for which see Note ad loc. The term *Σηίρ* has shifted in its reference, since it now refers to Edom, which lay south of Moab i.e. south of the Wadi el Ḥesa, the Biblical Brook Zered. The term *τὸ ὄρος τὸ Σηίρ* at times refers to the southern part of Palestine and at times to the territory of Edom. Some time during the Persian period the Edomites occupied Idumea in southern Judah; at least by Maccabean times they were firmly settled there.

V.4b describes the reactions of the Edomites to the passing through of the Israelites. They will not only be scared but also very wary — *εὐλαβηθήσονται σφόδρα*. A B *C b s* gloss has added *υμας* after the verb, but this is under the influence of *ὑμᾶς* modifying *φοβηθήσονται*.[3] The verb is unique as a rendering for the Ni of שמר, which is usually rendered by *προσέχω* (only in the Pentateuch). In fact, Deut uses *προσέχω* 10 times (and Gen once, and Exod four times as well as once for the Qal).

2:5 The Hithp of גרה occurs either with מלחמה as in vv.9,24 or without as v.19 and here, but in all cases LXX has *συνάψητε ... (+ εἰς) πόλεμον*.[4] The verb התגרה means "engage in conflict," with or without a word for war or battle modifying it. In Greek *συνάπτω* can also be so used, but it is unusual, so that the presence of *πόλεμον* does not presuppose that the parent text had מלחמה.[5]

---

2. According to BDB sub גבול, over against the singular 186 times.
3. See THGD 119 for the secondary character of the B reading.
4. Aq renders the clause by *μὴ ἐρίσητε ἐν αὐτοῖς* "do not quarrel with them," whereas Sym has *μὴ παροξυνθῆτε πρὸς αὐτούς* "do not irritate them."
5. Cf LS sub voce A.II.1.

The reason given for the divine prohibition is that God will not give them *ἀπὸ τῆς γῆς αὐτῶν*, a partitive construction in imitation of the Hebrew מארצם.[6]

Coordinate to the partitive phrase is *ουδὲ βῆμα ποδός* "not a footstep." What is meant is that not even as much land of Edomite territory as a footstep might cover will be given the Israelites. The parent text is picturesque: עד מדרך כף רגל "even up to the treading of a footsole." Hex has inserted under the asterisk the word *ιχνους* before *ποδός* to represent כף, which is, however, quite unnecessary.

The reason for the exclusion is that "*ἐν κλήρῳ δέδωκα* the hill country of Seir to Esau." The phrase *ἐν κλήρῳ* always modifies the verb *δίδωμι* in Deut,[7] and represents either ירשה (only in Deut) or נחלה. The use of an *ἐν* phrase is not based on the Hebrew, but is a set phrase "by lot" which means "as a portion, an inheritance." The Greek must be understood as equivalent to ירשה נתתי "I have assigned as an inheritance." In MT לעשו is inserted between the two words, whereas LXX has *τῷ Ἠσαύ* following the verb. Hex has rearranged the order to conform to that of MT. For *τὸ Σηίρ* see comment at v.1.

The majority text has inserted *τοις υιοις* before Ἠσαύ, for which there is no counterpart in MT; it has been added to level with *υἱῶν* Ἠσαύ of v.4.[8]

2:6 For MT's תשברו ... בכסף LXX simply used *ἀγοράσατε*, since one obviously bought with money in ancient Alexandria. As might be expected hex has added *αργυριου* under the asterisk[9] to equal the prepositional phrase.[10] Only *O* witnesses have the hex gloss placed in the MT position; an A F V *C''* *s*+ text has *αργυριου* before *βρώματα*, whereas the B *b f*+ text has it after the noun. Cod 963 supports the shorter text of LXX. The translator translated the first verb of the verse as an aorist imperative, i.e. "food buy from them."

In the coordinate clause the purchase of water is ordered, but for this MT uses a different verb, תכרו, also modified by בכסף. To differentiate from *ἀγοράσατε* LXX rendered freely by *μέτρῳ λήμψεσθε* "you shall take by

6. See SS 162.
7. See list 56 in THGD 99.
8. For the originality of LXX see THGD 119.
9. According to Cod M the addition stems from Aq.
10. SS 128 calls the preposition a ב of price, as an extension of the instrumental ב.

measure" — after all, that is how one receives water![11] — to which perforce an *ἀργυρίου* as a genitive of price had to be added, since the verb λαμβάνω does not mean "to buy." Origen, who approached his textual work in a purely quantitative fashion, equated λήμψεσθε with תכרו, and finding no equivalent for *μέτρῳ* placed it under the obelus. It should be noted that the translator does not use an imperative form here, but a future, which in the context has imperatival force.

2:7 This verse outlines the reason for the orders given in vv.5—6. MT gives this as יהוה אלהיך ברכך for which LXX has *κύριος ὁ θεὸς ἡμῶν εὐλόγησέν σε*. The first plural is used throughout vv.8—9, which seemingly influenced the translator to use *ἡμῶν*.[12] A popular A variant has *υμων*, but alternating plural and singular in second person is no improvement. A Byz+ reading has corrected to *σου* which equals MT.[13] The remainder of the verse is consistently in the singular. The plural *τῶν χειρῶν σου* renders ידך, but the plural is regular in LXX,[14] whereas MT vacillates between singular and plural.

The Masoretes vocalized ידע as third person with reference to Yahweh, i.e. "(Yahweh) knows," but LXX has understood the word as an imperative *διάγνωθι*,[15] either vocalizing the word as a free infinitive or an imperative. Its modifier is *πῶς διῆλθες* "how you crossed" for the neutral לכתך "your going, travelling."[16] LXX has amplified "this great desert" by *καὶ τὴν φοβεράν*, a gloss based on 1:19. Origen recognized its absence in MT and placed the words under the obelus. In the tradition the majority B V text has *εκεινην* for *ταύτην*, but this is also dependent on 1:19.[17]

The translator realized that זה was not used here as a demonstrative pronoun (as הזה immediately before it was), but as an adverb modifying a period of time (comp 8:2,4) and tried to convey this freely by *ἰδού* (though LXX omits זה ארבעים שנה at v.4). In any event, both texts are clear that the verse

11. Sym rendered תכרו by *ἀντλήσετε* (retroverted from Syh). Sym apparently thought of the homophonous root כרה "to dig," for which see Vulg *heurietis*.
12. See the discussion in THGD 108.
13. The Others all have *σου*.
14. See list no.21 in THDG 92; see also Tov 270.
15. Sym also understood it as an imperative as his *ἐννοήθητι* "consider, reflect" shows.
16. SS Inf 23 calls this a free translation.
17. See THGD 113.

divides at this point, the temporal expression modifying the nominal clause which follows, *κύριος ὁ θεός σου μετὰ σοῦ*;[18] this clause is then explicated by *οὐκ ἐπεδεήθης ῥήματος*. What is meant is that God's continual presence is demonstrated by the fact that you did not want for anything.

2:8 The opening verb in MT, נעבר, is modified by four מן phrases which have been variously interpreted by LXX. The first one, מאת אחינו, is realized as an accusative modifier: (*παρήλθομεν*) *τοὺς ἀδελφοὺς ἡμῶν*, and the second one, מדרך, by *παρὰ τὴν ὁδόν*. LXX takes the next two as modifying דרך, i.e "the way ... from Ailon and from Gasion Gaber," which is a possible interpretation of the Hebrew. The LXX understanding of the last pair modifying "road" is a sensible one, and it explicates the notion of v.3 *ἐπὶ βορρᾶν*; the journey is understood as being along the Araba road from Ailon and Gasion Gaber northward towards Moab.[19]

Both Ailon and Gasion Gaber were located at or near modern Aqaba at the head of the Gulf of Aqaba. The name Αἰλών occurs only here for אילת; whether it was influenced by the Classical Αἴλανα is doubtful. It is variously spelled in the tradition as *αιλωμ* (by N—M) confusion, *λαιων* (Α—Λ), *αιδων* (Λ—Δ), *αιδωμ*, *εδων*, *ελων*, *ελωμ*, *ιαλων* (by transposition), and changed to *ανατολων* in Byz, and in hex to *ηλαθ*. The transcription Γασιών for עצין is based on the /ġ/ phoneme represented by the grapheme ע. It showed much confusion in the tradition, particularly in the vowels, producing *γαισιων*, *γισιων*, *γισων*, *γαισειων*, *γεσσων*, *γεισων*, *γησων*, *γαεσιων*, but also *γεδσιων*, *σιγων*, *αισιων* and *εταιων*. Γάβερ remained more constant, only the *d* text by palaeographic confusion producing *γαμερ*, and individual mss attesting to *γαβηρ*, *βαγερ*.

The last clause represents two coordinate clauses in MT. The participle *ἐπιστρέψαντες* was chosen as critical text rather than the majority reading *επιστραφεντες* in view of its support by the oldest witness, cod B, with the passive variant attributed to the influence of v.1; either reading is sensible; cf comment at v.1. The main verb is again *παρήλθομεν* which an F *oII* variant

---

18. For the use of *ἰδού* as an emphatic see Bauer sub voce 1 b ε.
19. Sym interpreted the phrase as *ἀπὸ τῆς ὁδοῦ τῆς ἀοικητῆς ἀπὸ* Αἰλάθ (retroverted from Syh).

has attempted to improve in view of the northerly direction presupposed, by its *ανεβημεν*.

2:9 The verb צור means "to constrict, tie up," hence, "besiege." LXX uses *ἐχθραίνετε* "(do not) treat inimically, as an enemy," a translation used in LXX only here and in v.19. Since the coordinate verbal construction is *συνάψητε ... πόλεμον*, for which see comment at v.5, the translator probably interpreted correctly. Note that LXX uses the plural for the verse instead of MT's singular. The Greek has also interpreted את מואב as the people of Moab, i.e. as *τοῖς* Μωαβίταις, which is of course what "Moab" means. After all, in the next clause Moab is referred to by בם.

ἀπό is used in a partitive sense, thus "any of their land."[20] For *ἐν κλήρῳ* see comment at v.5. For the Moabites as *υἱοῖς Λώτ* see the story at Gen 19:36—37. *τὴν* 'Αροήρ represents את ער. The city of Ar occurs also at vv.18, 29 where it is also transcribed as 'Αροήρ. The name only occurs elsewhere in MT at Num 21:15 where LXX has Ἤρ, and at 21:28 where it was misread as עד (i.e. rendered by *ἕως*). It also occurs at Isa 15:1 but only in MT and not in LXX. The popular B 963 reading *σηιρ* both here and at v.18 cannot possibly be correct in view of v.5 (Seir was given to Esau).[21] LXX presupposes that ער and ערער are the same; cf 2:36 3:12 4:48.

2:10 Vv.10—12 constitute an antequarian note on the former inhabitants of the regions traversed. The earlier inhabitants were *οἱ* 'Ομμίν for the Hebrew האמים. The *—in* ending may well be due to Aramaic influence, since that is the Aramaic plural inflectional ending. Note also 'Ραφαΐν for רפאים in the next verse. The Greek understood the Ommin as dwelling *ἐπ' αὐτης*, i.e. on the land; בה of MT must refer to ארצו of v.9 (*τῆς γῆς* in LXX).

These people are called a people great and numerous and *ἰσχυρόν* as the 'Ενακίμ. MT has רם "tall" here, which hardly equals *ἰσχυρόν* "strong," and the equation is actually unique in OT. One suspects the influence of 9:14 where God said to Moses "and I will make you into a nation *μέγα καὶ ἰσχυρὸν καὶ πολύ*." In the Pentateuch ענקים occurs only here in ch.2 (vv.10,11,21), but as בני ענק it appears at 9:2, where LXX has *υἱοὺς* 'Ενάκ. In Num 13:33

20. See SS 162.
21. For the variant as palaeographically explicable see THGD 143.

the same phrase occurs, but it is omitted (because of homoiot) in LXX. In the same chapter הענק occurs (vv.22,28) but in a bound phrase with ילידי, and again it is transliterated as Ἐνάκ. In the tradition a B V+ text has *ισχυοντες* for ἰσχυρόν and *f* has *ισχυροτερον*, but these are obviously secondary.[22]

2:11 Ῥαφαΐν are also mentioned in v.20 where they are equated with the Ζομζομμίν, and in 3:11,13, according to which Og the king of Bashan was a remnant of the Rephain. Reputedly they were οἱ γίγαντες who were in Astaroth Karnaim, Gen 14:5; comp Deut 3:11. In the tradition Ῥαφαΐν is misspelled, aside from itacisms, as *ραφα(ε)ιμ* due to Hebrew influence (probably hex), as *ραφειν* in *f*, and as *ραφαειρ*. The future tense can hardly be taken as prospective, but must be potential, i.e. "the Raphain may be reckoned — even they — as the Enakim." For ὥσπερ Ἀνακίμ see comment at v.10.

In the second clause the verb is in the imperfect which is sensible, since customary action in past time is intended: "they were calling them Ommin."

2:12 An antequarian note on Seir parallel to that on the land of Moab. In earlier times the Chorrite inhabited Seir. LXX uses the singular ὁ Χορραῖος instead of the plural as MT, but it is taken as a collective since pronominal references to them (αὐτούς, ἀυτῶν) are in the plural; cf v.22 where MT does use the singular. In the tradition the name is often spelled with a single *rho*. Vowel change produced *χερραιος* and *χωραιως*, and one ms mistakenly prefixed an *alpha*, thus *αχορραιος*.

LXX correctly understood the verb in the second clause, יירשום, as an old preterite form which the context demands, rendering it by ἀπώλεσαν (αὐτούς). The translator rightly understood the Hebrew lexeme in the sense of "dispossess," hence "destroyed, killed." For οἱ υἱοὶ Ἠσαύ see comment at v.8. The coordinate verbs ἀπώλεσαν καὶ ἐξέτρεψαν (for יירשום וישמידום) are synonyms and simply emphasize the destruction: "destroyed them and rooted them out."

The ὃν τρόπον construction belies the proleptic setting of Moses' speech as a pre-Conquest occasion, since it describes Israel's action in past tense, i.e. the עשה of MT. LXX rendered לארץ by an accusative τὴν γῆν. In modifica-

22. See the discussion in THGD 133.

tion of ἐποίησεν it serves as an accusative of specification, i.e. "as Israel did with respect to the land." That this was the land τῆς κληρονομίας αὐτοῦ is typical of Deut,[23] as is the fact ἔδωκεν κύριος αὐτοῖς.[24] LXX follows MT exactly in the number for pronouns referring to ישראל; accordingly LXX has "the land of its (αὐτοῦ) inheritance, but "which the Lord gave αὐτοῖς." The *C''* *b s*+ tradition has leveled this by changing αὐτοῦ to αυτων, thereby attaining a consistent plural.[25]

2:13 The use of νῦν οὖν is rare in Deut; in fact, it only occurs elsewhere at v.24, where it has no counterpart in MT; here it represents עתה, though Sam has ועתה. In Gen the collocation regularly stood for ועתה; cf Note at Gen 27:43. Over against Gen the Deut translator usually translates ועתה by καὶ νῦν (five times) and only at 10:22 does he change to νυνὶ δέ. Since v.13 takes up where v.8 had left off, νῦν οὖν is a fitting introduction: "so now, now then."

In the place of ועבר לכם LXX has καὶ ἀπάρατε ὑμεῖς καὶ παραπορεύεσθε. This may reflect the Sam text which has סעו ועבר לכם, though LXX does begin with a conjunction; furthermore, ὑμεῖς which is presumably intended to reflect לכם (for which see comment at 1:7), follows ἀπάρατε rather than the last verb. What LXX says is "get up and pull stakes, even you, and cross over." Since MT did not have an equivalent for ὑμεῖς in its present position hex placed it under the obelus. Actually καὶ ἀπάρατε should also have been included under the obelus since MT has only two verbs. For τὴν φάραγγα Ζάρεδ see comment on Σηίρ at v.4. This was the unofficial boundary between Moab to the north and the Edomites to the south. In the tradition it also appears as ζαρε, αρεδ, ζερεδ, ζαδερ (*C''*), ζαρατ (B *b*) and ζαρεθ,[26] and even as γαζερ, ραζεδ and ρεθ.

2:14 LXX uses the same verb which had occurred in v.13 to render the root עבר to translate הלכנו here, παρεπορεύθημεν, and then has παρήλθομεν to render עברנו, which had been used in v.13 similarly for נעבר. The translator apparently wanted to follow the usage of v.13 rather than the Hebrew. For

23. That the land was inherited is clear from lists 13—14 and 56 in THGD 90,99.
24. See list 10 in THGD 88—89.
25. Sym also changed to αὐτῶν, whereas Aq Theod retain αὐτοῦ.
26. For the originality of Ζάρεδ both here and in v.14 see THGD 143.

Καδῆς Βαρνή see comment at 1:19. Syntactically the main clause is nominal with αἱ ἡμέραι as subject and τριάκοντα καὶ ὀκτὼ ἔτη as predicate.

The second ἕως οὗ clause is only connected to the main clause as a clause modifier, i.e. the days were 38 years, viz., until that .... Here MT has עד plus an infinitive, as in v.15.[27] Its verb is διέπεσεν which occurs only three times in the OT for the root תמם (also in vv.15 and 16), an odd translation since διαπίπτω means "to fall through, away or apart," whereas the Hebrew intends to convey the notion that the entire generation of warriors had "come to an end," i.e. "perished."[28] I would understand the clause to mean "until the entire generation of warriors had fallen (i.e. had died)." The verb is then modified by the prepositional phrase ἐκ τῆς παρεμβολῆς. The tradition found this modification lexically awkward, and tried to smooth out the text under the influence of v.16, adding either αποθνησκοντων modifying ἀνδρῶν as Byz, or a nominative αποθνησκοντες as a popular A B gloss.[29]

The tradition also had a problem with κύριος αὐτοῖς in the concluding καθότι clause. B *b*+ not only changed κύριος to ο θεος, but also changed the word order. A change in word order is also witnessed by 963(vid) and *f n*, whereas the popular variant used the double name κυριος ο θεος.[30]

2:15 For יד יהוה LXX has ἡ χεὶρ τοῦ θεοῦ. There is no obvious reason for changing the divine name to τοῦ θεοῦ. It does put the stress on the divine power being responsible for destroying them out of the camp, the αὐτούς referring to the warriors mentioned in v.14.[31] As in v.14 ἐκ renders מקרב, and in both cases hex has added μεσου to represent the second element קרב, the asterisk being attested in v.15 as well. For διέπεσαν see comment at v.14. A popular variant reads the Classical second aorist διεπεσον, but Deut uses only the Hellenistic inflection for this verb.

27. See SS Inf 113.
28. Aq rendered תם literally by ἐτελειωθῇ "was made complete, perfect." Sym had ἕως ἂν ἀναλωθῇ (retroverted from Syh). For the Aq reading see comment at SS Inf 199—200.
29. That these are secondary is clear from THGD 56.
30. See the discussion in THGD 128—129.
31. See Appositives 1.5.3.

2:16 καὶ ἐγενήθη introduces a temporal conditional clause, of which v.16 is the protasis, and v.17, the apodosis; for this usage see comment at 1:3. For διέπεσαν see comment at v.14. The marked infinitive למות modifies תמו, but an infinitive modifying διέπεσαν would be rather peculiar; accordingly, the translator made excellent sense by choosing a participle ἀποθνήσκοντες, which modifies the subject οἱ ἄνδρες. At v.14 מקרב was translated simply by ἐκ, but here both morphemes are represented in LXX as ἐκ μέσου.[32]

In the tradition a popular K reading has the long form επειδη for ἐπεί, but this is merely a free variant, which is never used in Deut. As in v.15 the Classical second aorist διεπεσον obtains for the Hellenistic inflection as a popular reading as well.

2:18 The nominal construction אתה עבר is as usual rendered by a present tense verb preceded by an otiose pronoun: σὺ παραπορεύῃ; it is best understood as a present of intention, "as for you, you are going to pass by." The verb is modified by two accusatives; τὰ ὅρια Μωάβ is the direct modifier; they are going to "pass by the borders of Moab," and the second one, τὴν 'Αροήρ, is an accusative specifying the particular point at which they are to pass along the borders. For τὴν 'Αροήρ see comment at v.9.[33]

2:19 The orders addressed to the people concerning the Ammonites are in the singular in MT for v.19 but then change at v.24 into the plural for the opening imperatives. LXX is plural throughout v.19 except for σοι modifying δῶ, but see comment at v.24 for a further change in number.

For קרבת מול "you shall come near in front of," LXX has προσάξετε ἐγγύς, but ἐγγύς glosses the verb, and is hardly a rendering of the preposition,[34] though the orders practically rewrite those of v.9, which see. Here, however, they pertain to the υἱῶν 'Αμμάν rather than to the Moabites. The "land of the Ammanites" lay north of M ab, with the river Arnon, modern Wadi Mojib, separating the two territories. The name 'Αμμάν represents an old vocalization which in Hebrew changed to עמון; some witnesses, *C''* *b* *s*+, have revised the spelling to αμμων so as to equal MT, but the spelling with /-

32. Aq illustrates his extreme literalism by his ἀπὸ ἐγκάτου.
33. See also THGD 143.
34. Not so Aq who rendered literally: ἐγγίσεις ἐναντίον.

-an/ is original. The basis for God's not allowing the Israelites to attack the Ammanites is the narrative of Gen 19:30—38, more specifically v.38.

2:20 Vv.20—23 interrupt the narrative with another antequarian notice (see also vv.10—12). For Ῥαφαΐν and λογισθήσεται see discussion at v.11 and comp especially 3:13. In contrast to v.11, where אף הם was rendered literally by *καὶ οὗτοι*, here אף הוא is changed to *καὶ γάρ*. What is meant is that their former occupation of Ammanite territory is the reason for its potentially being reckoned as *γῆ* Ῥαφαΐν. Misspellings of Ῥαφαΐν beyond those given in v.11 are limited to errors found in only one or two mss (except for *ραφασιν* found in four mss); these consist of *ραφιειμ*, *ραφιειν*, *ρεφαειν*, *ραφασι*, *ραφαραειν*, *ραφαει*, *ραφοι*, *ροφαειν* and *ραφαεις*.

Unusual is the change in word order from רפאים ישבו בה to *ἐπ' αὐτῆς κατῴκουν οἱ* Ῥαφαΐν, which constitutes LXX's attempt to parallel v.12 "in Seir there dwelt the Chorrite." This misled Origen into thinking that בה had no equivalent in LXX and so hex added *εν αυτη* after the imperfect verb. The majority text (hex?) had also transposed the verb and its subject so as to equal MT. The choice of an imperfect verb was excellent, since they used to be dwelling there *πρότερον*.

The masculine plural gentilic העמנים is rare, occurring only four times in OT, and LXX renders it correctly. MT vocalizes the name in accordance with the old Canaanite shift of "ā" to "ō," but LXX's vocalization is the older one and is quite legitimate. Only at 2Esdr 14:7 (=Neh 4:1) does LXX render the word as here (at 3Reg 11:5 *υἱῶν* Ἀμμάν calls the MT reading into question, and at 2Chr 26:8 *οἱ* Μιναῖοι seems to presuppose a different parent text). The usual designation is בני עמון, *οἱ υἱοὶ* Ἀμμάν. The Ζομζομμίν as the earlier inhabitants of Ammanite land is referred to only here, and nothing further is known of them. As might be expected the spelling received rough handling in the tradition; in fact, only four witnesses attest to the original spelling. Misspellings based on nasal confusion include *-ιμ*, *-ειμ* and *ζονζ-*; syncopation produced *ζωμμειν*, *ζομνειν*, *ζομφειμ*, *ζομμιν*, *ζουμμειν*; aphaeresis created *ομμειν*; dissimilation is seen in *ζομζομβειμ*, *ζομζομφειν*, *ζωμζομβειν*, *ζομζομπι*, *ζομζομπει*; vowel change appears in *ζαμζ-*, *ζηζ-*, *ζοζομεν*; assimilation of nasal, in *ζοζ-*, *ζηζ-*; confusion of *ζ* — *χ* in *ζοχομ(μ)ειν*, *ζοχαμμειν*, and some odd balls *οοζζομμην* and *νοζομμιν*.

The simplex verb *ὀνομάζουσιν* is changed into the compound *επονομαζουσιν* in the majority of witnesses, but the compound is due to the influence of v.11.[35]

2:21 V.21a in MT repeats v.10b exactly; see comment ad loc. LXX, however, has a different rendering for רם; instead of *ἰσχυρόν* it has *δυνώτερον* here.[36] A popular B gloss has added *υμων*, being impelled by the comparative to add a genitive pronoun, whereas the Byz text voided the difficulty by changing the word to *δυνατον*. The lectio difficilior is clearly original text.[37] The antecedent of *αυτούς* must be *οἱ Ἐνακίμ*, and of (*προσώπου*) *αὐτῶν* is Ῥαφαΐν, and of the last *αυτῶν*, *οἱ Ἐνακίμ*. This would be neatly clarified by interpreting *καὶ ἀπώλεσεν* as "whom (the Lord) destroyed."

The verb *ἀπώλεσεν* is modified by *ἀπὸ προσώπου αὐτῶν* which literally renders מפניהם. That the preposition *ἀπό* is original is also clear from this translator's preference for prepositional modifiers cognate with the prepositional element in the verb. A B *C'*' *s z*+ variant *προ* represents an inner Greek stylistic improvement.[38] The remainder of the verse in MT reads "and they dispossessed them and dwelt in their place." LXX has no equivalent for "them" and hex has supplied an *αυτους* to represent the pronominal suffix. In the tradition a majority B gloss, *εως ημερας ταυτης*, was added at the end. There is no basis in MT for it, and it was obviously borrowed from v.22 where עד היום הזה does occur in exactly the same context.[39]

2:22 Difficult is the rendering of the singular verbs עשה and השמיד as plurals. In MT Yahweh of v.21 is the subject of both, but LXX has plural verbs. It should be noted that the verse also continues with plural verbs: ויירשו וישבו תחתם as in v.21. That change to plural is internally quite justified in MT, since מפניהם immediately precedes and the pronominal suffix is the antecedent subject. The lack of a stated antecedent for *ἐποίησαν* was felt in the tradition. Both *εποιησα* and *εποιησεν* obtain, with the latter well supported by A F M *oI*

35. See the discussion in THGD 55.
36. Aq translates by λαὸς *μέγας καὶ* πολὺς *καὶ* ὑψηλός; i.e. רם is literally rendered by "high."
37. See also the discussion in THGD 56.
38. See THGD 61.
39. See THGD 119.

d t+. The second verb was also changed in the Byz text to the singular to agree with MT, but the more difficult text must be original. Another attempt at relieving the text is seen in the popular V variant which changed *τοῖς υἱοῖς* (Ἠσαύ) to *οι υιοι*. This had a real advantage, since it made the sons of Esau the subject of both verbs.

It is clear from v.12 that the sons of Esau had annihilated the Chorrite, which makes it obvious that the translator intended *τοῖς υἱοῖς* Ἠσαύ as the subject of *ἐξέτριψαν*. This then fits the historical picture consistent with what was said in v.12. But what about the plural *ἐποίησαν*? To the translator God had taken care of the Enakim, but the other peoples had been destroyed and their land taken over by still other peoples. The translator clearly had to avoid the singular of MT since that would make God the subject, so he chose the lesser evil of an indefinite plural verb. I would translate "as was done to the descendants of Esau, just as they had destroyed ...." For the remainder of the verse see comments at v.12.

2:23 V.23a is a pendant nominative which is then pronominally referred to in the main clause as *αὐτούς* and *αὐτῶν*. The Εὐαῖοι—עוים occurs only here in Deut (and elsewhere only in Jos 13:3 where העוים is coordinated with פלשתים, but in LXX *τῷ* Εὐαίῳ is coordinated with the five *σατραπίαις* of the Philistines). They are represented as dwelling *ἐν* Ἀσηρὼθ *ἕως* Γάζης. The name Ἀσηρώθ is peculiar, since in MT the masculine plural חצרים obtains; the Greek presupposes חצרות, a place name as at 1:1 which, however, LXX translates as Αὐλῶν; cf comment ad loc; comp also Num 11:35. The noun חצר can have either masculine or feminine plural inflectional endings and means "enclosure, court, unwalled settlement," thus "villages." LXX, however, took it as a place name; since it along with Gaza[40] determined the extent of the area occupied, it is presupposed that it lay in southwestern Palestine, i.e. the area later settled by the Philistines. In the tradition B plus two mss read *ασηδωθ*; this has nothing to do with Ashdod as BHS would suggest, but is due to confusion of *δ* and *ρ*.

The main clause is introduced by *καί* with no support in MT. In MT the subject of the verb is כפתרים who were emigrating מכפתור. Caphtor has tradi-

40. Which Aq transliterates as Ἀζά.

tionally been identified as Crete, but LXX identifies the place as Καππαδοκία and its inhabitants as οἱ Καππάδοκες. Wainwright with much learning has argued that the LXX identification is correct, viz. that Caphtor was not an island, but was in Asia Minor.[41] According to LXX (at Amos 9:7: τοὺς ἀλλοφύλους ἐκ Καππαδοκίας) the Philistines came from Cappadocia and so were originally Cappadocians.

2:24 With v.24 the address of Moses resumes from v.19. For νῦν οὖν see comment at v.13. MT connects only the third imperative ועברו by means of a conjunction; LXX connects all three with καί. For the first two imperatives see comments at v.13; the third one has παρέλθατε rather than the παραπορεύεσθε of v.13, but they are synonyms. A majority A F M V reading has the Classical παρελθετε, but LXX uses the Hellenistic form throughout the book. LXX also added ὑμεῖς after the verb, which has no justification from MT, but see the arbitrary nature of its use in v.13. For the Arnon see comment at v.19.

The next clause is introduced by ἰδού, a regular element used to call attention. Its usual equivalent in MT is הנה (Gen 83 times; Exod 25; Lev 21; Num 19 and Deut eight), but here MT has the imperative ראה which is quite rare in the Pentateuch (three times each in Gen and Exod, and four in Deut); see also v.31 11:26 30:15.[42] The divine promise of successful conquest is put into the perfect with fine feeling. Though the defeat of Seon is still future, the divine intent has been resolved on and the certainty of victory is absolute; God has spoken: παραδέδωκα εἰς τὰς χεῖράς σου. A *C'' s* variant has the aorist, but this can only be a mistake. Over against MT the prepositional phrase has the plural noun. Whenever LXX uses "into the hand(s)" to modify the verb παραδίδωμι it is never singular but always plural (see comment at 1:27), so this has no textual significance whatsoever.[43]

Seon, king of Heshbon, and his territory constitute an enclave within nominal Ammanite territory — note that Seon is called τὸν Ἀμορραῖον, and his land is therefore forfeit. Ἑσεβών is often spelled as εσσεβων through dittography. Other spelling errors are εσευων, επεβων, εσερων and των αβων.

41. G.A.Wainwright, Caphtor-Cappadocia, VT 6(1956), 199—209.
42. The count is based on HR.
43. See on this point SS 136.

LXX follows the pattern in number set by MT throughout with plural imperatives in v.24a, and singular forms *σου*, *ἐνάρχου*[44] and *σύναπτε*. For *σύναπτε ... πόλεμον* see comment at v.5.

2:25 LXX follows Sam's החל rather than the first person אחל of MT, again using the present imperative *ἐνάρχου*.[45] So the Israelites are ordered: "begin to place your terror and your fear upon all the nations which are underneath the sky." The change to an imperative is curious, since one expects God to be the agent; see 11:25. The infinitive *δοῦναι* is a calque for the Hebrew תת, which can mean both "give" or "place, set." So the people themselves (rather than God as MT) are to create terror and fear. The genitives in *τὸν τρόμον σου καὶ τὸν φόβον σου* are of course objective; it is the terror and fear of you which you are to impose. Note also that LXX read כל with העמים rather than with השמים as in MT.[46]

MT ties v.25b directly to the first part of the verse by its אשר, thus "the nations ... which will hear ... tremble and ...." LXX also uses an indefinite relative, but by using the nominative starts a new sentence, i.e. "whoever on hearing your name shall be troubled and undergo pains because of you." For "your name" MT has a cognate שמעך "report of you," but this need not presuppose a parent שמך. The word *ὄνομα* can mean "reputation, fame," as e.g. at Num 14:15. *ταραχθήσονται* translates רגזו somewhat loosely; the Hebrew means "they shall tremble." The last verb, חלו, often refers to the pains suffered in childbirth, and the use of *ὠδῖνας* is appropriate.[47]

2:26 Comp Num 21:21. The use of *πρέσβεις* to translate מלאכים is rare, occurring elsewhere only in Num 21:21 22:5, and is probably due to the parallel passage in Num. Just where the wilderness of קדמות lay is not certain, though it would probably be near the northern border of Moab, i.e. near the Wadi Mojib. Κεδμώθ was variously spelled in the tradition, either in two syllables or in three. For the former *κεδμωδ* (by dental confusion), *καδμωθ* and *κοδμωθ* (by vowel change), *κελμωθ* (Δ—Λ confusion in *z*), nasal infixation for

44. Aq prefers the simplex form *ἄρξαι*.
45. Aq follows MT with *ἄρξομαι*; cf f.n. at v.24.
46. Kenn 109 also read כל before העמים.
47. Aq translates the verb by *φρίξουσιν* "they will shiver, tremble," which is unusual; Aq normally uses *ὠδίνω*.

κεδμωνθ, and *κεδωμθ* by transposition. Three syllable realization reflects MT,[48] and include *κεδαμωθ* in Cod B,[49] *καιδαμωθ* (b), *κηδεμωθ* (*t*), *κηδεθμων* (*d*), *μακεδμωθ* (*n*), and hex *καδημωθ*. LXX interprets the second modifier for אשלח, viz. דברי שלום, sensibly by means of a dative of accompaniment, *λόγοις εἰρηνικοῖς*.

2:27 LXX follows MT in using the singular first person throughout the verse as over against its parallel Num 21:22. MT uses the long form אעברה "let me pass by, through,"[50] which LXX translates by a future showing volition, "I would pass through."[51] The coordinate futures, *πορεύσομαι* and *ἐκκλινῶ*, are different, and simply show intention.[52] MT repeats בדרך, presumably for emphasis.[53] In any event LXX wisely translates it only once. In the tradition *πορεύσομαι* is changed to *παρελευσομαι* in a well supported B F V text, but it is an error based on its occurrence in the preceding clause.[54] The final clause makes clear that the preceding clause does mean that Israel will not deviate from the main road. *δεξιὰ οὐδὲ ἀριστερά* are terminal accusatives showing direction towards which, modifying a verb of movement.

2:28 The prepositional phrase בכסף is twice well rendered by a genitive of price: *ἀργυρίου*.[55] The form *ἀποδώσῃ* is rare;[56] for LXX it only occurs in Deut (four times; see also 14:20,24). It occurs twice in this verse, but for different verbs: תשבר and תתן. Both ואכלתי and ושתיתי express result: "so that I may eat, ... drink," but LXX renders word for word by coordinate clauses *καὶ φάγομαι* and *καὶ πίομαι*, i.e. the syntactic patterns are Hebraic.

The last clause is a רק clause in MT: "only let me pass through on foot." LXX takes the particle as an exceptive particle presupposing a negative; *πλὴν ὅτι* means "except that," i.e. "(I will do nothing) except that I will cross

48. The Three all witness to Καδημώθ.
49. See THGD 143—144 for its secondary character.
50. See GK 108c for the cohortative use here.
51. See Porter 419—439.
52. *Idem* 424—425.
53. GK 123e speaks of "repetition to express an exceptional or at least superfine quality" and translates "only along by the high way"; comp also 133k.
54. See THGD 133.
55. See SS 128.
56. See Bl—D 95.1.

over on foot." For the nature of the tense see comment on *παρελεύσομαι* at v.27. The dative *τοῖς ποσίν* is peculiar Greek; it translates ברגלי though disregarding the suffix,[57] and can only be understood through the Hebrew meaning "on foot." The majority text, probably hex, makes the Greek even worse by adding *μου* to equal the Hebrew suffix.

2:29 The Greek is a literal rendering of MT. The first part is a *καθώς* clause explicating the request of vv.27—28. For Ἀροήρ see comment at v.9. V.29b is a *ἕως ἄν* with subjunctive clause indicating not only how long the Israelites wanted to be in Seon's land, but also why. What they were intending was to cross the Jordan. In the concluding relative clause the text changes to the plural "our God ... to us," in exact imitation of MT. In the tradition the *f* text begins the plural already in the *ἕως ἄν* clause with its *παρελθωμεν*, whereas a B+ text omits *ἄν*, which is contrary to LXX usage. Nowhere in Deut does LXX ever fail to include *ἄν* in a *ἕως* clause with a subjunctive.[58]

2:30 The phrase *δι' αὐτοῦ* modifies the infinitive *παρελθεῖν*; both it and the Hebrew בו must mean "through him," i.e. through his territory. One might well have expected בה, since *δι αυτης* refers to *γῆν*, but both texts have the masculine.

The reason for Seon's unwillingness is expressed in a *ὅτι* clause; it was due to divine interference. MT changes over to the second singular at this point, but LXX continues with the first plural of the last clause of v.29 with *ὁ θεὸς ἡμῶν*. The Lord our God hardened his spirit and encouraged his heart; what is meant is that God promoted within Seon the determination to withstand any crossing of his borders.

MT has למען תתו "in order to deliver him" with יהוה אלהיך as the subject continued from the main clause, and with the suffix as object. LXX, however, understood the suffix as the subject, and accordingly used a passive verb: *ἵνα παραδοθῇ* "that he might be delivered." In any event, it was the Lord your God who was responsible for it. For *εἰς τὰς χεῖράς σου* see comment at v.24. Note that LXX changes to a second person singular at this point. The phrase כיום is adequately rendered by *ὡς ἐν τῇ ἡμέρᾳ ταύτῃ* "as in this

57. See SS 101,121,127.
58. See THGD 124.

day." The tradition was troubled by the consecution ὡς ἐν and the 963 *C*'' *s*+ text omitted ὡς, but this is an attempt at improving the style, not as BHS = ביום; comp v.25 where ἐν τῇ ἡνέρᾳ ταύτῃ rendered היום הזה.

2:31 Vv.31—36 show the implementation of v.30b. The Lord begins by assuring Moses that he has begun to redeem his promise to give the people land. The perfect ἦργμαι shows that he has initiated the process of handing over Seon. LXX, however, follows Sam in describing Seon as *βασιλέα* Ἑσεβὼν *τὸν* Ἀμορραῖον as at v.24, which see. For *ἰδού* rendering ראה see comment at v.24.

In contrast to v.24 where a present inflection was used LXX now uses aorists: *ἔναρξαι κληρονομῆσαι*, but following the pattern of imperative plus infinitive. The use of the compound *ἔναρχαι* is simply a variant to the simplex *ἦργμαι*, both rendering the verb חלל. The Hebrew equivalent for the infinitive is a cognate expression רש לרשת, which LXX shortens as a single infinitive. Origen added a dative noun, *κληρονομια*, to represent רש, understanding *κληρονομῆσαι* to be the rendering for לרשת, which in view of the translation of v.24 is not at all certain. The Byz text has changed the aorist to the present infinitive *κληρονομειν*, but the tense of the imperative influenced the translator to continue with the aorist.

2:32 The majority text has added *βασιλεα εσεβων* to Seon, but this has no equivalent in MT and is clearly ex par;[59] it is significant that 963 follows MT in not supporting the descriptive title. The battle was joined at Ἰάσα which represents יהצה. The site has not been identified, though the general area in which it was located is clear; cf Bible Dictionaries sub *Jahaz.* In the tradition it has been misspelled in various ways: *ιασεα*, *ιεσσα*, *ισσα*, *σιασεα*, *σιασσα*, *σιεσσα*, but most witnesses have *ιασσα*, which cannot possibly be original since the final *he* represents the postpositional unstressed directional suffix.[60]

2:33 *παρέδωκεν* is modified as in v.31 by *πρὸ προσώπου* plus pronoun. The verb is often modified by *εἰς τὰς χεῖρας* plus a genitive (e.g. 1:27 2:30 3:2,3), which has led to its inclusion either as a doublet or as substitute in pop-

59. See THGD 56.
60. See the discussion in THGD 62.

ular variant texts, but other ancient witnesses all follow MT and the variants are to be judged as being ex par.

The victory was complete; the Israelites smote not only him but also *τοὺς υἱοὺς αὐτοῦ*, which supports the Qere בניו rather than the singular Kethib בנו "his son"; this is also consonant with all other ancient witnesses.

2:34 For נלכד LXX has *ἐκρατήσαμεν* "overcome, conquer," which is an unusual equivalent in LXX, occurring only four times (also at 3:4 Jdg 8:12 Hab 1:10). In fact, the usual equivalent in the OT is λαμβάνω or a compound of it.[61] It is modified by *πασῶν τῶν πόλεων*, i.e. without an *αυτου*, for the Hebrew את כל עריו in spite of the fact that all Greek witnesses do add *αυτου* (except one ms which has *αυτων*); in fact, only the Old Latin translation supports the LXX text. It is of course fine Greek to lack a genitive pronoun, since it is fully obvious from the context that the cities are those of Seon. This is a good example of how important it is to examine all the evidence. It would not have occurred to anyone to question *αυτου* as original LXX were it not for the fact that Syh has the word under the asterisk, thereby indicating that Origen's parent text did not have the pronoun. Its addition was of course not solely dependent on hex, since it would easily be added ad sensum as well.

The next clause has *ἐξωλεθρεύσαμεν* "we rooted out, destroyed" as translation of נחרם "we put under the extermination ban," an equation which had occurred at Exod 22:20(19), which see, and it also occurs twice at 3:6.[62] The verb חרם occurs three times with a cognate free infinitive in Deut. Twice (13:16 20:17) it is rendered by *ἀναθέματι ἀναθεματιεῖτε*, and once (7:2) by *ἀφανισμῷ ἀφανιεῖς*. Outside the Pentateuch it is more commonly translated by the root *ἐξολεθρεύω* (e.g. eight times in Jos, and seven in 1Reg), and the specific notion of placing under the extermination ban is often disregarded. In fact, the verb *ἀναθεματίζω* occurs in the Pentateuch outside the two Deut passages only twice (Num 21:2,3) as a rendition of the verb חרם. The verb is modified by *πᾶσαν πόλιν ἑξῆς* "every city in succession." LXX had apparently interpreted the Hebrew מתם as derived from the root תמם thus "completely, in total." The Hebrew is indeed peculiar. The preposition את

61. Aq has *κατελαβόμεθα* here. Sym has *ἐπορθήσαμεν* "we destroyed, plundered."
62. Aq rendered it literally by *ἀνεθεματίσαμεν* "we anathematized," i.e. put under the ban of extermination.

usually governs a definite noun, but עיר is indefinite. Then the "men and the women and the children" simply explicates what נחרם את כל עיר consists of, thus "we rooted out every city of men, women and children."

Since מתם was misunderstood, the second and third items are modified resp by *αὐτῶν*. It should be noted that grammatically *αὐτῶν* 1° and 2° have *πόλεων* as antecedent, and the LXX may well have intended its major cut after *ἑξῆς*. This would mean that "their women and their children" do not modify *ἐξολεθρεύσαμεν*, but rather *κατελίπομεν*. This would mean moving the comma after *αὐτῶν* 2° to follow *ἑξῆς*. Thus "their women and their children we did not leave alive." This differs from the Masoretic tradition which has the ethnach at והטף.

MT has a construction in the last clause which is only freely rendered by LXX. MT has לא השארנו שריד "not did we leave a remnant," whereas *ζωγρίαν* means "a taking alive," thus "we did not let any to remain alive."[63] That of course is what not leaving a remnant means!

2:35 In contrast to v.34 (*πλήν*) the non-human became booty, i.e. *ἐπρονομεύσαμεν* "we plundered, ravaged," i.e. we took as spoils of war. The verb originally was used in the sense of "to forage," i.e. to live off the land, but in LXX it is regularly used in the sense of the Hebrew בזז. In MT the verb בזזנו has a double modifier, the cattle and the spoils of the cities אשר לכדנו, but LXX has changed the intent of MT by omitting the relative pronoun, with the result that v.35b is a coordinate clause "and the spoils of the cities we took." Hex has added *ων* after *πόλεων* to equal MT.

2:36 *ἐξ* 'Αροήρ has as equivalent מערער, though at vv.9,18 and 29 the name was also used for ער; the translator did not distinguish between ער and ערער;[64] see comment at v.9. Aroer lay on the edge of the Arnon gorge. This is called a נחל or "wadi," and is translated first as (*παρὰ τὸ χεῖλος*) *χειμάρρου* 'Αρνών, i.e. "torrent, river" Arnon. In the coordinate construction the same word is translated by (*τὸν πόλιν τὴν οὖσαν ἐν*) *τῇ φάραγγι*, "(in) the ravine, valley." The usage in the book is peculiar. Only these two nouns are used to

63. The Three render שריד correctly, Aq by *λεῖμμα*, and Theod Sym by *ὑπόλειμμα*.
64. Aq Sym have *ἀπὸ* 'Αροήρ, as does the A F M *O*+ variant text, but Theod followed LXX.

render נחל. Prior to this verse only *φάραγξ* had been used, and after this verse only *χειμάρρους* is used up to 21:4—6 where נחל occurs three times but is translated throughout by *φάραγξ*. It is doubtful whether the translator distinguished these at all; to him both words meant נחל.

The conquered area extended northward *καὶ ἕως ὄρους τοῦ Γαλαάδ* "even to the mountainous area of Galaad," though MT simply has ועד הגלעד, probably under the influence of 3:12.

MT then states that there was no city which was too high (שגבה) for us, i.e. no city was unscalable. LXX has quite a different verb, *διέφυγεν* "escaped (from us)," which makes fine sense but is not what MT says,[65] though presumably LXX does not falsify what MT intended.

In the last clause LXX interprets את הכל as a plural *τὰς πάσας* referring presumably to cities, which may well be what MT intended. The verb נתן is modified by לפנינו as in v.33, but LXX has *εἰς τὰς χεῖρας ἡμῶν* which reflects Sam's בידנו.

2:37 MT suddenly changes to a second singular verb קרבת, i.e. "only to the land of the Ammanites[66] you did not draw near." All the ancient versions including LXX level to the first plural, *προσήλθομεν*. This land of the Ammanites is then defined in v.37b. For יד נחל "side of the wadi" LXX has the fine interpretation *τὰ συγκυροῦντα χειμάρρῳ* "the (territories) adjacent to the wadi." The area of the Ammanites lay to the east of the Jabok. This also included the cities of the mountainous area eastward, i.e. *τὰς ἐν τῇ ὀρεινῇ* for (the cities of) ההר.

In the tradition the *f* text read *παρηλθομεν* for *προσήλθομεν*, with only a slight difference in emphasis; the choice of the *παρα* compound may have been influenced by *συγκυροῦντα* which modified the verb. A B V 920 *f n z* variant witnesses to the genitive *χειμαρρου* for *χειμάρρῳ*, but the Classical dative is preferable.[67] The name Ἰαβόκ was often misspelled by copyists, the most popular being *ιακωβ* (by *C*ʼʼ *n s y z*). Others include *ιοβοκ*, *ιαρβοκ*, *ιαβος*, and even *αρνων* occurs.

---

65. Sym translates by *ὑπερίσχυσεν* "be stronger, prevailed (over)," also a free rendering, but this is similar to Pesh.
66. Theod and the Later Revisers follow the Masoretic vowelling with Ἀμμών rather than the Ἀμμάν of LXX.
67. See the discussion in THGD 58.

Instead of the coordinate construction "וכל that Yahweh our God commanded" LXX has *καθότι*, which is clearer. LXX also clarified by adding *ἡμῖν* after *ἐνετείλατο*, which is an ad sensum addition. An early (prehexaplaric) text omitted the pronoun under the influence of the Hebrew.

Chapter 3

3:1 Vv.1—2 are an exact repetition of Num 21:33—34 except that they are told in first person rather than in third; it is obvious that the translator simply took over the passage, only adding *αὐτός* before "and all his people" in view of MT's הוא, which had been omitted in Num (though added by hex); comp 2:30,[1] and changing *καθώς* to *ὥσπέρ*.

Bashan was the area to the east of the Sea of Galilee extending southward to the Yarmuk River. Its exact boundaries are unknown, but Edrei must have been at its southern boundary since Og and his army went out to meet the Israelites there, and its location is at modern Derʿa near the Yarmuk. אדרעי became Ἐδράϊν in LXX.[2] The nunation became mimation in B *f*, which in a number of instances was omitted, probably because of hex influence. An infixed *sigma* is probably due to uncial confusion of Ε—Σ, and obtains in *εσδραειν* and *εσδραει*. Vowel change appears in the *z* spelling *αδραειν*. Also in the tradition a popular A F M V gloss, *μετ αυτου*, appeared after "all his people," which is ex par, and lacks any Hebrew support.

3:2 For *εἰς τὰς χεῖράς σου παραδέδωκα* see the comments at 2:24. For the secondary character in 963+ of *παρεδωκα* see comment at 2:24 as well. LXX has added *πᾶσαν* before "his land" against MT, probably because of "*πάντα* his people" coordinate with it. The relative clause modifying Seon is a nominal clause in MT, but has an imperfect verb in Greek to render the participial predicate, as is usual for LXX. A popular A F M text has added *τω* before *Σηών*, but this is unnecessary; the appositive *βασιλεῖ* is sufficient to determine the case of the proper noun.

3:3 MT has no counterpart to *αὐτόν* as object of *παρέδωκεν*, but comp 2:33 where it does. For *εἰς τὰς χεῖρας ἡμῶν* see comment at 2:24. *καί* 2° ... *καί* 3° is a "both ... and" construction representing גם and ו in Hebrew. The name Ὤγ occurs ten times in the book, but only here and in v.10 is the name articulated. Here the article represents את but at v.10 the article is in the genitive

1. See SS 73 as well.
2. The diairesis is unnecessary in view of the placement of the accent.

and it may have been used because it is followed by ἐν τῇ Βασάν, which contrasts with v.4 where the unarticulated Βασάν is followed by ἐν Βασάν. The verb πατάσσω is the regular equivalent for הכה.[3]

The translation of לו modifying השאיר by αὐτοῦ is ambiguous. Does it modify καταλιπεῖν or σπέρμα? Actually two *O* mss represent a clearer and more literal αυτω.[4] The term שריד was rendered freely at 2:34 by ζωγρίαν, but here by σπέρμα.[5] The Hebrew word really means "survivor, remnant."

3:4 καί ... ἐκείνῳ are the identical words of 2:34; see comments ad loc. The victory was total; all his cities (60) were taken. The territory taken is defined as πάντα τὰ περίχωρα 'Αργὸβ βασιλείας Ὢγ ἐν Βασάν, from which it is clear that βασιλείας is in apposition to 'Αργόβ, not to περίχωρα which is accusative. In Hebrew, which in its Masoretic form does not inflect for case, this is not clear. Most witnesses, however, read βασιλεως for βασιλείας, which cannot be other than an unthinking copyist's error. So too LXX 'Αργόβ defines more exactly the actual kingdom of Og; this also seems to be the intent of the phrase "in Basan"; the kingdom was then not coextensive with Βασάν, but was within it. In the tradition the name has been confused with αρβοκ/αρβουκ of Gen 23:2 in *b y z* texts; other misspellings attested are αργω, αργωμ, αργη and even αρααρ βοκ.

Unfortunately this is no help to the modern reader, since the name Argob has not been identified with any assurance. All that is certain is that it was περίχωρα, plural of περίχωρον "something round about," hence an area. The Hebrew was חבל "a rope, measuring line," and so an area which has been measured out.[6]

3:5 MT has a nominal clause: "All these (were) cities fortified ...." but LXX by omitting אלה makes the verse a nominative pendant, which is then taken up

3. Problematic is Aq's ἀνεθεματίσαμεν which Aq uses elsewhere only and always for the root חרם. I suspect that the reading belongs to 2:34.
4. Which may have come from Theod or Aq; Sym retains αὐτοῦ.
5. Aq again has λεῖμμα, as at 2:34.
6. Aq renders the word by the plural σχοινίσματα, a word formed from σχοινίς "rope, cord," so lands measured out by a σχοινίς, a land measure used especially in Egypt according to LS s.v. Theod apparently read the singular (πᾶν) σχοίνισμα, whereas Sym translated by περίμετρον "circumference," i.e. the entire are by measure.

in v.6 by *αὐτούς*, thus "as for all these strong cities ... (we destroyed them)."[7] Hex has added *αυται* after *πᾶσαι* so as to equal MT. LXX has also interpreted MT's passive participle בצרות by an adjective *ὀχυραί* "secure, safe, strong."[8]

In MT the terms חומה גבהה דלתים ובריח "high wall(s), gates and bar(s)" are usually understood as defining בצרות, thus "fortified by high walls, gates and bars" (with חומה and בריח naturally understood as collectives). LXX has taken these as nominatives, "fortified cities, high walls, gates and bars." In sense, however, these three terms must describe the fortified cities. Actually the syntax of LXX here is similar to that of MT.

LXX misunderstood הפרזי entirely. It means "open land," hence in modifying ערי "cities of the open land," hence hamlets, unwalled villages. LXX confused it with the gentilic הפרזי, which is vocalized differently, and has *τῶν Φερεζαίων*.[9] Just what the Pherezites were doing in Basan is not clear, but then it is doubtful that the Alexandrians had any clear idea of the tribes that were said to inhabit Canaan before the arrival of the Israelites.

3:6 Incidentally most witnesses spell *ἐξωλεθρεύσαμεν* as *εξωλοθρ.*, a later form created by progressive assimilation. The earlier form has been adopted throughout the Pentateuch as original. LXX did not translate the initial conjunction of ונחרם but it added one in rendering the free infinitive החרם in v.6b. This does make good sense if v.5 is a pendant nominative as suggested ad loc.

LXX correctly understood the free infinitive as contextual, in which condition the infinitive in simply setting forth the verbal idea takes on the coloration of its context, in this case the first plural aorist active indicative, and so *ἐξωλεθρεύσαμεν* correctly repeats the form beginning the verse. For the translation of v.6b see 2:34 from which the translator borrowed his translation except for omitting the genitive pronouns (even where the Hebrew text differs such as הנשים occurring here without a conjunction). This was necessitated by there being no Hebrew equivalent for *οὐ κατελίπομεν ζωγρίαν*; see the discussion ad loc.

---

7. Obviously the punctuation at the end of the verse must be changed to a comma.
8. Aq has rendered more literally by *διηρμέναι* a middle passive participle of *διαίρω*, thus "lifted up, made exalted, high."
9. Aq quite correctly has *ἀτειχίστων* "unwalled," as do The Others.

3:7 Comp 2:35 as a parallel statement. For *τὰ κτήνη καὶ τὰ σκῦλα τῶν πόλεων* as well as for *ἐπρονομεύσαμεν* see comments at 2:35. For the verb the Byz text has *προενομευσαμεν*, i.e. augmenting the verbal element of the compound rather than the compound as a separate verb. It represents the later renewal of Classicism, a renewal which did not always fully take over the dynamics of the Classical Age. After all, *προνομεύω* means "to take as spoil," not "to graze beforehand."[10]

3:8 Instead of מיד LXX has the plural *ἐκ χειρῶν*; kings not only had hands; there were actually two kings involved. For the plural *τῶν Ἀμορραίων* see discussion at 1:4. For *πέραν τοῦ Ἰορδάνου* see comment at 1:1. The limits of the territories of the two Amorrite kings are defined as from the *χειμάρρου Ἀρνών* (for which see comment at 2:36) up to *Ἀερμών*, by which Mt. Hermon is meant. These constituted resp. the southern and the northern limits of the territory taken by the Israelites under Moses. The transcription of חרמון by *Ἀερμών* is constant in Deut and Jos, though here it becomes *ερμων* in *O*. MT defines Hermon as הר, which LXX disregards, but hex has inserted *ορους* to represent it. A majority B V 920 text has *και εως* for *ἕως*, but *καὶ ἕως*, which is normal for ועד, never occurs for עד in Deut.[11]

3:9 Instead of צידנים "Sidonians" LXX updates to its own time by *οἱ Φοίνικες* "Phoenicians."[12] LXX did recognize יקראו as an old preterite inflection and translated by an aorist *ἐπωνόμασαν*.[13] A popular old reading "corrects" the verb to the present tense *επονομαζουσιν*, but this may be an early attempt to reflect the more usual understanding of the prefix inflection. In contrast to v.8 *Ἀερμών* here appears articulated; in MT the name is governed by a preposition: לחרמון which permits a vocalization showing an article.

LXX presupposes the transposition of two consonants as parent text for *Σανιώρ*, i.e. שניר for שרין, thus consonantally the same as שניר in v.9b, though with a different vocalization. In the tradition only hex corrects to the

10. Aq understood בזונו well as his *διηρπάσαμεν* shows.
11. See THGD 56.
12. The Three correct LXX to *Σιδόνιοι*.
13. Not so The Three! Theod and Sym have the simplex in the present tense: *ὀνομάζουσιν*, whereas Aq has an imperfect *ἐκάλουν*.

Hebrew with *σαριων*. Other variants, excluding itacisms, in the tradition obtain as *σαναωρ*, *ανιωρ*, *σαυριων*, *σανιων*.

The Amorrite name for Hermon is adequately transcribed in LXX by Σανίρ. Non-itacistic variant spellings include *σαμιρ* (N—M confusion); infixed vowel: *σανιειρ*, *σανιηρ*, *σανιορ*; and aphaeresis: *ανιρ*, *ανειρ*, *ανιηρ*.

In the second clause MT has a singular (but collective) subject האמרי, but a plural verbal predicate. The Greek recognizes the singular subject, and perforce used a singular verb. For the tense see above.

3:10 LXX understood המישר "the plain" as a proper noun Μισώρ, being persuaded by the coordinate names Γαλαάδ and Βασάν.[14] The name Σελχά for סלכה is still extant in Selkhad in the Jebel ed-Druze. It constituted the northern boundary of the area of Basan conquered by the Israelites, whereas Edrain was its southern limit. For Ἐδράιν see comment at v.1. For *τοῦ* Ὤγ see comment at v.3. In contrast to v.4 Βασάν is here articulated. The phrase בבשן could theoretically be unarticulated (it also occurs at 4:43 where it, like 3:4, is unarticulated). Elsewhere in the book הבשן occurs 12 times, and only twice is it unarticulated in LXX (vv.1,11). For בני בשן at 32:14 see comment ad loc. Γαλαάδ refers roughly to the mountainous area between Heshbon and the Wadi Yarmuk, i.e. south of Bashan.

3:11 The *ὅτι*/כי clause apparently gives the reason why the Israelites could take possession of Basan, "because only Og ... was left of the Raphain." The preposition *ἀπό* "from" translates מיתר "from the rest of," and hex has added *λειμματος* under the asterisk to represent יתר. For the Ῥαφαΐν see comment at 2:11. Og was reputedly the last of the race of giants. His giant stature is immortalized by the antequarian note in this verse concerning his *κλίνη*. Its Hebrew equivalent is ערש "couch"; here it is usually thought to be metaphorically used for tomb. The Greek can be so used,[15] though the notion of an iron tomb is odd, and it may be best to take it as "bed" rather than as sarcophagus.

---

14. Not so The Three. Aq has a literal rendering: *τῆς εὐθείας*; Sym rendered by *τοῦ ὁμαλοῦ* "the level ground," and Theod has *τῆς ὑπτίας* "the flat, horizontal."
15. See LS s.v.2 and 3.

The particle הלה is more usually spelled הלא "is it not," but is rendered affirmatively by LXX as *ἰδού*, thereby forming two *ἰδού* clauses side by side. The translation of the proper name רבת "Rabba" by *ἄκρᾳ* is hardly reasonable; the parent text presupposed probably involved a transposition of consonants as ברת the bound form of בירה "fortress, citadel." The notice states that this *κλίνη* of Og was still in the *ἄκρᾳ* of the Ammanites as visible proof of his great stature.

The size of this bed was nine by four cubits measured according to the ordinary cubit: *ἐν πήχει ἀνδρός*, i.e. cir. 18" or 45 cm.[16] So the overall measurement of Og's iron bed was cir. 13'6" x 6' or 4.05 x 1.80m.

In the tradition *πήχεων* appears in its contracted form *πηχων* in B+, but the uncontracted form is probably original, though the contracted form is already attested as early as the third century B.C. in Egypt.[17]

3:12 LXX uses the demonstrative *ἐκείνην*, though MT has the pronoun of nearer designation, הזאת. This must presuppose a parent ההיא, since nowhere else in the book is הזאת or הזה rendered by *ἐκεῖνος*. The definite demonstrative pronoun of nearer definition occurs in the singular 107 times in Deut. In four cases the phrase כ(ה)יום הזה is translated differently (by *σήμερον* 4:38 8:18; *ὥσπερ καὶ σήμερον* 6:24, and at 29:27, by *ὡσεὶ νῦν*), once at 17:5 it is omitted due to homoioteleuton, and in 101 cases it is accurately rendered by *οὗτος*. The one case of *ἐκείνην* must then be based on a parent ההיא.

The area possessed is located *ἀπὸ Ἀροήρ*, i.e. only the one boundary is given, though it is more precisely described by the relative clause *ἥ ἐστιν παρὰ τὸ χεῖλος χειμάρρου Ἀρνών*. MT has no equivalent for *τὸ χεῖλος*, but the Greek supports Sam which has שפת; the clause is an exact copy of 2:36. At 4:48 the clause also occurs but with the preposition *ἐπί* (plus the genitive), which promoted the variant reading *επι* in B Byz+.[18]

Moses then assigned half the mountainous area of Galaad and its cities to Rouben and Gad. LXX has *ὄρους* unarticulated, though whether this is original or not is uncertain, since the majority text, apparently including 963, supports *του ορους*. The word *ἥμισυς* only occurs three times in Deut, but in no case

16. For *ἐν* used as measure see SS 128.
17. See Mayser I 1.267.
18. See THGD 118.

does the genitive following it have the article (see also v.13 29:8). MT names the recipients לראובני ולגדי here as well as at v.16 and 29:7, but LXX has τῷ Ῥουβὴν καὶ τῷ Γάδ (as at v.16) but at 29:8(7) it changed Γάδ to Γαδδί. The two prepositional phrases also occur at 4:43 where LXX has the diverse pattern of τῷ Ῥουβήν ... τῷ Γαδδί. A *z* variant text actually has γαδδι here as well.

3:13 By τὸ κατάλοιπον of Galaad is undoubtedly meant the northern half of Galaad, i.e. north of the Jabbok River; cf v.16. Over against MT LXX adds καί before πᾶσαν τὴν περίχωρον Ἀργώβ, which constitutes the translator's attempt to clarify a difficult text. According to v.4 all the area of Argob apparently constituted the extent of Og's kingdom. The καί then defines καὶ πᾶσαν τὴν Βασάν over against "the rest of Galaad." I would translate: "even all the area of Argob, all that Basan — (as) land of (the) Raphain will it be reckoned."[19] MT has the major cut in the verse at המנשה, and the translator seems to have been influenced by that reading tradition as well, even though the Greek syntax goes its own way.

3:14 Vv.14—17 constitute another account of the territories in Transjordan assigned to the Israelites. Yair, Manasseh's son, is presented as having taken "all the area of Argob," for which see vv.4,13; comp Num 32:41 for another version of Yair's military exploits, viz. taking τὰς ἐπαύλεις αὐτῶν rather than all the area of Argob. LXX follows Sam rather than MT in introducing the account with καί. The Byz text has changed Ἀργώβ to ιαβοκ, which can hardly be taken as a serious variant. Other spellings attested are αρβοκ, αρβοβ, αρβοη and αριοβ. The area taken is limited ἕως τῶν ὁρίων Γαργασὶ καὶ Ὀμαχαθί, whereas MT has עד גבול הגשורי והמעכתי. The translator must have had הגרגשי in mind for the first name, which obviously would be wrong; the Girgashites were a Canaanite tribe living in Canaan before the Israelite conquest. The spelling was corrected by hex and *f* to γεσουρι. Misspellings include the suffixing of *nu*, dittography of *sigma, gamma* read as *tau* in γαρτασει, or as *beta* in γαρβασι.

19. Instead of λογισθήσεται Aq renders יקרא by κληθήσεται.

The second name was completely misunderstood by the translator who took the definite article as part of the name to be transcribed.[20] The tradition has dealt wildly with the word, not only producing such variants as *ομοχατη*, *ομαχεθι*, *ομαχθι*, *οχαματι*, *ομαχαθην*, but also *μαχειρ*, *ομαιαειρ*, and even *ο ιαειρ* with internal variants as the A F M V majority variant text, a reading based partially on the name יאיר rather than on MT. The two Aramaean tribes are said to have been spared by the invading Israelites at Jos 13:13.

In the last clause the nominal *τὴν* Βασάν must, like its Hebrew equivalent את הבשן, be taken as an explicating appositive of the pronoun *αὐτάς*, i.e. "named them ... i.e. Basan." The nominal is syntactically odd in both languages, and the translator simply aped the Hebrew text. What is presumably meant is "he named them according to his name — I mean Basan — Αὐὼθ Ἰαίρ." It should be noted that neither אתם nor its translation *αὐτάς* has an antecedent. A majority A F M text has tried to fix up the translation by substituting *αυτο*; this at least makes the reference singular which is sensible, but it too does not have a proper anaphoric referent.

The name given is correctly transcribed as a proper noun. Αὐώθ, however, bewildered copyists, as a list of their attempts at copying the name shows: *αωθ*, *αβωθ*, *αυωβ*, *ανωθ*, *δυωθ*, *διωθ*, *δηωθ*, *δυκιθ*, *ναβωθ*, *ναυω* and *υιωθ*, most of which can be explained palaeographically, or as in the case of the first three spellings as rooted in auditory confusion.

The phrase *ἕως τῆς ἡμέρας ταύτης* is zeugmatic; it presupposes not only "he named them," but also "and it has continued to be called such" until this day.

3:15 Μαχίρ, the eldest son of Manasseh, is now represented as being alloted Galaad. Though according to Num 26:33 Machir is said to be the father of Galaad, vv.12—13 did say that Moses assigned half of the mountainous area of Galaad to Rouben and Gad, and only the remainder to the half tribe of Manasseh, but this seems to be contradicted by this verse. The problem lies with MT, however, since LXX translated MT faithfully.

---

20. The Revisers correctly understood the Hebrew words as an articulated gentilic and read *τοῦ* Μαχαθί.

In the tradition the *C''* *s* group has substituted the compound *παρεδωκα* for the simplex, but Moses' assignment of the land is throughout represented by *ἔδωκα*; cf vv.12,13 and 16.

3:16 Vv.16—17 state in more specific fashion than in v.12 what the heritage of Rouben and Gad was to be. For *τῷ Ῥουβὴν καὶ τῷ Γάδ* see comment at v.12. The two verses are intended to give the four boundaries of the land given these two tribes. In v.16 the southern, northern and eastern boundaries are given. I would change the punctuation of the verse by removing the first and second colons. Then the clause demarcated by the third and fourth colons can be taken as a parenthetical remark, which incidentally defines the eastern border as well. The collocation *ἕως χειμάρρου Ἀρνῶν* defines the southern border of the territory with the double accusative *μέσον ... ὅριον* modifying the verb *ἔδωκα*, i.e. "the middle of the torrent as boundary." For the B+ variant compound *παρεδωκα* see comment at v.15.

The second boundary is the northern one, *καὶ ἕως τοῦ Ἰαβόκ*. But the Yabok stretches eastward (from the Jordan) a considerable distance and then curves southward. It is the north—south stretch which elicits the parenthetical remark *ὁ χειμάρρους ὅριον τοῖς υἱοῖς Ἀμμάν*. Since the torrent refers to the Yabok I would insist on the deictic force of the article here and translate: "This torrent is (i.e. serves as) border for the Ammanites," and it also then serves as eastern border for the Israelite tribes.

In the tradition *χειμάρρου* (*Ἀρνῶν*) is articulated by the *C''* *b* *s*+ text, which is due to the influence of *τοῦ χειμάρρου* later in the verse. The Byz text attempted to simplify the syntax by adding a *και* before *ὁ χειμάρρους*, but the asyndetic character of the parenthetical statement must be original.

3:17 What remains is to delineate the western border. The Araba,[21] by which is meant the Jordan Valley on the eastern bank of the Jordan, and the Jordan itself are to serve as "border stretching (from) Machanarath down to the Sea of the Araba, viz. the Salt Sea, below Asedoth with Phasga to the east." Syntacti-

21. For והערבה Aq has *καὶ ὁμαλή* "and a level (area)," and Theod has *καὶ ἐν δυσμαῖς* "and in the west," while Sym has a doublet, *καὶ πεδινή, καὶ ἀοίκητος*, for which see Salvesen 143.

cally the subject is "the Araba and the Jordan," and the predicate is *ὅριον* modified in turn by the rest of the verse.

The translator misunderstood מכנרת "from Kenereth," and took the phrase as a name, hence *Μαχανάραθ*.[22] The tradition made a real mess of this name, changing vowels, dentals, infixing consonants, transposing them, aphaeresis of the first syllable, and syncopation of syllables, while the majority text prefixed the name with an *απο*. The preposition, though equalling MT, had nothing to do with the Hebrew; it was simply added for good sense to balance with the *καὶ ἕως* phrase which followed.

This western border extended southward to the Dead Sea, here called both the Sea of the Araba and the Salt Sea, its extent being defined by MT as תחת אשדת הפסגה "below the slopes of Pisgah";[23] cf also 4:49 where the same phrase occurs. LXX did not understand אשדת and took it as a place name *Ἀσηδώθ*, which is then variously spelled in the tradition as *ασιδωο*, *ασιδωδ*, *ασιδων*, *σηδωθ*. The place name *τὴν Φασγά* has not been identified but must have been near the mouth of the Arnon, i.e. on the slopes though which the Arnon flows. The genitive *ἀνατολῶν* has ablative force, i.e. "from the east," representing מזרחה "eastward."

In the tradition *τὴν Φασγά* becomes genitive as *της φασγα* in *n*+ or *της φαγαδ*, but as *την φασγαδ* in *C*'', and as *την σφαγα* in cod M. The word *ἀνατολῶν* is prefixed by *απο* in a *z* text, but by *εως* in some *y* mss. A popular variant has changed *ὑπό* to *απο*, but this cannot be correct. What is meant is "below," i.e. just south of Asedoth.

3:18 *ὑμῖν* does not refer to all the Israelites, but only to the people of Rouben, Gad and the half-tribe of Manasseh. Moses says: "The Lord your God *ἔδωκεν* you this land as a possession," but the majority of mss read *δεδωκεν*; the perfect certainly is appropriate in the context. The two forms are easily confused, but usage favors the aorist. The aorist form occurs with the Lord as subject or as speaker 23 times in Deut plus five cases for the compound *παραδίδωμι*, i.e. a total of 28 cases. For the perfect there are only eight cases plus four for the

---

22. For the original spelling see THGD 63.
23. For *καὶ ἕως ... Φασγά* Sym has *καὶ ἕως θαλάσσης τῆς πεδιάδος τῆς ἀοικήτου θαλάσσης ἁλυκῆς ἀπὸ ὑποκάτω Ἀσηδὼθ τῆς φάραγγος* (retroverted from Syh). For Ἀσηδώθ Aq has *κατάσχυσις*, and he translated הפסגה by <*η*> *λαξευτή*.

compound, thus a total of 12. In the immediate context of this chapter the aorist occurs seven times (6 + 1 compound), and the perfect only twice (1 + 1). Furthermore, the aorist is supported by both B and 963, and so is probably original. For *ἐν κλήρῳ* see comment at 2:5, though here the phrase translates לרשתה, as it does at 12:1.[24]

LXX makes the same first cut for Yahweh's statement as MT does after לרשתה (which has a zaqeph qaton accent). What every warrior, *πᾶς δυνατός* for כל בני חיל, is to do is to cross over (the Jordan) armed before the other Israelites, i.e. assist them in the conquest of Canaan itself. LXX translates carefully, only deviating on the number of the phrase, though the singular *πᾶς δυνατός* really does not differ in intent from MT, since there too the phrase constitutes an explicating limitation on the subject "you," thus: you, I mean every able-bodied male.

3:19 Only common sense tells the reader that *οἶδα ὅτι πολλὰ κτήνη ὑμῖν* is a parenthetical statement inserted between the subject "your wives and your children and your cattle" and the predicate *κατοικείτωσαν*. The Greek renders MT literally except for the word order of *πολλὰ κτήνη*, though 963 and hex have transposed the words, thereby conforming to MT. The *C*'' *s*+ text has also added *πασαις* before "the cities," as well as changed *ἔδωκα* to *δεδωκα*, for which comp the discussion in v.18. The Byz text has also added the preposition *εν* before the relative pronoun *αἷς*, which is hardly an improvement; it is simply a thoughtless mistake.

3:20 The men of the two and a half tribes settling the land east of the Jordan are to occupy their lands only after the remaining tribes have finished the conquest of the Promised Land west of the Jordan. This completion is put in terms of the Lord *καταπαύσῃ* "should give rest," equivalent for יניח. LXX has added *ὁ θεὸς ὑμῶν* to the subject, thus leveling with the occurrence of *κύριος ὁ θεὸς ὑμῶν* occurring in the *ἥν* clause later in the verse.

This giving rest is explicated by a coordinate clause put into the future, *κατακληρονομήσουνσιν*, the subject being "your brothers," and the object, *τὴν γῆν*. The M 963 *f*+ text has the verb in the subjunctive mood as determined

24. See SS Inf 56.

by ἕως ἄν, but LXX avoids the potential mood in favor of the prospective future, i.e. as something certain to take place. The relative clause, a typical Deuteronomic one for which see comment at 1:20, in turn modifies γῆν. In the tradition ὑμῶν in the relative clause appears in the majority A B 963 text as ημων, but this itacism has no support in MT any more than it did for ὑμῶν 2°, where it was also well supported in the tradition. These variants should normally not be taken seriously, since the change is only explicable in Greek and not in MT;[25] see particularly the discussion at 1:20—21.

The locative expression ἐν τῷ πέραν τοῦ Ἰορδάνου maintains the pretence that this is being spoken in Transjordan, and so refers to the land west of the river; cf 1:1 and see comment at 1:5.

A second clause in the future defines the return ἕκαστος εἰς τὴν κληρονομίαν αὐτοῦ. That inheritance was also a divine gift mediated by Moses, ἣν ἔδωκα ὑμῖν. A popular variant has the perfect δεδωκα, but the aorist is quite sufficient.

3:21 The orders given to Yesous are mixed in number. One might have expected, since the orders are in direct speech form introduced by λέγων/לאמר, the address to be in second person singular form, but neither LXX nor MT is consistent. MT does use the singular in עיניך as well as in the final relative nominal clause אשר אתה עבר, but refers to Yahweh as אלהיכם. LXX, on the other hand, has οἱ ὀφθαλμοὶ ὑμῶν as well as κύριος ὁ θεὸς ὑμῶν, but then in the ἅς clause has the singular σὺ διαβαίνεις. Admittedly the plural in "your eyes" is difficult, but it must be original text.[26] LXX has also simplified the Hebrew nominal structure עיניך הראות "your eyes which were seeing" as a verbal clause "your eyes ἑωράκασιν.[27] The Greek has simplified this considerably, but has rendered the intent of MT adequately.

The verb ποιέω occurs twice, but in different syntactic patterns. In the ὅσα clause ἐποίησεν is modified by the accusative (πάντα) ὅσα and a dative of indirect object τοῖς δυσὶν βασιλεῦσιν rendering a ל prepositional phrase. In the

25. See also THGD 108.
26. See the discussion in THGD 108.
27. Since the participle is articulated in MT the syntax is rather odd. One would prefer to take the participle as predicate, but it is apparently attributive. The כן clause must then be understood as "so (shall your eyes be the ones seeing how) the Lord shall do ...."

οὕτως clause which follows, *ποιήσει* (*κύριος*) is modified only by an accusative *πάσας τὰς βασιλείας*, which in MT is, however, again a ל phrase. What is meant is "so shall the Lord effect (dispossession) of all the kingdoms." An F *b z*+ text has simplified this by changing the accusative to the dative. Also in the tradition the majority of witnesses have added to *κύριος* the gloss *ο θεος ημων*.[28] Its secondary nature is emphasized by the mixture in the tradition: a few mss have *ο θεος υμων*, and the *d* text has *ο θεος*. LXX translates MT correctly here.

The final relative clause in MT is אשר אתה עבר שמה. LXX's attempt to render שמה results in awkward Greek: *ἐφ' ἅς ... ἐκεῖ*, and one might translate: "to which you are going to cross over," with the present tense *διαβαίνεις* translating the participle.

3:22 LXX renders the suffix of תיראום by the prepositional phrase *ἀπ' αὐτῶν*, whereas at v.2 the same verb is modified by an accusative *αὐτόν*. There, however, the pronoun represented אתו. The verb with pronominal suffix occurs only here in Deut, though modification by a מן phrase is common throughout the book, and the possibility of a different parent text must be borne in mind.

The use of the pronoun *αὐτός* is emphatic in the *ὅτι* clause, and imitates a common Hebrew pattern of a nominal clause: N as subject with the predicate a third person pronoun plus N. The Hebrew has "Yahweh your God" as subject, and הוא plus articulated participle הנלחם as predicate. LXX has imitated the Hebrew by its *αὐτός* and then rendered the participle by a future verb *πολεμήσει*. The verb is in turn modified by a prepositional phrase *περὶ ὑμῶν*. A popular variant changes the preposition to *υπερ*, which in this context is a synonym. The modification of this verb by a *περί* phrase is unusual. In the OT an accusative modifier is the most common; also often used are *ἐπί*, *πρός* or *ἐν* phrases, but *περί* is found elsewhere only at Exod 14:14 1Macc 3:21,43 and 2Macc 14:32.

3:23—24 Vv.23—25 present Moses at prayer on his own behalf. The vocative *κύριε κύριε* represents two different words in MT: אדני יהוה, a combination which occurs in Deut only here and at 9:26 where it is translated in the same

28. See THGD 119—120.

manner. This raises the question: Was the Qere actually read as *ʾdny ʾdny*? *ἤρξω* appears in a variant A F M *y*+ text as the perfect form *ηρξαι*, but an aorist is preferable. The translation of עבד by *θεράπων* was favored by the Exod translator, but seldom occurs in the rest of the Pentateuch (once in Gen, four times each in Num and Deut). The term עבד occurs only 22 times in Deut and is rendered eight times each by *παῖς* and *οἰκέτης*, and once each by *δοῦλος* and *υἱός*.

The divine revelation is shown by four nominals in LXX: *τὴν ἰσχύν σου καὶ τὴν δύναμίν σου* and the pair *καὶ τὴν χεῖρα τὴν κραταιὰν καὶ τὸν βραχίονα τὸν ὑψηλόν*. The first two are a doublet rendering for את גדלך. To the translator the divine instrument of divine redemption, גדל, needed explication. Greatness as an instrument was thought of in active terms of strength and power. For the latter two MT has only ואת ידך החזקה and LXX's pair is ex par.[29] Usually LXX does not reproduce the pronominal suffixes in this formula; in fact, it does so nowhere except at 9:26.

The interrogative clause is introduced by אשר here, used in a causal sense as LXX's *γάρ* shows.[30] The query is an ascription of praise of God as incomparable.[31] MT's question is a nominal one, מי אל, and LXX naturally uses the linking verb *ἐστιν*. The point of the comparison is twofold. In MT the two are both prepositional phrases, כמעשיך וכגבורתך. LXX does render the second one literally by (*καὶ*) *κατὰ τὴν ἰσχύν σου*, but the first one by *καθὰ σὺ ἐποίησας*. The majority of witnesses rendered the collocation by placing the otiose *σύ* at the end. The noun does occur 12 times in Deut, and elsewhere it is always rendered by *ἔργον* except at 11:3 where *τὰ τέρατα* occurs. In the tradition M Byz have the doublet phrase *και κατα τα εργα σου* between the two, and it is likely that this was ultimately based on the Hebrew text, probably through one of The Three. Furthermore, hex has changed *σῷ θεράποντι* to *θεραποντι σου* to conform to the MT word order. Hex has also added *σου* after *χεῖρα* and after *βραχίονι* to represent suffixes in MT.

3:25 The actual entreaty is that he (Moses) might be allowed to enter the Promised Land. LXX renders the cohortative entreaty by *διαβὰς* (*οὖν*) *ὄψο-*

29. See List 18 in THGD 91.
30. For its causal sense see BDB s.v. 8.c or KB s.v. B.b.
31. Aq renders אל not by *θεός* but as usual by *ἰσχυρός*, in which he is here followed by Sym.

μαι, i.e. using a volitional future, "so crossing over I would see." The οὖν ties the actual plea to the preceding; this was intended to sway God to cancel his prohibition of 1:37, which see. LXX has added a demonstrative to MT's "the good land," making it "this good land," probably under the influence of the phrase τὸ ὄρος τοῦτο τὸ ἀγαθόν later in the verse. Hex recognized the gloss by placing ταύτην under the obelus. The pronoun may, however, simply reflect the deictic force of the article in הארץ. For πέραν τοῦ Ἰορδάνου see comment at v.20.

This good land is then identified by τὸ ὄρος τοῦτο τὸ ἀγαθὸν καὶ τὸν Ἀντιλίβανον. For the latter term see comment at 1:7.

3:26 The Hebrew ויתעבר is usually understood as derived from a root meaning "be carried away by passion," thus here, "be infuriated with," i.e. the Lord was angry with Moses, but LXX considered the more commmon root meaning "to pass by," and translated by ὑπερεῖδον "overlooked," thus "disregarded," which is contextually sensible as well. What LXX says is "the Lord disregarded me (i.e. my entreaty) because of you."[32]

For the idiom רב לך and its translation by ἱκανούσθω σοι see comment at 1:6.[33] The idiom προσθῇς ἔτι plus infinitive is a Hebraism and simply means "any more," thus "do not speak about this matter any more."[34] LXX has placed ἔτι immediately after the verb since ἔτι simply reinforces the verbal idea, but hex has transposed it after the infinitive to which it also added πρός με in view of MT's דבר אלי עוד.

3:27 Moses is told to go up ἐπὶ κορυφὴν Λελαξευμένου. Why הפסגה, which is usually taken as a proper noun, Mt. Pisgah,[35] should be rendered by a perfect passive participle of λαξεύω is not at all clear. Presumably what is meant is a mountain which looked as though it were carved in stone, thus a stony mountain.[36] Comp also 4:49 where תחת אשדת הפסגה occurs and is rendered by ὑπὸ

32. Theod and Aq translated by ὑπερέθετο, i.e. reading the more common root.
33. Aq translates רב literalistically by πολύ.
34. See Bauer sub προστίθημι 1.c as well as Bl-D 435 f.n.4.
35. Aq rightly transcribes as Φασγά.
36. Dogniez-Harl simply translate as "la Pierre-Taillée" which is probably the wisest course.

'Ασηδὼθ τὴν λαξευτήν "under the hewn Asedoth," which is no clearer than this verse. At v.17 and 34:1, however, the translator transliterated as Φασγά.

LXX subordinated שא by means of a participle ἀναβλέψας, but introduced the main verb ἴδε with καί in imitation of MT's וראה. The Byz text has improved the Greek by omitting this barbarism. The four directions are ordered as west, north, south and east, thus across the Jordan directly west and then to the right, i.e. north; by south is probably meant the area of the Negeb, and by east the area to be occupied by the Transjordan tribes already alloted their inheritance must be intended. A popular A F V variant reads *νοτον* instead of λίβα, but both mean "south."[37]

3:28 The Lord continues with instructions to Moses to prepare his successor Yesous to take over as leader of the people. The name 'Ιησοῦς becomes 'Ιησοῦ in the dative (and genitive), and not *ιησοι* as cod B has it.[38] The Byz text has glossed the name with a dative article so that it could not be misunderstood as a genitive. MT continues with two imperatives וחזקהו ואמצהו which both mean "strengthen, make strong." LXX has distinguished the two by κατίσχυσον αὐτὸν καὶ παρακάλεσον αὐτόν "strengthen him and encourage him,"[39] which is contextually most fitting.

The ὅτι clause consists of two coordinate future clauses defining what Yesous will be doing, one introduced by οὗτος and the other by αὐτός, both translating הוא. The change in pronouns is probably made merely for variation, and the tradition has readily confused the two, *z* having transposed the two and *C'' s* having *ουτος* for both. The pronouns are used to contrast with Moses' future; he will not cross over nor assign the land of promise to the Israelites, but Yesous will do so. In the tradition "the land which you have seen" has been popularly changed by prefixing "all" to "the land."

3:29 This verse concludes the narration of the first three chapters with a statement about location: "We were dwelling in a valley near the house of Phogor." בית פעור was a place in Moab mentioned three times in Deut (also at

37. The source of the variant must have been The Revisers, though the tradition is divided. One ms attributes *νότον* to The Revisers, whereas another ms reads *ο´ οἱ λ´* λίβα. I suspect that the latter note has wrongly coalesced two notes into one.
38. See THGD 62.
39. Aq corrects the second verb to *κραταίωσον*.

4:46 34:6) and in each case the בית is translated; only at Jos 13:20 is the name recognized as Βαιθφογώρ. The name פעור also occurs singly at Num 23:28 in the Balaam story as a height in Moab — *ἐπὶ κορυφὴν τοῦ Φογώρ* — but this need not be the same as בית פעור at all. Whether the name is etymologically related to the Arabic "faġara" "to open wide," hence "to gape" is not certain. Note the derivative "fuġra" used to indicate the mouth of a valley, and the contiguity of *ἐν νάπῃ* "in a valley."[40] The valley lay מול "over against" Beth Peor, which LXX rendered by *σύνεγγυς οἴκου Φογώρ*, i.e. near the house of Phogor.

40. Aq and Sym render גיא by *φάραγγι*.

Chapter 4

4:1 Israel is initially addressed with a singular imperative *ἄκουε*, but then the verse follows in the plural, which is then continued through v.8. This is only partially in imitation of MT which also changes to the plural at this point, but it levels the text to the plural where the singular occurs at אלהיך מקרבך in v.3 and ראה in v.5. The pair *τῶν δικαιωμάτων καὶ τῶν κριμάτων* is a common one in Deut[1] as well as the Hebrew equivalents החקים and המשפטים.[2] The translations are not inappropriate. חקים are matters which are prescribed, things etched by limitations, and *δικαιώματα* are matters determined or circumscribed by what is right, hence divine commandments. משפטים are judgments, and derivatives of the root *κριν-* "to judge," either as *κρίματα* or *κρίσεις*, are good renderings.

MT's relative clauses are both nominal patterns with participles as predicates. LXX normally renders such by a present tense as here, but for the first one it has an otiose *ἐγώ* before *διδάσκω* in imitation of the Hebrew אנכי מלמד where the pronoun is of course necessary. Over against MT, LXX has added *σήμερον* after "I am teaching you," which hex accordingly placed under the obelus. The addition is ex par.[3]

The collocation *ἵνα ζῆτε* is a commonly recurring phrase in Deut.[4] In the tradition a majority B 963 text has added *και πολυπλασιασθητε*; this has no basis in MT but is ex par; cf 8:11 11:8. The notion of inheriting the Promised Land also recurs frequently in Deut. That it is "the land which the God of your fathers is giving to you" is a variant of the shorter "which the Lord your God is giving to you," for which see comment at 1:20. The longer designation also occurs at 12:1 and 27:3.

4:2 The formula "you may not add ... nor subtract" with respect to a divine word is commonly used to identify the immutable word of God; cf e.g. Apoc

1. See List 22 in THGD 92.
2. Aq renders the coordinate phrases by *πρὸς ἀκριβασμοὺς καὶ πρὸς τὰ κρίματα* (retroverted from Syh).
3. See particularly list 30 in THGD 95.
4. See List 27 in THGD 94.

22:18—19.[5] The use of *πρός* for על is determined by the compound verb it modifies. The Deut translator tends to reuse the prepositional element in modifying prepositional phrases. The clause "which I am commanding you (today)" is a common Deut formula occurring with slight variations throughout the book.[6] The order *φυλάσσεσθε τὰς ἐντολάς* occurs again and again throughout the book as well.[7]

In the tradition the *d* text has the future passive *προστεθησεται* instead of *προσθήσετε*. Also represented are the homophonic *προσθησεται* and the middle form *προσθησεσθε* in B F+, but the active notion "to add" is obviously intended here as a contrast to *ἀφελεῖτε*. A majority variant added *σημερον* after *ὑμῖν* 1°, but this is an obvious importation from its occurrence after *ὑμῖν* 2° (which follows Sam).

The use of *ὅσας* in the last clause contrasts with the earlier relative clause introduced by *ὅ* (i.e. referring to *ῥῆμα*). In the tradition the A B *C'' b y*+ text has *οσα*, but 963 plus the majority read the LXX form (referring to *ἐντολάς*); for such variants only the tradition can decide.[8]

4:3 For *ἑωράκασιν* translating the participle הראת see comment at 3:21. MT does not support *πάντα* but it is present at 3:21 with which LXX levels.[9] The subject of the *ὅσα* clause is *κύριος ὁ θεὸς ἡμῶν*, though I would now change the pronoun to the A+ reading *ὑμῶν*. At the end of the verse *κύριος ὁ θεὸς ὑμῶν ἐξ ὑμῶν* occurs, and I suspect that *ἡμῶν* is an itacistic error for *ὑμῶν*. MT is no help, since it has only יהוה as subject; hex rightly placed *ὁ θεὸς ἡμῶν* under the obelus. Admittedly *ημων* is heavily supported in the tradition for the two pronouns at the end of the verse as well, but MT has second singular pronouns: אלהיך מקרבך, and the first plural must be secondary there. Since *ὁ θεὸς ἡμῶν* in the *ὅσα* clause is the result of the translator's leveling with the fuller designation later in the verse the reading *ὑμῶν* is almost certainly to be preferred as LXX.[10]

5. For a fuller discussion see Dogniez-Harl 133.
6. See list 30 in THGD 95.
7. See list 23 in THGD 92—93.
8. See THGD 58 and 106.
9. Though Kenn 75 does read את כל.
10. See Appositives 1.4.

The reference τῷ Βεελφεγώρ recalls the narrative at Num 25:1—5 where לבעל פעור occurs (vv.3,5) rather than the בבעל פעור in MT here.[11] MT understands Baalpeor to be a place, but this is not as clear in LXX; a dative modifying *ἐποίησεν* usually intends an indirect object: "did to"; LXX was probably influenced by its second occurrence in the verse where it is governed by *ὀπίσω*; in fact, MT takes בעל פעור in two senses: first as a place name, and then as the Baal of Peor, i.e. as an idol.

The *ὅτι* clause begins with a pendant nominative "every man who walked after Beelphagor," which is then brought into the clausal structure by means of an accusative pronoun *αὐτόν*; thus "as for every man ... the Lord ... destroyed him." For the plural *ὑμῶν* see comment above.[12]

4:4 The attributive participle *οἱ προσκείμενοι* "those devoted, attached to" modifies the pronoun *ὑμεις*.[13] Most unusual is the phrase *ἐν τῇ σήμερον*; in fact, it occurs only here in Deut. The normal rendering for היום is *σήμερον*.

4:5 The opening *ἴδετε* is based on the Sam ראו. Highly unusual is LXX's choice of *δέδειχα* "I have shown, pointed out" for למדתי; in fact, it occurs elsewhere in the Greek OT only at Isa 40:14 *τίς ἔδειξεν αὐτῷ κρίσιν* and 48:17 *δέδειχά σοι τοῦ εὑρεῖν σε τὴν ὁδόν*. Elsewhere Deut normally uses the verb to render הראה. What Moses has shown are *δικαιώματα*[14] *καὶ κρίσεις*. At v.1 MT has the same pair as here, but the second one, המשפטים, was translated by *κρίματα*; cf comment ad loc.

The *καθά* clause has *κύριος* as subject, whereas MT has יהוה אלהי. The majority text does add *ο θεος μου*, but this is probably hex in origin. Unexpected is the purposive infinitive construction *ποιῆσαι οὕτως*; one expects a plural pronoun modifying the infinitive "to do them," but LXX follows MT's כן. The infinitive is modified by *ἐν τῇ γῇ* which translates בקרב הארץ, i.e. it disregards קרב.[15] The description of the Promised Land as one *εἰς ἣν εἰσπο-*

11. The Others have *ἐπί* as rendering of the preposition. It should be noted that Kenn 9,193,300 read לבעל as well.
12. For מקרבך Theod retains a plural pronoun: *ἐκ μέσου ὑμῶν*, whereas Sym has *ἐκ μέσου σου*, and Aq translates as *ἀπὸ ἐγκάτου σου*.
13. Aq has *προσκολλώμενοι*. Aq uses only this verb or the simplex as equivalent for the root דבק.
14. Sym translates by *προστάγματα*.
15. But not so Aq who has <*ἐν*> *ἐγκάτῳ τῆς γῆς*.

ρεύεσθε ἐκεῖ κληρονομεῖν αὐτήν[16] is formulaic (though its exact equivalent recurs only at v.14 and 28:63).[17]

4:6 The opening future verbs *καὶ φυλάξεσθε καὶ ποιήσετε*, are used absolutely, but the reference must be to the *δικαιώματα καὶ κρίσεις* of v.5. The futures here have imperatival force. The syntax of the verse following these verbs is somewhat loose. I would divide after *ἐθνῶν* (as the Masoretes did), and read the rest of the verse as a conditional sentence with the apodosis being introduced by *καὶ* (*ἐροῦσιν*) in imitation of MT. *ὅτι* introduces all of this, first with the nominal clause "this is your wisdom and understanding before all the nations." This is then explicated by the conditional: "whoever might hear all these ordinances will say: Behold a wise and intelligent people is this great nation." The point being made is that *πάντα τὰ δικαιώματα ταῦτα* are obviously so wise and intelligent that anyone hearing them will praise Israel as being *σοφὸς καὶ ἐπιστήμων*. It should be noted that MT does not have an equivalent for the *πάντων* modifying "the nations."

LXX fails to render the suffix of בינתכם, since *ὑμῶν* already modifies the coordinate *ἡ σοφία*, making a repeated pronoun otiose. Hex has, however, supplied an *υμων*. The root בין occurs twice in the verse, as בינת and נבון. LXX distinguished neatly by *σύνεσις* vs *ἐπιστήμων*.[18]

4:7 LXX translates the interrogative מי well both here and in v.8 by the interrogative adjective *ποῖον*, thus "what kind of great nation (is it)." The גוי of MT is modified by a relative clause in which the pronoun contains לו, i.e. "to whom." The translator rightly has the dative *ᾧ*, but continued with *ἐστιν αὐτῷ*; the *αὐτῷ* is otiose in Greek, and simply imitates the לו of MT.

MT has אלהים קרבים within the relative clause; the plural is used since the question pertains to a non-Israelite nation. LXX has made the clause singular with its ... *θεὸς ἐγγίζων* (*αὐτοῖς*), presumably on the understanding that gods in the singular are involved, i.e. each nation would have a god drawing near to it. The plural pronoun is an ad sensum interpretation for אליו. The

16. Only Aq follows LXX's present infinitive; Theod and Sym attest to the aorist *κληρονομῆσαι*.
17. For other instances of the formula see list 13 in THGD 90.
18. But Aq has *σύνετος* for the second noun here.

relative clause in MT contains two prepositional phrases, לו anδ אליו; the first one relates to the relative pronoun, i.e. "to whom there are gods." Then אלהים is modified attributively by קרבים אליו, "which are near to it." The antecedent for both phrases is גוי. LXX distinguishes the two in schizophrenic fashion by number, the first one as *αὐτῷ* (the nation), and the second one as *αὐταῖς* (nation as "peoples"), which is clever but at best confusing.

The comparison contrasts the *θεὸς* (*ἐγγίζων αὐτοῖς*) with *κύριος ὁ θεὸς ἡμῶν* .... The point is then made how the Lord our God draws near in all the things *οἷς ἂν αὐτὸν ἐπικαλεσώμεθα*, "about which we might invoke him."

4:8 The second point of comparison between other nations and the Israelites concerns the *δικαιώματα καὶ κρίματα δίκαια* received by the Israelites; this also made them unique. The initial format is the same as in v.7, but the pattern of comparison is a *κατά* phrase "according to this *νόμον*," by which the Deuteronomic code of instruction is meant; this is clear as the relative clause modifying *νόμον* shows, viz. "which I am setting before you today." Note the collocation *δίδωμι ἐνώπιον*, in which *δίδωμι* must be taken as a calque of נתן in the sense of "set, place."

4:9 With v.9 a new theme is introduced; this is marked by the change to a second singular discourse. This is even more obvious in MT which begins with רק "only," which LXX omits. The first two clauses use the same root in MT, but different stems: the Qal of שמר becomes *πρόσεχε*, whereas its Ni is translated by *φύλαξον*. The two clauses are strictly synonymous, since נפש with pronominal suffix simply equals the reflexive pronoun, thus "take care (for yourself), and watch your person."[19] This type of repetition is typical of the wordiness of Deut.

LXX renders the metonymy of הדברים אשר ראו עיניך literally by its (*πάντας*) *τοὺς λόγους οὓς ἑωράκασιν οἱ ὀφθαλμοί σου*. The expression "(the matters) which your eyes have seen" means "which you have experienced." The *πάντας* has no counterpart in MT, a fact which hex recognized by its obelus.[20]

---

19. For the formula *πρόσεχε σεαυτῷ* ... *μή* see list 31 in THGD 95.
20. The Others all read *μήποτε* instead of *μή* (before *ἐπιλάθῃ*).

The coordinate *μή* clause is parallel to the "lest you forget" clause. *μὴ ἀποστήτωσαν ἀπὸ τῆς καρδίας σου* means "lest they should leave your heart," i.e. disappear from your memory. *καρδία* like its Hebrew counterpart לבב refers to the mind, the intelligence. The subject of the verb must be the *λόγους* of the coordinate clause.

The last clause, though coordinated by *καί*, is contrastive, i.e. "but" you must teach your sons, so that the *λόγους* will remain throughout the generations; the notion of generations is expressed by "your sons and your sons' sons."

4:10 *ἡμέραν* must be understood as an adverbial modifier to *ἑωράκασιν*, thus "(experienced) ... at the time (day) that you stood ...."[21] The day is actually defined in LXX by *τῇ ἡμέρᾳ τῆς ἐκκλησίας*, i.e. a reference to the assembly of people at Khoreb when God spoke to them and gave them the Ten Words; cf 18:16 where ביום הקהל obtains. That phrase also occurs at 9:10 10:4 but is in both cases omitted by LXX, while here LXX adds it even though MT lacks it. The phrase recalls the day as the time of divine revelation at Mt. Khoreb. Hex correctly placed the phrase under the obelus to show its absence in MT.

On that occasion Moses was told "*ἐκκλησίασον* to me the people and *ἀκουσάτωσαν* my words." The use of *ἐκκλησίασον* reaffirms the time as "the day of the assembly." For the second verb MT has אשמעם "I will make them hear (my words)." LXX by its change to third plural imperative makes the people the subject, which is consistent with the third plurals within the *ὅπως* clause. Thus "they may hear my words in order that they may learn ... and may teach." The purpose of hearing God's words is twofold: a) to "learn to fear me all the days which they are going to live on the land," and b) to "teach their sons." What they are to teach their sons is not expressly stated, but it must be that which they are to learn, viz. *φοβεῖσθαι με κ.τ.λ.* It is then clear that the fear of the Lord is something that can be learned and taught; it is the divine instruction, particularly the Ten Words.

Instructive for understanding how the translator operated is his rendering of אשר. The relative pronoun occurs three times in the verse. The first one is rendered by (*ἡμέραν*) *ἥν*; the second one is taken as a purposive particle *ὅπως*

---

21. Hardly modifying *συμβιβάσεις* of v.9 as Dogniez-Harl, since the day is characterized as taking place in the past.

(plus the subjunctive), and the last one becomes (ἡμέρας) ὅσας; a B F *oI f*+ text changed ὅσας to ας, but the oldest witness, 963, witnesses to LXX.

4:11 For ἔστητε ὑπὸ τὸ ὄρος see Exod 19:17. The next clause has the verb in the imperfect which translates the participial predicate בער. ἐκαίετο shows what was happening while the people stood at the base of the mountain. The verb is modified by a dative of instrument, which translates the prepositional phrase באש of MT.[22] In MT this is also modified by עד לב השמים "to the center of the sky." לב is not separately translated in LXX, ἕως τοῦ οὐρανοῦ being deemed sufficient,[23] but hex has inserted καρδιας under the asterisk to represent it.

The verse ends with a list of three words, all signifying forms of darkness and all in the nominative, serving as a contrast to the fire burning up to the sky, i.e. "(but there was) darkness, gloominess, tempest." The second and third items, γνόφος, θύελλα, hardly translate ענן וערפל, their correspondents in MT, but are taken over from 5:22, and cf. Exod 10:22 where the three nouns also occur in LXX;[24] see comment ad loc. A popular B gloss has added φωνη μεγαλη at the end, but this was taken over from 5:22, where the three nouns also obtain.

4:12 The Lord speaking ἐκ μέσου τοῦ πυρός recurs often in the first part of Deut, thereby showing how he revealed himself.[25] A *C''* *s z* tradition has glossed κύριος by θεος but this is not to be taken seriously. The majority text has inserted εν τω ορει before "from the middle of the fire," as an obvious borrowing from 5:4. The revelatory mode is described positively as φωνὴν ῥημάτων ὑμεῖς ἠκούσατε and negatively as ὁμοίωμα οὐκ εἴδετε.[26] The stress is placed on God's invisibility by the concluding contrastive ἀλλ' ἢ φωνήν which is to be taken in the same sense as זולתי קול "save (only,) a voice." LXX fails to show the participial predicates אתה שמעים and אינכם ראים by imperfect

22. See THGD 117.
23. See SS 69.
24. The Others render ענן more appropriately by νεφέλη, whereas Aq renders ערפל by ὁμίχλη "mist, fog."
25. See list 35 in THGD 95—96.
26. Sym has μορφήν instead of ὁμοίωμα for תמונה; see a plausible explanation in Salvesen 146—147.

verbs as it normally does. The Greek simply recalls the fact of their occurrence, i.e. by verbs in the aorist, rather than the continuity of the verbal notion which might have been more appropriate. In the tradition the 963 *b n+* text does read the imperfect, *ηκουετε*, for the first verb, but does not do so for the second; it must therefore be secondary.

4:13 What had only been referred to as "my words" is here put into the theological context of God's covenant. That covenant is defined as *ἣν ἐνετείλατο ὑμῖν ποιεῖν*, thus as obligations imposed by God on his people.[27] Nothing is said here about God's side of the covenant; rather the people have had announced to them *τὰ δέκα ῥήματα*, for which see 5:6—21.

For God's writing the Ten Words on two stone tablets see Exod 32:15—16,19 and 34:1,4. The adjectival phrase *πλάκας λιθίνας* is also found in the Exod accounts; it simplifies the bound phrase לחות אבנים, though correctly understanding its intent.

4:14 Moses' role in the covenant is also divinely dictated; it is described as *διδάξαι ὑμᾶς δικαιώματα καὶ κρίσεις*. The Ten Words were spoken directly by God to the people; now Moses is to teach them how these are to be realized in their lives. What this means is that the *δικαιώματα καὶ κρίσεις* constitute the practical exposition of the principle demands laid down by God in the Ten Words. It should also be noted that *δικαιώματα* is the regular word for חקים in Deut,[28] whereas המשפטים is usually translated either by *κρίματα* or *κρίσεις*; for a discussion of these terms see comments at v.1.

The consecution *ποιεῖν ὑμᾶς αὐτά* follows MT's order לעשתכם אתם, i.e. the subject precedes the modifier. A B+ variant inverts the two as *αυτα υμας*, but this must be an error. LXX normally puts the accusative pronominal subject before the object.[29] For "into which you are entering there to inherit it" see comment at v.5. Undoubtedly this form of the formula influenced the translator to adopt *εἰσπορεύεσθε* for עברים rather than *διαβαινετε*.[30]

---

27. For a brief, but still relevant, discussion of "covenant" see Driver 67—68.
28. Aq corrects this by his *ἀκριβασμούς*.
29. See THGD 129.
30. For "cross over … inherit" see list 14 in THGD 90.

4:15 For the idiom φυλάξεσθε τὰς ψυχάς see comment at v.9. The future has imperatival force here. The ὅτι clause is presumably causal, and sets the stage for the prohibition of v.16. What the prolix language is meant to convey is: Take care ... that you may not make for yourselves γλυπτὸν ὁμοίωμα κ.τ.λ. The reason for this is expressed by the ὅτι clause "you did not see a likeness in the day that the Lord spoke to you in Khoreb in the mountain from the midst of the fire." The prepositional phrase ἐν τῷ ὄρει has no counterpart in MT and constitutes a leveling with its occurrence in a similar context at 5:4. For the Lord speaking "from the midst of the fire" see comment at v.12.

4:16 MT has "lest you should corrupt," which LXX renders by μὴ ἀνομήσητε "lest you should act lawlessly." LXX stresses the idea of disobedience rather than that of moral corruption.[31] Hex has μητοτε for μή so as to render פן more accurately. The use of the double pronoun ὑμῖν αὐτοῖς for לכם yields a reflexive sense "(make) for yourselves." This is made even more obvious by the popular B variant υμιν εαυτοις.[32] γλυπτός is the regular rendering for פסל in LXX, and means something engraved, fashioned, and usually refers to an idolatrous image; here its apposite defines it as ὁμοίωμα, a likeness. In MT this is bound to כל סמל, but LXX has πᾶσαν εἰκόνα[33] in apposition with γλυπτὸν ὁμοίωμα.

ὁμοίωμα occurs twice in the verse. As in vv.12,15 it translates תמונה literally, but in the collocation ὁμοίωμα ἀρσενικοῦ ἢ θηλυκοῦ it translates תבנית, as it does four times in the next two verses. תבנית/ὁμοίωμα is used only for specific forms (male, female, cattle, birds, creepers, fish).

4:17—18 More ὁμοίωμα which are forbidden; these are all on the level with the "ὁμοίωμα of male and female" in v.16.[34] Image making of cattle, birds, reptiles or fish is forbidden. Each one, in distinction from the "male or female" in v.16, is further defined. That of πάντος κτήνους is characterized as τῶν ὄντων ἐπὶ τῆς γῆς. The translator puts the modifier in the plural. As often he will sacrifice grammatical correctness for sense; του οντος might satisfy

31. Theod and Aq render literally by μὴ διαφθείρητε.
32. See THGD 111 and 96, list 37.
33. Aq translates סמל by εἰδώλου. The genitive reflects the syntax of the Hebrew as well.
34. Aq tried to render תבנית more exactly by his ὑπόδειγμα "pattern."

purists, but κτῆνος is a collective, hence τῶν ὄντων is used. The second likeness, πάντος ὀρνέου πτερωτοῦ, is defined as ὃ πέταται ὑπὸ τὸν οὐρανόν. The phrase "winged bird" translates the bound construction צפור כנף. MT defines this as that "which flies בשמים." Since שמים was thought of as a dome resting upon the earth the translator thought of the birds as flying beneath that dome. The third category, πάντος ἑρπετοῦ, is characterized by ὃ ἕρπει ἐπὶ τῆς γῆς, and the last one, πάντος ἰχθύος, is modified by ὅσα ἐστιν ἐν τοῖς ὕδασιν ὑποκάτω τῆς γῆς. Note that unlike the first one, the translator does not realize the collective by an ad sensum plural, but retains the more grammatical singular.

4:19 The καὶ μή ... προσκυνήσῃς καὶ λατρεύσῃς construction is coordinate with the μὴ ἀνομήσητε καὶ ποιήσητε one of v.16. As in v.16 hex has added ποτε to μή to represent פן, placing ποτε under the asterisk. MT has a succession of five coordinate verbs governed by פן: "raise (your eyes), see, be drawn away, worship, serve." LXX has subordinated the first three participially, placing the stress on προσκυνήσῃς καὶ λατρεύσῃς. These two verbs are similar in meaning; in fact, προσκυνέω occurs nine times in Deut, and in seven cases is coordinated with λατρεύω (also 5:9 8:19 11:16 17:3 29:26 30:17, but not at 26:10 32:43).

The first construction is simplified as ἀναβλέψας used absolutely;[35] of course, "looking up to heaven" involves eyes, and though not literalistic it is a good translation.[36]

The second construct is "seeing the sun and the moon and the stars καὶ πάντα τὸν κόσμον τοῦ οὐρανοῦ." In MT כל צבא השמים is in apposition to the named astral bodies, but LXX coordinates.[37] Hex has rightly placed the καί before πάντα τὸν κόσμον under the obelus. By taking צבא as κόσμος LXX stresses the ordered character of the sky; the Creator God had put the stars in their places, and they now serve not only as the decoration of the skies, but they also give order to the heavens.[38] The use of κόσμον also avoids the more

35. See SS 102 where it is called an example of "freie Wiedergaben." Sym corrects to ἄρας σὺ ὀφθαλμούς σου (as retroverted from Syh).
36. Cf Lee 26.
37. Aq renders כל צבא by πᾶσαν στρατίαν taking צבא in the sense of "host, army."
38. Schl makes the interesting observation about the phrase κόσμος τοῦ οὐρανοῦ "per quem stellae sunt intellegendae quibus κόσμος, *ornatus*, recte tribui potest, et quae ad modum ordinatissimi exercitus procedunt."

literal notion of an army of heaven, which might yield some notion of intelligent heavenly forces rather than objects created by God.

The third participle is *πλανηθείς* "being led astray" for נדחת, an intelligent choice to introduce the verb *προσκυνήσῃς*, thus "being led astray (by seeing the heavenly bodies) you would worship."[39]

These heavenly bodies are further characterized by a relative clause "which the Lord your God assigned (+*αὐτά* = אתם) to all the nations which are underneath the sky." This renders MT literally except for omitting כל (from "all the sky"), and adding *τοῖς* after "nations."[40] The verb *ἀπένειμεν* occurs only here for חלק; in fact, this verb occurs elsewhere in LXX only twice in 3Macc (1:7 3:16), but it is an accurate equivalent to חלק.[41]

4:20 This verse is contrastive with v.19 as the *δέ* shows. The subject of the verbs is *ὁ θεός*. Since in MT it is יהוה, hex has added *κυριος* before it and placed *ὁ θεός* under the obelus. Both Cod G and Syh have *κυριος ο θεος* under the obelus, but this is obviously an error. Origen would have put *κυριος* under the asterisk, and *ο θεος* under the obelus. Why LXX should have used *ὁ θεός* instead of *κυριος* is puzzling since *κύριος* (with or without *ὁ θεός σου*) is used throughout the context (vv.15,19,20,23,24).[42] The phrase *καμίνου τῆς σιδηρᾶς* recurs only once in LXX (Jer 11:4). The Hebrew equivalent כור הברזל does recur at 1Kgs 8:51, but LXX there renders the phrase by *χωνευτηρίου σιδήρου*. The figure is a striking one for the more usual *οἶκος δουλείας*.

The purpose of the Exodus is given as להיות לו לעם נחלה "to become a people as a possession for him." LXX interprets as "to be for him a people *ἔγκληρον*." The adjective means "having a share, sharing an inheritance," but here it has a passive sense, i.e. "a people possessed"; the dative must here be a dative of possession, and could hardly intend "(sharing) with him." The

---

39. Aq renders נדחת literally by *ἐξωσθῇς* "you would be thrust back."
40. The Three all have *λαοῖς* (*λαούς* in Sym) instead of *ἔθνεσιν τοῖς*. Sym translates תחת כל השמים by *ὑπὸ ὅλον τὸν οὐρανόν*, but Theod and Aq, by *κάτω παντὸς τοῦ οὐρανοῦ*. Note also that Sym used the indefinite relative pronoun *ἅτινα* for אשר, whereas Aq retained the *ἅ* of LXX.
41. Aq translates by *ἐμέρισεν*, and Sym as *διεκόσμησεν*; for the latter see Salvesen 148.
42. See Appositives 1.5.3.

adjective is a hapax legomenon in LXX.[43] For ὡς ἐν τῇ ἡμέρᾳ ταύτῃ see comment at 2:30.

4:21 For *κύριος ἐθυμώθη μοι* see comment at 1:37. The phrase על דבריכם "because of your words" is amplified as *περὶ τῶν λεγομένων ὑφ' ὑμῶν*, a direct reference to the people's murmuring at 1:27—28.

The verb *ὤμοσεν* is modified by two coordinate *ἵνα μή* clauses expressing the intent of the oath, viz. "that I would not cross ... nor would enter." LXX adds a demonstrative pronoun *τοῦτον* after *τὸν Ἰορδάνην* over against MT here as well as in v.22. This may well be due to the influence of 3:27 where MT has את הירדן הזה (as at 31:2).[44] In all other cases of *τὸν Ἰορδάνην* (4:26 9:1 11:31 12:10 27:2,4 32:47) no demonstrative pronoun obtains. LXX also differs from MT's designation of the land as הארץ הטובה in its *τὴν γῆν*; hex adds *την αγαθην* after *γῆν* to equal MT. For the relative clause ending the verse see comment at 1:20.

Unusual is the failure to render the suffix of אלהיך. The collocation יהוה אלהיך occurs 193 times in Deut, and only five times does LXX have only *κύριος ὁ θεός*, i.e. fails to render the suffix (also at 19:2,8 21:5 24:9). In the 123 cases in chh.1—18 that of 4:21 is the only case of the second singular suffix being omitted from the collocation. The omission does make a neat point, however. Since *κύριος* was also Moses' God the omission of *σου* is probably intentional.[45]

4:22 The Greek is an exact translation of MT except for adding *καί* before *οὐ* and for "this" modifying Jordan, for which see comment at v.21; the three participial predicates of MT are all rendered by a present tense: "I am going to die ... going to cross ... but you are going to cross," which are then followed by the future *κληρονομήσετε* for a contextual ירשתם. Note the fine use of a contrastive *δέ*. The collocation "cross over ... and possess the land" is a typical Deut pattern.[46] Hex has correctly placed *τοῦτον* under the obelus; that B omits the word along with Byz (as well as two *O* mss) could either represent

43. Aq uses the more common noun *κληροδοσίας*.
44. It should be noted that Kenn 605 adds הזה as well.
45. See Appositives 2.3.
46. See list 14 in THGD 90.

original LXX with Origen's parent text containing *τουτον* as a gloss or, as seems more likely, it could show post-hexaplaric revision. It should also be noted that MT (followed by LXX) has switched to the plural which then continues partway through v.23.

4:23 The initial warning השמרו לכם is translated by *προσέχετε ὑμεῖς*.[47] The nominative pronoun is unexpected and is basically otiose, but see comment at 1:7. The command is otherwise in the singular as *πρόσεχε σεαυτῷ* (4:9 6:12 8:11 11:16 12:13,19,30 15:9 24:8), except at 32:46 where, however, לכם does not occur in MT.

μὴ ἐπιλάθησθε again reflects a פן construction in MT as at vv.9,16,19 and hex corrects *μή* by adding *ποτε*.[48] In the tradition *C'' s z* attest to the genitive instead of to *τὴν διαθήκην*. The genitive follows Classical usage, whereas an accusative modifying *λανθάνομαι* is Hellenistic. The term is used, as in v.13, of the demands made upon the people by the covenant, for which see comment at v.13.[49] *διέθετο* rendering כרת when referring to God making a covenant with man is normal usage in OT, already occurring at Gen 15:18 which see. The equation was favored by Deut, occurring ten times in the book.

καὶ ποιήσητε continues the subjunctive, i.e. it is still governed by *μή*, thus "and that you should make." This is voided by an A 963 *O+* variant *και ποιησετε*, i.e. a future indicative verb, which contemplates that the people would disregard the prohibition against making images. In the tradition a popular text reads *και ανονησητε* before it which is, however, based on v.16 or v.25. The use of *ἑαυτοῖς* after *ὑμῖν* changes *ὑμῖν* into a reflexive; it is the plural equivalent of *σεαυτῷ*. For *γλυπτὸν ὁμοίωμα* see comment at v.16. Here *ὁμοίωμα* is modified by *πάντων ὧν*; the relative pronoun is genitive plural by attraction to its antecedent; grammatically it should be in the accusative, but this translator favors inflection of relatives by attraction rather than by grammatical relation. LXX translated צוך by *συνέταξέν σοι*; the verb occurs only nine times in the book for צוה, whereas *ἐντέλλομαι* is used 80 times (and

47. Aq translates the verb by *φυλάξασθε*.
48. The Others reflect this as well by *μήποτε ἐπιλάθησθε*.
49. The anonymous marginal reading *συνθήκης* is almost certainly Aq.

occurs for no other verb). It was probably chosen to avoid any possible notion that God had ordered the making of images.[50]

4:24 The text continues with the singular, which it uses through *υἱῶν σου* of v.25, imitating MT. The verse gives the basis for the prohibition of the making of images. The Lord is a *πῦρ καταναλίσκον*, a devouring fire, thus a destructive force which will destroy those who make images.[51] This receives its explanation in the nature of God as a *θεὸς ζηλωτής*. What this means is that in contrast to other gods he is jealous of his cult, which must be imageless; cf Note on Exod 20:5.

4:25 LXX renders the כי clause as a conditional *ἐάν* type. For בני בנים, LXX personalizes by adding *σου*, thus "your sons' sons"; the pronoun is placed under the obelus by hex to show its absence in MT. With the next clause the text changes to the plural, which is sensible since "sons and sons' sons" are now understood as included in the subject. The choice of *χρονίσητε* to render נושנתם is peculiar, since it simple means "to spend time," and so to linger, tarry, but the Hebrew means "to grow old."[52] Of course, growing old does involve the spending of time. Actually the Ni of ישן occurs elsewhere only in Lev 13:11 (of an old disease, as *λέπρα παλαιουμένη*) and 26:10 where ישן is rendered by *παλαιὰ παλαιῶν*. For *ἀνομήσητε* see comment at v.16.

The last clause is still part of the protasis, and the change of *ποιήσητε* to the future indicative, *ποιησετε*, in *d*+ is obviously wrong. Its modifier is the singular *τὸ πονηρόν* which stands for הרע, and not the plural *τα πονηρα* as in B V *n*; when *πονηρός* is used nominally for רע in Deut (13 times) it is always singular; in fact, the plural only occurs at 7:15 for MT's רעים, but in such contexts as "do evil, remove evil" the word occurs only in the singular (see also 9:18 13:5 17:2,7,12 19:19 21:21 22:21,22,24 24:7 31:29). Most of these refer to people, i.e. as *τὸν πονηρόν*, only here and 9:18 17:2 and 31:29 does the neuter obtain. The infinitival construction at the end of the verse can hardly be purposive, nor is it complementary; "to provoke him to anger" is hardly the purpose of doing evil before the Lord; rather it shows what doing

50. See THGD 57.
51. Aq translates אכלה more literally by *κατεσθίον*.
52. The Three all read *παλαιωθῆτε*.

evil involves, i.e. "thereby provoking him to anger." It has been suggested that such infinitives are really epexegetical in nature,[53] which makes good sense. What the infinitive actually intends is probably result; the result of doing evil in the Lord's presence is that it incites him to anger.

4:26 This verse constitutes the apodosis to the condition of v.25. Since the future tense continues in the following verses, it is possible to take them as part of the apodosis as well, but I would rather take those cases as an explication of v.26.

διαμαρτύρομαι is here used in the sense of calling witnesses to the truth of a statement. The witnesses called are *τόν τε οὐρανὸν καὶ τὴν γῆν* as personified bodies. The present tense correctly represents the neutral tense character of העידתי; this is itself made obvious by the presence of *σήμερον*. "I call heaven and earth to witness to you today." LXX has rendered בכם by a simple dative showing to whom or for whom the verbal action is directed. Presumably one might label this a dative of disadvantage,[54] and it might be translated "against you."

That to which these cosmic bodies are to witness is the reality of the divine statement of the *ὅτι* clause. The dire punishment on those who make images is stressed by the use of dative nouns preceding cognate verbs: *ἀπωλείᾳ ἀπολεῖσθε ... ἐκτριβῇ ἐκτριβήσεσθε*, which is one of the ways by which the translator renders free cognate infinitives. As in the case of the infinitives, the cognate datives stress the verbal idea, thus "you will really be destroyed ... you will certainly be annihilated." In MT the first verb, תאבדון, is followed by מהר "quickly," which LXX disregarded. I suspect this to have been due to homoiarchton, since the next word מעל also begins with *mem*. Exactly the same thing obtains at 9:16 where the word is followed by מן, but at 9:3 where מהר is not followed by *mem*, but by כאשר, the word is translated by *ἐν τάχει*. Hex adds *ταχυ* under the asterisk to represented the omitted word.

Within the relative clause modifying *γῆς*: "into which you are crossing the Jordan there to inherit," LXX renders אשר plus שמה in Hebraic fashion by *εἰς ἣν ... ἐκεῖ*, with the adverb being otiose in Greek. On the other hand, it

53. In SS 210.
54. The so-called "dativus incommodi."

fortunately did not render the suffix of לרשתה "to inherit it," though the majority text did add *αυτην*; comp vv.5,14.

The punishment is stated in negative terms by the Hebrew לא תאריכן ימים "not shall you lengthen days." For this LXX has created a neologism *πολυχρονιεῖτε* based on the adjective *πολυχρόνιος*; comp Gen 26:8 where the Hebrew idiom is rendered by *ἐγένετο πολυχρόνιος*. The verb occurs only here in the entire LXX. This is followed in MT by a כי clause, i.e. you will not live long because you will be completely annihilated. LXX makes the clause adversative, ἀλλ' ἤ, which is smoother.

4:27 What v.26 means in practical terms is outlined in vv.27—31. The diaspora is threatened: "the Lord will scatter you among *πᾶσιν* the nations.[55] MT has no equivalent for *πᾶσιν*, but it is supported by Vulg. Its omission by the Byz text could be recensional. By contrast an A *C b s*+ text has added *πασιν* in the next *ἐν* phrase as well. The phrase *ὀλίγοι ἀριθμῷ* "few in number" correctly interprets the Hebrew idiom מתי מספר literally "men of number," thus people that can be counted, a few. LXX has rendered both בעמים and בגוים by *ἐν τοῖς ἔθνεσιν*, rightly understanding the two phrases here as identical in meaning. For *εἰς οὕς ... ἐκεῖ* see comment at v.26. The verb in the relative clause in MT is ינהג; Yahweh will drive you out. LXX softens the active force of the verb by using *εἰσάξει* "will bring you in."

4:28 MT reads: and there you will serve אלהים; the word must refer not to the Lord, but to "gods," i.e. foreign or other gods.[56] LXX understood this and translated by *θεοῖς ἑτέροις* which may be due to the reading אחרים attested in some mss,[57] and is also supported by Pesh.[58] This is followed by the apposite phrase מעשה ידי אדם "the work of human hands." LXX makes this plural *ἔργοις* as it does with *ξύλοις καὶ λίθοις*. Thus for LXX the other gods are not just human products; they are sticks and stones.

That these gods are insensitive is a theme common to OT thought, particularly in the prophets. The negatives are expressed by *οὐδέ* rather than by

55. Aq has *διασκορπίσει* rather than *διασπερεῖ*, but these are synonyms.
56. For *λατρεύσετε* used to indicate idol worship see Daniel 67—68.
57. In Kenn 75, 146, 152 and 199.
58. Tar^O gets around this by its לעממיא פלחי טעותא "peoples who worship idols."

ουτε as B *z*+. This translator throughout preferred the *delta* to the *tau* forms, thus *μήδεν*, *οὐδεῖς*, *οὐδέ* rather than *μηθεν*, *ουθεις* or *ουτε*.[59] The senses mentioned are seeing, hearing, eating, smelling. In the tradition the urge to add speaking somewhere in the list is apparent especially in the *s* text, but this has no support in MT.

4:29 The punishment is, however, not absolute, and vv.29—31 provide an escape; repentance is possible. In exile "you (i.e. the people) will seek the Lord your God, and you will find (him) when you seek him ...." In contrast to LXX MT only has the first verb in the plural, then changing to the singular and not returning to a plural before v.34. LXX only changes to the singular after "seek him," and thereafter follows MT.[60]

The *ὅταν* clause is meant to modify *εὑρήσετε*, thus "you will find (him) when ...." Most witnesses agree with Sam and add *αυτον* after the verb, but LXX follows the earlier text of MT; the pronoun is added to simplify the text; the Sam text was probably influenced by the suffix of תדרשנו.

The modifier "with your whole heart and your whole person" is a typical Deut formula.[61] What the text is saying is that seeking him must be unreserved and complete as a condition for finding him. The reading of ב by *ἐξ* is idiomatic.[62]

V.29 has taken the opening words of v.30 בצר לך as a further modifier of *ἐκζητήσητε*, which interpretation is enhanced by the fact that the next word begins with *waw*. Making the cut with LXX after *θλίψει σου* is simpler than the versification of MT. It should also be noted that the compound verb contrasts with the simplex, which is LXX's way of distinguishing דרש from בקש of MT.

The tradition illustrates profusely how itacistic spellings can confuse the reader. One of the most common cases is that of the ending -*τε* vs -*ται*, both being pronounced as /tε/ in Hellenistic and Byzantine Greek. Occasionally the

59. See the discussion on negatives in THGD 113—115, as well as the comment on this verse at *ibid* 62.
60. Sam and Vulg have the first verb in the singular as well, which results in a consistent singular throughout. Tar^O follows MT, and Pesh consistently has plurals for the verse.
61. See List 19 in THGD 91—92.
62. See SS 127.

variant is sensible, but the reader is warned to be guided by the parent Hebrew where no such confusion is possible. The verbs in this verse are all second plural active, not third singular medio-passive, and the -*ται* spelling is simply a misspelling for -*τε*. Of course, the reverse is just as possible, but the Hebrew parent usually determines which spelling is correct.

4:30 The verse then begins with *καὶ εὑρήσουσίν σε* for ומצאוך, with *οἱ λόγοι οὗτοι* referring to the matters mentioned in vv. 25—29. The prepositional phrase *ἐπ' ἐσχάτῳ τῶν ἡμερῶν* here looks no farther ahead than to Israel's repentance. The phrase takes on eschatological significance in prophetic literature, but it is doubtful that the translator had anything more in mind than the indefinite future when in exile the people would repent and God would be good to them. The dative singular governed by *ἐπί* reflects the preposition ב of Hebrew. Most witnesses have the genitive *εσχατου*, but the dative testifies to the literalist tendency of the Deut translator.[63]

The second and third clauses change from third plural to second singular and show what will take place "at the end of the days." The use of the future passive has middle force: "turn yourselves," which adequately renders the Qal of שוב. It is modified by an *ἐπί* phrase, chosen by the translator to modify an *επι*- compound, rather than the popular B text reading *προς*, which constitutes a smoothing out of the text to equal "return to," but *ἐπί* is original.[64] The final clause *καὶ εἰσακούσῃ τῆς φωνῆς αὐτοῦ* means "and you shall obey him." The compound *εἰσακούω* is often chosen to convey the notion of obedience in LXX.

4:31 The *ὅτι* clause gives the basis for the repenting people's confidence. Israel's God is a *θεὸς οἰκτίρμων* "a compassionate God," in which the adjective intends to portray God as filled with feelings of compasssion. A popular gloss has added *και ελεημων*, but this is taken over from Exod 34:6.

This divine characteristic makes valid the assurances which constitute the remainder of thc verse: a) "he will not forsake you," a good rendering of the Hi verbal form ירפך; b) nor will he *ἐκτρίψῃ σε*, for which see comment at v.26. c) Over against MT this clause obtains in absolute form; MT has the

63. See the discussion in THGD 57.
64. See THGD 117—118 for the usage with *ἐπιστρέφω*.

clause in parataxis. By not coordinating this clause with the other two the translator has opened the way for understanding *οὐκ ἐπιλήσεται*—fin as a summary statement involving both a) and b). God will not forget the covenant of your fathers; this involves never forsaking you nor permitting your destruction. The genitive *τῶν πατέρων* is an objective genitive, the covenant which God made with the fathers. This is the other side of the covenant shown in vv.13 and 23; here it is not the demands of the covenant between God and his people, but God's promises that are proclaimed. This is clear from the relative clause modifier *ἣν ὤμοσεν αὐτοῖς* which refers to *διαθήκην*. That it was sworn gives quite a different point of view from the *διέθετο* of v.23 or of *ἐνετείλατο ποιεῖν* of v.13. The subject of *ὤμοσεν* is obvious from the context, but a popular reading adds *κυριος* at the end of the verse; this has no basis in MT and is quite otiose.

4:32 MT ties this verse to the preceding by כי; thus v.32 becomes proof for the statement of v.31. LXX has disregarded the כי and begins with the imperative *ἐπερωτήσατε* modified by an accusative, thus "inquire of former times, which happened before you."

The participle *γενομένος* is modified both temporally and spatially. The former is an *ἀπό* phrase: "from the day that God created mankind on the earth." The verb *ἔκτισεν* renders ברא, which is the usual Aquila rendering; the equation occurs only here in the Pentateuch, and is a literalistic one. The spatial modifier is *ἐπὶ τὸ ἄκρον τοῦ οὐρανοῦ ἕως ἄκρου τοῦ οὐρανοῦ*. In the con text it should mean "from the end of the sky to the end of the sky," or better said "from one end of the sky to the other." But *ἐπί* with the accusative does not ordinarily mean "from" in Greek. The translation represents the Hebrew למקצה, in which ל plus ועד means "from ... up to." Presumably the Greek can be understood as "to (or on) one end of the sky even to the other."

What they are to inquire after is given as a series of *εἰ* clauses which translate a number of interrogative clauses extending into v.34. The first is "whether there has (ever) happened (anything) like this great thing." The verb is an adequate translation of נהיה, the Ni of היה. The second query is *εἰ ἤκουσται τοιοῦτο* "whether such (a thing) has (ever) been heard." The subject represents a prepositional phrase in MT, כמהו,[65] and the Greek understood it

65. The Others render this literally by *ὅμοιον αὐτῷ*.

correctly. The majority text has the accusative form *τοιουτον*, which can only be the result of a thoughtless error.

4:33 A further question which, like the two in v.32, is also in the perfect tense: "Has a people (ever) heard the voice of a living God speaking from the middle of the fire as you have heard (even you) and lived"? MT has no equivalent for *ζῶντος*; LXX follows Sam's אלהים חיים,[66] as does Tar^O; the longer text is ultimately based on 5:26. Hex has rightly placed the word under the obelus signifying its absence from MT. LXX has an otiose *σύ* after the verb *ἀκήκοας*, but this is simply in imitation of MT's אתה. LXX changed to the aorist for the last verb with sensitivity. The continuation with a perfect verb would have given an incorrect sense. What is meant is "and lived," not "and has lived."

4:34 The last query is also not in the perfect but in the aorist tense: "Or did God, coming in, attempt to take for himself a nation out of the middle of a nation ...."?[67] The use of the singular *ἔθνους* reflects Israel's own history, i.e. Egypt was the nation out of which God had taken Israel. Did ever any God try something similar?

To make the comparison even more striking, this kind of redemption is signalized by a series of *ἐν* phrases. The first one is a singular *ἐν πειρασμῷ*. Since this modifies *ἐπείρασεν* the singular may well be an intentional change from MT catagorizing all the following ones.[68] Note that in MT the next one, באתת, in contrast to LXX, has no conjunction before it, whereas the first phrase is plural, במסת. The Hebrew could be interpreted to mean "by trials, viz. by signs and by wonders," etc., i.e. all the following ב phrases are summarized as being "trials." I would take *πειρασμῷ* as a collective, i.e. an overall cover term, followed by "even by signs and by ...." The pair "signs and wonders" is a common formula in Deut, occurring at least ten times in the book.[69]

The item *καὶ ἐν πολέμῳ* is again a singular one, probably because it refers to the "war" which the Lord fought with Pharaoh at the Red Sea; cf

66. This gloss also occurs in Kenn 184 and 196.
67. Instead of *μέσου* Aq has *ἐγκάτου* for קרב.
68. See the categorization in SS 125.
69. See List 50 in THGD 98.

Exod 14:14,25 15:1—12. This is followed by the wellknown Deut pair *καὶ ἐν χειρὶ κραταιᾷ καὶ ἐν βραχίονι ὑψηλῷ*, for which see comment at 3:23—24. It should be noted that "with a high arm" has become a regular equivalent for MT's בזרוע נטויה "with a stretched out arm."[70] The final modifier in the list is *καὶ ἐν ὁράμασιν μεγάλοις* "and by great visions." The Hebrew has ובמוראים גדלים "and by great terrors."[71] Obviously the translator took the noun to be derived from ראה rather than from ירא, and to refer to the divine appearances to Israel at Choreb.

The norm used was their experience of everything "which the Lord your God did in Egypt before you"; to this has been added a free rendering of the first two words of the next verse in MT, אתה הראת "as for you, you were shown," freely rendered by *βλέποντος* after *ἐνώπιόν σου*, thus "before you as you take note." LXX has combined the two structures "in your presence" and "as for you you were shown" into a single one characterizing the Choreb revelations, i.e. as taking place in the presence of the Israelites while they were looking on.

4:35 The verse is a *ὥστε* construction which summarizes the purpose of God's dealing with Israel in his special care for his people;[72] this purpose was to convince Israel that only their God is truly God; in other words, *οὐκ ἐστιν ἔτι πλὴν αὐτοῦ*. The first two words of the verse in MT had been joined to v.34; cf comment ad loc. This allows the translator to concentrate on the purposive infinitive לדעת as the sole point of the verse: Israel must be convinced of their monotheistic faith. LXX also makes this more pointed by adding *ὁ θεός σου* after *κύριος*. The statement is not merely an affirmation that the Lord is God, but the Lord is first identified as "your God."[73]

It is the second clause, however, that asserts the monotheistic faith. It is not enough to recognize that the Lord is God, but one must also affirm that he alone is God. In the tradition the *f* text has *θεος* instead of *ἔτι*, which makes the statement even more absolute. Also attested is the late form *ειδησαι* in Cod

70. Aq translated the participle literally by *ἐκτεταμένῳ*.
71. Aq has an unusual word, *φοβήμασιν* "things creating terror." According to LS the word is also found in Sophicles, *Oedipus Coloneus* 699.
72. See SS Inf 55.
73. See Appositives 1.1.4. for a possible exegetical point being made.

B. This definitively illustrates the danger of relying solely on the witness of one ms, even the best ms. The form is clearly secondary to *εἰδέναι*.[74]

4:36 How the Lord revealed himself to Israel, both "out of heaven"[75] and "upon the earth." The heavenly revelation has God as subject in MT: "he made you hear his voice." LXX has voided this by making "his voice" the subject in the rendering *ἀκουστὴ ἐγένετο ἡ φωνὴ αὐτοῦ*. It is hardly probable that the translator was avoiding making God the subject for theological reasons, since in the very next clause he is active in *ἔδειξέν σοι*. More probable is the translator's desire for a stricter parallel with the last clause in which a second person verb is used, *ἤκουσας*. This makes a triple distinction in subjects: his voice, God himself, the people.[76] The majority A F M V variant text has changed this by rendering the first one by *ακουστην σοι εποιησεν την φωνην*, an early borrowing from Theod.

The purpose of his heavenly revelation is stated infinitively: *παιδεῦσαί σε* "to instruct you," translating ליסרך. *παιδεύω* is regularly used to render יסר throughout the OT, and so it is really a calque for the Hebrew root, which basically has a moral dimension "to admonish, discipline, set straight." Instruction is not then first of all an intellectual exercise but is education in a way of life, a correction of faults, and the Greek must be understood in this way.

The earthly revelation is twofold, a visual and an auditory one. "He showed you his great fire" refers to the Choreb experience; cf v.11. But the auditory experience follows as "you heard his words from the middle of the fire." By "his words" is meant the Ten Words, for which see comment at v.13. For God speaking from the middle of the fire see vv.12,15,33.

4:37—38 In MT vv.37—38 are the condition for the "therefore" clause (paratactically expressed) in v.39. LXX has interpreted these verses quite dif-

74. See THGD 138.
75. Aq changes the preposition to *ἀπό*, whereas Theod retains the *ἐκ* of LXX.
76. The Three all made God the subject and *τὴν φωνήν* the object of the verb. Aq rendered השמיעך by a neologism *ἠκόωσέν σε*; The root *ἀκοόω* is a causative, denominative verb created from *ἀκοή*. Theod has the causative *ἠκούτισέν σε*, and Sym uses the verbal figure *ἀκουστήν σοι ἐποίησεν*.

ferently. The *διά* plus marked infinitive constitute the condition: "because he loved your fathers"; the construction represents תחת כי plus infinitive, a structure which occurs only here in OT.[77] This is, however, no justification for rewriting MT without evidence, as BHS does with its ותחי. The apodosis follows immediately in two coordinate finite aorist clauses, both introduced by *καί*.[78] Then v.38 follows with a series of three infinitives: "to destroy ... to bring in ... to give you their land to inherit," and ends with a comparative *καθὼς ἔχεις σήμερον*.

V.37 then sets the stage by its *διά* structure; all the divine action is based on the fact of *τὸ ἀγαπῆσαι αὐτὸν τοὺς πατέρας σου*. Divine love for Israel is only seldom mentioned as a basis for action in the book (also at 7:13, which see, and 23:5). Who the fathers were is not stated, though they are occasionally identified as Abraam, Isaak and Jacob (1:8 6:10 9:5,27 29:13 30:20 34:4).

This divine love is then activated by his election of "you their seed after them," and by his deliverance of the people from Egypt. The Hebrew modification of יבחר is peculiar, since it is singular: בזרעו אחריו.[79] The plural is certainly simpler. LXX makes a special point of this plurality by its unique addition of *ὑμᾶς*, thereby making sure that Israel might feel confident that they are the chosen seed. That this is hardly based on a parent text is clear from its context which is singular second person throughout this section (vv.35—39). Hex has quite rightly placed *ὑμᾶς* under the obelus. The tradition also found the *ὑμᾶς* odd, and Byz made an attempt to relieve it by adding *παρα παντα τα εθνη* "from all the nations."

In the second clause of the apodosis LXX also shows its own point of view by substituting *αὐτός* for בפניו, thereby stressing that God was personally responsible for the deliverance from Egypt, which is also implicit in the instrumental phrase *ἐν τῇ ἰσχύι αὐτοῦ τῇ μεγάλῃ*.[80]

---

77. See SS Inf 133.
78. See comment on the apodotic *καί* at SS 34.
79. Driver takes it as a reference to Abraham, and König as to Jacob, but most change the reference to the plural along with all the old witnesses except Tar^{O}.
80. See the statement in Dogniez-Harl 145; see also Prijs 106 which cites the Passover Haggada interpreting the redemption out of Egypt as follows: לא על ידי מלאך ולא על ידי שרף ולא על ידי שליח אלא הקדוש ברוך הוא בכבדו ובעצמו.

V.38 interprets the redemption by means of three purposive infinitives which interlock. The first one, "ἐξολεθρεῦσαι nations great and stronger than you before you"[81] has in turn an infinitive giving its raison d'etre, "to bring you in," i.e. into the Promised Land. This in turn is in order *δοῦναί σοι τὴν γῆν αὐτῶν κληρονομεῖν*. The blunt rendering of להוריש "to disinherit" by *ἐξολεθρεῦσαι* "to destroy" occurs here for the first time in OT, but it became popular especially in Deut (e.g. it occurs nine times in chh.13—14). All of this is then described as כיום הזה, which LXX interprets freely by *καθὼς ἔχεις σήμερον* "as you have (it) today."[82]

4:39 Along with v.40 this concludes a section with three coordinate futures serving as imperatives. The first two are more or less synonyms: *γνώσῃ* and *ἐπιστραφήσῃ τῇ διανοίᾳ* "know and bear in mind." Hex added *σου* to represent the suffix of לבבך. The passive of *ἐπιστρέφω* has the notion of constantly paying attention, of being turned inwards, and with *τῇ διανοίᾳ* "to keep in mind, be aware of."

The *ὅτι* clause defines what it is that is to be known and borne in mind. It constitutes a variant of v.35 expanding its *ὅτι* clause by substituting for *ἐστιν* two prepositional phrases: *ἐν τῷ οὐρανῷ ἄνω καὶ ἐπὶ τῆς γῆς κάτω*. The Greek has added *ὁ θεός σου* after *κύριος* ex par; MT simply has יהוה.[83] The last clause of the verse is taken over entirely, though the text of MT differs by omitting the מלבדו of v.35.[84]

4:40 The third imperatival clause orders the keeping of his *δικαιώματα* and his *ἐντολάς*,[85] for which see comment at v.2. The double phrase is modified by a *ὅσας* clause occurring frequently in the book, for which see comment at v.2 as well. The double phrase renders את חקיו ואת מצותיו. For the first element see comment at v.1. The second is the usual translation in OT; out of a total of

81. For the rendering of the comparative מן see SS 150. It should be noted that LXX only has the second adjective in the comparative although in MT מן refers to both adjectives.
82. Or as Rashi has it: כאשר אתה רואה היום. For *ἔχειν* in LXX see SS 181—188, and especially 185.
83. See Appositives 1.1.3.
84. See Appositives 1.1.4.
85. See list 23 in THGD 92—93.

202 occurrences of מצוה, 158 are rendered by ἐντολή.[86] The relative adjective agrees with its nearer antecedent ἐντολάς. A popular 963 variant witnesses to the pronoun ας, which may be due to homoioteleuton within the word.[87]

The remainder of the verse consists of a number of formulae common to the book. The notion "that it may be well for you," or some variant of it, occurs 16 times in the book,[88] and the next one "that your days may be long" obtains 12 times.[89] MT has this formula paratactically joined to the preceding, whereas LXX does not. Nonetheless it can hardly be taken as the purpose for the preceding clause. Note that this one uses ὅπως instead of ἵνα as in the preceding clause. Both clauses modify φυλάξῃ. LXX has rendered תאריך in the plural in spite of the singular context throughout the verse. This is probably due to the use of the hapax legomenon μακροήμεροι which would seem odd with a singular second person of γίνομαι. For the common formula "which the Lord your God is giving you" see comment at 1:20.

The verse ends with πάσας τὰς ἡμέρας, an accusative showing extent of time. Though separated considerably from φυλάξῃ it does modify it. Thus "you must guard ... all the time."

4:41 *τότε* introduces a new section which comprises vv.41—43. Moses set aside three cities of refuge in Transjordan. LXX understood אז יבדיל as referring to the durative past.[90] The verb ἀφώρισεν "defined, set apart," with an infinitive means "designated for a purpose." The three cities are πέραν τοῦ Ἰορδάνου, for which see comment at 1:1. That this refers to Transjordan is clear from ἀπὸ ἀνατολῶν ἡλίου for MT's "to (the) sunrise," but in either form it means "eastward." The use of ἀπό with a direction word represents a common Hebrew usage in which מן with a direction means "direction towards," here as "eastward," i.e. towards the sunrise. This is obviously intended here; comp Apoc 21:13.

4:42 The purpose of the special designation: to serve as cities of refuge. This is described by an unmarked infinitive φυγεῖν ἐκεῖ τὸν φονευτήν; the subject is

86. According to Dos Santos.
87. See THGD 106.
88. See List 28 in THGD 94.
89. See List 29, *ibid.*
90. See GK 107c for the imperfect after אז, טרם, בטרם and עד.

articulated since it is modified by a relative clause limiting "the slayer," and can not be used as support for Sam's הרוצח. This limitation is crucial for the passage, and excludes slayers who slew either knowingly or in hate. Slayers who can escape pursuit are described as *ὃς ἂν φονεύσῃ τὸν πλησίον οὐκ εἰδὼς καὶ οὗτος οὐ μισῶν αὐτὸν πρὸ ἐχθὲς καὶ τρίτης*. MT has את רעהו, but LXX never has an *αυτου* modifying *πλησίον* throughout the book.[91] Hex has added *αυτου* to equal MT. The negated participle *οὐκ εἰδώς* idiomatically represents the Hebrew בבלי דעת "without knowledge"; what is meant is "without foreknowledge."

The second qualificaiton is "not hating him previously." For the idiom *πρὸ τῆς ἐχθὲς καὶ τρίτης* see Note at Exod 4:10. The majority variant *χθες* is the Attic form.

The second part of the verse, which is presented in two paratactic clauses, explicates the first part, i.e. "he may flee to one of these cities and live."[92] The genitive *τῶν πόλεων τούτων* translates a partitive מן construction in MT idiomatically.[93]

4:43 The three cities named are assigned to the three tribes given territory east of the Jordan. Each of the cities is articulated by *τήν*, representing את in MT, as well as making clear that these are in apposition with *πολεῖς* of v.41. The first one is *Βόσορ*, said to be in the desert in the plain area assigned to Rouben.[94] As at 3:12 the Hebrew has the gentilic which the Greek disregards, as it does for מנשי at the end of the verse. It is mentioned in the Moabite Stone as being rebuilt by Mesha.[95] It is misspelled as *μοσορ* or *σοβορ* in the tradition.

The second city is *Ῥαμὼθ ἐν Γαλαάδ*, often mentioned in OT; cf Bible Dictionaries for its history. It is probably to be identified as Tell Ramith in northern Gilead near the modern Syrian border. It was assigned *τῷ Γαδδί* for לגדי. For the variation *Γαδδί* over against *Γάδ* see comment at 3:12. A *b n*+ text has substituted the tribal name *γαδ*. In the tradition *Ῥαμώθ* is variously realized, by vowel change as *ραιμωθ*, *ραμααθ* and *ραμαθ*; by infixation,

---

91. For *πλησίον* modified by genitive pronouns see the discussion in THGD 7778.
92. On the meaning of the future tense see Porter, Ch.7.
93. See SS 169.
94. Instead of *πεδινῇ* Aq translates מישר by *εὐθείᾳ*.
95. For its possible location see Bible Dicitionaries sub Bezer.

ραμαωθ; by dittography, *ραμμωθ*, and by consonant change as *ραβωθ* and *ραμων*.

The third city is Γαυλών in Βασάν and is assigned to Manasseh, representing גולן in MT. Its location remains much disputed both in ancient and in modern times, and various locations have been proposed.[96] The name was also unknown to copyists who spelled it in various ways: *γαυλην*, *γελων*, *γαιλων*, *γαυδων*, *γαυρων* or *αυλων* (Byz). The name Βασάν was articulated by Byz (with *τη* corrupted in some witnesses as *γη*); it was also misspelled at times as *βασσαν* by dittography, and even appeared in one ms as *βασανιτιδ*.

4:44 The relation of vv.44—49 to its context is by no means clear. Does it belong to chh.1—4 or does it introduce chh.5 ff.? It is also possible to view v.44 as a subscription to what preceded it, and vv.45—49 as a superscription to what follows. In any event, the problem is that of the parent text rather than of its translation.

There is one difference, however, between LXX and MT, which might be significant. MT begins v.44 with a conjunction, thus tying it with the preceding text, but LXX does not. On the other hand, v.45 does not start with a conjunction, either in MT or in LXX. It might then mean that MT makes a new beginning with v.45; the presence of a conjunction would have had meaning, though its absence is not overly significant.

Since התורה means "instruction," *νόμος* should also be taken in this wider sense, since it is the standard equivalent for תורה.[97] The term could apply equally to the speech by Moses in chh.1—4 or to that which is introduced by ויאמר in 5:1. It refers to the instruction "which Moses set before the Israelites" in either case.

4:45 The *f* text introduces this verse with *και*, but this is due to a scribal impulse to connect the two nominal clauses, and is not original. The matters about which Moses spoke to the Israelites are more fully characterized as *τὰ μαρτύρια καὶ τὰ δικαιώματα καὶ τὰ κρίματα*; the first item is a new characterization—for the other two see vv.1,8 and comp vv.5 and 14. The plural עדת

96. See especially the Anchor Bible Dictionary sub Golan Heights for a survey of these suggestions.
97. According to Dos Santos 204 times out of 232.

is only translated by *μαρτύρια* in the OT,[98] and must be understood as a calque for the Hebrew. It also occurs at 6:17,20 and nowhere else in the Pentateuch (at Gen 21:30 a singular עדה occurs); it is particularly common in the Psalter (especially in Ps 118 with 23 occurrences). Whether the plural is derived from the abstract עדות or is a plural of a presumed עדה is irrelevant, since LXX always translates this plural in the same way. It is a term that only applies to divine laws, and is usually translated as "testimonies." For the other two terms see comment at v.1.

The genitive absolute *ἐξελθόντων αὐτῶν* stands for בצאתם, with the suffix referring to בני ישראל, as *αὐτῶν* does to "Israelites."[99] A majority 963 tradition has the gloss *εν τη ερημω* inserted before it. It has no support in MT, but was imported from 6:4 in the same context. A popular F variant text has *ενετειλατο* instead of *ἐλάλησεν*, but this is contextually motivated by "the testimonies and commandments and judgments" which serve as referents for *ὅσα*. Furthermore, these are usually commanded by the Lord, but here Moses "spoke" them. Over against MT, LXX has *γῆς Αἰγύπτῳ* for מצרים.

4:46 The locative phrases modify *ἐλάλησεν* of v.45, and designate precisely where Moses spoke these testimonies and judgments and decrees. For *πέραν τοῦ Ἰορδάνου* see comment at 1:1. For *ἐγγὺς οἴκου Φογώρ* see discussion at 3:29, where, however, מול was rendered by *σύνεγγυς* rather than *ἐγγύς*.[100] Over against 3:29 בגיא, LXX has *ἐν φάραγγι* rather than *ἐν νάπῃ*, but these are synonyms. The third designation is "in the land of Seon." For the conquest of Seon's land and peoples see 2:30—36. For *(τῶν) Ἀμορραίων* and *Ἑσεβών* see comments at 1:4. The verb *ἐπάταξεν* is singular by attraction to the nearer member of the compound subject, *Μωυσῆς*. For both the concluding genitive absolute and "land (of Egypt)," see comments at v.45.

4:47 Vv.47—49 detail the conquest, not only of Sihon's land, but also that of Og, summarizing the accounts of 2:30—3:10. V.47 begins with "and they possessed his land," but the *n* text changes *αὐτοῦ* to *αυτων*, with *Ἀμορραίων* rather than *Σηών* as antecedent. This is not only against MT; it is also

98. According to Dos Santos 40 times.
99. See SS Inf 90.
100. Aq rendered it by *ἐναντίον*.

unlikely, since *καὶ τὴν γῆν Ὢγ* who was also an Amorrite is coordinate with it. It would be odd then to refer to the land of the Amorrites and the land of Og; the reading is simply an error.

These two kings and their lands were in Transjordan *κατὰ ἀνατολὰς ἡλίου*. This is obviously merely a variant of *ἀπὸ ἀνατολῶν ἡλίου* in v.41; both mean "eastward"; see comment ad loc. The full form of *κατά* before a vowel is almost certainly original, even though the elided *κατ* is found in B *C s t*+ here as well as in v.49.[101] In fact, elsewhere the full form is assured before words beginning with *alpha* (see 19:15,16 32:8). On the whole, the unelided forms are preferred in Hellenistic Greek.

4:48—49 The dimensions of the land taken in Transjordan. The opening prepositional phrase with the relative clause is taken over exactly in MT from 2:36, but LXX translated afresh with *ἐξ* becoming *ἀπό*, and *παρὰ τὸ χεῖλος* appearing as *ἐπὶ τοῦ χείλους*, but the intent is the same: it means "from Aroer which is on the edge." For further elucidation see comments at 2:36.

At 3:8 the other direction was described as *ἕως 'Αερμών*, but here for an expanded MT: ועד הר שיאן הוא חרמון, LXX reads *καὶ ἐπὶ τοῦ ὄρους τοῦ Σηὼν ὅ ἐστιν 'Αερμών*. Presumably LXX read ועד as ועל, though this is not certain.[102] Most confusing is the transcription *Σηών*, since this was also used for Seon, king of Basan. It is, however, distinguished from the king's name by being articulated. The *ἐπί* plus genitive must be taken to mean "to (the hilly area of the Seon)." For *'Αερμών* see comment at 3:8.

V.49 includes in the survey "all the Araba[103] beyond the Jordan eastward," which MT introduces with a conjunction. Instead of *τήν* the Byz text has *την γην* which is basically a dittograph. In fact, ארץ הערבה never occurs in MT, though comp Jer 2:6. MT also has a longer text. After "eastward" MT has ועד ים הערבה, which was probably omitted because of homoio-

101. See THGD 117.
102. Aq and Sym have *ἕως ὄρους Σηών* for עד הר שיאן, i.e. a word for word rendering.
103. The ms evidence for Sym is diverse and confusing, combining two readings which are probably *ἐν τῇ πεδιάδι* and the other *διὰ τῆς ἀοικήτου*. I suspect that a gloss explaining the root as meaning an uninhabited place is involved. Without its context its precise restoration is impossible; cf also f.n. at 1:7 as well as Salvesen 143.

teleuton, the previous word מזרחה also ending in *he*. A translation was added under the asterisk by hex as *και εως θαλασσης της αραβα*. The Byz text has a gloss here that was also influenced by MT: *και εως θαλασσης των δυσμων ηλιου*; note that ערב means "evening," and מערב "setting (of the sun)," hence west. For ὑπὸ Ἀσηδὼθ see comment at 3:17. The change of the preposition to *απο* in A B V *C d*+ was palaeographically conditioned, simply a copyist error, as the accusative *τὴν λαξευτήν* proves. The apposite *τὴν λαξευτήν* is a translation of the place name הפסגה, which was transcribed at 3:17 as *τὴν Φασγά* but translated at 3:27 as *Λελαξευμένου*; see comment at 3:27. In the tradition *λαξευτήν* was changed to *λελαξευμενην* by the Byz text under the influence of 3:27.

Chapter 5

5:1 It is clear that a new beginning is made here with Moses calling all Israel and addressing them. The imperative plus vocative, *ἄκουε* Ἰσραήλ, witnesses to a solemn statement; cf also 6:5 9:1 20:3 and comp 4:1 6:3. What they are to hear are *τὰ δικαιώματα καὶ τὰ κρίματα*, by which presumably is meant all that follows up to 32:45, which state that "Moses finished speaking to all Israel." For the pair see comment at 4:1. In the tradition, a popular variant text added *παντα* before *τὰ δικαιώματα*, but this is ex par; see 4:6 6:2,24 26:16.

The verb λαλῶ is modified by two *ἐν* phrases. The first one, *ἐν τοῖς ὠσὶν ὑμῶν*, illustrates how *ἐν* and *εἰς* are confused; what is here meant is "speak into their ears" rather than a locative *ἐν*, and one might well have expected *εἰς* plus an accusative.[1] The second phrase shows time when; MT simply has היום which is more commonly rendered by *σήμερον* (54 times); היום is uniquely rendered here by the phrase *ἐν τῇ ἡμέρᾳ ταύτῃ*, which occurs only six times elsewhere, and throughout it always has a הזה in MT as counterpart, either as כיום הזה (2:30 4:20) or as היום הזה (2:25 5:24 27:9 32:48). Obviously the parent text here must have been היום הזה.

The order to the people with respect to these ordinances and judgments is twofold, both to learn them (what is meant is to memorize them) and to carry them out; *φυλάσσω ποιεῖν* means to be precisely careful in following these orders, thus carry them out.[2] A 963 *C f+* tradition has the imperative *φυλαξασθε* which can hardly be correct, since it is coordinated with a future tense.

5:2 MT has the first person plural throughout vv.2 and 3, and then changes to second plural with v.4. LXX has levelled these verses and made them consistently second person, which makes equally good sense. The change must have been intentional; though the first and second personal pronouns were homophonous in Greek, they are quite distinctive in Hebrew. Furthermore, the distinction between Moses and the people is stressed in v.5, and this may well

1. See SS ch.11 "EN für ΕΙΣ in der Septuaginta," and especially p.136.
2. For this common collocation see list 25 in THGD 93—94.

have influenced the translator. That Byz+ has ημων for ὑμῶν is an itacism, not a correction, as its failure to change ὑμᾶς to ημας makes certain.

The basis for the commandments and the judgments which the people are to obey is the divine covenant made with them at Choreb.[3]

5:3 Emphasis is placed on the current constituency of Israel. The human partners in the covenant were not τοῖς πατράσιν ὑμῶν but rather πρὸς ὑμᾶς, who are then further defined as "you here all alive today." MT has the same preposition for both, i.e. את our fathers, and אתנו, but LXX changes from the dative to a πρός structure. The actual covenant is something that God grants "to us"—it is unidirectional, i.e. the partners are not on the same level, which the choice of διαθήκη rather than συνθήκη also makes clear.

The second part of the verse is a pendant nominative, though it is explicative of ὑμᾶς; the sense is probably something like—"(I mean) you here all alive today." The collocation is separated syntactically from the clause, and is only loosely connected rhetorically, somewhat like an afterthought. This is sensible in Hebrew where אנחנו can be understood as in apposition to the suffix of אתנו. For Greek which inflects for case one would really have to continue in the accusative plural. The nominative was probably promoted by the fact of the independent pronoun, which is commonly limited to the subject slot. But LXX also did not render MT literally, omitting אלה and reordering היום כלנו חיים as πάντες ζῶντες σήμερον. Hex added αυτοι after ὑμεῖς to equal the אלה, as well as υμεις after πάντες to equal the suffix of כלנו, and then rearranged the materials so that σήμερον preceded πάντες. The Byz text also transposed ζῶντες σήμερον, but hardly on the basis of MT.

5:4 Perforce MT had to change to second person, since the distinction between the Lord addressing Israel face to face and Moses' position in this contrasts in v.5. It is no problem in LXX which has a consistent second person reference. The idiom πρόσωπον κατὰ πρόσωπον also occurs at 34:10 where the preposition used is אל, whereas here it is ב. The Greek uses κατά because that is good Greek. Actually the translator could have simply used κατὰ πρόσωπον and it would have meant the same thing.[4]

3. See list 36 in THGD 96.
4. See Bauer sub κατά II.1.b.

5:5 The crasis form *κἀγώ* is preferred throughout to *καὶ ἐγώ*; in fact, the latter never appears in Deut (see also 10:10 12:30 32:21,39). LXX follows Sam rather than MT which lacks the conjunction. MT's participial predicate עמד is correctly taken as *εἱστήκειν*, formally pluperfect of *ἵστημι* but used as simple past tense, here to be understood as imperfect, thus "I was standing." Hebrew usage repeats the preposition, thus "between the Lord and between you," but Greek (as English) does not usually do so. LXX did not, and hex inserted *ανα μεσον* before *ὑμῶν* under the asterisk to equal the disregarded (ו)בין of MT.

Moses served as mediator, by which is meant that he told the people what it was that the Lord had said. By *τὰ ῥήματα κυρίου* the Ten Words are meant; they follow in vv.6—21; cf v.22 "These words the Lord spoke." MT, however, has the singular דבר, but Sam has the plural. Since the Hebrew word is followed by יהוה a *yodh* could easily fall out by haplography (or conversely be added as a dittograph). LXX presupposes the Sam text which in view of what follows is certainly simpler.

The reason for Moses' mediation is stated in the *ὅτι* clause as a twofold one: the people were afraid of the fire, and they did not ascend the mountain (of revelation); see Exod 20:18b—21 which describes the people's reaction to the Lord's theophany on the mount of revelation, and Moses' alone "entering the cloud where God was." The verse ends with a direct speech marker *λέγων*/לאמר, which proves that v.5 is a parenthetical statement; the *λέγων* presupposes the *ἐλάλησεν* of v.4.

5:6 It might be noted that the entire Decalogue is a second singular document inside a second plural context (with v.22 reverting to the plural both in MT and LXX). Here MT equals Exod 20:2 exactly. LXX is, however, not a copy but a new rendering. It has no *εἰμι* after *ἐγώ*, although hex does add it under the asterisk, possibly on the later notion that the long form אנכי should be rendered by *ἐγώ εἰμι*.[5]

Also translated differently is אשר הוצאתיך. Exod had translated this by means of a relative clause, *ὅστις ἐξήγαγόν σε*, shrewdly representing the original first person verb by *ἐξήγαγον*. The Deut translator changes the con-

---

5. See the statement in THGD 55.

struction to an attributive participle ὁ ἐξαγαγών σε. The popular Exod text influenced the tradition, and the majority text read the Exod version, with a V *C'' f s*+ subvariant reading the verb in the third singular.

5:7 MT equals Exod 20:3. LXX and Exod differ in their rendering of על פני. Exod had understood it as πλὴν ἐμοῦ; cf Note ad loc. LXX renders the phrase by πρὸ προσώπου μου "before me." Of the ancient versions only Vulg agrees with LXX, all the others supporting the majority text which has πλην εμου taken over from Exod.[6]

5:8 Sam equals Exod 20:4; BHS has כל, not וכל as Sam, but many mss do have וכל. LXX with its οὐδέ presupposes וכל. It also has γλυπτόν for פסל, but Exod has εἴδωλον; see Note at Exod 20:4. Cod B+ attest to ειδωλον, obviously taken from the Exod parallel. In the tradition a popular A M text has τω υδατι for τοῖς ὕδασιν for no apparent reason except that the singular is three times more frequent (in all cases) than the plural (15 vs 5 times) in the book. It may also have been influenced by the coordinate singulars ἐν τῷ οὐρανῷ and ἐν τῇ γῇ.

5:9 BHS differs from Exod 20:5 in having ועל rather than על before שלשים; many mss, however, follow the Exod text. LXX follows the Exod text for v.9a,[7] but then uses a ὅτι construction rather than γάρ as in Exod. It also differs from Exod's ἕως τρίτης καὶ τετάρτης γενεᾶς by its ἐπί plus accusative. In Deut the collocation is in apposition with ἐπὶ τέκνα, rather than showing the extent of God's repayment as in Exod.

As in Exod, however, it designates the subject of the "because" clause not as in MT "I Yahweh your God am a jealous God", but as ἐγώ, i.e. "I am the Lord your God, a jealous God ...." The *zaqqef qaton* on קנא makes the predicate אל קנא, whereas the rendering of אנכי by ἐγώ εἰμι makes clear that κύριος ὁ θεός σου is a predicate nominative. Thus the reason for prohibiting image worship is not that the Lord is jealous, but rather because he is the Lord your God. It is because of who he is, Israel's God, not what he is, that an imageless cult is to be practiced. See also the discussion at Exod 20:5.

6. Theod and Aq have ἐπί for πρό, whereas Sym has κατὰ πρόσωπόν μου.
7. Instead of λατρεύσῃς Aq has δουλεύσεις, for which see Daniel 113.

θεὸς ζηλωτὴς κ.τ.λ. is then in apposition to "the Lord your God." The Hebrew participle פקד is interpreted by ἀποδιδούς "a repayment" rather than by a "visitation."[8] The repayment will be exacted upon the third and fourth generations. This is followed by the dative τοῖς μισοῦσίν με which modifies ἀποδιδούς, and contrasts with τοῖς ἀγαπῶσίν με of v.10 which must modify ποιῶν (ἔλεος).

5:10 The Qere of MT equals Exod 20:6. The last word reads מצותו but the Qere מצותי is supported not only by LXX but by many Hebrew mss, Sam and the other old versions as well. LXX has taken over Exod word for word; cf Notes ad loc. In the tradition Byz has changed προστάγματα to the more usual rendering of מצות, εντολας.

5:11 Both MT and LXX equal Exod 20:7; cf Notes ad loc. "To take up the name" means to take it up on the lips, thus to utter.[9] Anyone so uttering the divine name will not be "declared pure, clean."[10]

5:12 Comp Exod 20:8 which has זכור instead of שמור. It also lacks כאשר צוך יהוה אלהיך. LXX is a careful rendering of MT with the imperative φύλαξαι "take care of (the Sabbath day)" plus the complementary infinitive ἁγιάζειν αὐτήν.[11] τῶν σαββάτων occurs only in the plural in the Pentaeuch, possibly initially as a transliteration of the Aramaic emphatic form שבתא. In some of the later books of the OT a singular σάββατον was formed on its basis, it being already adopted into Greek as a plural noun. The ὃν τρόπον clause is a literal rendering of the כאשר clause of MT, but has no equivalent in the Exod version.

5:13 Both MT and LXX equal Exod 20:9 exactly; cf Notes ad loc.[12]

8. Theod and Aq render פקד more literally by ἐπισκεπτόμενος. They also translate עון by ἀνομίας (retroverted from Syh).
9. For ἐπὶ ματαίῳ Aq has the literalistic εἰς εἰκῇ as in Exod.
10. Aq translates ינקה exactly by ἀθῳώσῃ "be guiltless, considered guiltless."
11. See SS Inf 62.
12. Aq translates תעבד by δουλεύσεις as expected. Aq only uses this root for the Hebrew root עבד.

5:14 Vv.14—15 constitute the elaboration of the Sabbath commandment; comp Exod 20:10—11. V.14 is much like its parallel in Exod but is longer. In the Hebrew the two versions are identical through ובתך, after which Deut expands. It continues paratactically with "and your maidservant and your cattle and your sojourner who is in your gates," which Deut expands considerably; it adds ושורך וחמרך after ואמתך.[13] It has also added כל in modification of "(and) your cattle," which follows. Furthermore, it has added a למען clause "in order that your male and female servants may rest like you." LXX is exactly the same as Exod through *ὁ προσήλυτος*; up to this point Exod supports MT of Deut. In both texts hex has added *σου* under the asterisk to equal the גרך of MT. The relative clause modifying it was freely rendered by *ὁ παροικῶν ἐν σοί* in Exod, but much more literally here as *ὁ ἐντὸς τῶν πυλῶν σου*.[14] As in the Exod passage *ἐν αὐτῇ* has no counterpart in MT, and hex has accordingly put the phrase under the obelus. An odd B *y*+ variant text reads the plural *οι υιοι*; its oddness is emphasized by the text's leaving *ἡ θυγάτηρ* in the singular; obviously the variant text was a thoughtless copyist error.

The למען clause is well rendered in literal fashion by a *ἵνα* construction. In the tradition "your male and female servant" has been popularly increased by *και το υποζυγιον σου*, (to which the *C* text has prefixed *ο βους σου*), obviously taken from the list earlier in the verse.

5:15 Exod 20:11 based the Sabbath commandment on the creation story of Gen 1—2:4a, i.e. God worked six days and rested from his labors on the seventh, and because of that he blessed and sanctified the seventh day. Deut, however, bases it on the great redemptive act of the exodus from Egypt. The Sabbath is then a weekly celebration of that event.

The verse begins with *καί* and it is not immediately clear with what this clause is coordinate. It is unlikely to be coordinate with the last clause of v.14 since the *ἵνα* introducing it would require a subjunctive form rather than a future, though admittedly the syntax of the Greek Deut is at times quite loose. It seems preferable to coordinate it with *οὐ ποιήσεις*, so that what is intended is "you shall not do any work ... and you shall remember"; these two things

13. Aq translated חמר by *ὄνος*, and Sym by *ὁ ὄνος*, in place of LXX's *τὸ ὑποζύγιόν*.
14. Theod made it *ὁ ἐν ταῖς πύλαις σου*, which Aq adopted but without *ταῖς*!

you must do. These are logically connected in that the rest from labor gives the opportunity for reflection on God's providential care and deliverance of his people.

The two things to remember are given in the *ὅτι* clause: a) your former estate as *οἰκέτης ἐν γῇ* Αἰγύπτῳ[15] and b) the Lord's deliverance of the people. The term *οἰκέτης* applies primarily to "household servants," but the domestic character of the servitude should not be pressed. Deut always uses the phrase "in Egypt-land," rather than "in the land of Egypt" as some *n z* witnesses have it.[16]

The act of deliverance is described by the common Deut phrase as being carried out "with a strong hand and a high arm," for which see comment at 3:23—24. *διὰ τοῦτο* ties the divine command to the immediately preceding clause stating the fact of God's deliverance. The order (*συνέταξέν σοι*) is modified by a *ὥστε* plus infinitival structure which in Classical terms should show probable result, but the *ὥστε* is actually otiose here, since all that is intended is a complement to the verb *συνέταξεν*. This is also clear from MT which has a marked infinitive לעשות. The collocation לעשות יום השבת is highly unusual; in fact, elsewhere only at Exod 31:16 *φυλάξουσιν ... τὰ σάββατα ποιεῖν αὐτά*, is *τὰ σάββατα* a direct modifier of *ποιεῖν*, which in turn modifies *φυλάξουσιν*. LXX may well have been influenced by that passage in its translation *φυλάσσεσθαι* "to guard (the day of the Sabbath)." Coordinate with this infinitive is a second one, *καὶ ἁγιάζειν αὐτήν*, which has no basis in MT whatsoever.[17] It is clearly based on v.12: (guard the day of the Sabbath) *ἁγιάζειν αὐτήν*.

5:16 Comp Exod 20:12. MT of Exod lacks כאשר צוך יהוה אלהיך after ואמך as well as ולמען ייטב לך as a second למען clause. LXX has as an equivalent *ὃν τρόπον ἐνετείλατό σοι κύριος ὁ θεός σου ἵνα εὖ σοι γένηται καί*, after which the translation of MT's first clause is given, i.e. *ἵνα μακροχρόνιος γένῃ ἐπὶ τῆς γῆς*. Exod also has the two *ἵνα* clauses, i.e. it is longer than MT, and the reordering of the two clauses in LXX may have been due to the Exod version. Exod also adds *τῆς ἀγαθῆς* after "upon the land," for which there is no basis

15. See list 32 in THGD 95.
16. See THGD 137.
17. See SS Inf 141.

in MT; cf Notes ad loc. Both render כבד idiomatically by τίμα "hold in honor, respect."[18] For the relative clause modifying γῆς see comment at 1:20. The relative pronoun ἧς is genitive by attraction to its antecedent γῆς.

5:17—19 equals Exod 20:13—15. The order of these three verses is problematic. MT has for both traditions the order: murder, commit adultery, steal, but the Greek traditions differ; Both begin with "commit adultery," and LXX of Exod then follows with "steal, murder," which LXX here transposes: thus "commit adultery, murder, steal." MT of Deut uniquely connects the three with conjunctions, but Sam does not, and LXX follows Sam. But in the LXX tradition vv.17 and 18 are transposed in most witnesses to equal the order of MT, presumably due to hex reordering.

5:20 equals Exod 20:16. The only differences between the two lie in the conjunction with which MT begins here, which Sam and LXX lack, and the שקר of Exod which becomes שוא, though some mss read שקר under the influence of the parallel passage.[19] LXX, however, is an exact copy of Exod; cf Note ad loc.

5:21(18) equals Exod 20:17. The Greek texts are identical, but not so MT. The Greek texts are much closer to MT of Deut than to that of Exod, and I shall only refer to MT of Deut here. It introduces the verse with a conjunction, but neither Sam nor LXX do. MT has two different verbs changing from תחמד to תתאוה; these are synonyms, and LXX uses ἐπιθυμήσεις for both. MT also introduces the second prohibition with a conjunction, and again neither Sam nor LXX do. LXX introduces the other modifiers with οὔτε but MT lacks a conjunction before שדהו and שורו. And over against MT, LXX adds οὔτε παντὸς κτήνους αὐτοῦ as a final item before "nor anything that belongs to your neighbour." MT of Exod is rather different, for which see Notes ad loc.

5:22(19) The use of συναγωγήν to render קהל in Deut is unusual; it occurs elsewhere only at 33:4. The word קהל occurs twelve times in the book and is more commonly translated by ἐκκλησία; see discussion at 4:10. The two

18. Aq preferred his more usual δόξαζε.
19. Kenn 17*,84,199,379,387,489*,595,607,618.

Greek words carry different emphases: *ἐκκλησία* stresses the calling together, whereas *συναγωγή* refers to the group gathered together. For *ἐκ μέσου τοῦ πυρός* see comment at 4:12.

This is followed by four nouns in the nominative without a stated predicate; this equals Sam; the first three also occur at 4:11, for which see comment ad loc. Here קהל גדול/*φωνὴ μεγάλη* is added. What LXX says is "there was darkness, gloominess, tempest, a great sound." Hex has placed *θύελλα* under the obelus as being without an equivalent in MT, though the actual one without an equivalent in MT is *σκότος*, i.e. MT lacks the חשך of Sam. That this completed the Lord's speaking "these words" (i.e. the speaking is limited to the Ten Words) is clear from *καὶ οὐ προσέθηκεν* "and he did not add," i.e. continue; in other words, he stopped.[20] The direct speaking of the Lord to the people began and concluded with the Ten Words. From then on Moses mediated the divine laws to the people.

That this was the intention is clear from the conclusion: "and he wrote them on two stone tablets and gave (them) to me." LXX does not translate the suffix of ויתנם, since that is obvious from the context. Hex did supply an *αυτας* under the asterisk to equal the suffix. A popular variant text had *κυριος* at the end, but this is otiose.

5:23(20) With v.23 a new section begins. For the rendering of ויהי by *καὶ ἐγένετο* to introduce a time designation see comment at 1:3. The idiom ויהי כ also occurs at 31:24, but there it is more idiomatically translated by *ἡνίκα δέ*. The *ὡς* introduces the protasis of the condition for the apodosis beginning with *καὶ προσήλθετε* and continuing with v.24. Over against MT, LXX has the voice[21] coming out of the midst *τοῦ πυρός* as at 4:12, but MT has החשך. MT can be defended, since the fire was surrounded by *σκότος*, *γνόφος*, *θύελλα*, but cf v.22; LXX "corrects" to agree with v.24 where the Lord spoke out of the midst of the fire; see also v.24.[22] The second clause within the protasis, *καὶ τὸ ὄρος ἐκαίετο πυρί*, is circumstantial as is its Hebrew counterpart.[23]

---

20. Tar^O has a different understanding: ולא פסק "and he did not stop." Rashi explains the Tar readings as: לפי שמדת בשר ודם אינן יכולין לדבר כל דבריהם בנשימה אחת ומדת הקב"ה אינו כן, לא היה פוסק ומשלא היה פוסק לא הוה מוסיף.
21. Aq has *σὺν τὴν φωνήν* for את הקול, whereas Theod Sym retain LXX.
22. Kenn 84 actually reads האש, whereas Kenn 81,109 have האש החשך.
23. See GK 141e.

The verbs in the apodosis, *προσήλθετε ... καὶ ἐλέγετε*, are in second person, but they are defined by "all the leaders of your tribes and your eldership." The noun *ἡγούμενοι* also occurred at 1:13 for ראשי, which see.[24] The term *γερουσία* occurs here for זקני for the first time. זקנים is normally rendered thus (16 times) in the book, and is translated otherwise only four times (*ἀνδράσιν* 21:20; *πρεσβύτεροι* 31:9 32:7,[25] and *φυλάρχους* 31:28, but see comment ad loc). The singular is used in the sense of "the council of elders."

5:24(21) The use of the imperfect *ἐλέγετε* is unusual for תאמרו as coordinate with the *προσήλθετε* of v.23, and would better suit the Hebrew participle אמרים, but that would then presuppose אתם/*ὑμεῖς* preceding it. It can, however, merely be the translator wishing to stress the continuity of their objection, which does go on through v.26; this would then contrast with the coordinate *προσήλθετε* which is not an imperfect, i.e. it hardly involves a process. What they say is "The Lord our God has shown *ἡμῖν* his glory.[26] The *ἡμῖν* is lacking in B* 963+, and is transposed after *ἡμῶν* in a popular variant. This might help to explain the reading of The Others referred to in the footnote. MT has the phrase ואת גדלו after "his glory", which has no equivalent in LXX. It was probably omitted because of homoioteleuton, since the next phrase in MT also begins with ואת. Hex has made up for it by adding *και την μεγαλωσυνην αυτου* under the asterisk. For *ἐν τῇ ἡμέρᾳ ταύτῃ* see the discussion at v.1. By *εἴδομεν* as a translation of ראינו is meant "we see" in the sense of "we recognize, realize." What we realize is that "God can speak to man and he (still) lives." The future in Greek expresses expectancy or potentiality.[27] What LXX is saying is that it is possible to hear the voice of God and not perish, even though it is dangerous (see vv.25—26).

5:25(22) *μὴ ἀποθάνωμεν* translates למה נמות freely but correctly; the *μή* plus subjunctive is used in the same sense as at 4:9,16,19,23 where it translated פן. The *b* text with its *μηποτε* correctly understood the text. The reason for the

24. Aq has *κεφαλαί*.
25. Which is also the reading of Aq here.
26. According to a marginal reading of ms 344 The Others lack *ἡμῖν*, which I find unbelievable in view of הראנו of MT.
27. See Porter 438—439.

fear is shown by the ὅτι clause: "this great fire will destroy us." The verb interprets תאכל "eats, devours."[28]

The ἐάν clause introduces a condition which is actually within the ὅτι clause as punctuated in the text, with the apodosis introduced by καί. The construction is rhetorically awkward, and it might be preferable to change the comma before ἐάν to a colon. By this change the conditional simply means "if we continue to hear the voice of the Lord our God (any more), we shall die." The Masoretes have interpreted it in this way by placing the first cut in the verse after הזאת. The first person second aorist verb is followed by an otiose pronoun, but it represents the Hebrew nominal clause: participle + pronoun. In the tradition the majority A F M V text has the active form προσθωμεν.[29]

5:26(23) MT begins with כי מי כל בשר "For who (of) all flesh," but LXX omits "all" in its τίς γὰρ σάρξ.[30] Hex supplies πασα under the asterisk before σάρξ to equal MT.

In MT the verbs in the relative clause are שמע and ויחי, both intended as past tenses. LXX, however, renders the first one by ἤκουσεν, but the second by (καὶ) ζήσεται. What LXX is saying is that no one "who has heard the voice of (the) living God speaking from the middle of the fire as we (did) can expect to live." MT asks for a historical example: "has anyone ever heard ... and lived," i.e. with the implication that such an experience has always been fatal. LXX by its ζήσεται declares by a rhetorical question that it is unreasonable to expect to remain alive under such a condition.

5:27(24) Note that the translator follows the Hebrew closely in using σύ twice, once with a singular imperative, possibly intending stress: "as for you, approach," and once before a future verb where it is fully otiose, though it does contrast between Moses as receptor and Moses as speaker. What Moses is asked to do is to listen to כל which Yahweh our God will say. LXX omits כל and simply has ὅσα, but hex inserts παντα under the asterisk, a reading that then dominated the tradition. Most witnesses have added προς σε at the end of

28. Aq has a literal φάγεται (retroverted from Syh).
29. Theod retains the LXX verb, but Aq changes to προσθῶμεν, whereas Sym has a different verb entirely, ἐπιμείνωμεν "remain, continue."
30. Aq prefers κρέας for בשר.

the first ὅσα clause, but this is a secondary gloss based on the second ὅσα clause without any basis in MT. Both ὅσα clauses contain ἄν which appears in a substantially supported tradition as εαν, which only became popular within relative clauses later than LXX, especially by the first centuries BCE and CE.[31] What the Israelites request is that Moses mediate and become the transmitter of God's demands on his people.

The Israelites on their part pledge καὶ ἀκουσόμεθα καὶ ποιήσομεν, both futures showing intention. Not only will they listen, but they will carry out what God demands; they will obey.

5:28(25) The translator has rendered in economical fashion what the Lord heard, דבריכם בדברכם "your words when you were speaking," by τῶν λόγων ὑμῶν λαλούντων "the words which you were speaking."[32] This is identified as τῶν λόγων τοῦ λαοῦ τούτου which the Lord says that he heard. In each case τῶν λόγων is preceded by τὴν φωνήν representing an את קול of MT; this hardly admits of translation into English: "the sound (or voice) of words" is tautological, and I would simply disregard τὴν φωνήν in translation. MT continues with היטיבו כל אשר דברו. LXX rendered היטיבו by the adverb ὀρθῶς "correctly,"[33] which one might translate: "correctly (spoken) are all the things they have spoken." The adverb serves as predicate of the construction. The *d* text was troubled by this and changed πάντα ὅσα to ο λαος ουτος, thus: "this people spoke rightly," but this has no basis in MT.

5:29(26) The collocation מי יתן is a Hebrew idiom expressing desire "O that, would that,"[34] and the Greek τίς δώσει can only be understood as a Hebraism. This first occurs in Num 11:29 as τίς δῴη. מי יתן also occurs in the Pentateuch at Exod 16:3, where it is rendered idiomatically by ὄφελον. At Deut 28:67 the phrase occurs twice and is rendered both times by πῶς ἂν γένοιτο; see comment ad loc. In MT the idiom is followed by והיה, a unique usage which LXX translated by the infinitive εἶναι. MT has the subject of היה as לבבם זה "this their heart," with להם modifying היה, thus "that this their heart might be to

31. See "ἄν versus ἐάν in relative clauses" in THGD 99—102.
32. For the part. conj. see SS Inf 91.
33. Theod and Aq have a more literal rendering: ἠγάθυναν "they have done well."
34. See GK 151a,b, KB sub נתן Qal 6, and BDB sub נתן Qal 1.f.

them," i.e. "they might have such a heart." LXX has rendered this by taking זה as an adverb: *οὕτως τὴν καρδίαν αὐτῶν ἐν αὐτοῖς*; this reordering is not fully certain since a popular reading has changed the position of *οὕτως* so that it precedes the infinitive. This would make the adverb modify *δώσει*.[35] The rendering of להם by *ἐν αὐτοῖς* is unusual, but may have been used to avoid using a simple dative *αὐτοῖς* in two senses, since in the *ἵνα* clause it is used to show an indirect object. Here a dative of possession would have translated the intent of MT exactly.

This construction is in turn modified by a *ὥστε* clause with coordinate infinitives: "so as to fear me and to guard my commandments all the time." LXX follows Sam rather than MT's "כל my commandments." Hex accordingly adds *πασας* before *τὰς ἐντολάς μου* under the asterisk so as to equal MT. The *ὥστε* construction translates marked infinitives, which may be simply complementary. I would translate LXX as "Would that their heart might be thus disposed in them to fear me and guard ...."

The verse ends with a *ἵνα* clause modifying the coordinate infinitives, i.e. the purpose of fearing the Lord and observing his commandments continually is "that it might be well for them and their sons for ever," for which see comment at 4:40. Highly unusual is the rendering of לעלם by *δι' αἰῶνος*. It also occurs at 12:28 in another "in order that it may be well" context, but elsewhere the phrase occurs in the OT only at Wis 4:19 Isa 60:21 and Jer 20:11. The usual translations are *εἰς (τὸν) αἰῶνα* and *ἕως (τοῦ) αἰῶνος*. The *δι'* phrase may best be rendered by "perpetually" rather than by "forever."[36] In thc tradition, *ᾖ αὐτοῖς* becomes *αυτοις γενηται* in the *z* text, but with no real change in meaning.

5:30*(27)* The imperative "say" should be accented as *εἶπον*.[37] What Moses is commanded to say to the people is שובו לכם לאהליכם. LXX found the לכם awkward to translate and used an otiose *ὑμεῖς* to show its presence in the Hebrew, for which see comment at 1:7. LXX updates the Hebrew which orders the people to return to their tents. This would be an odd statement in the Jewish quarter of Alexandria, and so LXX changes "tents" to *οἴκους*.[38]

35. But see THGD 129.
36. Comp LS sub *αἰών* II.1.
37. See footnote at 1:42.
38. Sym has the literal *σκηνάς*.

5:31(28) αὐτοῦ means "here" and correctly renders פה.[39] What God is saying to Moses is "Stay here with me." τὰς ἐντολὰς καὶ τὰ δικαιώματα καὶ τὰ κρίματα recurs often in the book.[40] For ἐντολάς see comment at 4:40, and for the other two see comment at 4:1. MT has כל המצוה, and hex has added πασας before τάς under the asterisk to equal MT. The singular of MT is correctly understood as a collective, as the coordinate plural nouns make clear. God will communicate these to Moses and in turn διδάξεις αὐτούς. For the verb see the comment at 4:14. In the tradition, all three nouns have been individually glossed by μου. These are all secondary, having no basis in MT; they simply make explicit what is already implicit.

The clause καὶ ποιείτωσαν with its third plural imperative shows a correct understanding of ועשו which expresses result, thus "so that they will do (them) in the land." A majority V gloss has added ουτως probably under the influence of v.29 for good sense, but the shorter text equals MT. What is understood is that they will do the commandments and ordinances and judgments. For the ἥν clause see comment at 1:20. In the tradition ἥν becomes η by attraction to γῇ in a popular text, but all the older witnesses have the grammatically correct accusative.

5:32(29) The number pattern is peculiar in LXX. MT is consistently plural for vv.32—33, but LXX only has the first verb, φυλάξεσθε, and the last two verbs, μακροημερεύσητε and κληρονομήσετε in the plural, and for the rest has a singular reference. A popular variant changed the initial verb to an imperative φυλαξασθε. The future itself already has imperatival force, and the imperative as a rendering for ושמרתם would be highly unusual indeed. The norm demanded for observance is expressed by the common Deut ὃν τρόπον construction (for כאשר).[41] LXX has ἐνετείλατο κύριος ὁ θεός σου, but MT has אתכם at the end, so hex has added σοι; a popular gloss, however, added σοι after the verb.[42] This must be secondary in view of the hex addition; Origen presumably would have transposed σοι, not added another one. It must be said

39. Aq makes it abundantly clear with ἐνταῦθα.
40. See list 22 in THGD 92 as well as comment at 4:1.
41. See list 9 in THGD 88.
42. See THGD 56.

though that the verb is usually accompanied by a dative of person (25 times) and only three times does it lack such (also in the next two verses).

The last clause continues in the singular with ἐκκλήσεις. B V *b*+ do change the verb to the plural, which is probably due to the plural verbs in vv.32 and 33, but the singular must be original.[43] Nor is the B F M *oI*+ gloss of εις before both δεξιά and ἀριστερά to be considered original text.[44] The prepositional phrases do occur often in the Greek OT, but the Deut translator never used the preposition in these contexts.

5:33(30) This verse syntactically continues v.32 in LXX, i.e. the κατά clause modifies ἐκκλήσεις: "you shall not incline ... on the way."[45] As in v.32, the tradition added σοι after ἐνετείλατο in a popular B F V variant, whereas hex added it after θεός σου; cf comment at v.32. The verb is modified by the infinitive πορεύεσθαι. MT has constructed v.33a quite differently; in MT the verse is not part of the preceding verse syntactically. Instead of the infinitive it has the finite verb תלכו, and the prepositional phrase with which the verse begins modifies it. Thus: "in all the way which Yahweh your (plural) God commanded you, you shall walk," a much clearer statement than the Greek.

The second part of the verse is a למען/ὅπως structure. It governs three clauses: תחיון "you may live," טוב לכם "it may be good for you," and הארכתם ימים "you may lengthen days," i.e. live a long life. It is the first two which are problematic. LXX has for the first verb καταπαύσῃ σε which hardly constitutes even a free translation of תחיון, but seems to presuppose the root נוח. Could the translator have misread the verb as תנחון "you might rest," and then interpreted it as "he might give you rest"? The idea that if one does not stray from the divinely ordered path one would be rewarded with God given rest (from one's enemies?), and εὖ σοι ᾖ does make sense.[46] The third verb, μακροημερεύσητε, is a neologism created to translate the expression "you shall make days long." It occurs four times in the book (also at 6:2 11:9 32:47) and is used only to translate this expression; it also occurs once in Judg 2:7, as well as in Sir 3:6 where unfortunately the Hebrew is not extant.

43. See THGD 60; Aq witnesses to <ἀπο> στήσεσθε for תסרו.
44. See THGD 61.
45. See LS sub κατά B.I.2.
46. The Others read ἵνα ζῆτε καὶ ἀγαθὸν ὑμῖν which renders MT literally.

Chapter 6

6:1 A superscription. For *αἱ ἐντολαὶ καὶ τὰ δικαιώματα καὶ τὰ κρίματα* see comment at 5:31. MT lacks the first conjunction, following the pattern: a b + c.[1] The verb *ἐνετείλατο* is modified only by a complementary infinitive, and with no personal object or infinitival subject in imitation of MT, but "me" must be understood, i.e. "commanded me to teach you." The infinitive is in turn modified by another infinitive *ποιεῖν* (*οὕτως*). The adverb has no counterpart in MT, and is borrowed from 4:5. For "your (God)" the majority A B M text read *ημων*, a good illustration of homophony creating a variant text. "Our God" makes excellent sense, but it is not original LXX as a glance at the Hebrew shows—after all, one could hardly confuse אלהיכם with אלהינו; see comment at 1:10.[2] For "enter to inherit" see comment at 1:8.

The *ὑμεῖς* plus inflected present tense is the usual pattern for translating the nominal clause with participial predicate. The infinitive *κληρονομῆσαι* occurs absolutely over against MT: לרשתה. Approximately half the witnesses follow the B text in adding *αυτην*; this could be hex, but it is probably ex par. לרשתה occurs 25 times in the book. LXX fails to translate it at 19:2; three times (3:18 5:31 12:1) it is rendered by *ἐν κλήρῳ*, and 13 times it is translated by an infinitive meaning "to possess" ($\sqrt{}$*κληρονομε* or its *κατα-* compound) plus *αὐτήν*, and eight times as here by such an infinitive without *αὐτήν* (also 4:26 7:1 9:6 19:14 21:1 25:19 and 32:47). The translator obviously did not feel obliged to render the pronominal suffix.

6:2 MT changes to the singular second person, but LXX continues with the plural through *θεὸν ὑμῶν*,[3] and again uses the plural for the last *ἵνα* clause. For the popular *ημων* variant see comment at v.1. The initial *ἵνα* clause must explicate the *διδάξαι ποιεῖν* of v.1, which is made doubly clear by LXX's putting the clause in the plural—note *διδάξαι ὑμᾶς*. The verb *φοβῆσθε* is modified by an infinitive *φυλάσσεσθαι* which equals MT's לשמר. Presumably the infinitive shows the consequence or result of fearing the Lord. If Israel truly

1. But Kenn 9,107*,129,167,172,193,199 do have והחקים.
2. See THGD 108.
3. Sym attests to the singular *ἵνα φοβῇ κύριον τὸν θεόν σου* (retroverted from Syh).

fears the Lord it will guard all his *δικαιώματα* and his *ἐντολάς*; in fact, the fear of the Lord is defined as the observance of all his ordinances and his commandments.

For the *ὅσας* clause see comment at 4:2; *σήμερον* in the clause is based on Sam, not on MT. This is followed by the nominative *σὺ καὶ οἱ υἱοί σου καὶ οἱ υἱοὶ τῶν υἱῶν σου* which serves to identify more precisely the subject of *φοβῆσθε*. MT has the singular for "sons" throughout; only Vulg follows LXX here.

MT ends the verse with למען יארכן ימיך, with the third plural subject referring to ימיך, i.e. "your days may be lengthened." LXX has the second plural as at 5:33; see comment ad loc.[4]

6:3 LXX renders the opening ושמעת ... ושמרת in unusual fashion by imperatives: *καὶ ἄκουσον ... καὶ φύλαξαι*, probably to prepare for the *shema* of v.4; it seems to impart greater solemnity to the divine order. It does not change the basic meaning, since these verbs are lexically imperatival as well.[5] For the collocation *φύλαξαι ποιεῖν* see comment at 5:1. Here the infinitival structure is used absolutely. What is intended, but not expressed, are the commandments and ordinances and judgments of v.1; these Israel must be careful to practice, i.e. to obey.

For the *ὅπως* clause see comment at 4:40. The Byz text has changed it to a *ἵνα* clause probably under the influence of the coordinate *ινα* clause; there is no difference in meaning. MT has ייטב לך for which LXX has *εὖ σοι ῇ*. A popular A F V text transposes *σοι* after *ῇ* which would be closer to MT, but LXX never has *σοι* after *ῇ* or *γένηται* in the book regardless of the Hebrew order.

The coordinate *ἵνα* clause is in second person plural, *πληθυνθῆτε σφόδρα*, in which it simply follows MT.

The *καθάπερ* clause has clarified the כאשר clause of MT, which reads "as spoke Yahweh the God of your fathers to you—a land flowing with milk and honey." LXX has supplied *δοῦναι* before "to you." The translator understood MT's דבר to mean "promised." LXX's *δοῦναι* makes this clear by its

4. SS 102 calls it a free translation.
5. Aq renders these verbs literally by *καὶ ἀκούσεις καὶ φυλάξεις* (retroverted from Syh).

ἐλάλησεν ... δοῦναι, which I would translate "promised to give (a land ...)." This interpretation reflects a true conception of what God's דבר involves. To the translator the Lord's speaking by itself constitutes a sure promise. The ῥέουσαν collocation occurs seven times in the book (also at 11:9 26:9,10,15 27:3 31:20), and was a cliché already found in Exod and Num (four times in each).

6:4 LXX introduces the *shema* by a superscription not present in MT: "and these are the ordinances and the judgments which the Lord commanded the Israelites in the desert as they were going out of the land of Egypt." Hex quite correctly placed all of this under the obelus to show its absence in MT. The collocation is apparently a version of 4:45 with the following differences: the addition of *καί* at the beginning; the omission of *τὰ μαρτυριὰ καί*; the substitution of *ἐνετείλατο* for *ἐλάλησεν*, and of *κύριος* for Μωυσῆς, and the addition of *ἐν τῇ ἐρήμῳ*; cf comments ad loc. It is undoubtedly intended to introduce vv.4—5 as is clear from v.6 which refers retrospectively to *τὰ ῥήματα ταῦτα*, viz. from שמע to the end of v.5.

ἄκουε is the solemn call to attention; it renders שמע which in its transliteration *Shema* is used as a title for the statement of faith which follows. It is often misused as including only the one statement *κύριος ὁ θεὸς ἡμῶν κύριος εἷς ἐστιν*, but its reference should include v.5 as well. It should also be noted that in contrast to v.3 the imperative is inflected from the present stem. The call to attention is then a process, not simply a call to hear but rather to remain in the listening mode; it really means something like "be hearing," although this sounds a bit odd in English.

The syntax of MT has been variously analyzed, and the apparent ambiguity can be applied to LXX as well. I would analyze the collocation as consisting of a) *κύριος ὁ θεὸς ἡμῶν* as a pendant nominative, whose chief purpose is to identify *κύριος* as Israel's covenant God—it is significant that in the second singular context in which *κύριος* is speaking to the Israelites as a collective singular the statement uses *ἡμῶν*, so that the statement is decontextualized with the community speaking in first person plural of "our God"; and b) *κύριος εἷς ἐστιν* containing the subject *κύριος* and the predicate *εἷς ἐστιν*. The Greek statement may be translated: "As for the Lord our God, the Lord is one." MT has for b) יהוה אחד which is more ambiguous. By adding the linking verb the translator excluded the possibility of understanding b) as the predicate of a).

6:5 Flowing from that statement of monotheistic faith is the command now stated in covenantal terms in second singular to love the Lord with complete devotion. This is the first mention of the people loving the Lord (see also 7:9 10:12 11:1,13,22 13:3 19:9 30:6,16,20). *ἀγαπάω* is the ordinary word for "love" in the Hellenistic period.[6] This complete devotion is shown in MT by three ב phrases which LXX, however, translates as three *ἐκ* phrases, i.e. designating not the means by which you are to love, but rather the source from which the love proceeds.[7] These three sources are the *διανοίας*, *ψυχῆς* and *δυνάμεως*, and in each case, so as to emphasize the completeness of the devotion, the articulated noun is modified by *ὅλης*. Instead of *διανοίας* the majority text has *καρδιας* as at 4:29 (see comment ad loc), but the much rarer rendering of לבב is original LXX.[8] The term stresses the intelligent center of an individual; it is that which propels one, it is understanding, intelligence, and refers to the world of thought, of reflection, of reason. The second term refers to the person, and the third means "strength, power." Together they mean "completely, without reserve." In the tradition the Byz text felt *ψυχῆς* to be inadequate in the triad and either substituted *ισχυος* or added it as a fourth source, but in essence it is really a doublet of *δυνάμεως*.

6:6 The reference in *τὰ ῥήματα ταῦτα* is to the *shema* amplified by v.5, i.e. the credo plus its response. For the *ὅσα* clause see comment at 4:2. For the two coordinate prepositional phrases see comment at 4:29. MT has only one phrase, על לבבך, as modifier of היו. That these words "shall be in your heart and in your person" means not only that you will always remember them (*ἐν τῇ καρδίᾳ σου*), but they will also become part of you, they will be in your *ψυχῇ*. The second phrase has been placed under the obelus in hex since it is absent in MT. Its addition, though it may have been influenced by the common collocation, does add a significant point. It might also be noted that the first phrase appears in *b z* as *επι της καρδιας σου*; this is closer to MT, which is either coincidence or was mediated by one of The Three.

---

6. See S.P.Swinn, *ἀγαπᾶν* in the Septuagint, SCS 28, 49—82.
7. See SS 127.
8. See the discussion in THGD 59.

6:7 Vv.7—9 detail how these words (see v.6) are to be imprinted in the memory of the community. MT orders in colorful fashion שננת "you shall sharpen, hone"; what is meant is "sharpen the consciousness, the memory," hence the more prosaic *προβιβάσεις* "you shall teach," a correct understanding of MT's intent.[9] The double accusatives refer to "what" and "whom" the verbal action applies resp. For the latter most witnesses have the second one as *τοις υιοις*, i.e. the dative showing indirect object.

The second clause adds a new dimension in that it insists on the constancy with which you are to speak with your children, viz. about *τὰ ῥήματα ταῦτα* of v.6. This is clear from the four nominative participles modifying the subject of λαλήσεις.[10] The Masoretes interpreted the verse differently; by placing the first cut after בם (by the ethnach), the four prepositional phrases modify the two coordinate clauses, which is a somewhat different way of putting it. LXX has made the first cut between *υἱούς σου* and *καί*.

MT has all four infinitives in the prepositional phrases with the second singular suffix, i.e. "when you are sitting, etc."[11] LXX has no *σου* at all, since these are unnecessary to the sense.[12] Similarly בביתך is rendered by *ἐν οἴκῳ*, i.e. without *σου*, since one normally sits in one's own house! Hex, however, added *σου* to equal MT more exactly.

The middle participle *κοιταζόμενος* is a neat rendering for שכב and only occurs three times in LXX (also 11:19 Lev 15:20), thus "laying onself down." Even more unusual is the rendering of בקומך by *διανιστάμενος* which is a seldom used Hellenistic word. In fact, it only occurs three times in LXX (also at 11:19 and Jud 12:15). Other compounds of *ἵστημι* are more commonly used for rendering the Qal of קום: *ἀνίστημι* 318 times; *ἐξανίστημι* 20; *ἐπανίστημι* 29, and the simplex form 28 times.[13]

9. Aq translates by *δευτερώσεις*, which presupposes the root שנה "to repeat, do a second time."
10. For attributive participles rendering ב plus bound infinitives see SS Inf 91.
11. The Others render v.7b by *ἐν τῷ καθῆσθαί σε ἐν οἰκίᾳ σου καὶ ἐν τῷ πορεύεσθαί σε ἐν ὁδῷ καὶ ἐν τῷ καθεύδειν σε καὶ ἐν τῷ ἀνίστασθαί σε*, thus a word for word translation.
12. See SS 102.
13. According to Dos Santos. See also the discussion in Dogniez-Harl ad loc.

6:8 MT's וקשרתם is translated by *καὶ ἀφάψεις αὐτά* in LXX.[14] The antecedent for the pronoun must again be *τὰ ῥήματα ταῦτα* of v.6. They are to serve "*εἰς σημεῖον* on your hand." LXX quite correctly has the singular *τῆς χειρός* rather than the plural of Sam which is hardly sensible.

The second clause, *καὶ ἔσται ἀσάλευτα πρὸ ὀφθαλμῶν σου*, is supposed to represent והיו לטטפת בין עיניך. The Hebrew noun refers to "frontlets, phylacteries," a rare word occurring only three times in O.T. (also 11:18 Exod 13:16), and its exact meaning is not certain. In Tar these are תפלין, the technical term for phylacteries. LXX did not understand the word at all, and used the adjective *ἀσάλευτα* "immoveable." The neuter plural is used since it has the same antecedent as *αὐτά*, viz. "these words" of v.6. These words being tied up as a sign on the hand will then "become immoveable before your eyes, i.e. they are constantly in your sight (on your hand).[15] See also Note at Exod 13:16. In the tradition *ἔσται* becomes the third plural imperative *εστωσαν* in *f*+, and A B *n*+ read the singular *ασαλευτον* as in Exod 13:16.[16]

6:9 LXX inexplicably changed the continued singular of the verse into the plural;[17] did the translator thoughtlessly read the final consonant of כתבתם twice, both as plural second person inflection, and then as a pronominal suffix, thus *γράψετε αὐτά*? Or, as is more likely, he read the verb as a plural and added *αὐτά* ad sensum. These (words) are to be written "on the jambs of your houses and of your gates," i.e. the jambs of both the houses and the gates. The Hebrew is different in that בשעריך is coordinate with על מזוות ביתך rather than with ביתך.[18] Note also that ביתך is singular which in view of the second singular context is possible, though the singular does refer to the Israelite community, not to the individual Israelite. LXX has the noun in the plural as does Sam, with which Pesh also agrees (but not Vulg). The plural is then also

---

14. Aq used *συνδήσεις* "you shall tie together" for the verb, which is somewhat more literal than *ἀφάψεις* "you shall fasten."
15. Aq has *καὶ ἔσονται εἰς νακτὰ μεταξὺ τῶν ὀφθαλμῶν σου* "and they shall become tightly pressed materials between your eyes." Sym agrees with Aq except for using *διεσταλμένοι* "defined, definite." Theod is closer to LXX with *καὶ ἔσονται εἰς σαλευτὰ ἀνὰ μέσον ὀφθαλμῶν σου*. For a possible explanation of the odd Sym rendering see Salvesen 151.
16. See THGD 136.
17. The Three witness to the singular *γράψεις*.
18. See Prijs 81.

carried through in the plural pronouns, i.e. (*τῶν οἰκιῶν*) *ὑμῶν* and (*τῶν πυλῶν*) *ὑμῶν*. In the tradition the *b* text has the verse consistently in the second person singular and also has the singular *του οικου*; it has also changed the second phrase to *εν ταις πυλαις σου*; in other words, the text has been changed to render MT exactly; see also the variant text of *b* in v.7. Its text was obviously influenced by the Later Revisers.

6:10—11 This is the first case in the book of והיה introducing a temporal clause, which LXX translates by *καὶ ἔσται ὅσαν*. והיה introducing some kind of conditional clause occurs 25 times in Deut. In one case it along with the כי clause it introduces is omitted (31:21). Of the remaining 24 cases three simply have *ἐὰν δέ*/*μέν* (for והיה אם at 11:13 20:11, and for והיה כי at 15:16). All the others translate והיה by *καὶ ἔσται*. Six of them add *ὅταν* (also 11:29 17:18 20:2,9 23:13); eight add *ἐάν* (8:19 21:14 24:1 25:2 26:1 28:1,15 29:19); two have *ἡνίκα* (7:12 25:19); another two add *ὡς ἄν* (27:4 30:1), 21:16 and 27:2 add *ᾗ ἂν ἡμέρᾳ*, and 28:63 has *ὃν τρόπον*. LXX now joins MT by returning to the second singular.

The *ὅταν* clause covers all of vv.10 and 11, with v.12 serving as its apodosis. *ὅταν* governs an aorist subjunctive since its action precedes that of the apodosis: thus "whenever the Lord your God brings you into the land." "Land" is modified by a relative clause in which the verb *ὤμοσεν* is accompanied by a complementary infinitive *δοῦναι* with five objects: *πόλεις*, *οἰκίας*, *λάκκους*, *ἀμπελῶνας καὶ ἐλαιῶνας*, in turn followed by two nominative participles which modify the subject of *πρόσεχε* which begins the apodosis in v.12; see below.

The indirect object of *ὤμοσεν* is *τοῖς πατράσιν σου*. In the Hebrew, לאברהם ליצחק וליעקב is in apposition with "your fathers". LXX connects all three with *καί*, and articulates only the first one, *τῷ Ἀβραάμ*, the other two obviously being dative as well.

The first object of *δοῦναί* (*σοι*) is *πόλεις*, which is described as "great and fine, which you did not build," an exact rendering of MT. V.11 continues with the second object *οἰκίας* without a conjunction, following Sam rather than MT's ובתים. This one also has an appositive: "full of all good things which you did not fill." The third is *λάκκους*, described as "dug which you did not dig out." MT has cognates חצבת ... חצובים, which LXX distinguishes nicely by the simplex λελατομημένους and the compound ἐξελατόμησας. Again LXX follows Sam in not introducing λάκκους with a conjunction. And finally, the coordinate objects, ἀμπελῶνας καὶ ἐλαιῶνας are modified by the relative clause "which you did not plant."

In MT this is followed by ואכלת ושבעת "and you shall eat and be filled," which are coordinate with יביאך of v.10. LXX connects this differently. By using nominative participles, καὶ φαγὼν καὶ ἐμπλησθείς, the collocation is subordinated as attributes to πρόσεχε σεαυτῷ of v.12. Lexically it means the same; it is still "you" who eat and are sated who are to be on guard, but it is structurally different; it might be translated "then when you eat and are full watch out lest ...."

6:12 The apodosis to the ὅταν clause (vv.10—11): a πρόσεχε σεαυτῷ μή construction,[19] for which see comment at 4:9. In the tradition hex has added ποτε to μή to represent פן.[20]

The appositive τοῦ θεοῦ σου is based on Sam; it has no equivalent in BHS.[21] For ἐξ οἴκου δουλείας see Note at Exod 13:3.[22] The warning not to forget their covenant God is carried forward in vv.13—15.

6:13 equals 10:20. It is obvious where the stress is being placed; each of the four clauses preposed the modifier to the verb in imitation of MT: κύριον τὸν θεόν σου, αὐτῷ, πρὸς αὐτόν and τῷ ὀνόματι αὐτοῦ. The third clause is absent in MT, but the longer text does occur at 10:20, of which LXX is an exact translation. In fact, LXX simply took over 10:20.

For "fear the Lord your God" see comments at v.2 and 4:10. This notion is a dominant one in the book, and the coordinate clauses explicate what fearing the Lord means. It involves his worship. The verb λατρεύω is used particularly in LXX for cultic service; in fact, only rarely is the verb used in LXX in any other sense but that of serving deity;[23] exceptions are ἄρχοντι

19. Aq has his usual φύλαξαι for השמר.
20. So too The Others read μήποτε.
21. See Appositives 1.
22. For τοῦ ἐξαγαγόντος σε ἐκ γῆς Αἰγύπτου see list 3 in THGD 87.
23. See Daniel 66—72 where she points out the non-sacerdotal character of λατρεύω.

at Lev 18:21 and Ναβουχοδονοσόρ at Jud 3:8. The Hebrew תעבד is much broader in scope, as the more common rendering, δουλεύω, shows.[24]

The second explication reads "to him you shall cleave." The verb is used metaphorically to express devotion to someone, in which case it is modified by a πρός phrase. It can also be used of malignant forces when it is modified by an ἐν phrase, such as plagues and diseases, 28:60, or curses, 29:20. It is more commonly modified by a dative which is neutral in character, and may be intended in a literal, physical sense as in "bones to flesh" at Ps 101:6 or the "tongue to the larynx" at Job 29:10 θ'.

The last way in which the fear of the Lord is shown is in adjuration, i.e. in an oath formula in which the divine name is used to validate an oath. An oath sworn in the Lord's name automatically brands the speaker as a devotee. The dative τῷ ὀνόματι is good Hellenistic usage,[25] as over against the Classical accusative.

In the tradition the A text represents the NT version,[26] in which προσκυνησεις obtains instead of φοβηθήσῃ. The reading is clearly inferior, since it is lexically much too close to λατρεύσεις to stand as the first verb; see comments above. Also well attested in NT is the A V 963 majority variant text, which adds μονω after αὐτῷ. It has, however, no basis in MT, and of the ancient witnesses only Vulg supports it. The gloss may interpret correctly, but its origin is exegetical and textual; cf vv.14—15. Another majority text is the addition of επι before the dative τῷ ὀνόματι (αὐτοῦ), which is good Hellenistic usage to designate that, or the one, sworn by. The accusative would be Classical usage, though the dative is also attested.[27]

6:14 The fear of the Lord your God means that you are not to go after foreign gods, i.e. "any of the gods of the nations which surround" Israel. The ἀπό is partitive, hence the translation "any"; it represents a partitive מן in MT.[28] The verse is in the plural in which it simply imitates MT, though why the writer should suddenly individuate in the context of the collective singular which both

24. According to the count in Dos Santos δουλεύω renders the Qal of עבד 114 times as over against λατρεύω 75 times and ἐργάζομαι 37 times.
25. See THGD 137.
26. Matth 4:10 Luc 4:8.
27. See LS s.v. III.
28. See SS 169.

precedes and follows the verse is not immediately clear. Of course, abandoning the Lord in favor of "other gods" is an individual rather than a communal affair, and the change may be based on some such notion.

Change in the tradition to the singular involves only the verb; neither the text of M *oI* with *ου μη πορευση* nor that of *z*+ with *ου μη πορευθης* can be taken seriously since ὑμῶν at the end is left unchanged. The change to *ου μη* plus the subjunctive reflects scribal uncertainty as to prohibitions; this is especially clear in the *C s*+ text which has *ου* with the subjunctive.

6:15 For θεὸς ζηλωτής see comment at 4:24.[29] As a jealous God the Lord will not tolerate idolatry, but he may in fury annihilate those of his people who stray in this fashion.

μή represents פן, and hex as usual has added *ποτε* under the asterisk to represent the Hebrew. LXX subordinates the first clause participially to the second so as to read "being angered should destroy." The Hebrew idiom has יחרה אף יהוה אלהיך, literally "the anger of Yahweh became hot," which LXX interprets well by rendering the verb by ὀργισθείς, subordinating the subject to a dative θυμῷ, and making κύριος ὁ θεός σου the subject.[30] In the tradition the A B F M *oP n y*+ text reads *θυμωθη* instead of θυμῷ. This change necessitated adding a *και* before ἐξολεθρεύσῃ which is supported by the majority text as well.[31]

Thc phrasc ἐν σοί occurs twice in the verse but in different senses. In the first instance it is purely locative: "the Lord ... is a jealous God in you," representing the בקרבך of MT. In the μή structure, however, the phrase modifies the participle ὀργισθείς, thereby designating with whom the Lord is angry; MT has בך. For the main verb, ἐξολεθρεύσῃ, see comment at 1:27.

6:16 MT switches to the plural for vv.16—17a, whereas LXX keeps the singular except for ἐξεπειράσασθε in v.16.[32] The distinction in number seems strange indeed. The only apparent difference seems to be that the singular is

29. The Three read ἰσχυρός, which is regularly used to render אל. The lemma in the second apparatus for the first note should be corrected to read θεός 1° (ind mend ad ζηλωτής]. The index in the mss is on the wrong word.
30. Aq and Sym retain the θυμῷ of LXX, but Theod supports the variant text θυμωθῇ.
31. That these are secondary corrections is argued at THGD 58—59.
32. The Three all have the plural πειράσετε instead of ἐκπειράσεις.

used in ordering the people as a whole, but a reference to the event in the desert is recalled in the plural, possibly because the event was an act of rebellion on the part of the Israelites, an action against Moses, i.e. they acted not as God's people but as Israelites. The verse introduces a new theme which continues through v.19. The verb *ἐκπειράζω* is an unusual word also occurring at 8:2,16, and otherwise only at Ps 77:18, always for נסה Piel.[33] V.4a is quoted literally in NT (Matt 4:7 Lk 4:12). The verb means "put to the test," something that the Israelites had done *ἐν τῷ Πειρασμῷ*; for its rendering of the place name מסה see Note at Exod 17:7. That the verb means "put to the test" is clear from the story in Exod 17:1—7; see in particular v.7b where the *πειράζειν κύριον* is defined as testing "whether the Lord is among us or not."

LXX changes the voice of *ἐκπειράζω* in the *ὃν τρόπον* clause to the middle, though with no change in meaning. That the tradition should try to level it to the active is not surprising. A popular variant has *εξεπειρασατε*; a *d* text reads *εξεπειρασετε*, and a *z* variant makes it *εξεπειρακατε*, but the middle must be original.

6:17 The positive counterpart to "not testing the Lord" is carefully guarding his commandments, testimonies and ordinances. Once again the order to Israel to guard is in the singular, for which see comment at v.16. MT is here also in the singular for the second part of the verse. The Hebrew pattern: cognate free infinitive plus finite verb is realized in the Greek by a present participle preceding a finite cognate verb,[34] presumably with the same intent as the Hebrew of putting stress on the verbal idea: thus "you must really guard"; the use of a present rather than an aorist participle is intended to show that the guarding is a continuous practice.

Unusual is LXX's failure to render any pronominal suffixes of nouns: אלהיכם simply becomes *τοῦ θεοῦ*,[35] and עדתיו and חקיו are translated by *τὰ μαρτύρια* and *τὰ δικαιώματα* resp. Admittedly most witnesses do read *του θεου σου*, but it should be noted that MT has the plural suffix, and not the singular.[36] Hex has added *σου* to both the other nouns to equal MT. The

33. According to Dogniez-Harl ad loc the verb is a neologism found only in LXX.
34. See for this usage A. Aejmelaeus, *Participium coniunctum* as a criterion for translation technique, VT XXXII (1982), 385—393.
35. See Appositives 3.0. for a possible reason for disregarding the suffix.
36. See THGD 56.

Hebrew also introduces the pair with a conjunction, and again the tradition has added *και* before *τὰ μαρτύρια*, possibly due to hex influence. For the use of *δικαιώματα* to translate חקים in Deut see comment at 4:1.[37] The *C*'' text has added an extra phrase with *και τα κριματα*, which is ex par, e.g. v.20. With צוך MT returns to the singular, and continues with it for the remainder of this section, as does LXX.

6:18 The verse is an amalgam of typical Deut structures. The first is "the good and the fine before the Lord your God."[38] These nominalized adjectives represent הישר והטוב "the upright (straight) and the good." It is, however, by no means clear which Greek word is intended for which Hebrew word, since neither one is a regular equivalent. ישר is usually rendered by *εὐθής* or *εὐθύς* (68 times), but by *ἀρεστός* only five and by *καλός* only three times. On the other hand, טוב is usual rendered by *ἀγαθός* (332 times), but by *καλός* 99 times, and by *ἀρεστός* only three times. Nor is the Hebrew text regular. For the five cases of *τὸ ἀρεστὸν καὶ τὸ καλόν* three are actually reversed, only 21:9 agreeing completely with our verse; in fact, most witnesses here also reverse the two, but B and 963 support LXX. In MT הישר והטוב occurs only here; at 12:28 the two are reversed, and for the other three, 12:25 13:18 and 21:9, MT has only הישר. Obviously no pattern obtains.[39]

For *ἵνα εὖ σοι γένηται* see comment at 4:40. For *καὶ εἰσέλθῃς καὶ κληρονομήσῃς τὴν γῆν* see comment at 1:8. The land is often called "the good land" (also at 1:35 3:25 8:10 9:6 11:17). For "which the Lord swore to your fathers" see comment at 1:8.

6:19 This verse belongs syntactically to the preceding relative clause; it is complementary to *ὤμοσεν*, i.e. which he swore ... *ἐκδιῶξαι* "to chase out (all your enemies before you as he said)."[40] LXX differs from MT in that the latter identifies the subject of "said" as יהוה. As expected, hex has added *κυριος* (under the asterisk) to make up for the omission.

---

37. Aq translates by *ἀκριβάσματα*.
38. See list 51 in THGD 98.
39. Theod translates the two in regular fashion by *τὸ εὐθὲς καὶ τὸ ἀγαθόν*.
40. Somewhat problematic is the explanation of *ἐκδιῶξαι* as "instrumental-modal: dadurch, dass; indem" of König ad loc. It is simpler to consider it complementary; it's what he swore to your fathers.

6:20 LXX follows Sam's והיה in its *καὶ ἔσται* introducing a *ὅταν* clause, for which see comment at vv.10—11; MT simply begins with כי; hex has placed *ἔσται* under the obelus (though the *καί* is erroneously not included). The *ὅταν* clause has as its apodosis the *καὶ ἐρεῖς κ.τ.λ.* of v.21. *τίνα ἐστίν* is a good rendering of מה, but *C'' s+* change to *τινος*.[41] For the coordinate nouns which here serve as subject in the question, see comment at 4:1 5:31.[42]

Problematic is the person of the pronouns in the *ὅσα* clause. MT reads "which commanded אלהינו אתכם," which should then become *ο θεος ημων υμιν*, but LXX reads *ὁ θεὸς ἡμῶν ἡμῖν*, which also makes good sense. But in Hellenistic Greek *υμιν* and *ημιν* were pronounced alike. I strongly suspect that the critical text should read *ἡμῶν ὑμῖν*, which is read by 12 scattered mss only, and that the consistent first plural text was probably a case of leveling, a response to an urge difficult to resist. I would now defend *ἡμῶν ὑμῖν* as original text. The distinction is intentional. The Lord is our God, but the son correctly asks: What did he command "you," not "us."

6:21 What *ἐρεῖς τῷ υἱῷ σου* continues through v.25. For *οἰκέται* for עבדים see comment at 5:15. The dative *τῷ Φαραώ* is one of possession, correctly translating לפרעה. For *ἐν γῇ Αἰγύπτῳ* see comment at 5:15. MT does not support *γῇ*, but the phrase ארץ מצרים is common and the translator read it ex par. Actually the phrase occurs 12 times in Deut, whereas במצרים occurs only six times. The statement that the Lord brought you out from there (i.e. Egypt) also occurs often in the book; see comment at 1:27. For *ἐν χειρὶ κραταιᾷ καὶ ἐν βραχίονι ὑψηλῷ* see comment at 3:23—24.[43] MT has only a single item ביד חזקה and the double phrase is ex par.

6:22 For *σημεῖα καὶ τέρατα* see comment at 4:34. Only here are these called not only *μεγάλα* (as 7:19 29:3) but also *πονηρά*. The collocation *ἔδωκεν* ...

41. The Three simply have *τί*, which B *b+* also read. For its secondary character in LXX see THGD 111.

42. For *τὰ μαρτύρια* Aq has the singular *ἡ μαρτυρία*, presumably vocalizing עדת as an abstract singular: ʿēdūt. Theod and Sym retain LXX. For *δικαιώματα* Aq substituted *ἀκριβάσματα* as at v.17, Sym has *προστάγματα*, and Theod read *ἠκριβασμένα*.

43. For the instrumental *ἐν* see SS 121.

ἐνώπιον ἡμῶν represents the Hebrew ויתן לעינינו, and must be understood as a calque meaning "he set before us." The modification of the verb by three ἐν phrases is one in which the preposition denotes "the object to which someth. happens or in which someth. shows itself."[44] I would translate: And the Lord set great and evil signs affecting Egypt, Pharaoh and his house before us.

6:23 The preposed (καὶ) ἡμᾶς equals MT and stresses "us" in contrast to those affected by the signs and wonders of v.22. In the tradition a popular A F M V text added the subject for ἐξήγαγεν as κυριος ο θεος ημων (or simply κυριος in *b*), but the subject is obvious and it has no support in MT. The history of redemption is restated: "he brought us out from there, to bring us in, to give us this land, which he had sworn to give to our fathers." This is a slightly amplified version of MT, which lacks the pronoun of "this land," as well as the second "to give." One might, however, argue that ταύτην does represent the deictic force of the phrase את הארץ, whereas the addition of δοῦναι to complement ὤμοσεν is ad sensum, simply making explicit what is already implicit.

In the tradition this expansionist tendency is further illustrated by a popular A F M text, which not only adds κυριος ο θεος ημων as the subject of ὤμοσεν, but also rearranges the text and adds a dative pronoun in its τοις πατρασιν ημων δουναι ημιν. This second δοῦναι was placed under the obelus in hex to show its absence in MT; its omission in *C'' s* equals MT and was probably mediated by one of The Three.

6:24 V.24a is translated word for word; in it the first infinitive, ποιεῖν, is complementary, but the second one, φοβεῖσθαι, may be understood in two ways, either as purposive or in apposition to the first one. The second alternative seems to me preferable, since it fits the theology of the book in which the fear of the Lord is guarding his commandments as at 5:29(26) and 6:2. One can then understand the Lord's command as "to do these ordinances, viz. to fear the Lord our God"; see comment at v.2.

For ἵνα εὖ ἡμῖν ᾖ see comment on καὶ εὖ σοι ᾖ at 5:33(30). The second ἵνα clause changes the syntax of MT by which "to preserve us" is changed to

44. Bauer sub ἐν I.2.

ζῶμεν, and כהיום הזה "as this day," which occurs only here in the book, is amplified by a καί in ὥσπερ καὶ σήμερον "as even today."

6:25 MT states that צדקה will be ours should we be careful to perform all these commandments before the Lord. This is interpreted as ἐλεημοσύνη, as well as at 24:13 where the returning of a pledged garment before nightfall will be an ἐλεημοσύνη σοι before the Lord your God. Here the notion underlying צדקה appears to be one of merit.[45] In later Hebrew צדקה comes to mean "mercy," and "deeds of mercy," and so "almsgiving," and this apparently influenced the translator. So what LXX is saying is that "we will have mercy (i.e. God will be charitably disposed towards us) if we diligently practice πάσας τὰς ἐντολὰς ταύτας before the Lord." The translator understood המצוה הזאת correctly as a collective.

In the tradition an F *f z*+ variant changes ταύτας to του νομου τουτου probably in the awareness that this section of admonition cautioning obedience ends here, with 7:1 changing to quite a different set of warnings and instructions. The majority B 963 tradition has added κυριος ο θεος ημων after "as he commanded us," against MT. This named subject is extremely frequent in the book, and is clearly secondary.[46]

---

45. See זכותא of Tar^{O}.
46. See the discussion in THGD 119—120.

Chapter 7

7:1 The conditional clause is introduced by כי and means "when," but LXX translates by ἐὰν δέ. Lexically, however, this can hardly mean "and if," but must intend "when."[1] A popular A F M V text has rewritten the conditional as *και εσται εν τω εισαγαγειν σε κυριον τον θεον* ..., the origin of which is not certain. It must have been rooted in an objection to ἐὰν δέ as calling into question the divine resolve to bring the Israelites into the Promised Land. It is not a recensional change, since it is not supported by MT; it must be an exegetical one. Much simpler is the Byz clarification which introduces the condition by *και εσται οταν*.

The use of ἐκεῖ in εἰς ἥν ... ἐκεῖ is a Hebraism, one which occurs frequently in the book. Hex has inserted *συ* before εἰσπορεύῃ to represent אתה (בא). For κληρονομῆσαι see comment at 6:1.[2] Hex has added *αυτην* to equal MT.

The apodosis is introduced by καί. The variant *εξαρη* for ἐξαρεῖ, supported by A F M V 963 *O*' *f*+, is an itacism, though it is the spelling of the aorist subjunctive; this would make it part of the protasis, with v.2 beginning the apodosis, which would also make sense. This is a possible interpretation of MT, though the absence of a conjunction before החרם in v.2b makes the choice for the onset of the apodosis with v.2b the likely intent of the Hebrew.

What is promised is that "when the Lord your God brings you into the land, which you are entering to possess (it), he (i.e. the Lord) will remove great and numerous nations from before you." Cod B lacks καὶ πολλά, but this is simply a case of omission through homoioteleuton.[3] MT's text is shorter; it has a single adjective רבים and LXX's doublet μεγάλα καὶ πολλά is an expansion. The Canaanite nations are then listed. This is the first mention of the seven in MT, which in turn influenced the Exod LXX text greatly;[4] see also Jos 3:10 24:11. Each is joined by καί, and everyone is articulated, thereby equalling MT. To be disregarded as secondary is the absence in B V+

---

1. See Bauer sub ἐάν 1.d. The Others all have ὅταν instead of ἐὰν δέ.
2. See THGD 121 for the usage in Deut.
3. See THGD 124.
4. See THGE 157—158.

of the article for all but *τὸν Χετταῖον*; this is an abbreviated version, not supported by 963.[5] The list represents the traditional tribes inhabiting pre-Israelite Canaan. These seven nations are described as *πολλὰ*[6] *καὶ ἰσχυρότερα ὑμῶν* "numerous and stronger than you"; note the comparative ממך in MT is rendered by the positive degree for the first one.[7] The text of LXX is only weakly supported. A popular B V 963 reading substituted *μεγαλα* for *πολλά*, and the majority A F M text added *μεγαλα και* at the beginning. The popular *μεγαλα* has entered the text under the influence of its earlier occurrence in the verse.

7:2 V.2a is still part of the apodosis, being joined by conjunctions; the first clause is parallel to the preceding one: "and the Lord your God will deliver them into your hands (i.e. into your power)," but the second is an instruction "and you shall smite them."

The first clause in MT has been simplified by the translator. MT has ונתנם יהוה אלהיך לפניך "and Yahweh your God should set them before you (so that you may smite them.)" By changing לפניך to *εἰς τὰς χεῖράς σου* "into your power," and rendering the verb by *παραδώσει*, a smooth translation is made. The change in subject to second person in the second clause then ensures its imperatival interpretation.

V.2b is syntactically separate from the preceding, and the interpretation would be simplified if the comma before *ἀφανισμῷ* were changed to a colon. The lack of an initial conjunction, which in MT had marked the onset of the apodosis, signals a syntactic break. What is intended is an explication of the *πατάξεις* clause, an explication which continues through v.5. This begins with the common Hebrew pattern: cognate free infinitive preceding a finite verb, החרם תחרים, which refers to the devotion of enemies to total destruction as a sacral vow in order to ensure protection of God's people against the idolatrous influences of the heathen. It is translated by *ἀφανισμῷ ἀφανιεῖς*, a verb meaning "to render unseen," hence to obliterate. I would translate: "you must

5. See THGD 59.
6. Sym understood the comparative ממך as applying to רבים as well: *πλείονα ἢ σύ* (retroverted from Syh).
7. Aq has an odd understanding of (ממך) עצומים which he understood as עצמים (more commonly עצמות) or more precisely as עצמיך — *ὀστόϊνα σοῦ* "your bones."

thoroughly wipe out."[8] The Greek translation is most unusual. The verb recurs as a rendering of חרם only twice elsewhere (Jer 27:21 28:3), and the noun as an equivalent for חרם is unique. *ἀφανισμός* actually occurs only here in the Pentateuch, but it later becomes the regular rendering for שמ(מ)ה in the prophets.

That the point of such extermination of the enemy was that of separation, of keeping the people apart from any association with non-Israelites, is clear from the next order, also given asyndetically: "not shall you make a covenant with them." In fact, "nor shall you deal mercifully with them." The root חנן "be gracious, merciful" is regularly rendered by *ἐλεέω* (see also 13:17 28:50).[9]

7:3 *γαμβρεύσητε* is a neologism based on *γαμβρός*, used throughout LXX to render חתן "in-law." At Gen 38:8 the verb also occurs but for יבם; see Note ad loc. Here it is used to translate the Hithp of חתן, thus "enter into an in-law relation, to intermarry," Since marriage is an individual affair, LXX uses the plural *γαμβρεύσητε* even though MT consistently uses the singular. One might have expected a dative modifier to render בם as at 2Esdr 9:14 *τοῖς λαοῖς*, but LXX has *πρὸς αὐτούς*; the mutual relationship is thereby emphasized. This is clear from the detailed prohibition explaining the interdict: "your daughter you must not give to his son, and his daughter you must not take for your son." LXX here returns to the singular of MT.

7:4 The reason for the prohibition of intermarriage with gentile tribes in v.3 is the inherent danger of idolatry. The Hebrew text is difficult to understand. It reads: "For he shall turn aside your son from after me and they shall serve other gods." But the subject of יסיר is vague; just who is "he"? The nearest antecedent is the suffix of בתו in v.3, i.e. the father-in-law; probably what is meant is the foreigner as represented in the list of seven nations in v.1. Note also the reversion to first person in מאחרי, i.e. as though God himself is speaking. But then עבדו is plural; who are "they"? Presumably בתך and בנך are meant. The Greek has simplified the statement considerably. It has

8. The Others translate the verb by their usual *ἀναθεματιεῖς*.
9. But Aq has his usual *δωρήσῃ* "give gifts" for the verb חנן.

λατρεύσει, i.e. the singular following the Sam text.[10] Since verbs in Greek do not inflect for gender, one can understand LXX as "For she (i.e. *τὴν θυγατέρα αὐτοῦ*) would turn your son from me, and he would serve other gods"; the clause fits perfectly in the context of the last clause of v.3.

For *ὀργισθήσεται θυμῷ κύριος* see comment at 6:15. The verb is modified by *εἰς ὑμᾶς* but the plural interruption imitates בכם of MT. The text follows MT closely in returning to the singular in the last clause. The change in number is as bewildering in the Greek as it is in the Hebrew. For *ἐξολεθρεύσει* translating השמיד see comment at 6:15. *τὸ τάχος* as an adverbial phrase correctly interprets מהר of MT.

7:5 Both MT and LXX change to the plural for this verse. The things they are to "do for them" are four in number, and the text is an exact copy of Exod 34:13: see Notes ad loc.[11] The only significant difference between LXX and MT is the explication of פסיליהם as *τὰ γλυπτὰ τῶν θεῶν αὐτῶν*,[12] for which see 12:3. Hex has rightly placed *τῶν θεῶν* under the obelus as having no equivalent in MT.

7:6 Both LXX and MT switch to the singular, probably because the reference is to λαός, and the unitary nature of the people makes the singular appropriate. The *ὅτι* shows the reason for the orders given in v.5. You cannot tolerate idolatrous objects, *βωμούς*, *στήλας*, *ἄλση*, *γλυπτὰ τῶν θεῶν*, because you are a λαὸς *ἅγιος* to the Lord your God. After all, being *ἅγιος* is being קדוש, which means to be separate, set aside to sacred purposes. A *ἅγιος* people is one that is dedicated to God, i.e. holy. It is the antonym of "profane, secular." A holy people could hardly abide idolatry.

The second clause is coordinate to the first one, as LXX makes clear by introducing it by *καί* over against MT. Not only are they a holy people, they are also the people of God's choice; they have, however, been chosen for a particular reason: *εἶναι αὐτῷ λαὸν περιούσιον παρὰ πάντα τὰ ἔθνη* which are on earth, i.e. "to be his special people rather than all the (other) nations." The choice of *προείλατο* to render בחר is highly unusual; in fact, it occurs else-

10. Also supported by Kenn 99 and the *serviet* of Vulg.
11. Instead of *τοὺς βωμούς* The Three witness to *τὰ θυσιαστήρια*.
12. The Others naturally lack *τῶν θεῶν*.

where only at Prov 1:29. The normal rendering for בחר is *ἐκλέγω*,[13] and it was probably used here to indicate preference; note its modification by *παρά*; the Lord preferred Israelites to all the (other) nations.

In the tradition B Byz have added *σε* to *εἶναι*, but this is otiose; as a complementary infinitive the subject is already stated in *σέ*. For the meaning of *περιούσιον* see Note at Exod 19:5[14]. A popular gloss in the phrase *ἐπὶ προσώπου τῆς γῆς* inserts *πασης* before "the earth," added under the influence of the common phrase "all the land"; but *γῆς* here refers to the earth, not just to the land (of promise).

7:7 Vv.7—8 belong together, with v.8 constituting the adversative of v.7; thus "not because you were more numerous ... but because ...." Both LXX and MT revert to the plural for vv.7—8a before returning to the singular in vv.8b—11. The *ὅτι* represents מן, i.e. "(not) from your multitude," which LXX translates by *ὅτι πολυπληθεῖτε*, which with *παρά* makes a comparative statement. The *παρά* also renders a מן, but that one must mean "from (all the nations)." So the Greek has restated what the Hebrew says in quite a different way: "not because you were more numerous than all the nations," which does render the intent of MT adequately.

προείλατο "prefer, deliberately select" translates חשק "dotes on, cling to."[15] The pair *προείλατο* and *ἐξελέξατο* are roughly synonymous, though *ἐκλέγω* is the usual rendering for Qal בחר; cf comment at v.6. I would translate: "did the Lord prefer and choose you." That Israel was the people of God's choice is a common theme in the OT.

The *πολυπληθεῖτε* statement is contrasted by the *γάρ* clause at the end of the verse. The articulated המעט plus מן is the Hebrew pattern for the elative, and is shown in LXX by the unarticulated *ὀλιγοστοὶ παρά*.[16] In the tradition the Byz text has the Classical form *προειλετε* for the Hellenistic *προείλατε*, and has also expanded *κύριος* by adding *ο θεος*; both are obviously secondary readings. 963 *oI+* have repeated *κύριος* for *ἐξελέξατο* from the preceding clause; this is quite unnecessary, since the subject is obvious.

---

13. According to Dos Santos 158 times.
14. Sym has *ἐξαίρετον*; cf Exod 19:5 and comment at Salvesen 96.
15. Aq translates the word by *προσεκολλήθη*. Aq distinguishes between חשק and דבק by *προσκολλᾶν* and *κολλᾶν* resp.
16. See SS 150.

7:8 ἀλλὰ παρά is used to render כי מן, with כי taken in the sense of כי אם. The reason for God's preference for or choice of Israel was twofold, first of all, because τὸ ἀγαπᾶν ὑμᾶς and διατηρῶν τὸν ὅρκον.... [17] The notion that God loved people already occurred at 4:37 with τοὺς πατέρας σου, but here his love for Israel is determinative for the people's election as his people, a theme which became central in the NT; comp John 3:16. The second compulsion for God's choice was "the oath which he swore to your fathers." Who the fathers were is not stated; it could be either Abraam, Isaak and Jacob (cf 6:10), or the generation brought out of Egypt which died in the wilderness.

The election of Israel was then actualized by ἐξήγαγεν κύριος ὑμᾶς ... καὶ ἐλυτρώσατό σε .... The former was done ἐν χειρὶ κραταιᾷ καὶ ἐν βραχίονι ὑψηλῷ; see comment at 6:21. As at 6:21, MT has only the first phrase. Accordingly, hex placed καὶ ἐν βραχίονι ὑψηλῷ under the obelus. The second clause changes to the singular σε, i.e. the stress is not on individuals but on the community of Israel. The exodus is here described as ἐλυτρώσατό σε, i.e. he redeemed you, he paid a ransom, representing יפדך. This was first used in the Pentateuch of the ransom of the firstborn at Exod 13:13, and λυτρόω is the standard word used for rendering פדה (40 times, followed by ῥύεσθαι - five times, and ἀλλάσσειν three times).[18] A popular gloss adding κυριος as subject for the second clause was probably created because the verb of the first clause was some distance from this one, but it is quite unnecessary. The land of Egypt from which the Lord rescued Israel is called οἴκου δουλείας, a common description,[19] first occurring at Exod 13:3.

7:9 The singular continues through v.11. The initial καὶ γνώσῃ follows hard on v.8; what is meant by "and you shall know" is that because the Lord loves you and keeps his oath ... you may safely conclude ὅτι ...; the ὅτι clause states what it is that you may now know. The lead clause represents the MT nominal pattern יהוה אלהיך הוא האלהים in which the subject is "Yahweh your God," and the predicate is the nominal clause "he is God," thus "Yahweh your God is God." LXX imitates this by a pendant nominative κύριος ὁ θεός σου, along

17. The occurrence of מן plus bound infinitives is rare; see SS Inf 107.
18. According to the count of Dos Santos.
19. See list 3 in THGD 87.

with the subject and predicate construction *οὗτος θεός*. The last word is then followed by a series of three appositional phrases, "the faithful God, the one guarding covenant and mercy ... (10) and the one repaying those who hate (him) openly so as to destroy them." *ὁ θεὸς ὁ πιστός* represents האל הנאמן "the God who is trustworthy, dependable.[20] The adjective seldom occurs for anything other than the Ni of אמן (29 times), which in turn is almost always translated by *πιστός* or the verb *πιστόω* (9 times). As Dogniez-Harl points out, the adjective is only rarely used of God in the OT, and it is generally reserved "à un homme ou à l'alliance de Dieu, à son jugement, à ses paroles."[21]

The second appositive represents God as one who keeps his promises, i.e. "the one who guards the covenant and mercy to those who love him and guard his commandments." This is a clear reflection of the rationale for the prohibition of the use of images in worship in the Decalogue, for which see comment at 5:10. The adaptation is here in third person and expands somewhat on the Decalogue form by adding *τὴν διαθήκην καί* before "mercy," changing *ποιῶν* to *φυλάσσων*, substituting *τὰ προστάγματα* for *τὰς ἐντολάς*, and interpreting and transposing to the end *εἰς χιλιάδες* as *εἰς χιλίας γενεάς*. This last change is significant in that it confirms the understanding that "thousands" means thousands of generations contrasting with the "third and fourth generation" of 5:9. Any rationalist attempt to limit the boundless extent of God's *τὴν διαθήκην καὶ τὸ ἔλεος* by considering the "thousand generations" a rhetorical amplification rather than an interpretation of the "thousands" of 5:10[22] should be withstood.

In the tradition B+ has omitted the articles modifying *θεός* 3°, *πιστός*, *διαθήκην* and *ἔλεος*, but not *φυλάσσων*, which is the exact opposite of MT, and obviously secondary.[23] The variant *b* reading of *τα προσταγματα* for *τὰς ἐντολάς* is due to the influence of the Decalogue (5:10). Also attested are the popular *αυτου* glosses on both *διαθήκην* and *ἔλεος*, which receive no support in MT. The Byz text attests to the Classical *τον ελεον* for the neuter of LXX, but the Hellenistic form is the more common throughout LXX.[24]

---

20. Aq as usual translates האל as <ὁ> *ἰσχυρός*.
21. P.163.
22. As e.g. by Driver ad loc.
23. For a discussion of these variants see THGD 104.
24. See Thackeray 158.

7:10 The third appositive to *θεός* 2° of v.9 is given in v.10a. This contrasts with God's reaction to those who love him: those who hate him he will repay openly so as to destroy them. The second part of the verse expands on the first part by two clauses introduced but not joined by a *καί*; BHS has no conjunction at all. Whether that text is earlier than that of mlt mss is impossible to determine since the word before אל ends with *waw*, and either haplography or dittography created a secondary text for the Hebrew. The first clause in MT reads לא יאחר לשנאו, which LXX translates by *καὶ οὐχὶ βραδυνεῖ τοῖς μισοῦσιν* following the plural of Sam.[25]

The emphasis in the verse is on requital, since the last clause again uses the verb *ἀποδίδωμι*, viz. in *κατὰ πρόσωπον ἀποδώσει αὐτοῖς*. In MT the prepositional phrase which I would render by "openly" is אל פניו, but in Sam is על פניו; it is not clear which text was parent to LXX which idiomatically leaves the suffix untranslated,[26] as it does in both cases of *τοῖς μισοῦσιν*. An *αὐτόν* is quite unnecessary in Greek, since the context makes it obvious that it refers to God.[27] Hex has added *αυτον* to both cases of *μισοῦσιν* as well as *αυτου* to both cases of *πρόσωπον*, all under the asterisk, to equal MT.

7:11 A summary statement soliciting obedience in all matters ordered. For *τὰς ἐντολὰς καὶ τὰ δικαιώματα καὶ τὰ κρίματα* see comment at 5:31. That *τὰς ἐντολάς* translates the singular המצוה should occasion no surprise. The Hebrew term is used throughout the book as a collective, and the articulated plural המצות never appears. Of the 13 cases of המצוה in the book, one is not translated (31:5), one is rendered by the singular *ἡ ἐντολή* (30:11), and all the others are interpreted as plural.

Over against MT, LXX has the demonstrative *ταῦτα* modifying *κρίματα* which is odd indeed; in any event, hex places it under the obelus. MT, on the other hand, has לעשותם, and LXX simply has *ποιεῖν*. Hex has added *αυτα* under the asterisk to equal the disregarded suffix of MT.

---

25. The MT text may well represent a compromise combining a double reading. Either the singular לשנאו or the plural לשנאיו was read twice and then the two readings were combined by the Masoretes. In fact, Kenn 157 reads לשנאיו in both cases, whereas Kenn 168 reads לשנאו for both; cf also Prijs 98.

26. See SS 102.

27. For the usage in Deut see the discussion in SS 101—102.

7:12 For καὶ ἔσται ἡνίκα ἄν see comment at 6:10—11. LXX follows MT faithfully in using the plural for v.12a, and then switching to the singular. The verse is a general statement intended to introduce a description of all the blessings attendant on adherence to his ordinances (ἀκούσητε πάντα τὰ δικαιώματα ταῦτα καὶ φυλάξητε καὶ ποιήσητε αὐτά). MT does not support πάντα, which fact hex recognized by placing it under the obelus. The overall statement on blessings then continues with v.12b in the singular, i.e. the adherence is seen as an individual matter but the divine blessings affect the collective "you," the community as a whole. LXX cleverly distinguishes between the שמרתם and the שמר of Yahweh your God. The first is translated by the simplex φυλάξητε, but the second one becomes the compound διαφυλάξει, which is lexically stronger than the simplex, thus "guard carefully, watch closely." For τὴν διαθήκην καὶ τὸ ἔλεος see comment at v.9. The καθά clause represents an אשר clause in MT and poses a problem. The Hebrew clause occurs 12 times in Deut and only here and at 26:15 is the אשר rendered by καθά; elsewhere it is always translated by a relative pronoun. Four cases of כאשר occur with the verb נשבע (13:18 19:8 28:9 29:12), but these are always rendered by ὃν τρόπον. At 26:15, however, the text is fully secure. Instead of καθά 963 *C*′′+ read καθο, whereas B+ read ο. The reading of 963 never occurs in Deut, and that of B has only weak support.[28] The LXX text is then clearly original.

A number of variant traditions may be noted. For the B V Byz+ εαν for ἄν see comment at 5:27. The Byz text glossed φυλάξητε with αυτα on the pattern of καὶ ποιήσητε αὐτά which follows immediately. The Classical τον ελεον occurs in the Byz text as well. Peculiar is the majority variant reading υμων for σου. The plural did occur in the protasis, but the singular is consistently used in the apodosis and equals MT.[29]

7:13 V.13a consists of three clauses: "and he will love you and bless you and increase you"; these are general statements. The promises only become specific with the fourth clause in which the verb εὐλογήσει has a series of modifiers, but the verb had already been used with σε and defined by the coordinate καὶ πληθυνεῖ σε, i.e. the blessing has already been defined as a matter

28. See the discussion in THGD 132—133.
29. See THGD 110.

of increase. The first two modifiers are both פרי in Hebrew, but LXX distinguishes between fruit of the body as *ἔκγονα* and that of the ground as *καρπόν*.[30] דגן is normally translated by *σῖτος* (36 out of 39 times).[31] The collocation *τὰ ἔκγονα τῆς κοιλίας σου* in coordination with a similar pattern is a common one in Deut.[32] LXX throughout the OT renders תירש by *οἶνος*.[33] So too when יצהר is translated, it usually appears as *ἔλαιον*, but that also appears far more often for the usual word for oil, שמן.[34]

The terms שגר and עשתרת are contextually nicely rendered by adapting them to their genitives, i.e. *τὰ βουκόλια* (*τῶν βοῶν*) and *τὰ ποίμνια* (*των προβάτων*). For the relative clause with which the verse ends see comment at 1:8, but see also the discussion at 7:12. LXX adds *κύριος* as named subject for *ὤμοσεν*, which is unnecessary in the context. It has been placed under the obelus by hex to show its absence in MT.

7:14 *εὐλογητός* can be used either of God or of man. It can not be contrasted with the passive participle, *ευλογημενος*, except that *εὐλογητός* can not be used of the non-human world; cf 28:4—5. In the Pentateuch *εὐλογητός* is used of human beings as often as of deity; see Note at Gen 12:2.[35] For the comparative expression *παρὰ τὰ ἔθνη* comp comment at v.7.[36]

MT distinguishes between the male עקר and the female עקרה. LXX not only follows this pattern but even chooses different adjectives to translate the two: *ἄγονος* and *στεῖρα*.[37] The last phrase is coordinated rather awkwardly at the end rather than after *ἐν ὑμῖν* where it logically belongs, but it equals MT.

---

30. Aq will have none of such distinctions, but has *καρπὸν γαστρός σου* instead of *τὰ ἔκγονα τῆς κοιλίας σου*.
31. But not by Aq who has *χεῦμα* which refers to that which flows (*χέω*) and seems odd, but recurs at 12:17. Is the Aramaic verb אידגן "be piled up" possibly related?
32. See list 40 in THGD 97.
33. But Aq distinguishes between יין and תירש reserving *οἶνος* for the former. Instead of *τὸν οἶνον* he has *ὀπωρισμόν*, a word known only from Aq. It must be related to *ὀπωρίζω* "to gather fruit," and so the early vintage rather than the mature *οἶνος*.
34. Aq uses *ἔλαιον* for שמן, and renders יצהר by *στιλπνότητα* which means "brightness" reflecting the root צהר, probably justified as indicating the shiny, glistening character of olive oil.
35. The distinction made by E.Bickermann, Studies in Jewish and Christian History, II (Leiden, 1980), 313—323 referred to by Dogniez-Harl, 285, simply does not fit the facts.
36. According to SS 150 the comparative *παρά* occurs three times in the book, though see v.7.
37. Aq does not, but has *στεῖρος* for the first one.

In the tradition Byz ties this verse to the preceding by means of *καί*, but MT does not support a conjunction. The *b n+* text read *και ευλογησει σε* instead of *εὐλογητὸς ἔσῃ*, but this comes from v.13. *C'*' introduces v.14b with a *και*, which is certainly secondary.

7:15 The majority of witnesses add the appositive *ο θεος σου* to *κύριος*, but this has no counterpart in MT. For *νόσους ... τὰς πονηράς* comp ἕλκει Αἰγυπτίῳ of 28:27. The Hebrew equivalent מדוי also occurs at 28:60, though in the singular where it is rendered by *τὴν ὀδύνην* (Αἰγύπτου) *τὴν πονηράν*, whereas חלים רעים in 28:59 is translated by *νόσους πονηράς*. It is doubtful whether LXX intended any distinction between the two words. These evil diseases are characterized by two relative clauses, *ἃς ἑώρακας καὶ ὅσα ἔγνως*, a doublet rendering for אשר ידעת. Hex has rightly placed *ἃς ἑώρακας καί* under the obelus as not being represented in MT.[38]

In the second part of the verse a negative and a positive statement contrast absolutely in LXX, i.e. *οὐκ ἐπεθήσει* contrasts with *ἐπιθήσει*. The Lord "will not place (*πάσας ... ἃς ἑώρακας καὶ ὅσα ἔγνως*) on you, and (i.e. but) he will place them (*αὐτά* referring to *ὅσα*) on all those who hate you." The Greek uses a direct modifier only for the second verb, and hex has supplied an *αυτα* under the asterisk for the first as being consonant with MT. The contrast is not as absolute in MT, which changes verbs: ישימם but נתנם,[39] though admittedly they are synonyms meaning "put, place."

7:16 LXX softened the harsh figure of MT's אכלת את כל העמים by inserting *τὰ σκῦλα*, i.e. "you shall eat all the spoils of the nations"; hex placed *σκῦλα* under the obelus since it has no basis in MT. The אשר clause which modifies העמים is rendered by a *ἅ* clause; this is ambiguous since the pronoun could refer either to *σκῦλα* or to *ἐθνῶν*, but since the Deut translator tends to inflect relative pronouns by attraction to the noun modified (which would be *ων* in the case of *ἐθνῶν*), he probably had *σκῦλα* in mind.

The collocation *οὐ φείσεται ὁ ὀφθαλμός σου ἐπί* is a set collocation which often obtains in Deuteronomic literature; in Deut see also 13:8 19:13,

38. Theod and Aq have *ὅσα ἔγνως*, whereas Sym has *ἃς οἶδας*.
39. For ישימם בך Theod and Aq have *οὐ θήσει αὐτά ἐν σοί* (The *θήσεις* in ms 344 should read *θήσει{ς}*). Sym had *οὐ ποιήσει{ς} ἐν σοί*.

21 25:12. It is always in a context where one is admonished to show no favor, to be unsparing in carrying out the divine will in some form of retribution or punishment.

The section ends with what is thematic in the book, the warning not to serve (in worship) their gods, to which is appended a ὅτι clause: "for this is a σκῶλον for you, i.e. "a stumbling block." The Hebrew has the picturesque מוקש "lure, snare," i.e. something that entraps.[40]

7:17 V.17 begins a new section in which the people are assured that their God will lead them to victory and eventually to a total conquest of the Promised Land. V.17 is the protasis for the assurance given in the following verses. The translator chose διανοίᾳ to render לבב since thought is involved: "if you should say within yourself," i.e. should you think; see comment at 6:5. διάνοια is used only six times for לב(ב) in Deut, whereas καρδία occurs 42 times. ὅτι is added to introduce what it was that one might think. Hex has placed it under the obelus to show that it has no counterpart in MT.

The comparative מן is rendered by ἤ following the positive degree,[41] thus "more numerous than I." LXX has changed the clause רבים הגוים האלה into a singular one πολὺ τὸ ἔθνος τοῦτο, thus dealing not with the whole mass of peoples but one by one: "this nation is more numerous than I am."

7:18 For the formulaic call to confidence οὐ φοβηθήσῃ see the comment at 1:21. The positive counterpart is the command to recall what the Lord did to Pharaoh and to all the Egyptians. This command is modified by a cognate dative representing the cognate free infinitive pattern of MT, whereby the verbal idea is emphasized, thus "simply remember clearly." For ἐξολεθρεῦσαι rendering להוריש see comment at 4:38.

7:19 The "great trials" (taken over together with "signs and wonders" by 29:3) must refer to the plagues; the signs and wonders refer to the plagues as well, see comments at 4:34. Over against MT these are described as τὰ μεγάλα ἐκεῖνα, which hex placed under the obelus; the words are probably taken over from 29:2. τὰ σημεῖα follows Sam rather than MT which has a

40. Sym chose σκάνδαλον, whereas The Others retained LXX.
41. See SS 150.

conjunction והאתת, and hex added a *και* to equal MT. Similarly the next phrase, *τὴν χεῖρα*, is supplied by an introductory *και* by hex to equal והיד of MT. For "the strong hand and the high arm" see comment at 3:23—24. As at 4:34 *ὑψηλόν* has נטויה as parent reading, since "high arm" has become formulaic for the translator.[42] All these accusatives modify the *ἐποίησεν* of v.18.

The Masoretes made the first cut in the verse with אלהיך 1°, and the critical text has been punctuated in the same way. A first reading might view the *ὡς* structure as finding its balance in the *οὕτως* one, but this is not what was meant. The Lord has no intention to bring the nations out (of Egypt) as he did you. Rather the *ὡς* structure serves as another nominal modifying *ἐποίησεν*, i.e. "how the Lord your God brought you out" is what he also did.

The *οὕτως* has then a broader reference; it calls to mind all the *πειρασμούς*, the signs and wonders, the mighty hand and high arm, how God brought out the Israelites. In this same way the Lord is going to deal with all the nations,[43] i.e. in the exercise of his power. With Israel he had acted strongly to save; with the nations of whom you are afraid he will act strongly to destroy. That this is what is meant is clear from the following verses (20—24). It should be noted that the translator has made the contrast between *οὕτως* and what went before even more definitive by a change which must have been exegetically determined. The Lord is not called אלהיך but *ὁ θεὸς ἡμῶν*.[44] This claim of communal acceptance of covenantal recognition of the Lord as "our God" who will make us victorious over the nations whom we are to displace serves as an avowal of full involvement; it is after all "our God" who will fight for us.

7:20 For the *σφηκίας* as a divine instrument of destruction see also Exod 23:28 Jos 24:12. The verb *ἐκτριβῶσιν* is a second aorist passive subjunctive: "until they be destroyed." The subjunctive is well chosen to represent the bound infinitive of the Hebrew, which has "until the perishing of those who are left ...." It contrasts neatly with the perfect participles which serve as sub-

---

42. Aq and Sym have the more literal *ἐκτεταμένον*. And instead of *κραταιάν* Aq has *ἰσχυράν* for חזקה (retroverted from Syh).
43. The Others read *λαοῖς* rather than *ἔθνεσιν*.
44. See THGD 109.

jects: "until those who have been left and those who have been hidden from you[45] be destroyed."

7:21 LXX has interpreted תערץ "tremble, be in dread of" by *τρωθήσῃ* "be wounded"; in context the assurance reads "not shall you be wounded because of them." The people will not merely be subject to psychological hurt; they are assured that they will suffer no physical hurt from those whom they are to displace.

This assurance finds its basis in the divine presence; their covenant God, the Lord, is *ἐν σοί*, characterized as an אל גדול ונורא which LXX translates by *θεὸς μέγας καὶ κραταιός*.[46] The latter term is hardly a translation of נורא which means "fearful, awesome.[47] The adjective *κραταιός* is the usual description for the Lord's יד חזקה, which contrasts with 10:17 where *ὁ ἰσχυρός* is coordinated with *ὁ φοβερός* to describe *ὁ θεὸς ὁ μέγας*; in both cases MT has (ה)נורא. In the tradition the *n t* text articulates the entire phrase so that *θεὸς μέγας καὶ φοβερός* is no longer predicate but an attributive to *κύριος ὁ θεός σου*, thereby making *ἐν σοί* the predicate.

7:22 MT uses the verb נשל "clear away," i.e. the Lord ... will clear away these nations; for this LXX uses *καταναλώσει* "shall use up, consume," a unique equation, but then the Hebrew verb is itself rare. This activity is to take place *κατὰ μικρὸν μικρόν*, a literalism for מעט מעט. The Hebrew repetition of the word represents a distributive function, thus "little by little, gradually," and the Greek has to be understood in the same way, i.e. as a Hebraism. V.22b then gives the explanation for this gradual consummation; you as God's human agent "will be unable to destroy them quickly." For *τὸ τάχος* see comment at v.4.

The reason given for avoiding a quick destruction of the inhabitants in favor of a gradual one is a double one in LXX, though only a single one in MT. The first one "lest the land become a desert (and)" has no basis in MT, and is thus marked with an obelus in hex; its source is Exod 23:29 where it

45. The Others insert *προσώπου* in the phrase *ἀπὸ σοῦ* to represent more literally מפניך.
46. As expected Theod and Aq render אל by *ἰσχυρός*.
47. Theod and Aq have *φοβερός*.

represented פן תהיה הארץ שממה. The translator has simply taken it over word for word. But not so for the second, where LXX has its own translation; comp the text ad loc.

The collocation πληθυνθῇ ἐπὶ σέ is probably intended in a comparative sense: should become too numerous for you. The verb is singular to agree with the neuter plural τὰ θηρία τὰ ἄγρια. "The wild beasts" is a good rendering of חית השדה, i.e. the beasts of the field contrast with domesticated animals.

7:23 The Hebrew has it that Yahweh your God will give them לפניך, which LXX simplifies by εἰς τὰς χεῖράς σου, i.e. rather than "before you"; see comment at v.2. The second clause is also a simplification on the part of LXX. In the context that "he will destroy them with a great destruction" does fit, but that is not what MT says. It has והמם מהומה גדלה "and he will confuse them with a great confusion," a somewhat odd action[48] which will then continue עד השמדם "until he has exterminated them." LXX has contextualized its rendering;[49] comp Exod 14:24 where LXX translated by συνετάραξεν (i.e. the camp of the Egyptians).

7:24 Some mss read בידיך instead of בידך of BHS. Greek also has the plural noun as do Pesh and Vulg. The phrase εἰς τὰς χεῖρας ὑμῶν signifies "into your power.[50] Why LXX should change from the singular to the plural for v.24a and then revert to the singular while MT has the entire verse in the singular is puzzling, but note that in v.25a both have the plural and for v.25b both have the singular. I can think of no satisfactory explanation.

The second clause gives orders to destroy their ὄνομα ἐκ τοῦ τόπου ἐκείνου. To destroy their name means to erase their memory. MT has: their name מתחת השמים "from under heaven," but LXX limits the extent of the erasure to "from that place." What "that place" refers to is not fully clear, but is probably ἡ γῆ of v.22, i.e. the land which they will be taking into posses-

48. Aq has καὶ φαγεδαινώσει αὐτοὺς φαγεδαίνῃ μεγάλῃ "and he will afflict them with great cancerous sores." Sym has καὶ ταράξει αὐτοὺς ταραχὴν μεγάλην, and Theod rendered by καὶ ἐκστήσει αὐτοὺς ἔκστασιν μεγάλην.
49. Theod has changed ἂν ἐξολεθρεύσῃ to ἐκτρίψει.
50. See SS 136.

sion.[51] Somewhat problematic is ἀπολεῖτε since a majority text including all the uncials has the third middle future απολειται; unfortunately -τε and -ται were homophonous and the context alone must decide, since MT is no help with its singular אבדת. Exegetically, however, the middle form would have τὸ ὄνομα as subject which would relate this clause to the preceding as its result. But that God would deliver their kings into your power so that their name should be destroyed could hardly have been intended. The second plural also fits in with the ὑμῶν of the first clause.[52] Furthermore, that Israel should be an active agent is clear from the context; note the verb in the ἕως ἄν clause.

The final statement is again in the singular: "no one will withstand you (i.e. be able to set himself up against you) until that you should destroy them." The plural αὐτούς must have the same reference as the ἀυτούς of v.23 and the αὐτῶν of v.24 rather than the βασιλεῖς of v.24.

7:25 Except for lacking an initial καί the first clause is exactly the same in v.5; see comment ad loc. Vv.25a—26 are once again in the singular. The verse begins with the prohibition: "you may not covet silver and gold ἀπ' αὐτῶν." Most witnesses join the two metals with ουδε rather than καί. That ουδε is better Greek is obvious, but καί must be original; no scribe would intentionally change an original οὐδέ to και.[53] The combination ἐπιθυμήσεις ἀπ' αὐτῶν refers to the γλυπτά, i.e. the pronoun refers to the heathen images which were often silvered or gilded. This is somewhat clearer in MT which has עליהם; thus the silver and the gold is "on them."[54]

Such desire has an attendant risk: μὴ πταίσῃς δι' αὐτό "lest you should stumble on account of it.[55] The αὐτό presumably refers to the gold (and/or silver). Hex as usual finds μή insufficient for translating פן and adds ποτε under the asterisk. MT has a slightly different verbal action. תוקש means "you should be snared, be trapped."

The justification for this prohibition is given in the ὅτι clause; it is "because it is an abomination to the Lord your God," a statement that often

51. Sym has ὑποκάτω τοῦ οὐρανοῦ.
52. See the discussion in THGD 139.
53. See THGD 132.
54. Aq has ἐπ' αὐτοῖς.
55. Aq translates μήποτε σκωλωθῇς ἐν αὐτῷ "lest you should be offended by it." Aq regularly renders the root יקש in this way.

recurs.[56] The word βδέλυγμα "abomination,filth" is the term used in Deut to render תועבה (17 times), but only once for שקוץ. The reverse is the case for Lev where it renders שקוץ nine times but תועבה only five times.[57] The bound form תועבת occurs nine times in Deut and one might expect βδέλυγμα to be modified by a genitive (as at 12:31 18:9), but the dative is the more common, occurring also at 17:1 18:12 22:5 23:18 25:16 27:15.

7:26 Here it is clear that a βδέλυγμα is something concrete; it is something that must not be brought into your house, a clear reference to an idolatrous object. The second clause, rendered paratactically in imitation of the Hebrew, gives the result of such action. Should one bring an abominable thing into one's house one would become ἀνάθεμα like it (i.e. like the abominable thing). That ἀνάθεμα should be read rather than αναθημα with B uniquely I have argued elsewhere.[58] The term means something devoted to deity. In LXX, however, it uniquely equals חרם, being used only to translate this root. So it is a calque for חרם, which refers to that which is under the ban, something devoted to destruction; cf Lexx. Not only goods, but people, cities and the like could be put under the ban and were then to be totally destroyed. What is implied is that if one should take an idolatrous object into one's house, one would also be subject to ἀνάθεμα.

This is then explicated by two emphatic constructions rendering cognate free infinitives plus finite verbs, the one a שקץ, the other a תעב structure. The former actually means "to detest," so the Hebrew clauses may be translated: you shall thoroughly detest it and completely abominate it because it is ἀνάθεμα. The parallel clauses in Greek are translated by the same pattern; a cognate dative noun preceding a future verb. In MT both verbs have a third singular masculine suffix, whereas LXX renders them absolutely. Hex has "corrected" the translation by adding αυτο under the asterisk to both verbs so as to equal MT. The first clause is rendered by προσοχθίσματι προσοχθιεῖς which means "with an offense you shall take offense," i.e. you shall really take offense.[59]

56. See list 52 in THGD 98—99.
57. According to HR.
58. In THGD 135.
59. Sym interprets strangely by ἰσχαίνων ἰσχαίνεις. The root means to hold in check, restrain, and so "holding back you hold back," not a luminous statement.

Chapter 8

8:1 The majority F V text has added ταυτας after πάσας τὰς ἐντολάς, but this has no support in MT and is based on ex par (see 6:25 11:22 15:5 17:19 19:9 27:1). For the ἅς clause see comment at 4:2. LXX has levelled the singular suffix of מצוך to the plural of the verse as ὑμῖν, which B V *O b n* have "corrected" to σοι (hex?). For φυλάξεσθε ποιεῖν see comment at 5:1. For ἵνα ζῆτε see comment at 4:1, and for εἰσέλθητε καὶ κληρονομήσητε τὴν γῆν see comment at 1:8. For the ἥν clause see comment at 1:8 as well. The verb πολυπλασιασθῆτε "you shall be multiplied" translates רביתם. It only occurs once elsewhere in LXX (at 11:8), but there it has no equivalent in MT, and its source is here; comp also the majority B 963 gloss at 4:1.

In the tradition εἰσέλθητε καί is popularly reduced to εισελθοντες under the influence of the oft-recurring "entering you shall inherit" as at 1:8. A popular A F M V text has added την αγαθην after γῆν, which is ex par. Cod B has added the gloss ο θεος υμων to κύριος, and *d* has added ο θεος σου, but these are both ex par.[1]

8:2 To "remember all the way which" means to remember in detail how (the Lord ... has led you). A *b* reading has the imperative μνησθητι instead of the future, but the future itself has imperatival sense. LXX did not translate זה ארבעים שנה, though it is translated at v.4. Hex has added a translation under the asterisk: τουτο τεσσαρακοστον ετος. That it is an import into LXX is clear from its own translation of the phrase at v.4: ἰδοὺ τεσσαράκοντα ἔτη.

The ὅπως ἄν structure contains three coordinate verbs in the subjunctive,[2] and it modifies ἤγαγεν, thereby indicating why the Lord brought Israel into the desert: it was to afflict them and test them and discover the things in their heart. In LXX God had a triple purpose in taking Israel into the desert. This differs considerably from MT; MT does have purposive marked infinitives, but does not join them by conjunctions. What MT says is that God afflicted Israel so as to test them in order to discern the things which were in

1. See the discussion in THGD 119—120.
2. See SS Inf 57.

their heart.[3] Thus in MT God's ultimate purpose is to discover whether Israel would obey him or not. But in LXX the three verbs are all on the same syntactic level and their internal lexical relations are obscured.

In the tradition a popular A F M text has the simplex instead of *ἐκπειράσῃ*. The simplex occurs at 4:34 13:3 38:8 with little or no variation in the tradition, whereas the compound also occurs at v.16 and 6:16 (twice) with little variation (except at v.16 where *y*+ does read the simplex). Both forms render the Pi of נסה exclusively, but the compound is rare; aside from the four occurrences in Deut it only occurs once elsewhere (Ps 77:18), whereas the simplex is common. The rarer compound, i.e. the more difficult reading, is to be preferred here.

8:3 The verb *κακόω* recurs here and is to be explained as part of God's testing of Israel, i.e. *καὶ ἐλιμαγχόνησέν σε καὶ ἐψώμισέν σε τὸ μάννα*. God's affliction is not for its own sake, but consists in trials which in turn had an educative end. The verb *ἐλιμαγχόνησεν*, a variant of *ελιμαγχησεν*, "to be wracked by hunger, deprivation" occurs only here in OT; it adequately renders ירעבך in the Hi, which obtains only twice in OT; at Prov 10:3 ירעיב occurs in the proverb: "Yahweh will not starve a righteous person," which LXX translates literally by *οὐ λιμοκτονήσει κύριος ψυχὴν δικαίαν*. But the Lord not only withheld food, he actually fed them with manna. The verb *ψωμίζω* means to feed by putting bits of food into the mouth; the picture is that of a nurse putting food morsels into a baby's mouth, a picturesque rendering of the Hi of אכל "cause to eat."[4] For *μάννα* see the explanation of the word as a variant of *μάν* in a Note at Exod 16:31.[5]

In MT המן is modified by a relative clause containing two coordinate clauses: "which you did not know and your fathers did not know." LXX has only a single relative clause; the first one, "you did not know and," has no counterpart in the Greek, a clear case of homoioarchon (ידע) causing parablepsis. An equivalent has been supplied by hex as *ο ουκ ηδεις και*. In the

3. See SS Inf 67.
4. Aq has rendered the word by *ἐβρωμάτισε*.
5. That it is the transcription of the Aramaic emphatic form is clear from מנא of Tar[O].

tradition a B M *b*+ text has for *ᾔδεισαν* the itacistic spelling *ειδησαν*, a late formation based on *εἴδω* (a first aorist form) which never occurs in Deut.[6]

The purpose of this threefold testing was that God "may show you that man can not live solely by bread, but by every word which goes out through the mouth of God man can live."[7] The word "man" refers to generic man and might better be rendered as "mankind." In MT the two clauses are both כי clauses, the first one negative, and the second one, positive. LXX simplified this by introducing the second one by the adversative *ἀλλ'*. MT has no equivalent for "word" and hex has accordingly placed *ῥήματι* under the obelus. The phrase *ἐκπορευομένῳ διὰ στόματος* is an idiomatic rendering for the bound structure מוצא פי of MT.[8] LXX has the "mouth" *θεοῦ*, whereas MT has פי יהוה.[9] To the translator the feeding of the people with manna was not strictly speaking a covenantal matter; it was rather a matter of divine sustenance, a display of power, and the use of *θεοῦ* was more appropriate.[10]

8:4 That your garments *οὐ κατετρίβη* "did not get used" means that they remained new, never became second hand, thus never wore out, i.e. לא בלתה. In MT the subjects of the two clauses are singular, שמלתך and רגלך. LXX has these in the plural: *τὰ ἱμάτιά σου* and *οἱ πόδες σου*. Undoubtedly this does not misrepresent what MT intends. The modification by *ἀπὸ σοῦ* is determined by the Hebrew מעלך, i.e. it represents a kind of zeugmatic construction for "wear out and fall away from you."[11]

The second clause states that your feet (i.e. plural as Sam) *οὐκ ἐτυλώθησαν* "did not become calloused." The verb is a hapax legomenon in LXX; its counterpart בצקה in MT is also rare occurring only twice (also in Neh 9:21). The verb means "to swell up," and so of the foot "to get blisters."[12]

---

6. See the discussion at THGD 138.
7. For "can live" as rendering of *ζήσεται* see Porter 421—424.
8. See SS 69.
9. Which Theod corrects to *κυρίου*.
10. See Appositives 263.
11. Sym renders the prepositional phrase by *ἀπάνωθέν σου*; comp the same usage in 29:5b.
12. Apparently Aq read *ὤδησαν* "became swollen" (retroverted from Syh).

For the rendering of הנה by *ἰδού* see comment at 2:7. This equation is rare, occurring elsewhere only three times (Ps 55:10 Zech 5:1 7:5); only the last one, "behold seventy years," is an exact parallel.

8:5 That לבב (and therefore *καρδίᾳ*) refers to one's intelligence is clear from its usage here; it is the seat of the verbal notion of ידעת/*γνώσῃ*, i.e. "you should know in your heart." LXX uses the dative for MT's עם "with (your heart)."

What you should know is given in the *ὅτι* clause which consists of a *ὡς*/*οὕτως* structure in which the *ὡς* clause contains the protasis, i.e. *εἰ* plus an optative showing a potential as the basis for the comparison. The optative is aorist since it is neutral: "should a man chastise his son." That the optative was no longer viable in later forms of Greek is clear from the variant texts which the tradition produced, either the popular *παιδευσῃ* (subjunctive) or an equally popular future which was clearly influenced by the future of the apodosis. The verb *παιδεύσαι* means to train a child, here through correction as representing יסר in the Piel. The subject of the *εἰ* clause is *τις ἄνθρωπος* in which the indefinite pronoun serves as the English indefinite article, hence "a man, someone."

MT makes the *οὕτως* clause nominal, with מיסרך, i.e. a participle, as predicate. One would then expect LXX to use a present tense verb, but actually a future obtains, thus "so will the Lord your God chastise you." A warning about what is going to happen is not amiss, except that MT makes it a general statement: "the Lord chastens you." MT has no equivalent for *οὕτως*, and hex has accordingly placed it under the obelus. LXX has added the adverb to make explicit what is implicit in MT.

8:6 Presumably the second part of the verse, i.e. the two infinitival structures, explicate the statement "you shall guard the commandments of the Lord your God." Guarding his commandments means a) "to walk in his ways," and b) "to fear him." The first defines a manner of life, one in which one's conduct is determined by *ταῖς ὁδοῖς αὐτοῦ*. Though these "ways" are not identified, they must be the contents of the Law Code, i.e. *τὸ δευτερονόμιον τοῦτο* of 17:18. The second aspect of guarding his commandments is the fear of the Lord. This verb also involves conduct; to fear the Lord means to live the life of a true Yahwist, one whose conduct reflects the demands of God's ordinances and commandments; cf comment at 6:2.

8:7 The verse begins with כי/γάρ setting out why Israel should guard the Lord's commandments (v.6); it is because the Lord is bringing them in to the Promised Land. The use of the present εἰσάγει is that of incipient action; the Lord is on the point of bringing them in. The present tense troubled copyists. Some followed the V *cI' n s* reading of an aorist subjunctive εισαγαγη, which is probably created by dittography, but most witnesses support the A M variant future form εισαξει, which constitutes a pedantic correction of fact. The present tense is, however, standard as a rendering for the participial predicate. The Promised Land is called a γῆν ἀγαθὴν καὶ πολλήν; MT has only ארץ טובה, but Sam adds ורחבה which the translator mentally heard as ורבה. The root רבב, or its adjective רב, רבה, is regularly rendered by πολύς. Presumably what is meant is "large, extensive." Hex has placed καὶ πολλήν under the obelus to show that it was not present in MT.

This land is then described by a series of descriptive appositives in MT introduced by ארץ, continuing through v.9. For the first ארץ the translator has substituted οὗ signifying place.[13] The pronoun introduces a nominal clause in which χείμαρροι ὑδάτων πηγαὶ ἀβύσσων serves as subject and ἐκπορευόμεναι as predicate agreeing with the nearer feminine subject πηγαί, thus "where streams of waters, springs of the depths, are flowing out." In a desert environment such a description would be paradisaic. The majority A F M V text has joined the two subjects by και, but LXX follows MT and is the more unusual text; it is clearly original. The phrase πηγαὶ ἀβύσσων has as its counterpart עינת ותהמת; the translator simplified the coordinate nouns by treating them as though they were a bound phrase, i.e. without the conjunction. The participle is in turn modified by two διά phrases: "through the plains and through the hilly areas," i.e. through hills and dales, thus comprising the entire country.

8:8 The agricultural products of the Promised Land. Seven products are mentioned, the first two and the last two in the genitive modifying γῆ 1° and 2° resp., and the middle three in the nominative, i.e. on a level with γῆ 1° and

13. See LS sub ὅς, ἥ, ὅ A b.2. and Bauer sub οὗ 1.a.β.

2°. What the Greek says is "a land of wheat and barley, (where there are) vineyards, figs, pomegranates, a land of olive trees of oil and honey." In MT the middle three are all preceded by a conjunction, while in LXX only the first two and the last two are thus coordinated. In the tradition, popular Byz readings have added *και* before *συκαί* and *ῥόαι*; these may have been recensional (from one of The Three?).

8:9 Other characteristics of the Land of Promise are described. The Hebrew word מסכנת is a hapax legomenon meaning "poverty," and is correctly translated by *πτωχείας*. The expression *οὐ μετὰ πτωχείας* is preposed within the clause in imitation of MT so as to focus on the main element in the clause. This is clear from the coordinate clause "and you shall be wanting of nothing on it." MT lacks an initial conjunction.[14] In MT "you shall eat" is modified by בה לחם; LXX omits the first word and renders the second by *τὸν ἄρτον σου*. These differences disturbed Origen who added *εν αυτη* under the asterisk after the verb, and placed *τόν* and *σου* under the obelus as not being present in MT.

The second part of the verse is also introduced by *γῆ*, in turn modified by a *ἧς* structure containing a nominal and a verbal clause. The former renders MT literally: (*ἧς*) *οἱ λίθοι αὐτῆς σίδηρος*.[15] The B V *C*'' *n s*+ text omits *αὐτῆς*, and I would now consider this original LXX, with the popular text adding *αυτης* as a recensional gloss, probably due to hex. It should be noted that all the usual followers of the hex text, *O*'' Arm Syh, witness to the longer text, which equals MT.[16] The second clause predicts the mining of copper from its hills. MT uses the verb תחצב "you shall mine, extract,"[17] which LXX adequately renders by *μεταλλεύσεις*.

8:10 The first two verbs summarize v.9a,[18] and the third one enjoins the positive response: "you shall bless the Lord your God." The verb *εὐλογέω* is most often used of God blessing people, but it also describes individuals blessing someone else such as a father blessing a son. Here, however, it is used of

14. Though Kenn 181 does read ולא תחסר.
15. Sym interprets freely by *οἱ λίθοι ὡς σίδηρος*; does this betray an awareness of a lack of iron mining in Palestine or is this simply a pedantic correction?
16. Against THGD 125.
17. Aq translated it somewhat more exactly by *λατομήσεις* "you shall quarry."
18. See list 33 in THGD 95.

people blessing God, which is unique in the Pentateuch. It can hardly mean "to bestow a blessing," but must be understood in its literal sense, "to speak well of," thus "to praise." It was of course promoted by the Hebrew ברכת. The verb is also modified by the prepositional phrase *ἐπὶ τῆς γῆς τῆς ἀγαθῆς* "for the good land (which he gave you)."[19] In the tradition a majority gloss has added *κυριος ο θεος σου* as named subject, but this has no basis in MT and is quite unnecessary in the context.

8:11 *πρόσεχε σεαυτῷ* introduces a complex syntactic structure which continues through v.16 (or v.17, though not as punctuated in LXX). It is then modified by *μή* in the sense of "lest" which governs the entire structure; the *μή* is actually repeated in v.12. For the initial warning see comment at 4:9. As usual hex adds *ποτε* under the asterisk to *μή* when it renders פן.

The warning against forgetting (*ἐπιλάθῃ*) the Lord your God is thematic, occurring not only at the beginning of this verse, but is repeated in v.14, (see v.19 as well); it contrasts with the command to remember (*μνησθήσῃ*) in v.18.

μὴ ἐπιλάθῃ is defined by an articulated infinitive *τοῦ μὴ ... φυλάξαι ...*, which imitates MT's לבלתי שמר. LXX normally does not articulate infinitives in this book (only v.18 and 17:12 elsewhere),[20] and here shows how forgetting the Lord manifests itself, i.e. by not guarding *τὰς ἐντολὰς αὐτοῦ καὶ τὰ κρίματα καὶ τὰ δικαιώματα αὐτοῦ*. Since MT has suffixed all three nouns, hex has added *αυτου* under the asterisk after *κρίματα* as well, so as to correspond fully to MT. For the common coordination see comments at 4:1 and 5:31, and for the *ὅσα* clause see note at 4:2.

8:12 As in v.11, hex has added *ποτε* after *μή* under the asterisk to equal פן. For the first two participles see comment at v.10. All the participles modify *ὑψωθῇς* of v.14; they are the conditions which promote the hybris resulting in forgetting the Lord.

The second pair of participles concerns adequate housing. The Greek has *ἐν αὐτοῖς* modifying *κατοικήσας* over against MT which hex shows by its obelus. The phrase is, however, stylistically necessary, since *οἰκίας* has been mentioned, and it would be odd to use *κατοικήσας* absolutely.

---

19. Sym has clarified the phrase by substituting *ὑπέρ* for the preposition.
20. See the discussion in THGD 103.

8:13 The translator was faced with a problem; he had rendered the verbs of v.12 by participles modifying the main verb, *ὑψωθῇς* of v.14; the subjects in v.13 are, however, no longer second person singular, but rather "your cattle, your flock, silver and gold, and everything which is yours"; this meant that participles were no longer viable. To solve this he went over to genitive absolute constructions with the aorist passive participle of *πληθύνω* being repeated three times (in imitation of MT): "And your cattle and your flock being multiplied for you, silver and gold being multiplied for you, and all things which shall be yours being multiplied to you." The participle is in all three cases modified by *σοι*, whereas MT has לך only for the silver and gold. The other two cases of *σοι* are dutifully placed under the obelus by hex to show their absence in MT. The Greek also differs from MT in that the middle construction lacks the conjunction before *ἀργυρίου*. A *και* has been supplied by a few witnesses, but this need not be hex in origin; it is probably an ad sensum gloss.

The change in construction does not obviate the relation of this verse to *ὑψωθῇς* of v.14, since as in the case of the participles of v.12 the genitive absolutes of v.13 also detail conditions leading to v.14.

8:14 Since the core of the complex structure occurs in the first two verbs *ὑψωθῇς* (*τῇ καρδίᾳ*) *καὶ ἐπιλάθῃ* (*κυρίου τοῦ θεοῦ σου*), the translator rightly disregarded the initial conjunction in MT. The first clause is put in second person, whereas MT has רם לבבך, i.e. "your heart" is subject of a third person verb.[21] LXX disregarded the suffix of לבבך though the A F M V majority text did add *σου*; the *σου* may have been added by Origen. In the tradition the participial form *υψωθεις* occurred in *d f*+, but this is irrelevant; it is an itacistic spelling of LXX as the retention of *καί* before *ἐπιλάθῃ* shows.

The second verb reverts to the theme of "forgetting God." The collocation *κυρίου τοῦ θεοῦ σου* is followed by a series of four attributive participles which describe the Lord's saving acts involving the people.

---

21. Aq treats רם as a participle, which is also possible, i.e. *καὶ ὑψωθείς* with *τῇ καρδίᾳ σου* "in your heart" as modifier. Both Theod and Sym have (*καὶ*) *ὑψωθῇ ἡ καρδία σου*, though the *καί* is not attested for Sym.

The first of these is the exodus itself. For bringing out from the land of Egypt see comment at 1:27. The descriptive phrase characterizing (out of) the land of Egypt, *ἐξ οἴκου δουλείας*, often accompanies "from the land of Egypt,"[22] but is particularly well-known from the Decalogue; cf 5:6 and Exod 20:2.

8:15 The second participial structure deals with the desert journey; the Lord is "the one who brought you through that great and fearful desert." MT has no demonstrative pronoun, and hex has accordingly placed *ἐκείνης* under the obelus. Note the fine understanding of the preposition in במדבר shown by *διά* with the genitive. As explication of (that) fearful desert, MT adds נחש שרף ועקרב וצמאון "fiery serpents and scorpions and thirsty ground," i.e. without prepositions. LXX clarifies this by introducing these by *οὗ* "where," viz., *ὄφις δάκνων καὶ σκορπίος καὶ δίψα* "biting serpents and scorpions and thirst"; the first two must be taken as collectives; in fact, plural nouns would have been a more accurate translation. LXX has taken שרף as *δάκνων*, i.e. interpreting in terms of the serpent's bite.[23] The word *δίψα* provokes another *οὗ* clause "where there was no water." For the adverbial use of *οὗ* (twice) see comment at v.7.

The third participle recalls the divine supply of water out of the rock, for which see Exod 17:1—7 Num 20:2—13. MT has "the one who brought out for you water from the rock of flint." LXX translates מים by *πηγήν ὕδατος* and places it at the end. Hex rearranges the text to fit the Hebrew order. Why LXX should have changed "water" to "a spring of water" is not clear; it may represent an explanation of how sufficient water for the Israelites could have come out of solid rock, i.e. it must have been a spring. The bound phrase צור החלמיש is well-rendered by an adjectival phrase in Greek, *πέτρας ἀκροτόμου*;[24] as applied to stone the adjective should probably be thought of as a "jagged (rock)," since it is a compound referring to the "end cut off."[25] In

22. See list 3 in THGD 87.
23. The meaning of שרף is not fully certain; in fact, NJPS translates it by "*seraph* (serpents)." Aq was not satisfied with LXX and translated it by *ἐμπρηστής*. Sym explains the term by *φυσήματι καίων* "burning by puffing," i.e. with burning breath; see Salvesen 150.
24. See SS 66.
25. Aq has his usual word *στερεός* for צור.

the tradition, hex has reordered ἐκ πέτρας ἀκροτόμου to the end to conform to the word order of MT.

8:16 The fourth attributive refers to God's feeding Israel with manna, for which see v.3, which parallels this one. For μάννα see comment at v.3. For the ὅ clause including the variant spelling ειδησαν for ᾔδεισαν also see comments at v.3.

V.16b in MT consists of two coordinate למען clauses followed by a marked infinitive plus a prepositional phrase. The למען clauses are realized in LXX by ἵνα plus coordinate subjunctives, i.e. "in order that he might afflict you and test you." A popular A F M V gloss has repeated ινα before the second verb, thereby making it formally equivalent to MT. The gloss (as far as its pattern of support is concerned) does not seem to be hex in origin; it could, but need not, be based on the Hebrew. For the relation of the two verbs see the discussion at v.3.

The marked infinitive which follows is translated by εὖ σε ποιῆσαι which follows the Hebrew pattern. In the tradition this has been simplified by prefixing a και (B *O* Byz+) and changing the infinitive to another subjunctive (also B *O*+), i.e. "and that he might prosper you,"[26] but this voids the intent of MT and of LXX in which the trials by which Israel was tested had their purpose in εὖ σε ποιῆσαι. MT's infinitive has a suffix which is clearly the object of the verbal action since the infinitive is Hi, thus "to prosper you." The Greek is, however, quite ambiguous, and I would take σε as subject, rather than as object of the infinitive, i.e. "that you might prosper."

The infinitive is modified by a temporal phrase, ἐπ' ἐσχάτων σου, which translates the Hebrew באחריתך. A *C*+ text has the singular noun εσχατου, and the A *O*+ text read the dative singular εσχατω, but either singular or plural can be used to signify the future "in your latter times." The B *C''* *b s*+ gloss has added των ημερων, i.e. in your latter days as at 4:30, but there the phrase represents באחרית הימים; the shorter phrase is original.[27]

8:17 This verse clearly contrasts with the following one. The point must be that should you mistakenly think that it was your own strength that performed

26. See the discussion in THGD 132.
27. See THGD 121.

all this you must recall that the Lord is the real source of that strength. But MT and LXX differ in how they say it. In MT v.17 must be understood as a protasis, i.e. the *waw* of ואמרת balances with the *waw* of וזכרת of v.18 as marking the onset of protasis and apodosis resp.; thus "should you say ... then remember." But the Greek introduces v.17 by *μὴ* (*εἴπῃς*), to which hex has prefixed a *και* to equal the *waw* of MT. LXX can be understood in one of two ways. It could be taken in the same sense as the *μή* of vv.11 and 12, and continuing as part of the vv.11—16 structure, thus "lest you should say." This is unlikely to have been intended in view of the character of that complex structure which seems to come to an end with v.16, nor has it an equivalent פן as in vv.11 and 12. More likely to have been intended is a prohibition "do not say in your heart," i.e. don't think. The initial *καί* of v.18 must then be understood as an adversative contrasting with v.17. The Byz text has made two changes in the text. It has added *οτι* to introduce what you should not say in your heart, which is quite unnecessary, and it has changed *ἐποίησεν* to the plural in view of the coordinate subject "my strength and the power of my hand," but MT has the singular עשה, which LXX follows.

LXX has translated את החיל הזה by *τὴν δύναμιν τὴν μεγάλην ταύτην*, and hex has placed *τὴν μεγάλην* under the obelus, since it is not found in MT. The term חיל is somewhat ambiguous, since it can mean "strength," as well as "wealth," and most moderns take it in this latter sense.[28] LXX is also ambiguous in its *δύναμιν* "power, ability," but that can be understood as referring to what was expressed by the attributive participles of vv.14—16, i.e. the power shown in the acts of deliverance accorded Israel.

8:18 The real source of strength for effecting power is the Lord your God, and Israel is enjoined to remember that fact. What they are to remember is that *αὐτός σοι δίδωσιν ἰσχύν*. This renders הוא הנתן לך כח,[29] in which the *αὐτός*/הוא serves to place contrastive emphasis on the Lord as the effective agent rather than on Israel itself. This strength which the Lord gives has as its purpose the infinitival structure *τοῦ ποιῆσαι δύναμιν*; for its meaning see the comment at v.17, and for the articulation of the infinitive see comment at

28. In fact, Aq attests to this sense with his *εὐπορίαν* for חיל in v.18.
29. See SS 81.

v.11.[30] Hex has transposed *σοι δίδωσιν* to conform to the Hebrew word order. Furthermore, a popular V variant has changed *αὐτός* to *ουτος*. Since הוא is translated by either in Deut (with *ουτος* the more common rendering) one can only decide on the critical text by examining the nature of its supporters. The *ουτος* seems to be a Byz reading, whereas *αὐτός* is LXX.

In LXX a second purpose obtains for the Lord's giving strength expressed by a *ἵνα* clause, which is coordinate with the infinitive structure. This differs from MT, which introduces the clause by למען, i.e. it constitutes the purpose for the infinitival structure, לעשות חיל. LXX, however, is based on Sam which read ולמען. In LXX God gave strength in order to establish his covenant. For the nature of the covenant *τῶν πατέρων σου ἣν ὤμοσεν αὐτοῖς* see the discussion at 4:31. A popular B gloss identifies the subject of *ὤμοσεν* as *κυριος*, but this is secondary.[31] That covenant was one of the promises which he gave to the fathers. The verse ends with *ὡς σήμερον* which adequately reproduces כיום הזה, which has only a loose rhetorical relation to the foregoing. What is probably intended is "as is still valid today." The Byz tradition has identified "your fathers" as *τω αβρααμ και ισαακ και ιακωβ*, and has also changed *σήμερον* to the more literal *η ημερα αυτη*, a reading ultimately based on the Hebrew.

8:19 The chapter concludes with a solemn warning in the last two verses. Its sternness is reflected in the reinforced verbs λήθῃ ἐπιλάθῃ and ἀπωλείᾳ ἀπολεῖσθε reflecting cognate free infinitives plus finite verbs. For the introductory *καὶ ἔσται* see comment at 6:10. What "actually forget the Lord your God" involves is defined by three coordinate clauses: "and you should go after other gods and serve them (cultically) and worship them." To both MT and LXX it is clear that being a faithful Israelite focused primarily on λατρεύσῃς and *προσκυνήσῃς*; forgetting the Lord your God meant engaging in foreign cult. For Deut idolatry was the central sin. This is even stronger in LXX where עבדת is defined not by *δουλευσῃς*, but by λατρεύσῃς "serve cultically."

The apodosis is a solemn charge found in an enlarged form in a similar environment (but also a broader context) at 4:26; see the comments ad loc. That enlarged form strongly influenced the tradition here. All but ten witnesses

30. See also SS Inf 34 for the genitive.
31. See THGD 119—120.

have added *τον τε ουρανον και την γην* after *σήμερον*,[32] and the Byz text has added *απο της γης* at the end of the verse. Neither gloss is supported by MT and both are imports from 4:26. With the apodosis the text changes to the plural which then continues through v.20, as does MT.

8:20 The concluding prediction of v.19 "you will certainly be destroyed" is enlarged upon. MT begins with כגוים "as the nations," but LXX amplifies by *καθὰ καὶ τὰ λοιπὰ ἔθνη* "as even the other nations"; the translator thereby stresses the contrast between the nations "which the Lord is about to destroy before your face" and the *ἀπολεῖσθε* which pertains to you. The present tense is the usual rendering for participial predicate and is incipient in nature; the future *απολει* of *O* must be rejected as secondary. Also secondary is the popular gloss *ο θεος* after *κύριος*. Only *κύριος*/יהוה is fitting here since Israel has rejected him as their God.

The reason for *οὕτως ἀπολεῖσθε* is restated as "because of the fact that you did not listen to the voice of the Lord your God." Though MT has the prefix tense תשמעון "you would (not) listen," the aorist *ἠκούσατε* is not a mistaken rendering; it relates the condition for being destroyed as factual, not as potential.

---

32. For its secondary nature see THGD 121.

Chapter 9

9:1 In MT vv.1—6 are addressed to Israel in the singular; though in v.1 *ὑμεῖς* does occur, and in v.5, *ὑμῶν*, LXX follows MT's singular for the rest. Israel is often addressed by *ἄκουε* absolutely (see also 6:4 20:3 27:9) or with modifier (4:1 5:1), or in the aorist (6:3 absolutely, and 5:27). When Israel is addressed absolutely it is followed by some statement as here about what Israel is going to do (as 20:3) or has done (27:9) or affirms (6:4). Here Israel is told that it is on the point of crossing the Jordan *σήμερον*; this is a nominal clause in MT, but the incipient present tense is used in LXX. The purpose of crossing is *εἰσελθεῖν κληρονομῆσαι*. The second infinitive modifies the first one and must mean, as its Hebrew parent לרשת does, "to dispossess," an extension of the notion "to become the heir of"; to become the heirs of peoples means to kill them off and take over their possessions. This is fully clear from vv.2—6.

The infinitive is triply modified, in v.1 by *ἔθνη* and *πολεῖς*, and in v.2 by *λαόν*. The *ἔθνη* are described as *μεγάλα καὶ ἰσχυρότερα μᾶλλον ἢ ὑμεῖς*;[1] see comment at 7:1. The comparative is based on its parent עצמים ממך.[2] The *πολεῖς* are also "great" as well as *τειχήρεις ἕως τοῦ οὐρανοῦ* "walled up to the sky," for MT's "fortified בשמים." The *ἕως* correctly shows that the walls are high reaching into the sky, a typical hyperbole of Hebrew style. In the tradition the two infinitives are coordinated by *και* in a popular A variant based on the common expression "go in and inherit," but it has no support in MT.

9:2 As in MT LXX distinguishes between גוים and עם, using *λαόν* "a people" for the latter; *λαόν* is further described by three adjectives: *μέγαν καὶ πολὺν καὶ εὐμήκη*. MT has only two, גדול ורם, but "and numerous" often follows "great" (1:28 2:10,21 7:1, and comp 9:14 26:5), and the translator levelled with these. Hex has correctly placed *καὶ πολύν* under the obelus. The word *εὐμήκης* occurs only here in OT, and one might have expected *ὑψηλόν* as at 12:2, but it is well-chosen, since the tallness of the sons of Enak is precisely

1. For the twofold comparative plus *ἤ* see SS 150.
2. Aq interprets עצמים as at 7:1 by *ὀστοϊνα*, and ממך by *ὑπέρ σε*. Theod retains LXX, but Sym simply has *σου* after the comparative. This is also the reading of *C'' s*.

what is intended by רם. For the "sons of Enak" see comment on Ἐνακίμ at 2:10. The phrase is modified by a relative clause with coordinate second singular verbs, each preceded by an otiose σύ in imitation of MT.[3] The second verb, ἀκήκοας, is modified by a question "Who can withstand over against the sons of Enak," which is what "you heard." Presumably the question was proverbial.

9:3 The ὅτι clause is an imitation of a common Hebrew nominal clause in which the predicate equals הוא plus nominal, thus "the Lord your God" has as predicate οὗτος plus a present tense verb (rendering a participle). The Hebrew "Yahweh ... is the one going before" translates into a pendant nominative *κύριος ὁ θεός σου*; οὗτος becomes the subject rendering הוא, and the predicate is *προπορεύεται*.

For *πῦρ καταναλίσκον ἐστίν* see comment at 4:24. The figure gives a rationale to the two clauses that follow: οὗτος will destroy them and οὗτος will turn them aside before you. The οὗτος/הוא is repeated to place the stress where it belongs, viz. on the Lord your God, who is the real actor in defeating the Canaanite nations.

Odd is the rendering of יכניעם by *ἀποστρέψει αὐτούς*. The Hebrew verb means "make to bow down," i.e. subdue. One might have expected a verb like *ταπεινόω* which is used in LXX five times for the Hi and 10 times for the Ni. The Hi form occurs only here in the Pentateuch (and the Ni also only once, at Lev 26:41 of the uncircumcised heart as *ἐντραπήσεται*). "He shall turn them aside" would seem to weaken what MT says.

Possibly the verb was chosen to place Israel's action in dramatic relief: *καὶ ἀπολεῖς αὐτοὺς ἐν τάχει*, i.e. God turns them aside (or back) so that the people can give them the coup de grace. The tradition apparently was disturbed at the change in person, which the parent text had fostered, and the majority text (all but B 458) changed the verb to third person. On the other hand, two mss (B 527) omitted *ἐν τάχει*, concerning which Dogniez-Harl suggests that this might be an attempt to avoid a contradiction with 7:22,[4] but this kind of harmonization presupposes conscious revision, and the combination B 527 shows no recensional traits elsewhere. The omission is just a simple mis-

3. For οἶσθα Theod and Aq have ἔγνως, and Sym has οἶδας.
4. P.175.

take; in fact, the B copyist was particularly careless in Deut (as over against Num).[5] In the tradition hex has reordered *σοι κύριος* to equal the יהוה לך of MT, but LXX generally attracts the dative pronoun next to the verb regardless of MT.[6]

9:4 For *μὴ εἴπῃς ἐν τῇ καρδίᾳ σου* see comment at 8:17. בהדף is rendered freely by *ἐν τῷ ἐξαναλῶσαι*. The Hebrew is much more colorful: "when (Yahweh) pushes out"; presumably in so doing he does destroy them.

What they are not to imagine is "On account of my righteousness has the Lord brought me in to possess this good land." The adjective *τὴν ἀγαθήν* has no basis in MT, and hex has put it under the obelus, but it is a common designation of *γῆν* (see e.g. 1:35 3:25 4:22 6:18 e.g.), and LXX has harmonized. The stress is placed on the preposed *διὰ τὴν δικαιοσύνην μου*, as the contrastive *ἀλλά* clause shows. This clause is not part of what you are not to imagine, but is the real reason for God's destroying these nations. Here the contrast is shown by the preposed *διὰ τὴν ἀσέβειαν τῶν ἐθνῶν τούτων*.

Surprising is the future verb *ἐξολεθρεύσει* since the Hebrew has a nominal clause with a participial predicate, מורישם. One might well consider the present tense, supported only by G 509, seriously as possibly original LXX, since that is the usual translation pattern of the translator. Similarly in v.5 where the participial predicate is again rendered by the future, cod G has the present tense *εξολθρευει*, and is supported by the Old Latin codd 100 and 104. Since in the uncial text ΣΕΙ is easily confused with ΕΙ the question remains open. For the singular *τὴν δικαιοσύνην* see comment at v.6. Problematic is the choice of Greek preposition for מפניך. One might have expected *απο προσωπου σου*, which is read by a popular V variant text. But *πρό* is not only the rarer translation, it is also supported by the oldest witnesses B A F, and must be LXX. The source of the variant is undoubtedly v.5, which see.

9:5 This verse simply elaborates what was already said in v.4. It is enhanced in two ways: by the negative *διά* phrase a second one has been added: *ουδὲ διὰ τὴν ὁσιότητα τῆς καρδίας σου*. The term *ὁσιότητα* "piety" renders ישר "straightness, uprightness" only here.[7]

---

5. See especially THGD 48, where this is discussed and illustrated.
6. The Others all follow the order of MT with *κύριός σοι*.
7. Aq renders more literally by *εὐθύτητα*.

And to the positive part a ἵνα clause has been added: "and in order to establish the covenant which the Lord swore to your fathers, Abraam and Isaak and Jacob." This differs from MT in that הדבר was interpreted as τὴν διαθήκην, and ליצחק becomes καὶ Ἰσαάκ; MT has no conjunction. Furthermore, the suffix for לאבתיך is singular, but LXX has ὑμῶν, for which see comment at v.1. For the unusual future ἐξολεθρεύσει see comment at v.5.

The subjects for the two parts of the verse are nicely contrasted as σύ vs κύριος, in which σύ represents the usual translation of the Hebrew pattern of pronoun plus predicate as an SP nominal clause.[8] The second subject, κύριος, follows Sam, which hex amplified by *ο θεος σου* to equal MT.[9]

In the tradition, a popular B tradition has added *αυτου* after διαθήκην, thereby showing that it is the Lord's own covenant, which is tautological indeed.[10] The *d* text has changed ὑμῶν to *σου* which does equal MT, but this is not to be trusted, since the same text also omits the rest of the verse. And for Ἰσαάκ and Ἰακώβ B V+ have repeated the dative article *τω*, but this is unlikely to be original as the pattern of usage in Deut shows.[11]

9:6 The inclusion of σήμερον is a case of leveling with v.3, since it has no support here in MT; hex has dutifully placed it under the obelus. That it was not because of your righteousness that the Lord is giving you the land is stated a third time. It should be noted that both here and in v.4 the majority of witnesses have the plural *τας δικαιοσυνας*, whereas at v.5 the plural has no support except in some Sahidic mss. The singular must then be original throughout.[12] Also in the tradition the negative οὐ is changed to the *ουχι* of v.5 in B V *C'' n s*+.[13] And the *b*+ text has added a pronoun *αυτην* after κληρονομῆσαι. This does equal MT, but is neither original nor hex; it constitutes an ad sensum gloss.[14]

The verse ends not with a positive counterpart as in vv.4 and 5, but with a ὅτι clause "because you are a stiffnecked people." The compound,

---

8. I find puzzling the statement in SS 82 that "das betonte σύ vermindert die Betonung von οὐχί ... ἀλλά ...."
9. As did The Others.
10. See the remarks in THGD 122.
11. See THGD 104—105.
12. See the discussion in THGD 136.
13. See THGD 113.
14. See the discussion in THGD 121.

σκληροτράχηλος,[15] represents rather unusually a bound phrase in MT;[16] cf also v.13. Highly unusual is the rendering of the pronoun אתה by εἶ. It is almost always represented by σύ, the only exceptions being in the clause "for you are a holy people ...," occurring at 7:6 14:2,20; i.e. it only occurs when λαός is the predicate.

9:7 With this verse begins a lengthy call to recollection, a μνήσθητι, continuing through 10:11 to introduce the divine requirements which the Lord makes of his people in 10:12ff. Sam has simplified the unusual זכר אל תשכח by inserting a conjunction before אל, but LXX supports MT, thereby continuing the sternness and intensity of the warning: Remember, don't forget! What they are to remember is how they enraged the Lord.

With v.7b LXX changes to the second plural with Sam, whereas MT still retains the singular in יצאת before giving way to the plural with באכם. The course of Israel's enraging the Lord is described as a continuous one during the entire wilderness wanderings: ממרים הייתם "you were continuously rebellious." LXX renders this neatly by a present participle and an imperfect verb: ἀπειθοῦντες διετελεῖτε "you continued being disobedient."[17] The verb in MT is modified by עם יהוה "against Yahweh," which LXX rendered by τὰ πρὸς κύριον. This usage is also found at v.24 and 31:27 in almost the same context. The consecution τὰ πρός plus deity occurs elsewhere in Deut only at 1:36 where it renders אחרי; cf comment ad loc. Hex was bothered by this rendering for the preposition עם and placed τά under the obelus. Instead of ἐξ (Αἰγύπτου) the majority text has εκ γης which does equal MT, but this is probably ex par in view of the frequency of the phrase "out of the land of Egypt."

9:8 Most of the recollections of vv.8—10:11 are to be found in Exod 32,34. The modification of ἐθυμώθη by an infinitive is in imitation of MT's יתאנף being modified by להשמיד, and can be rendered by "he was angry (enough) to destroy you." The verb ἐξολεθρεύω is a favorite one of the Deut translator,

15. Aq has -τένων instead of -τράχηλος.
16. See SS 70.
17. This was not literal enough for Aq who rendered the participle by προσερίζοντες "provoking to anger."

though it is the usual one for שמד (Ni or Hi 19 times), but it also occurs for השחית (4 times), החרים (3 times), הוריש (4 times), and once each for הכרית and האביד.[18]

9:9 The construction here is odd with the verse beginning with a genitive absolute, but this can hardly be part of the clause "I stayed in the mountain"; that would be neither sensible nor syntactically correct, since it has a first person singular subject just as the genitive absolute does. In fact, it must be taken with v.8, with *καὶ κατεγινόμην* beginning an entirely new structure. Rhetorically it is only loosely connected, thus "the Lord was angered against you sufficiently to destroy you, while I was (quite innocently) going up the mountain to receive the stone tablets, etc." Then v.9b and the following verses recall the Horeb event, an event which angered the Lord, in some detail, actually continuing through v.21. This is not what MT intended. It begins with a preposition plus bound infinitive plus suffix, בעלתי, i.e. "when I had ascended the mountain ... I remained, etc." For MT the two parts of the verse belong together. For the "covenant which the Lord covenanted with (toward) us" see comment at 5:2. The tradition has created an odd but old variant in reading *ας* instead of *ἧς* after *πλάκας διαθήκης*, supported by all the uncial witnesses. It can only represent a thoughtless scribal error, since the resultant text makes little sense.[19] Its reader would have had to take "tablets of the covenant" as representing the covenant itself.

The main clause of the verse reads *κατεγινόμην* for אשב. The verb occurs only three times in the Pentateuch (and only once elsewhere in OT), for שכן at Num 5:3 and for מושב at Exod 10:23. The word is attested as early as Demosthenes in the fourth Century B.C., but became more common in the Hellenistic period in the sense of "abide, dwell."[20] The "forty days and forty nights" recurs in vv.11,18,25 and 10:10. At v.18 "I ate no bread and drank no water" also occurs, and in both verses the text describes Moses' fasting during the forty day and night period; note that in both cases the close relation between the time period and the fasting is shown by the lack of a conjunction between the two.

---

18. According to HR.
19. See the discussion in THGD 107.
20. Sym preferred *παρέμεινα* as a more Classical term.

9:10 Much of v.10a reflects Exod 31:18, though in first person as spoken by Moses; cf comments ad loc. LXX reproduces MT exactly, whereas the remainder of MT is much abbreviated. The second part has a prepositional phrase as subject of a nominal clause, i.e. ככל הדברים (plus relative clause) with עליהם as predicate. LXX has changed this to a verbal structure by substituting *ἐγέγραπτο πάντες οἱ λόγοι* for ככל הדברים, and rendering MT's predicate as a preposed prepositional phrase modifying the passive verb. I suspect that the translator was simply trying to make good sense out of the Hebrew text; no different parent text need be presupposed. Entirely omitted by LXX are the two concluding prepositional phrases מתוך האש ביום הקהל, which hex restored as *εκ μεσου του πυρος εν ημερα εκκλησιας* under the asterisk. The two phrases add details not essential to the narrative, but comp 10:4 and 18:16 for their presence in similar contexts.

9:11 For *καὶ ἐγένετο* plus a timer see comment at 1:3. The time designation in LXX differs from MT, which has מקץ "at the end of (40 days and 40 nights)"; LXX uses *διά* plus the genitive. What LXX seems to say is "in the course of the 40 days and 40 nights," thus God's turning over the two stone tablets took place during this period, not necessarily at the end; *διά* can, however, also be used to refer to the end of the period, i.e. having passed through a period of time and then.[21] Note that the two bound phrases לחת האבנים and לחות הברית are differently rendered, the first as an adjectival phrase, *τὰς (δύο) πλάκας τὰς λιθίνας*, and the second, by a genitive structure, *πλάκας διαθήκης*. The genitive noun is articulated in A+, but this is a stylistic change, not a correction based on MT.

9:12 This verse corresponds closely to Exod 32:7,8a. This can be seen in what the Lord said. The Exod account has *βάδιζε* instead of *ἀνάστηθι*, *ἠνόμησεν γάρ* for *ὅτι ἠνόμησεν*, and *μόσχον* instead of *χώνευμα*. Over against MT the Exod text follows Deut in *ἐξήγαγες* (הוצאת), whereas LXX follows Exod in *ἐκ τῆς Αἰγύπτου* (מארץ מצרים rather than ממצרים of Deut). That the Deut translator was acquainted with the Exod LXX seems almost certain. The verb

21. See Bauer sub *διά* II.2. — "to denote an interval after."

ἠνόμησεν "acted lawlessly, transgressed" renders שחת rather freely.[22] The figure παρέβησαν "go alongside" is used five times in the book to render סור, but only once otherwise (תמרו at 1:43), and is an adequate rendering.[23]

9:13 LXX has inserted between "and the Lord said to me" and the direct speech marker the words λελάληκα πρὸς σὲ ἅπαξ καὶ δίς, the source of which is unknown. The words ἅπαξ and δίς occur only infrequently in LXX and joined as here they occur only at 1Reg 17:39 2Esdr 23:20 (=Neh 13:20) and 1Macc 3:30, none of which commending themselves as source for the insertion. If one examines the parallel account in Exod, one notes that the characterization of Israel as λαὸς σκληροτράχηλος occurs twice in Exod 33 (vv.3,5) as well as once in Moses' intercessory prayer on behalf of the people in 34:9. It is actually the case in the golden calf episode that God spoke not just once but twice accusing the people of being stiffnecked. At Exod 33:3 God says οὐ γὰρ μὴ συναβῶ μετὰ σοῦ διὰ τὸ λαὸν σκληροτράχηλόν σε εἶναι. Two verses later the Lord says to the Israelites: ὑμεῖς λαὸς σκληροτράχηλος. This strikes me as convincing proof that the Deut translator made use of the Exod account. The insertion is quite correctly placed under the obelus by hex. The direct speech introduced by λέγων continues through the next verse.

9:14 An elaboration of Exod 32:10. For the Hebrew "ease off from me and I will" LXX has ἔασόν με plus infinitive, a good idiomatic rendering.[24] The Byz text has the more Hebraic και εξολοθρευσω instead of the infinitive. This destruction will mean that "I will erase their name from under the sky," i.e. they will be completely forgotten in the world.

Over against this the Lord promises Moses that the covenantal promises will be transferred to him; he will "become a nation great and strong and numerous rather than this one." The *O* text has omitted "great and," which presupposes that the text which Origen inherited had already been revised to equal MT, since it is absent from the Hebrew. Here LXX uses three positive

---

22. Theod and Aq have used a more exact rendering for שחת in διέφθειρεν "corrupted."
23. But not to Aq who translated by ἀπέστησαν, which was his standard rendering for סור.
24. Though SS Inf 125 calls this "nicht korrekt."

grades plus *μᾶλλον ἤ* to show comparison[25] in contrast to v.1; cf comment ad loc. Unexpected is *τοῦτο* as a reference to the people, since the context had used plural references, *αὐτούς* and *αὐτῶν*, but MT had ממנו and the translation must reflect the translator's confusion between *ἔθνος* and λαός. The reference should have been to λαός, not to *ἔθνος*; cf v.13.

9:15 Comp Exod 32:15. The Exod account does not have the middle clause "and the mountain was burning with fire." In MT this is a circumstantial clause, i.e. a coordinate nominal clause with a participial predicate. The imperfect tense in LXX is fitting in the context of an aorist *κατέβην* to show circumstance as well.

For the last clause LXX follows MT in lacking a linking verb, i.e. the predicate is a prepositional phrase, but the clause omits הברית from the phrase לחת הברית, simply having *αἱ δύο πλάκες*. Hex has added *της διαθηκης* under the asterisk to equal MT,[26] but the majority A F M V text has added *των μαρτυριων*. The gloss undoubtedly reflects influence from the Exod account which reads *αἱ (δύο) πλάκες τοῦ μαρτυρίου* as in 31:18, but why the A text should read the plural is not immediately clear. It may well be due to the use of the plural in references coordinate with *δικαιώματα* and *κρίματα* at 4:45 6:20 (and comp 6:17), thus more appropriate than *τοῦ μαρτυρίου*, which Deut retains for אוהל מועד.

9:16 MT shows what "I saw" by הנה clauses, i.e. "And behold you had sinned ... and made ... you turned away ...," and then continuing with two clauses in the first singular in v.17. LXX translates this by the participle *ἰδών* with a *ὅτι* clause to render the content of the הנה clauses, then reducing the first clause of v.17 into a participle coordinate with *ἰδών*, and only finally making the first person references with *ἔρριψα*. The pattern is fully adequate for understanding MT.

What Moses saw is described in three coordinate clauses. The first is a general statement "you had sinned before the Lord your God." MT designates the one against whom one sins by ל, which Deut always renders by *ἔναντι* (see 1:41 20:18). This is the same as Num 32:23, while Lev 4:2 has added *ἔναντι*

25. See SS 150.
26. Whereas Aq has *τῆς συνθήκης*.

κυρίου (against MT) as modifier to *ἁμάρτῃ*. In Gen and Exod the pattern is different. The ל becomes *εἰς* at Gen 20:6,9 43:9 Exod 10:16, *ἐναντίον* at Gen 39:9 Exod 10:16, *ἐνώπιον* at Exod 32:33 and *πρός* at 23:33 and Gen 44:32.

The second clause reads "and you made for yourselves עגל מסכה for which LXX has only *χωνευτόν*. Most witnesses follow A F M V in adding *μόσχον* before it, a reading which was probably hex in origin.[27] The reference is of course to the golden calf episode of Exod 32.

The third clause characterizes what the Israelites did as "*παρέβητε* from the way which the Lord had commanded you." The verb *παραβαίνω* is regularly used by Deut to render סור (see also v.12 11:16 17:20 28:14), whereas elsewhere in LXX it is unusual (*ἐκκλίνω* is the most common rendering); elsewhere in the Pentateuch it occurs only in the parallel Exod 32:8. Over against v.12, however, LXX overlooked מהר, a failure rectified by hex which added *ταχυ* under the asterisk. The tendency in LXX to attract the dative pronoun to the verb is illustrated by (*ἐνετείλατο*) *ὑμῖν κύριος* even though MT has יהוה אתכם; the majority text (hex?) has transposed these to equal MT.

9:17 Comp Exod 32:19. For the syntactic pattern see comment at v.16. That a popular A F M V text should omit *δύο* from "my two hands" is not surprising. *δύο* had occurred in "the two tablets" just beforehand, and only a pedantic literalism, such as LXX often displays, would insist on "two hands" to render שתי ידי of MT. The two first person verbs occur in third person in the parallel Exod passage.[28]

9:18 אתנפל "I made myself fall down" is interpreted by LXX as *ἐδεήθην* "I besought," i.e. in prayer, for which also see v.25, where it becomes clear from v.26 that the falling down before Yahweh was a time of intercession for the sinful people.[29] MT follows with כראשנה "as the first," but LXX makes this more precise by its *δεύτερον καθάπερ καὶ τὸ πρότερον* "a second time as even the former," a reference to v.9 where the clause "forty days and forty

27. In any event Theod and Sym also read *μόσχον χωνευτόν*, whereas Aq has *μόσχον χωνεύσεως*.
28. But for Aq *συνέτριψα* was not literal enough for translating Pi of שבר, and he substituted *κατέαξα*, aorist of *κατάγνυμι*.
29. The anonymous reading *προσέπιπτον* could well be Aq; cf the attested Aq reading *συνέπιπτον* at v.25.

nights food I did not eat and water I did not drink" also occurs in exactly the same words; cf comment ad loc.

That ἐδεήθην means "to beseech in prayer" is clear from the second part of the verse. The περί structure modifies ἐδεήθην. The parent text for τῶν ἁμαρτιῶν ὑμῶν was probably the Sam text חטאתיכם rather than the singular of BHS, though the singular can, particularly since it is modified by כל, be understood collectively.[30] The relative pronoun ὧν is inflected by attraction to its antecedent, ἁμαρτιῶν, rather than grammatically, which would require an accusative as modifying ἡμάρτετε. The verb is in turn followed by an adverbial infinitive explicating how "you sinned," viz. "by doing evil before the Lord your God." MT does not have an equivalent for "your God," and hex has therefore placed the phrase under the obelus. That a few Hebrew mss do add אלהיך is irrelevant textually, since the context is plural throughout this section.[31] The final infinitive, παροξῦναι, shows the result of doing evil—it provokes him to anger. The infinitive renders להכעיס which is an unusual rendering, occurring elsewhere only at Ps 105:29 Isa 65:3. הכעיס is usually rendered by παροργίζω (33 times according to Dos Santos). παροξύνω renders קצף five times in Deut (and elsewhere only at Isa 47:6). The verb also translates נאץ (mainly in Pi), twice in Deut (31:20 32:19) and 11 times elsewhere (in the Pentateuch at Num 14:11,23 16:30).

9:19 Unusual is the rendering of יגרתי "I was scared, fearful" by the present tense εἰμι plus an adjective ἔκφοβος, since in the context one would have expected a past tense. What the translator probably wanted to say was "I was scared and I still am." The adjective only occurs once elsewhere in LXX, at 1Macc 13:2 where it is coordinate with ἔντρομος. I would render the opening words by "and I am (still) scared because of." MT introduced the verse with a causal כי "Because I was scared," but LXX voided a causal relationship by using καί. LXX simply affirms Moses' state of mind rather than giving his fearfulness as the reason for his prayer.

LXX also changed the אשר clause modifying האף והחמה into a ὅτι clause. Rather than identifying the anger and wrath, LXX gives the reason for

30. Kenn 18,69,107*,170*,196 also attest to חטאתיכם.
31. See Note b in BHS.

Moses' being scared; it was because "the Lord was provoked to anger against you enough to destroy you."

The *καί* introducing the second part of the verse must be understood in an adversative sense: "But the Lord listened to me also on this occasion." The compound *εἰσήκουσεν* is particularly appropriate, since it means listening in a positive sense; he reacted favorably. The term *καιρῷ* means a specific time and is the regular rendering for עת; here it is appropriate, since a specific time is intended.[32] The popular A M variant *εκεινω* for *τούτῳ* is a more exact equivalent for ההוא, and may be an early recensional change.

9:20 As in v.18, a verb is modified by an adverbial infinitive; *ἐθυμώθη* is explicated by *ἐξολεθρεῦσαι* indicating to what extent he was angered: "enough to destroy him." That Moses interceded specifically for Aaron as well is known elsewhere only from the text of Sam at Exod 32:10, where it is also found in three Greek mss. The Sam text there is, however, almost certainly based on this verse. In the tradition a popular A F M V text has articulated the infinitive, but Deut seldom articulated an infinitive (only three times); cf comment at 8:11.

καιρῷ recurs here as in v.19, but here it is modified by *ἐκείνῳ*, where it translates בעת ההוא, for which see the comment at v.19.

9:21 *τὴν ἁμαρτίαν* is singular since it refers specifically to *τὸν μόσχον*. LXX has *αὐτόν* after *ἔλαβον* against MT, which hex noted by putting it under the obelus. LXX reads "and (as for) your sin which you effected, the calf, I took it." The destruction of the idol is graphically described—"I burned it in the fire and cut it up, grinding (it) thoroughly until it became powdery, and it became like dust." MT interrupted the series of finite verbs by a free infinitive טחון plus an adverbial היטב. A contextual free infinitive takes on the verbal coloration of its context, which is here first singular preterite, and so it means "I ground (it) well." LXX attempted to preserve its unusual nature by using a participle *καταλέσας* plus *σφόδρα*, a good rendering of the intent of the Hebrew.[33] A popular F M V tradition added *αυτον* after the participle ad sensum.

---

32. Aq renders פעם by his usual equivalent *καθόδῳ*.
33. Sym used *ἐπιμελῶς* to render היטב adverbially.

LXX has expanded on עד אשר דק לעפר "until it was crushed into dust" by creating two clauses: *ἕως οὗ ἐγένετο λεπτόν* "until it became powdery" and *καὶ ἐγενήθη ὡσεὶ κονιορτός* "and it became like dust," the first explicating דק, and the second, לעפר. That the two aorists *ἐγένετο* and *ἐγενήθη* are actually interchangable is clear from this verse; both mean "became." Hex placed *καὶ ἐγενήθη* under the obelus, since it had no counterpart in MT.

The Greek, probably in the interests of style, disregarded the suffix of את עפרו, i.e. simply has "I threw *τὸν κονιορτόν* into the water." Hex added *αυτου* under the asterisk to represent the suffix.

9:22 Three more instances in which Israel provoked the Lord to anger. The first one was *at Taberah*, which LXX translated by *ἐν τῷ* Ἐμπυρισμῷ "at the Burning," for which see Num 11:3, where the noun is explained as *ὅτι ἐξεκαύθη ἐν αὐτοῖς πῦρ παρὰ κυρίου*, the antecedent of *αὐτοῖς* being *ὁ λαός*.

The second place was *at Massah.* LXX translated this by *ἐν τῷ* Πειρασμῷ "at the Temptation." This refers to the occasion described in Exod 17:1—7; at v.7 Moses gave a double name to the place, מסה ומריבה, translated as Πειρασμὸς *καὶ* Λοιδόρησις explained chiastically by *διὰ τὴν λοιδορίαν* of the Israelites and *διὰ τὸ πειράζειν κύριον λέγοντες* ....

The third instance took place *at Qibroth-hattaavah* translated by LXX as *ἐν τοῖς* Μνήμασιν *τῆς ἐπιθυμίας* "Tombs of longing." This was a reference to Num 11:34, where the name is interpreted as given *ὅτι ἐκεῖ ἔθαψαν τὸν λαὸν ἐπιθυμητήν*, "because there they buried the people even those with longing," a reference to the people who craved and demanded meat and were destroyed while eating quail.

At all three places *παροξύνοντες ἦτε κύριον*. I would now correct the critical text and add *τὸν θεὸν ὑμῶν*. Only B 58, two La codd and Arab lack the appositive. Furthermore, it is attested in both G and Syh as being under the obelus, by which hex witnesses, not only to its absence in MT, but also to its presence in Origen's LXX text. In fact, I can only explain my adoption of the shorter text as due to an undue regard for B equalling MT.

9:23 Another example of Israel's disobedience and rebellious attitude. For Καδὴς Βαρνή see 1:19. Note again the translator's tendency to place a pronominal modifier between the verb and the subject, even when MT has the pronoun after the subject. LXX has (ἐξαπέστειλεν) ὑμᾶς κύριος for MT's יהוה אתכם; hex transposed the words to equal MT.[34] The A majority text reads the shorter compound αποστειλεν rather than ἐξαπέστειλεν. There is very little difference between the two, and one is left to follow the oldest witnesses in choosing the critical text, in this case that of Cod B.

In the Lord's command to Israel to go up and possess the land, the land is characterized as ἣν δίδωμι ὑμῖν, though MT has אשר נתתי לכם.[35] In the tradition, a *y* reading has δεδωκα instead of δίδωμι, whereas a majority A M text reads εγω διδωμι. Relative clauses in which the main verb is δίδωμι occur 57 times in Deut, only five of which are in the present tense (always δίδωμι), and the remaining 52 all in past tense, usually aorist but occasionally perfect. The instances with present tense elsewhere in the book occur at 4:8 5:31 11:32 32:49. Each of these has נתן as participial predicate, and together with the strong support for the A variant it is difficult to avoid the conclusion that LXX's parent text read either אני נתן or only the participle instead of נתתי, and that the נתתי of MT was the result of the overwhelming majority of past tense readings in the book.

The verse is a conditional structure. The protasis of the ὅτε clause continues through the above relative clause, and the apodosis begins with καὶ ἠπειθήσατε, and consists of three coordinate clauses. The first one: "(and) you disobeyed the word of the Lord your God" is for MT's ותמרו את פי of the Lord your God. The verb ἀπειθέω is used for המרה throughout this chapter (see vv.7,24 as well as 1:26).[36]

This disobedience was rooted in the second clause: "and you did not believe him," which in turn resulted in the third one: "and you did not listen to (i.e. obey) his voice."

9:24 MT begins with ממרים הייתם עם יהוה as in v.7, but the verb is here rendered literally by ἦτε rather than διετελεῖτε. For the rest, LXX has the same rendering as at v.7; cf comments ad loc. The tradition was apparently troubled by the asyndetic structure, and an *O* C′′ *s*+ text introduced the verse

34. As did The Others.
35. The Others have the aorist ἔδωκα.
36. Theod is followed by Sym in taking תמרו את פי as derived from מרר in his rendering παρεπικράνατε τὸ στόμα.

by αλλ, whereas the Byz text introduced it by και. The LXX text simply followed MT. The temporal modifier in LXX reads ἀπὸ τῆς ἡμέρας ἧς ἐγνώσθη ὑμῖν, in which the relative is genitive by attraction to its antecedent. A majority A F M V variant text has αφ ης ημερας which represents an attempt at better Greek. The third person verb probably reflects the Sam text דעתו rather than the דעתי of MT, though LXX has tried to improve on it by using a passive verb with a dative modifier "was known to you" rather than "he knew you," but it does make good sense as referring to the time that God revealed himself to Israel.[37]

9:25 ואתנפל is translated here as in v.18 by καὶ ἐδεήθην; see the discussion ad loc.[38] The ὅσας ἐδεήθην dutifully renders MT's אשר התנפלתי, but it is oddly repetitive. It must modify "forty days and forty nights," and probably reflects the כראשנה of v.18 and its rendering in LXX; see comments ad loc. The verse would read equally well if it were not there, and a few scattered witnesses actually did omit it.

The reason for Moses' intercession is given in the γάρ clause. The Hebrew אמר at times means "thought," i.e. "said in this heart, said to himself." Here it is modified by a marked infinitive, and so must mean "he had thought to (destroy you)." The Hebrew connotation should also be taken over for the εἶπεν of LXX which is modified by ἐξολεθρεῦσαι ὑμᾶς.

9:26 For the augmented form ηὐξάμην B *b n* read the Attic unaugmented ευξαμην. The Hellenistic form only won acceptance in times later than LXX.[39] Why LXX substituted τὸν θεόν for יהוה as the object of intercession is problematic; after all, in v.25 κύριος is twice used, in one case in a similar context (ἐδεήθην ἔναντι κυρίου). Here LXX no longer uses ἐδεήθην as in v.25, but the actual verb meaning to engage in prayer, ηὐξάμην, reflecting the אתפלל of MT as at v.20. The equation also occurs three times in Num (11:2 21:7,8). In the later books of the OT the translation occurs only three times, and the compound, προσεύχομαι, becomes the standard rendering (69 times according to

37. Theod followed by Sym obviously reflects MT with ἔγνω ὑμᾶς.
38. Aq translated the verb by συνέπιπτον, reflecting the נפל root.
39. See THGD 142.

Dos Santos), a rendering occurring only twice in the Pentateuch (Gen 20:7,17).

For *εἶπα* the Byz text read the Classical *ειπον*, but Deut preferred the Hellenistic first aorist inflection throughout. For *κύριε κύριε* rendering אדני יהוה see comment at 3:24. The title *βασιλεῦ τῶν θεῶν* is not only unique in LXX; it has no equivalent in MT, as the obelus in the hex tradition also makes clear. Dogniez-Harl speculates that its source was the divine appelation of the Egyptian Amon-Ré,[40] which seems to me to be odd indeed, though I can think of no obvious other explanation. The title *θεὸς τῶν θεῶν* does occur elsewhere (10:17 Ps 135:2), and God is often called "king," especially in Pss, e.g. *ὁ βασιλεὺς τῆς δόξης* in 23:7—10, or as *βασιλεὺς μέγας* at 46:3, but the combination "king of the gods" occurs only here; it recognizes, as do the other titles, that Israel's Lord is supreme; its hyperbole suggests supremacy over against all other deities; it counteracts any suggestion that *παρὰ τὸ μὴ δύνασθαι κύριον εἰσαγαγεῖν αὐτοὺς εἰς τὴν γῆν* (v.28). In Deuteronomic terms the *τῶν θεῶν* are not real gods; they are the "other gods," the gods of the nations, and only the Lord is powerful, *οὗτος θεὸς τῶν θεῶν καὶ κύριος τῶν κυρίων* (10:17) i.e. "the supreme God and the supreme Lord." In the tradition an *s t+* reading changes *θεῶν* to *εθνων*, and the *b* text, to *αιωνων*, but neither God of the nations (created by palaeographic confusion?) nor God of the ages (a much later concept) is to be taken seriously.

Israel is called *τὸν λαόν σου καὶ τὴν κληρονομίαν σου*, with a relative clause following, which is introduced by *ἥν*, i.e. in agreement with the nearer antecedent. The verb in the clause is modified in MT by בגדלך, which LXX interprets as referring to great strength, i.e. *ἐν τῇ ἰσχύι σου τῇ μεγάλῃ*, which occurs later in the verse, as well as at v.29, where MT has בכחך הגדל. Note that cod G has mistakenly put *τῇ μεγάλῃ* instead of *τῇ ἰσχύι* under the obelus, clearly a copyist error.

The final relative clause is introduced by *οὕς*; the plural form has no proper grammatical antecedent, but must sensibly refer to *τὸν λαὸν ... καὶ τὴν κληρονομίαν*, a reference to the people of Israel. In MT "you brought out of Egypt" is modified by the single phrase ביד חזקה, which LXX amplifies considerably as *ἐν τῇ ἰσχύι σου τῇ μεγάλῃ καὶ ἐν τῇ χειρί σου τῇ κραταιᾷ καὶ*

40. 179: "elle refléterait l'influence de la religion ptolémaïque sur le tradacteur."

ἐν τῷ βραχίονί σου τῷ ὑψηλῷ, with only the middle phrase reflecting MT, the other two being placed under the obelus in hex to show their absence in MT. But even the single modifier "by a strong hand" is changed to equal the more usual בידך החזקה. Hex omits the article before χειρί and places σου τῇ under the obelus thereby equalling MT's text. For the typical Deut expression see comment at 3:23—24. Also an expansion over against MT is the γῆς before Αἰγύπτου, but this is obviously ex par.

9:27 A good example of a senseless scribal error is the addition by *C'*' of a dative singular article before Ἀβραάμ. Since the three patriarchs are defined appositively as τῶν θεραπόντων σου, i.e. in the genitive, the dative article is patently not sensible. The three names precede the appositive phrase in LXX, and are transposed by hex to equal the order in MT. The choice of θεραπόντων for עבדי reminds one of Exod where θεράπων is especially common for עבד. This is also translated by παῖς in Deut nine times (which is also used for נער(ה) six times). παῖς is the favored translation in Gen. Oddly δοῦλος occurs in the Pentateuch only three times, twice in Lev and once in Deut (32:36). "Your servants" is modified by a relative clause, οἷς ὤμοσας κατὰ σεαυτοῦ, which has no basis in MT, but was lifted word for word from its parallel Exod 32:13, for which MT had אשר נשבעת להם בך. The clause was omitted by A *O*+, probably under the influence of The Others who also omit it.

μὴ ἐπιβλέψης is modified by three ἐπί phrases, and is to be understood in the sense of "disregard." The nouns involved are all plural, though MT's nouns are all singular: "stubbornness, wickedness, sin." LXX understood these as collectives: σκληρότητα, ἀσεβήματα and ἁμαρτήματα, which is a legitimate interpretation. The last one is modified by αὐτῶν, but רשעו has a suffix which is not translated, and hex has added αυτου after ἀσεβήματα.[41] Because of this addition of αυτου some *O* mss have changed the final αὐτῶν to αυτου as well, which by coincidence happens to correspond to MT: חטאתו.

9:28 As usual LXX translated פן by μή and hex added ποτε. The subject of εἴπωσιν is οἱ κατοικοῦντες τὴν γῆν which presumably renders Sam's עם הארץ

41. The asterisks in G and Syh have been badly transmitted. They should only apply to αυτου.

rather than the הארץ of MT,[42] though the participle would be a free interpretation of עם. The presumption is no more than that, since MT would be metonymic for the inhabitants or for the people of the land as well. The construction *ὅθεν ... ἐκεῖθεν* is a Hebraism imitating אשר plus משם. LXX adds a direct speech marker, *λέγοντες*, which hex placed under the obelus to indicate that it has no counterpart in MT. It does make clear where the direct quotation begins.

The *παρὰ τό* construction translates מבלי quite correctly, and carries it over to the coordinate מן structure as well. What the inhabitants might infer is that Israel's God is powerless to redeem his promise to bring them into the land on the one hand, and that his exodus of the people into the desert was motivated by hatred, on the other. These possible attacks on God's honor are intended to sway the Lord from his destructive intent. The *ἀποκτεῖναι* is purposive; he brought them out in order to kill, to which hex has appended *αυτους* under the asterisk so as to represent להמתם more precisely. Since *αὐτούς* already occurred immediately before the infinitive, it becomes almost offensively repetitious in Greek, and the translator had wisely omitted it.

9:29 This verse is intended as adversative to what the Canaanites might say. The reality is that "these are your people and your heritage." The use of *κλῆρός σου* instead of *κληρονομίαν σου* as at v.26 for translating נחלתך is simply for variety's sake; the two nouns mean the same. "Whom you brought out of the land of Egypt," for which see comment at 1:27, is close to Sam; MT lacks "of the land of Egypt" entirely, and Sam has the shorter ממצרים; hex has placed *ἐκ γῆς Αἰγύπτου* under the obelus. For the two *ἐν* phrases see comment at 3:23—24. The two phrases also occurred at v.26, which see.

42. In fact, all the ancient interpretations agree with LXX.

Chapter 10

10:1 The phrase *ἐν τῷ καιρῷ ἐκείνῳ* occurs frequently for בעת ההוא (1:9,16,18 2:34 3:4,8,12,18,21,23 4:14 5:5), and has become a set phrase.[1] Here, however, *ἐκείνῳ* precedes the articulated noun to emphasize a change of theme; see also v.8. The phrase is here followed by *εἶπεν* without a direct speech marker which often accompanies the phrase when it marks a reference to speech of some kind. The command to hew out two stone tablets as on the first occasion also occurs at Exod 34:1 with one substantial difference; כראשנה is here translated by *ὥσπερ τὰς πρώτας* but in Exod by *καθὼς καὶ αἱ πρῶται*; See Notes ad loc.

The second clause has no counterpart in MT of Exod, but its Greek has taken it over from Deut. It renders MT word for word. The third clause, the order to make an ark, is, however, unique to our account. Here the order is simply to make a *κιβωτὸν ξυλίνην*,[2] and has none of the elaborate instructions found in connection with the *κιβωτὸν μαρτυρίου* in Exod 25:9—21.

10:2 V.2a is echoed in Exod 34:1b with minor differences. For (*ἐπὶ*) *τὰς πλάκας* Exod has *τῶν πλακῶν*, and for *ὅσα* Exod has *ἅ*; cf Notes ad loc. In the tradition *b* has *των πλακων* as well, and B *O*′′+ read *α* for *ὅσα*.[3] Whether the *O* Byz reading *επι* (*ταῖς πλαξίν*) instead of *ἐν* was influenced by the Hebrew על or is simply a rationalization that the words were "upon" not "in" the tablets can not be determined. Uncertain as well is the original case of the relative pronoun introducing *συνέτριψας*. The choice of *ἅς* follows B as the oldest witness, but the majority A F M V text reads *αις*. Since the translator often chooses the inflection of relative pronouns by attraction to their antecedents the *αις* could well be original. The Exod parallel also reads *ἅς*, but there a popular B variant has *αις*.

The point of making an ark is now clear: "you shall put *αὐτάς* into the ark." The pronoun refers to the *πλάκας*. The B *ol b*+ variant *αυτα* must refer

1. See list 4 in THGD 87.
2. Aq translates ארון as usual by *γλωσσόκομον* "chest, box."
3. See THGD 106 for a discussion of the relative pronoun vs the relative adjective.

to ῥήματα, which is peculiar. The variant is palaeographically determined; it is a haplograph based on the similarity of Σ-Ε in the uncial script, and is therefore not to be seriously considered.

10:3 Except for the reference to the ark, this verse is paralleled in Exod 34:4. Here the word שטים, probably "acacia (wood)," is defined as being *ἀσήπτων*,[4] a word reserved in the Pentateuch as translation for שטים. It was originally probably chosen for exegetical reasons. Since the ark was to be a permanent repository for the tablets, it was important that its permanence be assured, and a word was chosen meaning "not subject to decay";[5] see Note at Exod 25:5. כראשנים apparently gave translators trouble; comp v.1 where the accusative obtains. Here it becomes *ὥσπερ αἱ πρῶται*, whereas Exod has *καθάπερ καὶ αἱ πρῶται*. B *O n s*+ read *ως* rather than *ὥσπερ*,[6] but there is no lexical distinction; see also comment at v.1. The difference in case is based on what Bauer describes as "The *ὡσπερ*-clause is somet. shortened and needs to be supplemented."[7] For v.1 the phrase implies "as (you did) the first ones," whereas in v.3 it would mean "as the first ones (were) hewn)." Also in the tradition the phrase *ἐπὶ ταῖς χερσίν μου* is changed; a *b n*+ text read *εν* as the preposition, which by chance equals MT's בידי, and an F V *C f s* gloss has *δυσιν* before *χερσίν*, which is ex par, e.g. 9:15.

10:4 *ἔγραψεν* is given without subject, but the context is first person, and so the reference must be to the Lord (cf 9:10), and not to Moses as in Exod 34:28. The writing was a copy of that on the original tablets, i.e. *κατὰ τὴν γραφὴν τὴν πρώτην*.[8] For *τοὺς δέκα λόγους* see 5:6—21, and compare *τὸ δέκα ῥήματα* at 4:13. The term also occurs at Exod 34:28.

According to MT Yahweh had spoken "from the fire ביום הקהל." At 9:10 LXX had omitted both prepositional phrases as unnecessary to the narrative, and here LXX omits the second phrase only, possibly because it seems an obtrusive phrase in this context. Hex of course has added *εν τη ημερα της*

---

4. Aq transliterates as *σεττίμ*.
5. SS 64 simply says "wird hier falsch übersetzt."
6. See THGD 132.
7. Bauer sub *ὥσπερ* 2.
8. Aq understood the prefix of מכתב as instrumental, i.e. *τὸ γραφεῖον*, though without further context it makes no sense.

εκκλησιας under the asterisk to equal MT. At 18:16 the timer is useful after the locative *ἐν Χωρήβ*, and so the phrase does obtain.

10:6 Vv.6—7 are part of an itinerary which seems to be a scramble of part of the itinerary of Num 33; cf vv.30—33. V.6 mentions three names, Βηρώθ, (υἱῶν) Ἰακίμ and Μισαδαί. In MT these are בארת בני יעקן מוסרה, i.e. "(from) Beroth BeneYaqan to Moser." The translator translated בני יעקן by "sons of Yakim," thus "(they moved from) Beroth of the Jakimites to Misadai," misreading the nasal of יעקן as a *mem*. The location of either place is not known. Μισαδαί is more problematic; the *delta* is based on ר-ד confusion, but why the postpositional *-he* should be read as *yodh* to make -αι is not clear. The place has not been identified, neither as מוסרה nor as Μισαδαί.

Beroth does not occur in Num 33. The Israelites travelled from Μασουρούθ/מסרות to Βαναιακάν/בני יעקן (v.32), and from there to the hilly area of Γαδγάδ (v.32). The name *βηρώθ* is stable in the tradition, only *βηθωρ* being attested as a variant Greek spelling in one ms. The name Ἰακίμ appears as *ιακιν/ακιν* in *O*; by aphaeresis as *ακ(ε)ιμ*, *ακεμ*; as influenced by the better known name Joakim as *ιωακ(ε)ιμ*, *ιωκειμ* in *n z*+, and even as *ισακειμ* in one ms. Outside of various itacisms Μισαδαί appears by dittography as *μισαδδαι*, *μεσσαδαι*; by aphaeresis as *σαδαι*; by vowel change as *μησωδαι*; by infixation as *μισαγδαι* in *f*; by suffixing as *μεισαδαγ*, and by prefixing as *σμισαδαι*.

That Aaron died and was buried at Μισαδαί/מוסרה conflicts with Num 33:37 which identifies the place of Aaron's death and burial as Ὢρ τὸ ὄρος πλησίον γῆς Ἐδώμ and see also 20:22—28, where the transfer of the priestly garments (and thereby the office) to Eliezer his son is also said to have taken place. In our verse only the assumption of the priestly office by Eliezer is mentioned.

10:7 See Num 33:32b—33. The *d* text has added a number of way stations of the itinerary from Num 33:34—37 at the beginning of the verse, but this merely complicates the problem of the two verses here. In the Num itinerary the journey from the hill country of Γαδγάδ went on to Ἐτεβάθα, which is obviously the same as our Ἰετεβάθα for יטבתה. In the tradition both names, being totally unknown to scribes, suffered greatly. Without attempting to explain the process I give the following variant spellings (disregarding all itacisms) as occurring for Γαδγάδ: γαδγαδα, γαδαγαδ, γαγαδ, γαλγαλ, γαδιγαδ, αγαδγαδ, γαδδαδ, γαλγαδ, γαλδαδ, γαλααδ, γαδδα, γαλδαδ and γαδ. For the second name, note ιεταβαθα, ιεταβυθα, ιτεβαθα, ετεφαθα, ετεβαθα, ιετεβαδα, τεβαθα, ταιβαθα, ταβαθα, ισαβαθα, ρεταβαθα and γαβαθα.

The verse ends with a pendant nominative: "it is a land containing stream(s) of water." In MT presumably ארץ is in apposition to the name יטבתה; this would be shown by the variant reading γην in four mss, a reading which was intended to relieve the syntax.

At the end of the verse another Byz tradition has added the itinerary which the *d* strand had added at the beginning of the verse. The source is Sam, which it translates literally.

10:8 The word order (ἐν) ἐκείνῳ τῷ καιρῷ for בעת ההוא is unusual, and found elsewhere in Deut only at v.1; cf comment ad loc for the unusual order. With v.8 the theme changes to the setting aside of the tribe of Levi for sacred duties. This dedication is described as διέστειλεν "separated, set aside," which is a good rendering for הבדיל (see also 19:2,7 29:21).[9]

The collective הלוי is rendered by τὴν Λευί, "that of Levi," the article referring to φυλήν. In MT שבט הלוי is a bound phrase, and one might have expected a genitive article του before the proper noun as in four mss. The purposive infinitives describe the ends for which the Lord set them aside, with only the last one governed by a καί, which reproduces MT exactly. A Qumran text (2QDeut[c]) witnesses to a conjunction before the second infinitive as well (ולעמוד), but this finds no Greek support in the tradition. Exegetically it would make good sense, since one could then understand λειουργεῖν καὶ ἐπεύχεσθαι as modifying παρεστάναι. But both MT and LXX must be understood as intending all four infinitives to modify the main verb הבדיל/διέστειλεν.

The first duty of the Levites was to carry the ark of the covenant of the Lord; this is well-attested as carried out by the Levites (see Num 4:15 1Reg 6:15 2Reg 15:24 1Chr 15:2), or by priests and Levites in Jos 3:3, though in 3Reg 8:3 it is said that the priests carried the ark. Then they were παρεστάναι ἔναντι κυρίου, i.e. to stand in attendance before the Lord. Instead of the per-

---

9. But Aq used ἀχώρισεν.

fect infinitive, an F V *oII C*'' *s*+ text has the simpler aorist *παραστηναι*, but the more difficult reading of LXX is to be preferred.

The third reason for dedicating the Levitical tribe was *λειτουργεῖν* "to serve cultically," for MT's לשרתו. Hex has added an *αυτω* under the asterisk to render the suffix, which LXX had considered otiose, and so had disregarded.

The final modifier is *ἐπεύχεσθαι ἐπὶ τῷ ὀνόματι αὐτοῦ* "to pray in his name," or possibly "to give thanks in his name." The Hebrew has לברך, for which comp 21:5 where *εὐλογεῖν* also is used.[10] This was apparently a liturgical function of some sort in which a blessing was pronounced in the liturgy, as LXX fully understood, hence the use of *ἐπεύχεσθαι*. See especially 21:5. Rashi defines this as the priestly blessing.[11]

10:9 MT has a consistent singular throughout the verse, but LXX only has the singular for the second part. In v.9a the collective sense of לוי is shown by *ταῖς Λευίταις* and "among the brothers *αὐτῶν*." This inconsistency was bothersome to the tradition. Though the plural "to the Levites" is retained throughout, *O*+ does change *αὐτῶν* to *αυτου*, which conforms to MT. Conversely for (*κλῆρος*) *αὐτοῦ* a popular M variant witnesses to *αυτων*, and to *αυτοις* for *αὐτῷ*.

The notion of "the Lord is his heritage" must be a reference to their income as described in 18:1—4.[12] In the tradition *κύριος* has been glossed by *ο θεος* in the M *oI C*''+ text, which must be ex par. In the *καθά* clause LXX had not stated the subject, whereas MT has יהוה אלהיך. Hex has supplied the subject as *κυριος ο θεος σου* under the asterisk to equal MT.

10:10 The elided form, *κἀγώ*, is always used in Deut rather than *καὶ ἐγώ*, though crasis is otherwise rare in the book. The pluperfect *ειστηκειν* occurs in B+, but only the aorist (*εἰσήκουσεν*, *ἠθέλησεν*) occurs in the context, and must here be original as well.[13] MT has כימים הראשנים inserted before "forty days," which LXX does not recognize, thereby omitting the recognition that

10. Aq also uses *εὐλογεῖν* here.
11. He reads והוא נשיאת כפים.
12. This is how Tar^O interprets as well: מתנן דיהב לה יי אנון אחסנתה.
13. See THGD 141.

this is Moses' second lone stay on the mountain, though comp vv.1,3. Hex has filled in *ως ημεραι αι πρωται* under the asterisk to equal MT. The statement "I stayed on the mountain" refers to Moses' intercession, as the second clause makes clear; the fuller statement had occurred at 9:18—19.

Instead of the more common "on that occasion" the pronoun *τούτῳ* is used. This reflects בפעם ההוא rather than בעת ההוא. Though LXX used the same noun it differentiates by using *τούτῳ* rather than *ἐκείνῳ*; see also 9:19. In the tradition *O* Byz changed to *εκεινω*, thereby reflecting ההוא more exactly.

The divine change of heart is shown in the final clause, which BHS introduces without a conjunction. A well-supported Hebrew variant text does witness, along with Sam, to the conjunction, which tradition LXX also follows: "And the Lord was unwilling to destroy you." MT has changed to a singular reference for the people in השחיתך, but not LXX which renders by *ἐξολεθρεῦσαι ὑμᾶς*.[14] The verb *ἐξολεθρεύω* is a favored one in Deut, occurring 34 times as translation for at least six different verbs,[15] including the Hi of שחת, literally "corrupted," four times.

10:11 The divine command to Moses in MT קום לך למסע "Rise for travelling" is rightly rendered with no recognition of the לך as *βάδιζε ἄπαρον* "go, travel."[16] Instead of לפני העם LXX follows Sam with *ἔναντι τοῦ λαοῦ τούτου*,[17] which together with *ἄπαρον* means "lead this people." Hex has placed *τούτου* under the obelus since it has no basis in MT. The change of *βάδιζε* to the aorist *βαδισον* in *C'' s* is no improvement whatsoever.

The change to third person plural in the second part of the verse probably intended result or purpose in MT, i.e. "that they might enter and possess." LXX did well by using the third person imperatives "and let them enter and possess." For the relative clause ending the verse see comment at 1:8. In the tradition the *z* text read the compound *κατακληρονομειτωσαν*, but this is

14. The Others render literally as *διεφθεῖραί σε*.
15. According to HR.
16. Aq renders every word literally as *ἀνάστηθι σαυτῷ εἰς ἄπαρσιν* "rise for yourself for departure"; Theod understood לך as an imperative: (*ἀναστὰς*) *πορεύου εἰς ἄπαρσιν*, whereas Sym more idiomatically has *πορεύου εἰς το ἀπαίρειν*.
17. Aq retains only *ἔναντι τοῦ λαοῦ*, whereas Theod has *ἐναντίον τοῦ λαοῦ*, and Sym more elegantly has *ἔμπροσθεν τοῦ λαοῦ τούτου*; only Sym retains the pronoun of LXX.

palaeographically conditioned; the simplex verb of LXX is preceded by *καί*, and the compound variant is created by partial dittography.

10:12 *καὶ νῦν* usually introduces some change of direction in what is being said (see also 4:1 5:25 26:10 31:19). Here the change is to instruct the people in the lessons to be drawn from Moses' account of their desert experiences, which ended with v.11. With this verse both MT and LXX change to second person singular, i.e. 'Ισραήλ is addressed as a collective entity. The address is put in question form with *αἰτεῖται* as present tense being used to render the participial predicate שאל.[18] In the tradition an F *b f*+ text has the active *αιτει* which I suspect to be palaeographically inspired, since it is obviously not as appropriate as the middle form. The *C'' s* text has *ζητει*, which is probably a variant from *αιτει*, rather than from the middle form of LXX. The pattern followed is *τί κύριος ... αἰτεῖται ...* ἀλλ' ἤ plus five infinitives extending into v.13.

The first infinitive is *φοβεῖσθαι* the Lord your God. The fear of the Lord is a favorite demand in MT (5:29 6:2,13,24 8:6); it is something that can be learned (4:10 14:22 17:19 31:12,13); it is basic to the other demands, an awe which for the true worshipper is the base for worship and life. It should also be noted that all the infinitives are present infinitives; the demand is a continuous one on the people.

The second infinitive is *πορεύεσθαι ἐν πάσαις ταῖς ὁδοῖς αὐτοῦ*. In the tradition, B+ introduce this with *και*,[19] as do Pesh and Vulg. The collocation is a common Deuteronomic one.[20] The third one is coordinated to the second as *καὶ ἀγαπᾶν αὐτόν*. The two are mentioned together elsewhere (11:22 19:9 30:16), but in reverse order. For its interpretation see comments at 6:5.

The fourth infinitive is also paratactically given as *καὶ λατρεύειν κυρίῳ τῷ θεῷ σου ἐξ ὅλης τῆς καρδίας σου καὶ ἐξ ὅλης τῆς ψυχῆς σου*. The verb is most commonly used in the book to warn against "serving" other gods, but occasionally as here in the command to "serve" the Lord (6:13 10:20 11:13 and cf 28:47).[21] The verb is almost limited to rendering עבד, but usually in the

---

18. Sym has *αἰτεῖ*, but The Others follow LXX.
19. As do Kenn 5,84 and Tar^{P}.
20. See list 26 in THGD 94.
21. See Daniel 67.

restricted sense of cultic service (28:48 is the one exception in the book). This cultic service is to be done ἐξ your whole heart and your whole person, i.e. it comes out of own's inner being. This is expressed in MT with ב "with."[22] For the two common ἐξ phrases see comment at 4:29.

10:13 The final infinitive defining what the Lord your God is seeking of you is "*φυλάσσεσθαι* the commandments of the Lord your God and his ordinances." LXX follows the Sam text, rather than MT which lacks אלהיך. Hex notes this absence by placing *τοῦ θεοῦ σου* under the obelus. The verb occurs 54 times in Deut, first occurring at 4:2 with "*τὰς ἐντολάς* of the Lord your God," and together with *τὰ δικαιώματα αὐτοῦ* (at 4:40; see comments ad loc.[23] For the *ὅσα* clause see comment at 4:2, and for the *ἵνα* clause, a comment at 4:40. The *ἵνα* clause seems an afterthought, but it is still part of the question asked of Israel in v.12. The translator has used a common Deuteronomic structure to interpret MT's prepositional phrase לטוב in turn modified by לך, i.e. "for your good."

10:14 The preposed *κυρίου τοῦ θεοῦ σου* imitates MT in placing the stress on the predicate: "the Lord your God's is." The hyperbole of *ὁ οὐρανὸς τοῦ οὐρανοῦ* as distinct from *ὁ οὐρανός* 1° probably simply means "even the very heavens."[24] This contrasts with "the earth and all that is in it." In the tradition the *C''* *b* text joins this with a *και* to the preceding, but this is hardly to be taken seriously.

10:15 The collocation חשק לאהבה is somewhat tautologous "was attached (to ...) in love," i.e. love to love! LXX has neatly but freely differentiated by *προείλατο* ... *ἀγαπᾶν* "chose to love," and then by *ἐξελέξατο* to render יבחר, which also means "choose, select." For these two verbs see comment at 7:7. All of this is introduced by *πλήν*, thus "nonetheless, in spite of this, your fathers he chose to love ...." LXX changed to the second plural with the onset of the verse, whereas in MT the change is made only in the second part of the verse with בכם (*ὑμᾶς*). The levelling to the plural in LXX is sensible indeed.

---

22. See SS 127.
23. Theod renders חקת by *ἀκριβάσματα* (retroverted from Syh).
24. GK 133i calls this kind of construction a periphrase for the superlative.

The reference to "their seed after them" is identified as ὑμᾶς. It is Israel whom he selected "out of all the nations," For Israel as the Lord's elect people see comments at 7:7,8. The phrase כיום הזה is translated by κατὰ τὴν ἡμέραν ταύτην. For other translations of the phrase see 4:20,38 8:18 and for כהיום הזה, 6:24.

10:16 MT's bold figure ומלתם את ערלת לבבכם "you shall circumcize the foreskin of your heart" is translated by καὶ περιτεμεῖσθε τὴν σκληροκαρδίαν ὑμῶν, i.e. the foreskin is given a moral interpretation; it is the hardness of your heart which is to be cut away.[25] The notion of "hardness of heart" recurs in Sir 16:10 in a reference to the rebellious Israelites in the desert, τοὺς ἐπισυναχθέντας ἐν σκληροκαρδίᾳ αὐτῶν.[26] At Jer 4:4 σκληροκαρδιαν is the majority reading for ἀκροβυστίαν τῆς καρδίας, and is obviously borrowed from Deut. What the figure intends is to invite Israel to open their hearts to the Lord, the hardness of the heart having been removed.

So too the coordinate clause condemns Israel's stubbornness: "and your neck no longer stiffen" (literally: make hard). For stiffneckedness see comments at 9:6 and 13.

10:17 Vv.17—18 describe Israel's God in terms of titles, attributes and works. V.17 begins with a pendant nominative (ὁ γὰρ) κύριος ὁ θεὸς ὑμῶν. The unusual articulation is occasioned by γάρ, which must be postpositive. One might translate "For as for the Lord your God." The actual nominal clause is οὗτος θεός κ.τ.λ. This represents a typical nominal clause in Hebrew: "For the Lord ... is God of gods, etc." The titles given are both superlatives: ὁ θεὸς τῶν θεῶν καὶ κύριος τῶν κυρίων, i.e. "the supreme God and the supreme Lord." Both titles occur in the Great Hallel, Ps 135:2,3, and at Dan 2:47 θεὸς τῶν θεῶν occurs as well as κύριος τῶν βασιλέων in king Nabouchodonosor's recognition of Daniel's God; the first τῶν is lacking in the θ′ text. The phrase should not be taken as meaning the chief among the Gods, but rather as translated above.

---

25. Aq simply translates by ἀκροβυστίαν (καρδίας).
26. Tar^{O} fully removes the metaphor by תעדון ית טפשות לבכון "you shall turn aside the stupidity of your heart." Note also Rashi's comment on its meaning: אוטם לבבכם וכסויו.

His attributes are detailed as ὁ μέγας, ὁ ἰσχυρός and ὁ φοβερός. The middle one is a translation for הגבר.[27] According to Dos Santos this equivalent occurs 23 times in OT. The most frequent translation is δυνατός (73 times); also to be noted are μαχητής (18 times), and γίγας (17 times). It does accent the ability, strength, and warrior-like character of God. The majority text has a και joining the second attribute to the first, but omits the article. Sam does support a conjunction here,[28] but it is unlikely to have been original text, since the other two adjectives are both articulated, and the presence of the conjunction is tied to the loss of the article. The term φοβερός, like its Hebrew equivalent נורא, refers to the one held in awe; see also its use at 1:19 2:7 and 8:15 in describing the terrible desert.

Two negative attributes are then given: God is one ὅστις οὐ θαυμάζει πρόσωπον οὐδὲ μὴ λάβῃ δῶρον "one who does not respect persons nor takes a gift," i.e. a bribe; cf also 16:19.[29] The first of these translates לא ישא פנים, an idiom meaning "he does not play favorites," which LXX renders adequately.[30] Nor can God be bribed. The Hebrew word is שחד "bribe."[31]

10:18 Customary works of the Lord; he acts as protector of the proselyte, orphan and widow. This trio is mentioned here for the first time, but the combination is typically Deut.[32] These three have become symbols for those who are helpless in society, i.e. ones who cannot help themselves, and for whom there is no obvious defender or protector. MT lacks the first member of the trio, reserving τὸν προσήλυτον for the second part of the verse; hex accordingly placed προσηλύτῳ καί under the asterisk. Such protection is shown in upholding the cause of the helpless; God ποιῶν κρίσιν for them, effecting their case in court, and so becomes their effective defender, i.e. administers justice for them.

LXX has rendered the two participles of the verse differently. The first one, עשה, becomes a participle as well, and serves as a further attributive to v.17, but the second one, אהב, is translated as a participial predicate, i.e. by

27. Whereas it is the usual rendering for האל in Aq.
28. See THGD 131.
29. See Daniel 125.
30. The verb is literally rendered by Aq as ἀρεῖ, whereas Theod has λήψεται.
31. Aq renders this by δωροκοπίαν "bribery."
32. See list 43 in THGD 97.

the present tense ἀγαπᾷ; thus "and he loves the proselyte so as to provide for him food and clothing." For the term *προσήλυτον* see Note at Exod 12:48. The infinitive *δοῦναι* modifies ἀγαπᾷ adverbially, describing how he loves him; it is the practical demonstration of his love.

10:19 Here the proselyte alone is singled out for consideration; Israel is enjoined to imitate God by loving the proselyte, though its raison d'etre is different; Israel's love is historically conditioned; they themselves had been proselytes in Egypt land; see Note at Exod 23:9. That the G *n t*+ variant text *αιγυπτου* is secondary is clear from usage. In Deut, LXX always renders בארץ מצרים by ἐν γῇ Αἰγύπτῳ, i.e. not by *εν γη αιγυπτου*.[33]

10:20 This verse is exactly the same as 6:13; even the variants *προσκυνησεις* for *φοβηθήσῃ*, the addition of *μονω* after *αὐτῷ*, and the addition of *επι* before "his name" occur there as well. For its interpretation see comments ad loc. The Hebrew texts are, however, not identical. Only that of 6:13 has the conjunction representing *καί* 1°,[34] whereas the source of *καὶ πρὸς αὐτὸν κολληθήσῃ* is only present here. It should be noted as well that with this verse the second singular takes over.

10:21 הוא is in both cases rendered by *αὐτός*, though a well-supported B text in both cases reads *ουτος*. Which of these is original is difficult to determine. In fact, *αὐτός* occurs 22 times and *οὗτος* 26 times in Deut; in usage they also parallel each other; both recapitulate after a pendant nominative; both serve as subject for a nominal predicate or for a verb.[35] Here in both cases the pronoun is subject for a nominal predicate.[36]

The term *καύχημα* "dignity, pride" is an unexpected translation for תהלה "praise," and occurs only here in the Pentateuch.[37] The term תהלה is

---

33. See THGD 137.
34. Though many Hebrew mss do read ואתו as at 6:3. The conjunction is also present in Tar, Pesh and Vulg.
35. But see THGD 113.
36. See SS 79 where it is suggested that these are variants of the formula אני יהוה.
37. According to HR the equation recurs twice in Zech and three times in Jer.

probably taken here as that which is praiseworthy, thus that in which one takes pride, one's dignity.[38] *καύχημα* is used for various Hebrew terms as well.[39]

God is then described as one who perfomed in you "these great and *τὰ ἔνδοξα* things in you." The choice of *ἔνδοξα* "glorious" to render נוראת "fearful" is highly unusual,[40] occurring elsewhere only at Isa 64:3 where the translation is extremely free, and is of no help here. The translator found the notion of taking pride in "fearful" things strange, but by understanding the Lord's fearful actions as reflecting divine glory the notion of "glorious" becomes reasonable. In the tradition an A F M majority text has the Classical *ειδον* for *εἴδοσαν*, but Deut uses only the Hellenistic form (see also 7:19 11:2).

10:22 Instead of *ἑβδομήκοντα* a popular A F V text adds *πεντε*, i.e. 75, which is based on Exod 1:5 and/or Gen 46:27; cf Notes ad loc.[41]

The translation of ועתה by *νυνὶ δέ* illustrates the contrastive use of *δέ*. On the one hand, seventy; on the other, like the stars of the sky in multitude. In fact, *δέ* is only seldom used to introduce a clause in Deut.[42] For *ὡσεὶ τὰ ἄστρα τοῦ οὐρανοῦ τῷ πλήθει* see comment at 1:10.[43]

---

38. Aq renders the word by *ὕμνησις*.
39. See the discussion of the root in Dogniez-Harl.
40. Aq has a more obvious rendering *ἐπίφοβα*.
41. Aq witnesses only to *ἑβδονμήκοντα* to agree with MT.
42. According to Aejmelaeus 36 it is used only 34 times as opposed to *καί* 1273 times, thus 2.7% over against 97.3%.
43. See also THGD 84.

Chapter 11

11:1 For the first clause see 6:5. For clauses similar to the second one see 4:40 6:2,17 7:11 8:11 10:13,[1] all of them ordering the keeping of the divine laws. The list here is unique in that it includes *τὰ φυλάγματα αὐτοῦ*, translating משמרתו, both of which occur only here in the book. It is coordinated with the well-known nouns *δικαιώματα*, *ἐντολάς* and *κρίσεις*, and obviously belongs in the general class of things divinely ordered. Since it stands first in the list and is cognate with the verb *φυλάξῃ*, it must refer to that which must be guarded, presumably "charges," i.e. those things with which God has specifically charged the Israelites. After this general order the chapter continues in the plural.

In the tradition the Byz text added *τα προσταγματα αυτου* as an extra item in second place in the list. And hex has transposed *ἐντολάς* and *κρίσεις* to reflect MT's order: ומשפטיו ומצותיו.

11:2 The syntax of this verse is peculiar, and the critical text would be improved by a slight change in punctuation; a comma should be placed after *εἴδοσαν*. The collocation *ὅτι οὐχὶ τὰ παιδία ὑμῶν ὅσοι οὐκ οἴδασιν οὐδὲ εἴδοσαν* is parenthetical and contrasts with the subject of *γνώσεσθε*. The sense of the passage is "(it is) you (who) know today—for (it is) not your children who neither knew nor saw,—the instruction ...." LXX differs from the common understanding of MT in which the את in the כי clause is understood as "with," which promotes the understanding "For it is not with your children, who have neither known nor seen, (that I am speaking)."[2]

It is, however, possible to take the critical text without change in punctuation by taking the *ὅτι* clause to extend through v.3 *αὐτοῦ* 2° as the parenthetical section. This would still take the larger section as contrasting with the subject "you," but in this interpretation it is "the children who neither knew nor saw the instruction of the Lord your God and his great works ... and

1. And see also list 22 in THGD 92.
2. As in Rashi: כי לא את בניכם אני מדבר עכשיו שיוכלו לומר....

his wonders." What you should know are the four ὅσα clauses of vv.3—6, whereas in the alternative interpretation it would be παιδείαν through v.6.[3]

The terms παιδείαν/מוסר designate the divine instruction given through the manifestation of divine power both in Egypt and on the desert journeys. גדלו is here translated literally by τὰ μεγαλεῖα αὐτοῦ. The noun with suffix only occurs four times in Deut. At 5:24 it is not translated. At 3:24 9:26 the noun occurs as גדלך; at 3:24 it is rendered by the doublet τὴν ἰσχύν σου καὶ τὴν δύναμίν σου, and at 9:26, by τῇ ἰσχύι σου τῇ μεγάλῃ. It would seem that τὰ μεγαλεῖα is used in the sense of "great acts of the display of power." This understanding is enhanced by its context "strong hand, high arm, signs and wonders." For τὴν χεῖρα—τὸν ὑψηλόν see comment at 3:23—24. Both χεῖρα and βραχίονα disregard the suffixes of their Hebrew counterparts, and hex supplies αυτου for both under the asterisk.

11:3 For σημεῖα and τέρατα see comment at 4:34. τέρατα, however, hardly translates MT which has מעשיו. *O* has corrected this to εργα.[4] LXX apparently was influenced by the common pair, which is indeed fully appropriate as a designation for the plagues; cf e.g. Exod:7:3,9 11:9,10.

The first of the ὅσα clauses refers to the plagues "within Egypt to Pharaoh king of Egypt and to all his land." The plagues are not mentioned as such. Note that each of the four clauses is introduced solely by ὅσα ἐποίησεν. The *d* text has changed ἐποίησεν to the imperfect εποιει. Oddly it also did so for the last clause (v.6), but not for the two intervening ones. The change is arbitrary and clearly secondary.

11:4 The second ὅσα ἐποίησεν concerned "the host of the Egyptians, their chariots and their cavalry." This is inflected in the accusative, rather than in the expected dative which would better reflect MT's ל phrases. In fact, the Byz text has changed τὴν δύναμιν to the dative. That this is a secondary reading, however, is clear from the fact that the elaborations τὰ ἅρματα ... τὴν ἵππον are left in the accusative. The accusatives can be understood as pendant in anticipation of the αὐτούς later in the verse; i.e. they are accusatives of specification referring to the realms wherein "he acted." These two nominals

3. This is the interpretation of Dogniez-Harl 186 ad 11,2—6.
4. Which is based on Sym's ἔργα. Aq reads ποιήματα, while Theod retains LXX.

have transposed סוסיו and רכבו, and hex has corrected the word order to agree with MT. *τῶν Αἰγυπτίων* interprets מצרים "Egypt" as its people, which is a legitimate interpretation of the consonantal text. Meanwhile *ἐποίησεν* is explicated by the *ὡς* structure, which consists of two clauses, separated by a genitive absolute construction. The reference is to the Red Sea episode of Exod 14—15.

The first *ὡς* clause is ambiguous; is *ἐπέκλυσεν* to be understood intransitively, in which case the subject is *τὸ ὕδωρ*, or is it to be taken as a transitive with the Lord your God as its subject? Contextually it should be the latter, since *ὅσα ἐποίησεν* throughout reflects God's actions, and so this must mean "how he made the water of the Red Sea flow (note the Hi of הציף) over them." ים סוף is translated by *τῆς θαλάσσης τῆς ἐρυθρᾶς*;[5] cf also 1:40 2:1. The *αὐτῶν* refers to the three accusatives earlier in the verse, "host, chariots and cavalry," the pendant structure noted above. The clause is followed by a genitive absolute, "as they were pursuing *ἐκ τῶν ὀπίσω ὑμῶν*." This is the only case of אחרי being translated in this way in Deut. Naturally one would expect simply *ὀπίσω*, as e.g. at 19:6. What the *ἐκ τῶν* brings to the fore is the expressed intention, not just of chasing after, but of chasing after and catching, whereas at 19:6 it is the *καταλάβῃ* that adds that further dimension. It should be noted that articulation of an *ὀπίσω* phrase does occur at 24:20,21; comp similarly articulated *πρός* phrases at 1:36 9:7,24 31:27.

The second clause governed by *ὡς* puts it bluntly: "and the Lord destroyed them (utterly) up to the present day." Such an "up to" phrase might seem inappropriate after an aorist verb, but it imitates Hebrew usage in which a temporal עד phrase is often found in such contexts; such may not seem strictly logical, but all that is meant is that the effects (i.e. they are dead!) continue until the present day.

In the tradition *ἐπέκλυσεν* was easily misread as *επεκαλυψεν* by O' or as *εκαλυψεν* by *s*, which in turn led to *επεκαλυφθη* in *b*. In fact, the verb was even misread as *επεκαυσε* by one ms and as *ενεκαυσεν* by another, which must really have baffled their readers! The (*ἐπὶ*) *προσώπου* was popularly changed to the accusative, but all the old uncial texts support LXX; either case would be sensible. And *κύριος* has been glossed by a popular A F M V text

5. The reading is supported by Sym, but Theod and Aq remove the articles to correspond more closely to MT.

with *ο θεος*, but the majority B text supports LXX, which also equals MT, and must be original. היום הזה is rendered idiomatically by *τῆς σήμερον ἡμέρας* in LXX, but this did not satisfy Origen; hex accommodated to MT by its reordering to *της ημερας της σημερον*.

11:5 The third *ὅσα ἐποίησεν* deals with the events of the desert journey. It is put in general terms as "to you in the desert," modified by a *ἕως* structure, which in MT consists of a double עד structure, viz. עד באכם, in turn modified by עד המקום הזה. LXX wisely translated the second one by a prepositional phrase *εἰς τὸν τόπον τοῦτον*. thus "until you came to this place." The V *C''* *s*+ text changed the Classical *ἤλθετε* to the Hellenistic *ηλθατε* which Deut, however, did not use.

11:6 The fourth *ὅσα ἐποίησεν* concerns the single episode recorded in Num 16 concerning Dathan and Abiron. For Ἀβιρών with *nu* rather than *mu* for אבירם see Num 16. In the tradition only three mss change to -*ρωμ*. The majority F M V text has also repeated the dative article before the name, but Deuteronomic usage tends not to repeat the article in a list of names; i.e. the articulation of the first name establishes the case for any subsequent name as well. Also in the tradition Ἐλιάβ is spelled *ελιαμ* in most *C''* mss, but this is due to the similarity of cursive *β* and *μ* in tenth to twelfth century scripts.

The pattern *οὕς* ... *αὐτούς* is a Hebraism; good Greek would omit the *αὐτούς*, which, however, no scribe dared to do. The figure of the earth opening its mouth simply renders the Hebrew; the figure is engendered by the notion of יבלע/*κατέπιεν* "swallow." For what was included along with the two men see also Num 16:32, which lists "their houses and all the men who were with Kore and their cattle." The difference between *οἴκους* and *σκηνάς* is that of households and dwellings, whereas *τὴν ὑπόστασιν* here refers to substance, thus possessions. This is described as *τὴν μετ' αὐτῶν*, so "and all their substance which was with them." MT describes יקום as that אשר ברגליהם "which followed them, which was in their train"; this means that יקום may well refer to people who sided with the rebels; note the reference in the Num account to "the men who were with Kore." LXX, however, refers to goods, possessions, which Num identifies as *τὰ κτήνη αὐτῶν*.

11:7 The ὅτι clause gives the reason for γνώσεσθε of v.2 with which this section began, i.e. you shall know because you were experiencing all these things. The Hebrew clause is nominal, though the participial predicate is usually articulated, i.e. "your eyes were the ones seeing"; LXX disregarded the articulation, and simply used an imperfect verb, *ἑώρων*.

What your eyes were seeing was "all the great works of the Lord which he did for you *σήμερον*." MT is shorter here, simply having אשר עשה, and accordingly hex placed *ὑμῖν σήμερον* under the obelus to show its absence from the Hebrew. One might have expected a different timer such as "these past years," but *σήμερον* intends the *ἐποίησεν* to be understood as that which he has now effected. It would then appear that LXX is making an important exegetical point; the Lord's great deeds, though effected in the past, constitute a present, i.e. a permanent, reality.

11:8 Vv.8—9 constitute an amalgam of typical Deuteronomic expressions. For *φυλάξεσθε πάσας τὰς ἐντολὰς αὐτοῦ* see comments at 4:2,40. MT has no counterpart for *αὐτοῦ*, and so hex has placed it under the obelus. The addition of the pronoun makes clear the ultimate source of the commandments; it is not Moses the speaker, but the Lord. For "which I am commanding you today" see comment at 4:2. That this is a common pattern is clear from the fact that in spite of the plural context of the verse it uses *σοι*. The majority A F M V text levels this to its context by its *υμιν*. The *ἵνα ζῆτε* has as counterpart in MT למען תחזקו "that you may be strong,"[6] but *ζῆτε* is ex par.[7] In fact, it is quite clear that the entire *ἵνα* clause with its four verbs was not a translation of MT at all, but was simply taken over word for word from 8:1. This is especially clear from the second clause, *καὶ πολυπλασιασθῆτε*, which has no equivalent in MT here at all, but does have at 8:1. For the tandem verbs "enter and possess" see comment at 1:8. *ὑμεῖς*—fin represents a common formulaic pattern in Deut.[8] MT does not witness to *τὸν Ἰορδάνην* which is ex par (see 9:1 11:31 30:18 31:13); hex has placed the phrase under the obelus.

---

6. Aq and Sym translate the verb correctly as *ἰσχύσητε*.
7. See list 27 in THGD 94.
8. See list 1 in THGD 86—87.

11:9 The verse begins with a conjunction in MT, but not in LXX; a *και* has been supplied by the Byz text, however, which probably betrays recensional activity. For *ἵνα μακροημερεύσητε ἐπὶ τῆς γῆς* see comment at 4:40. For the relative clause see comment at 1:8. Unusual in the clause is the addition *καὶ τῷ σπέρματι ὑμῶν*; in fact, only 1:8 has the same pattern. Over against MT the Greek adds the prepositional phrase, *μετ' αὐτούς*, as at 1:8, and hex has accordingly put it under the obelus (see also 4:37 10:15). For *ῥέουσαν γάλα καὶ μέλι* see comment at 6:3.

11:10 This verse begins a new section extolling the glories of Canaan; it extends through v.12. The Hebrew clause pattern is nominal with הארץ as subject and the predicate as לא כארץ מצרים הוא, with the predicate in turn consisting of a nominal clause, of which הוא is the subject—thus "the land ... is not like the land of Egypt." LXX patterns differently: *ἔστιν γὰρ ἡ γῆ ... οὐχ ὥσπερ ἡ γῆ Αἰγύπτου ἐστίν*; it treats the Hebrew preposition as an adverb by its double use of the linking verb. For the relative *εἰς ἣν* clause see comment at 1:8. Both *εἰς ἣν ... ἐκεῖ* and *ὅθεν ... ἐκεῖθεν* are Hebraic syntactic patterns. All second person references in the verse are plural in LXX, whereas MT in v.10a has the singular in the first אשר clause: אתה בא, but then it reads יצאתם in the second אשר clause.

MT then changes to the second singular in v.10b (i.e. with the last אשר clause), making the reference collectively to the Israelites: "(in) which (which LXX simplifies by its *ὅταν*) you sowed your seed, and you watered (it) with your foot ("feet" in Sam) like a garden of herbage." This is a reminder of the hard agricultural work which the Israelites performed as slaves in Egypt. LXX postpones the change to the second singular to the next verse, and changes the verbs to third person plural for the entire *ὅταν* clause, and makes "your foot" the plural "feet," disregarding the suffix; the reference is thus entirely to the Egyptians themselves. The change is clearly intentional on the part of the translator. After all, reminding the Alexandrian Jews of their work as agricultural slaves in ancient times was not necessary, and in contemporary Egypt the Egyptians had to work their own land. Hex has added *σου* under the asterisk after both *σπόρον* and *ποσίν* to equal the pronominal suffixes in MT.

The notion of *ποτίζωσιν τοῖς ποσίν* remains puzzling in spite of various suggestions as to its meaning. That the dative is intended as instrumental seems to be clear,[9] and in an Egyptian context, where the Nile is the lifeline for farmers, it must be a reference to some ancient form of irrigation. Dogniez-Harl suggest that it refers to the shādūf,[10] which puzzles me since I know of no particular involvement of the feet in connection with it. Other suggestions are made by Driver, such as possibly a small watering machine turned by the foot, or the use of the foot for regulating the flow of water in the canals or for the purpose of opening and closing the sluices.[11] The fact is that one can only speculate on what practice this refers to. One possibility which has never been suggested to the best of my knowledge is that the dative is really a locative, i.e. "watered at the feet." Watering at foot level then contrasts with "the rain from the sky," which characterized Canaan according to the next verse. One thing seems certain; it was in some way related to the irrigation system.[12] The word *κῆπον* "garden" occurs only here in the Pentateuch. גן was more commonly rendered by *παράδεισος*, especially in Gen.

11:11 Since v.11 contrasts with v.10, LXX begins with a *δέ* construction. The *d* text makes this contrast even more obvious by changing *ἡ δέ* to *αλλ η*. For the *εἰς ἥν* clause see comment at 4:22.[13] MT has interpreted the second singular of vv.10—12 by using the plural, but LXX remains consistently singular. For אתם עברים LXX has *εἰσπορεύῃ*. The *O* Byz text not only has the plural, but hex has also rendered the pronoun under the asterisk as *υμεις*.

This land is then described in LXX as *ὀρεινὴ καὶ πεδινή* "hilly and level" rather than MT's "land of hills and valleys." *πεδινή* probably made more sense to an Alexandrian than the Hebrew בקעת, though a בקעה could refer to a plain area between hilly ridges as the term *biqʿa* still does in Arabic-speaking lands today. And even more of a contrast to Egypt is *ἐκ τοῦ ὑετοῦ τοῦ οὐρανοῦ πίεται ὕδωρ* "from the rain of the sky one can drink water."

9. See SS 121.
10. P.188 "allusion a une méthode d'irrigation très ancienne, san doute au moyen du *shaduf*.
11. P.129; see also Lee 121—122.
12. Sym translated the אשר clause by *ὅπου σπείρας τὸν σπόρον σου ποτίζεις τοῖς ποσί σου ὥσεὶ κῆπον λαχάνων*.
13. For והארץ אשר אתם עברים שמה Aq has *καὶ ἡ γῆ ἣν διέρχεσθε ἐκεῖσε*, whereas Theod reads *καὶ ἡ γῆ ἣν ὑμεῖς διαβαίνετε ἐκεῖ*. Sym renders the clause by *ἡ δὲ γῆ ἣν διαβαίνεις (κληρονομῆσαι αὐτήν)*, i.e. Sym does not render שמה separately.

11:12 A further elaboration of "the land" described in v.11: "a land which the Lord your God *ἐπισκοπεῖται* it." The verb means "to have watch over, to care for," and translates the participle דרש "seek after," so care for;[14] in other words, Yahweh looks after the land; it is something special.

This is elucidated by the rest of the verse: "always the eyes of the Lord your God are on it." *διὰ παντός* stands for תמיד "continually,"[15] The Masoretes have cut the verse at *αὐτήν*, and the critical text is punctuated in the same way, but *διά παντός* could just as well be taken with what precedes, in which case the comma would have to be moved after the phrase. In view of the tradition which preposes תמיד in emphatic position I would take the Greek in the same way.

The statement is modified by "from the beginning of the year to the end of the year." In MT the second "the year" is unarticulated in BHS and this oddity may represent a double tradition, one in which both are articulated and another in which both are unarticulated. It may be noted that Sam represents the former.[16]

11:13 For והיה plus אם see comment at 6:10. MT has vv.13—14a in the plural, whereas LXX has the singular throughout except for the first verb *ἀκούσητε*. A popular B variant has the compound *εισακουσητε*, but there is little leverage to help in determining which is original, except that the simplex is the more common in Deut for the Qal of שמע, occurring 54 times as opposed to 28 times for the compound. Lexically either one is adequate. Nor does its modification by *ἀκοῇ* seem to make much difference. This occurs six times in Deut, but each time a substantial variant obtains, except at 11:22 where the variant *εισακουσητε* is only weakly supported by *C*'' *s*+, but there MT has שמר תשמרו. In all others A and B contrast, and the variant is always substantially supported.[17]

LXX has *πάσας* modifying "his commandments" over against MT, but *πάσας τὰς ἐντολάς* often occurs (15 times) in the book including vv.8,22, and it is simply ex par. LXX has Moses speaking here, and refers to the

---

14. Theod and Aq have the literal *ἐκζητεῖ*.
15. Aq has *ἐνδελεχῶς*.
16. Many Hebrew mss level the text either with both as שנה or as השנה.
17. See THGD 143 for a discussion of this text.

ἐντολάς as αὐτοῦ (God's), but MT reads מצותי as though God is speaking, which is inconsistent, since v.13b speaks of Yahweh God in third person. LXX has removed the inconsistency by leveling the text as third person throughout. For the ὅσας clause see comment at 4:2. The *C*'' *s*+ text has the plural pronoun υμιν which incidentally equals MT.[18]

These commandments are shown by two infinitives: "to love the Lord your God and to serve him with your whole heart and person," for which see comments at 10:12.

11:14 Vv.14—15 constitute the apodosis for v.13; MT continues with God speaking with ונתתי, but LXX follows Sam's ונתן; cf comment at v.13.[19] The bound phrase מטר ארצכם is realized in LXX by ὑετὸν τῇ γῇ σου, which makes good sense, since the rain is for the ground, not of the ground.[20] A popular A variant does witness to τῆς γῆς, however, whereas *b* has επι της γης. It should also be noted that the *O* text reads υμων for σου; this could be a hex correction based on The Three. καθ' ὥραν renders בעתו by a fine idiomatic phrase meaning "on time."[21] In the tradition a popular Byz reading has κατα καιρον. The two terms πρόιμον καὶ ὄψιμον are adjectival nouns in apposition with ὑετόν, and refer to the early and the latter rains resp., i.e. the autumn rains or the יורה, and the gentler spring rains, the מלקוש.

The second clause shows the result of God's provisions: you will bring in your agricultural produce. With אספת MT reverts to the second singular, which is continued through v.15. The verb really means "you shall gather," rather than εἰσοίσεις "you shall bring in."[22] For the agricultural produce see comment at 7:13.

11:15 For δώσει see comment at v.14. An A F M majority text has changed the verb to second person, which changes the sense entirely; it then becomes an order for the Israelites to provide fodder in the fields for the cattle. This

18. The Others all read ὑμῖν.
19. Theod and Sym both witness to δώσω.
20. Only Sym has the genitive τῆς γῆς ὑμῶν; Theod has the articulated dative τῇ γῇ ὑμῶν, but Aq omits the article. All three "correct" the singular pronoun to ὑμῶν, as expected.
21. Aq naturally renders בעת by ἐν καιρῷ; The Others have κατὰ καιρόν.
22. The Others have συνάξεις.

presupposes a different kind of agricultural situation, one in which the drought-ravaged fields are so barren that the farmer must supplement fodder to feed the cattle. But the context demands a reference to God's providential care of the Israelites' cattle, and the variant must be a mistake. *χορτάσματα* "fodder" is unique as a translation for עשב which is most commonly rendered by *χόρτος*.[23]

11:16 MT changed to the singular briefly with v.15b: "and you shall eat and be sated," again reverting to the plural with v.15. It is thus an aside. LXX rendered this by singular participles subordinated to *πρόσεχε* of v.16. In MT this is a plural השמרו, but LXX does not change to the plural until v.16b (with *παραβῆτε*), and so it has added the participles to v.16. What LXX says is "While you are eating and being filled, watch yourself lest your heart be dilated (i.e. puffed up)."[24] This constitutes a contextual interpretation for יפתה "be enticed, naively fooled." The translator took the word in a moral sense, in which prosperity beguiled the Israelite into a sense of arrogance.

LXX makes the transition to the plural with *παραβῆτε*, (after the singular *ἡ καρδία σου*). This transition is judiciously made here, by which the two plural verbs explicate how the puffed up heart expresses itself. Such a heart on Israel's part means that the people of Israel turn away from the Lord and serve idols. LXX then retains the plural throughout the rest of the chapter except for v.29. MT also has v.29 in the singular, as well as vv.19b,20 which LXX levelled to the singular. The verb *παραβῆτε* also occurs at 9:12,16 17:20 28:14, always from God's ways or demands. The root סור is also often rendered by *ἐκκλίνω* with roughly the same sense, though it has a more concrete sense of inclining from a path (see 2:27 5:32 17:11 31:29). For *λατρεύσητε ... προσκυνήσητε* see 8:19. The two terms are closely related, but the former refers to engaging in cultic service, whereas the latter means bowing down in obeissance, i.e. worshipping.

11:17 The rendering of חרה אף by *θυμωθεὶς ὀργισθῇ* is unique in the book. Elsewhere (6:15 7:4 29:27 31:17) the noun is always rendered by *θυμῷ* and

23. Aq renders by *χλόην*.
24. Instead of *πλατυνθῇ* Theod and Aq have *θελχθῇ* "be charmed, beguiled," and *ἀπατηθῇ* "be deceived" was read by Sym. The Aq reading is retroverted from Syh.

the verb by ὀργίζω. The B F *ol*+ text reads θυμωθεις οργη, a participle plus a dative noun, but this can hardly be taken seriously for the critical text.[25]

The display of divine anger will have immediate consequences. The Lord will confine, restrict, hold back the sky, and there will be no rainfall of which v.14 had spoken. This means crop failure, i.e. "the earth will not yield its fruit." Unfortunately, LXX does not distinguish between אדמה "ground" and ארץ "earth," translating both by γῆ; here it is אדמה which is meant. In the next clause γῆς recurs, but there it is for ארץ; what is meant there is "you will quickly perish from the good land (i.e. Canaan)." This is defined by a relative clause ἧς ἔδωκεν κύριος ὑμῖν. The Masoretes vocalized נתן as a participle, but LXX understood it as a past tense; the participle would have required a present tense, διδωσιν. Incidentally a B F M *C'' f s*+ variant has wrongly articulated κύριος. This is completely contrary to LXX usage, not only for Deut, but for the Pentaeuch as a whole wherever κύριος stands for יהוה.

11:18 Vv.18—20 reflect 6:6—9. In v.18a the verb is the active ἐμβαλεῖτε, rather than the linking verb ἔσται of 6:6, and the prepositional phrase is εἰς plus an accusative, rather than the locative ἐν plus the dative. That LXX was influenced by 6:6 is clear from its failure to render the suffix of דברי; accordingly hex has added μου under the asterisk after ῥήματα.

The second clause is a copy of 6:8 except that it uses the second plural throughout instead of the singular. See comments ad loc.[26] The tradition shows popular support for the A B F M V reading ασαλευτον, which in spite of its impressive support must be secondary.[27]

11:19 Comp 6:7. V.19a is, however, considerably different from 6:7. It reads καὶ διδάξετε τὰ τέκνα ὑμῶν λαλεῖν αὐτά "you must teach your children to speak (i.e. recite) them." This differs from MT, in which the verb is doubly modified, both by אותם and את בניכם, i.e. you shall teach them to your children. This in turn means that the infinitive which follows is not com-

25. See THGD 133.
26. For ἀφάψετε Aq has συνδήσετε "to tie together." The last clause is also differently rendered by Aq and Sym. Aq has ἔσονται εἰς νακτὰ μετάξυ ὀφθαλμῶν ὑμῶν, and Sym translated by καὶ ἔσονται διεσταλμένοι μετάξυ τῶν ὀφθαλμῶν; see f.n. at 6:8.
27. See THGD 136.

plementary, but defines the verb in adverbial fashion, thus "by speaking about them." Hex has tried to "correct" the text by inserting *αυτα* after the verb under the asterisk. But the shorter text is best understood as intentional. What the children are taught is to recite the words, i.e. by repetition, which is precisely how children were taught in the East from time immemorial.

The accusatives of specification that follow find their exact counterpart in the nominative singulars of 6:7b; see comments ad loc.[28] Hex has tried to correct the participles by omitting the final *sigma* in each case and adding *σου* under the asterisk, thereby equalling MT.

11:20 This is an exact copy of 6:9, for which see comments ad loc.[29]

11:21 For ירבו ימיכם LXX has provided an excellent free rendering by choosing a second person plural verb, *πολυημερεύσητε*, "you may experience many days,[30] with an anacoluthon adding a coordinate reference *καὶ αἱ ἡμέραι τῶν υἱῶν ὑμῶν*. For the relative clause which follows see comment at 1:8. The *καθώς* structure compares the promise made to the days of sky over the earth, i.e. as long as the heavens remain above the earth may your days continue. Note how the *καθώς* is syntactically coordinated with the anacoluthon.

11:22 MT begins with כי, but LXX, with *καὶ ἔσται* which would presuppose והיה; cf comment at 6:10.[31] The protasis in MT contains the verbal structure שמר תשמרון, but LXX has *ἀκοῇ ἀκούσητε*, which would presuppose the root שמע for which see v.13.[32] LXX has levelled with that verse. Both are modified by *πάσας τὰς ἐντολάς*, though here modified by *ταύτας* rather than

28. The Three translate *καθημένου ἐν οἴκῳ σου καὶ πορευομένου ἐν ὁδῷ καὶ κοιταζομένου καὶ διανισταμένου*. That there is something wrong with this tradition is obvious as the reading of The Others at 6:7 shows. I suspect that Theod and Aq at least reflected the grammatical patterns of MT more or less as at 6:7. It is possible that Sym may be the real source of the genitive participial tradition, but then at least with some antecedent such as (*τέκνα*) *σου*. See also SS Inf 91 for the participial renderings of infinitives.
29. For מזוזות which LXX renders by *φλιάς* Aq has *σταθμούς*.
30. See the discussion of this passage in SS 30.
31. Instead of *καὶ ἔσται ἐάν* Theod and Aq have *ὅτι ἐάν*, and Sym has *ἐὰν γάρ*.
32. Theod and Aq have the literal *φυλάσσοντες φυλάξητε*, but Sym has *διατελέσητε φυλάσσοντες*.

αὐτοῦ in spite of the singular כל המצוה הזאת.[33] For the *ὅσας* structure see comment at 1:8; either Sam or the parallel v.13 must be the source for the *σήμερον* which has no equivalent in MT; hex has correctly placed it under the obelus. MT ends the structure with לרשתה, but LXX disregarded the suffix, which hex made up for with *αυτας* under the asterisk. Hex also has added a genitive article to the following infinitive under the same asterisk to represent the marker of לאהבה. The B+ variant *σοι* for *ὑμῖν* can in this plural context only be judged to be a thoughtless error.[34]

The three infinitives constitute "all these commandments," viz. "to love, to walk, and to cleave to." For the first one see comments at 6:5. The B *C'' b s*+ text added *και* before the second one, i.e. constituting an a+b+c pattern rather than the a b+c pattern of LXX. Since LXX agrees with MT, the variant is probably secondary,[35] though Pesh and Vulg also support the conjunction. For the second infinitive see comment at 10:12. The last infinitive is an unusual one in that the verb occurs in Deut only three times, but only here in the sense of cleaving to God; for use in a pejorative sense see 13:17 28:21.

11:23 The use of *ἐκβαλεῖ* to translate הוריש is unusual, though see also Exod 34:24 Num 21:32, but הוריש can mean either "make to inherit" or "to disinherit." With *κύριος* as subject, and modified by *ἀπὸ προσώπου ὑμῶν*, the verb *ἐκβάλλω* is more suitable than the usual *κληρονομέω* used in the second clause.

In the second clause *κληρονομήσετε* shows the difference between the Hi of ירש rendered by *ἐκβαλεῖ* and the Qal meaning "to possess (or dispossess)." The nations to be dispossessed are described as *μεγάλα καὶ ἰσχυρότερα μᾶλλον ἢ ὑμεῖς*. For exactly the same pattern see 9:1 and the comment ad loc.[36] The B *ol*+ misreading of *ἰσχυρότερα* as *ισχυρα* is a textbook case of parablepsis where the copyist's eye jumped from the first to the second *rho*.

11:24 The figure represented by the *οὗ* clause renders the Hebrew one correctly; MT has אשר תדרך כף רגלים בו but LXX omits בו as otiose; of course

33. Sym attests to the singular *πᾶσαν τὴν ἐντολήν*.
34. See THGD 111.
35. See THGD 131.
36. See SS 150.

hex has added *εν αυτω* under the asterisk. The text is much better without this Hebraism.

The definition of the boundaries are ideal ones. For 'Αντιλεβάνου and the great river, the river Euphrates, see comments at 1:7. The adjective *τοῦ μεγάλου* has no equivalent in MT, and is probably taken from 1:7. The opposite border is *τῆς θαλάσσης τῆς ἐπὶ δυσμῶν*, a roundabout way of saying "the Sea towards the west," i.e. the Mediterranean. The Hebrew simply says (עד) הים האחרון as at 34:2, which LXX renders by *τῆς θαλάσσης τῆς ἐσχάτης*; "the sea of the rear" would contrast with הים הקדמני as at Zach 14:8 Jl 2:20.[37]

11:25 The verb *ἀντιστήσεται* plus *κατά* means "to stand up against, oppose." God promises Israel that it will be invincible. *τρόμον* and *φόβον* are preposed in imitation of MT, thereby placing the stress on these nouns. The two are transposed in a majority A F M V reading, which more closely equals MT's פחד followed by מורא, and the reading is probably a hex (or prehexaplaric) correction. It is the Lord your God who will place this trembling and fear of Israel *ἐπὶ πρόσωπον* of all the land.[38] The majority text follows The Three in reading the genitive; it is impossible to be certain as to which is original, in which case one adopts the reading of the oldest witness, Cod B. Usage also tells us nothing; *ἐπὶ πρόσωπον* occurs only twice, and *ἐπὶ προσώπου*, four times. I suspect that the *προσωπου* text is here secondary, being influenced by v.4 where *ἐπὶ προσώπου* does occur.

γῆς is modified by a relative clause which starts out well with *ἐφ' ἧς*, but then ends with the phrase *ἐπ' αὐτῆς*, a Hebraism imitating אשר plus בה. *ὃν τρόπον* represents a favorite construction in Deut for rendering כאשר.[39] LXX specifies the subject *κύριος* for *ἐλάλησεν*, which hex has placed under the obelus since it has no counterpart in MT. It is hardly necessary since *κύριος ὁ θεὸς ὑμῶν* already occurs as subject of *ἐπιθήσει* in the main clause.

11:26 Vv.26—32 constitute a nice bridge between the paraenesis of chh.1—11:25 and thc Law Code of Chh.12—26. They constitute the alternatives facing Israel: the blessing if they are obedient, or the curse if they disobey.

37. For *ἐπὶ δυσμῶν* The Others have *ἐσχάτης*
38. The Three have *προσώπου*.
39. See list 9 in THGD 88.

This is stated bluntly in v.26. Moses is speaking: *ἰδοὺ ἐγὼ δίδωμι ἐνώπιον ὑμῶν σήμερον εὐλογίαν καὶ κατάραν*. The opening word represents not the usual הנה but ראה, which it translates literally. ראה occurs rather than הנה seven times (also at 1:8,21 2:24,31 4:5 30:15), but only at 2:24,31 and 30:15 is it also rendered by *ἰδού*. In the other three cases the plural *ἴδετε* obtains, but in two of these (1:8 4:5) LXX represents the ראו of Sam. The use of *δίδωμι* (for the participle נתן) shows how the meaning of נתן in the sense of "put or place" (as well as the usual "give") has been taken over by the Greek word for "give." Here *δίδωμι* means "I am setting, placing." To set before you means to present you with the alternatives. These are then explained in vv.27 and 28 resp.

In the tradition the majority A F M V text reads the plural nouns, *ευλογιας* and *καταρας*, rather than the singular both here and in vv.27 and 28, but it is the phenomenon of blessing and curse which is intended, not the particular blessings and curses of chh.27 and 28 at the end of the law code; the majority readings are secondary.

11:27—28 *τὴν εὐλογίαν* recapitulates the first choice. The blessing which had been explicated in the promises of vv.8—15 is conditional on *ἀκούσητε τὰς ἐντολάς* of the Lord your God. To "hear" the Lord's commandments means of course to obey them. For the *ὅσας* clauses see comment at 4:2. Instead of *ὅσας* 1° B *s*+ read *ας*; for *ὅσας* 2° B+ read *οσα*, but *ὅσας* is obviously original in both cases.[40]

The obverse is *τὴν κατάραν*. Again the word is in the singular, though the majority text for both words witness to the plural.[41] The singular not only equals MT; it is far more effective than the plural would be. The condition is the negative of the condition for the blessing, which exactly parallels it, even though MT does not, i.e. MT has אשר אנכי מצוה אתכם היום, not after "you hear the commandments of the Lord your God," but after הדרך in the next clause. Accordingly hex has placed the *ὅσας* clause under the obelus, since LXX does have *ἣν ἐνετειλάμην ὑμῖν* as a modifying clause for *τῆς ὁδοῦ*/הדרך. The actual situation is that LXX has transferred the *ὅσας* clause to parallel the

40. See THGD 106 for a discussion of the usage of relative adjectives versus simplex relative pronouns.
41. See THGD 136.

position in v.27, and then added the ᾗς clause to fill the void left by the transfer. The two clauses, however, differ in that the one modifying *ἐντολάς* is the usual one, with a present tense representing the participial predicate of the regular pattern,[42] but the second one modifying *ὁδοῦ* is in the aorist. Presumably the first one refers to the law code which follows in chh.12—26, whereas the aorist verb refers to the paraenetic materials of chh.5—11; cf 5:33 8:6 9:12,16 10:12 and 11:22.

The condition in v.28 is explicated by a clause detailing what not hearing the Lord's commandments actually consists of. It amounts to wandering away, straying from the way. LXX makes a moral judgement by translating סרתם by *πλανηθῆτε*. This way is described as one "which I commanded you." Hex has added *σημερον* to equal MT, but see the remarks above.

This straying/turning aside is defined in MT as ללכת אחרי אלהים אחרים "by going after other gods," but LXX makes this more explicit by its *πορευθέντες λατρεύειν θεοῖς ἑτέροις*;[43] i.e. going after other gods means engaging in their cultic service; it is idolatry. Furthermore, these "other gods" are not native to Israel; they are ones *οἷς οὐκ οἴδατε* "which you did not know." The *οἷς* is dative by attraction to the case of its antecedent *θεοῖς*.[44]

11:29 For *καὶ ἔσται* plus *ὅταν* see comment at 6:10. The verse changes to second singular, but in v.31 the text reverts to the plural in both MT and LXX. The *γῆν* is modified by an *εἰς ἥν* clause, in which LXX substitutes the verb *διαβαίνεις* for the participle בא, probably under the influence of the common lexeme "cross over to possess" (4:22,26 11:8 30:18 31:13 32:47); cf also v.31.

The apodosis is in imitation of MT introduced by *καί*. For the meaning of *δώσεις* see comment at v.26. For the performance of the ceremony of blessing and curse see 27:11—14. "Placing the blessing" refers to the blessings of 28:1—14, whereas placing the curse refers to the curses of 27:15—26.[45] The former were (recited?) on Mount Garizin and the latter on Mount Gaibal. The ceremony is also described in Jos 8:30—35 (=9:2a—f) as involving a sacrifice

42. As in list 30 in THGD 95.
43. See SS Inf 66,140.
44. The Three changed this to the grammatically correct accusative, *οὕς*.
45. Tar^{O} translates the words as ית מברכיא "those who bless" and ית מלטטיא "those who curse resp.

and a reading of the law. For the location of the two hills see Bible Dictionaries. In the tradition Γαριζίν is misspelled in various ways: as *γαρρ.* by dittography, with a final *mu* instead of *nu* in *O* as a recensional correction, as *ριζειν* or *ιδειν* by aphaeresis, as *-ζη* by apocopation, as *γαζιρ(ε)ιν* by transposition of consonants, and as *γαριτιν* by consonantal confusion. On the other hand, Γαιβάλ was quite stable in the tradition, only *γαβαλ*, *γαιγαλ* and *γεγαλ* being attested (i.e. outside of the itacistic *γεβαλ*).[46]

11:30 The sentence modifier *ἰδού* is not supported by MT, which simply has the negative question marker הלא. Here *πέραν τοῦ* Ἰορδάνου refers to Palestine, i.e. the speaker is understood to be east of the Jordan. The collocation is modified by *ὀπίσω*, thus "at some distance beyond the Jordan," as well as by the adverbial *ὁδὸν ἐπὶ δυσμῶν ἡλίου ἐν γῇ* Χαναάν "on the road toward (i.e. by way of) the sunset, (i.e. מבוא השמש, so again simply "westward") in the land of Canaan."[47] MT has מארץ הכנעני i.e. "in the land of the Canaanite."[48]

The structure *τὸ κατοικοῦν ἐπὶ δυσμῶν* "the area that lies to the west" has no specific antecedent, hence "the area." This misinterprets MT, in which הישב בערבה refers to הכנעני, i.e. "(the Canaanite) who dwells on the plain," a reference to the plain area which the two hills overlook. LXX has taken ערבה as derived from the root ערב meaning "to go in," hence of the sun "to set," i.e. the west, but the ערבה is based on another root ערב, and means "steppe, plateau."[49] The translator was probably misled by the context in which *ὁδὸν δυσμῶν ἡλίου* had just been mentioned.

The area is more precisely located as *ἐχόμενον τοῦ* Γολγόλ and *πλησίον τῆς δρυὸς τῆς ὑψηλῆς*. To copyists the name Γολγόλ meant nothing, and it suffered greatly at their hands as the following list (disregarding homophonous spellings) shows: *γολγων*, *γολγοδ*, *γολγω*, *γογγολ*, *γοδγοδ*, *χολγοδ*, *σολγολ*, as well as the hex correction *γαλγαλ*. The location of a Gilgal/Γολγόλ in the vicinity of Shechem remains baffling, since no such a place

46. Aq transcribed as Ἡβάλ; this represents a pronunciation considerably later than LXX in which the *ʿayin* grapheme had represented the two phonemes /ġ/ and /ʿ/; by the time of Aq only the /ʿ/ realization remained.
47. Aq translated מבוא by *εἰσόδου*.
48. The Others read *τῶν* Χαναναίων (retroverted from Syh).
49. Aq read *ἐν ὁμαλεῖ* (retroverted from Syh).

is known. Nor is the geographical description "near the high oak" at all helpful. The translator was probably baffled by the Hebrew אצל אלוני מרה "besides the oaks(?) of Moreh." The term also occurs in the singular at Gen 12:6, where it is also translated by "the high oak," and LXX may well be based on that passage. Apparently the translator(s), not recognizing the place name Moreh, tried to make sense out of the name by transposing it as רמה, hence ὑψηλῆς.[50]

11:31 Vv.31 and 32 change to second person plural again. The reason why Moses has given these instructions: "because you are going to cross the Jordan, going in to possess the land." MT has לבא as a purposive infinitive modifying the participle עברים, but LXX uses an attributive participle modifying ὑμεῖς.[51] The *b* text has changed the participle to *εισελθειν*, which equals MT exactly. Of course "entering to possess the land" is the whole point of crossing the Jordan.

The land is described by a relative clause, for which see comment at 1:20. Over against MT LXX has added ἐν κλήρῳ πάσας τὰς ἡμέρας, which was taken over from 12:1, where it represents לרשתה כל הימים. Hex has placed it under the obelus to show its absence in MT.

V.31b is in the future, consisting of two clauses which simply reaffirm that Israel will possess the land and inhabit it.

11:32 The concluding advice to be careful to carry out the divine precepts and judgements also serves as an introduction to the laws which begin with chapter 12. That ποιεῖν should not be articulated in spite of strong majority support for *του* is consonant with the prejudice against articulated infinitives shown by the Deuteronomic translator.[52] Both nouns, προστάγματα and κρίσεις, are modified by demonstratives, (ταῦτα and ταύτας resp.), for which MT has no counterpart, and hex shows this by placing them under the obelus. This makes their change to *αυτου*, in both cases by majority texts, obviously secondary.[53]

---

50. Aq made it into αὐλῶνος καταφανοῦς. Presumably מרה was understood as related to מראה(?), hence something clearly visible, conspicuous. As for αὐλῶνος he took אלוני as a Greek word, transcribing it as αὐλῶν and then Hellenizing it. And so the "oaks of Moreh" became "a conspicuous glen"!
51. See SS Inf 59.
52. See the discussion in THGD 102—103, and cf also *ibid* 59.
53. See THGD 58.

The relative clause is a nominal one in MT: אנכי נתן, which LXX renders in its usual fashion by *ἐγὼ δίδωμι*. For the meaning of *δίδωμι* see comment at v.26.[54]

---

54. For *ὅσας* rather than the majority reading *ας* see THGD 106.

Chapter 12

12:1 LXX begins the Law Code with *καί* over against MT. חקים is here (and at 11:32) rendered by *προστάγματα*. The three common terms for "laws" in MT are חקים/חקת, משפטים and מצות, and they are rather consistently translated in LXX. E.g. חקים occurs 21 times in the book, and is translated 18 times by *δικαιώματα*, and once by *ἐντολαί*. The Law Code as a whole is called *τὰ προστάγματα καὶ αἱ κρίσεις*, i.e. חקים והמשפטים. משפטים as a plural designation for the laws occurs 20 times in Deut; 10 times it is rendered by *κρίματα*, six by *κρίσεις*, twice by *δικαιώματα*, once by *ἐντολαί*, and one case, 26:17, ומצותיו ומשפטיו is rendered by *καὶ τὰ κρίματα αὐτοῦ*. The singular, which is irrelevant here since it refers to individual regulations, occurs 17 times, 14 of which become *κρίσις*, two *κρίμα*, and one, 21:17, is freely rendered. The majority A F M V text has *τα κριματα α* instead of *αἱ κρίσεις ἅς*, which as the usage pattern shows is almost certainly secondary.

The overall instruction concerning these precepts and judgements is given in a relative clause, *φυλάξεσθε ποιεῖν* "you must be careful to perform." The verb *φυλάσσω* generally appears in its middle form in Deut, but about one in four cases is in the active; in fact, two mss, B and V, have the secondary active here as well,[1] but there seems to be little discernible distinction between the two lexically. A popular A F M V text reads *του ποιησαι*, whereas B *z*+ have *του ποιειν*. Articulation of infinitives is on the whole avoided by the translator, which makes *ποιεῖν* almost certainly original text. For the *ἧς* clause see comment at 1:20. The word order of the clause has the order: S-P, whereas MT has the predicate before the subject. The order: S-P is formulaic in character. Hex has reordered the text by transposing the verb after the subject to equal MT. Oddly enough the MT counterpart is given in the singular second person, whereas LXX, followed by Pesh but not by Vulg, has the plural consistently throughout the verse. LXX also uses the present tense *δίδωσιν* in the clause, though the Masoretes have vocalized נתן as a past tense. Within this formulaic clause the present tense occurs 29 times, and *ἔδωκεν*, only six times in the book. The phrase *ἐν κλήρῳ* (for לרשתה) is a set phrase, which occurs 17 times in the book.[2]

1. See THGD 142.
2. See list 56 in THGD 99, and comp SS Inf 56.

12:2 The use of the cognate free infinitive with the root אבד occurs only here with Israel as the actor in destruction; its rendering by *ἀπωλείᾳ ἀπολεῖτε* otherwise refers to Israel suffering such a fate should they be disobedient to the laws imposed; see 4:26 8:19 30:18. What is to be destroyed are the heathen cultic places, places defined as *ἐν οἷς ἐλάτρευσαν ἐκεῖ τὰ ἔθνη τοῖς θεοῖς αὐτῶν*. Note that the text does not follow the Classical realization of the neuter plural as a collective, and so requiring a singular verb as predicate. The Greek follows the Hebrew in using a plural verb. The usage *ἐν οἷς ... ἐκεῖ* is a Hebraism for אשר ... שם as is the *οὕς ... αὐτούς* for אשר ... אתם in the next relative clause. Note too that LXX has transposed *τοῖς θεοῖς αὐτῶν* to its more logical place in the first relative clause. Hex has transposed the phrase after *αὐτούς* to equal MT. In the second relative clause the present tense *κληρονομεῖτε* (for the participle ירשים) is to be understood as incipient, i.e. "about to dispossess." The A F M V majority text has the compound *κατακληρονομειτε*, but Deut prefers the simplex for rendering the Qal of ירש; in fact, this is used 46 times, whereas the compound, which is a synonym, occurs only nine times.[3] The phrase *ἐπὶ τῶν ὀρέων τῶν ὑψηλῶν* is often called a Deuteronomic phrase in the sense of a place for idolatrous worship, but it occurs only here in Deut. As for the coordinate *καὶ ὑποκάτω δένδρου δασέος* as a similar cultic place, this is actually unique in the entire OT, though its Hebrew equivalent תחת כל עץ רענן, which also occurs only here in the book (but comp Isa 57:5 and Ezek 6:13), does occur in Kgs, Isa, Jer and Ezek. The coordinate phrase *καὶ ἐπὶ τῶν θινῶν* occurs between the two, and renders ועל הגבעות. The Hebrew phrase often occurs as a place of idolatrous worship, in fact, it occurs together with the next phrase in 1Kgs 14:23 2Kgs 17:10 and Jer 2:20. The Greek *θινῶν* does render גבעה in Gen 49:26 Job 15:7, but not as idolatrous places. One would hardly expect *θινῶν* for גבעות here, since it really means a heap, and so a sandbank, i.e. a beach or shore. Even if one were to render it by "dunes," the notion of "dunes" as a place of worship is unexpected.[4] Since it does occur for גבעה in the two passages mentioned above, the notion of "hills" seems secured for LXX.

3. According to HR.
4. The Three correct to *τῶν βουνῶν*.

The collocation *δένδρου δασέος* "a hairy, shaggy," hence "leafy or luxuriant tree" is a good rendering for עץ רענן. But MT has the phrase modified by כל, which may have been considered an exaggeration by the translator. Hex has, however, added *παντος* under the asterisk before *δένδρου* so as to equal MT.[5]

12:3 The first four clauses are similar to 7:5; in fact, the last two are exact copies. In the first and second clauses the verb and its modifier are transposed at 7:5, and in the first clause the verb is also different (though they are the same in MT). Here LXX has the more colorful verb *κατασκάψετε* "you shall chop down, hack in pieces," rather than the more general *καθελεῖτε*; see comments ad loc. LXX distinguishes between the מזבחת which are idolatrous, *τοὺς βωμούς*, and those which are acceptable, *τὰ θυσιαστήρια*.[6] That the translator borrowed from his rendering of 7:5 is clear from clauses three and four. At 7:5 תגדעון in the third clause and תשרפון באש in the fourth are correctly rendered, but at 12:3 the two are transposed in MT, and LXX has followed 7:5. Because of this, hex, rather than transposing to equal MT, added *πυρι* under the asterisk after *ἐκκόψετε*, which does not make much sense.

The last clause has no counterpart in 7:5, however; it renders MT literally: "You shall destroy their name from that place." To destroy the name means to erase from memory (these objects of pagan worship).

12:4—5 The two verses must be read together, since it is only from the adversative clauses of v.5 that one can understand what is meant by v.4: "not shall you do thus to the Lord your God." What LXX probably intended by *οὕτως* is to indicate a contrast with the last clause of v.3, i.e. "you are not to destroy the Lord's name from that place," but "to the place which ... you shall both seek out and enter there."

The relative clause modifying *τόπον* occurs in one form or another 19 times in Deut.[7] A constant in each case is *ἂν ἐκλέξηται κύριος* (except at 16:16 where *αὐτόν* is inserted before *κύριος*. Its most common modification is *ἐπικληθῆναι τὸ ὄνομα αὐτοῦ ἐκεῖ* (nine times) "for his name to be invoked

5. Aq attempted to improve on *δασέος* by his *εὐθαλοῦς*.
6. But not so Theod and Aq who use *τὰ θυσιαστήρια* here.
7. See list 15 in THGD 90.

there." In MT the verb is modified by מכל the tribes, but LXX makes this ἐν μιᾷ as a substitute for a partitive מן. The *b* text "corrects" this to εκ πασων. Incidentally, for φυλῶν B has πολεων, which is an auditory error. V.5 is somewhat amplified, probably because this is the first occurrence of the notion expressed. It has a different infinitive before "his name," ἐπονομάσαι, but then adds ἐπικληθῆναι at the end. MT has לשום, which LXX interprets contextually; after all, establishing his name is well interpreted by ἐπονομάσαι τὸ ὄνομα αὐτοῦ.[8] It is only after this that MT continues with לשכנו תדרשו "after his earthly presence you shall inquire." LXX takes the first word as part of the foregoing and introduces the verb with καί (possibly reading ותדרשו by dittography of the *waw* after לשכנו?). For לשכנו LXX has ἐπικληθῆναι ἐκεῖ "to be invoked there," a regular usage in Deut (see also 16:2,6,11 26:2). What LXX intends is the understanding that God's earthly presence signifies the reality of his invocation, with ἐκεῖ specifying its location.[9]

The pair of verbs at the end is modified by ἐκεῖ, which refers to the beginning of the verse, viz. τὸν τόπον. MT changes the second verb to the singular, but LXX follows Sam which levelled it to the plural context.

12:6 MT has a list of seven things which you are to bring thither: your holocausts,[10] your sacrifices,[11] your tithes, the offering of your hand (probably some contribution made from the products of the land), your vows, your voluntary offerings, and the first-born of your cattle and flock. LXX has only six. The first two and the last three are normal equivalents for numbers 1,2,5,6 and 7. In place of numbers 3 and 4, מעשרתיכם and תרומת ידכם, LXX has only ἀπαρχάς ὑμῶν which fits neither one particularly well, though in vv.11,17 it stands for תרומה, but it more reasonably equals ראשית (18:4 twice 26:2,10 33:21). In Exod 25:2,3 35:5 36:6 as well as Lev 22:12 Num 5:9 it stands for תרומה. Origen decided that it represented תרומת, and so added υμων under the asterisk to represent the absent ידכם. This then meant that מעשרתיכם ואת had no equivalent, and hex inserted και τας δεκατας υμων under the

8. Tar^O interprets לשום את שמו שם by לאשראה שכנתה תמן "to make his presence to dwell there."

9. Tar^O renders לשכנו by לבית שכנתה, i.e. the place of his Shekinah. Rashi identifies this as זה משכן שילה "This is the tabernacle at Shiloh."

10. ὁλοκαυτώματα only translates עלת in Deut; see Daniel 244.

11. For θυσιάσματα ὑμῶν as rendering for זבחיכם see Daniel 206, f.n.16.

asterisk, i.e. in third place, but Byz changed the noun to the compound *επιδεκατας*. A popular B doublet text, *και τας ομολογιας υμων* "and your vows," is added after "your voluntary sacrifices," but obviously has no justification; cf comment at v.17. For the laws concerning the firstborn of cattle and sheep see 15:19—23.

An odd variant occurs in *C*, which has *τα προβατα* instead of *τῶν προβάτων*, making the flock coordinate to "the first-born of the cattle"; this could only be the result of carelessness, since the text could hardly have intended all the flock to be sacrificed!

12:7 The clause "you shall eat there before the Lord" would apply only to certain offerings, viz. the communion sacrifices, in which the worshipper and his family would share in the food.[12] This was presumably the case with the *θυσιάσματα* as over against the *ὁλοκαυτώματα* (though the text does not make any such distinctions here), and may have included "vows" and "voluntary offerings" as well.

These were then occasions for a communal rejoicing, which concerned *πᾶσιν οὗ ἂν ἐπιβάλητε τὰς χεῖρας* "all matters to which you put (your) hands," thus the products of your work. The Hebrew reads כל משלח ידכם, and the plural *τὰς χεῖρας* is apparently based on the ידיכם of Sam.[13] Hex has added under the asterisk a rendering of the suffix by *υμων*. The unusual Hebrew phrase occurs elsewhere at v.18 15:10 23:20(21) 28:8,20(21) and, except for 23:21 for which see comment ad loc, is always translated as here though in the singular; the idiom is unique to Deut. In the tradition the collocation has been revised by Cod B, which preposed the modifier, and changed it to the singular, thus *την χειρα επιβαλητε*, whereas Byz not only transposed, but kept the plural and added the hex *υμων*; apparently Byz is a further revision of the B rendering, which is itself obviously secondary.[14]

The norm for this celebration is given in the singular "as the Lord your God blessed you," in which it simply follows MT. The plural then returns in v.8.

12. See list 34 in THGD 95.
13. Aq rendered it word for word with *πάσῃ ἀποστολῇ χειρός*.
14. See the discussion in THGD 136—137.

12:8 The Israelites are warned not to "perform all that which we are doing here today"; what is meant by *οὐ ποιήσετε* must be contextualized by vv.4—7, i.e. engage in cult in the way we have perforce been accustomed to do in our wilderness wanderings, since we had no centralized sanctuary, nor was the cult regulated as it will be in a settled environment (vv.9—12). In the tradition *ἡμεῖς ποιοῦμεν* becomes in the F M V majority text *υμεις ποιειτε*, which is secondary, it being due to two contributing factors: a) the itacistic *υμεις* for *ἡμεῖς*, and b) the second plural context. But the Hebrew is determinative; it has אנחנו עשים. The Greek has made the ככל structure a direct accusative, possibly reading כל by haplography. A popular text, probably Byz in origin, has inserted *κατα*, thereby equalling MT exactly; the reading is not hex, however, though apparently it is based on MT.

The desert practice, which is to be avoided once the Israelites are settled, is characterized as *ἕκαστος τὸ ἀρεστὸν ἐναντίον αὐτοῦ*. LXX has disregarded the כל before the noun הישר, but כל in this context is unique; in fact, כל modifies הישר only twice elsewhere, Jer 40:5 Mic 3:9, as well as three times before ישרי (Ps 32:11 64:11 94:15). The word *ἀρεστόν* is not a literal rendering of ישר "straight, right," but it occurs regularly in the Pentateuch (except for 9:5 *ὁσιότητα*, 32:4 *ὅσιος* and Num 23:10 *δικαίων*) as a translation for ישר; see Note at Exod 15:26.

12:9 The verse explains the reason for the chaotic practice referred to: "for up to now you had not come to the resting place and to the possession which the Lord your God is giving you." LXX has levelled to the singular the odd change in number of the relative clause in MT, following the consistent plural of Sam, as does Vulg. The popular A B F M change of *ὑμῶν* in "your God" to *ημων* is merely an itacism; note that only one witness changed the corresponding *ἡμῖν* to *υμιν*, which one might have expected to accompany the popular variant. The use of *κατάπαυσιν* for מנוחה I take to intend a "resting place."

12:10 The *κατάπαυσιν* and *κληρονομίαν* of v.9 are here explicated by a series of future verbs: You shall cross, you shall dwell, he shall give you rest, and you shall dwell. In the two parts of the verse the issue of the first action is *κατοικήσετε*. In other words, "you shall cross the Jordan" means that "you will dwell in the land which the Lord your God is causing you to possess"; in the second part, "he (the Lord your God) shall give you rest from all your enemies which are about" means that "you shall dwell *μετὰ ἀσφαλείας*," i.e. securely, safely. MT has בטח.[15]

In the tradition *κατακληρονομεῖ* has been changed by the A F M V majority text to the future *κατακληρονομησει*, but this is due to the pressure of the future verbs in the context. The present tense is regularly used to translate a participial predicate; here מנחיל is predicate of a nominal clause.

12:11 The first clause is ambiguous, and can be translated in various ways. The predicate is uncertain; the subject is *ὁ τόπος*, but what is it that is said about the subject? This depends on the extent of the relative clause. As punctuated it extends through *ἐκεῖ* 1°, but then the predicate is simply *ἔσται*, which is odd. It is also possible to understand the syntax to mean either "the place which ... shall be for the invocation of his name there," or "the place which ... shall be there." In favor of the latter is the fact that *ἐκεῖ* 2° follows immediately, thus "the place shall be there; there you shall bring." On the other hand, the relative is elsewhere never split in this way,[16] and though it is awkward it may well be best to take *ἔσται* absolutely. The verb is placed before the subject and might then be taken as an emphatic position: "And there shall be the place, etc." Hex has rather crassly added *εν αυτω* under the asterisk after "Lord your God"; this does equal בו in MT, but its translation results in outrageous Greek.

The second clause then identifies the central sanctuary as the place to which you are to bring all your sacrifices. Actually *πάντα* is defined by a *ὅσα* clause, for which see comment at 4:2, which is in turn identified by a list of various sacrifices somewhat similar to that of v.6, and which are to be offered up in the sanctuary. For the first two in the list see comment at v.6. The third one, מעשרתיכם, had been omitted by LXX in v.6, but is here correctly rendered by *καὶ τὰ ἐπιδέκατα ὑμῶν*. For *τὰς ἀπαρχάς* see comment at v.6; here it is defined by *τῶν χειρῶν ὑμῶν*. The entire phrase is singular in MT,

15. Aq has the adverb *πεποιθότως* "confidently." Aq normally reserves the verb *πείθω* for בטח.
16. See list 15 in THGD 90.

תרמת ידכם, but Sam, which lacks any reference to hands, does have the plural, ותרמתיכם.

The next sacrifice, *καὶ τὰ δόματα ὑμῶν*, must represent Sam's ונדבתיכם; at least, this equation does obtain elsewhere, at 23:23 where נדבה אשר דברת בפיך is rendered by *δόμα ὃ ἐλάλησας τῷ στόματί σου*. So it is a gift which has been voluntarily promised to God.

This is to be distinguished from the vow, which is here described as *πᾶν ἐκλεκτὸν τῶν δώρων ὑμῶν ὅσα ἂν εὔξησθε τῷ θεῷ ὑμῶν*. In MT "your gifts" are defined as נדריכם "your vows,"[17] but the translator used a generic term *δώρων*, which, however, he then described as "those which you vowed." Why he should have substituted *τῷ θεῷ ὑμῶν* for יהוה is not clear; in any event hex added *κυριω* before it and then placed *τῷ θεῷ ὑμῶν* under the obelus to show what MT actually had.[18] The characterization of the vowed gifts as *πᾶν ἐκλεκτόν* is in imitation of MT's כל מבחר, i.e. "all your choice gifts which you might vow to your God."

12:12 For "rejoice" before the Lord see comment at v.7. The statement here is much more complete, particularly in that *οἱ οἶκοι ὑμῶν* of v.7 are here fully defined as including "sons and daughters, male and female servants" as well as "the Levite who is at your gates." The only change made by LXX is a stylistic one; MT has a conjunction before "male servants," but in this LXX follows Sam in making two separate pairs. Hex has "corrected" this by adding *και* before *οἱ παῖδες* to equal MT.

The Levite is described as one who is in your gates, which simply means that he is in your cities, i.e. he is resident among you.[19] The reason for the Levite living in your midst is given as due to the fact that *οὐκ ἔστιν αὐτῷ μερὶς ουδὲ κλῆρος μεθ' ὑμῶν*. What is meant is that in contrast to the twelve tribes, that of Levi had no tribal fief assigned to it.

12:13—14 With v.13 LXX changes to the second singular, which continues throughout the chapter except for vv.16,17b and 24. MT is more consistently singular; in fact, v.16 is its only exception in the remainder of the chapter. For

17. The Others render literally by *τὰ ἑκούσια*.
18. Only Syh witnesses adequately to Origen's corrections.
19. See list 44 in THGD 97.

πρόσεχε σεαυτῷ μή see comment at 4:9. Since *μή* represents פן hex has, as usual, added *ποτε* under the asterisk so as to indicate that fact.

These verses order the single sanctuary of divine choice as the only legitimate place for sacrifice. V.13 puts it negatively: "watch out lest you should offer up your holocausts in any place which you might see." The *ἄν* in the relative clause has been changed in all the uncials as well as in most cursives to *εαν*, but *ἄν* is original; see comment at 5:27.

V.14 is a positive order to perform Israel's public cult in the place of the Lord's choice. For *τόπον* defined by a relative clause see comment at v.5. The relative clause is shorter in MT, and LXX has added after *κύριος* the words *ὁ θεός σου αὐτόν* ex par (14:24 16:2,7,11,15), though the otiose *αὐτόν* has support only in the בו of 16:7. Hex has placed the extra words under the obelus to show their absence in MT. This place is located *ἐν μιᾷ τῶν φυλῶν σου*. Only cod B *n* Latcod 100 and Eth have *φυλῶν*, all others witnessing to *πολεων*, an auditory error which has no basis in MT. The orders are two: "there you must offer your holocausts," for which see comments at v.11, and "there you must do all the things which I am today commanding you," a general comment with no specific reference. For the *ὅσα* clause see comment at 4:2. MT has no equivalent for *σήμερον*, and hex has it under the obelus; but *σήμερον* is usually present in this Deut collocation (30 out of 38 times), and it is here ex par.

12:15 MT begins with רק "only," whereas LXX has *ἀλλ' ἤ* "but."[20] In the preposed *ἐν πάσῃ ἐπιθυμίᾳ σου* the *ἐν* shows norm or standard "according to your every desire (you may slaughter)."[21] That this is contrastive to the slaughter for sacrifice is clear from the *ἀλλ' ἤ* at the beginning of the verse. Hex has added *ψυχας* under the asterisk after the noun in view of MT's את נפשך, but the נפש is the "self," the person, and its omission in translation shows that the translator realized that the Hebrew meant "the desire of your person," of yourself, i.e. your own desire, which can be expressed simply by the pronoun. Non-sacrificial meat then, may be freely eaten. A popular variant has stressed this even more by glossing *φάγῃ κρέα* by a doublet borrowed from v.21: *κατα την επιθυμιαν της ψυχης σου*. The LXX's *κατά* phrase means "according to the blessing of the Lord your God, which he gave you in

20. Theod has the more exact *πλήν* (retroverted from Syh).
21. Hardly an instrumental *ἐν* as SS 127.

each city." MT has for the last phrase בכל שעריך, but the translator realized that "your gates" means "your city"; cf also vv.17,18, 21. Hex has added *σου* under the asterisk after *πόλει* to equal the suffix in MT.[22]

The second part of the verse emphasizes the complete freedom of choice in the matter. Even ceremonial purity is not required: both "the unclean among you and the clean together may eat it as of the gazelle or the deer." MT lacks equivalents for *ἐν σοί* and *ἐπὶ τὸ αὐτό*, and hex has put them under the obelus. The additions in LXX are simply ad sensum, made for clarification. The *αὐτό* modifying *φάγεται* is grammatically inexact, since it refers to *κρέα* which is plural; the plural is, however, usually a collective in the sense of dressed meat,[23] and the singular is ad sensum. *ὡς* governs two words in the accusative, which I have tried to express by "of," i.e. the words are accusative as modifying *φάγεται*, and what is meant is "as one eats gazelle or deer meat."

12:16 Prohibition against bloody meat. This is individualized by placing the verse in the plural. The tradition has made some changes. Particularly the *b* text has made a number of changes: *ουκ εδεσθε* for *οὐ φάγεσθε* is simply a synonymous expression; *ἐκχεεῖτε* has been changed to the singular *εκχεεις*, probably because of the pressure of the singular in much of the chapter. And for *ὡς*, *b*, together with *oI*, has the long form *ωσει*, which does not change the meaning. An attempt to relate the two parts of the verse is already found in 963, which, along with *O*, has the adversative particle αλλ to introduce the second part.

12:17 Limitations set on the freedom expressed in v.15. For *ἐν ταῖς πόλεσίν σου* see comment at v.15. The first such limitation is the tithe on grain, wine and oil. The word for tithe is the compound *ἐπιδέκατον*,[24] for which compare also 14:21—22. *σῖτος* is the regular rendering for דגן (36 out of 39 times in OT).[25] *οἴνου* has תירש as its counterpart in MT. LXX does not recognize any

22. See SS 102 which calls the failure to render the suffix a free translation.
23. See LS sub *κρέας*.
24. The Three used the simplex *δεκάτην*.
25. *τοῦ σίτου σου* satisfied Theod and Sym, but not Aq who had *χεύματός σου*, for which see f.n. at 7:13.

distinction throughout OT between תירש and יין, both of which are regularly rendered by *οἶνος*.

Also limited are the firstborn of cattle and flock. MT introduced these by a conjunction, but not LXX. This is followed in MT by וכל נדריך, for which LXX simply has *καὶ πάσας εὐχάς*. Hex has added *σου* under the asterisk to render the suffix.[26] The *εὐχάς* are modified by a relative clause, which LXX changes to the plural, which is then continued with *ὑμῶν* modifying both *ὁμολογίας* and *χειρῶν*, but MT has the singular throughout. I can see no rationale for these plurals, except that vows, *ὁμολογίας* and first fruits are matters which are individually, not collectively, entered into. The term *ὁμολογία* means "agreement, contract," and so it refers to that which one performs in a voluntary way. It does occur a number of times for נדבה, and it has taken on the meaning of the Hebrew term. For *τὰς ἀπαρχὰς τῶν χειρῶν ὑμῶν* see comment at v.11.

12:18 The adversative *ἀλλ' ἢ* for כי אם contrasts with v.17. What was forbidden in v.17 may, however, be eaten *ἔναντι κυρίου τοῦ θεοῦ σου*, i.e. in the central sanctuary. For "the place *ᾧ* the Lord your God has chosen *αὐτῷ*," see comment at v.5.[27] *ᾧ* is dative by attraction to its antecedent *τόπῳ*. A popular A F M V text has *ου* as the more appropriate case. The *αὐτῷ* is a Hebraism, which is hardly improved by the Byz reading *εν αυτω*, which equals the בו of MT even more exactly.[28] LXX has *αὐτά* ad sensum for the singular suffix of תאכלנו. After all, v.7 spoke of a number of imposed limitations.

For those members of the household who may partake, see v.12, though here the members are in the singular number. As in v.12 LXX followed Sam in lacking a conjunction before the second pair "your male and female servants." The last member in v.12 had been "the Levite who is in your gates," which is repeated here in MT, but which appears as *ὁ προσήλυτος ὁ ἐν ταῖς πόλεσίν σου* in LXX. The proselyte was certainly of great concern to Deut,[29] and was accepted as a resident alien. The translator may also have taken into

26. As did The Others.
27. Instead of *ὁ θεός σου* The Others simply have *θεός σου*. The attribution to The Others is in my opinion suspect. The omission of the article is typically Aq; it could also be Theod, but hardly Sym.
28. See THGD 111.
29. See lists 43 and 44 in THGD 97.

consideration that the Levite comes up for special consideration in the next verse, and that his mention in v.18 as well was inappropriate. A popular A F M V doublet has *και ο λευιτης* before it, whereas Byz changed "the proselyte" to *ο λευιτης*, which would equal MT. For "in your cities" see comment at v.12.[30] This also occurs as גר(ך) אשר בשעריך at 14:21 31:12, and comp also 24:14, though only at 31:12 is the phrase rendered as here.

The second part of the verse again orders rejoicing, for which see comment at v.7, and for "everything *οὗ ἂν ἐπιβάλῃς τὴν χεῖρα σου*, also see comment at v.7.

12:19 For *πρόσεχε σεαυτῷ μή* see comment at 4:9. As elsewhere hex has added *ποτε* under the asterisk to represent פן more accurately. The general proscription against neglecting the Levite is rendered somewhat freely in LXX. The verb תעזב has both temporal and locative modifiers in כל ימיך על אדמתך. Neither suffix is rendered as such, i.e. the first modifier is generalized by *πάντα τὸν χρόνον*, but the second-person reference is neatly preserved by making the locative part of a relative clause with a second-person verb, *ὅσον ἂν ζῇς ἐπὶ τῆς γῆς*. Apparently hex did not tamper with this translation, though the Byz text did add *σου* after *χρόνον* as well as after *γῆς*. An A *ol*+ variant reads *ζῃ*, i.e. a third person verb, but this is the result of haplography due to confusion of Σ-E on the part of a copyist, and is not to be considered seriously.

12:20 Vv.20—28 constitute an expansion on the legislation concerning the eating of meat, particularly on vv.15—16. Vv.20—22 elaborate on permisssion to eat meat. The condition (*ἐάν*) discussed is the future expansion of Israel's borders, which in accordance with the spirit of Deut is the Lord your God's doing, "as he had said to you." The *σοι* is of course an indirect object, but a *C'' s*+ gloss adding *εν* before it is apparently rooted in a misunderstanding of *σοι* as a locative. This has no basis in MT, which has לך.

The next clause, *καὶ ἐρεῖς*, is in the future,[31] but is coordinate to *ἐμπλατύνῃ*, and is also part of the condition.[32] That the future is possible with

30. Aq has *πύλαις* rather than *πόλεσίν* as one might expect.
31. Theod accepted *ἐρεῖς* but The Others have an aorist subjunctive *εἴπῃς*.
32. For *ἐάν* with the future see Mayser II,1,285 and 3,91 in which the usage is attested already in a Zen. papyrus of the third century BCE.

ἐάν fits in with the nature of the future, which is qualitatively different from a mere temporal notion. The future was after all a relatively late development from the subjunctive.[33]

What one might say is *φάγομαι κρέα*. The future is a good translation of the long form of the imperfect אכלה, often used in Hebrew as a cohortative. Here the future *φάγομαι* is desiderative "I would eat meat."[34]

The second *ἐάν* clause elaborates on the *φάγομαι κρέα* as a restated condition: "should you (*ἡ ψυχή σου*) desire to eat food,"[35] which is then followed by the apodosis: "according to all your desire you may eat meat." The use of *ψυχή σου* as a substitute for *σύ* is a Hebraism, since נפש is commonly used to designate the person (twice in this verse), as it is in Arabic, i.e. נפשי would simply mean "I, me." See also comment at v.23.

12:21 A further elaboration on the permission to eat meat. The protasis is now specifically put as *ἐὰν δὲ μακρότερον ἀπέχῃ σου ὁ τόπος*; the verb "be away from" is adverbially modified by the comparative *μακρότερον* plus the genitive *σου*, i.e. "should the place be too far away from you" (viz. to visit conveniently). The Hebrew has כי ירחק ממך המקום, and LXX has rendered the sense correctly.[36] A *b y* reading has transposed *ἀπέχῃ σου* so as to make the syntactic relations clearer. The particle *δέ* has no counterpart in MT, but it is appropriate, since v.21 contrasts with v.20. For the relative clause modifying *τόπος* see comment at v.5. The *C'' s+* text substituted the second aorist *δωη* for *δῷ*, but this is merely a variant form.[37]

The apodosis introduced by *καί* in imitation of MT consists of two coordinate clauses, *καὶ θύσεις ... καὶ φάγῃ ....* Both futures are voluntative in character, thus "you may slaughter ... and you may eat." *θύσεις* is modified by two *ἀπό* phrases, which are partitive in nature.[38] The nouns in these phrases are in turn modified by a relative clause *ὧν ἂν δῷ σοι ὁ θεός σου*. The relative pronoun is genitive plural by attraction to its antecedent. MT's text is

33. For the future as potentially prospective see Porter 426.
34. See Porter 424—425 for the deliberative character of the future.
35. See SS Inf 41.
36. But The Others insisted on a literal rendering of ממך and have *ἀπὸ σοῦ* instead of *ἀπέχῃ σου*.
37. See Bauer sub *δίδωμι*.
38. See SS 162.

somewhat different: אשר נתן יהוה לך with נתן vocalized by the Masoretes as a past tense: "which Yahweh has given to you." Various attempts to "fix up" the text obtain in the tradition. B and Byz have omitted *σοι*, and changed *σου* to *σοι*. The majority of witnesses has added *κυριος* before *ὁ θεός*, which may have originated in hex. But the text of LXX is original.[39] Also modifying *θύσεις* is the *ὃν τρόπον* clause, which apparently refers to v.15.

The second clause of the apodosis states: "and you may eat in your cities according to your desire" (literally "the desire of your person"; see comment at v.20). For *ἐν ταῖς πόλεσίν σου* as rendering for בשעריך see comment at v.15. The preposition *κατά* to interpret ב is unusual, but is attested elsewhere.[40]

12:22 This verse restates v.15b; see comments ad loc. LXX correctly understood the passive transform of MT by making *ἡ δορκὰς καὶ ἡ ἔλαφος* the subject; the verb remains singular, however, by attraction to the nearer subject. The *αὐτό* modifying *φάγῃ* is neuter singular as an indefinite reference to meat; this reflects MT's suffix of תאכלנו as well.

The last clause has the subjects stated as in v.15. The Qumran Temple Scroll (11QT) now substantiates the Sam text, which has בך, as basis for *ἐν σοί*.[41] The *ἐν σοί* was already added at v.15 to show that *ἀκάθαρτος* refers, not to the animals, but to the Israelites. Since MT lacks בך hex has placed *ἐν σοί* under the obelus.

In v.15 the subjects were modified by *ἐπὶ τὸ αὐτό*, but here by *ὡσαύτως*. In v.15 it had no counterpart in MT, but here יחדו appears as the source; actually *ἐπὶ τὸ αὐτό* would be the more exact rendering.

12:23 MT begins the warning by רק "only (be sure not to)," which LXX does not translate, but then it renders the imperative חזק by *πρόσεχε ἰσχυρῶς*, thereby showing that two Hebrew words are involved.[42] The articulation of the

39. This is defended in some detail in THGD 125—126.
40. See SS 127.
41. See L.H.Schiffman, SCS 33, 280—281, where the interesting point is made that the prepositional phrase removes any possible ambiguity. The distinction between the impure and the pure applies to people, not to the kinds of meat that may be eaten.
42. Sym translated the imperative by *ἀσφαλίζου* "render yourself secure."

infinitive is rare in Deut but all witnesses support it here.[43] For "eat blood" see v.16.

The reason for prohibiting the eating of bloody meat is given in a *ὅτι* clause: *τὸ αἷμα αὐτοῦ ψυχή*.[44] The term *ψυχή* is a calque for the Hebrew נפש, often translated by "soul," which is itself an English calque for the Hebrew word. The word stands for the self, the person, the essence of the individual. Here then it refers to the person as the life principle; it is life itself; cf Exod 21:23 where *ψυχὴν ἀντὶ ψυχῆς* is required. So eating *ψυχή* with meat is actually desecrating life; this is eating living flesh.

12:24 LXX uniquely puts this verse in the plural, even though the context is singular throughout. Since the next verse forbids eating in the singular, it may be that the repetition got to the translator, and the plural was used simply for the sake of variety. The first verb is used absolutely, and one might feel that תאכלנו was misread as תאכלו as the notes in BHS seem to presuppose, but this is hardly correct, since for the second verb, תשפכנו, the suffix is correctly read; the translator has *ἐκχεεῖτε αὐτό*. Hex has added an *αυτο* under the asterisk to the first verb as well. The *b* text actually has the singular for the second verb, *εκχεεις*, but not for the first verb. The change is not significant; in fact, the *b* text also transposes *ἐπὶ τὴν γῆν* after *αὐτό*, thereby reading the two verbs together: *ου φαγεσθε εκχεεις*, which is certainly an odd collocation.

12:25 For the first *ἵνα* clause see comment at 4:40. The *ἐάν* clause is then loosely tied to the *ἵνα* clause before it as a condition for *εὖ σοι γένηται κ.τ.λ.*, which in turn is tied to the imperative *οὐ φάγῃ αὐτό*. The rhetoric is loose indeed! Hex has transposed *σοι γένηται* to equal the word order of MT, but LXX never has *γενηται σοι* in this expression (see 4:40 5:16 6:18 12:28 22:7). Unexpected is the A F M V majority text adding *εις τον αιωνα* after *μετὰ σέ*. This does not occur in a similar context elsewhere in the book, though *δι' αἰῶνος* is found at v.28 and 5:29.

For the collocation *ποιήσῃς τὸ καλὸν καὶ τὸ ἀρεστὸν ἔναντι κυρίου τοῦ θεοῦ σου* see comment at 6:18. MT has a shorter text with only a single

43. See THGD 102—103; its list is, however, not complete; 3:3 and 12:23 should be added to the list.
44. Over against Theod and Aq, Sym makes this a *γάρ* clause.

modifier, הישר, for the verb;[45] it also has no equivalent to *τοῦ θεοῦ σου*, but LXX has levelled with v.28, where MT does have the fuller text as well. Both *τὸν καλὸν καί* and *τοῦ θεοῦ σου* have been placed under the obelus in hex.

12:26 In contrast to v.23 רק is translated here by *πλήν*. *τὰ ἅγιά σου* is here a generic term for the list of sacrifices listed in v.17 except for *τὰς εὐχάς σου*, which is separately listed;[46] this is also clear from the relative clause *ἃ ἄν σοι γένηται*, which describes the *ἅγια* as those which are incumbent on you (as opposed to *τὰς εὐχάς σου* which are voluntary). Hex has also transposed *σοι γένηται* to equal the יהיו לך of MT.

These are all to be brought into the sanctuary (see v.18), which LXX typically orders as *λαβὼν ἥχεις*. For the relative clause modifying *τόπον* see comment at v.5. LXX has the full clause, whereas MT simply has אשר יבחר יהוה. LXX has added *ὁ θεός σου αὐτῷ ἐπικληθῆναι τὸ ὄνομα αὐτοῦ ἐκεῖ* ex par, which hex has placed under the obelus to show its absence in MT.

12:27 The opening clause states the general rule: "you shall perform your holocausts." In MT "your holocausts" has הבשר והדם in apposition, i.e. MT continues "(with) the flesh and blood upon the altar of Yahweh your God." The trouble with this statement is that it seems to conflict with the second part of the verse, where the meat and the blood receive separate treatment. So first of all, the translator removed "and the blood,"[47] and then added a verb *ἀνοίσεις*, by which a new clause is created: "the meat you shall bring up on the altar of the Lord your God."

"But the blood (note the use of the contrastive *δέ*) of your sacrifices (for ודם זבחיך) *προσχεεῖς πρὸς τὴν βάσιν τοῦ θυσιαστηρίου*." The choice of *προσχεεῖς* for ישפך "shall be poured out," as well as of the *πρὸς τὴν βάσιν* instead of על (מזבח), is clearly a deliberate change. The verb שפך is almost always rendered by *ἐκχέω* (100 times out of 119 cases), but never (except here) by *προσχέω*.[48] In fact, *προσχέω* is reserved for translating זרק (22 times out of 23, i.e. this is the only exception). But what makes this particularly

45. Kenn 146 actually reads הטוב והישר.
46. Aq apparently understood קדשיך as a passive participle, since he translated the noun as *ἡγιασμένα*.
47. The Others add *καὶ τὸ αἷμα* (retroverted from Syh).
48. The count is that of Dos Santos.

peculiar is that *προσχέω* is seldom used in the Pentateuch together with "towards/near/upon the base of the altar." In fact, it occurs only once with *ἐπὶ τὴν βάσιν τοῦ θυσιαστηρίου* (Lev 6:32), whereas *ἐκχέω* occurs eight times (Exod 29:12 Lev 4:7,18,25,30,34 8:15 9:9), and *στραγγιεῖ*, at Lev 1:15 and *καταστραγγιεῖ*, at 5:9. But as Dion points out,[49] 11QT does have וזרקו על יסוד מזבח העולה, which is textually, along with Lev 6:32, the closest parallel I could find to LXX. Neither is exact in that LXX uses *πρός*, whereas Lev and 11QT have *ἐπί*/על. Actually *πρός* occurs elsewhere in this context only at Lev 1:15 4:18. What this shows is that the translator here reflects an old Halachic tradition, which he has formulated in his own way.

And finally by contrast, *τὰ δὲ κρέα φάγῃ* "but the flesh you may eat," again using a contrastive *δέ* to render the Hebrew *waw*. The verse now presents a consistent contrast between the blood and the flesh.

12:28 LXX follows Sam in having *καὶ ποιήσεις* as a third verb of instruction: "be careful and hear and do"; hex has placed it under the obelus, since MT does not have ועשית. Unusual is the fact that the first two verbs are imperatives, and only the third one is a future (though with imperatival intent), particularly in view of the fact that the second one represents ושמעת, i.e. not morphologically an imperative form; one might have expected *και ακουσεις*. Presumably the translator took the *καὶ ποιήσεις* as a result clause, i.e. "be careful and listen so that you will do."

This verse concludes the first major section of the laws, and is thus a general warning. *πάντας τοὺς λόγους* refers to these laws just concluded. This is clearer in MT, which added האלה; hex accordingly added *τουτους* under the asterisk. For the *οὕς* clause see comment at 4:2. For the *ἵνα* clause followed by an *ἐάν* clause see v.25, which has almost exactly the same text with one exception; instead of *δι' αἰῶνος* v.25 has *μετὰ σέ*. MT has both here, reading אחריך עד עולם, so hex has added *μετα σε* under the asterisk before *δι' αἰῶνος* to equal MT.

In the tradition a popular M tradition has added *σημερον* at the end of the *οὕς* clause; this equals Sam, but the gloss is probably ex par. Also equall-

49. P.E.Dion, JBL 106(1987), 487—490. Dion also points to a number of interesting Mishnaic parallels which show the Jewish origins of the changes.

ing Sam is the transposition of *καλόν* and *ἀριστόν* in a *z* text, but the equation is mere coincidence.[50]

12:29 Vv.29—31 are a warning against the cultic practices of the native inhabitants. V.29 constitutes the protasis. Though כי is rendered by *ἐὰν δέ*, it is sensibly a temporal condition, and should be rendered accordingly. The addition of *δέ* is appropriate, since a new section is thereby indicated. The verb יכרית is translated by *ἐξολεθρεύσῃ*; this same verb is used in v.30 to render השמד. The translator does not distinguish between "cut off" and "annihilate"; in both cases God destroys completely in LXX.

The conditions then are a) that the Lord is going to destroy the nations. *τὰ ἔθνη* is modified in ungrammatical fashion by an *εἰς οὕς* clause. The *οὕς* has no expressed antecedent, and the tradition has tried to correct it; *O* has changed it to *ου* "where," which is sensible, but it is not LXX. The Byz text has changed it to *εις α*, thus referring to the nations, which is not sensible. The *οὕς* as well as *αὐτούς* later in the verse and in v.30 are ad sensum references to the members of the nations, i.e. as though *ἀνθρώπους* were presupposed. It is of course the land which *σὺ εἰσπορεύῃ*, i.e. Palestine. MT states the purpose of their entering as לרשת אותם (מפניך) "to dispossess them (from before you)." LXX has changed this to *κληρονομῆσαι τὴν γῆν αὐτῶν* (*ἀπὸ προσώπου σου*), i.e. "to possess their land," with *αὐτῶν* referring to *οὕς*.

The second condition is *καὶ κατακληρονόμῃς αὐτούς*. In MT the verb is the same, but ירש can mean "to possess" or "to dispossess." LXX distinguishes the two by changing to the compound verb, thereby showing that the meaning has changed; here it must mean "you should dispossess them." What is now problematic is the *ἀπὸ προσώπου σου*; does it belong with what precedes as in MT, or with what follows, or with the opening verb? Once the translator had substituted "their land" for אותם a literal rendering of the prepositional phrase which followed created an interpretive problem. The critical text has placed a comma before the phrase, since "to possess their land from before you" does not make good sense, whereas "from before you you shall also dispossess them" does. It must of course be remembered that punctuation is a modern innovation, and LXX had none originally.

---

50. Aq renders ישר more literally by *εὐθές* rather than *ἀριστόν*.

The third condition is straightforward: "and you should dwell in their land." Many witnesses read *κατοικησεις*, which is the future spelling; this would then be the apodosis, but this is clearly wrong; the apodosis follows in v.30, and the *-σεις* spelling is simply an itacistic spelling of the aorist subjunctive.

12:30 For *πρόσεχε σεαυτῷ μή* see comment at 4:9. As usual hex added *ποτε* under the asterisk to denote the פן of MT. What is being warned against is somewhat problematic in MT. תנקש is vocalized as a Ni of the verb נקש, the meaning of which is uncertain. It is often emended to תוקש,[51] but LXX clearly does not presuppose the verb יקש. The translator found the passage difficult and did what good translators do, viz. contextualized, hence his *ἐκζητήσῃς* (*ἐπακολουτῆναι*). This says nothing about the parent text, except that it was difficult. The translation *ἐπακολουθῆναι αὐτοῖς* was impelled by אחריהם, thus "you should seek to follow them."[52] In turn this is modified by a *μετά* plus marked infinitive construction, "after their being completely destroyed from before you." For *ἐξολεθρευθῆναι* see comment at v.29.

MT then continues with a paratactic פן clause: "and lest תדרש their gods." LXX has changed this to a direct prohibition without a conjunction: *οὐ μὴ ἐκζητήσῃς τοὺς θεοὺς αὐτῶν*. Hex has again added *ποτε* under the asterisk after *μή* to render the פן. דרש is commonly translated by *ἐκζητέω*, or by the simplex, (122 times out of 181 according to Dos Santos). Now it is clear why he chose the same verb to render the puzzling תנקש earlier in the verse. What the translator says is "do not search out their gods." But דרש often means to seek an oracle from, and this lies in the background of its use and that of the Greek here as well, since it is followed by the direct speech marker *λέγων*/לאמר.

The message sought in the enquiry is *πῶς ποιοῦσιν τὰ ἔθνη ταῦτα τοῖς θεοῖς αὐτῶν*, with the reason for the query given as: *ποιήσω κἀγώ*. The present tense interprets יעבדו, though I suspect this was originally intended as an old preterite: "how did these nations serve"? The verb *ποιοῦσιν* is an odd choice for יעבדו. In fact, the root עבד is rendered by *δουλεύω* 117 times, by *ἐργάζομαι* 44 times, *λατρεύω* 75, and by *ποιέω* only seven times. *ποιέω* is

51. Tar^{O} understood it in that way with תתקל.
52. See SS Inf 140.

rather the stereotype for עשה (2368 times, with the next in order of frequency *γίνομαι* 43 times).[53] Since *ποιοῦσιν* is modified by the dative *τοῖς θεοῖς* the verb must be understood in the sense of λατρεύω, i.e. doing service (in a cultic sense). So "how do these nations do service for their gods? I would also do (so)." The choice of verb is probably a matter of leveling; the verb עשה occurs in the final clause" "even I would do so, even I," as well as in the opening clause of v.31.[54] LXX has not rendered כן, and hex has supplied *ουτως* under the asterisk. In any event, the Greek would be understood in this way, since the dative would be supplied for the *ποιήσω*, i.e. "I would also do service (to their gods)."

12:31 The Israelite is bluntly forbidden to do *οὕτως κυρίῳ τῷ θεῷ σου*. The reason for this is given in the *γάρ* clause. For *βδελύγματα* see comment at 7:25. MT has כל תועבת "every abomination," for which LXX has the plural noun but without "all." Hex supplies this by changing *τά* to *παντα*. "The abominations of the Lord" is followed by *ἃ ἐμίσησεν*, which equals MT, but most witnesses transpose *κυρίου ἅ* which cannot be correct. Note that this follows *βδελύγματα*, and dittography would be the original impulse to place an *α* before *κυρίου*.[55]

The *ὅτι* clause illustrates the abominations,, and thereby gives a rationale for the divine hatred. The verb *κατακαίουσιν* is in the present tense to show customary action, which is also commonly expressed by the prefix inflection in Hebrew.[56] For the heathen practice of human sacrifice see Bible Dictionaries.

12:32(13:1) An exhortation to observe carefully everything commanded. For the *ὅ* clause see comment at 4:2. LXX adds *σήμερον* against MT, thereby following Sam. It is under the obelus in hex. MT has put the first part of the verse in the plural, thus אתכם and תשמרו, changing back to the singular for the second half. LXX levels the verse to a consistent singular.[57]

53. Count according to Dos Santos.
54. See also the discussion in Daniel 68.
55. See the discussion in THGD 129.
56. See e.g. GK 107f.
57. See on *σοι* at THGD 110.

The second part of the verse implicitly declares the Law to be canonical: "you may neither add to it nor subtract from it." The "it" (*αὐτό*, *αὐτοῦ*) refers to *πᾶν ῥῆμα*; comp Rev 22:18—19 for penalties attached to such adding or removing.

Chapter 13

13:1(2) Vv.1—2 constitute the protasis and vv.3—4 are the apodosis of a condition warning against following prophets or dreamers who would lead the people to idolatry. For Deut's conception of prophet see 18:15—22. Prophets and those who dreamt dreams were presumed to be vehicles of divine revelation who in turn communicated by *σημεῖον ἢ τέρας*, for which see 4:34.

The verse begins with a *δέ* structure, appropriate for introducing a new theme. The combination *δῷ σοι* easily gave rise to variants in the tradition by auditory confusion; witness *δωσει* or *δωση*, in turn leading to *δωσει σοι* and even *δωη σοι*, but only *δῷ σοι* can be original.

13:2(3) Signs and wonders are legitimate means for prophetic communication, but they can also communicate illegitimate messages. Such a message is *πορευθῶμεν καὶ λατρεύσωμεν θεοῖς ἑτέροις οὓς οὐκ οἴδατε*, for which see comments at 11:28. I would now change *οὕς* to *οἷς* as at 11:28. Only an undue reverance for cod B impelled me to adopt the accusative here as well as at vv.6 and 13, both of which were probably originally in the dative by attraction to the antecedent *θεοῖς*. In all three cases most witnesses, including all the uncial texts except B, support the dative. At 11:28 and 32:17 exactly the same situation obtains, i.e. *θεοῖς* modified by *οἷς* plus the verb "to know"; in both cases only three witnesses "corrected" to *ους*. Furthermore, this translator tended to make relative pronouns agree with their antecedents rather than accede to the grammatical demands of the clause. As at 11:28 the two verbs are closely connected; in fact, *λατρεύσωμεν* becomes the reason for the verb *πορεύθωμεν*. MT has a different construction: "Let us go after other gods ... that we may serve them," which LXX renders freely but well. Hex, however, was troubled by this reordering. Somehow *πορεύθωμεν καὶ λατρεύσωμεν* seemed inadequate for translating the Hebrew text, so it substituted under the asterisk *ακολουθησωμεν* for *καὶ λατρεύσωμεν* to equal אחרי, and then added *και λατρευσωμεν αυτοις* at the end of the verse to make up for ונעבדם. Byz followed hex in the addition, but simply omitted *και λατρεύσωμεν* earlier in the verse, and added *οπισω* (*θεων ετερων*) so as to equal MT exactly.

13:3(4) The apodosis is put into the plural; its continuation as such into the next verse defines the extent of the apodosis. Oddly enough, MT has the initial verb תשמע still in the singular, but then changes to the plural, which continues through to the end of the next verse. The prohibition shows full understanding of the prophetic forms, viz., the spoken (*τῶν λόγων*) and the visual (*τὸ ἐνύπνιον ἐκεῖνο*). These may not be heard (*ἀκούεσθε*), which hearing would involve heeding, following, obeying.

The *ὅτι* clause gives the raison d'être for the phenomenon of the false prophet or dreamer. It does not mean that the Lord God is not in control of Israel's affairs; rather it constitutes a divine test to discover (*εἰδέναι*) whether you love the Lord your God with your whole heart and person (*ψυχῆς*), for which see comment at 6:5. MT has the more usual subject for the *ὅτι* clause, viz. יהוה אלהיכם, and hex has added *υμων* under the asterisk after *θεός* to equal MT. Furthermore, the majority A F M V text has articulated the infinitive as well, but the articular infinitive is rare in Deut, and the oldest witness, cod B, does not witness to the article; it is clearly secondary. MT uses nominal constructions twice: מנסה יהוה which LXX renders in normal fashion by a present tense *πειράζει* plus subject, and in the question modifying לדעת: הישכם אהבים. LXX renders the question particle by *εἰ*, but does not translate ישכם separately, rather incorporating it into the second plural present tense verb *ἀγαπᾶτε*. More usual would have been an otiose *υμεις*, as the more common rendering for a pronoun plus participle. It should be noted that hex actually adds such a pronoun under the asterisk. For the *ἐξ* phrases see comment at 4:29.[1]

13:4(5) One might have expected the positive command as the alternative to the prohibition of v.3 to have been introduced either by some adversative particle such as *ἀλλ' ἤ* or by a *καί*, but neither MT nor LXX has such. This is probably due to the preposed modifier: "after the Lord your God" occupying the emphatic position: thus "after the Lord ... be going," i.e. with the present imperative *πορεύεσθε*. The tense is most appropriate since following the Lord must be a constant, continuous path of obedience; MT does not have an

1. See also SS 127 for the use of the preposition.

imperative, but has תלכו, LXX substituting the common pattern of imperative plus coordinate future tense verbs. Preposed modifiers are used five times in the verse in imitation of MT, and is most effective in centering attention on "him ... his commandments ... his voice ... to him," rather than on the verbal ideas: "fear ... guard ... hear ... be inclined."

The Hebrew has an extra clause before the last one: ואתו תעבדו "and him serve," for which hex has added *και αυτω λατρευσετε* under the asterisk. It is fully possible that LXX had this, and that it had been omitted by reason of homoioteleuton in the Greek text which Origen used, but this is purely speculative. We do know that his text did not have it, and in such cases it is textually the wiser course to follow the earliest evidence we have. The rendering of תדבקון by *προστεθήσεσθε* is highly unusual. In fact, it occurs only once elsewhere: at Josh 23:12 it obtains in a protasis "if you should turn *καὶ προσθῆσθε* to those nations remaining with you ..., know that *οὐ μὴ προσθῇ* the Lord to destroy those nations";[2] the choice may have been an intentional play on *προσθῆσθε*/*προσθῇ* used in two different senses. Here the future passive "be joined to" is less colorful than the more usual rendering which would have used either *κολλάω* or *προσκολλάω*.[3]

13:5(6) MT continues with the plural, and then changes to the singular with הפדך; LXX levelled to a more consistent singular. The false prophet or dreamer shall be killed. The reference to the dreamer differs from both v.3 and MT in placing *τὸ ἐνύπνιον* as an insertion within *ὁ ἐνυπνιαζόμενος*; hex reorders *τὸ ἐνύπνιον* to correspond to MT. There is, however, another difference between the LXX of vv.3 and 5 in the understanding of ההוא. In both cases the structure in MT is ח(ו)לם החלום ההוא, and it is not clear which word the pronoun modifies, since חלם is taken as a bound noun. At v.3 the translator took the pronoun to modify החלום, and so it becomes *ἐκεῖνο*, but here it is understood as modifying חלם, i.e. *ἐκεῖνος*. This makes it consistent with the coordinate *ὁ προφήτης ἐκεῖνος*. The change in word order also emphasizes the notion of "that one who dreams the dream," and demonstrates that the translator intended the change in modification.

2. Following the text of Margolis.
3. Which is what Aq used (*προσ*)*κολληθήσεσθε* (retroverted from Syh). It is not clear whether the simplex or the compound was used.

The basis for the capital sentence is given in the *γάρ* clause. MT has דבר סרה על "he has spoken apostasy against," which LXX renders neatly by *ἐλάλησεν πλανῆσαί σε ἀπό* "he has spoken to lead you astray from."[4] Note also that LXX keeps the singular consistent with the context: *σε ... τοῦ θεοῦ σου* (*τοῦ ἐξαγαγόντος*) *σε*, but MT oddly has the plural with אלהיכם and אתכם, and then returns to the singular for the rest of the verse. Why MT should suddenly have two cases of the second plural in the middle of an otherwise consistent singular context is baffling, whereas LXX simply makes much better sense.

What made the *πλανῆσαί σε* so appalling was the fact that the straying was from their redemptive Lord. For "the one bringing you out of the land of Egypt," see comment at 1:27. In MT the coordinate phrase is והפדך מבית עבדים (note the return to the singular). The phrase בית עבדים is usually rendered by (*ἐξ*) *οἴκου δουλείας* (see 5:6 6:12 8:14 13:10), but here *οἴκου* is absent, an omission which hex apparently did not fill. In LXX *τῆς δουλείας* is used by itself, because it modifies *λυτρωσαμένου*, and one is not ransomed or redeemed from a place (a house), but from a condition (servitude). This all serves *ἐξῶσαί σε* from the way, "to thrust, push you from the way," a literal rendering of הדיחך מן הדרך.

The verse concludes with a typical Deut demand for the removal of evil from *ὑμῶν αὐτῶν*.[5] The verb used is, however, unique in this formula which otherwise usually uses *ἐξαρεῖς*, not *ἀφανιεῖς*. In all cases of the formula the Hebrew uses the root בער "to burn," hence to purge. In any event, the notion of removal is central to the formula. The community must excise the evil one from itself. It should be noted that מקרבך is rendered by the emphatic plural form in which *αὐτῶν* is added to *ὑμῶν*. Whenever the formula occurs in second person the Hebrew has the singular מקרבך, whereas LXX always has *ἐξ ὑμῶν αὐτῶν*. The point that LXX makes is that the community (*σύ*) must officially remove ... from among you (i.e. from the Israelites as individuals). In the tradition the A F M V majority text has levelled the text by changing the verb to the plural, but the peculiar change in number is original to the formula. It should also be noted that הרע is ambiguous; it can be understood as the abstract "evil" or as the concrete "the evil one." LXX always makes it

4. Aq renders סרה על literally by *ἀπόστασιν ἐπί*.
5. See list 37 in THGD 96.

refer to the person: τὸν πονηρόν. To the translator it was the evildoer who had to be removed, made to disappear, from the community. A substantial number of witnesses actually have το πονηρον, but this is obviously a secondary reading.

13:6(7) The condition is set up in vv.6—7, with the apodosis detailed in vv.8—11. The ἐάν clause uses the verb παρακαλέσῃ "invite," to render יסית "incite, allure" only here, but then the Hebrew verb only occurs 18 times in MT and is translated by 11 different verbs (the most frequent is ἐπισείω - four times). LXX's choice is adequate in the context.[6] The subject presupposed is an intimate: "your brother from your father or (following Sam rather than MT) from your mother, or your son or your daughter, or the wife who is in your bosom, or the friend who is like you yourself." Hex has placed "from your father or" under the obelus to indicate its omission from MT. MT has רעך for "the friend" and a popular hex text has added σου. A σου has also been added by an A F M V majority text after γυνή, but there is no support for it in MT, and it is otiose in view of the ἡ ἐν κόλπῳ σου modifier. (What other γυνή would be so described!) The secret invitation by such an intimate is to idolatry, of going and serving other gods. In the tradition βαδίσωμεν becomes πορευθωμεν in the majority text, but this is clearly borrowed from v.2 (or v.13), where it occurs in exactly the same context. Either verb can translate נלכה, but B as the oldest witness has βαδίσωμεν and should be taken as LXX. For changing οὕς of the critical text in favor of οἷς see the discussion at v.2.

13:7(8) V.7 is dependent on v.6, since it modifies θεοῖς ἑτέροις. These other gods are from the gods of the nations.[7] These nations are described as being סביבתיכם/περικύκλῳ ὑμῶν, again a plural in the middle of a singular context; probably the plural is used because "surrounding you" invites the idea of individuals, whereas ἐγγιζόντων and μακρὰν ἀπό can be taken to refer to the community σοι/σου). The *b* text exaggerates by making the opening phrase "from παντων the gods," for which there is no basis.

6. Aq and Sym translate by ἀναπείσῃ "seduced, misled."
7. The ἀπό could be understood as a partitive; see SS 169.

The final modifier, "from (the) edge of the land up to (the) edge of the land," i.e. from border to border, must also modify ἐθνῶν. It might be noted that ועד has been rendered, not by και εως, but simply by ἕως.[8]

13:8(9) The sentence on such people. The first verb is unique in LXX; the simplex, θέλω/ἐθέλω is the most common rendering for אבה (33 times, followed by βούλομαι - 17 times).[9] The compound, συνθελήσεις, is used here, since there is common willingness or consent involved. For "and not shall your eye be sparing on him" see comment at 7:16. Coordinate with it, and lexically paired with it, is οὐκ ἐπιποθήσεις ἐπ' αὐτῷ "not shall you show longing for him," but MT has ולא תחמל "nor shall you be sparing"; comp Jer 13:14 for the same pair. To show longing presumably means "to be sparing, show leniency."[10] The failure to represent the conjunction may be based on a parent text reading לא created by haplography, since the word before it is עליו. LXX also added a prepositional phrase under the pressure of the coordinate clause - ἐπ' αὐτῷ had also obtained with the preceding clause.

The last clause reads οὐδὲ μὴ σκεπάσῃς αὐτόν "nor shall you shelter him" for ולא תכסה עליו "nor shall you hide him.[11] The Greek makes good sense, though it does soften the warning somewhat.[12]

13:9(10) MT begins with כי הרג תהרגנו "because you shall surely kill him," in other words not תכסה עליו. LXX makes quite a different contrast. It disregarded כי entirely and has ἀναγγέλων ἀναγγελεῖς περὶ αὐτοῦ. The translator realizes that a capital sentence is to be carried out; in fact, the rest of the verse along with v.10 describe how the sentence is to be carried out. But the judicial sentence on an intimate needs a charge to be brought in before a sentence can be imposed, and so instead of MT's order to kill, he substitutes "you shall actually make a charge, a denouncement, concerning him"; only thereafter may the sentence be carried out. This makes the practice consistent with 17:2—7.

8. See THGD 56.
9. According to Dos Santos.
10. Sym has οὐκ σπλαγχνισθήσῃ "not shall you show pity."
11. See Lee 77.
12. Not so Aq who translates literally by κατακαλύψῃς.

The carrying out of the capital sentence is to follow the rules of 17:7. The accuser begins the process of killing the guilty one, and the rest of the people are to follow. The process is described as "the hands ... shall be on him ... to kill him." In both cases, i.e. *αἱ χεῖρές σου* and *αἱ χεῖρες παντὸς τοῦ λαοῦ*, "hands" is in the plural in LXX, but singular in MT. In both cases popular variants have the singular *η χειρ* in LXX as well. But the change to the singular in its support pattern betrays support by a large group having the singular for *σου* but the plural for "all the people"; this wrongly contrasts the single individual *σου* and the many involved in "all the people," as though individuals would only use one hand in the process of stoning. Note that at 17:7 LXX has the singular *ἡ χείρ* for both with no variation in the Greek tradition at all. What LXX here intends is that people throughout use both hands. The majority reading for *ἐσχάτῳ* is *ἐσχάτων* which I would now consider to be original LXX in spite of uncial support for the dative singular; see discussion at 17:7.

13:10(11) LXX has changed the second singular verb סקלתו to the third plural, which is more consistent with the verdict of v.9 in which both you and all the people take part in the killing. On the other hand, for MT the second singular is addressed to Israel, and the translator may have preferred the third plural to avoid any idea that the accuser alone was to do the stoning. For such a major crime death by stoning was ordered; see also 17:7.

The reason for this verdict is given in the *ὅτι* clause: it is "because he sought to apostasize you from the Lord your God." The use of *ἀποστῆσαι* to render להדיח rather than *ἐξῶσαι* as in v.5 is probably due to the fact that סרה occurred in the earlier context; a סרה which led to להדיח meant *ἀποστῆσαι*. For the attributive of "God" as *τοῦ ἐξαγαγόντος σε ἐκ γῆς Αἰγύπτου ἐξ οἴκου δουλείας* see comments at v.5. Here, however, מבית עבדים is fully rendered in LXX.

13:11(12) The desired result: "All Israel on hearing (this) shall be frightened, and they will no longer act...." MT uses plural verbs as predicates for "all Israel": ישמעו, יראון and יוספו, but LXX only changes to the plural with the third verb, *προσθήσουσιν*; for *ἀκούσας φοβηθήσεται* "Israel" is understood as a collective singular. LXX also added *ἔτι* following Sam rather than MT, which had no עוד. M *z*+ change φοβηθήσεται to the plural, which would conform to MT; it was obviously secondary, since they failed to change ἀκούσας to the plural as well.

The standard for action is "according to this evil ῥῆμα ἐν ὑμῖν." ῥῆμα is simply a calque for דבר which here does not mean "word," but rather "matter, event, thing." Again LXX renders בקרבך in the plural by ἐν ὑμῖν; see the discussion at v.5 on ἐξ ὑμῶν αὐτῶν.

13:12(13) The ἐάν governs vv.12—13,[13] with the apodosis extending from v.14 to the end of the chapter. The verb is modified by a locative phrase, which seems odd, since "in one of the cities which ...." is semantically part of the rumour, i.e. it ought to be part of v.13. According to the text the condition means that the hearing is in one of the cities. MT has עריך, and hex has added σου under the asterisk to equal the suffix.

πόλεων is modified by a relative clause, in which the pronoun ὧν is genitive by attraction to πόλεων, a phenomenon characteristic of this translator. The nominal clause is as usual rendered by a present tense, δίδωσιν, and is modified by a purposive infinitive κατοικεῖν σε "for you to reside (there)." The σε has no counterpart in MT, but serves as the subject of the infinitive. Whether the popular A F M V omission of σε was recensionally generated is possible, but not demonstrable. A *C*+ text has changed the present infinitive to the aorist κατοικησαι, but the dwelling there is a continuous state, and the present tense was intentionally chosen. לאמר is here rendered by the genitive λεγόντων, since it is dependent on the verb ἀκούσῃς.[14]

13:13(14) This verse gives the content of the direct speech marker. For ἐξήλθοσαν I would now read the Classical form ἐξῆλθον. The support for the Hellenistic form is minimal, only B *b*, and at 26:13 where another compound, παρῆλθον, occurs, the Classical form has universal support. The simplex ἤλθοσαν occurs, however, at 1:24, which makes the change less certain, though *b n s*+ do read ηλθον there. The -οσαν ending only occurs elsewhere in the book as εἴδοσαν at 7:19 10:21 11:2 (all with an A F M majority text reading ειδον, however), and as ἐμάρτοσαν at 32:5. The men who came out

13. Aq interprets ἐάν as a temporal particle ὅταν (retroverted from Syh).
14. See SS Inf 72.

are called *παράνομοι* "lawless ones" for the Hebrew בליעל usually interpreted as "worthless ones," but always of people who stir up evil. The word occurs here for the first time, and recurs at 15:9, where it refers to דבר as *ἀνόμημα*; cf comment ad loc.[15]

These *παράνομοι* are *ἐξ ὑμῶν*, but MT has the singular מקרבך, though changing to the plural for ידעתם at the end of the verse. LXX has a consistent plural for the verse. These lawless ones "have apostasized *πάντας* those inhabiting their city." The word "all" has no counterpart in MT, and hex has placed it under the obelus, but כול does occur in 11QT55.[16] The word is also included in the penalty to be imposed in v.15, and was probably added in both places to avoid the imposition of the death penalty on anyone who was not guilty. For *ἀπέστησαν* see comment at v.10.

The words of enticement are similar to those in v.6, which see. For *πορεύθωμεν* see comment at v.6. The relative clause modifying "other gods" is in the plural as in MT. For changing *οὕς* of the critical text to *οἷς* see the discussion at v.2.

13:14(15) The apodosis (see comment at v.12) is in the singular, except for *ἐν ὑμῖν* in v.14 and *ἀναθεματιεῖτε* in v.15, whereas MT is consistently singular throughout. The phrase בקרבך occurs ten times in MT, and half the time it becomes plural in LXX (vv.11,14 16:11 19:20 23:16), and singular at 7:21 13:1 17:2 26:11 28:43. It should be said that whenever it is rendered by *ἐν σοί* it is Israel as community that is intended, e.g. at 7:21 "because the Lord your God is *ἐν σοί*." On the other hand, מקרבך also occurs ten times, and nine times LXX has the plural (once 18:15 it is omitted). The plural suffix only occurs once; at 1:42 בקרבכם obtains and LXX has *μεθ' ὑμῶν*. It would seem then that whenever *ἐν ὑμῖν* obtains the stress is on the people as a community of Israelites.

MT has three verbs of enquiry: דרשת וחקרת ושאלת, with the last one modified by היטב as an adverbial intensifier. LXX apparently has reordered these with the second and third reversed. The first one is well-translated by

---

15. . Tar[O] renders by בני רשעא; Rashi etymologizes rather fancifully with בלי עול "yokeless," which he then applies as "those who have thrown off his (i.e. God's) yoke."

16. See L.H.Schiffmann, SCS 33, 283—284 for a possible halachic source for the addition.

ἐτάσεις "test, examine." This has been omitted by B+ because of homoioteleuton, i.e. of *καί*,[17] but it is of course original. The second one, *ἐρωτήσεις*, is a stereotype for שאל; in fact, except for Exod 3:13 (for אמר followed by a question) it translates only שאל throughout the OT. On the other hand, חקר is variously translated by verbs meaning to search out, among which are both *ἐξερεύνω* and its simplex. It seems obvious that LXX transposed the two, and hex has actually retransposed the two verbs to equal MT. This means that in LXX *σφόδρα* (for היטב) modifies *ἐξερευνήσεις*, rather than *ἐρωτήσεις*.

The result of the thorough investigation was *καὶ ἰδοὺ ἀληθὴς σαφῶς ὁ λόγος*. *καὶ ἰδού* is a calque for והנה, a call to attention that: "the matter is clearly true," for the Hebrew אמת נכון הדבר "(it is) truth, the matter is sustained." What this matter consists of is the fact that "*γεγένηται* this abomination in you." "It has happened" interprets the passive נעשתה "it has been done." In the tradition the B M Byz text has changed *ἀληθής* to the adverb *αληθως*, but this is induced by *σαφῶς* which follows immediately, rather than being the work of the translator.

13:15(16) The penalty is to be total destruction. "You must totally destroy (kill off) all those inhabiting that city by the edge of the sword." This follows MT in using the singular second person. For "all" see the comments at v.13. LXX has changed the second part of the verse to the plural. MT simply has the imperative החרם "anathematize" in the singular. LXX not only changes the imperative to the plural but also has a dative cognate noun before it: "with an anathema anthematize it (i.e. the city)." Whether the parent text had a free infinitive חרם (or בחרם) before the verb, or that the translator on his own, on the analogy of the cognate participle rendering a free cognate infinitive in the first clause, added a cognate noun in the dative, cannot be determined. What the clause means is that you must totally devote the city to destruction. Just why LXX changed this clause to the plural is puzzling. It is of course true that people carry this out, but that is also true of the other verbs as well; it is people who destroy, gather, burn, yet these verbs are all in the collective singular.

Included in the anathema is not only the city, but also *πάντα τὰ ἐν αὐτῇ*, to which MT added ואת בהמתה לפי חרב "and its cattle at the edge of the

17. See THGD 124.

sword." Of course, this was already included in "all those things in it," and may have been omitted by LXX as unnecessary. Hex has added *και τα κτηνη εν στοματι μαχαιρας* under the asterisk to equal MT.

13:16(17) V.16a consists of two clauses which LXX presents chiastically: all its spoils you must collect ..., and you shall burn the city with fire. MT has באש between the verb and את העיר, and hex reorders the nominals to equal the word order of MT. The gathering of spoil is to be done *εἰς τὰς διόδους αὐτῆς* "into its passages, roads," which is a unique rendering for רחבה, a word which is almost always rendered by *πλατεῖα* "broad places," such as piazzas, squares. This is not improved greatly by the Byz variant *διεξοδους*, "passages leading out (of the city)."

The second command is to burn the city by fire,[18] along with all its spoils, *πανδημεί* before the Lord your God. *πανδημεί* renders כליל and here means "altogether, completely."[19] The Hebrew כליל ל sometimes means "a whole burnt offering for (God)," and is often so understood here as well.[20] But the ancients in my opinion understood this better.[21] Tar^O translated by גמיר; Vulg has *universa*, and Pesh has *lgmr*. The word obviously means "completely, fully."[22]

The second part of the verse refers to the future: "and it shall be uninhabited for ever; not shall it be rebuilt again." The Hebrew has תל "a mound, a heap," which LXX translated freely by *ἀοίκητος*. The תל is called a תל עולם in MT "a perpetual ruin." The Greek renders the second word by *εἰς τὸν αἰῶνα*, but this need not presuppose a parent לעולם.

Such tells are indeed uninhabited mounds, which exist to the present day, and they graphically remind one of this verse.[23]

---

18. For *ἐν πυρί* as instrumental see SS 117.
19. As Aq fully understood by his *ὁλοτελῶς*.
20. E.g. by Driver "*As a whole-offering*," and adopted by NRSV and ZurB et al, or as "a holocaust" by NJPS.
21. For כליל in other versions and in Tar see Daniel 270—272.
22. König rejects any notion of sacrifice, and translates "(ihre ganze Beute) gänzlich wegen Jahves." For an excellent discussion of *πανδαμεί* see Daniel 263—265.
23. Aq translated the word literally as *χῶμα*.

13:17(18) The subject of the opening clause is *οὐδέν*, modified by a partitive *ἀπό* phrase.[24] The notion that nothing shall adhere in the hand means to leave severely alone, take nothing for oneself. Matters which are anathema are banned, devoted to destruction. The purpose underlying the prohibition is given in the *ἵνα* clause governing four coordinate verbs, the first one being an aorist subjunctive and the next three all futures.[25] The subjunctive verb represents a negative notion, "that the Lord may turn away from his burning anger," and the future ones are all positive: "he may give you mercy, be merciful to you, and multiply you." The change to the future can also be interpreted differently; i.e. one can understand *ἵνα* as governing only the first clause, with the three futures then interpreting how God's turning away from anger would eventuate for the people in the promises given in the three future verbs. Presumably the *ὃν τρόπον* structure applies only to the last verb, and refers to the numerous divine promises of progeny to the patriarchs. The subject of *ὤμοσεν*, though obvious from the context, is given as *κύριος* in LXX, but not in MT; hex has indicated this by placing *κύριος* under the obelus.

In the tradition only B among the Greek witnesses added *και* at the beginning of the verse, which happens to equal MT, but this is mere coincidence. The Byz text has *ουθεν* instead of *οὐδέν*, but Deut always uses the spelling with *delta*.[26] Also in the tradition *C s* change *ὃν τρόπον ὤμοσεν* to *καθως ελαλησεν*, and a popular A F M V gloss adds *καθως ελαλησεν σοι* as a doublet immediately before it. For the source of the variant text comp 1:11 6:3,19 12:20 26:19 31:3.[27]

13:18(19) A general condition attached to the immediately preceding, i.e. to the promise to multiply as the Lord swore to the fathers, made up of typical Deut structures: a) "hear the voice of the Lord" occurs many times in Deut;[28] b) for "to guard all his commandments" see comments at 4:2,40; c) for "which I am commanding you today" see comment at 4:2, and d) for "to do *τὸ καλὸν καὶ τὸ ἀρεστόν* before the Lord your God" see comment at 6:18. For the last collocation LXX rendered Sam's הטוב ו, which is absent in MT, and

24. See SS 169.
25. For the future after *ἵνα* see Bl-D 369.2.
26. See the note at THGD 114.
27. See also list 8 in THGD 88.
28. See list 16 in THGD 91.

so hex placed *τὸ καλὸν καί* under the obelus. Also in the tradition the A F M V majority text read the plural *εισακουσητε* instead of the *ἀκούσῃς*, which equals MT, but LXX follows MT in a consistent singular throughout the verse. This is clear from the dwindling support for variant plurals throughout the verse. The first *σου* becomes *υμων* in *C* and Byz; *σοι* becomes *υμιν* only in *C*, and *σου* 2° becomes *υμων* only in *d t* of the Byz text. Only the singular throughout is defensible as original text.

Chapter 14

14:1 That Israel was acknowledged by the Lord as his son was noted at Exod 4:22—23, but here the Israelites are called *υἱοὶ κυρίου*. A *s z*+ variant has the future *εσεσθε* for the present *ἐστε*. Since MT has the nominal clause בנים אתם only *ἐστε* can be LXX. That a new section begins here is clear from the lack of an introductory conjunction in both LXX and MT.

Because of their sonship the Israelites are told *οὐ φοιβήσετε*, a hapax legomenon in LXX. The verb *φοιβάω* means "to cleanse, purify." MT has תתגדדו "cut yourselves," used of the Baal priests in their attempts to enlist Baal's help on Carmel (1Kgs 18:28). Here it is used to describe pagan customs in connection with mourning for the dead, as at Jer 16:6; there, however, it is rendered by *ἐντομίδας ποιήσωσι*; comp also Jer 41(48):5 47:5(29:6) and Hos 7:14.[1] The translator avoided the notion of gashing oneself in favor of the notion of purification. Possibly the substitution was an oblique reference to Egyptian funerary customs, in which the corpse was cleansed with various spices; such reverance for the corpse was pagan and was to be avoided by the "sons of the Lord."[2] I would translate: "you must not engage in purificatory rites."

Also forbidden was the placing of *φαλάκρωμα* between the eyes for the dead. MT introduces this second prohibition with a conjunction, and hex has added *και* before *οὐκ* to equal it. The prepositional phrase *ἐπὶ νεκρῷ* as well as its Hebrew equivalent למת are intended to apply to both clauses, though the lack of *και* in LXX makes its application to the first clause less certain. The *φαλάκρωμα*, or קרחה, means "baldness," and the practice referred to is the cutting off of hair on the forehead, i.e. the forelock (literally "between the

1. Aq translates the word by *κατατεμεῖσθε*.
2. Dogniez-Harl refers to an article by E.Degani, "Due note filologiche, I:Dt 14,1 LXX, Bolletin del Comitato per la preparazione dell' Ediz. naz. del Classici greci e latini 14 (1966),93—94, in which the verb is thought to be derived from Phoebus, epithet of Apollo. But this is irrelevant and incorrect. The fact is that the epithet *φοῖβος* was applied to Apollo; i.e. the verb is not a reflex of Phoebus, but is simply from the stem $\sqrt{}$*foiba-* meaning "be clear, bright."

eyes"). The same practice was forbidden the priests at Lev 21:5: *φαλάρκωμα οὐ ξυρηθήσεσθε τὴν κεφαλὴν ἐπὶ νεκρῷ*.

In the tradition the verb *φοιβήσετε* was often confused with the verb *φοβέω*, since the command "do not fear" is common in LXX, particularly as *φοβηθησεσθε* (here in *b d t*+), but this is not overly sensible in this context; it is simply a copyist error thoughtlessly perpetuated in the tradition.

14:2 As the initial *ὅτι* shows, this verse gives the basis for the prohibition of v.1: "you are a holy people to the Lord your God, and you the Lord your God has chosen that you should be for him a *λαὸν περιούσιον* from all the nations which are on the earth.[3] In MT this is word for-word the same as 7:6 except for the second "your God," which is absent here, though present in Sam. Hex has accordingly placed *ὁ θεός σου* under the obelus.

LXX, however, has some differences from 7:6 in the second clause. It has the synonym *ἐξελέξατο* instead of *προείλατο*; it also has the fuller *γενέσθαι σε* for *εἶναι*, and instead of *παρὰ πάντα τὰ ἔθνη ὅσα* it has *ἀπὸ πάντων τῶν ἐθνῶν τῶν*. This last named difference is much more Hebraic in its rendering of the מן of comparison by *ἀπό* rather than by *παρά*. The verse has changed from the plural of v.1 to the singular in both MT and LXX. The singular is probably due to the singular of 7:6, from which MT obviously took its text. The plural then continues through v.20a, i.e. throughout the section on permitted and forbidden foods. For the verse in general see comments at 7:6.

14:3 Vv.3—20 are largely a repetition of Lev 11:2—20, though on the whole abbreviated except for vv.4b—5, which are absent from Lev. V.3 constitutes a superscription: "you shall not eat any abomination." Only MT and Tar^{O} continue the singular from v.2 into v.3, all other ancient witnesses, i.e. including LXX and Sam, have the plural. Which is earlier is unknown; arguments for both seem convincing. LXX makes the superscription integral to the section by integrating its number with that of the section. For *βδέλυγμα*, the term that characterizes all the forbidden foods, see comment at 7:25.

---

3. Instead of *περιούσιον* Sym has *ἐξαίρετον*.

14:4 Vv.4—5 give a list of the cattle which may be eaten, whereas Lev 11:2 substitutes for the list "from all the cattle which are on earth." MT introduces the list with זאת הבהמה, which LXX correctly interprets as collective, and renders by the plural *ταῦτα τὰ κτήνη*. V.4 names three such: *μόσχον*, *ἀμνόν* and *χίμαρον* "calf, lamb and kid," each accompanied by an *ἐκ* phrase, resp. "*ἐκ βοῶν* ... *ἐκ προβάτων* ... *ἐξ αἰγῶν*." The latter two represent bound phrases in MT: שה כשבים and שה עזים,[4] with LXX differentiating quite properly between the two kinds of שה. The first phrase, *μόσχον ἐκ βοῶν*, is formulated on the analogy of the other two with an *ἐκ* phrase, though MT simply has שור.[5] The *O* text omitted *ἐκ βοῶν*, thereby equalling MT.

14:5 A list of seven animals legitimate for food, the first two of which, *ἔλαφον* and *δορκάδα*, being well-known equivalents for איל and צבי resp. The other five equations occur only here. The יחמור also occurs at 1Kgs 5:3 where the translator did not translate it. Its equivalent in LXX here is *βούβαλον*. Apparently the reference is to some member of the antelope family. The remainder are all hapax legomena in the Greek OT. The אקו "wild goat" is a hapax legomenon, and is rendered by *τραγέλαφον*, which also occurs in the Theod of Job 39:1 as a translation for יעלי "mountain goat." דישן is also a hapax legomenon, and is translated by *πύγαργον* "white-rumped antelope."[6] Also probably in the antelope family is the תאו (see also Isa 51:20 where, however, LXX has *σευτλίον* "beet"). It is translated by *ὄρυγα*, also some kind of antelope or gazelle. Similarly problematic is the last animal, זמר, also a hapax legomenon in MT, oddly translated by *καμηλοπάρδαλιν* "giraffe." Obviously the translator did not know the word.

14:6 This equals Lev 11:3 exactly in LXX, but not in MT; it is the Deut text which corresponds to LXX in both. LXX (along with Pesh Vulg) follows Sam in having no conjunction at the beginning of the verse. Permitted as food are land animals with three characteristics, the first two of which, *διχηλοῦν ὁπλήν* "parting the hoof" and *ὀνυχιστῆρας ὀνυχίζον δύο χηλῶν* "having hoofs cloven

4. See SS 69.
5. Aq has the list as *βοῦς βόσκημα ἐκ ἀμνῶν καὶ βόσκημα ἐκ αἰγῶν* (retroverted from Syh).
6. So translated from a list of inhabitants of nomadic Libya in Herodotus IV.192 by A.D.Godley (Loeb Classics, 1963).

in two parts (literally two hoofs),"[7] seem both in LXX and in the parent Hebrew to say the same thing. The only distinction that I can see is that the second defines the cleaving of hoofs more precisely as being *δύο χηλῶν*/שתי פרסות.[8]

The third characteristic is *ἀνάγον μηρυκισμόν* "bringing up cud," i.e. the animal must be a ruminant.

14:7 An abbreviated version of Lev 11:4—6. MT begins with the exceptive particle אך, which Lev translates by *πλήν*, but Deut omits (because of homoiarchon? — note אך את, though LXX does have *καί*). Forbidden are three animals: the camel, the *δασύποδα*[9] and the *χοιρογρύλλιον*. These last two are species of rabbits, so probably "hare and daman." These represent resp. the ארנבת and the שפן in MT of Deut, which are reversed in Lev. At Ps 103:18 and Prov 30:26 *χοιρογρύλλιος* renders שפן, whereas *δασύπους* occurs only here and in Lev.

The reason for the prohibition is given in the *ὅτι* construction: "these bring up the cud, but do not part the hoof." Note that of the three characteristics given in v.6 the second one is not mentioned, from which one might conclude that any distinction between מפרסת פרסה/*διχηλοῦν ὁπλήν* and שסעת שסע שתי פרסות/*ὀνυχιστῆρας ὀνυχίζον δύο χηλῶν* is of no fundamental importance. What is of central importance, however, is *ἀκάθαρτα ταῦτα ὑμῖν ἐστιν*. The notion of the "unclean" occurred at 12:15,22 for the first time in the book, but here the distinction, as applied to what may be eaten vs what is not allowed, is basic to the section; cf also vv.10,18. In fact, unclean things were defined in the superscription as *βδέλυγμα*, and in the Lev 11 parallel this is often stressed; see vv.10,11,12,20,23,41,42 and 43. The Byz text has changed *ἐστιν* to *εσται*, but MT has a nominal clause, and the future is a later rationalization. The structure *ὀνυχιζόντων ὀνυχιστῆρας* has only one word in MT as equivalent, השסועה, so hex placed *ὀνυχιστῆρας* under the obelus.

---

7. NJPS translates these two characteristics neatly by "that has true hoofs, which are cleft in two."
8. Aq apparently renders by *δύο χηλὴν καὶ δεδιχασμένον διχασμῷ δύο ὁπλῶν*. The *δύο χηλήν* as a rendering for מפרסת פרסה seems to me dubious. Aq would hardly have rendered פרסה by *χηλήν* and its plural פרסות by *ὁπλῶν*. I suspect that *δύο χηλήν* is not part of Aq, but merely a variant of the LXX text.
9. Aq has *λαγωόν* instead of *δασύποδα*.

14:8 LXX's text follows Sam rather than MT, which apparently lacks an equivalent for *ὀνυχίζει —— μηρυκισμόν*; this is placed under the obelus in hex to show its absence in MT; MT simply has ולא גרה "and not (the) cud," but Sam has ושסע שסע פרסה והוא גרה לא יגור. Furthermore, LXX largely corresponds to Lev 11:7—8, except that instead of *μηρυκισμὸν οὐ μαρυκᾶται* Lev has *οὐκ ἀνάγει μηρυκισμόν*; furthermore, MT, as well as LXX, adds the judgment "unclean are these to you" at the end in Lev, but this is lacking here.

Uncleanness means not only that the eating of such flesh is forbidden, but even the touching of *θνησιμαίων αὐτῶν* is not permitted;[10] this accords with Levitical understanding that this renders unclean, e.g. Lev 5:2.

14:9—10 These verses deal with creatures that live in the water, and considerably abbreviate their counterpart in Lev 11:9—12. Deut simply sets up the double criterion: the permitted species must have *πτερύγια καὶ λεπίδες* "fins and scales" for MT's סנפיר וקשקשת.[11] The Hebrew words are singular, but, as collectives, are correctly rendered by plural nouns throughout the section. In fact, the initial את זה is also rightly understood as *καὶ ταῦτα* (following Sam which also begins with a conjunction). Conversely, water creatures lacking such may not be eaten; "unclean are these for you." The omission of the subject *ταῦτα* in B+ is simply a careless mistake inspired by homoioteleuton (following *ἀκάθαρτα*).[12]

In the tradition of v.9 *ταῦτα* is followed by *α* in a V *b*+ reading; this makes good sense, but it is not supported by MT, and is merely a dittograph. In v.10 the majority A F M V text reads *ουδε* instead of *καί* before *λεπίδες*, but this is simply a stylistic improvement, and not original; the *καί* represents MT literally. The *ἐστιν* has no equivalent in MT, but is required as a linking verb for *ταῦτα*. Most witnesses (including A F M V) change to the plural *εσται*, which is, however, secondary.

14:11 Vv.11—19 deal with creatures of the sky; comp Lev 11:13—23, which deal with the same subject, but at times quite differently. In contrast to Lev

10. Aq renders the word נבלתם by *νεκριμαίων* <*αὐτῶν*>.
11. Aq substitutes *φολίδες* for *λεπίδες*.
12. See THGD 124.

Deut begins with a general statement approving the eating of any clean bird, which it repeats at the end of the section (v.19); Lev also ends with such a statement describing what characterizes clean creatures (v.21), and then proceeds to list such as well in v.22.

14:12 Vv.12—18 give a list of prohibited creatures; clean ones, though permitted, are not listed at all in Deut. As in vv.7 and 9 זה is correctly understood as a collective — ταῦτα. The phrase ἀπ' αὐτῶν is clearly a partitive expression.[13] The syntactical structure differs from that of MT in that the relative pronoun of MT is not rendered in Greek, so hex added α after ταῦτα. Translations will illustrate the differences; MT has "And these are ones from which you may not eat," whereas LXX has "As for these, you may not eat (any) of them." V.12 lists three such prohibited creatures: the eagle καὶ τὸν γρύπα καὶ τὸν ἁλιάετον as in Lev 11:13 where, as here, MT's nouns represented are resp. נשר, פרס and עזניה. γρύπα/פרס as well as ἁλιάετον/עזניה occur only in these lists in OT. All three birds are vultures of some kind. The last-named bird is variously spelled in the tradition, but the variants can easily be explained from an original ἁλιάετον.[14]

14:13 This equals Lev 11:14 in LXX, but here MT has three birds rather than two. The γύπα, some kind of vulture, and the ἰκτῖνα "kite" may represent the MT of Lev, i.e. דאה and איה, though the equations are quite uncertain. Apparently the first word in Deut, והראה was read as והדאה.[15] If this is correct, the third name in MT, הדיה, is a doublet for הדאה, but this is only a possibility. Origen thought that the first one was absent from LXX and so he added και τον ιξον under the asterisk in first position in hex.

The concluding למינה "according to its kind" is throughout this section translated by καὶ τὰ ὅμοια αὐτῷ "and those similar to it," as in the Lev counterpart; see also vv.14(twice) and 17. In all cases it is joined by καί over against MT; in other words, not just the species of fowl mentioned but all those which are like it are also forbidden.

13. See SS 169.
14. See the discussion in Walters 80—81.
15. Aq, however, has ἴξον as the first bird.

14:14(15) = Lev 11:14b—16 in LXX; the texts are identical except that Lev has an extra *κατὰ τὰ ὅμοια αὐτῷ* after λάρον, whereas the Hebrew texts differ only in that BHS of Lev lacks the initial *waw*, though Sam and many mss have it. MT continues throughout the section to prepose each creature with את, but LXX, which in vv.12 and 13 had articulated each one, no longer adds the article. Hex apparently, as represented by mss 376 and 426, did add the article for four of the nouns (excepting the first one). The first one, *κόρακα* for ערב "raven," is no problem,[16] since it has *πάντα* before it. The second fowl is בת היענה "ostrich" translated by *στρουθόν*, which normally means "sparrow" or at least some small type of bird, whreas a "*μέγας στρουθός*" is a more usual term for ostrich.[17] But see also Isa 34:13 43:20 where the equation also obtains (though in the latter case as *θυγατέρες στρουθῶν*).[18] In the Isa passages the context is that of the desert, of lonely places.

The equation תחמס "falcon" and *γλαῦκα* "some kind of owl" only obtains in these two lists. The next one is λάρον, which is unique to these lists; apparently it is some kind of sea-bird, possibly a gull; this also describes שחף, but nothing more is known about it. The last one is the *ἱέρακα* "hawk" for נץ, also some kind of hawk. The equation also occurs at Job 39:26.

In the tradition the word order of LXX is often disturbed in vv.14—17, in part stimulated by certain differences over against the list in Lev. Generally speaking, LXX seems to follow MT, and LXX usually has majority support in the tradition.[19]

14:15(16) LXX begins the list of three with *καί*, following the text of Sam as well as of many mss over against BHS. The Hebrew list has הכוס, הינשוף and התנשפת, apparently representing three different kinds of owl. Whether the translator knew all these birds is doubtful; his list consists of *ἐρωδιόν* "heron, stork," *κύκνον* "swan" and *ἶβιν* "ibis." Since the Lev text is now different, it is difficult to compare them. In Lev 11:19 *ἐρωδιόν* renders החסידה "stork," which is expected; see also Ps 103:17 *τοῦ ἐρωδιοῦ ἡ οἰκία ἡγεῖται αὐτῶν* where חסידה is the Hebrew counterpart. The second one, *κύκνον*, occurs in

16. Though Aq does render the את כל preceding the noun by *σὺν πάντα*.
17. See LS sub *στρουθός* 2.
18. Aq renders somewhat more precisely by *στρουθοκάμηλον*.
19. See THGD 129—130.

Lev 11:18 for הרחם. What a רחם is is not clear; in Arabic "*rakhk am*" is the Egyptian vulture, "Neophron percnopterus," but the translator of Lev did not understand it thus. The same bird appears, though with a feminine ending, in the next verse, where LXX has *ἔποπα*. Apparently the word was strange to both translators. The third one, *ἶβιν*, is also puzzling. It represents תנשמת, but in Lev as well as in Isa 34:11, which also had an Egyptian translator, it renders ינשוף. But then the distinction between the two types of owl, ינשוף and תנשמת, is quite uncertain.

14:16(17) Three more unclean birds are given here. In MT these are הקאת "pelican," הרחמה for which see רחם in v.15(16), and השלך apparently some kind of owl. The Greek list is *καταράκτην*, *ἔποπα* and *νυκτικόρακα*. The first one must be some kind of "swooping down" type of bird, possibly a cormorant. Like the pelican it is known for its diving for fish. In Lev 11:18 it is used to render חסידה "stork," but at Ps 101:6 it renders קאת. Both LXX and MT took the bird to be a long-necked fish-eating bird. The second bird, *ἔποπα*, is the hoopoe. In Lev 11:19 it renders דוכיפת, which is unknown, and here it stands for רחמה, equally uncertain. In Zach 5:9 it translates חסידה. שלך occurs only in the two lists in MT, and is in both cases translated by *νυκτικόρακα*, also some kind of owl.

14:17(18) Four more birds are forbidden as food. The list in MT contains החסידה "stork," האנפה possibly a "heron," to which is added למינה (for which see discussion at v.13), הדוכיפת (see v.16), and העטלף "bat." The first one is identified as *πελεκᾶνα* "pelican" here, but as *ἐρωδιόν* in Lev 11:19, for which see v.15. The אנפה, as well as its translation *χαραδριόν*, occurs only in the two lists. Neither one is identified with certainty.[20] LXX translated הדוכיפת by *πορφυρίωνα* "purple coot," a member of the rail family. Both words occur only in the two lists, but in Lev 11:18 *πορφυρίωνα* has התנשמת, for which see v.15, as its Hebrew counterpart. The last bird is העטלף, and is correctly translated by *νυκτερίδα* in both lists; the equation is elsewhere only made at Isa 2:20.

---

20. LS identifies the *χαραδριός* as "probably the thickknee or Norfolk plover ... it was very greedy hence prov. *χαραδριοῦ βίον ζῆν*, of a glutton."

14:18(19) Lev distinguished between *τῶν ἑρπετῶν τῶν πετεινῶν* which may be eaten in 11:21—22 and those which are unclean in vv.29—31, whereas in Deut *πάντα τὰ ἑρπετὰ τῶν πετεινῶν ἀκάθαρτα*, and "you may not eat any of them." The phrase *ἀπ' αὐτῶν* is a partitive one. In MT the first clause is a nominal one in which טמא הוא לכם constitutes the predicate. LXX changed the syntactical pattern by translating הוא by *ταῦτα ἐστιν*; i.e. "all the creeping things that fly" (literally "of flying creatures") is a pendant nominative, and the main clause is "these are unclean for you." Origen was puzzled by this and placed *ταῦτα* under the obelus in hex, i.e. he thought that only the *ἐστιν* equalled הוא.

The prohibition in the second part is also formally different. LXX follows Sam's לא תאכלו מהם, but MT lacks the prepositional phrase and vocalizes the verb as a third person plural Niph: "not shall they be eaten."

In the tradition *O* Byz have an initial *και*. This corresponds to MT, and could be hex in origin. A popular B F text omitted *ταῦτα* which simplified the text considerably; this was probably the stimulus for the omission. The omission is, however, post hexaplaric, as the hex text proves. Also under the obelus in hex is *ἀπ' αὐτῶν*, which formally equals MT, but its omission would make odd sense in view of the active *φάγεσθε*.

14:20(21) Over against MT LXX begins with *καί*. Its omission in B *O* Byz could be recensional. LXX has *πᾶν θνησιμαῖον* preposed; hex has reordered it after the verb to equal MT. The Israelites may not eat any carcass; what is intended is the carcass of an animal that has died of itself. It may, however, be given to a *πάροικος* "an alien," which renders גר of MT. The word גר occurs 21 times in the book, and it is always translated by *προσήλυτος* "proselyte, resident alien" except here, and at 23:7 where *πάροικος* is also used. In the latter case LXX reads "not may you abominate an Egyptian, because you were a *πάροικος* in his land." The translator makes a distinction not made by MT in that the foreigner or alien is distinguished from the proselyte, who had numerous rights in Israelite law. To the translator גר can be a proselyte, i.e. a resident alien, or merely a foreigner, a *πάροικος*.[21] By making this distinction the apparent contradiction of Deut with Lev 17:15, where the "proselytes"

---

21. Aq uses different terms for the two: *προσηλύτῳ* vs *ξένῳ*.

along with the native born Israelite may not eat *θνησιμαῖον*, is voided. Such a *πάροικος* is one who is *ἐν ταῖς πόλεσίν σου*; this translates בשעריך, i.e. correctly understanding gates as metonymic for cities; see comment at 12:15. Similarly such a *θνησιμαῖον* may be sold to a stranger. There is one difference between the *πάροικος* and the *ἀλλότριος* shown by the verbs; the *πάροικος* may be given the carcass, but it may be sold to the stranger, presumably someone outside Israel. For *ἀποδώσῃ* see comment at 2:28.

The *ὅτι* clause explains the raison d'etre for the regulation; "you are a holy people for the Lord your God." Being holy involved remaining cultically clean. For λαὸς ἅγιος see comment at 7:6.

The final prohibition against boiling an *ἄρνα*[22] in its mother's milk is exactly the same in Exod 23:19; see Note ad loc.

14:21(22) Vv.21—28 deal with the regulations concerning the tithe. MT has a cognate free infinitive before the verb, which LXX renders by the accusative noun *δεκάτην*, and then translates the verb by the compound *ἀποδεκατώσεις*. For the usage see Gen 28:22. The verb is a neologism created by the Gen translator to express the Hebrew notion of tithing. Since the verb already has an accusative modifier, LXX renders the את phrase by a genitive *παντὸς γενήματος τοῦ σπέρματός σου* modifying *δεκάτην*. An A+ reading has *παν το γενημα* instead of *παντὸς γενήματος*, which could be understood as a correction towards MT, though it more likely represents an attempt at leveling with *τὸ γένημα*; see below.

MT follows with היוצא השדה, but LXX supports Sam which lacks the first article, i.e. the collocation is a bound phrase. LXX, however, adds *σου*, thus *τὸ γένημα τοῦ ἀγροῦ σου* "the produce of your field," which in MT is in apposition to the את structure, thus "all the produce of your seed, (even) that which the field brings out." But LXX placed this in apposition to *τὴν δεκάτην* rather than in the genitive. Hex has placed *σου* under the obelus, since it is absent in MT. The final structure, *ἐνιαυτὸν κατ' ἐνιαυτόν*, correctly interprets the distributive שנה שנה of MT.

14:22(23) LXX follows Sam in its pronoun *αὐτό* modifying *φάγῃ*, whereas MT has מעשר as direct modifier, i.e. "and you shall eat … the tithe." LXX

---

22. Aq translates גדי literally by *ἔριφον*.

makes two clauses out of this by adding a verb *οἴσεις* before *ἐπιδέκατα*, thus "you shall eat it ... and bring the tithes." Both *αὐτό* and the verb have been put under the obelus in hex, since they have no counterpart in MT. The antecedent of *αὐτό* is *τὸ γένημα*. In view of this LXX has limited the eating to the produce of the field, whereas in MT the feast included meat, i.e. the first-born of your cattle and of your flock. In fact, MT has a conjunction before בכרת, which LXX omits (intentionally? comp 12:17), but a popular hex text has added *και*. The tithe is now called *τὰ ἐπιδέκατα* rather than *δεκάτην* as in v.21, but the Hebrew text is also different. Instead of עשר (see comment at v.21) MT has מעשר, as in v.27(28), where *ἐπιδέκατον* is the LXX translation; cf also 12:17. For "the place which the Lord your God chose to have his name invoked there" see comment at 12:5. LXX has added *κύριος ὁ θεός σου* as the expressed subject, though MT lacks it. LXX always has an expressed subject in this context. In fact, in 16 out of a total of 19 occurrences of this formula in the book the subject is as here, and in the other three (16:16 18:6 31:11) the subject is simply *κύριος*; never is the subject unexpressed as here in MT. Hex has of course placed the subject under the obelus.

The combination "grain, wine and oil" occurs six times in the book (also at 7:13 11:14 12:17 18:4 28:51); even more frequent is "cattle and sheep."[23] For *οἴνου* and *ἐλαίου* as renderings for תירש and יצהר resp. see comment at 7:13.

In the tradition *οἴσεις* obtains in a popular B text as the plural *οισετε*, or in the singular passive *οισεται*. Since the verb was added by the translator on his own it is unlikely that he would have made it plural, since the context is entirely in the singular. It is of course possible that *οισεται* was the source of its more popular homophone *οισετε*; at least that would fit the context.

14:23(24) MT has כי four times in this verse, which is rhetorically confusing. LXX has taken the first two as marking the protasis, thus *ἐάν ... καί*, and the third and fourth as causal, i.e. as *ὅτι*, distinguishing, however, between the latter two by rendering יברכך by a simple future. This means that the second *ὅτι* clause is to be taken as interruptive, i.e. "— because the Lord your God will bless you." The apodosis then follows in vv.24—26.

23. See list 42 in THGD 97.

The use of δέ as contrastive particle is appropriate, since what follows contrasts with vv.21—22. The clause μακρὰν γένηται ἀπὸ σοῦ renders ירבה ממך in the light of the third כי clause, ירחק ממך. In fact, רבה is never rendered in OT by μακρὸς γίνομαι elsewhere except at 19:6, which see.

The V *d t z*+ change of γένηται to απεχη is purely stylistic, i.e. a change from "be far from" to "be far away from." Similarly, the popular A F M V transposition of ἀπὸ σοῦ after ὁ ὁδός is probably merely an attempt to simplify the text for the reader.

LXX simplifies the second כי clause by changing it to καί, as though MT intended וכי. MT really means "and should the way be too much for you so that you can not bring it," whereas LXX has put the two clauses on the same syntactic level: "and should the road be distant for you and you cannot bring them up." The Greek sensibly renders the singular suffix of שאתו by the plural αὐτά, the antecedent being ἐπιδέκατα.

For the relative clause see comment at v.22. It is not surprising that the majority F M V text has simplified the last ὅτι clause by changing εὐλογήσει to the aorist tense. It would be quite possible to take יברכך as an old preterite, but the more common, though also the more difficult, understanding as a future is to be preferred. The clause interrupts the sequence by a promise. What is meant is "because the Lord your God will (indeed) bless you." What LXX is saying is that the regulation will certainly apply to you — the Lord will give you abundant prosperity, and so you will be giving tithes.

14:24(25) This introduces the apodosis: "then you shall sell them for money, etc." ἀποδώσῃ is a good interpretation of נתתה "give," i.e. give for money. ἀργυρίου is a genitive of price, correctly understanding the ב of MT.[24] MT has no pronominal suffix, and so hex has placed αὐτά under the obelus. LXX has also changed בידך to the plural ἐν ταῖς χερσίν σου, which is simply ad sensum, i.e. (take it) with you. For the relative clause see vv.22 and 23; for αὐτόν comp 12:14, 16:7,15,16.

14:25—26(26—27) Instead of the נתתה בכסף of v.25 MT now has נתתה הכסף, which LXX understood correctly as δώσεις τὸ ἀργύριον (ἐπί) "you shall give

24. See SS 128.

out the money (for)." The *C′* text substitutes the third person verb for *δώσεις*, which is hardly sensible; it is probably due to the fact that the verb is surrounded by verbal forms ending in -*σῃ*, and an unthinking scribe wrote *δωσῃ* (leading to *δωσει*). It is of course wrong. What the money is to be paid out for is *παντὸς οὗ ἂν ἐπιθυμῇ ἡ ψυχή σου*, a construction which occurs twice, first to introduce the possible ingredients for the sanctuary feasts, *βουσίν*, *προβάτοις*, *οἴνῳ*, *σίκερα*, and then at the end of the list as a further alternative. In MT the two structures are not identical, the first having the verb תאוה and the second, תשאלך; the distinction is minimal, "you might crave" vs "you might seek for yourself," and LXX has not tried to manufacture a distinction.

MT gives the list of possible purchases as a list of four all joined by *waw*, whereas LXX gives them as two logical pairs: *ἐπὶ βουσὶν ἢ ἐπὶ προβατοῖς* and *ἐπὶ οἴκῳ ἢ ἐπὶ σίκερα*. A majority B text does add *η* before the second pair, but it is to be doubted that this is recensional; it is clearly not hex (*O* nor Syh witness to it), and it was simply added for stylistic reasons.[25] It will be noted that *σίκερα* is indeclinable, a transcription of the Aramaic form שכרא.[26] For "you shall eat before the Lord your God" see v.22, though here it occurs without an *αὐτόν* as modifier. For the notion of "rejoicing" see comment at 12:7. That the Israelite was to rejoice occurs often in the book; see e.g. 12:7,12,18 16:11,14,15.

The celebration was a communal one, in which not only *σὺ καὶ ὁ οἶκός σου* were to take part, but also the Levite. But this is not what MT says. There the Levite is not necessarily part of those partaking of the annual tithes as in LXX; comp vv.28; rather the Israelite is commanded: As for the Levite who is in your gates לא תעזבנו; LXX omits this entirely, and hex adds *ουκ εγκαταλειψεις αυτον* under the asterisk to make up for the omission. MT then has a כי clause giving the reason for not forsaking the Levite, which in LXX becomes the reason for having him take part in the celebration. This is in line with 12:12, which also makes the Levite one who shares in the festivities: *ὅτι οὐκ ἔστιν αὐτῷ μερὶς οὐδὲ κλῆρος μεθ' ὑμῶν*; this only differs in the number of the final pronoun. For *πόλεσίν σου* see comment at v.20.

---

25. For the second pair Tar^{O} has an amusing interpretation: ובחמר חדת ועתיק, which hardly represents the difference between the fermented and the distilled grape.
26. Aq, however, translates the word as *μεθύσματι*.

14:27(28) After three years the tithes are to be disposed of in a different way. MT says: "at the end of three years you shall bring out all the tithe of your produce in that year," with a second clause added "and you shall deposit it in your gates (i.e. your cities)." LXX does not have a *καί*, which means that "in that year" is most naturally read with the second clause, thus "in that year you shall place it in your cities (see comment on *πόλεσίν σου* at v.20). The Byz text has added *και* before *θήσεις*, which is probably inspired ultimately by the Hebrew text. The Greek text by its omission stresses the contrast between the practice of the third year and that of the other two years much more clearly than MT does. The Greek also follows Sam in having a pronominal modifier, *αὐτό*, after *θήσεις*, which hex accordingly put under the obelus.

14:28(29) The *ὅτι* clause concerning the Levite is an exact repetition of the *ὅτι* clause of v.27, which see. The tithe of the third year is solely for the disadvantaged, not just for the Levite but also for the proselyte, the orphan and the widow, for which see comment at 10:18. For *πόλεσίν σου* see comment at v.20.

The purpose of the triennial disposal of the tithes for the disadvantaged is given in the *ἵνα* clause; it is "in order that the Lord your God may bless you in all the works which you do." MT has מעשה ידך. Hex has added under the asterisk *των χειρων σου*, the plural noun being ad sensum (so too in Pesh Vulg). The relative pronoun *οἷς* is dative by attraction to its antecedent *ἔργοις*, which is typical of the Deut translator.

Chapter 15

15:1 This verse introduces the regulations governing sabbatical years of release for debt. "Every seven years you shall effect release."[1] The term *ἄφεσις* means "release, exemption," and is used as a technical term to render שמטה, which also obtains at v.9 and 31:10 in the phrase "year of release," as well as to translate the cognate verb at vv.2,3; cf Exod 23:11. The word also occurs regularly to translate the term יובל in Lev, popularly known as the "jubilee (year)"; cf e.g. Lev 25:28. For *ἄφεσις* see Note at Exod 23:11.

MT states that this is to take place מקץ שבע שנים, but this does not mean "after seven years" (i.e. at the beginning of year eight), but rather "at the end of seven years," as the details of the regulations, e.g. v.9, make clear.

15:2 MT introduces the legislation by וזה דבר השמטה "and this is the matter of the release," which LXX interprets by *καὶ οὕτως τὸ πρόσταγμα τῆς ἀφέσεως* "and such is the ordinance concerning the release." *O* mss have "corrected" this to *κ. ουτος ο λογος τ. αφ*. One might think that *οὕτως* was an itacism for *ουτος*, but this cannot be correct since it would have to be neuter, and two mss actually do read *τουτο*. The translator freely introduces *τὸ πρόσταγμα* by "in this manner," i.e. this is how the ordinance must be carried out. The use of *πρόσταγμα* is astute in that the matter of the release is in reality a decree, a divine ordinance (see v.5). The ordinance is put in third person in MT: "every creditor must release what he has lent his neighbour." LXX personalizes this by putting it in second person: *ἀφήσεις πᾶν χρέος ἴδιον* which (your) neighbour owes you," thus a demand for cancellation of every personal debt owed by the neighbour. In accordance with good Greek usage LXX does not render the suffix of רעהו since the referent is obvious from the context.[2] Hex has added *σου* under the asterisk to equal MT. The free rendering in second person may well have been inspired by the free infinitive שמוט

1. Aq renders the verse in literalistic fashion by *ἀπὸ τέλος ἑπτὰ ἐτῶν ποιήσεις ὑποσπασμόν* (retroverted from Syh). The noun is a hapax legomenon derived from *ὑποσπάω* "to draw away," hence "removal, erasure," and so a removal of restrictions.

2. For Deut usage in the translation of רעהו and רעך see THGD 77—78.

which contextually takes on the structure of its context, i.e. of תעשה of v.1. Then כל בעל משה ידו was understood not as "every creditor," but as *πᾶν χρέος ἴδιον*.[3]

MT then continues with לא יגש את רעהו ואת אחיו "not shall he press his neighbour, even his brother." LXX has *καί* at the beginning, probably due to dittography in the parent text, since the preceding word, רעהו, ends in a *waw*. LXX continues in second person: *τὸν ἀδελφόν σου οὐκ ἀπαιτήσεις*, omitting את רעהו ו and preposing the accusative modifier. Hex has reordered the text to conform to MT and added *τον πλησιον σου* before *καὶ τὸν ἀδελφόν σου* under the asterisk, thereby exactly equalling MT. LXX had omitted reference to the neighbour in the second clause because it was repetitious, and by limiting the requirement not to demand payment from "your brother" has made two parallel regulations, one about the neighbour and a similar one about the brother.

The *ὅτι* clause gives the basis for the demand for remission: "because a release has been proclaimed for the Lord your God." *τῷ θεῷ σου* has no counterpart in MT, and was placed under the obelus by hex to make that clear. The use of the passive *ἐπικέκληται* correctly renders the indefinite קרא "one has called (a release)," i.e. a release has been called. The *b n* text has the genitive: "the Lord your God's release" rather than the dative of agent: "(release) by the Lord your God."

15:3 MT makes the first cut after תגש, i.e. "of the stranger you may demand payment." LXX disregarded the conjunction in ואשר, interpreting the relative clause as modifying *ἀπαιτήσεις*, thus "of the stranger you may demand whatever is yours from him." This then stands in contrast with "of your brother you shall effect a release of your debt," with the last *σου* to be understood as an objective genitive, i.e. the debt to you. MT has no equivalent for *παρ' αὐτῷ* in the relative clause, and hex placed it under the obelus. The phrase became necessary once the clause was taken to modify the first verb. MT also has no real counterpart for *τοῦ χρέους σου*, though ידך occurs in its slot. But "your hand" is probably to be taken as subject of תשמט, i.e. "your hand shall cancel (payment)." Hex did not place *τοῦ χρέους σου* under the obelus in view of the fact that its slot is occupied in MT by ידך.

3. Which SS 102 classifies as a free translation, but see Tar^{O}, which renders by תשמט כל גבר מרי רשו "you must release every debtor."

A majority text has introduced the last clause with the adversative particle *δε* to make clear that the two clauses are contrastive. *τοῦ ἀδελφοῦ* modifies *ἄφεσιν*, i.e. you must effect the release of your brother with respect to his debt to you. Most witnesses change to the dative *τω αδελφω*; this would constitute a simplification of the text. For the secondary nature of the majority reading *εαν* instead of *ἄν*, see comment at 5:27.

15:4 LXX simplifies the clausal structure of MT by disregarding the first word of אפס כי. The first *ὅτι* clause then gives the reason for the regulation in v.3, i.e. "you must cancel the debt owed you by your brother because there must not be anyone in need among you." This in turn can be asserted because of the fact that the Lord your God will certainly bless you in the land. *ὁ θεός σου* is placed under the obelus since it has no counterpart in MT, the translator having followed Sam's אלהיך. What LXX is saying is that there must be no *ἐνδεής* among you, which there would be if debts were never cancelled. But such release will not really be a burden in view of the second *ὅτι* clause. In the tradition a popular V reading has *εστιν*, but MT has יהיה. A present tense defeats the point being made, viz. that there should not be anyone who is needy among you.

The relative clause is introduced by a dative pronoun *ᾗ* which is inflected by attraction to its antecedent *γῇ*. For the phrase *ἐν κλήρῳ* see comment at 12:1.

15:5 The verse is a protasis in familiar Deut language, but it has no obvious apodosis. Since the translator uses a *δέ* construction it seems to me unlikely that, as some scholars maintain for MT,[4] the translator intended the apodosis to be found in v.4a, with v.4b then taken as a parenthetical remark. The apodosis must rather be found in v.6b with v.6a a parenthetical statement of fact; see comment at v.6. The "if" clause is strengthened in MT by a cognate free infinitive, translated in LXX by a dative noun *ἀκοῇ* as at 28:1; for the clause in general see comment at 13:18. The translator has rendered v.5a idiosyncratically in the plural, but then reverts to the singular in the *ὅσας* clause. I can see no pattern underlying this change. For the coordinate com-

4. E.g. Driver.

plementary infinitival pattern "guard and do" in which LXX follows the Sam text,[5] see comments at 4:2,40, and for the ὅσας clause see comment at 4:2.

15:6 The verse begins with a ὅτι clause with an aorist verb; this does not fit well in the context which is either future or conditional, a fact which could suggest that v.6a might have been intended as a parenthetical statement. Note that it contrasts with the second ὅτι clause of v.4. The statement includes the ὃν τρόπον clause (for which see comment at 11:25) as well.

The remainder of the verse is then the apodosis for v.5, introduced by an apodotic *καί*. It consists of two pairs of contrasting clauses. The first of these contrasts in voice. δανίζω in the active voice means "to lend," but in the middle, "to borrow." What is promised is: "(if ...,) then you will *lend* to many nations, but (δέ) you will not *borrow*, with hex correcting "but you" to *και συ*. Unfortunately this kind of literalism not only destroys the fine crafting of the translator, it also weakens the statement. In the parallel pair of clauses the contrast is solely in the subjects "you" vs "they," thus: "and you (σύ) shall rule over many nations, but (δέ) they will not rule over you." MT does not support the σύ, but the translator has added it to balance with the preceding clause, σὺ δὲ οὐ δανιῇ, thereby showing where the contrast in the second pair is centered. The two pairs are present chiastically with mention of the "many nations" in b and b′ of the a:b::b′:a′ pattern. It might be noted that the σύ of b′ is placed under the obelus in hex to show its absence in MT. The B *y z* text omits the σύ, which omission might be due to mediate Hebrew influence.

15:7 Vv.7—11 detail the proper treatment of the poor ordered for Israel. The protasis in MT defines אביון as מאחד אחיך which seems an awkward construction; it would be simpler if the preposition were with the second word rather than the first. LXX clarifies this considerably by a simple genitive τῶν ἀδελφῶν σου,[6] which must be what MT intended; hex tried to "fix it" by adding an *εκ* before it. For πόλεων as interpretation of שעריך see comment at 12:12. For the ᾗ clause see comment at v.4. In the tradition a popular V reading changed the pronoun to *ην*, which constitutes a grammatical correction, but the dative by attraction to its antecedent is original Deut.

---

5. Kenn 9,136*,181 and 674 also read ולעשות.
6. See SS 169.

The apodosis begins with *οὐκ ἀποστέρξεις* and continues through v.8. The pattern used is *οὐκ* + verb and *ουδὲ μή* + verb, followed in v.8 by two positive verbs *ἀνοίξεις ... δανιεῖς*. The initial verb is a hapax legomenon in OT; it constitutes the negative or privative (*ἀπο*) of *στέργω* "to love." Used with *καρδίαν* in the clause it could be translated: "not shall you empty your heart of love," an interesting rendering of תאמץ "harden (your heart)."[7] The unusual verb puzzled copyists, who changed it to *αποστρεψεις* (by palaeographic confusion), which became the majority reading in the tradition; this makes sense, but it is not LXX as MT makes clear.

The second prohibition is "nor shall you *συσφίγξῃς* your hand from your *ἐπιδεομένου* brother." The verb occurs only here with *τὴν χεῖρά σου* but its intent is clear: "you shall not clench, close up tight, your hand over against your impoverished brother." The middle participle renders אביון, which in the protasis had been translated by *ἐνδεής*.

15:8 In fact, the exact opposite is demanded: *ἀνοίγων ἀνοίξεις* your hand to him; this disregards the initial כי, which is probably short for כי אם "but," and also changes the singular ידך to the plural "your hands." Hex has duly introduced the verse with *οτι* under the asterisk to represent MT, and also has the singular *την χειρα*, which was also inspired by the Hebrew. In the present context this is clarified by the second clause: *δάνειον δανιεῖς αὐτῷ ὅσον ἂν ἐπιδέηται καθ' ὅσον ἐνδεεῖται* "you shall freely lend him whatever he might be in want of, according to what is lacking." LXX follows Sam in beginning the clause without *και*; a popular text does add it, which then equals MT, but the pattern of support makes it almost certainly not hex. Whether Sam or MT was earlier cannot be determined, since it represents a case of haplography/dittography, (ו) לו. What is hex, however, is the insertion of *ικανον* under the asterisk after *δανιεῖς αὐτῷ*; this is intended to render די, which LXX rendered as though it were the Aramaic די, i.e. by *ὅσον*. It might also be noted that instead of *ἐνδεεῖται* most witnesses have *υστερειται* which in the middle inflection is a synonym; it only occurs here, however, in Deut, whereas

7. The tradition that Aq read *ουδὲ μὴ οἰκτειρήσῃς* (retroverted from Syh) is clearly wrong. It is more likely to be a gloss on *οὐκ ἀποστέρξεις*. Theod accepted the LXX as correct.

ἐνδέομαι also occurs at 8:9; either form would be satisfactory, in which case one follows the oldest witness, cod B.

15:9 For *πρόσεχε σεαυτῷ* see comment at 4:9. Hex as usual adds *ποτε* after *μή* under the asterisk to equal פן of MT. LXX defines דבר more fully as a *ῥῆμα κρυπτόν*; hex placed *κρυπτόν* under the obelus, since it has no counterpart in MT. This is also called an *ἀνόμημα*, a lawless matter, which translates בליעל.[8] This secret *ἀνόμημα* is given voice by the direct speech marker לאמר,[9] introducing the evil thought. In view of the regulation on the year of release the Israelite might well be tempted not to lend his impoverished brother as the seventh year draws near. For *ἐπιδεομένῳ* rendering אביון, see comment at v.7. The construction *πονηρεύσηται ὁ ὀφθαλμός σου τῷ* simply means "you should look with disfavor towards," thus "be unfavorably disposed towards." This might well result in his outcry "to the Lord against you and it will be *ἁμαρτία μεγάλη* in you." The adjective has no basis in MT, and it is put under the obelus by hex. Its addition simply serves to intensify the fault. Note the consecution of verbal forms: present *ἐγγίζει* which is the situation for the aorist subjunctive *πονηρεύσηται* showing the potential evil, followed by three future tense verbs showing the result of the potential subjunctive state.

15:10 The verse begins in MT with נתון תתן לו which LXX interprets satisfactorily by means of an intensifying cognate participle plus verb: "you must freely give to him." But according to LXX this is not an outright gift. According to v.8 *δάνειον δανιεῖς αὐτῷ ὅσον ἂν ἐπιδέηται*, i.e. "you shall freely lend him whatever he needs," and LXX has taken this over word for word as a definition of *διδοὺς δώσεις αὐτῷ*. Naturally hex has placed this under the obelus. In this way LXX avoids any possible notion that the Israelite is to give a free handout to his impoverished fellow countryman. B and Byz have gone a step further and added *καθο ενδεειται* based on the next clause in v.8 as well, but this is clearly secondary as a glance at v.8 shows, it being a variant text for *καθ' ὅσον ἐνδεεῖται*.

---

8. Aq is hardly satisfied with this free rendering and substitutes *ἀποστασίας*.
9. Aq always renders לאמר by *τῷ λέγειν*.

LXX makes a fine idiomatic translation of ולא ירע לבבך בתתך לו. The verb had been literally rendered in v.9 by *πονηρεύσηται* but here the translator chose *λυπηθήσῃ*, the second singular future passive of *λυπέω* "to grieve," modified by a dative: "not shall you be grieved in your heart." And the prepositional phrase with infinitive is translated by a genitive absolute *διδόντος σου αὐτῷ* "when you give him (something)."[10]

The *ὅτι* clause outlines the reason why the Israelite should be generous over against the needy; it will be to his own advantage; precisely *διὰ τὸ ῥῆμα τοῦτο* the Lord will make you to prosper in all your labors. It is a case of investing for the future, of "do ut des." LXX makes an interesting translation of the idiom משלח ידך "the enterprise of your hand(s)" by its *οὗ ἂν ἐπιβάλῃς τὴν χεῖρά σου* in which the verb *ἐπιβάλλω* reflects the root notion of שלח of the noun משלח;[11] the idiom is unique to Deut; see comment at 12:7.

15:11 A good exegetical case might be made for the originality of the popular A F V variant spelling *εκλειπη* instead of its homonym *ἐκλίπῃ*, since the present subjunctive would stress continuity of the verbal idea: For not shall the poor be (ever) wanting from the land. But it is the *fact* of their always being present, not the *continuity* of their presence that is intended, and the variant must be judged as an itacistic spelling of the aorist. The word *ἐνδεής* is of course a collective referring to the class of those who are in need. The *γάρ*/כי clause gives the general basis for the demand for generosity.

The *διὰ τοῦτο* then restates the commandment of v.8: *ἀνοίγων ἀνοίξεις τὰς χεῖράς σου αὐτῷ*, though identifying *αὐτῷ* as "your poor and needy brother who is in your land." The two nominals *πένητι* and *ἐπιδεομένῳ* are synonyms. Over against MT the Greek adds the words *ποιεῖν τὸ ῥῆμα τοῦτο* after *ἐντέλλομαι*, which hex correctly placed under the obelus.[12] The addition was probably intended to reflect the *διὰ τὸ ῥῆμα τοῦτο* of v.10, which in turn reflects the three clauses constituting v.10a.

15:12 The term *ἀδελφός* is here used as a general term for kinsman, as its modification by *ὁ Ἐβραῖος ἢ ἡ Ἐβραία* proves. The apodosis is not intro-

10. See SS Inf 90.
11. See the comment in SS 70.
12. See SS Inf 141.

duced by a conjunction, which accords with Greek style over against Hebrew usage. In MT, because of this usage, it might be possible to identify the onset of the apodosis with ובשנה, as the Masoretes did by marking the preceding שנים with an ethnach, but LXX, by recognizing a conjunction only with ובשנה, makes this impossible. The apodosis has two clauses: "he/she will serve you for six years, and in the seventh you shall send him away free (from you)." Unclear is the modifier of the prepositional phrase; it could modify *ἐξαποστελεῖς*, i.e. you shall send him away from you as a free (person), or it could modify the adjective showing how you shall send him away, viz. free from you. Since it is a matter of *ἄφεσις* I suspect that the former was intended. MT adds "year" after "seventh," which is unnecessary in the Greek, though hex does add *τω ετει* under the asterisk to equal MT.

15:13—14 LXX with sensitivity renders וכי here with *ὅταν* rather than with *ἐὰν δέ*; after all, the rule of v.12 is absolute, and *ἐάν* would relativize it. The freedman is not to be sent off empty-handed. Note that the protasis uses a present subjunctive, since the release from bondage is a process. One might well render it by "but when you are sending him off ...." For *ἀπὸ σοῦ* see the discussion at v.12.

V.14 defines what not sending him off empty-handed means. It involves *ἐφόδιον ἐφοδιάσεις* "you must provide him with provisions," which renders the unique העניק תעניק. The verb is based on ענק "neck," hence "to encircle with gifts," and so to supply with gifts. The Greek uses a cognate accusative to translate the cognate free infinitive. The change in figure is contextually accurate; note the modifying *ἀπό* phrases.[13] LXX renders these literally, except for the second one, מגרנך "from your threshing floor," which is realized as *ἀπὸ τοῦ σίτου σου*, i.e. from the products of the threshing floor, which is of course what MT meant. It does not, however, fit as well with the third one, the wine press. In MT, threshing floor and wine press constitute a regular pair, but *σίτου* and *ληνοῦ* do not.

LXX rightly understood the אשר clause as presenting the norm for the master's liberality, hence *καθά*: "as the Lord ... prospered you, you must give to him." Since Sam has כאשר it is quite possible that this was the translator's parent text, in which case it was literally rendered.

13. Which SS 162 takes as partitive.

15:15 καί 1° — Αἰγύπτῳ is exactly the same as in 5:15; cf comments ad loc. In the next clause LXX has added ἐκεῖθεν at the end for good sense; cf 24:18 which repeats this entire verse word for word, but in its Hebrew משם is present as parent; here hex has put it under the obelus as not being in MT. The clause is coordinate with οἰκέτης—Αἰγύπτῳ, i.e. it too is part of the ὅτι construction. The verb λυτρόω is used only for פדה in Deut.

In the "therefore" clause MT is nominal: אנכי מצוך, which is as usual translated by LXX by ἐγώ plus the present tense, but to which LXX adds the complementary infinitive ποιεῖν, following the Sam and 1Q5 reading לעשות.[14] For the clause in general see comment at 4:2. Hex has made a number of inroads on this clause. σοι ἐντέλλομαι has been transposed to equal מצוך; ποιεῖν was placed under the obelus, since לעשות does not obtain in MT but only in Sam, and σημερον at the end was added under the asterisk to represent the היום of the Hebrew.

In the tradition B *b f z*+ read αιγυπτου instead of the dative after ἐν γῇ, but Deut always reads the dative in this context (11 times) and only Αἰγύπτῳ can be viewed as LXX.[15]

15:16 For the failure to render an introductory והיה see the discussion at 6:10—11. The ἐάν is, however, followed by δέ. This has no textual significance whatsoever, since when specific laws begin with ἐάν (with the possible exception of 23:10) they always appear as ἐὰν δέ except for 20:11 where ἐὰν μέν obtains to balance with the ἐὰν δέ of v.12. If, on the other hand, ἐάν does not begin the law, i.e. when καὶ ἔσται precedes it, naturally no δέ can be used.

V.16 is the protasis of a condition for which the apodosis appears in v.17. The actual protasis is "but should he say to you I will not go away from you," to which the text attaches two ὅτι/כי clauses explaining the reason for the refusal. The first is the actual reason: "because he loved you and your household"; this in turn is occasioned by the fact that εὖ ἐστιν αὐτῷ παρὰ σοί.

In the tradition, the Byz text added a recitative οτι before "I will not go out from you," which is otiose, as well as unsupported by MT. A B *n* reading

14. But see SS Inf 138.
15. See the discussion in THGD 137.

transposed *ἐστιν αὐτῷ*, but since MT simply has לו there is no good reason for adopting this sparsely supported minority reading.[16]

15:17 As at Exod 21:6, the ritual of ear-piercing voids the disenfranchment of the slave refusing freedom. The master is to take a small awl, an *ὀπήτιον*, the diminuitive of *ὄπεας*, and pierce *τὸ οὖς* of the servant *πρὸς τὴν θύραν*. For the latter phrase MT has ובדלת which is usually interpreted as the ובקיר at 1Sam 18:11 19:10 as "into the door." I would suggest that for the Greek, where the conjunction does not obtain, it would be more sensible to compare the parallel Exod passage where "door" or "doorpost" merely signify the location of the ritual. Bringing the servant to the door is significant, since he is a servant of the house—in fact, Deut calls him an *οἰκέτης*—and I would suggest that *πρὸς τὴν θύραν* simply means "at the door." The B *O* Byz text substitutes *ωτιον* for *οὖς*, but this does not accord with Deut usage at all.[17]

The result is that the servant becomes an עבד עולם "a perpetual servant"; LXX translates the bound phrase by *οἰκέτης εἰς τὸν αἰῶνα* using the common LXX *εἰς* phrase.[18]

The last clause uses an accusative: *τὴν παιδίσκην*. The verb *ποιήσεις* can take an accusative plus an adverbial modifier: thus "and your maidservant you shall treat likewise."

In the tradition the majority A F V text omits the apodotic *καί* at the beginning of the verse, which improves the Greek, but is secondary. An F *C'*' *f s*+ text has *επι* instead of *πρὸς* (*τὴν θύραν*), and a popular gloss adds *επι τον σταθμον* as a second prepositional phrase, which is borrowed from Exod 21:6. A further stylistic change is that of A F M *oI' f*+, in which *οικετης σου* occurs for *σοι οἰκέτης*.

15:18 This verse is clearly a continuation of vv.13—15, which is what *οὐ σκληρόν* refers to; it is the regulation of the seventh year release of the Hebrew slave which should not be hard or difficult. The Hebrew construction allows for the subject to be taken as (בשלחך אתו (חפשי מעמך, but LXX has

16. See THGD 130.
17. See THGD 133—134.
18. See SS 69.

changed this to a genitive absolute rewrite with *αὐτῶν* modified by a passive participle "when they are sent off (free from you)."

The *ὅτι* clause gives good reason for consolation: "*ἐφέτειον μισθὸν τοῦ μισθωτοῦ* he served you for six years." The word *ἐφέτειον*[19] means "annual," thus "annual salary of a hired servant" is intended.[20] What it means is that the master ought not to grumble, since he had had a slave for six years for room and board!

The last clause promises a divine blessing *ἐν πᾶσιν οἷς ἂν ποιῇς*, presumably as a reward for following these regulations. Note again that the relative pronoun is dative by attraction to its antecdent *πᾶσιν*. For *ἄν*, rather than the majority reading *ἐάν*, see comment at 5:27.

15:19 Vv.19—23 deal with regulations concerning the firstborn. The verse begins with a pendant accusative: "As for every firstborn which is born among your cattle and among your sheep"; this introduces the general area of discourse which will be regulated in some detail in what follows, viz. "the males you shall devote to the Lord your God." MT has the singular הזכר, which LXX correctly understood as a collective, hence *τὰ ἀρσενικά*. The Hi verb תקדיש means "to make holy," i.e. to devote, and so to set aside solely to deity, and *ἁγιάσεις* is to be understood in the same way.

What this means in practical terms is ordered negatively in v.19b and positively in vv.20—23. Negatively this means that you may not work with the firstborn *μόσχος*. The young bull or ox was usually used as a work animal, whereas sheep were kept for their wool, but neither may you shear the firstborn of your sheep.

15:20 Positively put, such firstborn are to be sacrificed. The emphasis in the verse is not, however, on *φάγῃ αὐτό*, but on the location. The preposed locative *ἔναντι κυρίου τοῦ θεοῦ σου* means that the communal sacrifice is to be eaten in the sanctuary, and that annually, *ἐνιαουτὸν ἐξ ἐνιαυτοῦ*. In the tradi-

---

19. Not *εφετιον* as most mss have it; see THGD 135.
20. Many ancients took משנה to mean "double," though this makes the interpretation difficult. Aq read *δευτερούμενον*, and Tar^{JN} read בכפולא or בכפלה, but Vulg correctly as *iuxta mercedem mercenarii.* Aq also used *μισθίου* instead of *μισθωτοῦ*, but the two words mean the same.

tion B *b d* have omitted τοῦ θεοῦ σου, but this is due to homoioteleuton after κυρίου.[21]

The location is not just any sanctuary; it is the place ᾧ ἂν ἐκλέξηται κύριος ὁ θεός σου, for which see comment at 12:5. MT simply has יהוה as subject, and hex has put ὁ θεός σου under the obelus. The relative pronoun is dative by attraction to its antecedent. For the originality of ἄν in favor of the majority B reading εαν see comment at 5:27. The tag σὺ καὶ ὁ οἶκος σου is in apposition to the subject of φάγῃ.

15:21 Such sacrifices must be of unblemished animals. χωλόν always equals פסח just as עור is always rendered by τυφλός when understood as a noun. The reverse is also true; τύφλος only renders עור (or the feminine עורת). These are not the only blemishes possible, as Lev 22:21—24 (see also 21:17—21) makes fully clear, which fact is covered by ἢ καὶ πᾶς μῶμος πονηρός (in this context πονηρός is quite tautological). MT has neither conjunction, but Sam has או. LXX probably read Sam, and added καί for good sense, i.e. "or even (actually) any bad blemish."

In the tradition hex has omitted ἤ from ἢ καί, though MT has an equivalent for neither word. Byz has substituted θυσιασεις as the Hellenistic equivalent for θύσεις, but with no difference in meaning.

15:22—23 Vv.22—23 no longer refer to the sacrificial animals, but to those firstborn which have a blemish. For πόλεσίν σου as interpreting שעריך see comment at 12:15.[22] The pronoun αὐτό shows that the reference is still to a firstborn, in contrast to animals in general as at 12:15. V.22b—23 are almost word for word the same as in 12:15—16. Instead of ὡσαύτως here the parallel has ἐπὶ τὸ αὐτό,[23] and in 12:15 αὐτό is added after φάγεται. V.23 is exactly the same as in 12:16, except that the verbs are singular rather than plural; see comments ad loc. That this passage was dependent on 12:15—16 is clear from φάγεται. MT does not have the יאכלנו of 12:15, and the presence of the verb is convincing evidence of dependency. Hex of course has φάγεται under the obelus.[24] Most witnesses also add αυτου after αἷμα; this corresponds to MT's דמו, and the plus may well be hex.

21. See THGD 126.
22. Aq translates the noun literally as πύλαις.
23. And Aq has ὁμοῦ which is his regular rendering for יחדו.
24. That the εδεται of Cod B is not to be taken seriously is clear from THGD 134.

Chapter 16

16:1 Vv.1—8 deal with the festival of the Pascha ("Passover"). The initial order is φύλαξαι, an imperative correctly representing the isolate free infinitive שמור. For the consecution φύλαξαι ... ποιήσεις see comment at 5:1. The term חדש means "new moon," and by extension for the lunar calendar, "month." LXX correctly understood it in the latter sense, μῆνα, and specifies the month as τῶν νέων. The accusative is used to specify the time when the passover was to be observed; see Exod 13:4. Since האביב means the newly ripened grain, the translator probably intended τῶν νέων in the same sense, i.e. the time of the harvest of the new grain; see Note at Exod 13:4. What the Israelites are to do is τὸ πάσχα.[1] In MT it is simply called פסח, both here and in v.2. The article does appear in v.5 (את הפסח). What is meant by the term throughout (see also vv.2,5) is the passover sacrifice. Parallel accounts obtain in Lev 23:5—14, where it becomes the ἑορτὴ τῶν ἀζύμων, and in Num 28:16—25, where it is called πάσχα, i.e. without an article. Cf also Exod 12 for the account of the establishment of the feast.

The reason for the feast is given in a ὅτι clause, viz. that this was the time that ἐξῆλθες ἐξ Αἰγύπτου νυκτός. MT has הוציאך יהוה אלהיך ממצרים לילה. LXX, however, harmonized the account with vv.3,6. In v.3 reference is given as "you went out from (the land of) Egypt, and v.6 refers to the καιρῷ ᾧ ἐξῆλθες ἐξ Αἰγύπτου. The Byz text has εξηγαγεν σε κυριος ο θεος σου instead of the verb, the ultimate source for which must have been MT. For LXX what is recalled by this sacrifice is the departure of the Israelites from Egypt rather than the divine deliverance; cf the comment at v.3.[2]

16:2 What the Pascha sacrifice is to consist of is πρόβατα καὶ βόας rendering the collective singulars צאן ובקר correctly. For the place of the sacrifice in the formulaic pattern see comment at 12:5. LXX has followed Sam in its ὁ θεός

1. The ancients usually adopted the Hebrew word. Aq called it φεσε, and Sym made it φασεκ (retroverted from Syh), and Vulg, *Phase.*
2. Prijs 81 suggests that this change was made to avoid any contradiction with Exod 12:17,51 ἐν τῇ ἡμέρᾳ ἐκείνῃ and Num 33:3 τῇ ἐπαύριον τοῦ πάσχα as the time of the Exodus from Egypt.

σου, which MT does not have, and hex has the phrase under the obelus. Also without correspondence in MT is the *αὐτόν* which follows it, but see vv.7,11,15; only v.7, however, attests to the בו as an equivalent.

16:3 The phrase *ἐπ' αὐτοῦ* occurs twice, and is probably intended in the sense of "with it" as at Exod 12:8; cf Note ad loc. Since the Pascha is a communal sacrifice the phrase means that they are not to eat *ζύμην* with it,[3] but only *ἄζυμα* or מצות "unleavened cakes," for which see Exod 12:8. This is called "bread of *κακώσεως*," i.e. bread of oppression, distress,[4] to symbolize the period of Egyptian slavery. In fact, the reason given in the *ὅτι* clause is that you went out of Egypt *ἐν σπουδῇ*, i.e. in such haste that you took along your dough before it was leavened, Exod 12:34.[5] Note that at 12:11 the Israelites were told to eat the Pascha *μετὰ σπουδῆς*.

Oddly LXX renders v.3b entirely in the plural over against MT, which remains consistently singular, whereas Sam has v.3a in the plural, but the rest of the verse in the singular. In the following verse LXX reverts to the singular. The reason for the second plural is not immediately obvious. Possibly the exodus is here viewed by LXX as a matter of individual recall; you as individuals left Egypt in a hurry. So too the *ἵνα* clause giving the purpose of the feast is given as "in order that you (as individuals rather than as people) may recall your *ἐξοδίας* from the land of Egypt all the days of your life." On the other hand, the phenomenon of Sam seems to indicate that there was no particular rationale underlying the change in number. The use of *ἐξοδίας* for the exit from Egypt is highly unusual, recurring only at Mic 7:15, where it also refers to the departure from Egypt.[6] It usually means a going out on a military expedition, which is hardly fitting here, where it simply means "going out" as does the Hebrew צאתך. The paschal sacrifice was intended to impress indelibly on their individual memories the conditions under which they left the land of Egypt. It reflects on the story of the Exodus as described in Exod 12; thus *ἐν σπουδῇ* calls to mind *μετὰ σπουδῆς* of v.11; cf also *ἄζυμα* of v.8, and comp v.34; see vv.3—11.

---

3. Aq has *ζυμωτόν*.
4. Aq preferred *κακουχίας*.
5. Aq rendered בחפזון by *ἐν θαμβήσει* "with astonishment."
6. See SS Inf 25.

16:4 The verse begins asyndetically in LXX, but *C'' b s+* add *και*, which does agree with MT, but this is probably not recensional. The use of *σοι* after *ὀφθήσεται* is a literalism for לך, and is probably to be taken as a dative of instrument, thus "leaven may not be seen by you in all your borders"; what it means is that leaven is not to be present within your borders. The accusative *ἑπτὰ ἡμέρας* is an accusative of extent of time, thus "for seven days." The use of *κοιμηθήσεται* is a Hebraism for ילין "stay for the night," and the same sense must have been intended by the Greek. The *ἀπό* is a partitive one, thus "not may there remain overnight any flesh." The relative clause modifying *κρεῶν* is introduced by *ὧν*, genitive plural by attraction to its antecedent. The last phrase, *εἰς τὸ πρωί*, is not part of it, but modifies *κοιμηθήσεται* directly. It would be helpful to place a comma after *πρώτῃ* in the Deut text. For the secondary character of the B Byz reading *εαν* for *ἄν* see comment at 5:27. The popular A F M V variant plural, *θυσητε*, is of course secondary. It was created under the influence of the plural in v.3, but with v.4 LXX had reverted to the singular of MT.

16:5—6 These verses consist of regulations concerning the location of the sacrifice. The sacrifice may not be made in any of your cities, but only in the central sanctuary. The verb *δυνήσῃ* must here indicate permission rather than ability. For the relative clause modifying *τόπον*, see comment at 12:5. A popular Byz reading repeats *ἐκεῖ*, i.e. the adverb modifies both the infinitive *ἐπικληθῆναι* as well as the *θύσεις* which follows. This is probably an import from 12:11 rather than from Sam, both of which support the repetition of the adverb in similar contexts.

The Pascha is to be sacrificed *ἑσπέρας*, defined as *πρὸς δυσμὰς ἡλίου*, i.e. at dusk, at the going down of the sun, unusual for כבוא השמש.[7] In MT this is called a מועד צאתך ממצרים, the precise time of your departing from Egypt. The bound phrase is translated by a prepositional phrase *ἐν τῷ καιρῷ* "on the occasion" plus a relative clause *ᾗ ἐξῆλθες ἐξ Αἰγύπτου* "which you went out of Egypt," a free, but not incorrect, rendering of the Hebrew.

---

7. See SS Inf 98.

16:7 Over against MT's ובשלת LXX has two verbs, *καὶ ἑψήσεις καὶ ὀπτήσεις*, hex placing *καὶ ὀπτήσεις* under the obelus to show its absence in MT. On the other hand, Exod 12:9 says *οὐκ ἔδεσθε ἀπ' αὐτῶν ὠμὸν οὐδὲ ἡψημένον ἐν ὕδατι, ἀλλ' ἢ ὀπτὰ πυρί*. I suspect that the doublet is an intentional attempt at reconciling the two texts. Here MT specifically commands בשלת, i.e. *ἑψήσεις*, but Exod 12:9 forbids *ἡψημένον ἐν ὕδατι*, and so LXX adds what is commanded, viz. *ὀπτήσεις*; comp also 1Reg 2:15. Does it possibly then mean that the meat was first boiled in a pot, and then roasted in the fire? Could this then have reflected local practice in Alexandria? For the formula "place which the Lord your God has chosen *αὐτόν*" see comment at v.2.

16:8 Over against v.3 Deut has *ἕξ* days you shall eat unleavened cakes, which contrasts with the *ἐξόδιον* as the seventh day. To the translator this was not contradictory, since at v.3 it was already clear that the seventh day was also a day on which one had to eat *ἄζυμα*, but the seventh day was a special day over against the first six in that it was also an *ἐξόδιον* to the Lord your God; see Exod 12:16. MT has עצרת, whereas Sam has חג, and LXX apparently combines both traditions.[8] The term עצרת is a rare word. It occurs only six times in OT, once (Jer 9:2) in a non-technical sense of an assembly (of treacherous men), where LXX translates it by *σύνοδος*. Otherwise it refers to a solemn festival and is always translated by *ἐξόδιον*. In the Pentateuch it also occurs at Lev 23:36, where it is the eighth day of the *ἑορτὴ σκηνῶν*, and similarly, at Num 29:35. Obviously the *ἐξόδιον* is a special day.

MT simply says about it לא תעשה מלאכה. LXX expands this considerably in terms of Exod 12:16 though adapting it to the word order of MT. The Exod passage reads *πᾶν ἔργον λατρευτὸν οὐ ποιήσεται ἐν αὐταῖς* for the main clause. Our passage lacks *λατρευτόν*, reads *ποιήσεις* for the verb, and has the singular *αὐτῇ* since it applies only to the eighth day, whereas in Exod it pertains to the first and eighth days. The *πλήν* collocation is also taken from Exod though lacking *πάσῃ* modifying *ψυχῇ*. This is obviously a case of harmonization. For the meaning of the collocation see Note at Exod 12:16.[9]

---

8. Aq has *ἐπίσχεσις* "restraint, a holding back," i.e. a rendering based on the root עצר. Possibly Aq thought of the seventh day as a day in which one not only ate unleavened bread, but also held back from work on the pattern of the Sabbath commandment.
9. See Daniel 331,332.

In the tradition, hex has ἐν αυτῇ πᾶν as well as the πλήν clause under the obelus to indicate their absence from MT. The πασῃ gloss (mistakenly as the nominative πασα in Byz) of the M *C* Byz text is based on the Exod parallel.

16:9 Vv.9—12 deal with the Feast of Weeks, ἑορτὴν ἑβδομάδων. V.9 particularly defines the date of the festival. The Israelite is ordered to count out for himself seven ὁλοκλήρους weeks. The ὁλοκλήρους "full, complete" has no equivalent in MT, but is taken from Lev 23:15. The point is to include 50 days, as Lev 23:16 makes clear. Thus the feast begins and ends with a Sabbath day. The word ὁλοκλήρους is placed under the obelus in hex.

δρέπανον means "sickle, scythe." MT has "from the beginning of the sickle in the קמה (i.e. the standing crop)"; LXX interprets by means of a genitive absolute construction "when you begin the sickle (i.e. the cutting) of the crop," i.e. when you begin putting the sickle to the grain. This does not necessarily presuppose Sam's מהחלך since LXX may well have added σου ad sensum as did Pesh Vulg. The construction was probably impelled by the מן, i.e. "from the beginning of the sickle" thus "when you begin the harvesting of the grain."[10] The construction is by Classical standards ungrammatical, since its σου as subject corresponds to the subject of ἄρξῃ. The main construction is straightforward: you must begin to count seven weeks.

16:10 In MT the Israelite is told to make the feast of weeks to Yahweh your God מסת נדבת ידך which you must give. The term מסת is a hapax legomenon in MT, but may well be correctly interpreted by καθότι.[11] But the remainder is a very free rendering. Instead of נדבת LXX has ἰσχύσει with ἡ χείρ σου as subject, thus "according as your hand is strong."[12] This must be seen in the light of the ὅσα clause which follows: ὅσα ἂν δῷ σοι "whatever he might give you." So the καθότι clause must roughly mean "according to whatever you are able." This in turn is substantiated by the concluding καθότι clause: "according as the Lord your God has blessed you." LXX has followed Sam in

---

10. See SS Inf 107.
11. Compare Aram כמסת "according to sufficiency," i.e. according to measure.
12. Aq interprets מסת נדבת as ἔπαρσιν ἑκουσίων taking מסת as from נשא, thus "a raising of voluntary offerings."

reading ברכך instead of יברכך. The Deut translator seemed to have great trouble with נדבת, which occurs four times in the book. At 12:6 it is quite properly rendered by *τὰ ἑκούσια*, but at v.17, by *ὁμολογίας* for which see comment ad loc., and then at 23:23(24), where the נדבה is the result of a vow, it becomes *δόμα*.

One might well question the correctness of the *ὅσα* clause as a rendering of MT: אשר תתן "which you shall give." It is admittedly quite different from "whatever he (i.e. the Lord) gives you," and it is impelled by the rendering *ἰσχύσει ἡ χείρ σου*. It would make little sense to speak of "what you are able" alongside "what you will give," whereas "what God gives you" denotes the realm in which you are able.

16:11 The first part of the verse as far as "your cities" is the same as 12:12 (cf comments ad loc), except that it is all in the singular, and it has *ἐπὶ τῶν πυλῶν* instead of *ἐν ταῖς πόλεσίν*, the more usual rendering for בשעריׄ(ך) in Deut; see comment at 12:15. LXX follows Sam in not reading a conjunction before *ὁ παῖς σου*, over against MT. The *C n z* text does have *και*, but that is unlikely to have been recensional. To the list of those who are to rejoice before the Lord this verse adds "and the proselyte and the orphan and the widow who is among you." Here LXX uses the plural *ἐν ὑμῖν* ad sensum, even though MT has the singular בקרבך.

For v.11b see comment at 12:5. For the addition of *αὐτόν* over against MT, see comment at v.2. It has been changed to *αυτω* and placed under the obelus in hex to show its absence in MT.

16:12 V.12a is an exact copy of 5:15 (in the Decalogue), following it, as well as Sam, in "land of" Egypt over against MT, which simply has במצרים; hex placed *γῇ* under the obelus so as to indicate its absence in MT. For *φυλάξῃ καὶ ποιήσεις* see comment at 5:1. The A F M popular change of *φυλάξῃ* to *φυλαξεις* was undoubtedly due to the influence of the coordinate *ποιήσεις*.

16:13 Vv.13—15 deal with the *ἑορτὴν τῶν σκηνῶν*. V.13 is a word for word rendering of the Hebrew, even in its imitation of the באספך construction by its *ἐν τῷ συναγαγεῖν σε*. Unlike at 15:14, LXX here translates גרנך literally by (*ἐκ*) *τῆς ἅλωνός σου*. Of course, what comes from the threshing floor is *σῖτος* just as *ἀπὸ τῆς ληνοῦ σου* is *οἶνος*, but LXX keeps to the Hebrew idiom.

The gender of ἅλων is variable,[13] and B *O*+ read *του αλωνος*. What makes this particularly confusing is that the synonymns ἅλως and ἅλων are often confused and become mixed in the text; furthermore, the gender of the former is also uncertain. Thus in Ruth 3:2,14 τὸν ἅλωνα occurs, but τὸν ἅλω in vv.3,6 (but with *την* variants in Lucianic mss); at Jdg 6:37 ἅλωνι is almost equally divided between the articulation τῇ (with B) and τῷ (with A M N). Similarly in 1—4Reg, forms of ἅλων and ἅλως are equally divided (four for each). In three of the former the masculine articulation predominates (A and Lucian attesting to the feminine), but at 4Reg 6:27 τῆς ἅλωνος obtains with no masculine witnesses (B and i omit the article). In 1Chr τῆς ἅλωνος is attested throughout. In 2Chr only ἅλω obtains, but with uncertain gender. In Job 39:12 τὸν ἅλωνα occurs with Lucian and *c*+ reading *την*. In Jl 2:24 αἱ ἅλωνες obtains with no variation recorded. It is thus clear that confusion reigns, and that here, where the feminine article clearly dominates, it is probably original.

16:14 This verse is analogous to v.11. Here too the Israelite is called on to rejoice, but instead of "before the Lord your God," v.14 has ἐν τῇ ἑορτῇ σου; on the other hand, A F M *C'' s*+ do change to *εναντι κυριου του θεου σου*, and V *f*+ add the phrase as a doublet. Those who are included along with σύ are identical to the list in v.11, but the Levite is not characterized by ὁ ἐν ταῖς πόλεσίν σου, and the widow is described as ἡ οὖσα ἐν ταῖς πόλεσίν σου instead of ἐν ὑμῖν. Both changes equal MT, except that οὖσα has no equivalent in MT, and hex has it under the obelus. For πόλεσιν both here and in v.11 see comment at 12:12. Again LXX does not follow MT's ועבדך, but rather Sam, in the omission of the conjunction.

16:15 As in the case of the Pascha, so too the feast of tents is to be observed for seven days; the verb for observance is ἑορτάσεις, i.e. you shall feast. For the relative clause modifying τόπῳ, see comment at 12:5. Over against MT LXX has added ὁ θεός σου αὐτόν. The ὁ θεός σου follows Sam, and for αὐτόν see comment at v.2. In the tradition the majority A F M V text has *επικληθηναι το ονομα αυτου εκει* ex par.[14]

13. See Thack 144—145.
14. See SS Inf 141.

V.15b in LXX is an exact rendering of MT, except for the omission of אך in the apodosis, which hex has taken care of by adding *πλην* under the asterisk after *ἔσῃ*.[15] The addition of *δέ*, though not in MT, is normal with *ἐάν* when introducing a protasis throughout Deut. This is a simple future condition: "If the Lord ... shall bless you ..., (*καί*) you shall be rejoicing." LXX correctly rendered תבואתך as a collective by *τοῖς γενήμασίν σου*. Even the apodotic *καί* reflects MT, as does the future verb *ἔσῃ* plus the participle *εὐφραινόμενος*, an unusual construction for the book; the continuity of the rejoicing is stressed by the use of a present participle, which is fully appropriate in the context.

16:16 The term פעמים is rendered by *καιρούς* seven times in the Pentateuch; comp especially Exod 23:17 34:23,24, which all refer to three annual occasions; see also 2Chr 8:13.[16] Unusual is the Hebrew structure יראה את יהוה, in which the Masoretes twice vocalized the verb as Ni; LXX confirms that tradition by its *ὀφθήσεται* (*πᾶν ἀρσενικόν σου*) *ἐναντίον κυρίου* and its *ὀφθήσῃ ἐνώπιον κυρίου*; comp also 31:11, where לראות את פני יהוה becomes *ὀφθῆναι ἐνώπιον κυρίου*. The LXX preposition for the first one is uncertain in that the majority F M text has *εναντι*, but LXX is supported by both A and B plus eight ms witnesses, and is probably original. That the three prepositions *ἔναντι*, *ἐναντίον* and *ἐνώπιον* are semantically synonymous is clear from their usage in the above contexts.[17] Every male Israelite is to appear annually before the Lord (i.e. engage in worship) in the central sanctuary. For the *ᾧ* clause modifying *τόπῳ* see comment at 12:5. The *αὐτόν* within the clause follows the בו of Sam, but *κύριος* has no support in other ancient witnesses. Only *κύριος* is under the obelus in hex in the tradition according to cod G, since *αὐτόν* was apparently not present in the parent text of hex.

The three feasts are here called *τῶν ἀζύμων*, *τῶν ἑβδομάδων* and *τῆς σκηνοπηγίας* resp. The first refers to the *πάσχα* sacrifice of vv.2—8, since the eating of *ἄζυμα* is stressed as mandatory during the entire festival; cf v.3. The third feast had been called the *ἑορτὴν τῶν σκηνῶν* in v.13, but הסכות

15. Sym added *καθόλου* (as retroverted from Syh.)
16. Aq regularly translates by *καθόδους*; see also 9:19 Exod 34:24.
17. See the discussion in THGD 115—116, and for these semiprepositions in general see Sollamo, passim.

becomes τῆς σκηνοπηγίας "the setting up of tents," an appropriate term in view of its being celebrated by all male Israelites at the central sanctuary.

The last clause begins asyndetically in LXX, possibly because LXX changed from the indefinite third person verb יראה to the second person ὀφθήσῃ as well. LXX has also added τοῦ θεοῦ σου after ἐνώπιον κυρίου as well over against MT, which reinforces the change to a second person clause; hex placed the addition under the obelus to signal its absence in MT. That you should not appear before the Lord your God κενός is explicated in v.17.

16:17 The verse is rhetorically only loosely connected with the context, with the grammatical antecedent of ἕκαστος being the subject of ὀφθήσῃ, thus "each one (of you). What is meant is that "each one (of you must present an offering on the occasion of the three feasts in the central sanctuary) κατὰ δύναμιν κ.τ.λ." The phrase κατὰ δύναμιν τῶν χειρῶν ὑμῶν "according to the ability of your (plural) hands" is a free rendering of מתנת ידו "the gift of his hand." MT uses the third person suffix to agree with איש. Since יד does mean ability, power, a rendering δύναμιν in connection with "hands" is sensible.[18] LXX also changes to the plural τῶν χειρῶν ὑμῶν. Having personalized the clause by changing it to second person, the plural becomes meaningful in the first κατά clause, since the plural individualizes. Here it is the individuals who are being assessed, i.e. each one of you, and so both ὑμῶν and τῶν χειρῶν are used.

The second κατά clause reverts to the singular, and renders MT literally. It means "according to the blessing of the Lord your (singular) God which he gave to you (singular)." Now the singular is apt, since the divine blessing is bestowed on the people as a whole.

16:18 Vv.18—20 deal with the appointment of judges and legal interpreters throughout Israel. The κριτάς were those who decided cases of dispute, i.e. they were judges. Just what function the γραμματοεισαγωγείς had is not clear, but they must have been some kind of "introducers of cases," at least an εἰσαγωγεύς was a magistrate who brought cases into court;[19] see comment at

18. Aq translated מתנת literally as δόσιν.
19. See LS sub εἰσαγωγεύς II.

1:15.[20] For πόλεσιν see comment at 12:5. For the αἷς (attraction to its dative antecedent) clause see comment at 1:20.

The phrase κατὰ φύλας must modify καταστήσεις, i.e. you must appoint judges ... according to tribes; what is meant is that the judicial officers are not to be appointed extra-tribally. MT has a suffix, לשבטיך, which LXX idiomatically disregarded, but hex has added σου.

The final clause introduces the theme for vv.19—20: "and they shall judge the people with righteous judgments." LXX imitates MT by using a double accusative modifying κρινοῦσιν, τὸν λαόν designating who are to be judged, and the cognate accusative κρίσιν δικαίαν, the type of judgment to be made.

16:19 Making righteous judgments involves avoidance of three common practices in ancient Israelite society. LXX presents all three in third person plural, i.e. refers to the judges and legal interpreters of v.18, whereas MT uses the second singular throughout. LXX changed this intentionally to make these grammatically secure in the context. a) "not shall they turn aside (i.e. pervert) justice." At Exod 23:6 for תטה in the same context LXX has διαστρέψεις. b) οὐκ ἐπιγνώσονται πρόσωπον. Recognizing a face means showing favoritism, partiality. Justice involves strict impartiality, no prejudice. c) οὐδὲ λήμψονται δῶρα "nor shall they take gifts," i.e. bribes. The Hebrew שחד occurs twice, and is correctly understood as a collective.[21]

Only the last named is singled out for explanation, probably because bribery was such a common practice in ancient Hebrew society. The γάρ clause explains why bribery is so heinous. Even the σοφοί are affected: "bribes blind the eyes of the wise, and remove (i.e. annul) the words of the righteous."[22] The statement is proverbial in nature; note the lack of articulation and its apodictic style. The Byz text has "bribes" in the singular, δωρον, which does correspond technically to the שחד of MT, but see comment above.

---

20. Aq translated שטרים by ἐκβιαστάς "exactors," i.e. those who enforced the penalties exacted by the judges. Sym has a gentler notion, παιδευτάς "instructor." The tradition assigning this reading to κριτάς as well is simply wrong.
21. See the note in THGD 137.
22. Instead of ἐξαίρει "remove" Sym has συγχέει "confound."

16:20 The section ends with a general exhortation. MT repeats צדק in preposed position to the verb תרדף, which LXX interprets by a cognate adverb plus noun, thus: "justly you shall pursue justice," a fitting summary command. LXX now turns to the second singular of MT; see comment on the third plural in v.19.

The section ends with a purpose clause containing typical Deut patterns. The clause is the same as at 4:1 up to the relative clause which imitates the *αἷς* clause of v.18. That the *ἵνα* clause itself is a copy from 4:1 is clear from its plural second person format, whereas MT is not only singular throughout, but also has no equivalent for *εἰσελθόντες*; hex accordingly placed it under the obelus. Only the *b* text seemed disturbed by the bewildering change in number, and changed the pronouns in the relative clause to the plural *υμων* and *υμιν* resp.

16:21 Forbidden is the planting of *ἄλσος*, which is then identified as *πᾶν ξύλον*. The term *ἄλσος* meant "a grove" in Classical times, but cannot possibly mean that in LXX. It almost always renders אשרה (32 times according to Dos Santos) in OT. Exceptions are Isa which renders the word only by *δενδρά* (17:8 27:9), במה at Mic 3:12 Jer 33(26):18 and עב at Jer 4:29, as well as three cases in 1Reg where it was confused with עשתרת. Since אשרה/*ἄλσος* was not to be planted beside the Lord's altar, its identification as some kind of tree, or possibly some wooden pole, makes sense. In fact, it is here, and on the whole throughout OT, a stereotype for אשרה. Clearly it was a wooden cult object which was forbidden as an object of worship.

The relative clause, *ὃ ποιήσεις σεαυτῷ*, could theoretically refer either to *ἄλσος* or to *θυσιαστήριον*, but probably refers to the latter as the nearer neuter singular noun. It should be noted that *ὅ* is a conjectural restoration by Grabe, which has no ms or versional support, all of which support *ου*. The preceding word is *σου*, and, since MT follows with אשר, the conjecture is almost certainly original LXX. The Byz text has omitted the relative clause entirely; since it undoubtedly also read *ου*, it is simply a case of parablepsis based on homoioteleuton, the next verse beginning with *οὐ*.

16:22 It is possible to understand this verse as a further explication of v.21, i.e. *στήλην*/מצבה could be understood as explicating אשרה of v.21. On the other hand, a מצבה is almost always of stone, i.e. a stone stele, though at Isa 6:13 the word occurs twice, first as part of a felled אלה or an אלון, of which Isa says מצבה בם, and then makes an application: זרע קדש מצבתה. LXX unfortunately does not translate these structures at all, but Aq renders the last word by *στήλωσις αὐτῆς*, and Theod, by *στήλωμα αὐτῆς*. Most likely, however, the order not to set up a *στήλην*, as well as its Hebrew counterpart, forbids the erection of a stone stele.

The verse ends with a relative clause: "which things the Lord your God hated." The pronoun *ἅ* must refer to both vv.21 and 22, i.e. to *ἄλσος*, *ξύλον*, *στήλην*. The choice of an aorist tense is not overly fitting. Since שנא is stative in character, a present tense would have represented more accurately the parent text, and would have been more sensible.

Chapter 17

17:1 Sacrifices to the Lord must be without blemish of any kind. Comp 15:21 where a similar prohibition is made with respect to the sacrifices of the first born. Here the prohibition extends to any animal sacrificed, i.e. *μόσχον ἢ πρόβατον*. What such a *μῶμος* might be is undefined, but at 15:21 it is defined illustratively as *χωλὸν ἢ τυφλὸν ἢ καὶ πᾶς μῶμος πονηρός*, for which see comments ad loc. Here it is called *πᾶν ῥῆμα πονηρόν* "any bad matter," which is syntactically in apposition with *μῶμος*. That *ῥῆμα* is merely a calque for דבר here is obvious. Instead of *θύσεις* the majority A F text reads *προσοισεις*, but *προσφέρω* is never used in OT to render זבח, whereas *θύω* is the normal rendering (83 times for the Qal, and 13 for Piel).[1] An obvious Hebraism is the *ἐν ᾧ ... ἐν αὐτῷ* structure, which imitates the Hebrew relative clause containing בו.

The reason for this prohibition is given in the *ὅτι* clause: it is an abomination to the Lord your God.[2] For the oft recurring statement see comment at 7:25. This verse is a good example of *ἐστιν* being used both to render יהיה and הוא (in a nominal clause).

17:2 Vv.2—7 constitute the regulations concerning the idolator. Vv.2—4 are a multi-tiered protasis, and v.5 is the apodosis. V.2 introduces the conditions in general terms. It concerns someone *ὅστις ποιήσει τὸ πονηρόν ... παρελθεῖν τὴν διαθήκην αὐτοῦ* (i.e. of the Lord your God). The *ὅστις* refers to the *ἀνὴρ ἢ γυνή* who might be found in one of your cities, (for which see comment at 12:15). For *ἐὰν δέ* rendering כי see comment at 15:16. *τὸ πονηρόν* is actually not defined until vv.3—4 as being idolatry. For "which the Lord your God is giving to you" see comment at 1:20. "The evil (matter)" is explicated by the infinitival structure "*παρελθεῖν* his covenant." The verb *παρέρχομαι* is regularly used for עבר in its basic sense of "to pass by." Here for the first time in the Pentateuch the verbs are used figuratively with "covenant" in the sense of "pass by, disregard," and so "break, violate the covenant"; see also 26:13 and 29:12. The Lord's covenant with Israel demanded his sole worship. He will be

1. According to Dos Santos.
2. For the use of the dative to render the free element of a bound phrase see SS 68.

their God, and the Israelites, his people, but this is predicated on there being no other gods in the picture, 5:7. Breaking the covenant on Israel's part is then defined in v.3.

17:3 What breaking the Lord's covenant entails is detailed. In the popular B text *ἀπελθόντες* appears in the simplex form, but this contravenes Deut usage. The verb הלך is never rendered by *ἔρχομαι*, which normally translates בוא, whereas הלך is also rendered by the compound at 16:7 24:2 and 28:41.[3] Breaking the covenant is done by *λατρεύσωσιν θεοῖς ἑτέροις καὶ προσκυνήσωσιν αὐτοῖς*; note the use of the aorist subjunctive to show the potential nature of the verbal actions. In MT these are preterite, but LXX makes these verbs subjunctive in view of *ἐάν* in v.2. For these other gods as *τῷ ἡλίῳ ἢ τῇ σελήνῃ ἢ παντὶ τῶν ἐκ τοῦ κόσμου τοῦ οὐρανοῦ*, see comments at 4:19.[4] Note that MT introduces these by a conjunction ולשמש, as though those guilty of idolatry worshipped both other gods and astral bodies. 11QT 56 alleviates this by changing the conjunction to או, an interpretation shared by the Byz text, which has *η* (*τῷ ἡλίῳ*), but LXX identifies the "other gods" as the astral bodies, for which see 4:19.[5] לכל צבא is unusually rendered by *παντὶ τῶν ἐκ τοῦ κόσμου*, i.e. "anyone of those from the host (of heaven)"; LXX tries for greater accuracy; rather than worshipping all the heavenly host it individualizes. The relative pronoun *ἅ* in "which I had not ordered" has no specific antecedent; note, however, that *τὸ πονηρόν* has been interpreted in various settings, and the plural neuter simply refers in general to the evil things described. The Byz text has simplified the text by changing the pronoun to the singular *ο*. Another attempt at simplification is seen in the majority A F V variant, in which (*παντὶ*) *τῶν* is changed to *τῳ*—of course under the influence of *παντί*. Also in the tradition is the attempt to harmonize the person of the context. LXX follows MT in its first person *προσέταξα*, but the context is third person, and a B+ text has *προσεταξεν*. Another variant text, F M V *oI' f z*+, has added *σοι* after the verb, which is ex par.

---

3. See THGD 142—143.
4. For *τῶν ἐκ τοῦ κόσμου* Aq has *στρατιάν* as at 4:19.
5. Against L.H.Schiffman, SCS 33, 285—286, who prefers the Byz text because it is easier, but *lectio difficilior preferendum est* must apply here.

17:4 The second stage of the protasis: you are made aware of this idolatrous practice. LXX continues the aorist (passive) subjunctive "and it would be reported to you." In MT this is followed by ושמעת "and you should hear." LXX lacks this, possibly because it is otiose—presumably if it was reported to you, you heard it! Hex has added *και ακουσης* under the asterisk to equal MT. The A V+ variant *ανηγγελη*, a second aorist passive indicative, makes the verb past tense, which must be a thoughtless error.

There is an interruption at this point within the protasis, in that LXX follows with a future *καὶ ἐκζητήσεις σφόδρα* "and you shall search out diligently." The Masoretes also followed this interpretation; at least they marked the first cut in the verse immediately before ודרשת היטב. This is then the third tier in the protasis—a) a man or woman served and worshipped other gods; b) you were informed about it; c) you will of course determine whether the report fitted the facts; and d) in fact, it did: *ἰδοὺ ἀληθῶς γέγονεν τὸ ῥῆμα* "behold the matter actually happened." Or if one prefers, "this abomination had taken place in Israel," a clause in apposition to the *καὶ ἰδού* clause. The adverb modifies *γέγονεν*, whereas a *b z* variant reading *αληθες* would be an adjective modifying *ῥῆμα*. A rather odd variant reading of *C'' s* is one in which *τοῦτο* (*βδέλυγμα*) is changed to *αυτου*. This is difficult, since the antecedent must then be *ἀνὴρ* (*ἢ γυνή*) of v.2. It is of course not to be taken seriously.

17:5 Finally comes the apodosis. All of vv.3—4 having taken place, and the report fully verified, the judgment on the idolators is carried out. LXX introduces the apodosis with *καί* in imitation of MT. MT is considerably longer than LXX which has "and you shall bring out that man or that woman and you (plural) shall stone them with stones and they shall die." MT has after "woman" אשר עשו את הדבר הרע אל שעריך את האיש או את האשה "who have done this evil thing, to your gates, the man or the woman." The Hebrew is certainly verbose, and if it actually was LXX's parent text the translator tried to simplify the text.[6] Hex has added *οι εποιησεν το ρημα το πονηρον τουτο προς πυλαις σου τον ανδρα η την γυναικα* under the asterisk to equal MT. I am not sure how readers of the hex text made sense out of the text.

6. Vulg represents only part of the longer text: *qui rem sceleratissimam perpetrarunt ad portas civitatis tuae*, i.e. it does not render the את האיש או את האשה.

That LXX intentionally simplified the text seems clear from the fact that it rendered סקלתם by the plural λιθοβολήσετε αὐτούς. The translator occasionally interrupts a singular context when he wants to individuate a verbal action. Here it means that more than one person is involved. By the plural he avoids any possibility of misunderstanding the stoning of an idolator as an individual affair. The translator was obviously trying to clarify the judgment.

Of some interest is the fact that he has thereby omitted the place of execution as well. Again it is clear why he has done so. LXX interprets the word שעריך normally by πόλεσίν σου—see comment at 12:15; this would mean that אל שעריך would set the site of the execution within the city, whereas the intent of MT was to set it at, or just outside, the city gates.[7]

17:6 MT reads על פי שנים עדים which LXX translates by disregarding פי, i.e. ἐπὶ δυσὶν μάρτυσιν.[8] At 19:15 LXX has the same rendering as Aq does here. The preposition ἐπί is of course an abbreviation for על פי throughout. It is used with the dative in a figurative sense "of that upon which a state of being, an action, or a result is based."[9] The participle ὁ ἀποθνῄσκων is best rendered by "the one who is to die," i.e. the one who is under judgment.

17:7 Over against MT, LXX begins with a conjunction, καί, as does Pesh. Unusual is the singular ἡ χείρ with the plural genitive τῶν μαρτύρων, since Deut normally uses thc plural for "hand" with plural modifiers, but see 11:18 32:27. Here it is contrastive with ἡ χεὶρ παντὸς τοῦ λαός.[10] The use of the dative with ἐπί is intentional as a locative: "The hand of the witnesses shall be upon him." That the witnesses should themselves be the first to institute death by stoning is a principle of justice in which "all the people" simply follow the example of the accusers; they merely act ἐπ' ἐσχάτων, i.e. afterwards. In the tradition an A V+ text elided the final *nu*, i.e. reading επ εσχατω. In Deut the singular dative is only to be read in 4:30 in the phrase ἐπ' ἐσχάτῳ τῶν ἡμέρων. When it occurs without a modifier the genitive plural is used

7. The Tar are interesting in this connection. Tar^{OJ} have "to the gate of the house of (+ your Tar^{J}) judgment, whereas Tar^{N} has the puzzling לגו קורייכון.
8. Aq rendered word for word by ἐπὶ στόματος δύο μαρτύρων. Dogniez-Harl interpret ἐπί as *sur la foi de* throughout.
9. Bauer sub ἐπί II.1.b.γ.
10. See THGD 136—137.

throughout. Since either is possible, the tradition shows a confused picture. At 13:9(10) the majority read *ἐσχάτων* which is probably to be preferred. The dative singular does have the support of the uncials A B G V plus 13 cursive mss, whereas M 527 have the genitive singular. At 8:16 the variant *εσχατω* is supported only by A plus six mss, and at 32:20 only F has the dative singular, and ms 618 the genitive singular, all others supporting *ἐσχάτων*. Throughout the LXX in general the idiom *ἐπ' ἐσχάτων* occurs far more frequently than *ἐπ' ἐσχάτῳ* which is attested in critical editions only at Ezek 35:5, but elsewhere usually as *ἐσχάτων*, six times as *ἐσχάτου*, and once (at Job 23:8) as *ἐσχάτοις*.

For the formulaic last clause see the discussion at 13:5(6). In the tradition the majority A F M V text has substituted the plural *εξαρειτε* for *ἐξαρεῖς*, but only the latter can be original, both by reason of its formulaic character and its support in MT.

17:8 Vv.8—13 deal with complex juridical cases. For the predicate of the protasis MT has יפלא ממך, probably in the sense of "more complex than you can handle," which LXX has interpreted by *ἀδυνατήσῃ ἀπὸ σοῦ*[11] "impossible for you (i.e. to deal with)."[12] The subject of the verb is דבר למשפט "a matter for judicial decision," which LXX renders by *ῥῆμα ἐν κρίσει* "a case *sub iudice.*"

The subject is then modified by four cases of *ἀνὰ μέσον* plus an accusative and a cognate genitive, whereas MT has only the first three. The parent for the pattern is בין + noun for *ἀνὰ μέσον* + accusative, and ל + noun for the genitive noun. What is meant in each case is a type of case. Thus *αἷμα αἵματος* would be a case of bloodshed, i.e. manslaughter (either with intent or by inadvertence); *κρίσις κρίσεως* would be a case involving judgment (possibly appeal to a judgment, i.e. a dispute as to how a law is to be interpreted); *ἁφὴ ἁφῆς*, a case involving bodily injury. The Hebrew equivalent is נגע which means "a smiting, a wound." The Greek has added a fourth, *ἀντιλογία*

11. I find the suggestion in SS 151 that *ἀπὸ σοῦ* means "from your side" rather implausible.
12. Aq has (*ὅταν*) *θαυμαστωθῇ ἀπὸ σοῦ*. Aq always renders the root פלא by this Greek stem. The apparent exception at Jer 39:17 where ms 86 attests to Aq and Sym as reading *οὐκ ἀδυνατήσει*, is clarified by Syh which attributes *οὐ θαυμαστωθήσεται* to Aq and *οὐκ ἀδυνατήσει* to Sym.

ἀντιλογίας; this would be a case involving a dispute or controversy between two parties, admittedly a type of case which might be "impossible for you to deal with." Hex has rightly placed this one under the obelus. The translator apparently realized that quarrels were particularly difficult to settle, and need not involve any of the first three types of cases; it should certainly be mentioned separately. All these are then characterized by the apposite phrase, *ῥήματα κρίσεως ἐν ταῖς πόλεσίν σου*; for *πόλεσίν σου* see comment at 12:15.

The apodosis begins with v.8b, i.e. with "*καὶ ἀναστὰς ἀναβήσῃ* to the place which the Lord your God might choose for the invocation of his name there." For the formulaic characterization of the *τόπον*, see comment at 12:5. The formula is considerably shorter in MT: אשר יבחר יהוה אלהיך בו, though LXX does not translate the בו, for which hex has supplied an unnecessary *αυτω* under the asterisk. LXX has the fuller form, adding *ἐπικληθῆναι τὸ ὄνομα αὐτοῦ ἐκεῖ* ex par, which hex quite correctly placed under the obelus.[13]

17:9 The verse informs what is to be done in the place—you are to go to the *τοὺς ἱερεῖς τοὺς Λευίτας*, for which see comment at 18:1, and to the *κριτὴν ὃς ἂν γένηται ἐν ταῖς ἡμέραις ἐκείναις*. What seems to be meant is some kind of tribunal at the central sanctuary consisting of Levitical priests and the judge "who would be in office in those days." At 19:17 the tribunal includes "judges," i.e. in the plural. The Byz text "corrects" the text by changing *καί* to *η*, i.e. gives a choice between an ecclesiastical and a civil court.

In MT v.9b begins with ודרשת "and you shall consult, seek out," but LXX follows Sam's ודרשו in its *καὶ ἐκζητήσαντες* modifying *ἀναγγελοῦσίν σοι τὴν κρίσιν*. The verb דרש is here used in the sense of "inquire of"; it is not an oracle that is sought but a judgment, thus "to inquire of the judicial panel." The aorist participle was well-chosen to show that the tribunal is to pronounce judgment after having investigated the matter, i.e. *ἐκζητήσαντες*.

17:10 The appellant is to act according to the tribunal's judgment. This judgment in LXX is called "the *ῥῆμα* which they would relate to you." In the tradition B+ have *πραγμα*. דבר can mean either "word" or "matter," but here it is something announced, and only *ῥῆμα* can be correct.[14] For the formula

13. See SS Inf 141.
14. See also THGD 134.

characterizing *τοῦ τόπου*, MT is even shorter than at v.8, which see; it has אשר יהוה יבחר. LXX has the full formula: *οὗ ἂν ἐκλέξηται κύριος ὁ θεός σου τὸ ὄνομα αὐτοῦ ἐκεῖ*, with hex placing *ὁ θεός—ἐκεῖ* under the obelus to show its absence from MT. LXX did not render the pronoun in the phrase מן המקום ההוא, and so hex dutifully added *εκεινου*.

This order is then paralleled in v.10b by "and you shall be *σφόδρα* careful to act according to everything which *νομοθετηθῇ* to you." The intensifier has no counterpart in MT and hex has placed *σφόδρα* under the obelus to indicate that fact. The text of the uncials B V plus seven cursives omits the word, but this is hardly recensional. The passive verb in the *ὅσα* clause means "ordered by law"; it thus means that that which had been given out by the tribunal is a legal pronouncement. This is contextually motivated and stronger than MT's יורוך "they might instruct, teach you."[15] The verb occurs in OT only as a rendering for יורה, and may be considered as a calque for the Hebrew word; comp also Exod 24:12.

17:11 MT begins with "according to the law אשר יורוך, and according to the judgment." LXX has disregarded the relative clause entirely, which had also appeared at the end of v.10 in modification of ככל. This may represent the same tendency on the part of LXX to eliminate repetitive or unnecessary phrases as was seen in v.5. The clause modified תורה and was admittedly otiose; hex has, however, inserted under the asterisk *ον φωτιουσι σοι* to equal MT. Just what is meant by *τὸν νόμον* here is not obvious; elsewhere it refers to the "law" which Moses is presenting to the people; see especially the discussion at 1:5. It probably is here intended in general to reflect the priestly instruction—note the constitution of the central tribunal in v.9—along with the *κρίσιν* which is the actual judgment pronounced in the particular case, i.e. *ἣν ἂν εἴπωσίν σοι*, thus a judgment in which the priestly lawgivers shared as majority members of the court.

For the secondary character of the majority reading *εαν* instead of *ἂν* 1° and 2° see comment at 5:27.

17:12 The penalty for disobedience. Such a disobedient one is called "the man who would act arrogantly so as not to obey the priest ... or the judge *ὃς ἂν ᾖ*

15. Aq has *φωτίσωσιν* which is his regular rendering for the Hi of ירה.

ἐν ταῖς ἡμέραις ἐκείναις." The relative clause has no counterpart in MT, and hex has placed it under the obelus; its source is v.9, with which the translator levelled, though using ᾖ rather than γένηται. The word "arrogantly" translates ἐν ὑπερηφανίᾳ for בזדון "with presumption, insolence." What is meant is that disobeying the judicial order is insolence, arrogance. For the unusual articulated infinitive, see comment at 8:11. For τοῦ παρεστηκότος λειτουργεῖν, see the comment at 10:8. Here, however, ἔναντι κυρίου is absent after "standing," and the cultic service is characterized as being ἐπὶ τῷ ὀνόματι κυρίου τοῦ θεοῦ σου, a combination which recurs only once elsewhere in the OT (at 18:7, but without ἐπί). The name of the Lord is to be understood as surrogate for "the Lord"; in fact, λειτουργεῖν τῷ κυρίῳ does occur fairly often. This is of some consequence, since MT has לשרת שם את יהוה "to serve there Yahweh." That LXX read את שם for שם את is possible, except that I can find no case of שרת modified by את שם יהוה anywhere. שרת בשם יהוה does occur twice (18:5,7). Furthermore, the use of ἐπί is not thereby explained. I suspect that the translator wanted to harmonize with 18:7, but indicated that the text was somewhat different by adding ἐπί before τῷ ὀνόματι.

The apodosis is given in the second half of the verse, introduced by an apodotic καί: "and that man shall die." For the formulaic concluding clause see comment at 13:5.

17:13 The hoped for result: "And when all the people hear (this), they shall be afraid (i.e. fear God). MT goes on with ולא יזידון עוד "and not shall they be insolent any more." The translator found this an odd conclusion, and changed the verb to ἀσεβήσει "act impiously,[16] which is used only once elsewhere, at 18:20 where, however, it seems more fitting of a prophet who speaks a word in God's name which God had not ordered him to speak. The rendering is free, but not incorrect; insolence over against a judgment given in God's name is certainly acting impiously. The *O* text has changed the verb to the plural ασεβησουσιν, which corresponds to MT, and this could be recensional (hex).

17:14 Vv.14—20 deal with regulations concerning a ruler in Israel. V.14 is the protasis; the conditions are: entering the land, possessing it, dwelling on it

16. Aq rendered more literally by ὑπερηφανεύσονται.

and saying: "I would set over me a ruler, even as the other nations which are around me." The land is characterized by ἣν κύριος ὁ θεὸς δίδωσίν σοι, for which see comment at 1:20. Unusual is ὁ θεός for אלהיך, a choice made on the basis of support for the shorter text by ms 848 plus three cursives, all other Greek witnesses adding σου to equal MT. 848 is, after all, a witness from cir 50 B.C.E., 500 years older than the next extant ms, Cod B. Furthermore, the addition of σου is much easier to explain than its deletion in the tradition. The evidence for ὁ θεός for אלהיך rather than the more popular ο θεος σου in 848 also obtains in v.15 (where 848 and B alone support the shorter text), as well as at 19:8 21:5 24:9.[17] The support of 848 (and B 58) for σοι after δίδωσιν without the popular gloss εν κληρω (supported by all other Greek witnesses) again identifies the original LXX; here, in fact, the gloss is prehexaplaric, as the obelus in hex proves.[18]

The term מלך occurs frequently in Deut, and is always rendered by βασιλεύς except when it refers to Israel (five times: cf also v.15-twice 28:36 33:5); in such cases LXX consistently uses ἄρχων.[19] Obviously LXX is intentionally avoiding the use of βασιλεύς, since to the translator only God can be Israel's king, and hence the מלך becomes merely "a ruler."[20] The translator is also more precise in the comparative statement: ככל הגוי (אשר סביבתי). Rather than "as all the nations" LXX has καθὰ καὶ τὰ λοιπὰ ἔθνη, "as even the rest of the nations." The translator divides sharply between Israel as God's people and all other peoples; they have kings; only rulers are permitted for us.

In the tradition most witnesses have the κατα- compound instead of the simplex κληρονομήσῃς, but the latter must be LXX. Not only is the simplex supported by A B F M 848 + 19 cursives, but for the root ירש the Deut translator prefers the simplex; in fact, he used the simplex 47 times, whereas the compound was chosen only 10 times.

---

17. See THGD 76 as well as Appositives 267.
18. See THGD 78.
19. Aq, of course, corrects to βασιλέα (retroverted from Syh).
20. A. Rofe, Textus XIV (1988) 169—174 maintains that one might infer "that the LXX translated here from a Hebrew Vorlage that read נשיא throughout the king's law" (170), but this is quite unnecessary. It rather shows that the translator represented an interpretation by which the term βασιλεύς was denied to the kings of Israel, and the use of ἄρχων obtained "to lower the king's stature in the presence of the only true king, the Lord God of Israel" (171).

17:15 The verbal figure *καθιστῶν καταστήσεις* is best understood as a volitional future: "you may actually establish,"[21] rather than as a future expressing prospect. The participle is often used to render the free cognate infinitive which serves to intensify the verbal idea. The future is then permissive, not imperatival. For *ἄρχοντα* 1° and 2° see comment at v.14.[22] Such a potential ruler is to be one *ὃν ἂν ἐκλέξηται κύριος ὁ θεὸς αὐτόν*, i.e. not by popular election, but one to be chosen by the Lord God. The relative clause is formulaic when applied to *τόπος*; cf e.g. 12:14 14:24. For the majority *σου* modifying *θεός* see comment at v.14 as well. The awkward and otiose *αὐτόν* is Hebraic, a rendering of בו; a few copyists (V plus three mss) could not resist the impulse to omit it.

The second part of the verse specifies that only an Israelite may become ruler, i.e. someone *ἐκ τῶν ἀδελφῶν σου*. In fact, it is specifically said that "you may not establish over yourself a foreign person." Though MT uses a different infinitive, לתת, "to put, place," LXX continues with the same verb, *καταστῆσαι*, which root had already occurred three times (for the root שום) in the verse. This kind of harmonization makes it fully clear that the Lord will only consider an Israelite as candidate for *ἄρχων*. The reason for the prohibition is restated in a *ὅτι* clause: *οὐκ ἀδελφός σού ἐστιν*, in which the copula is used to render the pronominal subject הוא of a nominal clause (quite correctly).[23] In MT no such reason is given, since it has a relative clause, i.e. "who is not your brother." The translator apparently found this overly repetitive, and made it into a causal (*ὅτι*) clause.

17:16 LXX begins with *διότι* "because,. since," whereas MT has רק, which means "only, except." A popular A F M text has corrected the *διότι* to *πλην*, but the more difficult *διότι* must be original. LXX understands the verse as giving the reason for appointing native rather than foreign rulers, i.e. "because he would not multiply for himself a cavalry, nor return the people to Egypt." This is quite different from MT, in which v.16 begins to catalogue what the king is not to do as well as to do, with no organic connection to the orders given in v.15. The translator tied the two verses together by means of a *διότι*

21. See Porter 413—418.
22. For *ἄρχοντα* 1° The Others have *βασιλέα*.
23. See SS 76.

construction, a sensible statement, though it does not equal MT, as the variant A text does do.

But it is fully clear that the statement *οὐ πληθυνεῖ ἑαυτῷ ἵππον* is more than simply a reason for setting up a native ruler; it is also a regulation limiting the ruler's authority. The translator is suggesting that the three futures governed by *διότι* show how an Israelite, in contrast to a foreign, ruler would act: he would not amass a cavalry, nor wives, nor riches, an idealistic notion of authority hardly consistent with historical reality.[24]

"Nor shall he return the people to Egypt in order to amass for himself cavalry" is also governed by *διότι*, and also constitutes a limitation on the ruler's authority. Egypt was traditionally a place for buying horses from Solomon's reign onwards, according to 3 and 4Reg. But returning the people to Egypt (as slaves to pay for horses?) was another; that would undo the great act of divine rescue from the house of bondage. In fact, "but the Lord said to you: Not may you again return by this way (any more)." The translator has added a contrastive *δέ* to clarify the relationship of this clause to the preceding. The text is now in the second person plural as in MT, but the plural is unexpected; after all, what the Lord said is addressed to you as people, not to you as individuals. Unusual is the use of *αὐτῷ* after *πληθύνῃ* in a reflexive sense, but, with both B 848 supporting it, its originality seems assured. That most witnesses change it to *εαυτω* is a simplification of the text impelled by its use after *πληθύνει* in vv.16—17 (three times).[25]

Also problematic in the tradition is the omission of *ὑμῖν* in B *C'' n s*+, but the word is strongly supported, and it does equal MT. אמר is usually followed by an indication of the addressee, and LXX seldom fails to render such either by a dative or by a *πρός* construction.[26] Almost all witnesses support the *ὅπως* clause as adding *μη* before the verb. This is, however, clearly secondary, created under the influence of the various negative clauses in the context. Here it is also not sensible. Avoiding a return to Egypt so as not to increase the cavalry could not possibly have been intended.

---

24. Dogniez-Harl try to get around the plain meaning of *διότι* by rendering it by *donc*, but that is not what *διότι* means.
25. See THGD 78.
26. See also THGD 127.

17:17 Actually three negatives obtain here. After "and not shall he amass for himself wives," LXX continues with *οὐδὲ μεταστήσεται αὐτοῦ ἡ καρδία* "nor shall his heart be changed."[27] The use of *οὐδέ* instead of *και ουκ* used for all the other limitations is clearly intended to tie it to the preceding as part of a single statement, and the interpretation of the clause as a result or purpose clause seems warranted; this is also what MT intends.[28] In fact, the majority A F M V text has simplified this by changing *οὐδέ* to *ινα μη* (*μεταστη*), making the interpretation as a purpose clause certain.

The final limitation is in the amassment of silver and gold, but the prohibition is not absolute—only as *σφόδρα*/מאד is it wrong! In the tradition, hex has reordered *αὐτοῦ ἡ καρδία* to fit the Hebrew order. The *z* text had *μεταστη* for *μεταστήσεται* (for which see above), and changed "his heart" to *την* (*σ*)*εαυτου καρδιαν*. This understands *μεταστη* as second singular aorist subjunctive with "your own heart" as its modifier.

17:18 For *καὶ ἔσται ὅταν* see comment at 6:10. Over against the limitation of authority described in vv.15—17, the ruler is also positively instructed. "Whenever he sits on *τοῦ δίφρου τῆς ἀρχῆς αὐτοῦ*" renders כשבתו על כסא ממלכתו. In the tradition Byz changed *τοῦ δίφρου* to *του θρονου*, but this is secondary; the translator is intent on avoiding the notion of kingship for Israel's rulers entirely, and *θρονου* involves kings. Note how scrupulous LXX is in avoiding any hint of king or kingship by using *ἀρχῆς* rather than something like *βασιλεία*, the usual translation for ממלכת. In the tradition the B V *b n*+ text has omitted *τοῦ δίφρου*, possibly because of homoiarchon, i.e. from *τοῦ* to *τῆς*.[29]

The apodosis is introduced by an apodotic *καί* in imitation of MT: וכתב. When a ruler occupies his *δίφρος* he is to write for himself *τὸ δευτερονόμιον τοῦτο εἰς βιβλίον*. This *δευτερονόμιον* "second law" reflects MT's את משנה התורה הזאת "the copy of this law." Presumably "this law" means the Deut set of laws beginning with Ch.12. The term משנה can mean either "copy" or "second," and LXX has taken it in the latter sense. It is in this sense that the word has also been adopted as the name for the entire LXX book; Deut is a

---

27. Sym has *μήποτε ἐκκλίνῃ ἡ καρδία αὐτοῦ* (retroverted from Syh).
28. This is supported by Tar^{J}: דלא יטעיין ליביה, but not by Tar^{NO} which have ולא.
29. See THGD 124.

second law over against the תורה of Exodus—Numbers, a repetition of the law by God to Moses in Transjordan; cf 1:1. The word also occurs at Jos 8:32, where it is identified as the *νόμον Μωυσῆ*.

The book in which the ruler was to write the Deuteronomic law was (received) *παρὰ τῶν ἱερέων τῶν Λευιτῶν* "from the Levitical priests," i.e. the law to be copied was taken from the law which had been entrusted to the Levitical priests, (for which see comment at 18:1). *παρά* with the genitive "nearly always ... denotes a pers., and indicates that someth. proceeds fr. this pers."[30] MT has מלפני "from before." The Greek seems somewhat clearer, but I suspect that it has correctly understood the intent of MT.

17:19 The point of making this personal copy is detailed: it is to remain with him, and he must read in it daily for instruction. This instruction has practical ends: *φοβεῖσθαι κύριον τὸν θεὸν αὐτοῦ*, for which see comment at 4:10.[31] The B *b n+* text has changed the *αὐτοῦ* to *σου*, which is a thoughtless error created under the influence of the frequent occurrence of *θεός* modified by *σου*. Here it is inappropriate. A second purposive infinitival clause follows asyndetically. It must be understood as such, rather than as modifying *φοβεῖσθαι*, which would hardly be sensible. This is clarified by the B *b+* text, which has actually added *και* before the infinitive. For *φυλάσσεσθαι κ.τ.λ.* "(and) to be careful to do (i.e. obey) all these commandments and these ordinances," see comment at 5:1. It does not, however, render MT correctly. Instead of "all these commandments" MT has את כל דברי התורה הזאת. Admittedly the pattern: these commandments and these ordinances is a common one,[32] but this Hebrew phrase does not occur elsewhere until after the Law Code has been fully presented. It occurs at 27:3,8,26 (without כל) 28:58 29:28 31:12 and 32:46. It is throughout rendered by "all the words of this law" including 27:26, except at 27:8 where it becomes "all this law." Did the translator avoid such a literal rendering here since it would be fully appropriate only after the Code was completely presented? In any event, he chose a common pattern.

30. Bauer sub *παρά* I; comp also LS idem A.II.2.
31. See also list 24 in THGD 93.
32. See List 22 in THGD 92.

17:20 Structurally this verse has two *ἵνα μή* clauses giving negative purpose clauses following v.19b, i.e. "learn to fear ... to guard ... lest ... lest ...," followed by a positive purpose clause, *ὅπως ἄν* .... As in the case of the two asyndetic purposive infinitives in v.19, so too the two *ἵνα μή* clauses are not joined by a *και* in LXX, although MT does have a conjunction. Since the word before ולבלתי in MT is מאחיו, LXX's parent text may well have lost the conjunction by haplography. The *d* text does join this by a *και*, but this only as a substitute for *ἵνα μή* 2°.

The first *ἵνα μή* clause represents a word for word rendering of MT's רום לבבו מאחיו. The prepositional phrase *ἀπὸ τῶν ἀδελφῶν αὐτοῦ*, as well as that of MT, raise the question what "be raised *ἀπό*/מן" can mean. If one's heart is raised "away from" it must be in an upwards direction, hence probably "above" his brothers.[33] The ruler is not to be arrogant over against his fellows.

The second clause also contains an *ἀπό* phrase: lest he deviate from the commandments to the right or to the left. LXX has rightly understood המצוה as a collective, and so uses the plural *τῶν ἐντολῶν*. The structure *δεξιὰ ἤ ἀριστερά* obtains in v.11 with *οὐδέ* as conjunction representing *waw*; here the *waw* becomes *ἤ*, but this hardly means that its parent text necessarily had או.

The point or result of all this is expressed in the *ὅπως*/למען clause: "so that *μακροχρόνιος ᾖ* on his *ἀρχῆς*, he and his sons *ἐν τοῖς υἱοῖς* Ἰσραήλ." The verbal phrase adequately represents the Hebrew יאריך ימים "he may lengthen days." In the tradition B 82 substitute the verb *μακροχρονισῃ* for the phrase, which would render the Hebrew equally well, but its meagre support militates against accepting it as LXX.[34] Once again LXX avoids speaking of "kingdom" for ממלכת, rather using *ἀρχῆς*.[35] As for the prepositional phrase MT has בקרב ישראל "in (the midst of) Israel." LXX usually does not translate קרב at all and would simply use *ἐν*. But to speak of "his sons in Israel" would be somewhat odd. The translator avoids this by using *τοῖς υἱοῖς*, not because he had a parent text בבני ישראל, but to explicate "in Israel" as meaning "among the Israelites." Most witnesses add *μετ αυτου* after "his sons," which is an ex par gloss.

33. But not as SS 151 which renders "so that his heart would not rise up from (the side of) his brothers."
34. See THGD 139.
35. Aq naturally uses *βασιλείας*.

Chapter 18

18:1 Precisely what the term לכהנים הלוים means is much disputed, but LXX took the two nouns to refer to the same group, i.e. as "the priests, the Levites," or perhaps better "the Levitical priests," which is followed by an apposite construction ὅλῃ φυλῇ Λευί. For LXX the latter phrase defines the realm of the former. The phrase "the Levitical priests" also occurs at 17:9,18 21:5 24:8 27:9 as over against one case of "the priests, the sons of Levi" at 31:9 (those who carry the ark). One can conclude that all priests were from the tribe of Levi, but not that all Levites served as priests.

In any event, the Levites, whether as priests or as lower ranks in the sanctuary service, had no tribal μερὶς οὐδὲ κλῆρος as other tribes had; the "share or inheritance" refers to tribal land. The two nouns occur coordinately in the context of the Levites/Levi as well at 10:9 12:12 14:26,28 as a set phrase; in all these cases the words are synonyms, and no particular distinction was intended. This is undoubtedly also true of their Hebrew counterparts חלק ונחלה.

V.1b then continues in MT with אשי יהוה ונחלתו יאכלון "sacrifices of Yahweh and his rightful portion they shall eat." I have translated אשי by the general word "sacrifices," since אשי יהוה was some kind of generic term for a variety of sacrifices. Its translation by καρπώματα is no great help, since that word basically means "fruits."[1] But the verb καρπόω may mean "to enjoy the fruits of," and so simply "to enjoy something." The term may well have been chosen by earlier translators (Exodus—Numbers) as a term for sacrifices, either for the Lord to enjoy, or those which the Levitical priests might use.[2]

The translator, however, changed the sense of MT by disregarding the conjunction of ונחלתו entirely and making the suffix refer to the priests rather than to the Lord, i.e. καρπώματα κυρίου ὁ κλῆρος αὐτῶν and then adding a pronominal modifier to the verb: φάγονται αὐτά. This does make fine sense:

---

1. Aq translated אשי by πυρά, deriving the word from אש "fire." For a discussion of אשה and its translation in the Pentateuch see Daniel 155—164.

2. See the discussion in P.Harlé et D.Pralon, Le Lévitique, Bible d'Alexandrie 3 (1988), 39—40, where the rare word *apanage* is suggested as a translation. But to use such a rare word hardly promotes understanding. It is also rather overly distant from the root meaning of *karpo-*.

"the fruit offerings of the Lord are their portion; they shall eat them." The term "fruit offerings" is not overly luminous either, but by it I mean *καρπώματα* as offerings which in some way are fruitful, and so enjoyed. For the phrase *καρπώματα κυρίου* the A *f*+ text has the singular *καρπωμα* (probably due to homoioteleuton), and A *b*+ read the dative *κυριω*, but neither variant is to be taken seriously.

18:2 The first clause restates the first clause of v.1 in different words. The antecedent of *αὐτῷ* must be *Λευί*. The nominal sentence יהוה הוא נחלתו remains nominal in LXX, but הוא, which in such contexts is usually rendered by *οὗτος*, here becomes *αὐτός*. The construction apes that of MT with *κύριος* as subject, and *αὐτὸς κλῆρος αὐτοῦ* as predicate. דבר is commonly translated by *ἐλάλησεν*, but *εἶπεν* does occur, and in this context is somewhat more appropriate. The verse from *ἐν* to the end is, except for *καθά* becoming *καθότι*, an exact repetition from 10:9.

18:3 Though MT has a verbal clause: זה יהיה משפט, LXX in unusual fashion forms a nominal clause by not translating יהיה; hex supplied *εσται* under the asterisk to equal MT. The משפט/*κρίσις* of the priests refers to the custom or regulation concerning the priests. Their portion of the people's sacrifices was variously set out; comp 1Reg 2:13—16, where it is called *τὸ δικαίωμα τοῦ ἱερέως παρὰ τοῦ λαοῦ*, and Lev 7:22—24 where *τὸ στηθίνιον τοῦ ἐπιθέματος καὶ τὸν βραχίονα τοῦ ἀφαιρέματος* are the rightful portions for the priests.

Here the priests' allotment is described as מאת העם מאת זבחי הזבח. LXX renders the first מאת by *τὰ παρά* but the second simply by *παρά*; in this way the *κρίσις* is defined as *τά*, i.e. "portions from the people, (i.e.) from those sacrificing sacrifices," by which apparently any sacrifices are intended. LXX also has a cognate expression *παρὰ τῶν θυόντων τὰς θυσίας*. In the tradition a popular B Byz variant calls the sacrifices *τα θυματα* but LXX is preferable.[3] A popular variant has added *τα* before the phrase so as to ensure that the two phrases would be viewed as appositives, but that assurance is not necessary. In the Greek the second *παρά* phrase is intended to delimit the broader first phrase. What is meant is "the portions from the people (or more specifically) from those sacrificing sacrifices."

3. See THGD 134.

The sacrifices are then described as animal sacrifices, *ἐάν τε πόσχον ἐάν τε πρόβατον* "whether bullock or sheep."[4]

The verb in v.3b, *δώσει*, has no named subject, though the context makes it clear that it is the sacrificing Israelite who is intended. What LXX (and MT) says is "And one shall give (to the priest)." A popular variant text has simplified this by its *δωσεις*, but MT's נתן demands the third person. The portion due is defined as "the shoulder and the fleshy parts of the jaw (*τὰ σιαγόνια*) and the *ἔνυστρον*." The *ἔνυστρον* (more commonly written as *ἤνυστρον* as in M *oI*+) is the fourth stomach of animals that chew the cud; apparently this was edible.[5]

18:4 Not only portions of animal sacrifices, but also the firstfruits of grain, wine and oil, as well as the first cuttings of the sheep's fleece, are to be given to the priest. LXX begins syndetically over against MT, but *O b* omit the *καί* to equal MT. Though ראשית occurs twice, LXX translates the first occurrence by the plural, *τὰς ἀπαρχάς*, and the second by the singular, *τὴν ἀπαρχήν*, the number being chosen to indicate the number of genitive modifiers which follow; the second one is modified by a single one, *τῶν κουρῶν* rendering the collective noun גז. In the tradition the genitives *σίτου*, *οἴνου*, *ἐλαίου*, *προβάτων* are followed by *σου* in almost all witnesses, thereby following MT. Originally, however, as 848 (cir 50 B.C.E.) shows, the text was shorter without any *σου* at all, which good Greek style would indeed prefer.[6]

18:5 LXX's parent text was much closer to Sam than to MT; in fact, only three textual differences between LXX and Sam obtain. The subject of "chose" in LXX is *κύριος*, but in Sam, as well as in MT, it is יהוה אלהיך. In fact, all Greek mss except B 848 add *ο θεος σου* as well, but the combined witness of B 848 is definitive.[7] Sam also has a suffix in ולשרתו but LXX does not, though the *t* text does add *αυτω*; nor does LXX support the conjunction introducing the marked infinitive of Sam. This text is considerably expanded over against MT which does not support *ἔναντι τοῦ θεοῦ σου* nor *καὶ εὐλογεῖν*. Both of

4. Sym renders by (*ἐάν τε*) *βοῶν ἐάν τε βόσκημα*.
5. See LS sub *ἤνυστρον* with references.
6. See the discussion in THGD 78.
7. See THGD 76—77.

these structures are under the obelus in hex to show their absence in MT. It should be noted that both of these expansions are supported by 11QT60 as well.[8] LXX also has "in his name" after *εὐλογεῖν* with Sam (and see 11QT60 "in my name" as well) instead of בשם יהוה of MT. A majority text does change *αὐτοῦ* to *κυριου*, however.[9] One might well query the source of such a variant, which is not only widely supported, but is also a revision towards MT, especially since it is apparently not hex, the *O* group supporting *αὐτοῦ*. Two possibilities need consideration: a) Early copyists of the text may have been acquainted with the text of The Revisers, especially that of Theod. b) A more likely source is early recensional activity.[10] Such activity is attested e.g. in fragmentary early papyri, as the Greek Qumran fragments of Exod, Lev and Num show. On the other hand, Hebrew influence may have been present in the case of bilingual copyists, who probably knew their Hebrew Torah text much better than the Greek.[11]

This verse gives the reason (*ὅτι*/כי) for the allotment to the priests. The preposed *αὐτόν* refers to *ἱερεῖ* of v.3. Him the Lord chose out of all your tribes for a threefold purpose: a) *παραστῆναι*, for which most witnesses substitute the perfect infinitive *παρεσταναι*.[12] The notion *παραστῆναι ἔναντι κυρίου* means to be present in the sanctuary. This presence is then described by b) *λειτουργεῖν*. In MT this is modified by בשם יהוה, which is an unusual collocation. Used absolutely it means to serve in any kind of cultic activity such as sacrifice, intercessory prayer, or receiving gifts for the sanctuary. c) *εὐλογεῖν ἐπὶ τῷ ὀνόματι αὐτοῦ* "to bless in his name," probably a reference to "blessing the people" as with the Aaronic blessing, and so "to pronounce the benediction."[13]

That the priestly office is dynastic is clear from *αὐτὸς καὶ οἱ υἱοὶ αὐτοῦ πάσας τὰς ἡμέρας*. The collocation is syntactically separate from the verse, a kind of nominative pendant together with an accusative showing extent of time. Between these M Byz *f*+ insert *εν τοις υιοις ισραηλ* which was imported from 17:20.[14]

---

8. See the discussion in L.H.Schiffman, SCS 33,288—289.
9. See THGD 73.
10. See my PreOrigen recensional activity.
11. As was the case with 848; see my Attitudes for an analysis.
12. See note at THGD 79.
13. As SCS 33, 288—289.
14. See also THGD 134.

18:6 Vv.6—8 deal with the rights of Levites who live elsewhere. In MT the protasis consists of vv.6—7, with v.8 as the apodosis, i.e. on the analogy of vv.3—5 the center of attention is directed to the portion which the Levite is to receive. LXX has a different understanding. By disregarding the initial conjunction in v.7 the apodosis begins with v.7, and the stress falls on the absentee Levite's equal rights to engage in cultic service when he comes to the central sanctuary, along with equal access to the emollument due the priests.

The Levite referred to is one who comes from one of your cities, from all the Israelites. MT as usual has realized the synecdoche of שעריך as *τῶν πολέων ὑμῶν*; cf comment at 12:15. The plural pronoun was probably due to the same impulse that led the translator to add *τῶν υἱῶν* before "Israel," i.e. to distinguish Israelites from Israel, and so also *ὑμῶν* rather than a collective *σου*.

The relative clause modifying "the Levite" in MT is אשר הוא גר שם; LXX idiomatically interprets אשר plus שם by *οὗ*, i.e. "where he sojourns," but hex pedantically adds *εκει* under the asterisk to represent the שם. A similar pedantry on the part of hex follows immediately. MT continues with ובא בכל אות נפשו "and he comes in with all the desire of his person," which LXX with fine feeling renders by *καθότι ἐπιθυμεῖ ἡ ψυχὴ αὐτοῦ* "as his person (i.e. he himself) desires.[15] Origen found no counterpart for ובא and adds, still under the asterisk, *και ελευσεται*, creating thereby a peculiar Greek clause quite at odds with what either MT or LXX intended: "and he shall come as he himself desires." For the relative clause modifying *τόπον* see comment at 12:5. The majority B text has added *ο θεος σου* after *κύριος*, but this is not supported by MT, and must be ex par.[16]

18:7 The majority text does add a *και* at the beginning, but see the discussion at v.6.[17] The future tense is best understood as permissive: he (i.e. the visiting Levite) may cultically serve the name of the Lord his God. The dative after *λειτουργήσει* denotes whom or what is being served. The "name of the Lord" is then merely the surrogate for the Lord.

15. I find the reference in SS 127 (*καθότι* for ב) overly mechanical.
16. See also THGD 73.
17. See also THGD 79.

So the visiting Levite has the same rights to cultic service "as all his brothers, the Levites *οἱ παρεστηκότες ἐκεῖ ἔναντι κυρίου*." For the descriptive phrase see the comment in v.5 on *παραστῆναι*. These brother Levites are the priests who serve regularly in the sanctuary (*ἐκεῖ*); after all, the priests are all Levites.

18:8 MT reads חלק כחלק יאכלו "Like portions shall they eat," i.e. local Levite and visiting Levite alike. LXX has a singular verb following Sam and interprets חלק כחלק as *μερίδα μεμερισμένην*, "portion apportioned," i.e. an alloted share.[18]

The second part of the verse is obscure in MT, and LXX made a noble attempt to make sense. The Hebrew reads לבד ממכריו על האבות. The phrase לבד מן is rendered literally by *πλήν* "besides," and מכריו is understood as based on the root מכר "to sell," hence *τῆς πράσεως τῆς* "the sale of that which," and the prepositional phrase is interpreted as *κατὰ τὴν πατρίαν* "concerning the paternal inheritance." So probably "the sale of goods inherited from one's father." The general sense seems to be that the visiting Levite is to receive a due portion besides any heritage or proceeds from anything such as he might own.[19] In the tradition *C''* has *πραξεως* for *πράσεως* which is an obvious copyist error. Hex has added *αυτου* to represent the suffix.

18:9 Vv.9—22 deal with forbidden forms of divination and with prophecy. Vv.9—12 deal with what is forbidden. For the relative clause modifying *γῆν* see comment at 1:20. Over against MT, LXX does not have a pronoun introducing the verb in the protasis, and hex added *συ* before *εἰσέλθῃς* to equal MT. For *βδελύγματα* see comment at 7:25. The term *τῶν ἐθνῶν ἐκείνων* must refer to the indigenous peoples, though there is no immediate reference to them in the context.

---

18. Theod is more literal though also having a singular verb: *μερίδα ὡς μερίδα φάγεται* (retroverted from Syh^{m}).

19. The ancients tend to paraphrase in some way. Tar^{O} e.g. reads for the line בר ממטרתא דייתי בשבתא כבן אתקינו אבהתא, Tar^{J} elaborates by בר ממותרי קורבניא דיכלון כהניא דאוריתו להון אלעזר ואיתמר אבהתהון, and Tar^{N} has בר מן מותרי קורבנוי די אחסינו להון אבהתהון, and Vulg has *excepto eo quod in urbe sua ex paterna ei successione debetur*. Aq has ... *τῶν πράσεων αὐτοῦ ἐπὶ τοὺς πατέρας*, and Sym reads ... *τῆς κτήσεως ἐκτὸς τῆς κατὰ τὰς πατρίας*.

18:10 Vv.10—11 list nine forbidden practices which *οὐχ εὑρεθήσεται ἐν σοί*. It should be said that for most of these, precise distinctions among them, i.e. exactly how they differed from one another, are quite beyond the modern reader, either of the Hebrew or of the Greek terms, and their renderings are throughout only approximate.

The first one is *περικαθαίρων τὸν υἱὸν αὐτοῦ ἢ τὴν θυγατέρα αὐτοῦ ἐν πυρί*. The verb *περικαθαίρω* means "to purify thoroughly, completely," and the participle is used to render מעביר "one who causes to pass through." LXX gives the Hebrew action a cultic interpretation; presumably "cleansing by fire" is an attempt to ameliorate the horror of the notion of burning, for which see 12:31.[20] All the participles used in this list of forbidden practices are in the present tense, chosen to show a practice rather than an action. The conjunction *ἤ* correctly renders the intent of the *waw* of MT; the practice is not one involving both a son and a daughter, but rather one or the other. Cod B actually has *και* here, but I suspect this to be a careless mistake rather than an intended revision.[21] The practice of cleansing a son or daughter by fire is here not understood as a sacrifice, but rather as a means of invoking deity for discovering its will or intent.

The second is *μαντευόμενος μαντείαν* "divining an oracle or a divination." The Byz text introduces this with *και*, for which there is otherwise no textual support. The verb *μαντεύομαι* is the Classical term for divining, consulting an oracle; it is the general term for divination, whereas those that follow were presumably intended as more specific forms.

The third practice is *κληδονιζόμενος* "receiving or looking for an omen," a verb formed from the noun *κληδῶν* "a sign or omen." The Hebrew word is מעונן "practice soothsaying."[22] The verb occurs elsewhere only at 4Reg 21:6, and is used of Manasseh, where MT has the same verb as here. In the tradition the majority A F M V text introduces the participle with *και*, but this has no support in MT.

The next abomination is *καὶ οἰωνιζόμενος* "one who divines by interpreting the flight of birds," though not necessarily to be taken more specifically

20. Aq renders the participle literally by *διάγων*.
21. On the carelessness of the B copyist in Deut see THGD 48.
22. Sym interprets this as *σημειοσκοπούμενος* "one who observes signs," for which see Salvesen 152.

than divining from omens. MT has מנחש another word for some kind of divination. At Gen 44:5 it is used for divining by using a beaker, and there נחש ינחש is rendered similarly by *οἰωνισμῷ οἰωνίζεται*.

The last word is wrongly accented in the edition; the word is proparoxytonic, i.e. *φάρμακος*, not *φαρμακός*, and it means "sorcerer, magician," more particularly one who mixes magical potions. As at Exod 7:11 it renders מכשף "sorcerer"; see Note ad loc. MT has the word joined with the preceding by *waw*, but LXX follows Sam where it is asyndetic.

18:11 The first and second forbidden practices are syndetic in MT, but LXX follows Sam which lacks conjunctions, both for חבר and שאל. The sixth abomination is *ἐπᾴδων ἐπαοιδήν* "one who charms a spell or charm," rendering חבר חבר "to tie on a spell"; see also Exod 7:11, where *ἐπαοιδοι* translates חרטמי; see Note ad loc.

This is followed by *ἐγγαστρίμυθος* "ventriloquist," i.e. "a word in the belly," here rendering שאל אוב "one who inquires of a medium." The word אוב is uncertain of meaning. Presumably a medium was thought of as one who produced ghostly sounds as by ventriloquism.[23]

The eighth forbidden form for seeking answers was that of a *τερατοσκόπος* "a diviner of portents" for ידעני "(a consultant of) familiar spirits," i.e. one who consults spirits which have special knowledge. In MT שאל is understood with both אוב and ידעני, which LXX perceived correctly.[24]

The last one is an *ἐπερωτῶν τοὺς νεκρούς* "necromancer," which renders דרש אל המתים.[25] For an example of consulting the dead see the case of Saul and the Endor medium, 1Reg 28:7—19.

18:12 Everyone practicing such forms of divination and magic is once again said to be an "abomination to the Lord your God";[26] in fact, it is because

23. Dogniez-Harl is probably correct in translating as *oracle ventriloque.* Aq translated the phrase by *ἐπερωτῶν μάγον* "one who interrogates a wizard," whereas Theod has *θελητής* "wizard."
24. Aq translates by *γνωριστής* and Sym by *γνώστης*, both of which meaning "one who pretends to know the future"; Theod renders by *θεατής* "one who goes to see, who watches."
25. Aq read *ἐκζητῶν τοὺς νεκρούς* (retroverted from Syh).
26. For the dative expressing the relationship of the elements in a bound phrase see SS 68.

(*γάρ*) of this that such forms *οὐχ εὑρεθήσεται ἐν σοί* "may not be found in you" (v.10). LXX follows Sam's אלהיך, which MT lacks;[27] hex has accordingly put *τῷ θεῷ σου* under the obelus.

The second clause begins with *waw* in MT, ובגלל "and because of," but LXX changes this to another *γάρ*, *ἕνεκεν γάρ*, which is unusual; one might rather have expected a "therefore" construction. Actually a few cursives have omitted the *γάρ*, which also makes good sense. No Greek witness recognizes the initial conjunction of MT. In any event, the Lord hates those who practice such abominations; it is because of them that "he will destroy *αὐτούς* from before you." The antecedent of the pronoun is *ἐθνῶν* of v.9. In the tradition there are two instances in which B *n*+ represent a text shorter than LXX, neither of which equal MT. The omission of *ὁ θεός σου* after *κύριος* seldom represents LXX over against MT, since the translator is remarkably careful in this regard, and it is unlikely to be original LXX here either.[28] In the second case *ἀπὸ προσώπου σου* of LXX literally represents the מפניך of MT. The shorter text omitted *προσώπου*. Of course, *απο σου* is better Greek, and the change is stylistic.[29]

18:13 The adjective *τέλειος* means "perfect, without any spot, blameless," and correctly renders תמים (see also Gen 6:9 Exod 12:5), which also means "perfect" in the sense of without spot; specifically it means "complete," i.e. without imperfections. The future verb is imperatival, "you must be perfect." In MT this is modified by an עם phrase, thus be perfect in association with, i.e. towards the Lord. LXX here translates עם uniquely by *ἔναντι* "before," i.e. in the presence of.

18:14 The reason for the command to be *τέλειος* is the difference between these nations and you. LXX has changed the straightforward S—P pattern of MT to a more complicated one. The verbal in both cases is "will listen," but in LXX the subject is *οὗτοι*, a demonstrative with its anaphoric reference in a nominative pendant "as for these nations who ..., these will listen." The writer is here overly careless with gender; though *ἔθνη* is neuter he makes

27. Also found in Kenn 4,48,140.
28. See THGD 126.
29. See THGD 127.

pronominal references to it in the masculine (as though the antecedent were λαοί): οὓς ... αὐτοὺς οὗτοι. The οὗτοι has no equivalent in MT, and this has been indicated by an obelus in the hex text. The relative clause modifying ἔθνη contains a nominal clause consisting of pronoun plus participle, which as usual LXX renders by pronoun plus inflected present tense: σὺ κατακληρονομεῖς "you are disinheriting." LXX faithfully renders the אותם which follows, and only four mss in the tradition show the good sense of leaving it out, and making better Greek out of it. The verb ἀκούσονται is modified by two genitives, which tie the whole section, vv.9—14, together; they hear the κληδόνων καὶ μαντειῶν; for the two nouns see the comments at v.10. A majority A F M V variant has changed κληδόνων to κληδονισμων, which must have been rooted in palaeographic confusion, since the variant text is much less sensible.

By contrast—note the use of δέ—σοὶ δὲ οὐχ οὕτως ἔδωκεν κύριος. MT begins with ואתה, "but as for you," and then comes the clause "not thus did the Lord ... grant לך." This may have promoted the change in construction of the first clause with its preposed pendant nominative. By combining לך and אתה in a preposed σοί, LXX presented the intent of the Hebrew more economically.

18:15 The remainder of the chapter deals with the prophet in Israel. The term προφήτης is a calque for נביא; it is almost entirely limited to its translation, and the reverse is also thc case. So προφήτης equals the Hebrew נביא, and for its use cf Lexica of Biblical Hebrew. The term is preposed to the verb ἀναστήσει, which it modifies, thereby highlighting it as thematic. In MT נביא is doubly modified by two prepositional phrases מקרבך מאחיך which LXX simplifies by omitting the first one entirely; hex has added εκ μεσου σου under the asterisk to make up for the omission, but rhetorically speaking, making one phrase out of it is a tighter statement. Actually the parent reading for the translation may well have been the מקרב אחיך of Sam; comp also v.18. This prophet whom the Lord will raise for you will be ὡς ἐμέ; by this Moses is himself identified as a prophet.[30] What is not at all clear from this passage is whether a particular prophet (possibly Joshua) is meant as Moses' follower, or prophets in general. Later in the discussion it is the second that is meant, since

30. Not uninteresting is the Tar^J expansion: דדמי לי ברוח קודשא. To the Targumist a real prophet is imbued with a divine (holy) spirit.

prophets in general are referred to, and the possibility of not being a true prophet is discussed. The verse ends with *αὐτοῦ ἀκούσεσθε*, but this is syntactically connected with v.16. The verb is now in the plural in imitation of MT.

18:16 This verse must be taken as modifying the verb at the end of v.15, since it sets the norm for listening to him (i.e. to the prophet of the future). It fits the norm set up at Khoreb. What is meant is that it was there that the people discovered that it was too much for them to hear the voice of the Lord directly—they needed someone to mediate the Lord's word, so *αὐτοῦ ἀκούσεσθε*.

For *τῇ ἡμέρᾳ τῆς ἐκκλησίας* see comment at 4:10. The direct speech marker is now plural: *λέγοντες*, which ties it directly to the *ἀκούσεσθε* at the end of v.15.[31] What the people said is best understood as a deliberative future: "We would no more hear ... and this great fire we would not see any more (lest we should die)." The verbs are consistently put into first plural, i.e. LXX harmonizes the entire passage in the plural, which fits better in the context than the singulars of MT over against תשמעון in v.15. Note also that LXX is more in line with the plural (third person) of vv.17—18. The Masoretic interpretation of אסף as a short form "Let me (not) add" also confirms the above interpretation of the future verbs as deliberative. What the translator has done in the matter of number was intentional; *ἀκούσεσθε* is plural, and between it and *λέγοντες* a *ὅσα* clause is put in the singular (as in MT). The request made of the Lord was a popular response, a vox populi, and so a collective singular is justified: *ᾐτήσω ... θεοῦ σου*. In the tradition, hex has added the article *του* under the asterisk before *ἀκοῦσαι* to represent the infinitival marker of לשמע.

The last clause, ולא אמות, is not taken by LXX as a simple paratactic statement; rather by interpreting it as (*οὐδὲ*) *μὴ ἀποθάνωμεν*, i.e. *μή* plus the subjunctive, it understood this as a negative result clause: "so that we might not die."

18:17 *ὀρθῶς* "correctly, rightly" does get the point of היטיבו, which is often used adverbially. I would render what was said as "all that they have spoken is

31. Which SS Inf 73 apparently failed to do; at least reference is made to the marker being "in Inkongruenz zu seinem Hauptwort."

correct."[32] The word *πάντα* has no counterpart in BHS, and hex has placed it under the obelus.[33]

18:18 The first clause largely repeats the content of v.15, but it is put into the mouth of the Lord, and addressed to Moses, with references to the people changed to third person plural, along with some reordering of text. It reads "a prophet I will raise up for them out of their brothers like you."[34]

The role of the prophet is then defined: *δώσω τὸ ῥῆμά μου* in his mouth, and he will speak to them as I would order him." The verb takes on the meaning of נתתי in the sense of "put, place." The Masoretes have vocalized דברי as plural "my words," but LXX uses the singular, since it is God's spoken word; cf comment on λόγων in v.19. One might have expected an *εἰς* phrase after *δώσω* with action involved, i.e. "I will put into," but the translator understood בפיו as a locative; it informs where God placed his word: "in his mouth."[35] In fact, an *f* text, supported by G, has actually changed *ἐν τῷ στόματι* into *εις το στομα*.

The prophet is thus the one who transmits what God tells him to the people; he is the intermediary between God and man. LXX, however, has changed the את כל plus relative clause somewhat. MT says "everything which I shall order him," but the Greek disregards the כל, and changes את אשר to *καθότι*. LXX speaks of the norm for the transmission of God's word over against MT's content of that transmission. Oddly enough there is no record of hex having glossed the text with a *παντα*.

18:19 The verse is introduced by והיה, but LXX only has *καί*. Normally when והיה introduces a condition it becomes *καὶ ἔσται* in LXX; cf discussion at 6:10—11. Admittedly the construction differs, since the structure *καὶ ὁ ἄνθρωπος ὃς κ.τ.λ.* is a pendant nominative construction set up as an antecedent for *ἐξ αὐτοῦ*. As in the case of כל in v.18, no record of a hex correction is extant. Within the relative clause MT again has דברי as in v.18, but LXX follows Sam's דבריו. Over against *τὸ ῥῆμά μου* of v.18 the translator has *τῶν*

---

32. Theod and Aq have rendered the verb literalistically by *ἠγάθυναν*, and have also omitted *πάντα*.
33. Kenn 84 also added כל as did Tar^N Pesh and Vulg.
34. For *ὥσπερ σε* Aq reads *ὅμοιόν σοι* (retroverted from Syh^m).
35. Though SS 136 takes it in the sense of "into."

λόγων αὐτοῦ. What the Lord spoke in v.18 is τὸ ῥῆμα, but now it is the words of the prophet, and so the plural λόγων is used.[36]

The ὅσα clause represents אשר ידבר בשמי, and is potentially ambiguous as to the subject of the verb; it could be האיש which is the nearer possibility, or it could be the נביא of v.18. LXX voids any confusion by adding ὁ προφήτης after the verb.[37] The Hebrew clause modifies דברי immediately before it, but in LXX this is problematic. Theoretically this could be part of the pendant construction, but one can also take it as modifying ἐκδικήσω. Thus "I will exact punishment of him for whatever the prophet would speak in my name," which seems to me preferable. Somewhat unusual is the direct accusative modifier ὅσα for this verb, but the usage is attested elsewhere. The verb ἐκδικήσω translates אדרש "I will seek, require." I would translate the line: "I will require of him whatever the prophet might speak in my name."

In the tradition, ἄνθρωπος is made more specific by the A F M V *oP f y*+ gloss εκεινος. The gloss is ad sensum. Hex placed ὁ προφήτης under the obelus to show that it is absent in MT. For the popular εαν instead of ἄν 1° (as well as of 2°) see comment at 5:27.

18:20 For the translation of יזיד by ἀσεβήσῃ, see the comment at 17:13.[38] The first kind of "false prophet" is one who with deliberate intent speaks as a prophet, i.e. "speaks ῥῆμα in my name which I did not order (+ him MT) to speak." LXX does not have "him," though the majority text does have it; good Greek does not need to translate the "him." The addition of αυτω is probably ad sensum rather than recensional, added to make sure that the divine order had been made to the "prophet." Here ῥῆμα occurs in the singular as in MT; though this is not a divine word, it is proclaimed as though it were such; cf comment at v.18. Such an impious action constitutes a bastardization of the prophetic office, and ἀποθανεῖται ὁ προφήτης ἐκεῖνος.

But there is also a second type of false prophet to whom the penalty will apply, viz. "one who would speak in the name of other gods." This is equally

36. For an interesting discussion of the distinction intended see Dogniez-Harl, 41—43 as well as ad loc, where the two are defined as "On voit ici la spécialisation acquise par *rhéma* pour désigner l'enseignement révelé la bouche de YHWH ... et l'usage de *lógoi* pour les paroles qui seront mises par écrit" (p.231).
37. Tar^J also makes this clear: פיתגמי נבותי "words of my prophecy."
38. Aq again translates by ὑπερηφανεύσηται; see 17:13.

heinous for the monotheistic faith of Deut. In the tradition B V *n z* have reordered ῥῆμα after ἐπὶ τῷ ὀνόματί μου, thereby bringing ῥῆμα immediately before the relative clause "which I did order ...," which modifies it. This is probably an intentional reordering, and is secondary.[39]

18:21 The protasis raises a problem: "But suppose you say to yourself: How shall we identify (literally recognize) the word which the Lord did not speak?" LXX uses a δέ for the introductory *waw*, since it contrasts with what precedes, i.e. a possible objection to realizing v.20. In the tradition, εἴπῃς appears as the present subjunctive λεγης in F *C*'' *f s*+, but there is no need to express a process; the aorist is not only sufficient, but the translator normally uses the aorist in Deut, unless he particularly wants to insist on a present or perfect aspect. And the Byz text has added ο θεος after κύριος, but this is ex par.

18:22 The objection is answered. When μὴ γένηται τὸ ῥῆμα καὶ μὴ συμβῇ, that is a false prophet; the Lord did not speak that ῥῆμα. MT has ולא יהיה הדבר ולא יבוא which can be translated: "the word does not happen and does not come about." In other words, events prove that the prophetic prediction was a false one. It is identified as τὸ ῥῆμα ὃ οὐκ ἐλάλησεν κύριος. It should be noted that the translator throughout this section consistently used ῥῆμα for the word which was presented as the prophetic word from God. For the majority εαν reading see comment at 5:27. MT adds a suffix in דברו, but fortunately LXX did not reproduce it. The Byz did add an αυτο after ἐλάλησεν 1°, which can only be recensional in origin. Purely secondary are the *C*'' *s* gloss ο θεος or the Byz ο θεος σου amplifying κύριος. These are unsupported by MT, and are ex par.

In v.22b this action is branded for what it is: ἐν ἀσεβείᾳ spoke the prophet ἐκεῖνος. The term ἀσεβείᾳ "impiety" is unique as a translation of זדון "insolence, arrogance" for which see comment at 17:12. To the translator a word such as ὑπερηφανίᾳ was not strong enough to characterize speaking a word which the Lord had not spoken; such an action was impious; it was an ἀσέβεια. A majority A F K M V text has omitted ἐκεῖνος, but the shorter text is not LXX, since hex has placed it under the obelus to indicate that MT had

---

39. See THGD 130.

no pronoun. Once again LXX rendered דברו simply by *ἐλάλησεν*, and this time hex did add *αυτο* to represent the suffix of MT. For *ἐν ἀσεβείᾳ* see comment at 17:13.[40]

The section concludes with *οὐκ ἀφέξεσθε ἀπ' αὐτοῦ* "not shall you hold yourselves away from him"; what is meant is that you shall not refrain from inflicting the death penalty on him; you shall not spare him. The verb is put in the plural over against MT, since it is individuals who will have to carry out the death penalty. MT has the verb תגור "to be afraid of, to stand in awe of," for which see comment at 1:17, where it was rendered by *ὑποστείλῃ*.

---

40. Aq translated בזדון by *ἐν ὑπερηφανίᾳ* (retroverted from Syh).

Chapter 19

19:1 Vv.1—13 constitute regulations about the cities of refuge. V.1 is the general protasis introducing the section. The Hi of כרת is most commonly rendered by ἐξολεθρεύω, as e.g. at 12:29, but here the translator used ἀφανίσῃ. The only other occurrence of ἀφανίζω for הכרית occurs at Exod 8:9(5) where it is used for making frogs disappear from the land of Egypt.[1] The construction of the relative clause is Hebraic with its ἅ ... τὴν γῆν αὐτῶν for "whose land"; the relative pronoun is as usual for Deut attracted to the inflection of its antecedent, ἔθνη. Far more sensible is the Byz variant reading *ων* instead of ἅ. For the relative clause in general see comment at 1:20.

Usually the translator is careful to render יהוה אלהיך, but within the relative clause LXX has only ὁ θεός σου as subject; hex does add *κυριος* before it to equal MT. For κατακληρονομήσετε in the sense of "to disinherit," see also 18:14. Why the Greek should change to the plural in v.1b is not at all clear; in fact, the majority A F K M V text changes to the singular to equal וירשתם וישבת, but B 963 support the more difficult change to the plural, which is probably original LXX.

19:2 LXX translates תבדיל by διαστελεῖς "separate," which is regularly used in Lev and Num as well, but not in Gen and Exod.[2] For the relative clause see comment at 1:20. Unusual is ὁ θεός for אלהיך, and the support for the shorter text, probably shortened for stylistic reasons,[3] is limited to five cursive mss, but the *σου* of the majority text is under the asterisk, proving that it was a hex addition.[4] The clause ends in MT with לרשתה, which LXX omits.[5] It too has been supplied by hex under the asterisk as *του κληρονομησαι αυτην*.

---

1. Theod uses the more usual ἐξολεθρεύσῃ (retroverted from Syh^{m}.)
2. Aq has χωρίσεις, which is also used in Gen.
3. See Appositives 267.
4. See THGD 122.
5. See SS Inf 60.

19:3 MT begins with תכין "you must prepare," but LXX contextualizes with an imperative *στόχασαι*.[6] Since the next clause reads *καὶ τριμεριεῖς τὰ ὅρια τῆς γῆς σου*, which means "and you shall divide the borders of your land into three sections," it does take some advance planning; this probably determined LXX's choice of verb: "figure out, calculate." One might also have expected a future indicative to render תכין rather than an imperative, but the lack of a conjunction may well have impelled Deut's choice.[7] The imperative is modified by *σοι*, which the majority text has changed to *σεαυτω*; either would be adequate for rendering לך, but support by A B F as the oldest witnesses is determinative. The change of *σοι* to *συ* by M *C'' f*+, though sensible, is simply an itacistic spelling, as the Hebrew makes clear. LXX realized that dividing up the border into three equal parts might be difficult. The imperative is modified by an accusative *τὴν ὁδόν*, so "figure out the road."

The verb *καταμερίζει* occurs only here for ינחיל, though it does occur once for the Pi and twice for the Hithp (all in the Pentateuch). It means "divide up into sections," and is an odd choice in the context of the Lord's ינחילך the land. One might have expected the root *κληρονομέω*, but the translator avoided this in view of *κατακληρονομήσητε* in v.2 in the sense of "disinherit." Here the translator probably uses it in the sense of "which the Lord your God apportioned to you." Unexpected is the use of a present tense over against the future of the context. Presumably the translator viewed the apportioning of land by God as prior to that of *τριμεριεῖς* and of the last clause.

The last clause is the point of the entire exercise: "And it shall be a refuge there for every manslayer." MT is structured somewhat differently in that כל רצח is the subject of the infinitive לנוס, but the Greek does represent the sense adequately, though it must be admitted that rendering an infinitive by a noun is unusual.[8]

19:4 This verse introduces *τὸ πρόσταγμα τοῦ φονευτοῦ*. For *πρόσταγμα* see comment at 15:2. LXX identifies this decree as relevant for the future by

6. Possibly reflecting the root תפן rather than כון, as P.E.Dion suggests in his Deuteronomy 19:3; Prepare the Way, or Estimate the Distance? in Église et Théologie 25(1994), 333—341
7. Aq translates תכין literally by *ἑτοιμάσεις*.
8. See SS Inf 37.

adding *ἔσται*, whereas MT has a nominal clause: זה דבר הרצח. In this way LXX adjusts to the setting of the book, in which the laws are to regulate Israel's life after they enter the Promised Land. Hex has correctly placed *ἔσται* under the obelus.

The first *ὅς* clause is closely tied to the opening clause, i.e. it limits the application of the *πρόσταγμα* to the slayer "who may flee there (i.e. to a city of refuge), and live." Not every *φονευτής* qualifies for refuge (see vv.11—13), but only those who fulfil certain conditions, which are given in vv.4b—6. The basic condition is that the killing was done involuntarily, *ἀκουσίως*, contracted from *ἀεκουσίως*. This is a somewhat different emphasis from MT, which has בבלי דעת "unknowingly." The Greek prefers to accent the fact that intent was not involved, whereas MT stresses ignorance. At 4:42, however, *οὐκ εἰδώς* was used to translate the Hebrew phrase. The one killed is called את רעהו, but LXX disregarded the suffix in the interests of good Greek style. After all, whose neighbour could it be but "his neighbour." The majority text does add *σου*, but 848 consistently lacks a genitive pronoun after *πλησίον* and the shorter text is clearly original.[9]

Furthermore, relations had previously been in good order. Unusual is the literalistic rendering of the Hebrew pattern: pronoun plus participial predicate. This type of nominal clause is usually rendered in LXX by pronoun plus present (or imperfect) verb, but here it is rendered by *οὗτος οὐ μισῶν (αὐτόν)* because its modifiers mean "previously"; see also 4:42.[10] For *πρὸ τῆς ἐχθὲς καὶ πρὸ τῆς τρίτης* see Note at Exod 4:10. The popular variant spelling *χθες* for *ἐχθές* is the Classical form.

19:5 This verse is an example of *πατάξῃ τὸν πλησίον ἀκουσίως* rather than a further regulation, though it is presented paratactically. The syntactic pattern is a relative pronoun with four coordinate clauses as a pendant construction, which in turn serves as an antecedent for the *οὗτος* introducting v.5b. To show the pattern in translation it could be rendered as "And as for someone who enters ..., he (i.e. *οὗτος*) may flee ... and live." The circumstances are: he goes with the neighbour into the woods to collect some wood, and his hand is drawn back while cutting the tree with an axe, and the iron falling from the

9. See the discussion in THGD 77—78.
10. See SS 83.

wooden (haft) happens (i.e. to strike) the neighbour, and (i.e. so that) he dies. The text of MT is somewhat different. LXX has interpreted לחטב "to hew" as not really expressing the purpose of entering the woods; surely it was to gather firewood—*συναγαγεῖν ξύλα*.[11] And the movement of the hand is described as ונדחה "is impelled" rather than *ἐκκρουσθῇ* "drawn back." What LXX is thinking of is the way one handles an axe; one swings it back in order to send it forward on to the wood. In that backward swing the iron slipped off and struck the neighbour.[12] The action described is בגרזן לכרת which the Greek translates with a different pattern, viz. omitting the preposition, and using a participle *κόπτοντος* modifying *αὐτοῦ* (i.e. the one wielding the axe); see the translation above.[13] In MT the marked infinitive modifies נדחה, showing purpose.[14] The iron in MT נשל "slips off" the handle, whereas the Greek has *ἐκπεσόν*. Note how idiomatically LXX renders מצא את רעהו by *τύχῃ τοῦ πλησίον*. For *πλησίον* (twice) without *σου* see comment at v.4.

19:6 The phrase *ὁ ἀγχιστεύων τοῦ αἵματος* is a calque for גאל הדם, and must be understood in the sense of the Hebrew. The "avenger of blood" refers to the nearest male relative of someone who has been hurt or killed, and on whom lies the obligation to seek redress, i.e. to activate the lex talionis.[15] The verse begins with פן in MT, which LXX translates by *ἵνα μή*. A פן construction occurs 26 times in Deut and is usually translated without *ἵνα*, but *ἵνα μή* does occur in four cases (also at 7:22 22:9 32:27), and cannot be faulted. The opening verb is downgraded to a participle, *διώξας*, and is subordinated to (*καὶ*) *καταλάβῃ*, for which the Hebraic *καί* is, however, retained.

The pursuit is undertaken *ὅτι παρατεθέρμανται τῇ καρδίᾳ* "because he is heated (in) heart)," i.e. the LXX retained the figure of heat in MT's יחם לבבו, though in the interest of good Greek did not render the suffix. The majority A F M V text does add *αυτου*, thereby equalling MT, though the

11. Aq renders by *ἐκκόψαι*.
12. Aq has the more literal *ἐξωσθῇ* from *ἐξωθέω*.
13. SS Inf 60 calls this "a free translation."
14. Aq translates more literally by *ἐν τῷ πέλυκι τοῦ κόψαι*. Note how Aq distinguishes between לחטב and לכרת, using the simplex *κόψαι* for the latter but the *ἐκ*-compound for the former.
15. Only at 2Reg 14:11 is the Hebrew term translated differently. The majority A B M V text has *ἀγχιστέα τοῦ αἵματος*, though the Lucianic text does read *οι αγχιστευοντος το αιμα*; what the Old Greek read is uncertain.

gloss is probably ex par rather than recensional. For *διώξας* ... *καταλάβῃ* see Exod 15:9. *καταλάβῃ* is conditioned by the *ἐάν* clause "if the way was too long." LXX strengthens the Hebrew text by using the comparative adjective plus *ἦν* for the verb ירבה. It should be noted that the majority A F M V text has changed *ἦν* to the Classically more acceptable subjunctive *ῃ*.

What makes the situation perilous is that a capital sentence might be carried out before judgment is made. The execution is described as *καὶ πατάξῃ αὐτοῦ τὴν ψυχήν* "and he should smite his person"; the נפש/*ψυχήν* is the actual living being, the individual; in other words, he smites a mortal blow. To make sure that the idiom should be fully understood, LXX added *καὶ ἀποθάνῃ*, which is not supported in MT, and hex has correctly placed it under the obelus. In this case, however, it was not a *κρίσις θανάτου*/משפט מות, a case for a death sentence, since intention was not involved; it was an accident. For the last *ὅτι* clause see comment at v.4.

19:7 The conclusion: "therefore I am ordering you *τὸ ῥῆμα τοῦτο* saying." MT lacks an equivalent for "this matter," and hex has placed it under the obelus. Also hex has transposed *σοι ἐντέλλομαι* to equal the order of morphemes in מצוך of MT.

19:8 Vv.8—10 constitute a postscript: Suppose the Lord God should enlarge your borders, what then? The subject of the *ἐάν* clause is *κύριος ὁ θεός*; i.e. אלהיך is rendered without regard to the suffix. The evidence for the shorter text is sparse, but it includes 848 and that must be determinative, even though all other uncials, as well as most other mss, support the addition of *σου*.[16] The clause *ὃν τρόπον ὤμοσεν τοῖς πατράσίν σου* recurs at 28:9 29:13. For the enlarged borders extended "from the Red Sea to the sea of the Philistines, and from the wilderness to the Euphrates" promised, though not by an oath, see Exod 23:31, and Note ad loc. For the discussion of the ideal land of promise see the fuller discussion at 1:7. LXX renders MT literally, except that דבר is more commonly rendered by *ἐλάλησεν* than as here by *εἶπεν*.

19:9 The conditional structure follows on, and should be understood as part of, the condition of v.8; i.e. the *ἐάν* clause of v.9 introduces a further condi-

16. See the discussion in THGD 76 as well as Appositives 267.

tion for v.8. The Lord will only consider expanding Israel's borders "if you obediently perform all these commandments, etc." LXX has translated תשמר by *ἀκούσῃς*, as at 11:13 31:12. This does not necessarily mean that LXX read תשמע, since the two roots are similar in meaning. The majority text has the compound *εισακουσῃς*, but 848's support for the simplex is convincing.[17] For the *ἅς* clause see comment at 4:2. For *ἀγαπᾶν* see comment at 6:5. This infinitive plus the coordinate *πορεύεσθαι* are both present infinitives, since a process is intended, and the two together explicate *ἀκούσῃς*, showing how you are to show your submission. Most witnesses omit the *καί* joining the infinitives, probably ex par (comp 11:22 30:16), but the *καί* is supported by 848, and equals MT.[18]

The apodosis is introduced by an unnecessary *καί*, which reflects MT. The point of vv.8—9 is that under certain conditions "you may add still three more cities to these three (i.e. as ordered in v.7).

19:10 This verse is a general conclusion to vv.1—9; i.e. it has no immediate connection with vv.8—9, but rather with the section on cities of refuge for the innocent *φονευτής* as a whole, i.e. with vv.1—9. The future tense is then to be taken as prospective; it is what will be the case if the cities of refuge are in place, in other words the verse shows result. One might then interpret the clause as "and (so) guiltless blood will not be shed."[19] For the relative clause see comment at 1:20. For *ἐν κλήρῳ* rendering נחלה comp 4:21.

The last clause not only parallels the first one, but also serves as a transition to vv.11—13, which deal with what is to happen to the one who is *αἵματος ἔνοχος*. The Hebrew clause reads והיה עליך דמים "and bloodshed would be on you," and LXX has interpreted דמים "shed-blood" by *αἵματι ἔνοχος* "liable for blood," thus "and not shall there be one liable for blood within you."[20] In this way LXX makes "bloodshed" a legal matter.

For *ἐν τῇ γῇ* the *f* text has *επι την γην*, a rationalistic attempt at improving "be poured in the land," by "... on the land," but MT has בקרב ארצך, and בקרב is more commonly rendered by an *ἐν* phrase in LXX. The

17. See THGD 73.
18. See THGD 79.
19. Instead of *ἀναίτιον* Aq has *ἀθῷον* "innocent," which renders נקי somewhat more accurately.
20. The Others have "blood" in the plural *αἵμασιν* (retroverted from Syh).

dative *αἵματι* is changed to the genitive *αιματος* in *cl d+*, but *ἔνοχος* is more commonly modified by the dative.

19:11 The condition here described is the opposite of the case in vv.4—5, i.e. of an *ἄνθρωπος μισῶν τὸν πλησίον*. For the failure to render the suffix of רעהו see comment at v.4.[21] This man then *ἐνεδρεύσῃ αὐτόν* "lay in wait for him," and rose up against him, and smote his person (*πατάξῃ αὐτοῦ ψυχήν*); for the meaning of the collocation see comment at v.6. This is followed directly by *καὶ ἀποθάνῃ καὶ φύγῃ*, without any indication of change of subject, first to the victim, and then with *φύγῃ*, back to the slayer. Common sense, however, makes it all clear.

19:12 The subject is now *ἡ γερουσία τῆς πόλεως αὐτοῦ*. The term *γερουσία* "council of elders" is often used instead of *πρεσβύτεροι* in the Pentateuch (25 times, of which 16 occur in Deut, whereas *πρεσβύτεροι* occurs only four times in Deut). The predicates (*ἀποστελοῦσιν ... λήμψονται ... παραδώσουσιν*) are, however, in the plural, as in MT. Here the term *γερουσία* is fitting, since the elders function in a juridical fashion. This council is not that of the city to which the murderer fled, but *τῆς πόλεως αὐτοῦ*. The council must hand him over *εἰς χεῖρας τῷ ἀγχιστεύοντι τοῦ αἵματος*. Syntactically there is a break after *εἰς χεῖρας*, i.e. *εἰς χεῖρας* is in doublet fashion paralleled with a dative of indirect object. I would translate "they shall hand him over into the hands—(viz.) to the avenger of blood;[22] "hands" is metonymic for power, authority, control. For "avenger of blood" see comment at v.6. In the tradition, as one might expect, the dative has been changed to the genitive *του αγχιστευοντος* in *b f n+*, whereas B *z* have changed the dative singular to the genitive plural by adding a *nu* at the end, which is bizarre, since there is only one person who functions as the "avenger of blood." The more difficult dative is clearly to be preferred as LXX.

19:13 For the first clause see comment at 7:16. The next clause has בערת, which is explained in a comment at 13:5(6). The Deut formula is normally "you will purge the evil one from you." The usual rendering of בערת is

21. Theod and Aq add *σου*; Sym does not.
22. The critical text should have a comma after *χεῖρας*.

ἐξαρεῖς, but here it is uniquely καθαριεῖς, i.e. "you shall cleanse, purify."[23] The verb is modified by τὸ αἷμα τὸ ἀναίτιον, which follows the Sam text rather than the דם הנקי of MT. The translator was faced with the problem of making sense out of his parent text: ובערת הדם הנקי מישראל. What the Hebrew probably means is to purge (the stain of) innocent blood from Israel, but the intent is not at first blush apparent. LXX interpreted the burning as a cleansing, purifying element. Innocent blood has rendered Israel impure, and it has been cleansed by the execution of the murderer. Israel was impure as long as innocent blood cried out for vengeance, but it is now released from that impurity.

19:14 This verse maintains the inviolability of property boundaries. The verb μετακινέω is used only here for the Hi of סוג, but it is adequate. "You may not change ὅρια of a neighbour." MT has the singular גבול as a generic concept, which the plural interprets correctly. For πλησίον without σου to render רעך, see comment at v.4.[24]

The word ὅρια is modified by a relative clause, ἃ ἔστησαν οἱ πατέρες σου ἐν τῇ κληρονομίᾳ. ἔστησαν is contextually correct for גבלו "set borders,"[25] whereas οἱ πατέρες σου is a free rendering for ראשנים "those of former times"; these were indeed the ancestors, and hence LXX's "your fathers." The A M V *O*+ text does have προτεροι, which must be based (probably mediately) on MT; it may actually be a hex correction. The prepositional phrase renders בנחלתך without regard for the suffix. Only B supports the lack of a σου, which is otiose in the light of the ῇ clause, which modifies the noun.[26] The majority reading was easily created ex par. The relative clause makes it clear that it is your inheritance, since κατακληρονομήθης is second person. The use of the compound is merely for variety's sake, though the verb has the same root as that of the antecedent noun. The heritage which you will inherit is ἐν τῇ γῇ, which is also defined by another ῇ clause: which the Lord your God is giving you κληρονομῆσαι. Both relative clauses are introduced by ῇ which are inflected in the dative to agree with their dative antecedents. Note

23. Theod has ἐξαρεῖς (retroverted from Sym^m).
24. Aq translates the clause as οὐ προσλήψῃ ὅριον ἑταίρου σου (retroverted from Syh^m). Sym renders לא תסיג by οὐκ ἐπελεύσῃ.
25. Aq more literalistically minded has the neologism ὁριοθέτησαν.
26. See THGD 122.

how LXX places extra stress on the notion of inheritance by using the same root three times: "in the inheritance ... you will inherit ... to inherit." MT, however, changes the root to לרשתה for the last case. LXX fails to render its suffix in the interest of good Greek, but hex dutifully added *αυτην*.[27] The majority read *εν κληρω* instead of the infinitive, but that is an error created ex par.

19:15 The use of *ἐμμενεῖ* for יקום is a good choice, since it means "to last, abide," hence stand fast. The point is that a single witness against a person has no validity.[28] In the tradition, *μαρτυρησαι* occurs immediately after *μάρτυς εἷς*, in fact, in all mss except three, but 848 lacks it, as does MT, and the explanatory infinitive may well be due to v.18. It has been put under the obelus by hex, so the gloss must be prehexaplaric. The verb is then modified by four prepositional phrases, in which MT changes prepositions from ב to ל, to ל, to ב, but the translator used *κατά* throughout. One might keep the effect of the repetition in LXX by translating the first preposition by "against" and the other three by "as regards," since for the first one a genitive is involved, but an accusative for the other three. MT also lacks a conjunction before the last phrase, but LXX has smoothed out the text by adding *καί*. The Byz text has shortened the text by omitting the last phrase, *καὶ κατὰ πᾶσαν ἁμαρτίαν*; that this was not simply a thoughtless mistake is clear from the fact that the pronoun *ἥν*, which follows, was changed to *ο*, i.e. referring to *ἁμάρτημα*. For the popular A F V *εαν* variant instead of *ἄν*, see comment at 5:27.

V.15b makes a general rule out of the regulation concerning minimum witnesses at 17:6 for capital offenses. At least two are necessary for any kind of charge to stand. MT again uses יקום, as in the first clause, but LXX contextualizes neatly by the passive *σταθήσεται*, and the subject דבר has been fully expanded to *πᾶν ῥῆμα* "every case," i.e. any charge (shall be established). The *πᾶν* has been placed under an obelus in hex to show its absence in MT.

19:16 For *ἐὰν δέ* see comment at 15:16. Though MT again uses יקום (see comment at v.15), LXX uses a third equivalent, *καταστῇ*, since in the context

27. See THGD 79.
28. Aq uses the literal *ἀναστήσεται* "stand up."

the unjust witness stands up against, makes a charge against. The translation of עד חמס "a witness of violence" by *μάρτυς ἄδικος* weakens the notion of violence, but the translator is thinking of this as a legal issue; *δίκη* is involved, and a witness who promotes violence is in a legal situation unjust, i.e. guilty. For *κατὰ ἀνθρώπου* see comment at v.15. The charge made is לענות בו סרה "to accuse him of turning aside, i.e. of apostasy; see 13:6(5) דבר סרה and the comment ad loc. LXX uses a present participle, *καταλέγων* (*αὐτοῦ ἀσέβειαν*).[29] The translation of סרה by *ἀσέβειαν* is an interpretation in a personal sense. The charge is not one of a transitive action, a turning something or someone aside, but rather of an improper relation to God, of *ἀσέβειαν*.

19:17 The two men involved are defined as *οἷς ἐστιν αὐτοῖς ἡ ἀντιλογία* "who have the dispute,"[30] i.e. the one charged and the one making the charge are required to appear (*στήσονται*) "before the Lord, and before the priests, and before the judges who would be in those days." Unclear is the referent in *οἵ*; it could be the *κριτῶν*, or it could also include the *ἱερέων*. The Masoretes have made the first cut after יהוה, so that both priests and judges would seem to be intended. But since LXX continues with *καὶ ἐξετάσωσιν οἱ κριταὶ ἀκριβῶς*, i.e. excluding the priests, a straightforward reading of the Greek text might favor making only *κριτῶν* serve as anaphoric referent for the pronoun. On the other hand, see 17:9 where priests and a single judge make judgments. What further confuses the issue is that the Greek has *καί* before *ἔναντι τῶν ἱερέων*, whereas MT does not.[31] In MT "before the priests and judges" explicates what "before Yahweh" means. The Greek by its "*and* before the priests and *before* the judges" has made it possible to understand the phrases either as "before the Lord, both before the priests and before the judges" or as intending a triad of judges: the Lord and the priests and the judges. The appearance before the Lord and the priests makes it clear in any event that the dispute is to be settled at the central sanctuary.

19:18 For the opening verb, *ἐξετάσωσιν*, comp *ἐτάσεις* at 13:14(15) and see comment ad loc. The verb is an aorist subjunctive "let (the judges) examine,

29. See SS Inf 59.
30. See SS 58.
31. But Kenn 17,69,80*,84,158 and 184 do read ולפני.

investigate," which a variant *ol C'* *s*+ text has changed to a future, *εξετασουσιν*, but the subjunctive is intended, together with the adverb *ἀκριβῶς* inviting a thoroughgoing investigation. This opening clause does not really solve the problem raised about the *ἔναντι* phrase of v.17, since *οἱ κριταί* need not refer solely to the *κριτῶν* of v.17, but could refer to the judicial tribunal or triad as well.

καὶ ἰδού introduces the results of that inquiry: "a false witness has testified falsely (literally false things); he has stood up against his brother." The word העד has been taken by the translator as a verb (as Hi of עוד) rather than as an articulated noun.[32] The Masoretes have a different understanding. The noun העד is accented with a *zaqeph qaton*, and the break there makes שקר ענה באחיו a separate clause: "he has replied (i.e. testified) falsehood against his brother"; the preceding clause is then to be taken as meaning "the witness is a false witness."[33] The Tar have interpreted the line as "a false witness has witnessed a false witness against his brother."

19:19 The penalty is presented paratactically. The text changes to the plural, since exacting the punishment is done by individuals, LXX following MT. What you are to do is *ὃν τρόπον ἐπονηρεύσατο ποιῆσαι τῷ ἀδελφῷ αὐτοῦ*. The verb *ἐπονηρεύσατο* used with *ποιῆσαι* means "acted wickedly." The Hebrew verb זמם is neutral "to purpose, intend," though in this context "plotted" with its pejorative overtones would fit as a rendering for the Hebrew verb, whereas LXX more obviously adds a moral dimension to the intention.[34] In other words, the lex talionis is to be applied. In the tradition the dative phrase appears in the A B F M V majority text as *κατα του αδελφου αυτου*, an intrusion from v.18. It should be noted that 848 supports the dative, which also equals MT. That cir 30 witnesses wrote *ποιησεται* instead of *ποιήσετε* has nothing to do with a presumed parent ונעשה, as BHS maintains, is obvious; it is simply an itacistic spelling.

---

32. 11QT also reads העיד. A.Rofe, Textus XIV(1988), 164—165 argues, in my opinion quite rightly, that MT is the earlier and better reading.
33. Aq has *μάρτυς ψευδὴ* (*ὁ μάρτυς*) *ψεῦδος ἀπεκρίθη εἰς τὸν ἀδελφὸν αὐτοῦ* (retroverted from Syh^{m}), which does not account for העד, clearly an error of transmission in the Syriac text.
34. Aq renders זמם more exactly by *ἐνενοήθη* "had in mind."

For the last clause see comment at 13:5. LXX has exactly the same formulaic pattern, including a singular verb but plural pronouns as in 17:7 21:21 22:21,24 24:7, and says nothing about its parent text; it is strictly formulaic. The statement in BHS that LXX Pesh Tar^{J} (to which Tar^{N} could also be added) support the second plural is technically true, but it is irrelevant and misleading, since Pesh and Tar have the verb in the plural as well.

19:20 The carrying out of the penalty will have exemplary effect. "When those who are left over hear (about this), they will be afraid," i.e. be fearful in a good sense. This will result in their not again repeating to act in this evil fashion *ἐν ὑμῖν*. MT has the singular בקרבך, but Pesh follows LXX in the plural. Hex transposed *ἔτι ποιῆσαι* to correspond to MT's לעשות עוד. In the tradition 848 has the present infinitive *ποιειν*, also supported by A M and most cursives, but *ποιῆσαι* occurs in the parallel 13:11.[35]

19:21 The first clause follows Sam in its asyndetic character, and adds *ἐπ' αὐτῷ* over against MT, which hex has placed under the obelus; see the discussion at 25:12. The lex talionis which follows is appropriate here, since the preceding section as epitomized in v.19 gives an excellent illustration of the underlying principle. The rule is an exact copy of Exod 21:23b—24; see Note ad loc.

In the tradition most witnesses follows A M in adding *καθοτι αν δω μωμον τω πλησιον ουτως δωσετε αυτω*. This has no basis in MT, but is imported with a few changes (*πλησιον* for *ἀνθρώπῳ* and *δωσετε* for *δοθήσετε*) from Lev 24:20, where it also follows the lex talionis (though in an abbreviated form).

---

35. See the discussion at THGD 66—67.

Chapter 20

20:1 In the event of war the Israelites are instructed to trust in the Lord who brought them out of the land of Egypt. Instead of seeing horses and chariots LXX has *ἵππον καὶ ἀναβάτην* (the nouns are of course collective), i.e. vocalizing רכב as a participle.[1] The third element is *καὶ λαὸν πλείονά σου*, following Sam which also read a conjunction over against MT.

The apodosis is put in formulaic terms *οὐ φοβηθήσῃ* (*ἀπ' αὐτῶν*) for which see comment at 1:21. It differs from 1:21, however, in that here the future passive is employed (as at 7:18), whereas at 1:21 (and at 20:3) the present middle subjunctive obtains. Aorist subjunctives occur at 1:29 3:2, and present imperatives, at 31:6,8. These variations show the flexibility of such formulae. The reason for confidence is given in the *ὅτι* clause, which assures the Lord's presence in battle, an assurance symbolized in the period of the Judges and the early monarchy by the ark of the covenant accompanying the Israelite army.

20:2 For *καὶ ἔσται* plus a condition see the discussion at 6:10—11. The condition is a *ὅταν* clause which interprets the Hebrew pattern: preposition plus bound infinitive plus personal suffix, כקרבכם. MT has already changed to the plural, a switch which LXX delays to the next verse. In the tradition an *s* marginal reading has *εν τω εγγιζειν σε προς τον πολεμον*, which patterns like the Hebrew כקרבכם אל המלחמה. This tradition is obviously another and more Hebraic rendering of the Hebrew, and my own guess would be Theod, since Theod is the only one of The Three who certainly revised LXX; note that the singular *σε* does not equal MT but seems based on LXX's *ἐγγίσῃς*. Also in the tradition is the exegetical variant of V Byz which changed the verb to the present tense *εγγιζης*, i.e. understanding the drawing near as a process: "when you are coming near." Either an aorist or a present subjunctive makes sense, but generally speaking, unless the translator specifically wishes to call attention to the verbal notion as a process, he tends to use the neutral aorist. The verb here takes a dative rather than a preposition such as *πρός* or *εἰς* to

1. The Others read *ἅρμα* (retroverted from Syh^{m}).

represent the אל phrase. The verb can govern either a dative or a prepositional phrase.

The apodosis is introduced with an apodotic *καί*, and reduces the first verb to a participle, correctly putting the stresss on λαλήσει τῷ λαῷ, which is then elaborated in vv.3—4.

20:3 LXX changes to the second plural with the address by the priest to the people, which is sensible, since the instructions are intended for the individual fighters rather than for the army as a corporate whole. MT had already anticipated this by the plural suffix of כקרבכם in v.2, but LXX changed this to the singular, since the army as a whole was approaching the enemy. The imperative *ἄκουε* is, however, in the singular, since the addressee is Ἰσραήλ.

The Hebrew nominal pattern: pronoun plus verbal adjective is translated in the same way as the pronoun plus participle pattern, i.e. by the pronoun *ὑμεῖς* plus the present tense, *προσπορεύεσθε*. The adjective קרבים is carefully distinguished in LXX from the cognate verb. The latter occurs 11 times in Deut and is translated eight times by *προσέρχομαι* (1:22 2:37 4:11 5:23,27 20:10 22:14 25:11), by *ἐγγίζω* three times (15:9 20:2 31:14), and once by *προσάγω* (2:19), but never by *προσπορεύομαι* which is reserved for the one case of the verbal adjective in Deut.[2] A popular variant reads *προπορευεσθε*, but this variant is due to uncial misreading of *οσ* as *ο*. The simplex form is also attested, though not widely (by B *C*+), and *oI* has changed the verb to another compound, *εισπορευεσθε*, but the originality of LXX remains undoubted.

LXX changes the figure for the first words of encouragement; The verb רכך means "to be soft, tender," so "let not your heart become soft"; LXX uses the passive *ἐκλυέσθω*, "(let not your heart) become unloosed," hence faint. This is a good rendering. For *μὴ φοβεῖσθε* see comment at v.1. The verb תחפזו "to be alarmed" is translated by *θραύεσθε* "be shattered, broken up," an unusual equation, but then the Hebrew verb is not consistently translated throughout the O.T. Certainly no other text is implied.[3]

---

2. Aq has *ἐγγίζετε*; Sym uses *προσέρχεσθε*, and Theod leaves LXX unrevised.
3. Aq, followed by Sym, translated *θαμβεῖσθε* (retroverted from Syh); this is a literal rendering of MT.

The last encouragement is *μηδὲ ἐκκλίνητε ἀπὸ προσώπου αὐτῶν*, but MT has ואל תערצו מפניהם. The same Hebrew occurs at 7:21, but there the verb used in LXX is the singular *τρωθήσῃ*, and a singular also obtains at 31:6 as *πτοηθῇς*; it is used absolutely at 1:29, where it is rendered by *πτήξητε*, thus each time in some sense of being terrified, scared. But here LXX has "nor turn aside from before them." Possibly the translator felt that not having the heart faint, nor being afraid, nor being shattered, ought finally to issue in standing up to the enemy, i.e. not turning aside. But that is not what MT says.

20:4 The basis for the encouragement of v.3 is given in a *ὅτι* clause in which the predicate is an articulated participle modified by two purposive infinitives. The Hebrew predicate is ההלך עמכם "the one accompanying you," but LXX has the rather odd *ὁ προπορευόμενος* plus *μεθ' ὑμῶν*, an attempt to combine the idea of "leading (in battle), going before," along with that of accompaniment "with you."[4]

The first infinitive in MT is להלחם "to fight (for you with your enemies)," which is rendered by the compound *συνεκπολεμῆσαι* "to defeat in battle together (with you your enemies)." The *συν-* compound suggests a common onslaught,whereas the Hebrew has Yahweh fighting on your behalf. The second infinitive is given asyndetically as *διασῶσαι ὑμᾶς* "to rescue, save you," an exact translation of MT's להושיע אתכם. What both intend to show is that the purpose of God's fight alongside Israel is "to save" them. The majority reading has added a *και* before it which is rooted in an attempt to simplify the text, i.e. from "to fight ... to save" to "to fight ... and to save," but B 848+ quite correctly render the Hebrew.[5] The same impetus which motivated the majority text also impelled Sam's ולהושיע, but it is secondary.

20:5 Vv.5—8 give a series of exemptions from military service presented by *οἱ γραμματεῖς* to the people. The term translates the difficult השטרים, some kind of official who officially organized affairs for the government, or who carried out and interpreted governmental regulations; see comment at 1:15.

4. Sym renders the structure in better Greek as *ὁ προερχόμενος ὑμῶν*. Theod and Aq retain the prepositional phrase of LXX, but the participle, presumably *ὁ πορευόμενος*, has not survived in the tradition.
5. See THGD 73.

The word occurs three times in this chapter (also vv.8,9) and is throughout rendered by *οἱ γραμματεῖς* "scribes." It occurs four times elsewhere in the book where it is always translated by *γραμματοεισαγωγεῖς*, but is always mentioned together with rulers over 1000s, 100s, 50s and 10s (1:15), with judges (16:18), along with *οἱ ἀρχίφυλοι* and *ἡ γερουσία* (29:10), or along with *φυλάρχους* and *πρεσβυτέρους* (31:28). In this chapter *οἱ γραμματεῖς* apparently are the ones who keep the role for the army. Each exemption is introduced by *τίς ὁ ἄνθρωπος* "who is the man (that ...)." The first one is "the one building a new house and he did not *ἐνεκαίνισεν*," a neologism chosen to render חנכו "dedicated it," presumably determining its meaning thereby for the Greek as well.

Exemption is throughout declared by the scribes in formulaic terms: *πορευέσθω καὶ ἀποστραφήτω*, correctly representing the Masoretic tradition of vocalizing the verbs as short forms ילך וישב, thus "let him go and return." The second verb of the formula is changed to the *επι*— compound in the majority A F M V text, not only here but in vv.6—7 as well; the variant compound also occurs in v.8 but with much less support in the tradition (only in M *C*''+). No change in meaning is signalized by the variant text. The translator quite correctly rendered לביתו by *εἰς τὴν οἰκίαν αὐτοῦ*, rather than using *οικον*; *οἰκία* is the broader term including the domestic household. In v.5 it might otherwise be thought to mean "a new house" *οἰκίαν καινήν*, but what he returns to is "the household," as its use in vv.6—8 makes clear.

The reason for the exemption given is *μὴ ἀποθάνῃ ἐν τῷ πολέμῳ καὶ ἄνθρωπος ἕτερος ἐγκαινιεῖ αὐτήν*. The *μή* represents פן of MT, and here as well as in vv.6 and 7, hex has added *ποτε* to equal MT. The fear is that such a one might die in battle, and another person would dedicate it. Note that the second clause is a future, whereas the first is an aorist subjunctive since it is governed by *μή*. Once the builder has died, the *μή* no longer applies—another person will dedicate it. In the tradition the Attic future *ἐγκαινιεῖ* appears in a Hellenistic inflection in *b*+: as *εγκαινισει*.

20:6 An exemption is allowed for someone who has planted a vineyard ולא חללו, which LXX renders by *καὶ οὐκ εὐφράνθη ἐξ αὐτοῦ*. At first blush the two seem to be quite different texts, but this is not the case. The Hebrew means "and he had not rendered it profane," i.e. common. The firstfruits had to be brought to the sanctuary as an offering, and only then could the fruit of the vine be enjoyed. What *εὐφράνθη* means is "he had (not yet) enjoyed it himself," i.e. had not yet enjoyed the wine from the vineyard.[6] The offering was usually brought in in the fourth year, only after which the fruit could be used for common use.[7] It is thus clear that LXX is more or less in line with Jewish interpretation: "and he had not (yet) had enjoyment of it," but someone else would be enjoying the fruits of the vineyard. For *πορευέσθω—πολέμῳ* see comment at v.5.[8]

20:7 The third exemption permitted is of a man who has betrothed a woman and he had not (yet) take her (i.e. have sexual relations with her); in other words, he is engaged, but not yet married. The *b* text has added *εαυτω* after the verb, but this is an epexegetical gloss, which not only has no basis in MT, but is also quite otiose. For *πορευέσθω—πολέμῳ* see comment at v.5.

20:8 The three exempt cases are followed by an exemption of quite a different kind; this is apparent from its introductory statement: *καὶ προσθήσουσιν οἱ γραμματεῖς λαλῆσαι πρὸς τὸν λαὸν καὶ ἐροῦσιν*, "and the scribes shall speak further to the people and say." For *γραμματεῖς* see comment at v.5. The exemption is to be given to any person *ὁ φοβούμενος καὶ δειλὸς τῇ καρδίᾳ αὐτοῦ*. For the combination *φοβούμενος καὶ δειλός*, see the discussion at 1:20—21. For *πορευέσθω καὶ ἀποστραφήτω εἰς τὴν οἰκίαν αὐτοῦ* see comment at v.5.

The stress is not on the combination, but specifically on *δειλιάνῃ τὴν καρδίαν* i.e. making the heart cowardly. The danger of having a soldier who is cowardly, fearful at heart, is that this attitude might spread. MT says ולא ימס את לבב אחיו כלבבו. The verb means "to melt," which LXX fully understood as meaning "to make afraid, scared, cowardly." Instead of repeating לבב in

6. Aq translated the verb literally by *βεβηλώσει (αὐτόν)*, whereas Sym interpreted it by *λαϊκώσει (αὐτόν)* "rendered it common, fit for lay use."

7. Rashi comments: לא פדאו בשנה הרביעית. Tar^{N} interprets as ולא אפרק פירוי "he had not redeemed its fruit"; Tar^{J} is similar with ולא פרקיה מן כהנא. Vulg expands by an explanation: *et necdum fecit eam esse communem de qua vesci omnibus liceat*. Pesh simply contextualizes freely: "had not yet trampled, squeezed it."

8. Prijs 54 suggests the change of חללו to הללו but this is not necessary.

the final prepositional phrase LXX neatly encapsulates it by its ὡς ἡ αὐτοῦ. Hex has inserted *καρδια* under an asterisk to represent MT more exactly.

20:9 For καὶ ἔσται ὅταν see the discussion at 6:10—11. The prepositional phrase with bound infinitive is, as at v.2, translated by a ὅταν plus subjunctive clause: "whenever the scribes should stop speaking," thus only when the membership of the army is completely determined, καὶ καταστήσουσιν; this constitutes the apodosis introduced by an unnecessary καί. That it is the apodosis is clear from the change to a future indicative verb. It would appear that the scribes would then appoint commanders, though one might for good sense take the plural verb as being indefinite, i.e. "they shall appoint" with no specific antecedent intended. It might then be preferable to render this by a passive "and commanders of the army shall be appointed," thereby avoiding any notion that the γραμματεῖς actually appointed army commanders, which was hardly intended.

MT ends with בראש העם "at the head of the people" as modifier of the verb. LXX renders this by a second accusative modifying καταστήσουσιν, thus "they shall appoint commanders of the army as leaders of the people." Note that the translator has wisely rendered the plural צבאות by the singular τῆς στρατιᾶς; the "hosts" constitute "the army." The variant spelling *στρατειας* in F M *C''* *f s*+ is of course an itacistic spelling; the appointees led the army, not the expedition.

20:10 This verse introduces a section on rules regarding aggressive warfare. The verse begins without a conjunction in MT, but LXX begins with ἐὰν δέ; see comment at 15:16. For the apodosis MT has קראת אליה לשלום, i.e. call out to it (i.e. the city) peaceably, but LXX has ἐκκαλέσῃ αὐτοὺς μετ' εἰρήνης, with the pronoun grammatically without antecedent, but common sense dictates that αὐτούς must refer to the inhabitants of the city. The collocation ἐκκαλέσῃ μετ' εἰρήνης means a demand for surrender; before actually attacking the city the Israelites must seek voluntary surrender, i.e. without resistance.

20:11 As at 11:13 the היה of והיה אם is omitted; see discussion at 6:10—11. A popular variant has added *και εσται* at the beginning of the verse, under the mediate influence of the Hebrew; it is not, however, hex, as the pattern of support shows. The translator used a contrastive *μέν ... δέ* pattern to contrast vv.11 and 12. V.11 represents the peaceful alternative, viz. "should they reply peaceably to you, and open up to you." LXX continues with third person plural referring to the *αὐτούς* of v.10, whereas MT is also consistent with its third feminine singular verbs referring to עיר.

The apodosis demands that "all the people which are found in it shall be *φορολόγητοι* to you and *ὑπήκοοί σου*," i.e. tributaries to you and your subjects.[9] The syntax of the apodosis is somewhat peculiar, though it apes that of MT. It begins with *ἔσται πᾶς ὁ λαός* "all the people shall be," but then it defines who all the people are by "those found in it" (i.e. in the city), and continues with a repetition of "shall be," but now in the plural as *ἔσονται* in view of the restated subject "those found in it." Any modern translator must of course avoid the repeated "shall be." The first term renders למס "for the corvée," i.e. for forced labor. That מס may mean "tribute" in later Hebrew seems clear from Est 10:1 in which Ahasuerus imposed מס on the land and on the coastlands of the sea, as well as in Aram.[10] The second term represents a free rendering of עבדוך "they shall serve you."[11]

20:12 The alternative (*δέ*) is resistance. MT has ואם לא תשלים עמך "and if it should not make peace with you," but LXX plays on the last noun in v.11, *ὑκήκοοι*, and interprets "but if not *ὑπακούσωσίν σοι*," i.e. become subject to you.[12] After all, making peace in this context is by LXX definition becoming tributaries and subjects.

The alternative is not only negative, i.e. not becoming subject to you, but also positive: *καὶ ποιήσωσιν πρὸς σὲ πόλεμον*. The use of *πρός* in the sense of "with" is well-known (MT has עמך); cf e.g. John 1:1.[13] The B *oI y*+ text has the present subjunctive inflection, *ποιωσιν*, but the aorist coordinates with *ὑπακούσωσιν*, and must be original.

---

9. See Daniel 61 who calls it a faithful, but not a word-for-word rendering.
10. See the Tar: למסקי מ(י)סין.
11. The Three render the word by *δουλεύσουσίν σοι* (retroverted from Syh^{m}); cf also Daniel 112—113.
12. Aq translates literally by *καὶ ἐὰν μὴ εἰρηνεύσωσίν σοι*," (retroverted from Syh^{m}).
13. See also usage in LS sub *πολεμέω*.

The apodosis is not introduced with a conjunction over against MT: *περικαθιεῖς αὐτήν*. A variant *C*'' *b s*+ text does have a *και*, but this is more likely to be ex par than recensional. The verb is well-chosen to translate צרת "besiege." A variant A+ text has misread the verb as *περικαθαριεις* "you shall purge (it) away"; this would make sense, but it is based on a copyist error.[14]

20:13 The siege will be successful; the Lord "will deliver it into your hands." LXX has the plural *τὰς χεῖράς σου* over against BHS,[15] as does Pesh, though Vulg supports the singular. There is very little difference between בידך and בידיך; both mean "into your power."

The use of the singular is contextually unexpected for *πᾶν ἀρσενικὸν αὐτῆς*, and is a reflection of the Hebrew את כל זכורה. The plural *παντα αρσενικα* would have been more appropriate, since זכור is clearly a collective noun.

20:14 *πλήν* governs *τῶν γυναικῶν καὶ τῆς ἀποσκευῆς*, and a comma should be placed after it in the critical text, since what follows modifies *προνομεύσεις*. *ἀποσκευή* is a calque for the Hebrew טף, and so must be rendered in the Hebrew sense; the term first occurs at Gen 34:29; see Note ad loc for a discussion of the term.[16] So: women and children are not to suffer the fate of the males.

There are three preposed modifiers to *προνομεύσεις*: all *τὰ κτήνη*, and everything which is in the city, *καὶ πᾶσαν τὴν ἀπαρτίαν*. MT does not have "all" modifying הבהמה, and hex has placed the *πάντα* under the obelus accordingly. The last one represents כל שללה "all its spoil" in BHS, though numerous mss do read an initial conjunction, i.e. וכל. The שלל "spoil" is

14. Aq has rendered the verb as *περιέξεις*. According to Masius the Syh attributes *π. αὐτὴν περιοχῇ* to Aq (by retroversion), but the dative noun strikes me as a gloss rather than an Aq reading. Note that at v.19 *περιοχῇ* renders מצור in Aq.

15. Eight Kenn mss have ידיך. Tar[N], but not Tar[OJ], also supports the plural noun.

16. Aq translates טף by *νηπίων*. Lee 105—106 is convinced that it means more than children, but can include the entire family, and that *ἀποσκευῆς* should be translated by "family." I must admit to some scepticism. Out of a total of 39 occurrences טף is rendered by words meaning children 20 times, plus another 11 times by *ἀποσκευή*, i.e. 31 out of 39 times (the count is that of Dos Santos).

defined as ἀπαρτίαν "goods, chattels."[17] Hex has added αυτης to represent the suffix of שללה.

The futures are deliberative, thus "you may plunder ... you may eat."[18] The use of φάγῃ is a literalism for אכלת; to "eat booty" means to take and use the booty for one's own advantage. For the ὧν clause see comment at 1:20. The ὧν betrays carelessness on the part of the translator. The intent of the relative surely should have been to refer to προνομήν rather than to ἐχθρῶν, to which ὧν is attracted. What LXX actually says is "whom the Lord your God is giving you"; the translator must have intended ην. Within the relative clause the subject κύριος ὁ θεός σου precedes the verb, but hex reorders the two to equal MT.

20:15 The regulations given in vv.10—14 were to apply to all the cities at a great distance, τὰς μακρὰν οὔσας ἀπὸ σοῦ σφόδρα, i.e. those which were not ἀπὸ τῶν πόλεων τῶν ἐθνῶν τούτων; by this are meant the Canaanite peoples, for whom harsher rules (vv.16—18) were to apply. MT uses a ל phrase modifying תעשה to show to whom or what the Israelites are to do οὕτως, but LXX follows good Greek usage with its accusative modifier πάσας τὰς πόλεις.

The relative clause is a nominal one in MT, with אשר as the subject and a partitive מן as predicate.[19] The predicate ends with הנה, i.e. the predicate reads: "they are not from the cities of these nations." A B V *b*+ variant reads εκ for ἀπό, but the latter is preferable.[20] The translator, however, has read the pronoun as הנה "behold, lo" and taken it with the next verse. Origen with his quantitative approach took ἰδού of v.16 as filling the slot for רק, so that to his mind הנה was omitted.[21] Accordingly hex added εισιν under the asterisk.

20:16 In MT the verse begins with רק, which LXX commonly renders by πλήν, e.g. at v.14, but here it is omitted, LXX beginning with ἰδοὺ δέ; cf comment at v.15. A popular variant has changed δέ to δη, i.e. "behold, pray,"

17. Aq translates the noun literally by λάφυρα; Theod and Sym translate the modifier by καὶ πάντα τὰ σκῦλα αὐτῆς (retroverted from Syh); both support the καί of LXX against BHS.
18. Instead of προνομεύσεις, Aq has διαρπάσεις "seize (as booty)."
19. See SS 159.
20. See THGD 118.
21. As does SS 80.

but this is simply a copyist error and in the context is certainly no improvement; the δέ should be understood as contrastive, i.e. "but behold." By rendering הנה by ἰδού LXX calls attention to the difference between the treatment of enemies distant and those near at hand; the stress on this contrast adequately deals with what MT intended by רק.

For the ὧν clause see comment at 1:20. The antecedent, to which the inflection of the relative pronoun is attracted, is presumably the nearer ἐθνῶν, not πόλεων; since ὧν ... τὴν γῆν αὐτῶν must mean "whose land," the antecedent must be the peoples, not the cities. MT simply has נחלה at the end of the relative clause: "which the Lord ... is giving you as a heritage." LXX has expanded this with a purposive infinitive plus modifier, κληρονομεῖν τὴν γῆν αὐτῶν "to inherit their (i.e. the peoples') land." Hex has placed the modifier under the obelus as having no support in MT.

The rule is: οὐ ζωγρήσετε ἀπ' αὐτῶν πᾶν ἐμπνέον "you shall not let live from them anything breathing." LXX has changed the singular תחיה to the plural, i.e. it is an order to Israelites rather than to Israel, and it continues with the plural to the end of the section, whereas MT only changes to the plural with v.18. The greater consistency of LXX is attractive. The neuter participle ἐμπνέον means anything breathing, i.e. human beings and cattle. MT reads כל נשמה "all breath," and LXX has probably met the intent of the Hebrew. In the tradition a majority F V reading has changed the present infinitive κληρονομεῖν to the aorist κληρονομησαι, but the present is more fitting. The infinitive modifying δίδωσιν intends not simply a takeover from the native population, but a continual possession, a notion that the present infinitive promotes. The phrase ἀπ' αὐτῶν is also supported by מנהון of Tar[N], but by no other old witness, and hex has put it under the obelus to show its absence from MT. The phrase is an epexegetical filler, and hardly reflects a different parent text.

20:17 MT makes v.17a the reason for the order in v.16 not to let anything breathing live; it is because you must really put under the חרם, i.e. devote to complete destruction as a sacral trust, all the Canaanite nations. LXX simplifies (and changes) כי by means of the adversative particle ἀλλά. Either ἀλλά or the B variant, αλλ η, is possible, but in view of the sparse support for B's text ἀλλά is to be preferred.[22] Thus "you shall not let live ... but you

22. See THGD 138.

shall actually anathematize them." For *ἀναθέματι ἀναθεματιεῖτε* see discussion at 13:15(16). The *αὐτούς* is further explicated by the list of seven nations, all in the collective singular, articulated, and joined throughout by *καί*. MT has only six; LXX has added *καὶ τὸν Γεργεσαῖον* at the end. At 7:1 (which see) the list is also complete, both in MT and LXX though ordered differently. Sam also has seven nations here, though arranged in a different order as well. In MT the list of six lacks *waw* before the third (the Canaanite) and the fifth (Hivite), but LXX follows Sam in joining all those in the list with conjunctions.

In the tradition, B+ omit the article for all but the first nation, though LXX follows MT in articulating all seven.[23] In the tradition hex has placed *καὶ τὸν Γεργεσαῖον* under the obelus to show that it had no equivalent in MT. The Byz text has transposed it with "and the Jebusite" for no clear reason.

The *ὃν τρόπον* clause at the end is treated by LXX as a formulaic pattern, as the *ὁ θεός σου* proves. LXX has used the second person plural throughout the context (vv.16b—18), and the translator's retreat to the singular represents using a pattern, rather than translating afresh. See also 5:12,16.[24]

20:18 MT begins with the conjunction למען אשר "to the end that," which LXX renders simply by *ἵνα*. When followed by a negative particle, as here, *ἵνα μή*, it more commonly represents פן. The destruction of the populace must be total, "lest they should teach you to practice all their abominations"; MT has ככל תועבתם i.e. "according to all their abominations," but LXX is an adequate rendering; it certainly does not necessarily presuppose a different text, although it is possible that the translator read כל rather than ככל; for *βδελύγματα* see comment at 7:25. These *βδελύγματα* are then characterized as *ὅσα ἐποίησαν τοῖς θεοῖς αὐτῶν* "which they performed for their gods." It should be noted that MT has only this verse in the plural.

What makes all this so dangerous is that the Israelites might be persuaded by this teaching, with the result that *ἁμαρτήσεσθε ἔναντι κυρίου τοῦ θεοῦ ὑμῶν*. After all, the greatest of sins is idolatry, practicing abominations in the service of other gods.

23. See THGD 105.
24. See also List 9 in THGD 88.

20:19 For ἐὰν δέ see comment at 15:16. Vv.19—20 forbid destroying fruit trees during a siege. The condition given is "but should you besiege a city many days by making war against it to capture it." ἐκπολεμῆσαι is purposive, i.e. the purpose of the siege is to engage in warfare. The prepositional phrase which I have translated by "to capture it," has as parent text לתפשה, i.e. a marked infinitive, which LXX has understood as a preposition plus noun,[25] i.e. literally "for its capture."

The order in such a case is that "you may not destroy[26] its trees ἐπιβαλεῖν ἐπ᾿ αὐτὰ σίδηρον. τὰ δένδρα αὐτῆς translates עצה quite adequately, though only here in Deut does the plural occur, whereas the singular obtains at 12:2 22:6 as well, MT throughout having עץ. The infinitive equals a Hebrew marked infinitive, which defines attendant circumstances,[27] and determines specifically how the destruction takes place. The Greek can also be taken in this way, thus "by laying an iron (i.e. an axe) upon them.[28]

MT continues with a כי clause: "for from it you shall eat, and it you shall not cut (down)." LXX contrasts the first clause, i.e. the "laying an iron on them," with an adversative ἀλλά, thus in contrast to destroying the trees ἀπ᾿ αὐτοῦ φάγῃ "but from it (i.e. a fruit tree) you can eat, (and it you must not fell)."

The remainder of the verse is a μή question, i.e. one that expects a negative answer. This could possibly be translated as "Does a person (use) the tree which is in the field to go from you into the entrenchment"? In other words, ἄνθρωπος is taken as the subject, and what is predicated of him is τὸ ξύλον τὸ ἐν τῷ ἀγρῷ. Here עץ is rendered by the much more common (than δένδρα) word ξύλον (14 times in Deut). In this verse δένδρα refers to trees in general, but ξύλον to a specific tree. Instead of ἀγρῷ the A F M V majority text has δρυμω "thicket," which is a rationalization that trees do not grow in the open field but in a copse. Since B 848+ support the common rendering for שדה, viz. ἀγρῷ, this is certainly original text. The word order might seem at first reading to support this interpretation. MT is somewhat difficult at this point. It

25. See SS Inf, 56.
26. Instead of ἐξολεθρεύσεις Aq and Sym read διαφθερεῖς (retroverted from Syh^{m}).
27. See GK 114o.
28. For σίδηρον Aq has ἐν πελέκει "with an axe."

reads כי האדם עץ השדה.[29] Apparently LXX has disregarded כי, and understood the first letter of האדם as an interrogative prefix, hence *μή*.

But it is also possible to make *ἄνθρωπος* the predicate with "the tree which is in the field" the subject. Then it would mean "Is the tree which is in the field a human being that it should go into the entrenchment from you (i.e. because of you)?" This seems to me to be what LXX means.[30] LXX does well with a difficult passage,[31] though the rendering *χάρακα* "a palisade" is unique for מצור in LXX. It was probably chosen by the translator, however, to indicate that trees as poles might constitute a palisade or entrenchment for defence. Note also that *χαράκωσιν* occurs (also uniquely) for מצור in v.20. מצור also obtains at 28:53,55,57, but there it is translated by *στενοχωρίᾳ*.

20:20 For רק LXX uses the adversative *ἀλλά*, which is semantically possible since רק is also contrastive. The contrast here referred to is a non-fruitbearing tree. The unarticulated עץ is exactly reproduced by *ξύλον*, though most witnesses prepose *το*, i.e. "the tree"; the articulation is due to stylistic pressure. עץ is limited by a relative clause: "which you know not to be fruitbearing," and one might indeed expect an articulated antecedent. But both B and 848 follow MT in lacking an article. The collocation *ξύλον* plus its relative clause is a preposed accusative pendant which is brought into the main structure by *τοῦτο*, i.e. "this (or it) you may destroy, and fell, and build a *χαράκωσιν* against the city." The Hebrew word is מצור, the same word which was translated by *χάρακα* in v.19, but here by *χαράκωσιν* "palisade," which is normally made of wood.[32]

The "city" is characterized by a *ἥτις* clause, which is verbal in LXX (*ποιεῖ*), but nominal (הוא עשה) in MT. The participle of MT is reflected by the present tense in LXX. The final *ἕως* clause is best understood as modifying *οἰκοδομήσεις*, thus "you may build ... until it (i.e. the city) would be delivered up," i.e. until it has surrendered, which is a good rendering for רדתה "it is

29. For the bound phrase Aq has *τὸ ξύλον τῆς χώρας*, whereas Theod and Sym use *τοῦ ἀγροῦ* for השדה.
30. Tar^O also interprets it thus: לא כאנשא אילן הקלא למעל מקדמך בצירא.
31. Aq translates במצור by *ἐν τῇ περιοχῇ*. Sym has *ἔσω τῆς πολιορκίας* and Theod, *εἰς τὸν συγκλεισμόν* (both by retroversion from Syh).
32. Aq makes no such distinction but uses *περιοχήν*. Sym has *περίφραγμα* (retroverted from Syh), a term similar in meaning to LXX.

overcome, reduced." In the tradition *ποιεῖ* is changed by a popular V text to the future *ποιησει*, but the present tense is normally used by Deut to render a participial predicate.

Chapter 21

21:1 Vv.1—9 describe an expiation rite for an anonymous murder. The problem faced is that of a *τραυματίας*/חלל found in an open field for which the slayer is unknown. The term *τραυματίας* "wounded" is the regular rendering for חלל "pierced one," hence "slain," and the word here refers to a corpse. For its regular use as such see Note at Gen 34:27, where it first occurs.[1] This takes place *ἐν τῇ γῇ*, i.e. באדמה. Unfortunately LXX does not distinguish between אדמה and ארץ, translating both by *γῆ*.[2] In the tradition *C'' b s+* have added *σου* for which there is no textual basis in MT; it was added ex par. The relative *ᾗ* is dative by attraction to its antecedent *γῇ*, as is common for this translator, but the majority reading, including 848, has changed it to the grammatically correct accusative *ην*.[3] The infinitive *κληρονομῆσαι* is used absolutely, and hex has added an *αυτην* to equal MT.

The body is described as *πεπτωκὼς ἐν τῷ πεδίῳ* "fallen in the open field." בשדה is here used as antonym of בעיר, thus a rural area, which *πεδίῳ* represents adequately. What makes this of regulatory significance, however, is *καὶ οὐκ οἴδασιν τὸν πατάξαντα*. The verb is indefinite plural, which correctly renders the passive נודע, for which מי הכהו is the subject. LXX is simply an active transform of the clause. BHS has no equivalent for the conjunction, but Pesh and Vulg support the *καί*.[4]

21:2 The apodosis begins with *ἐξελεύσονται ἡ γερουσία* (*καὶ οἱ κριταί*), thereby disregarding the conjunction of ויצאו in MT. Most witnesses change the verb to the singular, but the plural is original. Though *γερουσία* is grammatically singular, it is a collective, and Deut always treats the noun as plural. Here 848, our oldest witness, has the plural and points the way to the original text.[5] Both *γερουσία* and *κριταί* are glossed in the majority of witnesses by *σου* which corresponds to זקניך ושפטיך of MT. In both cases 848 witnesses to a

1. Aq and Sym read *ἀνηρήμενος* "killed" (retroverted from Syh^{m}).
2. Aq usually uses *χθών* for אדמה and *γῆ* for ארץ which makes one question the correctness of the note in ms 344 stating that *α´ σ´ θ´* all read *ἐν τῇ γῇ*.
3. See THGD 67.
4. As do Kenn 129,181,186,193 all of which read ולא.
5. See the discussion with complete usage at THGD 140.

text without suffixes, and because of its great antiquity its text has been taken as LXX. Elsewhere throughout the book these two words have been carefully rendered as far as suffixes are concerned in accordance with MT, and Dion may have good reason to believe that the parent text must have read הזקנים והשפטים.[6] Elsewhere the elders are called "elders of the/his/that/this city" (19:12 21:3,4,6,19 22:17,18 25:8) or "of Israel" (27:1) or simply "the elders" (22:15 [against MT],16 25:7,9). Twice "your (plural) elders" are also mentioned (5:23 29:10). As for "judges" the word occurs absolutely at 16:18, as "the judge" at 17:9,12, as "the judges" at 19:17,18 25:2, and as your (plural) judges at 29:10 31:28. In fact, שפטיך occurs only here in Deut, whereas זקניך occurs elsewhere only once; at 32:7 it is, however, translated by *τοὺς πρεσβυτέρους σου*. The evidence given here makes Dion's suggestion attractive.

In the tradition the *d* text glossed (your) elders with *οι πρωτιστοι*, i.e. your chief or principle judges. Just who these chief judges were thought to be by the Byzantine glossator is unknown.

The elders and judges must measure the distances to the cities which are about the corpse.[7]

21:3 The opening clause in LXX in imitation of MT is a kind of pendant clause which has no other purpose than to define an antecedent for (*τῆς πόλεως*) *ἐκείνης*; that city will be the one which is nearest to the victim;[8] its elders are to take a *δάμαλιν ἐκ βοῶν* "a heifer from the cattle"; admittedly the *ἐκ βοῶν* is unnecessary, but it does interpret בקר as the source. For the plural verb with *γερουσία* see comment at v.2; here 848 alone attests to the plural verb although in the Classical spelling, *λήψονται*.[9] The Göttingen editions have consistently followed the Hellenistic spelling in view of the fact that, though in Ptolemaic times both forms are attested, the Hellenistic form dominates throughout the old uncials, A B and S. The *δάμαλιν* is described as "*ἥτις οὐκ εἴργασται*, nor had drawn a yoke." The Hebrew has quite a different construction: אשר לא עבד בה, the subject being impersonal: "with

6. P.E.Dion in De Septuaginta, 152—153.
7. Aq and Sym again have *τοῦ ἀνῃρημένου*.
8. Aq again has *ἀνῃρημένῳ*.
9. For a good discussion of the infixed nasal see Thackeray 108—111.

which (i.e. the heifer) there had not been worked." The Greek restated it more simply by taking the *δάμαλιν* of the previous clause as the subject.[10]

21:4 Those elders are to bring the heifer down into a נחל איתן. Just what an איתן wadi was is not fully certain; LXX makes it a *φάραγγα τραχεῖαν* "a rugged wadi," an interpretation which NJV has adopted.[11] The wadi is described as *ἥτις οὐκ εἴργασται οὐδὲ σπείρεται*. The clause is odd in its tense structure with the first one perfect and the second one present, but for a field to be sown it should first be worked up as any farmer knows full well. Note that, though עבד obtained in v.3, here the prefix tense is employed in MT, יעבד, but LXX uses the same tense as before, possibly for the reason given above.[12]

What they are to do with the heifer is *νευροκοπήσουσιν* "hamstring" it. But MT has ערפו, a denominative verb based on ערף "neck," and so "break the neck." LXX avoids killing the heifer, mereby hamstringing it. At Exod 13:13 (and 34:20) the verb also occurred and killing the animal was also avoided; see Note ad loc. The translator may well have found this old rite overly severe, and ameliorated the penalty, thereby retaining the use of the animal in a limited way. Over against MT, LXX does not represent שם, somewhat otiose in view of בנחל which fully defines the location. Even hex has apparently not deemed it necessary to add an *εκει* to make up for it.

21:5 The Levitical priests are to approach (and take part in the ritual of v.6; cf the opening statement at v.6). The reason for the Levitical priests taking part is given in a fulsome statement on their divinely appointed role in general. They are engaged because the Lord God has chosen them for a triple role: a) *παρεστηκέναι αὐτῷ*; b) *εὐλογεῖν ἐπὶ τῷ ὀνόματι αὐτοῦ*, and c) *ἐπὶ τῷ στόματι αὐτῶν ἔσται πᾶσα ἀντιλογία καὶ πᾶσα ἁφή*.

10. SS 121 dubs it "eine freie Wiedergabe."
11. NRSV has "a wadi with running water," which follows BDB ("ever flowing wady") and KB. ZürB has "Tal eines Wildbachs." Vulg: *vallem asperam.*
12. Dion, op cit., 154 (n.13) seems to agree when he says that "the translators may have wanted to suggest that the ground … must be one which *at the appointed time for the ceremony,* has not been ploughed, and is not receiving any seed."

It should be noted that LXX does not render the suffix of אלהיך, though the majority of witnesses do add *σου*.[13] The failure of LXX to render the suffix of אלהיך (seven times in Deut) in this context is, however, assured by the support of both B and 848. The verb *ἐπέλεξεν* is sparsely supported by the mss, though it is supported by B. Its originality is by no means certain, though exegetically the active is appropriate. Most witnesses support the middle form either of the compound with *επ-* or with *εξ-*, since the middle became common in the sense of "choose, select." The active is more usual in the specific sense of choice as "to call by name," which is appropriate in the Lord's selection of the priests for service. The two compounds are synonyms.

The first duty of the Levitical priests, for which term see the discussion at 18:1, was to stand at attention, to be present for him (i.e. for the Lord). The verb is an unusual rendering for לשרת, occurring only five times in the O.T., twice as a participle describing Joshua as "minister, attendant" to Moses (Exod 24:13 Num 11:28), once of Joseph being in attendance on Pharaoh's butler and baker in prison at Gen 40:4, and once at Isa 60:10. The usual translation is *λειτουργεῖν* (66 times, of which 18 occur in the Pentateuch).[14] But *λειτουργεῖν* refers to cultic service, and so *παρεστηκέναι* was chosen to indicate that the service here described, though priestly, was not cultic.[15] In the tradition the perfect infinitive is changed to the aorist *παραστηναι* in *C'' s z*, but with no real semantic change.

The second duty is *εὐλογεῖν ἐπὶ ὀνόματι αὐτοῦ* for MT: לברך בשם יהוה. The repetition of יהוה rather than a suffix to שם is intentional, since the specific task was to pronounce the blessing in the divine name; cf comment at 18:5. Of course, that is who is referred to by *αὐτοῦ*,[16] probably used for stylistic reasons.

The third duty refers to two areas in which the Levitical priests had to make pronouncement, that of disputes, and that of infections, more specifically that of leprosy. Making pronouncement is indicated by על פיהם יהיה "according to their utterance (literally mouth) shall be ...," which LXX renders word for word by *ἐπὶ τῷ στόματι αὐτῶν ἔσται*. The term *ἁφή* is used

13. For a discussion of the shorter text as original see THGD 76, as well as Appositives 267.
14. This was also used here by The Three; see Daniel 116.
15. See Daniel 95—96.
16. The Three do have *ἐν τῷ ὀνόματι κυρίου* (retroverted from Syh^{m}).

for נגע throughout Lev 13 and 14, but see also Deut 24:8 for ἁφή τῆς λέπρας, and 17:8 for ἀντιλογία.

21:6 Since the verse begins with καί I suspect that what is joined are "the Levitical priests (shall approach)" and "all the eldership of that city"; ἐκείνης refers to the city designated in v.3, i.e. both are to take part in the ceremony of washing the hands.[17] In MT they wash את ידיהם, but LXX simply has τὰς χεῖρας, since that they are to wash their own hands is obvious. Hex has of course added αυτων under the asterisk. This is done according to MT על העגלה הערופה "over the heifer whose neck was broken," which might be understood as an expiation ceremony, an action by which the washing of hands constitutes a declaration of innocence in the presence of a sacrificed heifer. But LXX has ἐπὶ τὴν κεφαλὴν τῆς δαμάλεως τῆς νενευροκοπημένης. The insertion of "the head" is probably on the analogy of Exod 29:10,15 and 19, where the priests place their hands on the heads of animals before they are slaughtered, as a symbolic transfer of guilt on to the beast. The insertion is also attested in the Temple Scroll (11QT 63:5) as על ראוש העגלה. I suspect that as far as the Greek is concerned the addition is an exegetical matter. After all, as Dion astutely points out[18] "once the heifer has been killed, there is no sense in transferring to it a community's objective blood guilt!" But in the Greek interpretation the transfer does make sense, since the heifer is not killed, but merely crippled, i.e. hamstrung.[19]

21:7 The accompanying declaration of innocence. The opening coordinate verbs "and they shall answer and say" are rendered by a single syntagm by subordinating the first clause as a participle: "and in answering they shall say." The subject of the declaration is the Levitical priests and the eldership; see comment at v.6. In the final clause ἑωράκασιν occurs absolutely, since what our eyes did not see is obvious; they have neither committed the crime,

---

17. Lee 37—40 sugegsts that νίπτω means to wash by rinsing or pouring, as distinct from πλύνω which means to wash by rubbing in water, hence commonly used of washing clothes.

18. in De Septuaginta, 156.

19. Aq corrects this by his τετενοντωμένης (retroverted from Syh); comp Aq's reading at Exod 13:13.

nor seen it being done. The Byz text has added an *αυτο*, an indefinite "it," but this is quite unnecessary even in good Greek style.

21:8 A concluding prayer which asks the Lord for mercy "in order that there may be no guiltless blood" in Israel. But MT has ואל תתן דם נקי "and do not place innocent blood," which, as Dion points out,[20] seems contradictory; there has been a washing of hands, and a declaration of innocence; and now "they must ask his forgiveness for what they have just emphatically claimed they had *not* done." LXX has avoided such contradiction by changing the prayer in MT not to charge Israel with the crime to a prayer that such may not happen, i.e. spare us from doing such a thing.[21]

LXX ends with confidence in a good result: "And the blood (i.e. bloodshed) shall be propitiated," a general conclusion that all is now well.

In the tradition, an A F M V majority text has an early prehexaplaric expansion: *εκ γης αιγυπτου* after *ἐλυτρώσω*. This is a gloss without any support in MT. That it is not original LXX seems clear from the support of the shorter text by B 848. That it is an early plus is proven by hex having placed it under the obelus.[22] Its source is, however, obscure. The verb *λυτρόω* is never modified in the Greek OT by this phrase; it is a phrase which commonly modifies *ἐξάγω*; for modification in the context of *λυτρόω* see 9:26 13:5 15:5 24:18.

21:9 For the formulaic "but you shall remove ... from your midst" see comment at 13:5. Its only variation is *τὸ αἷμα τὸ ἀναίτιον* for the usual *τὸν πονηρόν*, which would be senseless here. For the meaning of "remove innocent blood" see comment at 19:13. The term is metonymic for the stain of innocent blood being shed; comp the comment at v.8 as well. In the tradition, a popular gloss, *και εν σοι εσται*, has been added ex par.

The *ἐάν* clause has expanded the text of MT somewhat; the latter simply says: "if you do the right thing in the sight of Yahweh." Instead of הישר LXX has *τὸ ἀρεστὸν καὶ τὸ καλόν*, for which see 6:18. This is the order in 848, and therefore was adopted as LXX. On the other hand, the reverse order, which is

20. Op cit 157.
21. Theod and Sym had *καὶ μὴ δῷς αἷμα ἀθῷον* (retroverted from Syh[m]).
22. See THGD 80.

also the majority reading, follows the order of 12:25 13:18. Origen felt that the τὸ καλόν was secondary, and so it was placed under the obelus (presumably including καί). LXX also expanded κυρίου by adding του θεου σου, obviously ex par; hex placed the gloss under the obelus to show that it was not in MT.[23]

21:10—11 These verses are the protasis for the apodosis of vv.12—14. LXX had a difficulty with ונתנו (איביך) which is certainly problematic; in fact, a Genizah text has changed "your enemies to איבך to make it agree with the suffix of נתנו. LXX avoided this problem by its παραδῷ σοι, i.e. "(the Lord your God) will deliver (them) to you."[24] Admittedly this created a new problem, since LXX translated בידך by εἰς τὰς χεῖράς σου.[25] The phrase must then be taken as an expansion of σοι, i.e. "delivered (them) to you, into your power." The majority reading, αυτους for σοι, probably has nothing to do with the Hebrew, but constitutes an attempt to smooth out the text: τοὺς ἐχθρούς σου ... αυτους ... εἰς τὰς χεῖράς σου.

The last clause in v.10 is καὶ προνομεύσῃς[26] τὴν προνομὴν αὐτῶν "and you should take their booty as plunder" for MT's ושבית שביו, which refers to taking into captivity, with the odd שביו "its captives."[27] The free rendering of LXX is an attempt to make clear what MT probably intended.

V.11 then particularizes: "and should you see among the booty a woman fine in appearance, and you desire her, and would take her for yourself as wife." MT has בשביה "among the captives," which seems somewhat more fitting than ἐν τῇ προνομῇ, although see v.10. It might also be noted that the reflexive pronouns are not used in contracted forms in Deut, and so B's σαυτω must be secondary.[28]

23. See Appositives 260.
24. See THGD 73.
25. For a parent text בידיך as some mss?
26. That only the subjunctive can be correct seems obvious in spite of support for the future in the A B V C'' y+ text; the -σεις form is simply an itacistic misspelling of the subjunctive; see THGD 141.
27. The Three translate literally as αἰχμαλωτεύσῃς αἰχμαλωσίαν αὐτοῦ (retroverted from Syh^{m}).
28. See THGD 112.

21:12 The apodosis is introduced by *καί* in imitation of MT.[29] The rendering *ἔνδον εἰς* for את תוך is unique to Deut, occurring only here and at 22:2; the adverb seems rather otiose, but what LXX stresses by it is the intimacy of the new surroundings; one might render the clause "you must bring her home, into your house." That this is what is meant seems clear from the continuation of second person verbs: *ξυρήσεις* ... *περιονυχιεῖς* ... (v.13) *περιελεῖς* as over against third feminine verbs in MT. There the captive bride is to shave her own head, pare her nails, remove her garments of captivity, but LXX follows a tradition, also found in the Temple Scroll, 11QT63:12—13,[30] in which the Israelite man is to shave her head, pare her nails, and remove her garments. In LXX the hopeful husband is to signalize the end of her captive state in favor of a new status as wife, whereas in MT the captive is to symbolize her acceptance of her new status.

The compound *περιονυχιεῖς* is a neologism and a hapax legomenon, whereas the simplex does occur in 14:6 (and in Lev 11:3,4,7,26), where it refers to the hoofs of animals as "cloven."

21:13 For *περιελεῖς* see comment at v.12. Before assuming her wifely role, however, she is to dwell, *καθιεῖται*, hardly *καθιεται* as B,[31] for ישבה, in the man's house, and bewail her parents who are now lost to her; whether they were killed in the *πόλεμον* of v.1, or are simply distant, and hence foreign, is not said. The translator disregarded the suffixes of אביה and אמה in the interests of good Greek style, but hex dutifully added an *αυτης* under the asterisk to both nouns. The period of seclusion and mourning is to last a *μηνὸς ἡμέρας*, a Hebraism meaning a full lunar month, thus thirty days.

At the end of the mourning period "you may go in to her and cohabit with her"; the two verbs mean to have sexual intercourse. *καὶ ἔσται σου γυνή* adequately renders והיתה לך לאשה, and the change of pronoun to the dative *σοι* in A *b*+ is an unnecessary correction to the Hebrew.

21:14 For *καὶ ἔσται ἐάν* see the discussion at 6:10—11. The translation *θέλῃς αὐτήν* "want her" for חפצת בה "take pleasure in her" occurs here for the first

29. Though see THGD 79.
30. See the discussion by L.H.Schiffman, in SCS 33,290—291.
31. See THGD 138.

(and only) time in the Pentateuch. In the later O.T. books θέλω often renders חפץ. The nuance is somewhat different in LXX.

The issue is clear: you must send her away free. The Hebrew has לנפשה which LXX renders by ἐλευθέραν. The term נפש can mean "desire, passion, appetite," since these all reflect the person as he is within; cf also 24:15 where ἐλπίδα is used. The translation is a free but correct one; she is to be sent away according to her own desire, i.e. entirely free.[32]

This is explicated in the rest of the verse, in particular by "she may in no way be sold for money."[33] As a rejected wife she may not be treated as a slave. As long as she was ἐν τῇ προνομῇ this would have been possible. But now οὐκ ἀθετήσεις αὐτήν "you may not break faith with her." The Hebrew text has לא תתעמר בה. The meaning of the verb is unknown, and it occurs only once elsewhere, at 24:7, where the meaning is equally uncertain;[34] there the translator used καταδυναστεύσας. In both cases the translator rendered contextually.

The reason given is διότι ἐταπείνωσας αὐτήν "because you humbled her," an idiom used of having had sexual relations with someone. The verb is commonly used to translate ענה in the Piel.[35]

21:15 For ἐὰν δέ see comment at 15:16. Vv.15—17 concern the rights of the firstborn. The protasis sets up the case of a man with two wives, the one loved and the other one hated; both bear sons, but the son of the hated wife was born first. MT has האחת for both "the one" and "the other one," and LXX translates both by μία αὐτῶν. In both cases hex has placed the pronoun under the obelus to indicate the absence of an equivalent in MT.

For the second clause LXX does not render בנים, but simply has τέκωσιν. Hex supplied υιους under the asterisk after αὐτῷ to render the omitted word. That both children were male can only be inferred in the Greek from

32. See Daniel 332.
33. ἀργυρίου as a genitive of price renders בכסף throughout Deut according to SS 128.
34. Tar all render by תתגר "engage in trade, sell," which Pesh also follows, but this is read from the context rather than based on תתעמר. Vulg has *opprimere per potentiam* which may have been influenced by LXX.
35. Aq translates as ἐκακούχησας "you maltreated," which is his regular rendering of ענה Pi.

the last clause, which reads *καὶ γένηται ὁ υἱὸς ὁ πρωτότοκος τῆς μισουμένης*. The genitive nominal represents לשניאה of MT.[36] All but two mss, 848 and 767, support the articulated phrase, all others omitting the article to read *υιος πρωτοτοκος*. Admittedly an unarticulated nominal would be smoother Greek, but LXX imitates the Hebrew הבן הבכור and is original.[37]

21:16 *καὶ ἔσται ᾗ ἂν ἡμέρᾳ* occurs only twice in Deut, but at 27:2 MT's והיה ביום is followed by אשר plus a verb, and here by a bound infinitive plus suffix, הנחילו. This is rendered by *κατακληρονομῇ* which must be taken as a causative "make to receive," hence "bequeath,"[38] rather than "to receive" (the usual intent of this verb). The majority text has simplified the verb as *κατακληροδοτη*, which does refer to the distribution of an inheritance, but the Hi of נחל is usually translated by the *-νομέω* verb, either by the compound as here, or in the simplex form.[39] The distribution is *τοῖς υἱοῖς* for את בניו. LXX is supported only by 848 and Phil, all other Greek witnesses adding *αυτου* to the noun to equal MT. It is of course not impossible that 848 (cir 50 B.C.) and Philo (1st Century A.D.) should both have omitted an original *αυτου*, but that the otiose *αυτου* should have been added ex par is far more likely.[40] What he bequeaths is *τὰ ὑπάρχοντα αὐτοῦ*, which is an excellent interpretation of את אשר יהיה לו.[41]

What he is not able to do is "to give firstborn inheritance status to the son of the beloved one, bypassing the firstborn son of the hated one." That is certainly what MT means as well, though expressed a bit differently. The infinitive *πρωτοτοκεῦσαι* is a neologism formed on the basis of *πρωτοτοκεῖα* "birthright of the firstborn."[42] It occurs only here in LXX, though Aq also used it at Lev 27:26 as *πρωτοτοκευθήσεται*. The *ὑπεριδών* structure is a free interpretation of MT's על פני בן השנואה הבכר.[43] The על פני is odd, but *ὑπεριδών* is a good paraphrase of what was intended. That it must be idiomatic

36. But only Sym changes to the dative *τῷ μισουμένῳ*, whereas Theod and Aq retain the genitive of LXX.
37. See THGD 80.
38. This is given as its first meaning in Bauer sub voce.
39. See THGD 80.
40. See THGD 78.
41. See SS 183.
42. See Walters 52—53; cf also Lee 52.
43. Theod (and Aq?) read *ἐπὶ προσώπου (τοῦ) υἱοῦ τῆς μισουμένης*.

is clear from modern renderings: RSV "in preference to"; NJPS "in disregard of"; ZürB "zum Nachteil des"; Dogniez-Harl "en dédaignant."

21:17 For the initial כי LXX simplifies by an adversative ἀλλά, for which see comment at 20:17. LXX contrasts what the man with the two wives must do (v.17) with what he cannot do (v.16), which is sensible. What he is to do is to recognize the firstborn son of the hated one so as to give (i.e. by giving) him a double portion.[44]

The relative clause is introduced by *ὧν*, which is hardly feasible grammatically, but its number and case were determined by attraction to its antecedent *πάντων*. The singular passive verb *εὑρεθῇ* ought presumably to presuppose a neuter plural subject, i.e. *ἅ*. The clause simply means "(double for everything) which he possesses."

The *ὅτι* clause gives the reason for this right. MT has כי הוא ראשית אנו to which is added לו משפט הבכרה. The first clause is translated as *ὅτι οὗτός ἐστιν ἀρχὴ τέκνων αὐτοῦ* "for that one is the beginning of his children." But און hardly means "children" as such but rather "strength, power," hence "generative power," and the clause means "for he is the onset of his generative prowess." LXX simplifies by concretizing the notion of generative power by *τέκνων*, which is the creation of אנו.[45]

The final clause is neatly interpreted as *καὶ τούτῳ καθήκει τὰ πρωτοτοκεῖαν* "and to this one belongs the rights of primogeniture," for the Hebrew "his is the right of primogeniture." *καθήκει* is an unusual rendering for משפט, but it does occur twice in the Pentateuch; at Lev 5:10 9:16 כמשפט is rendered by *ὡς καθήκει* "as is proper." LXX follows Sam in introducing the clause with *καί*.

21:18 For *ἐὰν δέ* see comments at 15:16. For יהיה לאיש LXX transposes as *τινι ᾖ*, but hex "corrects" to the Hebrew word order. The son is called

44. The suggestion "frt l יבכר cf Vulg" in BHS for יכיר is completely fanciful. Vulg has *agnoscet primogenitum.* Jerome rendered יכיר literally by *agnoscet* and then added *primogenitum* for clarification, a common practice in Vulg.
45. Aq has ὅτι αὐτὸς κεφάλαιον λύπης αὐτοῦ (retroverted from Syh); λύπης presupposes "ʾāwen" rather than the "ʾōn" of MT; cf also Gen 49:3, and Note ad loc. Sym, however, read ὅτι οὗτός ἐστιν ἀρχὴ τῆς ἰσχύος αὐτοῦ (also from Syh); see the discussion in Salvesen 153.

ἀπειθής "disobedient" and ἐρεθιστής. The former translates סורר only here; it also translates מורה (Num 20:10 Jer 5:23), whereas ἐρεθιστής "perverse, rebellious" is a hapax legomenon translating מורה, though the root is well-known. For אביו and אמו LXX in good Greek style has simply πατρός and μητρός. Hex has of course added αυτου in each case to represent the suffixes.[46]

Furthermore, the parents chastise him, but he does not obey them.[47] The first verb is in the neutral aorist subjunctive, and the second is in the present, since not obeying is a process. This has, however, influenced the tradition, with the A F M V *O n z*+ text reading the present for the first one, παιδευωσιν, as well. Note that MT uses the same root שמע with respect to the voice of father and mother as in the last clause ולא ישמע אליהם, but LXX distinguishes them by different compounds; for the participle, ὑπακούων is used—note the present inflection used to stress the continuous failure to heed—and for ישמע LXX translates by εἰσακούῃ, again a present tense. The majority reading has changed the verb to the aorist εισακουση, but the present is exegetically correct.

21:19 The apodosis is divided into two parts; vv.19—20 constitute the juridical procedure, and v.21, the imposed sentence. The parents, ὁ πατὴρ αὐτοῦ καὶ ἡ μήτηρ αὐτοῦ, are to take him, and bring him to the council of elders (τὴν γερουσίαν) of his city. This is expressed by subordinating the first verb to a participle, συλλαβόντες, and the rendering of והוציאו literally by καὶ ἐξάξουσιν, which is such unidiomatic Greek that most witnesses have omitted the καί, only B and three scattered mss supporting the Hebraic Greek of the original text. The verb "shall bring him out" presumably means bring him out of the house. The majority reading substitutes αυτων for the αὐτοῦ modifying πόλεως, a rationalistic correction of antecedents; after all, the city is the parents' city, rather than that of the rebellious son. The same variant obtains for (τόπου) αὐτοῦ; the antecedent could hardly be different for the two pronouns.

---

46. Theod and Aq do likewise, but Sym, with greater reverence for Greek style, retains the LXX text.
47. See Prijs 16.

In the tradition *συλλάβοντες* becomes *συλλαμβανοντες* in the *b* text under the influence of the present tenses in v.18, but here only the aorist can be correct. The *f* text has substituted the simplex form, but both father and mother join in taking their son, which makes the compound particularly appropriate. A popular variant tradition has changed *ἐξάξουσιν* to the simplex, but the Hebrew dictates the compound.

21:20 LXX follows Sam's אנשי in its *ἀνδράσιν*, rather than MT's זקני. LXX identifies those adddressed as the same ones who carry out the death penalty in v.21, whereas Sam agrees with MT in v.21 that "all" the men of the city did the stoning. Here MT read אל זקני העיר.[48] As in v.19, *αὐτοῦ* (after *πόλεως*) is popularly changed to *αυτων*.[49] Another popular variant text has substituted *του τοπου* for *τῆς πόλεως* under the influence of v.19.

The parents then verbalize the son's behaviour described in v.18. There he was called סורר ומורה, which is repeated by the parents with זה as subject, thus a nominal clause, but LXX makes them verbal with *οὗτος ἀπειθεῖ καὶ ἐρεθίζει*.[50]

Furthermore, he does not heed our voice, i.e. he does not obey us. The popular text introduces the clause with *και*, but this has no support in MT; furthermore, the asyndetic clause is stylistically superior; note the lack of conjunction in the next clause as well. To these charges MT adds זולל וסבא "he is gluttonous and a drunkard." LXX renders the first by a present participle *συμβολοκοπῶν* "given to feasting," and the second, by a present tense verb *οἰνοφλυγεῖ* "he is a drunkard."[51]

21:21 MT has כל אנשי העיר take part in stoning the rebellious son, but LXX omits כל, thereby identifying the men as coincident with those to whom the parents brought their charge in v.20. Hex has added *παντες* under the asterisk to make up for the omission. The stoning is of course done *ἐν λίθοις*, i.e. by

48. Aq renders literally as *πρὸς πρεσβυτέρους πόλεως αὐτοῦ* (retroverted from Syh^m).
49. See also THGD 110—111.
50. Aq renders the first one by *ἀφίσταται*, and the second by *προσερίζει*, both present tense verbs "he revolts and rebels."
51. Aq renders סבא by *συμποσιάζει* "drink together, drink in company."

means of stones.[52] The verb used is a descriptive one, λιθοβολήσουσιν "they shall hurl stones."[53]

For the ἐξαρεῖς clause see comment at 13:5. The *C'' s* variant plural verb, εξαρειτε, is rooted in an attempt at leveling the text with the plural ὑμῶν αὐτῶν; MT has the singular throughout. A few scattered mss read το (πονηρόν) for τόν, but this occurs in a formula in which it is "the evil one" rather than the abstract "the evil," which obtains throughout.[54]

The last clause differs from MT in that MT has כל ישראל as subject of ישמעו ויראו, but LXX has οἱ ἐπίλοιποι; LXX made no new translation but lifted the entire clause from 19:20. The difference has no textual significance.[55]

21:22 V.22 is the protasis of a conditional structure, for which v.23 is the apodosis. The condition is that of someone who has committed a crime (ἁμαρτία) under sentence of death (κρίμα θανάτου), who is put to death (ἀποθάνῃ), whom you hanged on a stake (ξύλου). MT has the singular תלית, but LXX makes this plural κρεμάσητε; the translator makes the hanging as well as the subsequent burial (see v.23) the work of Israelites rather than of corporate Israel. It is clear that this is not a case of death by hanging in view of the consecution of clauses: "he is put to death, and you hang him," i.e. the hanging is the public display of the corpse, proof positive that the law has been upheld.[56]

21:23 MT begins with "not shall his body spend the night on the stake." The Greek renders the verb by ἐπικοιμηθήσεται "shall remain," i.c. for the night.[57] Its positive counterpart is given contrastively by an ἀλλά rather than

52. For the instrumental ἐν see SS 121.
53. This is too descriptive for Aq who has χερμαδιοῦσιν from χερμαδίζω. The verb, not listed in LS, is a denominative from χερμάδιον "large stone, boulder," The verb is factitive, hence, "to stone with stones, boulders."
54. Theod and Sym retain ἐξαρεῖς, but Aq changes to ἐπιλέξεις.
55. Aq translated the clause as καὶ πᾶς 'Ισραὴλ ἀκούσονται καὶ φοβηθήσονται (retroverted from Syh^{m}).
56. Jerome has preserved this verse and the next one in their entirety in Latin for The Three. Aq has *et cum fuerit in viro peccatum in iudicium mortis, et occisus fuerit, et suspenderis eum super lignum;* Sym has *si autem fuerit homini peccatum ad iudicium mortis, et occisus fuerit, et suspenderis eum super lignum,* while Theod reads *et quia erit in viro peccatum in iudicium mortis, et morietur, et suspendes eum in ligno.*
57 Aq has the more exact αὐλισθήσεται.

the כי of MT; see comment at 20:17. The verse continues the plural throughout which began with κρεμάσητε of v.22, whereas MT retains a consistent singular. The positive order is "but you must actually bury him on that day."

The reason for these orders is given by MT as כי קללת אלהים תלוי, which admits of more than one interpretation. The bound phrase could be interpreted as understanding אלהים as the subject, i.e. God does the cursing, or as object, i.e. cursing God.[58] LXX has opted for κεκατηραμένος ὑπὸ θεοῦ in which God is the one who curses. LXX has also clarified תלוי by insisting on πᾶς κρεμάμενος; hex has placed πᾶς under the obelus. Nor does MT have an equivalent for ἐπὶ τοῦ ξύλου, which MT has also placed under an obelus. It constitutes a leveling with v.22 where the phrase does occur; see also v.23a. Vulg, but not Pesh, supports the addition as well.

The last clause speaks of defiling the land. Leaving the corpse hanging overnight was apparently also a defilement of the land, whereas burial cleansed it. For the relative clause see comment at 1:20.[59]

---

58. Sym understood it thus with his ὅτι διὰ βλασφημίαν θεοῦ ἐκρεμάσθη, i.e. it is on account of blaspheming God. Theod and Aq have ὅτι κατάρα θεοῦ κρεμάμενος. For the various ways in which the Hebrew can be understood see the lucid discussion in Dogniez-Harl 248—249.

59. Jerome has given us the entire verse as translated by The Three in Latin. Aq had *non commorabitur morticinium eius super lignum, sed sepeliens sepelies eum in die illa, quia maledictio dei est, qui suspensus est: et non contaminabis humum tuam quam dominus deus tuus dabit tibi haereditatem.* Sym translated as *non pernoctabit cadaver ipsius super lignum, sed sepultura sepelies eum in die ipsa, quia propter blasphemiam dei suspensus est: et non contaminabis terram tuam quam dominus deus tuus dabit tibi ad haereditatem.* Theod reads *non dormiet morticinium eius super lignum, quia supultura sepelies eum in die ipsa, quia maledictio dei est suspensus: et non comtaminabis adama tuam quam dominus dei tuus dederit tibi haereditatem.* For a thorough discussion of these two verses in The Three see Salvesen 153—157.

Chapter 22

22:1 In MT the negative לא covers both תראה and התעלמת. LXX subordinates the first verb as ἰδών, has μή before it but not before the main verb ὑπερίδῃς, which could certainly mislead a reader. Cod B tried to improve it by adding μη before ὑπερίδῃς as well, but it would have been better simply to transpose the μή. What LXX intended was μή governing ἰδών ... ὑπερίδῃς, and it means: "not when you see ... should you overlook," i.e. when you see ... don't overlook.

The isolate meaning of נדחים would be "thrust aside, forced away," but in context LXX is precisely correct with its πλανώμενα "gone astray, wandered away."[1] This is clear from its modifier ἐν τῇ ὁδῷ; the animal was wandering about on the road, i.e. lost, astray. This phrase has no specific equivalent in MT, since the translator intended πλανώμενα ἐν τῇ ὁδῷ to interpret נדחים; hex placed the prepositional phrase under the obelus to show that it was a plus over against MT. One might have expected a singular participle since the reference is to μόσχον ἢ πρόβατον, but LXX follows MT exactly in using the plural for both πλανώμενα and αὐτά. In the tradition a popular F V text has succumbed to this expectation, and reads the singular πλανωμενον, though retaining αὐτά. The main clause, ὑπερίδῃς αὐτά, represents the more colorful התעלמת מהם "hide yourself from them"!

The cognate dative noun of the apodosis represents the cognate free infinitive of MT, hence "you certainly must return (them to your brother)." There is no textual basis for the well-supported doublet for the apodosis, reading αποδωσεις αυτω (or αυτα τω αδελφω σου); this is rooted in an attempt to correct ἀποστρέψεις to αποδωσεις as a more appropriate verb to indicate "return, give back"; cf.v.2. The shorter text[2] is clearly presupposed by 848, and is original.[3]

1. Both Theod and Sym retain LXX, but Aq pedantically renders by ἐξωσμένα.
2. See THGD 80.
3. According to HR the Hi of שוב is rendered three times by ἀποστρέφω and three times by ἀποδίδωμι in Deut, though in the OT as a whole the ratio is 87 to 50 (according to Dos Santos).

22:2 This verse makes clear that the term ἀδελφός is not to be taken literally; here it simply means "fellow Israelite" or "fellow clansman"; a "brother" might be μὴ ἐγγίζῃ, but hardly μηδὲ ἐπίστῃ αὐτόν. Should such be the case, however, you must bring them together (for αὐτά see comment at v.1) into your house. For ἔνδον εἰς see comment at 21:12. The A F M V majority text reorders as προς σε ο αδελφος σου, this being a more usual Greek word order, but B 848 support the order of MT, and indicate the original text.

The animal(s) must stay with you until your ἀδελφός goes looking for them (again αὐτά). Most witnesses, including A B F M, have αὐτά before ὁ ἀδελφός σου, but 848 supports the order of LXX (and of MT). The transposition is rooted in the natural urge to have the pronominal modifier αὐτά immediately follow the verb. The important thing is καὶ ἀποδώσεις αὐτῷ; MT reads והשבתו לו, i.e. LXX does not translate the suffix. The support for the shorter text by both 848 and B makes it likely that the majority text, which inserts αυτα before αὐτῷ, is hex in origin.

22:3 The same rule is to apply to anything else belonging to your "brother" which you happen upon. LXX follows the text of Sam in lacking an initial conjunction.[4] Specifically mentioned are "his ass" and "his garment," as well as κατὰ πᾶσαν ἀπώλειαν τοῦ ἀδελφοῦ σου. Why the translator changed the construction from a straightforward accusative to a κατά phrase is not at all clear. All three cases represent a ל phrase in MT, except that the last one is modified in MT by an אשר clause; in LXX the ὅσα clause is in apposition to the entire ποιήσεις 3° clause.

In fact, I would suggest that the translator intended the first cut to come between σου and ὅσα. It would be much clearer if the punctuation symbols after the σου and εὕρῃς were transposed. This would more accurately show the intent of LXX, an understanding promoted by the fact that the translator did not render the suffix of ומצאתה. The ὅσα clause then becomes the modifier for ὑπεριδεῖν. Translate: "whatever is lost by him and you should find (it), you may not overlook (i.e. fail to return).

In the tradition the majority text reads a secondary εαν for ἄν, for which see comment at 5:27. Furthermore, the majority of witnesses add αυτα after

4. Kenn 18,80 and 150 also read כן.

εὕρῃς as well as after ὑπεριδεῖν. The former at least had the justification of a suffixed verb in MT, מצאתה, though I doubt whether that had anything to do with the tradition; cf comment above; the verb εὑρίσκω commonly, though not necessarily, has an accusative modifier. The popular αυτα at the end of the verse is probably due to the influence of ὑπερίδῃς αὐτά in v.1.

22:4 This verse is based on an intuition similar to that of vv.1—3, viz. to help a person in need. The occasion is that of seeing the ass or ox of a fellow Israelite fallen on the road. As in the preceding verses, references to "the ass or the ox" are made in the plural, thus πεπτωκότας, (they are) "fallen";[5] the participle in MT is, however, also plural as was נדחים in v.1, and LXX simply imitates its parent text. Most witnesses follow the A F M V reading of the singular, but in view of plural references in vv.1 and 2, the plural of B+ must be original. For μὴ ὑπερίδῃς αὐτούς see comment at v.1. Here too the influence of pronominal usage in vv.1 and 2 has influenced the majority tradition reading αυτα for LXX's αὐτούς; the latter must be correct, however, since it refers to the masculine ὄνον and μόσχον.

In the last clause MT's cognate free infinitive is rendered by a participle. Since this kind of construction is foreign to Greek, the intent must be taken from the Hebrew structure in which the free infinitive serves to stress the verbal idea. I would translate the structure by "you simply must help him raise (i.e. the animal)." The tradition has tried to clarify the unusual absolute use of ἀναστήσεις triggered by תקים by adding either αυτα as *oII C*+ or αυτους with *cI' s*+, but the more difficult text is certainly original.

22:5 "A man's accoutrements may not be on a woman." The term σκεύη/כלי can refer to anything that is worn by a man, whether apparel or arms or even adornments.[6] What is meant is that a woman may not use a man's outfit. The obverse prohibition is more specific: "nor may a man don a female garment." The adjective phrase στολὴν γυναικείαν interprets the intent of the bound phrase שמלת אשה.[7]

5. Theod and Sym (and possibly Aq) change to the singular πεπτωκότα.
6. Dogniez-Harl translates by "d'équipement d'homme."
7. See SS 66. Aq translates שמלת by ἱματισμόν.

The ὅτι clause gives the reason for disallowing transvestitism: "anyone doing these things is an abomination to the Lord your God." Usually βδέλυγμα refers to an abominable practice, but occasionally by metonymy it refers to the practitioner of such; see also 18:12 25:16. In the tradition the Byz text has transposed ἐστιν after βδέλυγμα, but this is a matter of taste, since the ἐστιν has no equivalent in MT; hex has put it under the obelus. For βδέλυγμα see comment at 7:25.

22:6 MT has יקרא Ni with קן as its subject, i.e. "if a nest ... be chanced upon before you," which LXX translates into a second person verb συναντήσεις, thus "should you encounter a bird's nest in front of you along the way." The verb is normally modified by a dative as here, though the accusative variant in *C*'' *b*+ is also possible, especially in late texts. The V *n* text has ὀρνέων changed to the singular ορνεου, which formally agrees with MT's צפור, but the latter can be taken as a collective as well. The nests might be ἢ ἐπὶ παντὶ δένδρει ἢ ἐπὶ τῆς γῆς. The change in case reflects a change in Hebrew preposition; the local character of the dative reflects בכל עץ, whereas the second renders על הארץ, thus "in any tree or on the ground." MT only has a single או between the two, which then clearly means that along the way the nests are either in a tree or on the ground. The added ἤ before "in any tree" could mean a choice of three: "along the way or in some tree or on the ground," though ἤ ... ἤ could also mean "either ... or," which I suspect was intended. In the tradition δένδρει appears as δενδρω in a popular F M V variant. The LXX reading reflects the dative of δένδρεον, whereas the variant derives from δένδρον, but these are variants with no semantic differences. Furthermore, the mother bird is brooding on the nestlings or on the eggs. The verb is well chosen here, since brooding is what רבצת "crouching, sitting" actually implies.

In such a case you may not take the mother along with the offspring, a sensible order, since such a prohibition allows for the preservation of the species. In the tradition the words for nest and nestlings, νοσσία and νόσσος, appear in numerous texts in the Classical form of νεοσσ-, but this represents a later pseudo-Classical trend among copyists.[8]

8. For the νοσσ- stem as original throughout the Pentateuch see Walters 80—81.

22:7 This verse summarizes the regulation: "you must actually send the mother away, but the young ones (παιδία) you may take for yourself." Here the nestlings (בנים) are called παιδία, whereas in the previous verse בנים became τέκνων; there is no difference intended; both refer to the baby birds.

For the ἵνα clause see comments at 4:40.[9] In the tradition B *O*+ read γενη for ἔσῃ. The contraction σαυτω in *C'' s* is never found in Deut, which always uses the uncontracted forms of the reflexive pronouns.

22:8 MT does not begin with a conjunction, so hex has placed δέ under the obelus, but see comment at 15:16. Anyone building a new house must make a railing for the rooftop. The rooftop of Palestinian houses was flat, and in regular use, and a railing (στεφάνην) would keep one from falling over the edge.[10] MT has a conjunction to introduce the apodosis, but LXX fortunately does not. Hex has, however, introduced a και; this gained wide support in the tradition, which support included B and F.[11]

Lack of such a protective rail might occasion דמים "bloodshed," which is translated by φόνον "murder, manslaughter." When wilful neglect causes someone's death, this makes one responsible for the death; this is φόνος; see also Note at Exod 22:2(1). This φόνον is characterized as being ἐν τῇ οἰκίᾳ σου; the builder has occasioned manslaughter in his own house.

Note the care with which LXX has translated each word in "should the one falling fall"; one might have preferred a simpler "should someone fall," but repetition is characteristic of Deut. In the tradition an A+ variant has αυτης instead of αὐτοῦ, but the antecedent must be δώματί, not οἰκίᾳ.

22:9 The prohibition disallows sowing one's vineyard διάφορον, "in hybrid fashion." What is meant is that one may not mix species; the seed used must be all of one kind. MT prohibits כאלים "two kinds."[12]

---

9. That these clauses are simply Deuteronomic formulae is clear from lists 28 and 29 in THGD 94.
10. Sym calls it a κώλυμα "hindrance" (retroverted from Syh).
11. For evidence of recensional activity in Cod B see THGD 48—51.
12. Aq used εἱργμόν "prison," reflecting the root כלא "to restrain, imprison"! This is indeed an extreme case of non-contextual isolate translation. Theod also thought of this root as his κώλυμα shows. Sym alone interpreted accurately with ἀνομοιογενές "of different kind of species."

The reason given is ἵνα μὴ ἁγιασθῇ τὸ γένημα καὶ τὸ σπέρμα "that the produce and the seed may not be rendered holy," i.e. be removed from common use. MT does not join τὸ γένημα and τὸ σπέρμα with a conjunction at all. It has המלאה הזרע;[13] in fact, MT probably intends only המלאה as the subject of תקדש, with the rest of the verse explicating המלאה, i.e. "the seed which you sowed and the produce of the vineyard." MT is much clearer than LXX here; in MT המלאה refers to the full produce, i.e. the product of both kinds of seed, whereas תבואה refers only to the product of the vine. LXX does not distinguish between the two words, translating both by γένημα (-ματος). This failure has resulted in a confusing relative clause explicating σπέρμα as ὃ ἂν σπείρῃς μετὰ τοῦ γενήματος τοῦ ἀμπελῶνός σου. The μετά phrase stands for ותבואת כרמך, which MT intended to be coordinate with הזרע. The situation might be improved by placing a comma after σπείρῃς in the critical text.

In the tradition B *f n*+ have διφορον instead of διάφορον, thereby changing the intent entirely; this would prohibit the Israelite farmer from harvesting second crops. This is simply a scribal error; vineyards do not yield second crops, though second pressings are common. An interesting variant in 848 reads και το γενημα for μετὰ τοῦ γενήματος. This clearly shows Hebrew influence on the bilingual scribe, who obviously knew his Hebrew text thoroughly.[14]

22:10 "You may not plow[15] with an ox and an ass together." MT repeats the preposition with "ass" as well, but this would be otiose in Greek. ἐπὶ τὸ αὐτό "together" is a good rendering for יחדו.[16] Why harnessing an ox and a donkey together is wrong is not clear, except that it is admittedly foolish to do so since a donkey will let the ox do all the pulling.

22:11 MT forbids wearing שעטנז, a word occurring only here and its parallel in Lev 19:19; there it is defined as בגד כלאים "garment of two kinds (of cloth)," but here as צמר ופשתים "wool and flax," so it apparently means cloth made of mixed material. LXX translates the word in both places by κίβδηλον

13. Which Theod and Aq translate by τὸ πλῆρες τὸ σπέρμα (retroverted from Syh^{m}).
14. See THGD 70—71.
15. For ἀροτριάσεις see discussion in Lee 113.
16. But not good enough for Aq, who regularly uses ὁμοῦ to translate יחדו.

"adulterated, spurious."[17] LXX follows MT in making the spurious goods of "wool and flax" ἐν τῷ αὐτῷ for יחדו, a clever variation from v.10's ἐπὶ τὸ αὐτό, where יחדו meant "placed or added together," whereas here it means mixed up together in the same piece of goods; cf Lev's rendering of כלאים: ἐκ δύο ὑφασμένον. A popular A variant does substitute επι το αυτο, but this is due to the influence of v.10.

22:12 The Israelite is ordered to make for himself στρεπτά. This translates גדלים "twisted cords." These are to be on the four κρασπέδων of your περιβολαίων, i.e. the four borders of your wrap-arounds, presumably your loose outer cloak, at least they are defined as ἃ ἂν περιβάλῃ ἐν αὐτοῖς "with which you wrap around." The peculiar Greek is in imitation of MT: אשר תכסה בה; LXX has obviously taken the antecedent כסותך as a collective. The περιβολαίων stands for כסות "covering." The term could just as well refer to bed coverings; in fact, the poor used their cloaks as blankets at night. κρασπέδων translates כנפות "wings," hence edges. The wings of such garments must refer to the four borders or sides of the cloak.

22:13—14 A new section which extends through v.19 is introduced by δέ; this has no equivalent in MT, but see comment at 15:16. The protasis extends through v.14. The section deals with the bride, who after cohabitation, is accused of not having been a virgin. LXX has the subject τις before the verb λάβῃ, though MT has יקח איש. Accordingly, hex transposed the two words to equal MT. Once having cohabited with her, the husband μισήσῃ αὐτήν "he hated her," and charged her עלילת דברים, a phrase of uncertain meaning, but probably meaning "baseless charges." The word עלילת has the sense of willfulness, arbitrariness, and together with דברים leads to the notion of wilful or baseless charges.[18] LXX translates by προφασιστικοὺς λόγους "pretentious

17. Theod either did not know any Greek equivalent or did not know the Hebrew word, so he transliterated it as σατανας (from Syh^{m}); Aq created a neologism ἀντιδιακείμενον "of different kinds," whereas Sym made a neat choice with ἑτερογενές.
18. Tar are of little help in explaining עלילת. Tar^{O} has תסקופי "artifices," thus verbal artifices; Tar^{J} has ערר, so "objection, pretext," whereas Tar^{N} uses the same root as MT: עלילן. Vulg explains (*quaesieritque*) *occasiones quibus dimittat eam*, avoiding a direct translation.

words," i.e. specious charges. The adjective is a neologism occurring here and in v.17.[19] LXX has probably done well in its rendering.[20]

Furthermore, he has *κατενέγκῃ αὐτῆς ὄνομα πονηρόν* "brought against her a bad reputation," which is then defined by the man's actual charge: "This woman I took (i.e. married), and when I went in to her I did not find her *παρθένια*." The word means "virginity," but here it must mean evidence of virginity, i.e. "(to find her) virginity" must mean the same as the Hebrew בתולים "tokens of virginity."

αὐτῆς represents the Hebrew לה, where it meant "(I did not find) for her (tokens of virginity)." The tradition changed the pronoun to the dative *αυτῃ* in an *oI n* variant and to *εν αυτῃ* in *b*, but the genitive of possession is correct and original.

22:15 The parental reaction is to "bring the girl's *παρθένια* to the eldership at the gate." The parents are called *ὁ πατὴρ τῆς παιδὸς καὶ ἡ μήτηρ*. Hex has added *αυτης* after *μήτηρ* to show that MT had a suffix (אמה), but this is quite unnecessary; *ἡ μήτηρ* could hardly refer to someone else's mother. *τὴν γερουσίαν* is LXX's rendering for זקני העיר, to which hex has added *της πολεως* under the asterisk to equal the Hebrew העיר. For the use of *γερουσίαν* for זקני see the discussion at 19:12.

22:16—17 The father of the accused bride presents the case for the defence to the eldership. He begins with *τὴν θυγατέρα μου ταύτην*, though MT has no demonstrative pronoun, and hex has placed the *ταύτην* under the obelus. The use of the perfect verb *δέδωκα* is particularly fitting, and the change to the aorist *εδωκα* in *O* Byz is a mistake commonly made. The two are often confused in the tradition, and the aorist is far more common in Deut.[21]

The subordination of the last verb in v.16 to a participle *μισήσας* is unexpected before the onset of v.17, but a tenseless form does fit in subordination to the present tense verb *ἐπιτίθησιν*, in contrast to the past tense וישנאה of MT. MT has the verb coordinate with נתתי, i.e. "I gave her but he hated her." LXX has "I gave ... and since he hates her (he now charges her)." The

19. Aq translates the phrase by *ἐναλλακτικὰ ῥήματα* "perverse, wanton words."
20. SS 66 speaks of the translation as "ein gutes Resultat."
21. See THGD 140—141.

participle שם is correctly rendered by the present tense ἐπιτίθησιν, to which LXX added a dative pronoun αὐτῇ; this has no counterpart in MT, and is therefore placed under the obelus in MT.[22] For προφασιστικοὺς λόγους and παρθένια see comments at vv.13—14. The change of והנה to νῦν is contextually determined. The Greek is still contrasting the past action of the father, δέδωκα/נתתי, to the present atttiude and action of the bridegroom. In this way LXX points out the causal relation of the hatred to the subsequent action of the husband; what the father suggests is that the charge was motivated by the husband's dislike of his bride. The transposition of νῦν αὐτός by A F M *oI f y+* is a stylistic variation, by which the νῦν is brought immediately next to the verb, but it is obviously secondary.[23]

22:18 The stained cloth was proof positive of the falsity of the bridegroom's charges. LXX follows the Sam text which reads האיש ההוא, rather than MT which lacks the pronoun; hex has correctly placed ἐκεῖνον under the obelus. The verb παιδεύσουσιν means "discipline, chastise"; the Hebrew יסר is almost exclusively rendered by παιδεύω, and usually involves physical beating.[24] Note that the subject of the plural verb is the singular ἡ γερουσία, but this is understood as a collective throughout the book.

22:19 The phrase מאה כסף is interpreted as ἑκατὸν σίκλους. The term כסף as a metal is always rendered by ἀργύριον in Deut, but twice it is governed by a number, and is then understood by the translator as a coin, here as a shekel, and in v.29 as a δίδραχμα ἀργυρίου; cf comment ad loc.[25] σίκλος almost always has שקל as Hebrew equivalent throughout the OT. The word שקל does not occur anywhere in Deut, but it is common in the rest of the Pentateuch (twice in Gen 23; 13 times in Exod; 11, in Lev; and 20 times in Num).

The second clause might better have been rendered by a ους clause rather than a paratactic one, but LXX imitates MT, even to the extent of an absolute δώσουσιν. Oddly the translator now changes to νεάνιδος, which continues through v.21. נערה had occurred three times up to this point and was

22. Kenn 69,80,103,109 all add לה after שם.
23. See THGD 130.
24. See Prijs 16.
25. The Three read ἑκατὸν ἀργυρίου.

translated by ἡ παῖς throughout, but the next three become ἡ νεᾶνις. Thereafter the translator varies; apparently the two were completely synonymous as far as נערה was concerned. The rendering by παῖς is limited in Deut to this chapter (six times), and elsewhere in the Pentateuch it occurs only in Gen (three times).

The reason given for the fine is given in a ὅτι/כי clause: "he brought dishonor (i.e. a bad name) on an Israelite virgin." Not only shall she remain his wife, but he will never be able to divorce her. The Hebrew כל ימיו "all his days," i.e. for the rest of his life, is translated idiomatically by an accusative showing extent of time: τὸν ἅπαντα χρόνον, which is repeated in v.29. The use of χρόνος to translate ימים is nicely defined by 12:19 as (πάντα) τὸν χρόνον ὅσου ἂν ζῇς ἐπὶ τῆς γῆς. The rendering is in general limited to the freer translations: Gen (26:1,15), Jos three times, Job four times, and Prov. three times.[26]

22:20 The possibility that the charge be sustained is raised in vv.20—21. The predicate אמת היה "was truth" is rendered by ἐπ' ἀληθείας γένηται rather than by a predicate adjective, probably to bring out the notion that "this charge was based on truth," i.e. had a legal foundation. This foundation was a negative one, i.e. the παρθένια for the girl were not found. The two clauses are joined by καί in LXX, supported by Pesh and Vulg, but they are asyndeton in MT.

22:21 The penalty: death by stoning. MT states "they (i.e. the זקני העיר of v.18) shall bring out the girl to the door of her father's house." LXX also uses a plural verb, though its antecedent is γερουσία, but see comment at v.18. The *C'' s* text has εξαρουσιν, but this is secondary. The verb never occurs in OT for the Hi of יצא, whereas ἐξάγω occurs 170 times.[27]

Furthermore, LXX renders פתח by the plural (ἐπὶ τὰς θύρας) and omits "house," i.e. the translator has "doors of her father" though obviously referring to his house.[28] In the tradition most witnesses add (του) οικου after θύρας. The more difficult shorter text is supported by B and 848, and must be original

26. According to HR.
27. According to the count in Don Santos.
28. Aq translates אל פתח בית literally by πρὸς ἄνοιγμα οἴκου.

text.[29] Most witnesses add the unarticulated form; a good case could be made for suggesting that LXX originally read *του οικου* and that the B 848+ text was created by parablepsis. This remains a possibility, though the support for *του οικου*, including as it does 72-426-*oI*, looks suspiciously like a hex correction; actually all the other members of the hex group also support *οικου*, but without the article. A substantial number of the witnesses supporting the *οικου* gloss also support the omission of *τοῦ* articulating *πατρός*, but LXX always articulates "father" throughout this section.[30]

The subject changes for the next clause to "the men of her city." Parenthetically it might be noted that the evidence of 848 is not always to be followed. It omits *ἐν λίθοις*, but usage shows that the verb λιθοβολέω is modified by *ἐν λίθοις* throughout the book, and must be original, even though the phrase is tautological.[31]

On the other hand, its evidence for a shorter text is followed in the *ὅτι* clause, where *ἐν Ἰσραήλ* is supported by 848 plus very few mss over against *εν υιοις ισραηλ* of most witnesses. But LXX again follows MT. Admittedly the *υιοις* is under the obelus in hex, and were it not for 848 this evidence would probably swing the balance towards accepting *υιοις* as original. But 848 is over 300 years older than hex, and all that the obelus proves is that the gloss was already there in Origen's time.[32] The *ὅτι* clause gives the reason for the capital sentence; it is because she committed *ἀφροσύνην ἐν Ἰσραήλ*.[33] This *ἀφροσύνη* "foolishness, senselessness" refers to lack of sense or thought with respect to moral uprightness, which is then defined more particularly by the "gerundive" infinitive[34] *ἐκπορνεῦσαι* i.e. "prostituting her father's house." The *O* group simplifies the construction by changing the infinitive to a participial *εκπορνευσασα*.

For the formulaic last clause see comment at 13:5. Though *τὸν πονηρόν* actually refers to the girl guilty of fornication, the masculine is retained because of its formulaic nature; see also v.24. Note also the formulaic *ἐξ ὑμῶν αὐτῶν* for מקרבך.

29. See THGD 80.
30. See THGD 105.
31. See THGD 67.
32. See THGD 81.
33. Aq translates נבלה by *ἀπόρρευσιν*, for which see 1Reg 25:25.
34. The term is that of SS 209.

22:22 For ἐὰν δέ see comment at 15:16. Those committing adultery are to be killed. The condition is described as that of a man lying with a woman συνῳκισμένης ἀνδρί "one who was made to dwell with a man," thus a married woman. It renders בעלת בעל "one married to a husband."

The penalty: ἀποκτενεῖτε ἀμφοτέρους which translates מתו גם שניהם "both of them shall die." The Greek puts it into second person plural, i.e. orders the execution as a positive action on "your" part.[35] "Both" is then defined as "the man lying with the woman, and the woman." The definition is in the accusative, since it is in apposition to ἀμφοτέρους.

For the formula see comment at v.21. The formula differs from the usual formulaic ἐξ ὑμῶν αὐτῶν as in v.21 by reading ἐξ Ἰσραήλ, representing מישראל.[36] The majority text does read εξ υμων αυτων; this is not LXX, but rather ex par (v.21).

22:23 Vv.23—29 deal with cases of seduction. For ἐὰν δέ see comment at 15:16. The first case is that of a man who seduces a virgin betrothed to some one else, the seduction occurring in an urban area. This is dealt with in vv.23—24. V.23 constitutes the protasis: "Should there be a virgin (παῖς παρθένος) betrothed to a man, and should someone, finding her in a city, lie with her." For παῖς see comment at v.19. The Greek leaves πόλει unarticulated, whereas the Masoretes vocalized בעיר as articulated. The Greek sensibly leaves the first mention of "city" without an article, but thereafter throughout v.24 is quite naturally articulated. Since LXX has subordinated εὑρών, the translator does not translate the conjunction of ושכב in the interests of normal Greek.

22:24 The penalty begins with an asyndetic imperative ἐξάξετε "bring out" for the Hebrew והוציאתם "and you shall bring out." Hex has duly prefixed the verb with a και to equal the conjunction in MT. The verb is modified by the prepositional phrase ἐπὶ τὴν πύλην τῆς πόλεως αὐτῶν. MT has אל שער העיר ההוא, but LXX uses αὐτῶν instead of αυτου for ההוא, which the V Byz text

35. Aq and Sym translate by καὶ ἀποθανοῦνται ἀμφότεροι "both shall die." Theod has ἀποθανοῦνται καί γε δύο αὐτοί.
36. Both Theod and Sym retain LXX, whereas Aq changes the preposition to ἀπό.

changed to *εκεινης* to equal MT, a change probably mediated through one of The Three. The change to *αὐτῶν* makes possible the change of סקלתם אתם "you stone them" to the third person plural passive "(and) they shall be stoned." Since Byz had changed *αὐτῶν* to *εκεινης* it perforce also had to introduce *αμφοτεροι* as subject for *λιθοβοληθήσονται*.

ἀμφοτέρους is further explicated by *τὴν νεᾶνιν*[37] ... *καὶ τὸν ἄνθρωπον*, each with a *ὅτι* clause attached to give the reason for the death penalty: the girl "because she did not call out in the city," and the man "because he violated the wife *τοῦ πλησίον*."[38] The majority text added *αυτου*, which does equal רעהו of MT, but throughout the book LXX never renders the suffix of רעהו.[39] LXX has adequately rendered על דבר אשר (1° and 2°) by a simple *ὅτι*, but this was not good enough for Origen; hex changed both instances to *επι λογοι οτι*, which is rather peculiar Greek.

For the formulaic clause ending the verse see comment at v.21. A popular reading has changed *ἐξαρεῖς* to the plural *εξαρειτε*, thereby levelling to the plural *ὑμῶν αὐτῶν*, but LXX retains the usual formula.

22:25 The *δέ* is contrastive. The previous case took place in the city, but here it is *ἐν πεδίῳ*, i.e. in a rural area, an open field. The noun is anarthrous, since *πεδίῳ* occurs for the first time; this differs from the Hebrew usage, where בשדה is vocalized with an article.

LXX sensibly condenses the account for the second clause to *καὶ βιασάμενος κοιμηθῇ μετ' αὐτῆς* "and forcibly lies with her" for MT's והחזיק בה האיש ושכב עמה. Hex attempted quantitative equivalence by adding under the asterisk *αυτην ο ανθρωπος* after *βιασάμενος*, but LXX is a concise and much neater statement.

The judgment in MT is "only the man ... shall die," which the Greek interprets in transitive fashion as *ἀποκτενεῖτε τὸν ἄνθρωπον ... μόνον* "you shall kill only the man." The verb is sensibly in the plural, as in v.24, which see; presumably the sentence is understood to be the same, viz. that the men of the city will stone the man with stones, though the text does not actually say

37. Aq translates as *παῖδα*. Aq always rendered נער(ה) by the root *παιδ-*.
38. The Three all add *αὐτοῦ*.
39. See the list and discussion in THGD 77—78.

so. The relative clause identifying the man as אשר שכב בה is well-translated by an attributive participle in LXX.

22:26 The girl goes free in this case; she committed no capital offence (ἁμάρτημα θανάτου). The verse opens with καὶ τῇ νεάνιδι, a literal rendering of ולנער. Most witnesses, however, read the smoother τη δε νεανιδι, which is a stylistic improvement in bringing out the contrast between "you shall kill the man" and "but to the girl you shall do nothing." The Greek follows Sam in its use of the plural ποιήσετε.

The ὅτι clause argues by analogy: "as though some man should rise up against (his) neighbour and wound him fatally, so is this matter." The clause καὶ φονεύσῃ αὐτοῦ ψυχήν renders ורצחו נפש "and slay him with respect to person," i.e. רצח is doubly modified by the suffix and by נפש. LXX, by rendering the suffix by a genitive pronoun, has simplified it as "and slew his person." Though not stated, this can only refer to an accidental, rather than to an intentional killing; compare 19:4—10 with vv.11—13. The point of the analogy is that lack of intention means no imposed penalty. For πλησίον as rendering for רעהו see comment at v.24.[40] Most witnesses do add αυτου, but this is secondary. The analogy is drawn by οὕτως τὸ πρᾶγμα τοῦτο. τὸ πρᾶγμα translates הדבר in the sense of "the matter," which is what the Hebrew intends.[41] The *C'' s* text has το ρημα which is also the reading of Aq, but τὸ πρᾶγμα is much more fitting in the context.

22:27 The ὅτι clause explains why no blame attaches to the girl. The betrothed girl called out (i.e. for help), but because she was in the field there was no one to help her. Here בשדה is translated, not by ἐν πεδίῳ as in v.25, but by ἐν τῷ ἀγρῷ; the *t* text does read πεδιω, but the two nouns are synonyms. Note that in view of an earlier ἐν πεδίῳ the reference to "field" is now articulated.

The last clause in MT is a nominal one, with אין מושיע as subject, and לה as predicate. LXX renders the participle by an articulated future participle, and introduces the copula ἦν to make it a verbal clause. The future participle is exactly right here; what she did not have was someone who was to come to her aid. A popular A text has the present participle βοηθων, but the more

40. The Three again all add αὐτοῦ.

41. Aq renders the word by <τὸ> ῥῆμα, whereas Theod and Sym use ὁ λόγος.

unusual future is original. The transposition of the articulated participle after οὐκ ἦν is a hex correction to the word order of MT.

22:28 The δέ introduces another case, though MT lacks an initial conjunction; see comment at 15:16. Suppose the attacked girl is not betrothed, what then? The ἐάν introduces τις εὕρῃ (τὴν παῖδα τὴν παρθένον), i.e. with the subject pronoun before the verb. This reverses MT's order ימצא איש, and so hex transposes the Greek to conform to the Hebrew. MT has the modifier unarticulated, as in v.23, but LXX articulates the phrase because virgin girls have already been mentioned. What is different here is ἥτις οὐ μεμνήστευται. The conditions of v.25, καὶ βιασάμενος κοιμηθῇ μετ' αὐτῆς, are repeated word for word in LXX, though MT's language differs; instead of החזיק בה v.28 reads תפשה, but the translator quite correctly understood that the only difference between that case and this one was the status of the attacked girl, i.e. of betrothed vs not betrothed, and using identical language sharpens the distinction.

Two further distinctions between LXX and MT are a) LXX fails to render the suffix of תפשה, which hex "corrects" by adding αυτην after the participle, and b) the rendering of the concluding clause, ונמצאו, in the singular, καὶ εὑρεθῇ, "and he is discovered." Again LXX changes the text to the singular to put the stress where it belongs, viz. on the man who is violating the virgin.

22:29 That this stress is proper is clear from the judgment; it is only the man who is judged, not the victim. LXX disregarded the opening conjunction introducing the judgment in the interests of good Greek.

The penalty is twofold, a payment of a fine to the girl's father, and an indissoluble marriage. The fine is defined in MT as חמשים כסף, which is interpreted in unusual fashion as πεντήκοντα δίδραχμα ἀργυρίου. Much more common would be defining the fifty as σίκλους as at v.19; see comment ad loc. The defining of כסף as δίδραχμα occurs elsewhere in the Pentateuch only at Gen 20:14,16; see Note at Gen 20:14.

She shall also be his wife, correctly interpreting לו by a possessive αὐτοῦ. The reason given is the same as that in 21:14, though here תחת אשר is translated, not by διότι, but by ἀνθ' ὧν. In both cases the verb ταπεινόω is used to translate ענה Pi.[42] For the final clause see comment at v.19, where the same stricture is made on divorce in exactly the same terms; see comment ad loc. In view of the Hebrew ימיו hex has added *αυτου* after *χρόνον*. For *δίδραχμα*, as well as its variant spelling *διδραγμα*, see Note at Gen 20:14.

22:30(23:1) What is forbidden here is marriage with a (widowed) stepmother. The text does not specify "widowed," but that is obvious. At 27:20 the second clause is given as the reason for the curse on the one who lies with his stepmother, whereas here it is paratactic to the prohibition itself. Here יגלה is translated by *ἀνακαλύψει*, which the B *b z*+ tradition has changed to *αποκαλυψει*. The two compounds are synonyms, and the variant is due to 27:20, which has *ἀποκαλύψει* with unanimous support.[43] What may not be uncovered is the *συγκάλυμμα* of his father, i.e. the covering. This translates the Hebrew כנף "wing," a word used to symbolize protection. The figure is that of the mother bird, which guards and protects her chicks under her wings. The protection intended is the garment provided by the husband.[44]

---

42. As at 21:14 Aq translates differently: by *ἐκακούχησεν*.
43. See the discussion of the variant in THGD 143.
44. Aq simply translates by *πτερύγιον* "wing."

Chapter 23

23:1(2) Vv.1—6 list those who are to be excluded from Israelite fellowship. The first ones not allowed entrance into the Lord's assembly are eunuchs. They are differentiated as *θλαδίας καὶ ἀποκεκομμένος*. These refer to the testicles a) as crushed; comp *θλάω* "crush, bruise," and b) one cut off, i.e. castrated. The Hebrew terms are bound phrases: פצוע דכא "bruised by crushing"[1] and כרות שפכה "the male organ cut." Entering the Lord's assembly specifically refers to taking part in sanctuary worship. Eunuchs may not enter an Israelite sanctuary.

23:2(3) The same prohibition pertains to *ἐκ πόρνης*, i.e. one born of a harlot. The phrase's equivalent is ממזיר, a word of uncertain meaning, though usually understood as the product of an illegitimate union, e.g. of incest, thus a bastard.[2] MT has a further limitation: גם דור עשירי לא יבא לו בקהל יהוה. Presumably LXX's parent text was defective due to homoioteleuton. In any event, hex added under the asterisk *και γενεα δεκατη ουκ εισελευσεται εις εκκλησιαν κυριου* to equal MT. A similar statement obtains in the next verse where LXX did translate it.

23:3(4) "Neither Ammanite nor Moabite may enter the Lord's assembly." For Ammanite see comment at 2:20. The second clause in LXX differs considerably from MT. MT says: "Even (גם) a tenth generation may not ever (עד עולם) enter the assembly of the Lord." LXX begins with *καὶ ἕως δεκάτης γενεᾶς* and ends with *καὶ ἕως εἰς τὸν αἰῶνα*. The Greek says: "even to the tenth generation may he (i.e. either Ammanite or Moabite) not enter the Lord's assembly, (not) even for ever." It is difficult to find a rationale for the *καὶ ἕως εἰς* which occurs nowhere else in the book, though *ἕως εἰς* does occur at 31:24,30. In all three cases MT has עד. I suspect that the *καί* is not original, and would now omit it from the critical text. The text of 848 is rather sparse here, but what is clear is that either *κυρίου* or *καί* was lacking; i.e. the

1. Aq translates literally by *τραυματίας ἐπιτριμμοῦ*.
2. The Three all had their problems with the word. Aq adopted Theod's transliteration *μαμζήρ*, and Sym transliterated the Aramaic form as *μαμζιρα* (from Syh).

line length presupposes three or four less letters. The omission of *κυρίου* would be senseless but that of *καί* improves the text considerably.[3] The dominance of the *καὶ ἕως* tradition was then due to the occurrence of the collocation before *δεκάτης*. The clause may then be translated as "even to the tenth generation he may never enter the Lord's assembly." In the tradition hex has transposed *δεκάτης γενεᾶς* to equal the דור עשירי of MT. The addition of *αυτω* after the verb in the second clause by *O* also seems to be a correction towards the Hebrew's להם. LXX wisely did not translate the phrase, since it is largely untranslatable; cf also v.8.[4]

23:4(5) This eternal enmity against the Ammanite and the Moabite is explained by vv.4—5, i.e. it is על דבר אשר "because of the fact that" (for which see comment at 22:24), followed by לא קדמו. This is translated by a prepositional phrase, i.e. by *παρά* plus an articulated infinitive: *παρὰ τὸ μὴ συναντῆσαι αὐτούς* "because of their not meeting (you)."[5] The charge is lack of hospitality; they did not provide you with food and drink on the road when you were going out from Egypt. This is probably a reference to 2:30; though at 2:24 Sihon is called an Amorite, his territory did cover part of Ammanite land. The genitive absolute renders well the Hebrew ב plus bound infinitive construction.

The second reason (i.e. the *καὶ ὅτι* clause) also uses a plural subject, i.e. *ἐμισθώσαντο* presupposes both peoples being involved, though the hiring of Balaam only applied to Moab; see Num 22—24. MT, however, has a singular verb שכר, which contrasts with the plural קדמו. LXX has rendered consistently by the plural, leaving it to the intelligent reader to unscramble the references, viz. that the first charge pertains to the one party, and the second one to the other. I would suggest that the translator read שכר vocalized as a free infinitive, which would then automatically be taken in the context as a plural. Actually it is difficult to justify the inconsistent MT text.

For *Βαλαὰμ υἱὸν Βεώρ* see Num 22:5. For his coming *ἐκ (τῆς) Μεσοποταμίας* see Num 23:7. MT locates Balaam's home at (מ)פתור ארם

3. See THGD 71.
4. Driver calls this a ל of relation and refers to BDB 5a, but I am not at all sure what that means.
5. See SS Inf 133.

נהרים, but LXX omits the name of the town, for which see Num 22:5, where LXX transliterates by Φαθούρ(α).[6]

23:5(6) A reflection of the Balaam story of Num. Not only was the Lord unwilling to listen to Balaam, he actually turned the curses into blessings. MT is somewhat different in that "the Lord your God turned לך את הקללה לברכה." LXX did not translate לך, and hex provided for it by a *σοι* under the asterisk. The omission was probably palaeographically conditioned, since the word before it, אלהיך, has the same end consonant. The omission could hardly have been intentional since the notion that the Lord operated "on your behalf" is basic to the book as well as to the immediate context, as the *ὅτι* clause makes clear. LXX has also taken the two nouns as collectives: "curses ... blessings." In the tradition B *C'* *n*+ have *ευλογιαν* instead of the plural, but retain the plural *κατάρας*. The variant is obviously secondary.[7]

The *ὅτι* clause identifies the impulse for the Lord's action. It is because he loved you, a notion which is thematic in the book.

23:6(7) *οὐ προσαγορεύσεις* "not shall you address" renders לא תדרש, which is a good idiomatic translation; with שלמם וטבתם what is meant is "not shall you greet them nor wish them well."[8] LXX renders the nouns as *εἰρηνικὰ αὐτοῖς καὶ συμφέροντα αὐτοῖς*, thus "address them with greetings and good wishes," literally "peaceful words and benefits."[9] The repetition of *αὐτοῖς* is tedious, but it does equal MT. So too the accusative denoting extent of time, *πάσας τὰς ἡμέρας σου*, hardly needs *εἰς τὸν αἰῶνα* after it; Byz actually adds *εως* before *εἰς*, thereby reflecting v.3.

23:7(8) In contrast to the Ammanite and the Moabite, the Idoumaean and the Egyptian are not to be despised. The verb *βδελύσσω* is the standard rendering for תעב Pi, thus "abhor, feel a loathing towards," so despise. *'Ιδουμαῖον* occurs only here in Deut; the Idoumaeans were the descendents of Esau dwelling in Seir; cf 2:4 where they are called *τῶν ἀδελφῶν ὑμῶν*. The Egyptian is

6. Aq accounts for every word by *ἀπὸ Φατοὺρ Συρίας ποταμῶν*.
7. See THGD 136.
8. Aq translates literally by *οὐκ ἐκζητήσεις* "you must not seek out."
9. See Daniel 292.

also not to be despised, "because you were a *πάροικος* in his land." The גר is a resident alien, and as such had certain rights; he is then a *προσήλυτος*, which in all but two passages translates גר. But at 14:21 and here, *πάροικος* is intentionally used instead; cf comment at 14:21. In the tradition the majority of witnesses have changed *αὐτοῦ* to *αυτων*, an easy mistake in view of *αὐτοῖς* in v.8. But the reference can only pertain to *Αἰγύπτιον*, not to both Idoumaean and Egyptian.

23:8(9) MT makes בנים with its relative clause modifier the subject, and יבא, the predicate. What seems uncertain is the extent of the relative clause. The Masoretes have made the first cut after שלישי, i.e. "which are born to them in the third generation." It would be more straightforward to have דור שלישי as a modifier of יבא. Were it not for the Masoretic punctuation one would read "children which will be born to them" as a pendent construction, with דור שלישי as the subject and יבא as the predicate.

LXX rather unfortunately rendered אשר by *ἐάν*, but this seems to support the Masoretic division,[10] though LXX simplified the interpretation by making the verb plural, i.e. *υἱοί ... εἰσελεύσονται*. I would translate: "As for children, should they be born in the third generation, they shall enter the assembly of the Lord." The translator must have intended *γενεᾷ τρίτῃ* to modify *γενηθῶσιν*, since otherwise he would be saying "sons if (or when) they are born to them" which is not at all sensible. Apparently Origen intended to render the להם modifying יבא by adding *αυτοις* (changed to *αυτοι* in some mss), but this is not particularly meaningful either; cf comment at v.3.

23:9(10) For *ἐὰν δέ* see comment at 15:16. Vv.9—14 deal with regulations ensuring the clean status of soldiers in the camp. V.9 is a general warning: "Should you go out to encamp against your enemies, you must watch out for any evil matter." The infinitive *παρεμβαλεῖν* represents the noun מחנה "a camp," which modifies the subject of תצא, thus "if you go out as a camp." The use of *παρεμβαλεῖν* as a complementary infinitive is highly unusual in OT, occurring elsewhere only in 1Macc 5:27 with *τάσσονται*, at 5:42 with *ἀφῆτε*, 15:39 after *ἐνετείλατο* and in 3Macc 4:11 modifying *προσέταξεν*. It

10. Sym does understand אשר as a relative pronoun with his *οἱ υἱοὶ γεννώμενοι αὐτοῖς* (retroverted from Syh^{m}).

never renders מחנה elsewhere. The verb ἐξέλθῃς would more commonly be modified by εις πολεμον; in fact, *C'' s+* add it as a gloss before the infinitive, whereas Byz add it after it, but the unusual construction without the doublet εις πολεμον must be original LXX.

The apodosis is introduced by a και in most witnesses but not by 848, and in spite of MT's ונשמרת it is secondary.[11] A popular F M text transposes ῥήματος πονηρός, which is probably more common after παντός, but both are normal, and LXX follows the order of MT.

23:10(11) For ἐὰν δέ see comment at v.9. V.10 particularizes as to what an unclean state might be: Should there be among you someone who ἔσται not be clean (καθαρός "ritually clean") ἐκ ῥύσεως αὐτοῦ νυκτός." This stands for מקרה לילה "from an accident at night"; the Greek interprets the delicate allusion quite correctly as a man's involuntary ejaculation of sperm during sleep;[12] such a "flow during the night" renders a person unclean, and he must go outside the camp, and may not enter it. The apodosis is introduced by a conjunction in MT: ויצא, but the Greek is not, though in the tradition the majority of witnesses do add και, but see comment at v.9. The last clause is also asyndetic in MT over against LXX, but the καί may have a textual basis.[13]

In the tradition most witnesses change ἔσται to εστιν, but this is a stylistic change. Deut usually translates the prefix inflection (here יהיה) by the future, and this is supported inter alia by A B 848; the more literalistic rendering is original.[14]

23:11(12) For καὶ ἔσται rendering an introductory והיה see discussion at 6:10—11. The phrase τὸ πρὸς ἑσπέραν is an adverbial construction specifying the time at which the man is to bathe; this renders the idiom לפנות ערב "at the turn of evening," i.e. at dusk.[15] This is to be distinguished from δεδυκότος ἡλίου, a genitive absolute "when the sun has gone down," which is subsequent

11. For the use of the apodotic και see THGD 79.
12. Instead of ἐκ ῥύσεως αὐτοῦ Aq has ἐν συναντήματος "in an encounter, happening, accident."
13. At least 15 Kenn mss read ולא. The conjunction is also supported by Pesh and Vulg.
14. See THGD 73.
15. See SS Inf 31.

to τὸ πρὸς ἑσπέραν "at a time towards dusk." Here it might best be translated: after the sun has gone down. The Hebrew has כבא השמש "as the sun goes down."[16]

ירחץ is used intransitively, but LXX specifies the object as τὸ σῶμα αὐτοῦ. Hex attests to its absence from MT by placing the phrase under the obelus. In the tradition ἡλίου has been popularly articulated; the article was probably supplied by hex to equal MT.

23:12(13) LXX translates יד correctly by τόπος.[17] The τόπος refers to the toilet area, which must be outside the camp. The second clause translates MT word for word by καὶ ἐξελεύσῃ ἐκεῖ ἔξω, and is a euphemism for "and you shall defecate there (outside). In the tradition a popular attempt at improving the text reads εστω instead of ἔσται, but both MT and LXX state what must be, not what is proposed. See v.13 as well.

23:13(14) "And you shall have a πάσσαλος on your belt." A πάσσαλος is the standard translation for יתד "a tentpin or stake." Obviously it must be a small instrument which can be used for digging a small hole in the ground to hold and hide the feces, and may be translated by "spike." The phrase ἐπὶ τῆς ζώνης σου seems to presuppose אזרך "your belt" rather than אזנך of MT, but since the word is a hapax legomenon it is dangerous to emend. It is usually thought to mean "weaponry," an interpretation based on Tar.[18]

For καὶ ἔσται plus ὅταν see discussion at 6:10—11.[19] For בשבתך "when you sit" LXX has διακαθιζάνῃς "you sit down apart," a euphemism for "defecate."

The apodosis is introduced by καί in imitation of MT, and is indicated by a change to the future: "you shall dig with it (i.e. the πάσσαλος), and ἐπαγαγὼν καλύψεις." The participle probably refers to turning back, i.e. returning the soil and in so doing cover τὴν ἀσχημοσύνην σου ἐν αὐτῷ. The ἐν αὐτῷ has no equivalent in MT and hex has rightly placed the phrase under the obelus. But the phrase is made necessary by the choice of ἀσχημοσύνην to

16. See SS Inf 97.
17. As do Tar with אתר, as well as Pesh and Vulg: *locus*.
18. Tar[O] has על זינך; Tar[J] has על מאני זייניכון and Tar[N], במאזני זייניכון (mend pro במאני). Vulg follows LXX with *in balteo*.
19. See also SS Inf 86.

render צאת; that which goes out refers to feces, but without *ἐν αὐτῷ*, *ἀσχημοσύνην σου* would easily be understood as your *pudenda*.[20]

23:14(15) As usual LXX translates a participial predicate, מתהלך, by the present tense *ἐμπεριπατεῖ*, which is in turn modified by two purposive infinitives: *ἐξελέσθαι σε* "to save you," and *παραδοῦναι τὸν ἐχθρόν σου πρὸ προσώπου σου* "to deliver up your enemy before you." The MT counterpart for the latter reads ולתת איביך לפניך "and to set your enemies before you," i.e. put them into your power. LXX translates the plural noun by a collective singular *τὸν ἐχθρόν*.[21]

The next clause I would take as a therefore clause; one might render the Hebraic *καί* by "so (your camp must be holy)." Then the next two clauses, again hebraically each introduced by *καί*, must mean "there may not appear among you any shameful matter lest he should turn away from you." The collocation *ἀσχημοσύνη πράγματος* renders ערות דבר "nakedness of a matter," i.e. feces lying about openly.[22]

In the tradition an A M *ol n y* gloss *σοι* appears after *παραδοῦναι* to round out the infinitive. (God is in the camp to deliver) to you (your enemies before you), but the epexegetical gloss is otiose in view of the prepositional phrase, nor does it have a basis in MT.[23] A majority text changes the prepositional phrase to *εις τας χειρας σου*, but this is due to the influence of the common idiom "to deliver into your hands," and is obviously secondary.

23:15(16) Vv.15—16 contain regulations about the escaped slave. V.15 is a negative order, and v.16, a positive one. "You must not deliver a servant to (his) master." LXX does not translate the suffix of אדניו since it could only be "his" master who is referred to.[24] The verb *παραδώσεις* is a contextual trans-

20. Aq renders literally as *τὸ ἐξελθόν σου*, whereas Theod and Sym have *τὸν ῥύπον σου* "your filth."
21. Aq renders word for word: *τοῦ δοῦναι ἐχθρούς σου εἰς πρόσωπόν σου*, which Theod also has except for having *κατά* instead of *εἰς*. Sym has *δοῦναι τὸν ἐχθρόν σου καὶ ἔμπροσθέν σου (ἔσται οὖν)*, i.e. takes the prepositional phrase with what follows. The *καί* is admittedly surprising, and since the *καὶ ἔσται* of the next clause is changed to *ἔσται οὖν* it must be an error of transmission.
22. See SS 66.
23. See THGD 74.
24. See THGD 78.

lation of תסגיר Hi of סגר which means "to close up, shut up," but here the Hi is probably well-rendered by LXX.[25].

In the tradition *προστέθειταί* (*σοι*) "has added himself (to you)," i.e. has fled (to you), is changed by V *cI d*+ to *προστεθησεται*, but the future passive was hardly intended. The variant was probably palaeographically inspired.

23:16(17) The Greek text differs considerably from MT. Both texts begin with "With you he shall dwell." MT then continues with בקרבך for which LXX has *ἐν ὑμῖν* and then repeats the verb *κατοικήσει* which hex has correctly placed under the obelus. For MT's במקום LXX has *ἐν παντὶ τόπῳ*, i.e. has inserted "every"; as usual the word is put under the obelus in hex.

MT then continues with אשר יבחר באחד שעריך בטוב לו, but the Greek only has *οὗ ἂν ἀρέσῃ αὐτῷ*, i.e. omits יבחר באחד שעריך entirely. Hex has tried to repair this by adding under the asterisk after *τόπῳ*, *ου αν εκλεξηται εν μια των πυλων σου*, i.e. repeating the relative as though אשר was also missing. That this could not possibly be taken as LXX is clear from *πυλων*. LXX throughout renders שערי by *πόλεων*; see comment at 12:15.

What the Greek translator has done is to shorten the text considerably without substantially changing the message. The phrase "in one of your gates (cities)" is taken care of by making במקום "in every place," whereas "which he might choose" is really another way of saying *οὗ ἂν ἀρέσῃ αὐτῷ* (בטוב לו).

Such an escaped slave is not only to be allowed to live wherever he pleases, but this freedom is to be unhampered. "You may not afflict him," since he is a freedman, no longer a slave.

In the tradition the majority of witnesses read *εαν* for *ἄν*, but see comment at 5:27. And instead of *ἀρέσῃ* most witnesses including A F M read the present subjunctive *αρεσκη*. Either is possible, and so the oldest witness, cod B, was followed for the critical text.

23:17(18) LXX has a doublet translation for the Hebrew which forbids קדשה among the daughters of Israel, and קדש among the sons of Israel. The first translation is "Not shall there be a *πόρνη* among the daughters of Israel and not shall there be *πορνευών* among the sons of Israel. Throughout the verse

25. The Tar all use the root מסר "to deliver up, hand over. Theod and Aq, however, render the verb etymologically as *οὐ συγκλείσεις* (retroverted from Syh^{m}).

these nouns are modified by ἀπό phrases designating source, which I have rendered by "among."[26] The two terms mean female prostitute and male prostitute resp.[27] This is then repeated word for word but with *τελεσφόρος* in the first clause and with *τελισκόμενος* in the second. The entire doublet has been placed under the obelus in hex. The first term means "an initiate" and the second "one initiated." The translator was obviously not satisfied with a ban on prostitution; it was therefore connected with religion by means of the second rendering (possibly an allusion to mystery religions in which cult prostitution was practiced?). In other words, a *πόρνη* as *τελισφόρος* is a female cult prostitute, whereas a *πορνευών/τελισκόμενος* was a male who made use of such a prostitute. An A M *C'' b s+* gloss, *προς πασαν ευχην*, has been added at the end of the verse; for its source see v.18.

23:18(19) MT now refers to the female and male prostitutes as זונה "harlot" and כלב "dog," i.e. male prostitute; the two terms are rendered literally as *πόρνης* and *κυνός* resp. One may not bring a harlot's fee nor the price of a "dog" into the Lord's house *πρὸς πᾶσαν εὐχήν*, i.e. in the performance of a vow; the Byz text has added a *σου*, but this merely makes explicit what is already implicit. The Lord your God will not take "dirty money"! This is clear from the *ὅτι* clauses. Such money is not acceptable because "an abomination to the Lord your God are both." For *βδέλυγμα* see comment at 7:25. The *ἀμφότερα* refers to the *μίσθωμα* and the *ἄλλαγμα*, rather than to the *πόρνης* and *κυνός* as the neuter plural makes clear. This is a nominal clause in MT, and LXX adds *ἐστιν* for good sense; hex has dutifully placed the copula under the obelus.

It should be noted that vv.17 and 18 are not connected by conjunctions, except secondarily by the *b* text, which adds *και*; these are independent ordinances, even though both refer to people who promote and engage in illicit sexual relations. The references in v.18 are not necessarily to cult prostitutes as was the case in v.17.

---

26. See Bauer sub ἀπό IV.1.b.

27. Aq has translated קדשה by ἐνδιηλλαγμένη, which Schl defines as *immutatam quod meretrices vestem immutare solerent, ut vel ad prostibula vel ad constituta loca concederent.*

23:19(20) Vv.19—20 deal with money lending. V.19 forbids exacting any kind of interest from a fellow Israelite for money lent; comp Exod 22:25(24) for use of the term *τόκον*. Three types of *τόκον* are listed: *ἀργυρίου*, *βρωμάτων* and *παντὸς πράγματος οὗ ἂν ἐκδανείσῃς*, i.e. money, food or "anything which you might lend out." The relative *οὗ* is genitive singular by attraction to its antecedent *πράγματος*. The Hebrew word נשך probably refers to a form of return in which the interest was deducted from the capital loan in advance. The term is always translated by *τόκος* in LXX; this term refers to interest in general, i.e. that which a loan produces. MT's verbs derive from the root נשך. The Hi and the Qal are neatly distinguished in the Greek by *ἐκτοκιεῖς* "charge interest," and *ἐκδανείσῃς* "lend."

The Greek differs from MT in connecting all three cases of *τόκον* by a *καί*, whereas MT lacks a connective between the first two cases. The difference is a matter of style. For the popular *εαν* for *ἄν* see comment at 5:27. The Byz text has added the gloss *τω αδελφω σου* after *ἐκδανείσῃς*, an intrusion from the main clause.

23:20(21) An important distinction is made: you may exact interest from a stranger (i.e. a non-Israelite), but (*δέ*) not from your fellow-Israelite (*ἀδελφῷ*).[28] The *δέ* was popularly omitted erroneously, probably under the influence of *τῷ ἀδελφῷ σου* of v.19. It is appropriate as a contrastive conjunction, and is textually supported by a *waw* in MT.

The *ἵνα* clause which follows is intended to apply only to the prohibition "but of your fellow-Israelite you may not charge interest." It is "in order that the Lord your God may bless (i.e. prosper) you in all *ἔργοις σου* on the land." The Hebrew term משלח ידך also occurs at 12:7,18 15:10 28:8,20 where it is always rendered by *οὗ ἂν ἐπιβάλῃς τὴν χεῖρά σου* except at 12:7 where the plural obtains as *οὗ ἂν ἐπιβάλητε τὰς χεῖρας*; for the meaning of the structure see comment at 12:7. The Hebrew phrase does mean the undertaking (literally the sending forth) of your hand, which is what "your labors, words" interprets. For the *εἰς ἥν* clause modifying *γῆν*, see comment at 1:8.

28. Cf Lee 92—93.

23:21(22) Vv.21—23 deal with vows to the Lord your God. The initial *δέ* has no basis in MT, in contrast to the *δέ* of v.22 (for וכי), where it is expected,[29] but see comment at 15:16. Vows should be carried out without delay. The infinitive לשלם is rendered by *ἀποδοῦναι*, for which see also 7:10 (twice). Elsewhere this translation occurs in the Pentateuch only at Gen 44:4. The verb, when it occurs in the Pentateuch elsewhere (13 times in Exod and twice in Lev), is rendered by *ἀποτίνω*. Within Deut the verb also occurs at 32:45, but it is translated by *ἀνταποδώσω*.

The reason for this is given in the *ὅτι* clause; it is twofold: a) "the Lord your God will certainly require (it) of you." LXX has rendered the cognate free infinitive by a present participle, and it must be rendered in the sense of the parent text as placing stress on the verbal idea. Actually this sense is neatly communicated by the present participle plus a future cognate verb. Over against MT's ידרשנו LXX uses *ἐκζητήσει* absolutely, which is idiomatic in Greek; hex has provided *αυτην* to represent the suffix of the Hebrew verb; and b) "and it would be sin in you," i.e. you would incur guilt. The word *ἁμαρτία*, like its MT equivalent חטא, can mean "fault, sin" as well as "guilt" incurred by the sin. Here it must mean "guilt."

23:22(23) The *δέ* is properly contrastive: "but if you do not wish to vow." MT is somewhat different with its תחדל which is a more neutral concept; it means to fail, i.e. "but if you fail to vow"; thus if one did not make a vow, there will be no guilt. But *θέλῃς* involves the desire, the will;[30] it is unique in OT as a rendering for חדל. The point which the translator is making is that there is no compelling reason for making a vow in the first place; a vow is only made if one wishes to do so, and only if one has made such a voluntary promise is there an obligation to carry it out.

The apodosis reads *οὐκ ἔστιν σοι ἁμαρτία* "you have no guilt." MT, however, has the prefix inflection יהיה plus בך. It differs from the same statement in v.21 only in that והיה occurs there instead of יהיה; there it was the second reason why one should not delay paying one's vows to the Lord. A popular variant does read *εσται*, but this is probably influenced by v.21. And

29. But וכי is supported by Kenn 181.
30. Sym is also more neutral with *ἐὰν δὲ ἀπόσχῃ τοῦ εὔχεσθαι* (retroverted from Syh[m]).

over against MT (and v.21) LXX has no preposition for בך, but simply *σοι*, which 848 supports.[31] The addition of *εν* in the tradition is probably hex in origin.[32]

23:23(24) The preposed modifier, *τὰ ἐκπορευόμενα διὰ τῶν χειλέων σου*, renders the bound phrase מוצא שפתך, for which comp the similar phrase at 8:3.[33] The מוצא is of course understood as a collective, and its translation is excellent: "as for (the words) that go out through your lips," i.e. the things you say, *φυλάξῃ*, of these you must be careful.

What you must do is whatever *δόμα* you vowed to the Lord your God. The word *δόμα* simply means a gift, any kind of gift, but here it renders נדבה "a free will offering," which is normally translated by *ἑκούσιον*.[34] In fact, only at 2Chr 31:14 does *δόμα* translate נדבה elsewhere in OT; the reference there is to Kore who is in charge of the *δομάτων*, which are then detailed as *τὰς ἀπαρχάς* and *τὰ ἅγια τῶν ἁγίων*. The notion of gifts is not inappropriate, since a נדבה is of course a gift, i.e. the translation is not wrong; it is simply less specific. This *δόμα* is, however, not a spontaneous gesture; it is *ὃ ἐλάλησας τῷ στόματί σου*, i.e. it was promised as an *εὐχή*.

In the tradition only cod B represents the late Hellenistic lack of augmentation for the verb, *ευξω* instead of *ηὔξω*.[35]

23:24(26) This verse is transposed with the following one in MT, and hex has placed it after v.25 to equal MT. I can see no good reason for the transposition of these verses; v.24 refers to the grainfield, and v.25, to the vineyard, but the same principle is made mandatory for the two cases. Both verses start with *ἐὰν δέ*, even though both are asyndetic in MT; cf comment at 15:16. The word *ἀμητόν* usually means "harvesting, crop," but here it must mean the standing grain in the field, as does קמת in MT. Unusual is the translation of the suffix of רעך both in this verse and in v.25, since *πλησίον* is normally used absolutely without a genitive pronoun, but in these two verses *πλησίον σου* occurs three times.[36]

---

31. Theod and Aq read *ἔσται ἐν σοί*. Sym translates בך by *κατὰ σοῦ*.
32. See THGD 81.
33. See SS 69.
34. As it is by The Three.
35. See THGD 142.
36. See the discussion in THGD 77—78.

The apodosis is introduced by an apodotic *καί*, and consists of two parts: a) you may collect *στάχυς* with your hands;[37] *στάχυς* is here the accusative plural of *στάχυς* and means "ears or stalks of grain," and b) but "you may not cast the sickle (or scythe) on the standing grain of your neighbour."[38]

In the tradition the first case of *ἀμητόν* is articulated in a popular V text. There is, however, majority A B F M support for the anarthrous noun, and the popular variant is probably secondary, and due to the analogy of *τὸν ἀμητόν* in the last clause as well as of *τὸν ἀμπελῶνα* of v.25. Instead of *συλλέξεις* the A *b n* text has *συνάξεις*, which is a synonym, but here the weight of strong support is decisive for *συλλέξεις*. And hex has changed the word order of *ἐν ταῖς χερσίν σου στάχυς* to correspond to מלילת בידך of MT, while a popular M V variant has the more usual *σταχυας* as the accusative plural of *στάχυς*.

23:25 The principle of "eat as much as you like, but don't carry away the products of the land" is now applied to "your neighbour's vineyard." "You may eat grapes (*σταφυλήν* = cluster of grapes) — whatever would satisfy your person, but you may not put (them) into a pail (*ἄγγος*)."[39] MT has כליך, and the addition of *σου* by ms 767 and Syh is probably hex in origin.

Over against the pattern of v.24 the apodosis is asyndetic, i.e. in good Greek style, which contrasts with the ואכלת of MT. A popular Byz text has, however, added *και*, which is ultimately based on the Hebrew text. The *ὅσον* clause does meet the apparent intent of the difficult כנפשך שבעך; what it means is "as much as you like."[40]

---

37. Sym translates by *καὶ συντρίψεις τὰ θρύμματα ἐν τῇ χειρί σου* (retroverted from Syh[m]).
38. For *οὐ μὴ ἐπιβάλῃς* Theod has the future *οὐκ ἐπιβαλεῖς*, whereas Aq and Sym have *οὐκ ἐξαρεῖς*.
39. Aq has his usual *σκεύη* for כלי.
40. See SS Inf 154.

Chapter 24

24:1 Vv.1—3 constitute a complex protasis with v.4 as the apodosis. The protasis presents the case of a woman who is twice divorced. V.1 describes the circumstance of the first divorce, and it is the person who first divorces the woman who is the one to whom the law applies. The general condition is: Should someone take a wife and cohabit with her. LXX has included a conjunction *δέ* over against MT. In fact, all כי conditions in the chapter are asyndetic, whereas each one becomes *ἐὰν δέ* in LXX. For the general phenomenon of *ἐὰν δέ* for כי throughout this chapter, see comment at 15:16. Hex has reordered *τις λάβῃ* to agree with יקח איש of MT.

The specifics are: a) she finds no favor before him because he had found an *ἄσχημον πρᾶγμα* in her. Just what such a shameful thing was is not stated. The Hebrew has ערות דבר, for which see discussion at 23:14(15), where the same expression occurs, but is rendered somewhat differently. Whether the phrase refers to something sexual is not clear; it could hardly be unchastity, for which not divorce but death was decreed.[1] A popular A F M V text has the perfect *ευρηκεν* instead of the aorist, but the aorist is supported by the second century BCE fragment 957, and together with B+ must represent the original LXX. b) He would write for her a *βιβλίον ἀποστασίου* and put (it) into her hands. Neither MT nor LXX have "it." MT has the singular "her hand," which makes better sense, but in general LXX is not overly careful with the number of יד in ביד. "The document of separation" is a legal document which must actually be served by the husband on the wife. The Hebrew term is slightly different; a ספר כריתת means a document of cutting off or away.[2] and c) He would send her away out of his house. It appears that neither LXX nor MT spoke of any recourse which the wife might have!

Note that the three conditions following the *ὅτι* clause are all in the simple future as an interim apodosis, though the verse in its entirety is in turn part of the overall protasis, for which v.4 is the apodosis. This subpattern

1. See SS 33 and 66.
2. For Aq this is (*βιβλίον*) (*ἀπο*)*κοπῆς*, and Sym has *βιβλίον διακοπῆς*. Theod is more ruthless with his *βιβλίον ἐξολοθρεύσεως*; presumably the genitive noun refers to the marriage, thus "of annulment, annihilation."

within the protasis is repeated in v.3. The Byz text has confused the issue by its change of the third verb into an aorist subjunctive, *εξαποστειλη*; this is obviously wrong.

24:2 The next condition is that the rejected wife should marry another man. LXX has a shorter text than that of MT. MT had ended v.1 with מביתו, and then began v.2 with ויצאה מביתו, which the translator overlooked through homoioteleuton. That this shorter text is original is obvious, since it begins with a participle *καὶ ἀπελθοῦσα* for the clause והלכה. Hex has prefixed a translation of the omitted clause under the asterisk: *και εξελθη εξ οικιας αυτου*.

24:3 The third condition: the last husband would hate her, etc. (repeating *καὶ γράψει ... οἰκίας αὐτοῦ* from v.1; see comment ad loc). As in v.1 (*εὕρῃ*) the first verb is in the aorist subjunctive, and the paratactic clauses which follow are all in the future.[3] For the plural *τὰς χεῖρας* see comment at v.1. As in v.1 *δώσει* is used absolutely; an F M V popular gloss added *αυτη*, but this is an unthinking mistake, a doublet for the prepositional phrase, *εἰς τὰς χεῖρας αὐτῆς*, modifying the verb.

Alternatively, "the last husband who took her for himself as wife should die." MT repeats the כי particle after או, but LXX does not, it being quite unnecessary in Greek. In the tradition the majority F M V text adds *αυτης* after "the last husband"; this is not only otiose, it also has no support in MT. The reflexive pronoun *ἑαυτῷ* is idiomatic for לו with *ἔλαβεν αὐτήν*, and the B *C'' s*+ variant *αυτω* is secondary.

24:4 The apodosis: the former husband cannot remarry his former wife. The term for "her husband" in MT is now בעלה, but LXX retains *ὁ ἀνήρ*, and does not translate the pronominal suffix; the *C''* *b* text does add a secondary *αυτης*, but this only incidentally equals MT; it is hardly recensional. MT has successive marked infinitives in modification of יוכל, "able ... to return to take her to be (for him a wife)," i.e. able to take her again. LXX renders the first infinitive by a subordinate participle *ἐπαναστρέψας* modifying *ἀνήρ*,

3. For *βιβλίον ἀποστατίου* Aq, Sym and Theod translate as in v.1, which see.

which in turn is modified by the complementary infinitive *λαβεῖν*. LXX has no equivalent for להיות, and hex has added *του ειναι* after *λαβεῖν* to equal it.[4] The compound structure אחרי אשר is translated by *μετὰ τό* plus a passive verb "after she has been defiled,"[5] but MT has an odd form which seems to be a blend of a Hoph and a Hithp form, הטמאה, which I would interpret as a double reading, to be taken either as passive as per LXX, or reflexive as Hithp.[6] The point is that as far as the first husband is concerned, his former wife is now defiled by remarriage. Such a remarriage is by definition a *βδέλυγμα* before the Lord; for the term see comment at 7:25.

Unique in the OT is the interpretation of תחטיא "make sinful, guilty" by *μιανεῖτε*.[7] The plural agrees with the Sam text. Apparently the translator found the idea of making the land חטא peculiar—a land could hardly be such, but what one could do to the land was to defile it, render it unclean. For the *ἥν* clause see comment at 1:20. The clause is formulaic, and *σοι* must be original; the majority A F M V reading of the plural *υμιν* is a case of leveling with the plural verb *μιανεῖτε*.[8]

24:5 The collocation *τις λάβῃ* is transposed by hex to equal MT. Suppose that someone should take a wife *προσφάτως*; in MT the latter is an adjectival phrase, "a new wife."[9] LXX really says "should someone have recently taken a wife." He is therefore not to be drafted into the army according to MT; LXX interprets this by "he shall not go to war."

The next clause is peculiar in MT; it reads ולא יעבר עליו לכל דבר, probably meaning "not shall there pass over on him as regards anything," i.e. no assignments of any kind are to be given him for the army. LXX does quite well with this peculiar structure; *οὐδὲν πρᾶγμα* is made the subject of a passive verb, *ἐπιβληθήσεται*, plus a dative pronoun, thus "and not shall any matter (i.e. job, business) be put on him."[10]

4. See also SS Inf 60.
5. See SS Inf 130.
6. GK 54h is not an explanation, but a description.
7. see Daniel 309, footnote 34.
8. See THGD 112.
9. Aq has *καινήν*.
10. Kenn 18,129,181 read כל, which could be parent to LXX.

He shall go scot-free, i.e. be immune from public service of any kind, and remain in his home for one year. The final clause has a transitive verb according to the Masoretes, a Pi vocalization of שמח, thus "he shall gladden his wife whom he had taken";[11] LXX has also understood the verb as transitive.

24:6 The mill was in daily use for the preparation of food. Should it, or the upper millstone without which the mill could not function at all, be taken as security for a loan, meals could not be prepared. Their removal as pledge was forbidden because these would take *ψυχήν* in pledge. Here *ψυχήν* means the very person, one's life. The *ὅτι* clause is in the present tense, representing the Hebrew participle as predicate of a nominal clause.

24:7 ἁλῷ, an aorist subjunctive of *ἁλίσκομαι*, "be taken, caught," represents the Hi of מצא "find" correctly; someone is found stealing an individual *ἐκ τῶν ἀδελφῶν αὐτοῦ τῶν υἱῶν* Ἰσραήλ. MT repeats the preposition before "the Israelites," but this would be otiose in Greek, (and is really unnecessary in Hebrew as well). Then "having enslaved him he should sell (him)." The participle *καταδυναστεύσας* is used to translate התעמר, the meaning of which is unknown. It only occurs here and at 21:14 where it is also contextually translated; see comment ad loc.[12] LXX uses *ἀποδῶται* absolutely, since *αὐτόν* had already occurred with the participle. Hex, however, added *αυτον* under the asterisk to equal מכרו.

The apodosis is presented asyndetically, only *b* adding a *και* to equal MT. The penalty is "that thief shall die." The verse concludes with the *καὶ ἐξαρεῖς* formula, for which see comment at 13:5.[13] The majority A F M V text has changed the verb to the plural, thereby leveling the text with *ὑμῶν αὐτῶν*, but the formula throughout Deut reads the singular verb.[14]

---

11. Aq and Sym understood the verb as a Qal as their translation *καὶ εὐφρανθήσεται σὺν γυναικὶ αὐτοῦ* shows.
12. Tar^{ON} and Pesh read יתגר, while Tar^{J} has יעביד. Rashi interprets: אינו חיב עד שישתמש "he is not liable (for the death penalty) until he has placed him in servitude." Vulg renders the word by *vendito eo*.
13. Aq has the formula as *καὶ ἐπιλέξεις τὸν πονηρὸν ἐξ ἐγκάτου σου* (retroverted from Syh^{m}). How Theod and Sym rendered the verb is unclear from the tradition, but it seems likely that both retained LXX; see 21:21 for comparison.
14. As list 37 in THGD 96 makes clear.

24:8 LXX translates the Ni of שמר by *πρόσεχε σεαυτῷ*, but the Qal, by *φυλάξῃ/φυλάξεσθε*. In fact, in Deut the only exceptions to this are at 4:15 and 23:9, where the Ni is rendered by *φυλάσσω*. *πρόσεχε(τε)* plus an appropriate second person dative pronoun occurs 10 times for the Ni, and *φυλάσσω* for the Qal occurs 52 times.[15] The regulation concerns the plague of leprosy. That the נגע הצרעת was not actually leprosy is now recognized, but to the translator it was *ἁφῇ τῆς λέπρας*. For *φυλάξῃ σφόδρα ποιεῖν κατὰ πάντα* see 17:11, where the collocation also occurs, except for the tense of the infinitive. Here the present rather than the aorist infinitive is employed, possibly to stress the constancy of observance of the *νόμον*. LXX follows the text of Sam: לעשות ככל התורה rather than MT's ולעשות ככל.

The law is characterized as "one which *ἀναγγείλωσιν ὑμῖν* the Levitical priests." LXX follows MT in using the plural (second person) for the remainder of the verse. The choice of verb to render יורו may well have been influenced by 17:11, where the same expression is found though referring to *ῥήματος*. Only here is יורו ever rendered by *ἀναγγέλλω* in the Pentateuch; in fact, it only occurs elsewhere as such in free renderings at Job 27:11 Isa 2:3 28:9. The priests proclaim the law to you, rather than teach you, according to LXX. The last sentence renders MT word for word. In the tradition a popular B reading has the aorist imperative, *φυλαξασθε*, instead of the future *φυλάξεσθε*, but MT has the future.[16]

24:9 The isolate free infinitive is correctly understood as imperatival *μνήσθητι*. The translator interpreted it as singular, which, in view of the plural בצאתכם later in the verse, may well not have been so intended by the Hebrew writer; at least a plural is an equally valid translation. The *f*+ text does have the plural, but this is hardly recensional; it is simply a transcriptional error.

That LXX did not always translate the suffix of אלהיך is clear from the evidence of 848. That most witnesses add *σου* is not necessarily due to recensional activity; it is more likely due to the popularity of *ο θεος σου* in the book over against *ὁ θεός*.[17] For the tale of Mariam stricken with leprosy see Num ch.12.

---

15. The count is based on HR with (11b) corrected to (11a) for 24:8.
16. See also THGD 140.
17. The Three of course have added *σου*; see the discussion at THGD 76.

The genitive absolute is part of a locative construction ἐν τῇ ὁδῷ, and states when this took place.[18] The construction translates a prepositional phrase containing a bound infinitive, "at your going out from Egypt." The subject of the infinitive is plural, hence ὑμῶν in the Greek construction; this is inconsistent with the singular imperative, which introduces the verse, and is addressed to Israel as a people, but the translator (as well as MT) was not consistent in the use of number. Possibly the change to the plural is intentionally meant to refer to the exodus of the Israelites before they were constituted as a people at Mt. Horeb.

24:10 Vv.10—13 concern security against loan repayment. In MT the protasis uses the verb תשה Hi plus a cognate modifier משאת, but LXX translates the verb by the noun ὀφείλημα plus ᾖ, and משאת by another ὀφείλημα, which is somewhat confusing. Then מאומה becomes ὁτιοῦν τι; thus "Should there be a debt with the neighbour, whatever it be."[19] πλησίον is supported only by 848, all others having added σου, but the shorter text is now certainly original LXX.[20] B+ omits the δέ as well as τι, but neither is original.[21]

The apodosis forbids the creditor's entering the house of the debtor to collect the pledge. MT has לעבט עבטו; the Greek does not render the suffix—after all, it can only be the debtor's pledge—but hex has added αυτου to represent the suffix in MT.

24:11 Rather you must stand outside. The debtor is identified in MT simply as אשר אתה נשה בו "to whom you extended a loan," which LXX translated rather oddly by οὗ τὸ δάνειόν σού ἐστιν ἐν αὐτῷ "of whom your loan is with him," i.e. where you have your loan. This is a rather round about way of translating the Hebrew. The adverbial οὗ makes the clause refer to the ἔξω, with which the verse begins. Why the translator avoided his usual practice of translating the nominal pattern of pronoun plus participle by pronoun plus present tense verb is not clear, but at v.10 he also avoided using a verb to render the verb תשה, and rather used a verbal figure; see comment ad loc.

---

18. See SS 177 and SS Inf 90.
19. Sym has ἐὰν ἀπαιτήσῃς τὸν πλησίον σου ἀπαίτησιν ἡντιναοῦν (retroverted from Syh^m).
20. See the discussion in THGD 77—78.
21. See THGD 81.

It is the right of the debtor not to have the pledge seized, but rather for himself to bring it outside to his creditor.[22]

24:12 The initial *waw* is rendered by *δέ* to show contrast: "but if the man should be poor." The Hebrew has a nominal clause: "and if he is a poor man." LXX makes this into a verbal clause, omitting the pronominal subject,[23] and rendering the adjective by the verb *πένηται*.

The apodosis prohibits a creditor from going to sleep in the poor man's pledge. What this means is that the pledge given was a person's outer garment, which at night would do double duty as a coverlet. This is clear from v.13, where it is called *ἐν τῷ ἱματίῳ αὐτοῦ*, which became the source for the F V *C'' f s+* text, which substituted *ιματιω* for *ἐνεχύρῳ*.[24]

24:13 Positively stated: "you really must give back his pledge at sunset." MT has no equivalent for "his" in "his pledge," but has "to him the pledge." Accordingly hex has added *αυτω* after the verb to render the לו. Instead of *ἐνέχυρον* most witnesses read *ιματιον*, but that is due to the fact that in the next clause it is called *τῷ ἱματίῳ*. The cognate free infinitive becomes a cognate dative noun in LXX, hence my translation "you must actually give back." The Byz text has changed the dative noun to the cognate participle *αποδιδους*. The same text changed *περὶ* (*δυσμὰς ἡλίου*) to *πρός*. Either idiom is possible; at 16:6 *πρός* is used, and it recurs at Jos 10:27, but at Gen 15:12 *περί* obtains. In any event, this is idiomatic for כבוא השמש.[25] The strong support for *περί* is determinative here. I suppose *περί* suggests "around the time of," whereas *πρός* would simply mean "at."

The next two clauses, though paratactically presented, are the result of the creditor's humanitarian gesture: the debtor may sleep in his garment, and will bless you. The pledge is now identified as *τῷ ἱματίῳ* "his garment." [26]

---

22. Aq prefers to translate העבוט by *τὴν χρεοδοσίαν* "payment of debt."
23. See SS 81.
24. Theod retained the LXX text; Sym has *ἔχων τὸ ἐνέχυρον αὐτοῦ*, and Aq has *ἐν χρεοδοσίᾳ αὐτοῦ*.
25. See SS Inf 98.
26. Aq, however, still has *ἐν χρεοδοσίᾳ αὐτοῦ*, thus presupposing עבטו rather than שמלתו.

An even more important result will be "and there shall be *ἐλεημοσύνη* for you before the Lord your God." In MT this is צדקה, which is more commonly rendered by *δικαιοσύνη*,[27] but here it is the word for mercy, compassion, i.e. the translator understood the Hebrew word in the later sense of the word.[28] For a discussion of *ἐλεημοσύνη* for צדקה see the discussion at 6:25. In the tradition most witnesses have transposed *ἔσται σοι*, thereby agreeing with MT. I suspect that *σοι ἔσται* is actually original LXX, and that the B V *b t z*+ *εσται σοι* is a stylistic change to the more usual order. The whole point of the clause is that you will receive divine compassion; i.e. the Lord your God will smile on, be kind to you. The order gives proper stress to *σοι*, and it equals MT.

24:14 תעשק שכיר "oppress the wages" must mean "to cheat with respect to wages." LXX translates this by *ἀπαδικήσεις μισθόν* "deal with wages in unjust fashion." The A F M V majority text considerably simplified this by changing the verb to *αποστερησεις* "defraud, rob," but the more difficult *ἀπαδικήσεις* must be original.[29] In any event, it is clearly prohibited to deal in any crooked way with the wages of the poor and needy. And this applies to "fellow-Israelites as well as to the proselytes, who are in your cities." MT characterizes the proselytes as גרך אשר בארצך בשעריך. LXX has rightly taken גר to be a collective, and so rendered it by the plural *τῶν προσηλύτων*, thereby making a *σου* unnecessary; this also becomes otiose in view of the modifying clause *τῶν ἐν ταῖς πόλεσίν σου*. For *πόλεσιν* see comment at 12:15. LXX has, however, omitted בארצך probably due to homoiarchon, the next word beginning with the same consonant. Hex has inserted between *τῶν* and *ἐν* the phrase *εν τη γη σου*.

24:15 *αὐθημερόν* "immediately, on the very day" is an excellent rendering for ביומו.[30] So "on the selfsame day you must pay his wages." In fact, "not may the sun set over it"; i.e. you must pay before sundown. MT introduces this clause with a *waw*, which LXX omits as unnecessary, though the *waw* may

27. Aq makes it *δίκαιον*.
28. Lee 108 thinks that it means "kind deed," but this does not fit the context as well.
29. The Three all have *συκοφαντήσεις*, which renders תעשק more literally.
30. Much better than Aq's literalistic *ἐν ἡμέρᾳ αὐτοῦ*.

have been absent from the parent text by haplography after שכרו. LXX has the subject ὁ ἥλιος before the prepositional phrase ἐπ' αὐτῷ; hex transposes them to correspond to MT: עליו השמש. The antecedent of αὐτῷ is the same as that of αὐτοῦ; it is the poor laborer.

The ὅτι clause gives the rationale for immediate payment: "he is poor and he has ἐλπίδα in it," in other words, he depends on it, his expectations reside in his wages. MT has ואליו הוא נשא את נפשו. For this unusual use of נפש see the discussion at 21:14.[31] The Greek is a free rendering but does give the general sense of the clause.[32]

Furthermore, he might otherwise "complain against you to the Lord, and ἔσται ἐν σοὶ ἁμαρτία." The use of καταβοήσεται for יקרא is idiomatic Greek, but ἐν σοί is a literalism for בך. An M *C'*' *s*+ text omits ἐν, which is somewhat better Greek.[33]

24:16 LXX has ἀποθανοῦνται instead of the passive יומתו (twice).[34] The only difference is that MT presupposes execution: "shall be put to death," whereas LXX simply says "shall die." Deut insists on individual responsibility, a theme taken up at some length by Jer and Ezek.

In the last clause, the verb ἀποθανεῖται is singular over against יומתו in MT;[35] this makes better grammatical sense with ἕκαστος as subject. It is then modified by the prepositional phrase ἐν τῇ ἑαυτοῦ ἁμαρτίᾳ. Almost all witnesses omit ἐν, but it is original. Deut never uses a simple dative in modification of this verb in spite of MT's בחטאו.[36] For the meaning of ἁμαρτία see comment at 23:21.

24:17 MT lacks the equivalent for καὶ χήρας, which Origen noted by placing it under the obelus. The triad "proselyte and orphan and widow" is, however, a set pattern, and LXX throughout has all three.[37] One might note that MT has "proselyte orphan" in place of the triad, i.e. it has no conjunction joining the

31. See also Daniel 332.
32. See SS 87 and 102.
33. Theod and Aq retain ἐν σοί, but Sym improves on it by ἐπί σε.
34. As do Tar^{ON} and Pesh; Tar^{J} follows MT throughout.
35. As in Tar^{N} Pesh and Vulg.
36. See THGD 127.
37. See list 43 in THGD 97.

two.[38] One may not subvert the cause of the traditionally defenseless members of society. The specific application of this general principle is given in the second clause: "you may not take a widow's garment in pledge."

24:18 This verse is an exact copy of 15:15; see comments ad loc. It gives the basis for the protection demanded for the helpless members of Israelite society: you "were a house-slave in Egyptland, and the Lord your God ransomed you from there." In other words, you yourself were the helpless in society, hence the call to remember. LXX has *ἐν γῇ Αἰγύπτῳ*, but MT has במצרים; accordingly hex has placed *γῇ* under the obelus.[39] In the tradition the *f n*+ text reads *αιγυπτου* instead of *Αἰγύπτῳ*, but Deut never has the genitive after *ἐν γῇ*, but only the dative.[40] In the tradition hex has transposed *σοι ἐντέλλομαι* to equal the word order of MT.

24:19 Vv.19—22 order harvest time gleanings not to be taken, but rather to be left for the helpless in society to collect. The verse begins asyndetically in MT, but LXX, as throughout this ch., has *δέ* after *ἐάν*. Its omission in the A M F V majority text is probably due to the new section, which obviously begins with v.19. The condition in v.19 has two parts: *ἀμήσῃς ἀμητόν*[41] *ἐν τῷ ἀγρῷ σου* and *ἐπιλάθῃ δράγμα ἐν τῷ ἀγρῷ σου*. Hex has added *σου* after *ἀμητόν* to equal MT's קצירך.[42] The second condition is that you should forget a *δράγμα* for עמר "sheaf."[43] The prepositional phrase modifying it is the same as that modifying the first condition in LXX, though MT lacks a suffix: בשדה.

The regulation forbids returning to gather *τὰ ὀπίσω σου*, i.e. the overlooked sheaves. The gleanings are for the proselyte *καί* the orphan and the widow. MT lacks the conjunction before "the orphan"[44] The majority text added *τω πτωχω και* before *τῷ προσηλύτῳ*, but this is due to the influence of the parallel injunction at Lev 23:22. That it is secondary here is clear from the

38. But Kenn 17,181 Tar^{JN} Pesh and Vulg all support the conjunction.
39. The text is not certain; Kenn 17,181 and MT at 15:15 do read בארץ מצרים, as does Tar^{J}.
40. See THGD 137.
41. Aq uses *θερίσῃς θερισμόν* to translate תקצר קציר.
42. See SS 102.
43. Aq uses a rare word *οὖλον* with the same meaning; see LS sub *οὖλος*(D).
44. But Kenn 80* 109 do read וליתום, and this is presupposed by Pesh Vulg as well. See also THGD 81.

support for the shorter text by B and 848, as well as by MT.[45] For the *ἵνα* clause see comments at 14:28(29). MT has the singular כל מעשה, which LXX rendered by *πᾶσιν τοῖς ἔργοις*. In the tradition the *O* Byz text has changed to the singular *παντι εργω*; this may well be recensional.

24:20 A similar regulation obtains for the olive harvest. MT's regulation has "when you beat down your olives לא תפאר after you." The verb is usually taken to be a denominative form from a word for "boughs," so presumably "to shake the branches," i.e. go over them again. LXX interprets freely but sensibly by "if you should gather olives (*ἐλαιολογήσῃς*), you may not return to glean what was left behind (you)."[46] LXX took זית in the sense of "olives" rather an "olive tree," and made it part of the protasis.[47] In the tradition a popular variant for *ἐλαιολογήσῃς* changed the first element to *ελαια-*, which can hardly be correct; one can gather olives, but not olive trees.[48]

As in v.19 *τῷ προσηλύτῳ* is preceded by *τω πτωχω και* in *f n t+*, for which see Lev 19:10. Also over against MT's ליתום, LXX has a conjunction: *καὶ τῷ ὀρφανῷ*.[49]

LXX ends with two clauses, which are taken over word for word from v.22; see comment ad loc. These were omitted, however, by *O* and Byz, obviously under the influence of the Hebrew, which lacks both clauses. The clauses are, however, original LXX; at least they were already present in 848. For the first clause, which also occurs in v.18, see comment at 5:15. The *διὰ τοῦτο* clause at the end also occurs in exactly the same form at v.18.[50]

24:21 The same rule applies to vineyards. When you harvest your vineyard, *οὐκ ἐπανατρυγήσεις αὐτὸν τὰ ὀπίσω σου*, which I would translate: "not may

45. See THGD 81.
46. Aq's literalism led him to a highly peculiar rendering: (*ἐὰν*) *ῥαβδίσῃς ἐλαίαν σου οὐ στεφανώσεις* "(if) you should beat down your olive tree, you may not crown (or decorate)." Aq misunderstood תפאר as being the well-known verb פאר "to glory, honor." To Aq it was more important to give an equivalent for a Hebrew word than to make sense!
47. Both Theod and Sym read it with the apodosis. Theod read *ἐλαίαν σου καλαμήσῃ*, and Sym had *τὴν ἐλαίαν σου οὐ τρυγήσεις* "not shall you gather from your olive tree."
48. See THGD 138—139.
49. But Kenn 80* 109 170 do read וליתום.
50. See also S Inf 141.

you second-harvest it as to that which remained." The verb occurs only here and in Lev 19:10, and was probably coined by the Lev translator specifically to designate "reharvesting" for this context.[51] MT has no equivalent for *αὐτόν*, and a popular A F M V text omits it; this is unlikely to be due to Hebrew influence, but it is rather a stylistic improvement (thereby voiding a double accusative modifier). For the second clause see vv.18,20.

24:22 The verse consists of two clauses, both of which are found in exactly the same form in v.18; see comments ad loc. Hex has reordered *σοι ἐντέλλομαι* to agree with MT.

---

51. Theod and Aq translate תבצר by *ἐπιφυλλίσεις* (or -λλιεῖς) "you will glean grapes," whereas Sym has *ἀρεῖς τὰς ἐπιφυλλίδας*.

Chapter 25

25:1 All the verbs in the verse are in the subjunctive mood, since they are part of a general protasis, which is presupposed by the more specific condition of v.2. Good sense tells us that the subject changes with *κρίνωσιν*, though there is no indication of it in the text; it was the *ἀνθρώπων* who *προσέλθωσιν*, but with the next three verbs they are the objects of the verbal activity. This is clearer in MT, where the first of these three verbs has a pronominal suffix ושפטום; LXX does not translate this, but hex has added *αυτους* under the asterisk to render it. The understood, though unstated, subjects are the judges, presumably the elders at the gate, who traditionally assumed the role of judges in the case of a dispute—*ἀντιλογία*; see comments at v.2.

The three verbs are all paratactically presented in imitation of MT, though clearly the last two clauses are in apposition to *καὶ κρίνωσιν*, i.e. the judging consists of *δικαίωσιν τὸν δίκαιον* "declaring innocent the one in the right" and *καταγνῶσιν τοῦ ἀσεβούς* "condemning the guilty one (literally the impious one)." The Hebrew has והרשיעו את הרשע "and they declare wicked the wicked one."

25:2 For *ἔσται ἐάν* see comment at 6:10—11. The protasis pertains specifically to הרשע, which is now translated by *ὁ ἀσεβῆς*, though most witnesses have *ο ασεβων*, which is a synonym. But *ἀσεβῆς* was chosen on the basis of support by 957, a second century BCE fragmentary text. The impulse towards *ασεβων* was undoubtedly stimulated by its occurrence (*τοῦ ἀσεβοῦς*) in v.1. The predicate is *ἄξιος ᾖ πληγῶν* "be worthy of beatings," which is a good interpretation of the idiom בן הכות.[1]

The apodosis is introduced by *καί*; its omission by B Byz is a secondary stylistic improvement. The Hebrew text is not at all lucid, since it says "and the judge shall make him lie down והכהו לפניו." This only makes sense if one assumes that the subject changes for הכהו, i.e. "and one shall flog him before him (i.e. in his presence)." LXX has changed this considerably. It has changed והפילו to second person singular "(and) you shall make him lie down," and

1. See also SS Inf 26.

then substituted ἔναντι τῶν κριτῶν for השופט . The reasoning underlying these changes probably involved the fact that, though the Hebrew presupposes one judge, a judgment of this sort should presuppose a consensus of legal opinion. Furthermore, the Hebrew seems to say that "the judge" shall make him fall and flog him, but throughout the preceding verses the second singular has been used. Note two verses earlier: "remember ... that you were ... I am commanding you," and so LXX continues here with καθιεῖς;[2] comp also comment at v.1. The changes are both contextually and exegetically driven.

The translator deliberately changed the law so as to differentiate carefully between those who impose the sentence: κρίνωσιν ... καταγνῶσιν (which verbs presuppose κριτῶν, not the singular שופט) and those who carry out the sentence. LXX accordingly changed והכהו to a plural verb as well, μαστιγώσουσιν αὐτόν, and realized לפניו as ἐναντίον αὐτῶν, i.e. before the judges, all of which is sensible, having removed all the ambiguities, though it does not represent MT's text.

This is all to be done κατὰ τὴν ἀσέβειαν αὐτοῦ "according to his impiety." This renders MT's כדי רשעתו "according to the sufficiency of his wickedness," i.e. as much as his wickedness warrants.[3]

25:3 The first word of LXX, ἀριθμῷ, represents the last word of v.2 in MT, במספר, but in the Greek it belongs with the next word τεσσαράκοντα, which modifies μαστιγώσουσιν αὐτόν.[4] By leaving במספר as part of v.2, MT presumably leaves indefinite the number of lashes to be applied (i.e. proportionate to the severity of the offence), and then in v.3a makes an absolute statement on the upper limit of lashes which may be applied in any case. The Greek naturally continues with the plurals for the carrying out of the punishment, whereas MT carries on with singulars; see comments at v.2. The number refers to the number of lashes which may be administered, to which is added οὐ προσθήσουσιν, i.e. they may not exceed (i.e. the number).

V.3b begins with פן in MT and it governs the rest of the verse; LXX changes this to a separate condition in which ἐάν ... πλείους is the protasis,

2. Aq rendered literalistically by πτωματίσει "shall make him fall."
3. Aq translates כדי by πρὸς ἀρκετόν "according to sufficiency," a literalism which is not overly illuminating; the lemma in the second apparatus of the edition should include only κατά!
4. Prijs 100—101 speaks of enjambment, but I suspect there is more to it.

and the remainder of the verse, the apodosis. This does not change the "lest" notion; rather it explicates it by means of a separate condition. The protasis also changes the Hebrew somewhat. MT has "(lest) one should flog him beyond these מכה רבה," i.e. with more flogging. LXX simplifies this with "Should they flog him more than (or beyond) these complete floggings." The πλείους means "full, complete," and refers to the forty. What it means is "should they flog him beyond the maximum number allowed."

The apodosis is given without an apodotic και over against MT, which has ונקלה. The Greek ἀσχημονήσει "shall be dishonored, disgraced" is exactly correct. The one punished is called ὁ ἀδελφός σου, and means "your fellow-Israelite." Such a disgrace is particularly shameful, since it occurs in your presence, ἐναντίον σου.

25:4 LXX uses an attributive participle ἀλοῶντα to render the prepositional phrase בדישו, "in its threshing," i.e. a preposition plus bound infinitive plus suffix. The rendering "a threshing ox" is a fine translation.

25:5 Vv.5—10 regulate the levirate marriage. For a practical example of the principle of the levirate, see Gen 38. The protasis gives the conditions under which the levirate applies, viz. brothers are dwelling together, and one of them dies, but leaves no offspring. The Greek uses the tenses accurately with the first verb being a present subjunctive—"they were living together," but the second one, ἀποθάνῃ, is an aorist, since death is seen as an event rather than a process. The third condition is expressed nominally in MT, with בן as subject and אין לו as predicate. To bring this under the ἐάν clause the translator used ᾖ, i.e. he created a verbal clause with the subjunctive of εἰμί.

The apodosis is not introduced by a conjunction in either MT or LXX. The widow may not be married ἔξω, i.e. "to a man not a near relative." MT has לאיש זר "to a strange man." The interpretation ἀνδρὶ μὴ ἐγγίζοντι identifies the זר as someone not in the immediate family circle. The translator probably used this free rendering to focus attention on the only relative who was a candidate for the levirate, namely the brother.[5]

It is the brother-in-law who "must go in to her and take her to himself as wife and have sexual relations with her." LXX defines the יבם as ὁ ἀδελφὸς

5. The Three follow the Hebrew closely with ἀνδρὶ ἀλλοτρίῳ.

τοῦ ἀνδρὸς αὐτῆς.[6] The translator has also interpreted the cognate verb יבמה by *συνοικήσει αὐτῇ*, i.e. not literally as "he shall perform the levirate duties for her," but by what it involves; he must live with her, i.e. have relations with her, as the next verse makes clear.[7]

In the tradition *αὐτῶν*, which is supported by only three mss, B 848 and 29, appears in all other witnesses as *εξ αυτων*, which equals the מהם of MT. One suspects this to be an early correction based on the Hebrew text, but in view of the united support of B and 848, not original LXX. The 376′ *C′*' variant adding *εις* before *γυναικα* does equal the לאשה of MT; this could, in view of its support by 376′ (as representing the *O* group), be hex in origin, though *εις γυναικα* is common in the context of "take someone as wife," and it could simply be ex par.

25:6 The *ἔσται* is otiose, since the main verbal idea is *κατασταθήσεται*, but it does equal MT. The subject in MT is הבכור אשר תלד but LXX has *τὸ παιδίον ὃ ἂν τέκῃ*. It should be noted that Sam reads הבן before הבכור, which the Byz text supports with its *το παιδιον το πρωτοτοκον*.[8] LXX then translates יקום על by *κατασταθήσεται ἐκ* "shall be established from," which is an idiomatic rendering of the Hebrew, the point being that the child (the firstborn in MT) shall be reckoned as belonging to the dead brother, i.e. he will be considered the son of the first husband. LXX shortens the *ἐκ* phrase by disregarding אחיו, simply reading *ἐκ τοῦ ὀνόματος τοῦ τετελευτηκότος*. Hex has added *του αδελφου αυτου* between the two nominals under the asterisk.[9] The shorter text of course also refers to his (deceased) brother.

The raison d'etre for the levirate becomes clear from the last clause "and not shall his name be wiped out from Israel." In the tradition the middle form *τέκῃ* becomes the passive *τεχθῃ* in most witnesses, but LXX is supported by B and 848, and must be original.[10]

---

6. Aq translates the word here and in v.7 by *ὁ ἐπιγαμβρευτής*. The word occurs only here. For the verb from which it was created see Note at Gen 34:9.
7. Aq of course now uses the verb *ἐπιγαμβρεύσει*.
8. Aq equals MT with *τὸ πρωτότοκον ὃ τέξεται* (retroverted from Syh^{m}); Sym has the same verb as LXX.
9. As do The Three, who, however, also change the last nominal to *τοῦ τεθνηκότος*.
10. See THGD 74.

25:7 But suppose the brother does not want to perform the levirate for his dead brother. This is triply expressed in Hebrew: לא יחפץ, מאן and by לא אבה. LXX renders the first by *μὴ βούλεται*, but then uses the same verb for the next two: *οὐ θέλει* and *οὐκ ἠθέλησεν*, showing thereby that for the translator מאן is simply the negative of אבה.

The apodosis has the sister-in-law as subject who is simply called *ἡ γυνή*, having already been identified as being *τὴν γυναῖκα τοῦ ἀδελφοῦ αὐτοῦ*. Hex of course added *του αδελφου αυτου* under the asterisk, so as to equal MT more precisely.

She is to go up to the gate to the *γερουσίαν*. The gerousia was the judicial court for settling disputes, and met in the square inside the city gates. It was in this setting that she was to announce: "my brother-in-law does not wish to set up the name of his brother in Israel; my brother-in-law did not wish (i.e. to do so)." MT made no tense distinction between the two clauses, but used מאן "he refused" in the first clause, and then used לא אבה "he did not want to" absolutely, which is tautological. LXX tried to make sense of this tautology by using the present, *θέλει*, for the first one, and the aorist, *ἠθέλησεν*, for the second.

It might also be observed that LXX changed the modifier of *ἀναστῆσαι* over against the Hebrew. MT has "to raise up לאחיו שם," i.e. to his brother a name, but LXX stylized this with *τὸ ὄνομα τοῦ ἀδελφοῦ αὐτοῦ*, thereby voiding the indefiniteness of שם "a name." It will also be seen that throughout this account יבמה/יבם are realized not by a single nominal in LXX but by a nominal phrase: the brother of (my) husband/ the wife of (his) brother.[11] For *γερουσίαν* translating זקנים see discussion at 19:12.

25:8 The court proceedings: "The gerousia of his city shall summon him and say to him." The verb *ερουσιν* is used absolutely, i.e. it is not said what "they shall say to him," but presumably the elders are to interrogate the man as to his intentions. Most witnesses contextualize "of his city as *της πολεως εκεινης*, but the *αὐτοῦ* is original as the joint support of B and 848 makes likely; furthermore, MT has עירו.

11. Not so, however, in Aq who used *ἐπὶ γαμβρευτῆς μου*. See the footnotes in vv.5 and 9.

The response is introduced in MT by ועמד ואמר which LXX interprets as *καὶ στὰς εἴπῃ*, i.e. not by future verbs but by a subordinate participle and a subjunctive verb, both properly aorist. By *στάς* "standing up" the man makes it public, so "publicly (or openly) he would say." The conditional notion is nicely noted by LXX's subjunctive verb, i.e. it is not incumbent on the man to make the declaration, but should he make it, then the procedure outlined in v.9 takes place, and the levirate is not executed. The declaration is his renunciation "I do not wish to take her," by which the stative nature of חפצתי is shown by a present tense *βούλομαι*.

25:9 The widow now performs the rite of renunciation, by which the brother-in-law is released from the levirate, but through a public humiliation.[12] LXX subordinates the first verb נגשה to a participle, *προσελθοῦσα*, but then still retains the *καί* before the main verb *ὑπολύσει*. It should occasion no surprise that a popular variant omits the Hebraic *καί*.[13] The verb נגשה in MT is modified by two prepositional phrases אליו and לעיני הזקנים, but LXX omits the first one which is somewhat harsh, although the majority of witnesses do add *προς αυτον*. There is no obvious reason why copyists would omit such a phrase, whereas the impulse to add such is understandable. Furthermore, B and 848 both support the shorter text, which must be judged original.

The ritual consists of three parts: a) "she shall unloose his one sandal from his foot." The *αὐτοῦ* throughout the verse refers to the remaining brother, which of course good sense dictates. MT speaks of removing, חלצה, his sandal, though unloosing it, such as untying the straps from the sandal, would have the same effect. LXX specifies *τὸ ἕν*, i.e. the one (sandal); this has no counterpart in MT, though it is obvious from the singular of both "sandal" and "foot" that only one could be involved. Hex accordingly put *τὸ ἕν* under the obelus. For an actual case of removing the sandal and giving it to another to attest transfer of property, see Ruth 4:7—10. b) "And she shall spit in his face" constituted an act of scorn, which the brother-in-law had to undergo. The *C*ʾ *n s*+ text has *εμπτυσει* instead of *ἐμπτύσεται*, but both forms are attested as future inflections of *πτύσσω*. c) her public proclamation

12. Aq substitutes for "the wife of (his) brother" *ἡ ἐπιγαμβρευτής* (retroverted from Syh).
13. See THGD 74.

of her brother-in-law's refusal: "so shall they do to the man who will not build up the house of his brother." This is introduced by *καὶ ἀποκριθεῖσα ἐρεῖ*. In the tradition the F *d f*+ text has omitted the *ἀποκριθεῖσα* as a stylistic improvement, but the word is fitting as indicating a response to the man's declaration made in v.8; furthermore, MT requires it.[14] LXX's use of the indefinite plural *ποιήσουσιν* is a good interpretation of the Ni יעשה.

25:10 The section is concluded by stating the epithet by which he will be known from then on: "the house (i.e. the family or sept) of the one who had the sandal loosened." MT has a bound phrase חלוץ הנעל in which the free element corresponds to an objective genitive in Greek. This was clear to the translator who made the free element into an accusative *τὸ ὑπόδημα* modifying the genitive *τοῦ ὑπολυθέντος*.[15]

25:11 Vv.11 and 12 constitute a regulation applying the lex talionis, with v.11 as the protasis, and v.12 as the apodosis. The situation obtaining is that of persons fighting together, a man with his fellow. The fighting is described as *ἄνθρωποι ἐπὶ τὸ αὐτό*.[16] Most witnesses designate the "men" as *δυο*; this has no Hebrew equivalent, nor is it necessary, since this is obvious. In the course of the struggle "*ἡ γυνὴ ἑνὸς αὐτῶν* might come near to save her husband from the hand of the one beating him." MT simply reads "the wife of האחד," and hex has accordingly placed *αὐτῶν* under the obelus. In the tradition B F M V *O n z*+ omit the article before *γυνή*, but the preceding word is *προσέλθῃ* and the omission is a case of haplography.[17] Since *ἑνός* is modified by *αὐτῶν* it is not articulated; its articulation in MT is made up for by the pronoun.

What is objectionable is not that a wife should help her husband, but rather the way in which she does it: *ἐκτείνασα τὴν χεῖρα ἐπιλάβηται τῶν διδύμων αὐτοῦ*. LXX does not translate the suffix of ידה, since it is obviously her hand, not someone else's, that she extends;[18] hex, however, does add

14. See THGD 74.
15. For Aq the participle in LXX was not an accurate rendering of חלוץ and it required *ἐξαιρεθέντος* "removed."
16. The Three all use *ἄνδρες* instead of *ἄνθρωποι*. Theod retains *ἐπὶ τὸ αὐτό*, whereas Aq has his usual rendering of יחדו *ὁμοῦ*, and Sym has the freer but more idiomatic *πρὸς ἀλλήλους*.
17. See THGD 103.
18. See SS 101.

αυτης to represent the suffix. The Hebrew word for "his testacles" is מבשיו which is a hapax legomenon, but its meaning is clear; an instrumental *mem* prefix to the root בוש would produce an instrument of shame.[19]

25:12 The apodosis is introduced by a *waw* in MT, but LXX improves the text by an asyndetic construction. The penalty for the woman's immodest behaviour is severe: "you must chop off her hand," which constitutes an application of the lex talionis. The penalty must be exacted: *οὐ φείσεται ὁ ὀφθαλμός σου ἐπ' αὐτῇ*. The prepositional phrase has no equivalent in MT nor in 19:21. Normally the verb חום is modified by an על phrase, and when it is used absolutely it is, except for these two cases, always paralleled by another absolute clause, ולא (א)חמול, or as in Ezek 24:14 by ולא אנחם. The translator both here and at 19:21 must have been swayed by his knowledge of Hebrew usage. In the tradition the dative becomes *αυτην* in *O*, and *αυτης*, in *C'' s*+, but the rarer dative is original.

25:13 Vv.13—16 detail a demand for accurate weights and measures. V.13 deals with weights, which MT calls "stones"; these you may not have in your bag. These stones are correctly called *στάθμιον*, which is a weight used on balance scales. What is prohibited is *στάθμιον καὶ στάθμιον*, i.e. two kinds of weights, a heavy one for buying, and a lighter one for selling, or as LXX has it *μέγα ἢ μικρόν*. MT uses the more logical *waw* as conjunction.[20] In the time of the writer stones were used for determining weights; by the time of the Alexandrian translator not only stones, but cast metal weights were also used, especially among the wealthier merchants, hence the indefinite *στάθμιον*. In the tradition *oII C'' s*+ have *και* instead of *ἤ*, which does equal MT, though the variant is hardly recensional. It might be noted that Cod B and Eth add *σοι* after *ἔσται*; this equals the לך of MT, its source is hardly hex, but it is probably ex par; for the idiom *ἔσται σοι* for "you shall have," see 15:17 23:12,13 and comp 15:3.

25:14 Parallel to v.13 is the regulation on measures. The standard measure was the ephah, which roughly equals a half bushel, or cir 18 liters. One may

19. Aq etymologizes with *ἐν* for the preposition ב and the noun as *αἰσχύναις*.
20. Theod and Aq translate אבן ואבן literally as *λίθος καὶ λίθος*.

not have two ephahs of different sizes in the house, one large, and the other smaller, which is what MT also says. The Hebrew "ephah and ephah" is then translated by LXX as *μέτρον καὶ μέτρον*. As in v.13 a general term is used, since it is the principle, not the particular measure, that is of importance.[21] As in v.13, *ἤ* is changed to *και* in the tradition; in fact, it became the majority reading, but, as in v.13, the more difficult text of B is probably original. For the failure to render לך, and the variant gloss in ms 426 Eth, see comment at v.13.

25:15 Both the weights and the measures must be *ἀληθινὸν καὶ δίκαιον* "accurate and just." The first term translates שלמה which means "complete,"[22] and with וצדק might well be translated by "completely honest" as in NJPS. The LXX adjectives probably distinguish the two as "true" as to an agreed-on standard, thus "accurate," whereas *δίκαιον* is intended as "honest, just," i.e. one that is beyond criticism. The two clauses are connected by *καί*, whereas the two are asyndetic in MT.

For the *ἵνα* clause see comment at 4:40. MT's יאריכו ימיך "your days may be long" is neatly rendered by *πολυήμερος γένῃ* an accurate interpretation of the Hebrew.[23] For the relative clause see comment at 1:20. Over against MT the Greek adds *ἐν κλήρῳ* at the end, and so it is placed under the obelus by hex to show that it has no MT equivalent. It is, however, often part of this popular formula (ten times in the book) and it is ex par.

25:16 For *βδέλυγμα* see comment at 7:25. The free element in the bound phrase is rendered by a dative *κυρίῳ*.[24] BHS adds אלהיך, which LXX does not represent.[25] 848 and Philo are the only Greek witnesses to the shorter text, all the others adding *τω θεω σου*.[26] The subject is doubly stated: *πᾶς ποιῶν ταῦτα* in which *ταῦτα* refers to *στάθμιον* and *μέτρον* which are not accurate and just.

21. Aq sticks to *ἠφὰ καὶ ἠφά*. The Hebrew term obviously had no exact Greek equivalent in Aq's time, hence the transliteration.
22. Aq translates the word by *ἀπηρτισμένον* which means "completed."
23. SS 102 calls it a free translation as well as an example of the Greek disregarding the suffix; the latter is hardly accurate since *γένῃ* is second person singular.
24. See SS 68.
25. But Kenn 9,80,111,150,177,199 also omit אלהיך.
26. See THGD 76—77.

And secondly, it is also defined as πᾶς ποιῶν ἄδικον, "anyone doing something that was not right," i.e. anyone acting dishonestly. In the tradition 848 supports the popular change to the plural αδικα, but this probably became plural by attraction to ταῦτα; the reverse, i.e. from plural to singular, would be highly unlikely.[27]

25:17 Vv.17—19 constitute instructions to exterminate Amalek in due course. For μνήσθητι ὅσα ἐποίησεν, see 24:9 and comment ad loc. "What Amalek did to you on the way" reflects the event described in Exod 17:8—16, where Amalek made an apparently unprovoked attack on Israel at Raphidin, an event which evoked the divine intent to destroy Amalek completely from the face of the earth (v.14).

This is temporally defined by a genitive absolute construction: "as you (singular) were coming out of the land of Egypt." The Hebrew text is also temporal: a preposition plus a bound infinitive plus pronominal subject, though the pronoun is in the plural, בצאתכם. It should be noted that the next word is ממצרים, i.e. there are three *mems* in a row. Either MT is the result of dittography, or LXX, of haplography. Since the context is thoroughly singular throughout one suspects that LXX represents the earlier text. A popular Byz reading has a plural construction: εκπορευομενων υμων, which may well be recensional in origin. But LXX has ἐκ γῆς Αἰγύπτου. Here only B and 848 (and Eth) witness to γῆς, all others having εξ αιγυπτου, which represents MT. The two phrases are practically interchangeable, and in view of the joint support of B 848, the longer text is probably original.[28]

25:18 For אשר קרך "that he met you" is nicely interpreted by πῶς ἀντέστη σοι "how he withstood you"; this is contextually appropriate in view of what follows.

In MT the next clause is particularly difficult in that the verb ויזנב only occurs once elsewhere (at Jos 10:19, where with reference to "your enemies" Israel is told וזנבתם אותם, which LXX translates by καὶ καταλάβετε τὴν οὐραγίαν αὐτῶν). It seems to be a denominative from the noun זנב "tail." LXX confirms this with its καὶ ἔκοψέν σου τὴν οὐραγίαν "and he cut off your

27. See THGD 66.
28. See THGD 82.

tail," i.e. your rear guard. In MT the verb is modified by כל הנחשלים אחריך. The participle is a hapax legomenon and one can only guess at the meaning. Contextually it must refer to all those who tagged along behind, i.e. the stragglers. The translator contextualized, not on the basis of the verb זנב, but on what followed in the next (nominal) clause, and so interpreted as *τοὺς κοπιῶντας ὀπίσω σου*. Hex has added a *παντας* under the asterisk before *τούς* to render the untranslated כל. So to the Greek the *οὐραγίαν* or rearguard consisted of those who were worn out.[29]

The next clause in MT is nominal, with the pronoun אתה as subject, and the coordinate verbal adjectives עיף ויגע "faint and weary" as predicate. The two adjectives are synonymous. LXX interprets the first one as *ἐπείνας* "you were hungry," and the second one literally by *ἐκοπίας* "you were weary."[30] The use of the imperfect is normal for this translator, who understood the verbal adjectives to be analagous to participial predicates. The clause is nicely introduced by a *δέ* structure showing contrast.[31]

This might have been a plausible structure for the last clause as well, since the subject changes to "Amalek," who "did not fear God," but it has *καί*. The change by cod A of *τὸν θεόν* to *τον κυριον* is obviously secondary; the tetragrammaton would have required an unarticulated *κυριον*.

25:19 For *καὶ ἔσται* plus *ἡνίκα* see comment at 6:10—11.[32] The pronominal modifier *σε* is set immediately after the verb, which is common practice in Deut. Hex transposed it after the subject ,"the Lord your God," to equal the word order of MT. The relative clause is introduced by a dative pronoun *ᾗ*, dative by attraction to its antecedent *γῇ*. For the clause in general see comment at 1:20. For *ἐν κλήρῳ κατακληρονομῆσαι* see comment at 15:4.

The apodosis has two parts: a) "you must wipe out the name of Amalek from under heaven"; b) "and do not forget." Actually the Masoretes make the first cut in the verse between these two, which, though unexpected, is possible in MT, since both parts are asyndetic; thus "do not forget" is part two of the verse. The translator did not take it in that way, since he has added *καί* before

---

29. Aq interprets with *ἀπορρέοντας* (retroverted from Syh^{m}) "those fallen off, away," thus the stragglers.
30. Sym has *παρειμένος ἐγένου* (retroverted from Syh^{m}) "you were weakened."
31. See SS 81.
32. See also SS Inf 86.

οὐ μὴ ἐπιλάθῃ. In the a) part LXX used *ὄνομα* for the Hebrew זכר "memory." In the psychology of the Greek the name is that which concretizes memory.[33] If the name is forgotten, the person or tribe is forgotten. All trace of Amalek will be erased from under heaven, if ever the name is lost.

In the tradition certain corrections have been made to bring the text into line with MT. The Hebrew describes your enemies as מסביב, whereas LXX has *τῶν κύκλῳ σου*, but the *σου* has no counterpart in MT, and a popular F M V text (which includes *O*′⁾ Syh) omitted it, probably under Hebrew influence. By contrast לרשתה is rendered by *κατακληρονομῆσαι*, to which the popular hex text has added *αυτην*, so as to equal the suffix. The Byz text has articulated ᾿Αμαλέκ with a genitive article *του*; this serves to ensure that the proper name not be taken as in apposition to *ὄνομα*, but rather as its genitive. On the other hand, the name of Amalek is modified by *ἐκ τῆς ὑπὸ τὸν οὐρανόν*, rendering the prepositional phrase מתחת השמים. A popular variant text omitted the articulation of "heaven," reading *υπ ουρανον*. This is completely contrary to Pentateuchal usage. In Deut the unarticulated noun occurs only in poetic passages (32:1 33:13; also in Gen 49:25); elsewhere it occurs only at Gen 1:8, where God called the firmament *οὐρανόν*, and at 2:4 in the title *βίβλος γενέσεως οὐρανοῦ καὶ γῆς*.

33. See Daniel 229—230.

Chapter 26

26:1 Vv.1—11 concern the bringing in of firstfruits to the central sanctuary and the rite of confession accompanying it. V.1 is the protasis, and vv.2—11 constitute the apodosis. For *καὶ ἔσται ἐάν* see comment at 6:10—11. The *O* Byz tradition has preferred *οταν* to *ἐάν*, possibly to avoid any doubt attached to *ἐάν*; after all, it is when you will enter, possess, and dwell, and not "should you ...." *ὅταν* occurs only five times in the laws (chh.12—26), but only at 15:13 for כי; four times it renders a preposition (with bound infinitives), for כ at 17:18 20:2,9 and for ב at 23:13. The normal rendering is, as here, *ἐάν*, and the variant is an attempt at improving the text.

The three verbs are progressive: *εἰσέλθῃς* ... *κατακληρονομήσῃς* ... *κατοικήσῃς*, i.e. you will enter the land, then take possession of it, and finally, dwell on it. The preposition phrase *ἐπ' αὐτῆς* renders בה. Presumably to the translator the people were to dwell on the land rather than dwell in the land (country), though *κατοικέω* is more commonly modified by an *ἐν* phrase in Deut than by an *ἐπί* one. In the tradition the majority A F M V majority text substitutes *κατακληρονομησαι* for *καὶ κατακληρονομήσῃς*, but this is taken from 25:19, and does not represent a translation of MT.

26:2 That the apodosis begins with v.2 is clear from the change to the future tense. The apodotic *καί* is of course otiose, but it is not misleading. The first verb is *λήμψῃ*, which is the Hellenistic form which the Göttingen critical editions throughout have accepted as the original spelling, rather than the popular Classical *λῃψῃ*. Both are well-attested in the Egyptian papyri of the third century BCE, but codd B and A testify rather consistently to the Hellenistic form with the infixed *mu*. 848 from cir 50 BCE, however, consistently uses the Classical form, and this does call the originality of the Hellenistic form into question. Since both are attested for the period, the Hellenistic form ought probably to be retained, with the prevalence of the Classical spelling among the later cursive mss being understood as the product of the archaizing tendency of medieval scribes.

The verb is modified by an ἀπό phrase, which is clearly used in a partitive sense.[1] What you are to take is some of τῆς ἀπαρχῆς τῶν καρπῶν τῆς γῆς σου. The Hebrew has ראשית כל פרי האדמה. LXX follows the Sam text which lacked כל,[2] and hex has added παντων under the asterisk before τῶν to equal MT. Incidentally the Byz text has changed ἀπαρχῆς to the plural. Since ראשית can be taken as a collective, this is possible, but unlikely, as LXX. Though MT distinguishes between ארץ and אדמה, LXX unfortunately does not usually do so. The products (καρπῶν) here are of the soil, the ground, and LXX simply has γῆς. For the ἥν clause see comment at 1:20. In the tradition the formula has εν κληρω added at the end by the A F M V *oI' f z*+ text, but this is ex par.[3] MT has another אשר clause preceding it, however, which the translator apparently overlooked because of homoiarchon. It reads אשר תביא מארצך "which you shall harvest from your land." Hex has included it as οσα αν (or εαν) ενεγκης απο της γης σου.[4]

Secondly, you are to put it into a κάρταλλον "basket" for טנא.[5] The Byz text has articulated the noun, but the basket is mentioned here for the first time, and the text of LXX is more appropriate. The *b* text has the simplex βαλεις rather than ἐμβαλεῖς, but its modification by an εἰς phrase makes the compound the more fitting verb.

And "you are to go to the place which the Lord your God will choose ...." The ὅν clause is a typical Deut formula, for which see comment at 12:5. It occurs in exactly the same form at 16:6 17:8; and it constitutes a reference to the central sanctuary, which is a cornerstone of Deut thought.

26:3 On arrival he must go to the priest ὃς ἔσται ἐν ταῖς ἡμέραις ἐκείναις. The relative clause refers to the priest who is in charge of the service at the time. Most witnesses, however, make this a subjunctive clause by changing ἔσται to (ε)αν η; either makes sense, but B and 848 support the future, and it is to be preferred.

---

1. See SS 162.
2. As do Kenn 80,109.
3. See THGD 74.
4. Origen probably took it from Theod, since Aq read ὅσα οἴσεις ἀπὸ γῆς σου, and Sym had οὗ ἐὰν εἰσενέγκης ἀπὸ τῆς γῆς σου.
5. Aq preferred to call it by its more common designation ἀγγεῖον. For κάρταλλον see discussion in Lee 115—116.

That the suffix inflection is in Classical Hebrew basically neutral in tense is clear from הגדתי, which is defined by היום, hence LXX quite correctly has *ἀναγγέλλω* (*σήμερον*), i.e. a present tense. In the tradition the verb has been changed in the majority of witnesses to *αναγγελω*, but this is a case of haplography; the future is obviously wrong. The declaration is to the Lord *τῷ θεῷ μου*; thus the declaration becomes a personal confession, detailing the great redemptive activity of Israel's God, interrrupted by v.4, and then continued in vv.5—9. The personal nature of the confession is much clearer in LXX than in MT which has אלהיך.[6] The difference between the two is rooted in the Hebrew text; since the next word is כי the difference between the two is a case of haplography/dittography, not one of intentional change. I suspect that אלהי was original, but that is based on my interpretation of the passage and not on textual evidence.[7] In the tradition this has been corrected from *μου* to *σου* by F M *O f*+ to agree with MT.

What is confessed is "I have entered the land which the Lord swore to our fathers that he would give to us." The content of the divine oath is given in a complementary infinitive *δοῦναι ἡμῖν*. For the relative clause see comment at 1:8.

26:4 The priest (see comment in v.3) is to take the basket *ἐκ τῶν χειρῶν* (*σου*) for MT's ידך.[8] I suppose the question of singular vs dual depends on the size of the *κάρταλλον* (for which see v.2), i.e. whether it took one or two hands to carry it. But the number of יד with suffix is quite unsteady in Hebrew tradition.

The priest then must *θήσει* it *ἀπέναντι τοῦ θυσιαστηρίου* of the Lord your God. In the tradition another text arose; by itacism *θήσει* easily became the homophonous *θυσει* "sacrifice" in *C*ʹʾ *d*+. Since the notion of sacrificing firstfruits before the altar is not particularly meaningful, the *d* tradition made a further revision of the preposition to *εναντι* and deleted *τοῦ θυσιαστηρίου*, thus "and shall sacrifice it before the Lord your God," a fully meaningful statement, but also at variance with LXX (and MT).

---

6. The Three all attest to the second personal pronoun (*τῷ θεῷ*) *σου*.
7. See also Tov 291.
8. But this could be textual since Kenn 158,167,193,271,283 read ידיך.

26:5 The verse begins with ועניח ואמרת/*καὶ ἀποκριθεὶς ἐρεῖς*, which really continues the declaration of v.3, and the notion of "answering" here means "furthermore," or "and continuing." Actually vv.5—10a are the content of what "I declare today to the Lord my God" of v.3. This content is a narrative review of the redemptive acts of the Lord, involving us his people, and issuing (v.10a) in the present offering of the firstfruits of the land's produce. In the tradition the majority text has substituted for *ἀποκριθείς*, which is supported by B and 848, *αποκριθηση και*, which equals MT literally. But Deut never rendered "answered and said" in this way, but always by participle plus verb.[9]

Somewhat problematic is the first clause of the declaration in MT: ארמי אבד אבי. The second word is a participle presumably modifying ארמי, but the word usually means "to perish." Moderns interpret אבד in the sense of "perishing," hence fleeing.[10] One might compare Ps 119:176 for a possible parallel: I wandered כשה אבד "like a lost (i.e. perishing) sheep." Jewish interpreters tended to understand ארמי to refer to Laban who sought to destroy Jacob.[11] LXX was also troubled by אבד, and reads *Συρίαν ἀπέβαλεν ὁ πατήρ μου* "My father cast off Syria," which is a contextualized attempt based on the next clause "and he went down to Egypt."[12] In the tradition the majority text has transposed *beta* and *lambda*, thereby simplifying the text by its "my father left Syria (and went down to Egypt)," but this rationalizes the more difficult reading of LXX. What LXX is saying is that my father rejected Syria, i.e. refused to stay with Laban any longer, insisting on his return home to Palestine, but then went down to Egypt.

The Egyptian stay is characterized as *παρῴκησεν* "sojourned," i.e. a temporary stay as aliens; cf 18:6 of the Levites in Israelite cities. The emphasis is, however, on numerical growth. When he arrived in Egypt, it was *ἐν ἀριθμῷ βραχεῖ*, but there he became (*ἐγένετο εἰς*) a nation *μέγα καὶ πλῆθος, πολὺ καὶ μέγα*, a chiastic construction "great and numerous, many and great," whereas MT has גדול עצום ורב "large, powerful and numerous," In the tradition the Byz text changed *πλῆθος* to *ισχυρον και* and omitted *καὶ μέγα*, which

9. See THGD 82.
10. E.g. Driver, König, Mayes; NRSV has "wandering Aramean; NJPS, "fugitive Aramean."
11. So Tar and Rashi. Cf also Vulg: *Syram persequebatur patrem meum*. Pesh had a different reference with its "To Syria my father was driven." Comp also Prijs 225.
12. Theod retained LXX, but Aq has *ἀπώλλυτο*, and Sym, *ἀπώλλυεν*.

fits MT exactly, except for the first *καί*, which has no equivalent in MT. Hex merely placed *καὶ μέγα* under the obelus as having no counterpart in MT. The omission of *καὶ μέγα* by B Byz+ may simply represent an attempt to avoid the repetition of *μέγα*.[13]

26:6 The Egyptian bondage is characterized threefold: *ἐκάκωσαν* ... *ἐταπείνωσαν* ... *ἐπέθηκαν ἡμῖν ἔργα σκλήρα*. The first two represent וירעו and יענו resp.; these are close semantically; in fact, the latter is often rendered by *κακόω* (16 times). The rendering *ἐταπείνωσαν* is, however, the common rendering for ענה (56 times; others recurring are כנע - 15 times, דכא/דכה - 10 times, שפל - nine times.) *ταπεινόω* is practically a stereotype for ענה, especially in the Piel.[14] The third characterization does differ in LXX in that it rendered עבדה קשה "hard labor" by the plural *ἔργα σκληρά* "harsh tasks."[15]

26:7 "When we called out to the Lord the God of our fathers, the Lord heard our voice (i.e. our call),[16] and saw our *ταπείνωσιν*, and our *μόχθον* and our *θλιμμόν*." The three norms are more or less synonymous: humiliation, trouble, oppression, representing resp. עני, עמל and לחץ.[17] All three occur but once each in Deut, though the reading *ταπείνωσις* for עני is common elsewhere (18 times out of 34 occurrences). *μόχθος* for עמל occurs elsewhere only in Eccl where it is a stereotype. The last one occurs only twice in the entire corpus; at Exod 5:9 it also occurs for לחץ.

26:8 The great redemptive act of the Exodus—*ἐξήγαγεν ἡμᾶς κύριος ἐξ Αἰγύπτου* (for which see comment at 1:27) is strongly stressed by six *ἐν* phrases, one more than in MT, LXX adding *ἐν ἰσχύι μεγάλῃ καὶ* at the beginning of the phrases. The phrase occurs in similar contexts at 4:37 9:26,29. That LXX is enthusiastic in stresssing the great redemptive act even more strongly than MT is clear from its addition of *αὐτός* as subject of *ἐξήγαγεν* in

---

13. For similar grouping of adjectives see List 20 in THGD 92.
14. It is then hardly justified to insist on a difference in meaning between the Greek and the Hebrew as suggested by Dogniez-Harl.
15. This is "corrected" by The Three to *δουλείαν σκληράν* (retroverted from Syh^{m}). Cf also Daniel 113 and 59.
16. For the 848 readings see THGD 67,69.
17. For the first of these Aq has *πενίαν* "poverty, want."

front of the first ἐν phrase, which word hex placed under the obelus. So LXX adds "even he by great strength and (by a strong hand, etc.)."[18] For *ἐν χειρὶ κραταιᾷ καὶ ἐν βραχίονι ὑψηλῷ* see comment at 3:23—24. The majority A F M text has added *αυτου* after *βραχίονι*, and another A F M majority variant has articulated *ὑψηλῷ*, but LXX represents the usual idiom. For ובמורא גדל "and with great terror" LXX has *καὶ ἐν ὁράμασιν μεγάλοις* "and with great spectacles." LXX undoubtedly understood the root ראה rather than ירא. For the plural LXX may have been influenced by 4:34, where MT had ובמוראים גדלים. The phrase also occurs at Jer 29(32):21 in a similar context, but that was probably based on acquaintance with Deut. For *καὶ ἐν σημείοις καὶ ἐν τέρασιν* see comment at 4:34.

26:9 The gift of the promised land is the culmination of the divine acts of redemption. The collocation *γῆν ῥέουσαν γάλα καὶ μέλι* occurs particularly often in Deut (seven times, but also four times each in Exod and Num). Outside the Pentateuch it occurs but seldom (twice in Jer and Ezek, and once each in Bar and Sir).

26:10 The verse is rather obviously composed of two parts. The first part is in first person, and recalls the occasion for this declaration, which vv.2 and 3 had outlined, viz. the bringing of the firstfruits to the central sanctuary. That this is the conclusion of the declaration is clear from *καὶ νῦν ἰδού*. It differs from the orders in v.3, however, in translating פרי, not by *καρπῶν* "fruits," but by *γενημάτων* "produce (of the land)," though no distinction in meaning is apparently intended. *γῆς* is modified by a relative clause: "which you gave me, o Lord." The relative pronoun *ἧς* is genitive by attraction to its antecedent. A popular F text has changed the clause into third person: *εδωκεν μοι κυριος*, but the direct address marks the close of the address begun in v.3, and it also equals MT. Over against MT, the Greek added the formulaic *γῆν ῥέουσιν γάλα καὶ μέλι*. That the phrase is formulaic is clear from the accusative case, which does not fit well here, the reference being to *τῆς γῆς*. The tradition was understandably troubled by it, and simplified it in one of two ways: the *n t+* tradition changed the structure to the genitive, whereas the *b*

18. For *αὐτός* see also Prijs 106.

d+ text omitted it. That it was added under the influence of the preceding verse is obvious, but the addition does apparently hark back to the translator.

The second part of the verse, along with v.11, reverts to the initial second person singular future of vv.1—3. These consist of three clauses, the last of which constitutes v.11. First of all, "you must *ἀφήσεις αὐτά* before the Lord your God." MT reads הנחתו "you must lay it down," with the suffix referring to the טנא of vv.2 and 4. LXX has a different reference with *αὐτά* referring to *γενημάτων* earlier in the verse. Since the reference to "basket" is quite distant, a nearer reference to "produce" is simpler.[19] An F M V *oI f z*+ text does change *αὐτά* to *αυτο*, though it is doubtful that this was a recensional change; it was probably an attempt to change the reference to "basket," rather than to the "produce." The order to leave the produce before the Lord does not fully agree with v.4, where it is the priest who does the actual setting of the basket before the Lord. This may well have impelled the use of *ἀφήσεις* here, as well as the variant *αυτο* text; the worshipper leaves them, though it is of course the priest who does the actual placement. After all, *ἔναντι κυρίου* means at the sanctuary, but at v.4 the priest set it (the basket) before the altar of the Lord; cf comment at v.4.

The second order is *προσκυνήσεις ἔναντι κυρίου τοῦ θεοῦ σου*. The verb means "to bow down, prostrate oneself, do obeissance," in other words, to worship. What is unusual is the modification by *ἔναντι κ.τ.θ.σου*. Elsewhere throughout Deut the verb is always modified by a dative. In fact, the verb normally takes a dative of person. Throughout the OT I have found only one case of modification by *ἐναντίον* (*τοῦ λαοῦ*) at Gen 23:12, two of *ἐνώπιον* plus pronoun (Ps 21:28 85:9), and comp Ps 137:2 with its *πρὸς ναὸν ἅγιόν σου*. It does, however, equal MT לפני יהוה אלהיך. In the tradition most witnesses add *εκει* after the verb, which is both unnecessary, and without an equivalent in MT.[20]

26:11 The third component was that "you should rejoice in all the good things which the Lord your God gave to you and to your household," rightly understanding בכל הטוב as a collective; to this is appended *καὶ ὁ Λευίτης καὶ ὁ προσήλυτος ἐν σοί*. This is to be understood as coordinate to the subject

19. The Three do have the singular *αὐτό*.
20. See THGD 123.

"you"; i.e. you, as well as Levite and proselyte among you, are to rejoice. This is much clearer in MT, which has אתה before "and the Levite." Hex has introduced *σου* to represent the omitted pronoun.[21] In the tradition the LXX text was felt to be somewhat odd with the two nominative nominals tacked on at the end, and the majority B V tradition changed *τῇ οἰκίᾳ σου* to the nominative *η οικια σου*. This is, however, secondary as MT shows with its ולביתך, i.e. it is coordinate with לך.

26:12 Vv.12—15 concern the tithe of the third year. For *ἐὰν δέ* see comment at 15:16. The protasis of v.12 differs in LXX from that of MT. The latter has the ethnach on המעשר, i.e. "when you finish tithing, all the tithe of your produce in the third year, the year of the tithe." The apodosis then begins with ונתתה. But LXX ends the protasis with *ἐν τῷ ἔτει τῷ τρίτῳ*. The שנת המעשר ונתתה is understood as beginning the apodosis. שנת is understood as "second," i.e. "the second of the tithe," which means the second tithe, and the conjunction is disregarded, so that the apodosis begins with "the second tithe you shall give (to the Levite, etc.)," which makes fine sense.[22] To the translator 14:21—22 constituted the first tithe, whereas the reference here is to the second tithe, which was apparently collected only every third year; comp 14:27—28. This interpretation also solves the use of נתתה occurring without a direct modifier; in the Greek this is supplied by "the second tithe." In the tradition most witnesses add *της γης* after *γενημάτων*, but this is ex par. Both B and 848 support the shorter text, which also equals MT.[23]

So you are to give the second tithe to the Levite *καὶ τῷ προσηλύτῳ καὶ τῷ ὀρφανῷ καὶ τῇ χήρᾳ*, for which see comment at 10:18. MT has no equivalent for the first two *καίs*, coordinating only the last noun: "and the widow."[24] As for the Levite, he had no separate portion in Israel (cf

---

21. See THGD 119.
22. Rashi also understood two tithes being involved annually, but only one was designated for the Levite and the helpless in society, distinguishing this one as the first tithe, whereas the second tithe is the one which you yourself eat; cf 14:21—22. According to Rashi, in the third year only one of the two tithes due is collected, the one to be given to charity, and instead of the second tithe, יתן מעשר עני "he shall give a tithe for the poor." This does not mean, however, that he misread MT, but simply that it reminded him of two different tithes.
23. See THGD 82.
24. Kenn 4,150^{c},170* read ולגר instead of לגר and Kenn 4,80*,170*,199 and 232 have וליתום for ליתום.

14:26,28), and was therefore included in the list of those who were helpless; cf also 16:11,14.

As in the case of the regular tithe (14:22), it is to be eaten, though not by you, but rather by the Levite, proselyte, orphan and widow. They shall eat (it) in your cities (for which see comment at 12:15), and be sated; i.e. they will eat their fill. In the tradition B *C''* *s*+ read *ευφρανθησονται* instead of *ἐμπλησθήσονται*. The notion of eating and rejoicing is common in Deut; see chh.12,14,16, but here it has no basis in MT. The variant text was probably influenced by v.11.

26:13 LXX uses *ἐξεκάθαρα* (aorist of *ἐκκαθαίρω*) "I cleared out" for בערתי "I have exterminated," which makes good sense.[25] The Greek rightly interpreted הקדש as a collective in *τὰ ἅγια* "the consecrated things or portions." What is meant is that "I have cleared out the consecrated portions from my house by giving them, etc." That this tithe should be called *τὰ ἅγια* is not surprising. It had been ordered in v.12 as set aside, not for personal use, but as a tithe for charity, and so being set aside, it became consecrated for sacred use; these offerings are now *ἅγια*.[26] LXX has correctly interpreted הבית as *τῆς οἰκίας μου*; though MT has no pronominal suffix, it can only be "my" house.

The reference to *πάσας τὰς ἐντολάς* follows Sam in reading the plural, though the suffix of מצותך is not translated; it is otiose in view of the *ἅς* clause, which identifies the laws as those which you (i.e. the Lord) commanded me. Hex has, however, added *σου* to equal MT. Oddly in the next clause LXX has a singular accusative for ממצותיך, rather than the plural. Its omission of the preposition was simply a case of haplography;[27] the translator's use of the singular is probably a reference to the *ἐντολήν* at 14:27—28.

Over against MT LXX joins the recipients of the *τὰ ἅγια* by conjunctions, whereas MT lacks a conjunction before ליתום. LXX follows the pattern set in the preceding verse.[28]

---

25. Aq used *ἐπέλεξα* as at 21:21. Did Aq often confuse בער and בחר? But see Daniel 168.

26. Which Rashi calls the מעשר שני, in contrast to that which "I gave them to the Levite ...," which he calls the מעשר ראשון.

27. See SS 162.

28. Once again Kenn mss do testify to a conjunction. The following mss read וליתום: Kenn 17,69,132,150,170*,186 and 198.

26:14 An asseverance of innocence and full obedience. The verse divides into two parts: the first part asserts in three clauses what I did not do. The second part has two positive clauses. Oddly enough, only the first statement is syndetic in LXX, which is the precise reverse of MT, in which only the first clause is without a conjunction.[29]

The negative statements all have to do with the tithes referred to in v.13, viz. *τὰ ἅγια*. In each statement *ἀπ᾽ αὐτῶν* constitutes a reference to these consecrated portions. In each case MT necessarily has the singular ממנו, since the antecedent, הקדש, is singular. The first statement reads "I did not eat in my grief (or distress) from them." The *ἀπ᾽* is to be understood as partitive in each case, i.e. as "any of them."[30] The phrase *ἐν ὀδύνῃ μου* translates באני which on the basis of Ugaritic probably means "in my mourning."[31] It is not fully clear how this actually applies, since the tithe was intended for charity, and not for personal consumption. In any event, what is stressed is the *ὀδύνῃ μου*. It should be noted that each of the three clauses deals with some form of contamination, which contravenes the holy or consecrated nature of the tithe.

The second asseveration reads *οὐκ ἐκάρπωσα ἀπ᾽ αὐτῶν εἰς ἀκάθαρτον* "I have not enjoyed the use of any of them for an impure end."[32] MT has quite a different notion: ולא בערתי ממנו בטמא "And I have not removed any of them in uncleanness." MT seems to refer to the removal of the tithe in order to give it to those for whom it was meant, but not doing so while in an impure state. LXX interprets בטמא by an *εἰς* phrase.[33]

Except for disregarding the conjunction in MT, the third asseveration translates MT literally, which is not all that helpful. What does giving למת/*τῷ τεθνηκότι* mean? Does it mean funeral food or does it refer to the pagan practice of food for the dead? In the tradition hex has *ουδε* rather than *οὐκ*, i.e. equalling ולא of MT.

---

29. But Kenn 17,84,199 do read ולא.
30. See SS 162.
31. Aq did understand it in this way with his *ἐν λύπῃ μου*; similarly Sym has *ἐν πένθει μου*.
32. See Daniel 167—169 fpr the use of *ἐκάρπωσα* to render בערתי. She makes the point that the translators of the Pentateuch "connaissaient le sens que revêtait *καρποῦν* dans la langue cultuelle, — mais dans cette langue exclusivement."
33. Aq again interprets בערתי by *ἐπέλεξα*, for which see v.13, and בטמא, by *ἐν μιασμῷ* "in pollution."

The second part of the verse assures the Lord that "I have obeyed the voice of the Lord my God; I have done as you commanded me." The use of *ὑπήκουσα* is a fine touch on the part of the translator. שמעתי means more than simply "I heard"; it means subservience, obedience, which the Greek compound conveys. The only difference between LXX and MT is that ככל of MT is rendered by *καθότι*. Hex has "corrected" LXX by adding *παντα* before *καθότι*. There is no difference in meaning between *καθότι* of B 848 and the majority text *καθα*, but *καθότι* must be LXX.[34]

26:15 A prayer for divine blessing. God is implored to "look down from מעון קדשך (your holy abode)," which is rendered uniquely by the adjectival phrase (*ἐκ*) *τοῦ οἴκου τοῦ ἁγίου*.[35] The term מעון is a poetic word of infrequent occurrence in MT, which is variously translated, but only here prosaically by "house," though the appositive of the phrase, *ἐκ τοῦ οὐρανοῦ*, makes the reference fully clear.

The prayer is "bless your people *τὸν* Ἰσραήλ and the land ...." The unusual articulation of Ἰσραήλ represents the preposition את of MT. The "land" is modified by a relative clause, "which you gave them," with the pronoun in third person, whereas MT has לנו, which is consistent with the reference to "our father" in the next clause, and this is followed by a *καθά* clause modifying *ἔδωκας*. In the *καθά* clause LXX has added in modification of *ὤμοσας* the complementary infinitive plus pronoun *δοῦναι ἡμῖν*. The reason for the plus in LXX is to provide easy modification for *γῆν ῥέουσαν γάλα καὶ μέλι*, which comes at the end. In MT this simply refers to האדמה, i.e. "bless the land, ... even the land flowing with milk and honey." Since it is separated from its reference by two subordinate clauses, the *ἥν* and the *καθά* clauses, the addition gives the reader a crutch for the *γῆν* structure. Furthermore, the addition serves to clarify precisely what the Lord did. He gave it to our fathers in the past (i.e. *αὐτοῖς*), as he had sworn to them that he would give the land flowing with milk and honey to us; i.e. we are the beneficiaries; God has kept his sworn promise.

34. See THGD 82.
35. See SS 65.

26:16 Vv.16—19 constitute an exhortation to observance of the laws; this is a fitting conclusion to the Law Code of chh.12—26. *ἐν τῇ ἡμέρᾳ ταύτῃ* refers to the day on which the giving of the law was concluded. Only 848 witnesses to the original present tense *ἐντέλλεται*, which accords with Deut's consistent pattern of translating a participial predicate, מצוך, all other witnesses having the aorist *ενετειλατο*.[36] For *πάντα τὰ δικαιώματα ταῦτα καὶ τὰ κρίματα*, see comment at 4:1. The *πάντα* has no equivalent in MT, and its inclusion is ex par (see 4:6 6:2 7:12). LXX idiosyncratically renders all of v.16b in the second plural, whereas MT consistently has the singular throughout the verse. Why LXX should have done this is not clear, since it reverts to the singular for the rest of the chapter (as in MT). For *φυλάξεσθε καὶ ποιήσετε* see comment at 5:1. In the tradition these verbs are changed to the imperative, *φυλαξασθε και ποιησατε*, in F *C*'' +, but Deut normally renders the contextual suffixal inflections by the future.[37] The *C*'' *s* text reads *ταυτα* instead of *αὐτά*, but MT has אותם. For *ἐξ ὅλης τῆς καρδίας ὑμῶν καὶ ἐξ ὅλης τῆς ψυχῆς ὑμῶν*, see comment at 4:29.

26:17 MT has an odd text with the verb as the second masculine singular Hi of אמר, and את יהוה as its preposed modifier, thus "Yahweh you made to say (today)." What is clear in MT, is that a statement as to Israel's actions is intended. NRSV translates "you have obtained the LORD's agreement: to be ...," whereas NJPS has "you have affirmed this day that the LORD is your God, that you will ...." LXX obviously was puzzled by this text, and interpreted it contextually as *εἵλου* "you chose," which also seemed to fit in with v.18; see comment ad loc. Furthermore, the translator also avoided the notion that the people chose Yahweh; he substituted *τὸν θεόν* for Yahweh, thus "God you chose today to be your God." The hex text has changed this to *τον κυριον* to agree with MT, but this is purely recensional; Deut would never have used the article to render the tetragrammaton.[38] That האמרת is uncertain in meaning here is clear from the coordinate marked infinitives: וללכת ... ולשמר ...

36. See THGD 82.
37. See THGD 74.
38. Aq also found האמרת difficult and rendered the verb by *ἀντηλλάξω* "you exchanged, took in exchange." It is not clear to me how Aq understood this passage. Both Tar[OJ] follow the interpretation of LXX by using the verb חטב, whereas Tar[N] has אמלכתון עליכון יומנא הדין "you have crowned (him) king over you today."

ולשמע, all coordinated with להיות לך לאלהים. **The** האמרת can sensibly apply in the causative sense to the להיות construction, but the next infinitives all must have "you" as subject. LXX has nicely solved this by making the main verb *εἵλου*.

Accordingly, you have also chosen "to walk in his ways, and to observe his ordinances and judgments, and to obey his voice." Each of these recurs many times in the book. For "to walk in his ways" see comment at 10:12; for "to observe his ordinances and judgments" see comment at 4:40, and for "to obey his voice" see comment at 13:18. In the tradition hex has added *αυτου* after *δικαιώματα* to represent the suffix of חקיו in MT. The majority of witnesses has three coordinate nouns, with *και τας εντολας αυτου* either in second or third place; this is probably hex as well, since MT also has three: חקיו ומצותיו ומשפטיו, the translator having omitted the second word because of homoioteleuton.

26:18 The counterpart to Israel's choice of God as their God: "the Lord has chosen you today to be a special people for him." Again MT has האמירך "has made you say," which LXX interprets by *εἵλατο*, for which see discussion at v.17. For λαὸν *περιούσιον* see comment at 7:6, but especially the Note at Exod 19:5. In the tradition most witnesses add *σε* as subject of the infinitive after *γενέσθαι*, but this is quite unnecessary in view of *σε* (*σήμερον*) immediately before the infinitive. Furthermore, the second century BCE papyrus 957 lacks it.[39] In the *καθάπερ εἶπεν* clause most witnesses add *σοι*, which does equal the לך of MT, but it is not needed in the context, and B 957 both witness to its absence; LXX left it out as otiose.[40]

Appended is another infinitival structure: *φυλάσσειν πάσας τὰς ἐντολὰς αὐτοῦ*; it expresses the purpose of divine choice; they are chosen to be the Lord's people in order that they may observe all his ordinances. God will be their God, but they, as his people, must be an obedient people whose lives accord to his law.

26:19 MT begins with "ולתתך high over all the nations אשר עשה," i.e. "and to set you high over all the nations which he made." LXX translated the

39. See THGD 121.
40. One Kenn ms, no.6, does omit לך.

marked infinitive simply by *εἶναι* (*σε*), which is understandable in view of the *γενέσθαι* of v.18; the Greek avoids the notion that God had האמירך ... "in order to set you high over all the peoples." The relative clause was also reinterpreted by the translator, not as a relative clause defining all the nations as אשר עשה "whom he had made," but by *ὡς ἐποίησέν σε*, which is tied to what follows (rather than to *τῶν ἐθνῶν* which precedes). To the Greek, that you were *ὑπεράνω* all the nations, was convincingly shown by "how he made you *ὀνομαστὸν καὶ καύχημα καὶ δοξαστόν*," terms describing how God had "set you עליון over all the nations." In MT those are לתהלה ולשם ולתפארת "for praise and renown and glory." The second term is translated by a noun which means "boasting," or rather something or someone to boast about, hence a reputation, a שם. The other two Greek words are adjectives: "renowned ... glorious."

The remainder of the verse is a fitting conclusion to the Law Code: "that you might be, as he said, a holy people to the Lord your God." MT introduces this with a conjunction, as though this were a second purposive infinitive, and hex has also added *και* to introduce it. But the Greek intends the divine exaltation of his people to issue in their constituting a people *ἅγιον* to the Lord, i.e. holy, separate, apart, just as the *ὑπεράνω πάντων τῶν ἐθνῶν* had already implied.

Chapter 27

27:1 Vv.1—8 enjoin a rite in which all the words of the law are permanently inscribed on large stones, and accompanying sacrifices are carried out. The orders are made by Moses and the elders of Israel; only here in the book do the elders of Israel join Moses in instructing the people. In fact, *ἡ γερουσία* 'Ισραήλ never recurs in the book, though comp *τοῖς πρεσβυτέροις τῶν υἱῶν* 'Ισραήλ at 31:9, where they, together with the Levitical priests, are recipients of the book containing the law. In MT this is followed by את העם, who are designated as the ones receiving the order. Hex has added *τω λαω* to represent this designation. Why the translator should have omitted naming those who were supposed to receive these commandments is puzzling. That the statement is not overly clear is due to the inclusion of "and the eldership of Israel" in the opening clause, since the nominal, "all these commandments," is modified by a *ὅσος* clause in which "all these commandments" are defined as ones which I, not I and the eldership, am commanding you. It should be noted that the order is quite properly put into the plural. The plural imperative, *φυλάσσασθε*, is correctly plural; the free infinitive, which admits of no inflection, allows for adaptation to the context. That context is plural; note that "I am ordering" is modified by *ὑμῖν*. Its modifier in MT is in the singular, את כל המצוה, but in view of the כל the collective interpretation of LXX is sensible.[1]

In the tradition Byz has glossed the imperative with the infinitive *ποιειν*. It has also, along with *C*'' *s*, changed the *λέγων* in pedantic fashion to *λεγοντες*. And for *ὅσας* V *C*'' *s*+ read the simple relative *ας*.

27:2 For *καὶ ἔσται* plus temporal condition see comment at 6:10—11. Here the timer *ᾗ ἂν ἡμέρᾳ* introduces the protasis *διάβητε* the Jordan into the land ...." The verb is in the plural, which contrasts with the singular of the apodosis in vv.2b—3aα. For "cross the Jordan" see comment at 4:22, and for the *ἥν* clause, a comment at 1:20. Note that the *ἥν* clause already uses the singular. It might also be noted that this formula occurs 44 times in the book,

1. Aq uses the singular throughout: *φύλασσε σὺν πᾶσαν τὴν ἐντολήν*, as does Theod but in somewhat better Greek as *φυλάσσου τὴν πᾶσαν ἐντολήν*. Sym is best with *φυλάσσετε πᾶσαν τὴν ἐντολήν*.

but that after 12:9 it always has *σοι* after "give/gave" in the formula, regardless of MT.[2]

The apodosis is introduced by *καί*, and consists of three coordinate future singular clauses: *καὶ στήσεις* ... *καὶ κονιάσεις* ... (v.3) *καὶ γράφεις* .... The change in number follows that of MT. The setting up for yourself large stones may well refer to a boundary stele of some kind to be erected once you have crossed the Jordan. The Byz tradition limits the stones to *δυο*, undoubtedly being inspired by the two tablets of the decalogue; see 5:22. These are then to be plastered with plaster, i.e. a surface is prepared to permit writing on it.

27:3 MT has the entire verse in the singular, whereas LXX begins with the singular, but then has two clauses in the plural under the influence of v.2a, and then reverts to the singular for the remainder of the verse. Much of vv.1—8 is repetitive, and LXX has been affected by this, at times creating a text slightly at variance with MT. And instead of עליהם LXX realizes the pronoun by *ἐπὶ τῶν λίθων*. Then instead of בעברך it has the plural plus a modifier, *ὡς ἂν διαβῆτε τὸν Ἰορδάνην*,[3] as in v.4, continuing against MT with the plural in *ἡνίκα ἂν εἰσέλθητε εἰς τὴν γῆν*, but then changing with the *ἥν* clause back to the singular. Instead of "which the Lord אלהיך is giving to you, for which see comment at 1:20, LXX reads *ὁ θεὸς τῶν πατέρων σου*, for which see below. For "land flowing with milk and honey" see comment at 6:3.

Deut often uses a *ὃν τρόπον* clause to render כאשר. For an exact parallel, but in the plural, see 1:21, and for *ὃν τρόπον* clauses see comment at 11:25. The source of "the God of your fathers" earlier in the verse is the אלהי אבתיך in this clause.

In the tradition a *z* text changed the plural verbs *διαβῆτε* and *εἰσέλθητε* to the singular, thus agreeing with MT. This may, however, have simply been inspired by an urge for consistency in the verse. On the other hand, some of these same *z* mss also omitted the first *τῶν πατέρων*, thereby equalling MT in this as well. Why the translator should have changed the number of the verbs to the plural over against MT, and then back to the singular is baffling.

---

2. Aq added *ἐν κλήρῳ* after *σοι* over against MT!
3. For this rendering of ב plus a bound infinitive see SS Inf 86.

27:4 What was ordered in v.2 is substantially repeated here, but in the plural. For the initial *καὶ ἔσται ὡς* see comment at 6:10—11. Somewhat odd is the use of *οὕς* in the relative clause; it is of course attracted to *λίθους τούτους* immediately before it; what is meant is "concerning which." The clause, for which see comment at 4:2, occurs 38 times in Deut, and is usually in the singular (*σοι* rather than *ὑμῖν* 29 times), and this has influenced the tradition as well, since the A B F M V majority tradition also reads *σοι*, but the plural is original, and agrees with MT. In fact, LXX adheres strictly to the number of MT from vv.4 to the end of the section, reverting to the singular in the last clause. The order to raise these stones in mount Gaibal was a sore point with the Samaritans, who insisted on reading mount Garizin. The spelling Γαιβάλ for עיבל shows the *ʿayin* grapheme to have represented the *ghain* phoneme in the time of the translator. Oddly enough an Old Latin codex also reads *garzin.*

27:5 Also ordered was the building of an altar to the Lord your God. The altar was to be of unhewn stones, unlike the stele where the stones were to be plastered. MT refers to "an altar of stones"; LXX interprets this as being an altar *ἐκ λίθων*, i.e. an altar (composed) of stones.[4] For the tradition that an altar should be made of rough stone see Note at Exod 20:25. According to that tradition putting a handtool on the altar would defile it. What is here forbidden is putting an iron (tool) *ἐπ' αὐτούς*, i.e. on the stones. A B *z*+ tradition has *επ αυτο*, i.e. on the altar, but this is due to the influence of the Exod law which reads *ἐπ' αὐτό*.

27:6 The last clause of v.5 is explicated further by the statement that you must build the altar of *λίθους ὁλοκλήρους*, i.e. of "whole, complete stones," for אבנים שלמות, thus unchipped, raw stones.[5] See comment at v.5. Over against v.5 MT has a bound phrase מזבח יהוה, "the altar of the Lord (your God)"; in v.5 MT had מזבח ליהוה translated literally by *θυσιαστήριον κυρίῳ* (*τῷ θεῷ σου*). LXX does not distinguish the two, using a dative referent in both cases.

In the second clause MT uses a cognate modifier, i.e. העלית עולת. Since עולת is usually rendered by *ὁλοκαυτώματα*,[6] no attempt is made to render the

4. *See SS 63.*
5. Aq uses *ἀπηρτισμένους* for שלמות, for which compare his usage at 25:15 in connection with *στάθμιον*.
6. See Daniel 246.

expression by cognates, and the translator used *ἀνοίσεις* for the verb. *ἀναφέρω* is by far the most common rendering of העלה in the sense of "to offer up (sacrifices)" throughout the OT. In the tradition B Byz articulate the noun, but LXX correctly has it without an article, since this is the first mention of holocausts. The change to the singular in F *C*'' *s*+ is sensible, but it is a palaeographically inspired copyist error, though made easier by the following clause which speaks of a singular *θυσίαν*.

27:7 Most mss have *ἐκεῖ* after both *θύσεις* and *ἐμπλησθήσῃ*, but hex omits both, and has added it after *φάγῃ*, which equals MT. It seems somewhat unlikely that the translator should have rendered שם twice; it is only the second one that must be original, since the translator rendered אכלת by a doublet *φάγῃ καὶ ἐμπλησθήσῃ*; i.e. *ἐκεῖ* is correctly placed in LXX.[7] The collocation "eat and be filled" is a common one in Deut; cf 6:11 8:10,12 11:15 14:28 26:12 32:15.

MT reads for its first clause וזבחת שלמים. The noun almost invariably occurs in the plural (of abstraction), and refers to a type of communion sacrifice which throughout the Pentateuch is rendered by *σωτήριον*, here with the class definition *θυσίαν* (*σωτηρίου*). The term is hardly intended as a salvatory sacrifice; it is simply one of well-being.[8] Basically it is a celebratory rite; it is explicated by "and you shall eat, and be sated there, and rejoice (i.e. celebrate) before the Lord your God."

In the tradition hex has placed *συτηρίου* under the obelus under the presupposition that only one word may equal one Hebrew word; the designation is of course false; according to hex equations it could only have been *θυσίαν*, which was the extra item over against MT. A majority A 963 variant reading has added a dative of person to the first clause, *κυριω τω θεω σου*, which is ex par, presumably from v.6.[9]

27:8 A doublet on v.3; again Israel is ordered to write on the stones all *τὸν νόμον τοῦτον*, for which MT has דברי התורה הזאת. Hex did not try to render דברי; writing "the words of this law" does not differ much from "writing this

7. For the hex reading see notes at THGD 74 and 83.
8. See the discussion of the term in Daniel 275—281.
9. See THGD 120.

law." A popular variant tradition has added *τουτων* aftr *λίθων*, but this expansion has no support in MT, nor does it add anything significant, since the stones have been present in the context from v.2 onwards. The only thing new that this verse adds is *σαφῶς σφόδρα*, which renders the free infinitives באר היטב correctly.

27:9 The Levitical priests join Moses in a solemn pronouncement to all Israel; this continues in v.10, which is another admonition towards obedience with respect to the law. The *C'* text has *παντι τω λαω* instead of "to all Israel," possibly created to avoid the repetition of "Israel" in the verse. An A Byz variant distinguishes between the priests and the Levites by adding *και* between them, but this cannot be original LXX. Whenever "the priests" is followed by "the Levites" in Deut, the two are never joined by *και*. For *οἱ ἱερεῖς οἱ Λευῖται* see comment at 18:1.

The pronouncement begins with *σιώπα* "be quiet" plus *καὶ ἄκουε*. Obviously what is to come is of grave importance.[10] The actual pronouncement is: "today you have become a people to the Lord your God." What is meant is that now that God's law has been given to Israel, they have become the Lord's people. The use of the perfect is significant and well-chosen to render the unusual Ni verb נהיית, since the fact of becoming the Lord's people involves remaining such. The use of an *εἰς* phrase modifying *γέγονες* represents the Hebrew idiom היה plus a ל phrase in the sense of "to become." This literalism is frequent in LXX and simply means "become."

27:10 What the future verbs intend to show is that what results from having become the Lord's people is: "you shall obey the voice of the Lord your God, and perform all his commandments and his ordinances." This is clear from the parataxis which joins this verse to v.9, where the last clause is interruptive of *σιώπα καὶ ἄκουε ... καὶ εἰσακούσῃ ....* LXX has *πάσας* before "his commandments" over against MT. For the *ὅσα* clause, with which the verse ends, see comments at 4:2.

---

10. Aq translates הסכת by *πρόσχες* "pay attention, listen"; this follows the same Jewish interpretation as the Tar, which use the Aphel of צות; Tar[J] has ציתו which is the Pael form, but with the same meaning.

27:12 Vv.12—13 reflect 11:26—29, in which Israel is told by God that he is placing blessing and curse before them, the former if they obey the Lord's commandments, the latter, if they do not. On entering the promised land they are to place the blessing on Mount Garizin, and the curse on Mount Gaibal. V.12 specifies which tribes are to stand to bless the people. The subject for the two tribal groups is in each case *οὗτοι*, which might well be translated by "the following." Those who are to stand to bless the people are to be על הר גרזים, which LXX translates by *ἐν ὄρει Γαριζίν*, rather than by *επι* as one might have expected, but see v.13. The name of the mountain is spelled with a final *nu* as at 11:29, i.e. with an Aramaic plural ending. Hex mss. have changed the final consonant to *mu*. By dittography some mss have repeated *γαρ-* or *γαρι-*; two mss have lost the final consonant, and another one shows consonantal change in *γαρηβην*.

The *οὗτοι* is modified by *διαβάντες τὸν Ἰορδάνην*, which translates בעברכם though disregarding the suffix. The rendering of ב plus bound infinitive by an attributive participle is highly unusual in the book, though it also occurs at 5:28 6:7 and 11:19.[11] This is more exactly and more elegantly rendered in Byz by a genitive absolute construction *διαβαντων υμων*. The list of six tribes comprise "Symeon, Leui, Ioudas, Issachar, Joseph and Benjamin." These constitute the actual sons of Leah (except for Rouben and Zaboulon) and of Rachel. In LXX only the last two are connected by *καί*, whereas in MT a *waw* obtains between all the members. Sam has three pairs, i.e. the pattern "a+b c+d e+f." In the tradition cod A also adds a *και* before Λευί.[12] Misspellings other than itacisms are infrequent. For Λευί one ms reads λεβει. For Ἰσσαχάρ haplography easily created *ισαχαρ* in a number of mss, and Βενιαμίν shows up as *βενιαμειμ* in one ms, and as *βενιαμη* in another.

27:13 The other six tribes are to stand *ἐπὶ τῆς κατάρας ἐν ὄρει Γαιβάλ*. This renders literally the Hebrew על הקללה בהר עיבל. I would take *ἐπί* with the genitive in the figurative sense of "over" of power, authority, control of;[13] it is intended to contrast with the complementary infinitive *εὐλογεῖν* of v.12,

11. For the participle used to render ב plus bound infinitive see SS Inf 91.
12. Kenn 9,69,80,84,109 and 150 lack the conjunction on ולוי; For וישׂשכר Kenn 5,84,181 are without a conjunction, and Kenn 136 and 181 also lack it for ויוסף.
13. See Bauer sub *ἐπί* I.1.b.α.

thus "(they shall stand) for the curse," i.e. in control of the curse. בהר contrasts with על הר of v.12, but the translator has levelled the phrases by *ἐν ὄρει*. The transcription Γαιβάλ presupposes the /ğ/ phoneme representing the grapheme ע as in v.4, which see. It has been misspelled as *γαβαλ* by syncopation of the *iota*, by consonant confusion as *γαιβακ*, by uncial confusion of Λ—Δ as *γεβαδ* and *γεδαβ*. Ῥουβήν through nasal confusion became *ρουβημ*, *ρουβιμ*, *ρουβειμ*, as well as through ν/λ confusion as *rōbēl* in Eth and *rūbīl* in Arab and Syh. Ἀσήρ by dittography became *ασσηρ* as well as *ιασηρ*, and Νεφθαλί in most witnesses ends in a closed syllable, either with *nu* or more commonly with *mu*. Ζαβουλών has no conjunction before it as MT does, but it follows the text of Sam.[14]

27:14 It is now the Levites, i.e. the Levitical priests, for which see v.9, who are to proclaim vv.15—26. These are not to be confused with the tribe of Leui, which according to v.12 stand *εὐλογεῖν*, not to proclaim "curses." The collocation *ἀποκριθέντες ... ἐροῦσιν* means "take up the discourse." The participle signifies the onset of *ἐροῦσιν*; there is, after all, no sense of answering or responding here; comp 21:7 for a similar case. The addressees are *παντὶ Ἰσραήλ*, though MT has אל כל איש ישראל.[15] For the adverbial קול רם "with raised voice" LXX has a dative of means *φωνῇ μεγάλῃ* "with a big voice." Both mean "out loud." In the tradition hex added *ανδρι* before Ἰσραήλ to equal MT.

27:15 Vv.15—26 constitute a series of 12 curses, to each of which the popular response is the optative *γένοιτο*, which translates the "Amen" of MT as "may it be (so)." The first one accursed, *ἐπικατάρατος*, is "the person who might fashion *γλυπτὸν καὶ χωνευτόν* ..., and set (it) up in secret." It should be noted that the first and the last (v.26) curses are reflected by the indefinite relative *ὅστις* used to represent the Hebrew pronoun אשר (plus a verb in the future). All other curses lack the pronoun in Hebrew, but have a participle. These are all represented in LXX by participles as well, except for vv.19 and 25, which render the participle by a relative clause: *ὃς ἂν* plus a subjunctive verb. The

---

14. Also found in Kenn 1,181.
15. Theod has *πρὸς πάντας υἱοὺς Ἰσραήλ*, which Aq corrects to <*πρὸς*> *πάντα ἄνδρα Ἰσραήλ*; cf also Sym with *πρὸς πάντα ἄνδρα Ἰσραήλ*.

subject I have translated as "the person," since LXX has rendered האיש, not by ὁ ἀνήρ, but by ὁ ἄνθρωπος. The adjectives refer to man-made idols, either "sculpted" as forbidden by the Decalogue (5:8), or "molded" as the golden calf made by Aaron in the wilderness (9:12,16). Such images are characterized as a βδέλυγμα κυρίῳ, for which see comment at 7:25, and as ἔργον χειρῶν τεχνίτου "the work of a craftsman's hands."

The second clause refers specifically to an individual who sets (it) up secretly, ἐν ἀποκρύφῳ. Presumably, if it were done openly, it might be subject to some judicial process. On the whole, it is characteristic of the twelve verses that the practices accursed are particularly of secret violations of the law, i.e. not easily proven before the elders at the gate, and so are pronounced accursed by the Levites. Such a pronouncement was not easily revoked once it was spoken, and was considered fully effective.

In the tradition the article of ὁ ἄνθρωπος has been omitted by B 848 Byz *z*+, but in spite of this impressive support it is secondary; it represents an early haplography through confusion of the uncials O and Σ; note the consecution of ΟΣΟ. Throughout this catalogue of the accursed the subject is always articulated.[16] A majority A B F M V variant text has glossed θήσει with αυτο, which is hardly surprising, since the verb expects an accussative modifier. But MT's שם lacks a suffix, and here 848 follows MT in representing LXX's more dificult shorter text.[17]

Since this is the first of the curses, the popular response is described, not simply by ... ואמר, but by וענו כל העם ואמרו אמן. Both verbs are plural, and the popular "Amen" is described as "all the people responded by saying." LXX, as expected, uses the participle ἀποκριθείς modifying ἐροῦσιν. The אמן response throughout becomes γενοῖτο in LXX.[18]

27:16 The one accursed is the one who disobeys the commandment of 5:16; ὁ ἀτιμάζων is the antonym of τίμα, i.e. he is the one who dishonors his father or his mother. The popular response follows Sam in using the plural verb ἐροῦσιν over against the אמר of MT. This pattern is set throughout vv.16—26.

16. See the discussion in THGD 59.
17. See THGD 78.
18. Aq translates etymologically by πεπιστωμένως, whereas Theod and Sym transliterate by ἀμήν.

Note that it is no longer called a response, but simply *καὶ ἐροῦσιν πᾶς ὁ λαός*/ואמר כל העם. In the tradition throughout vv.16—26 *b s*+, often accompanied by *f*, do read *ερει* instead of *ἐροῦσιν* of LXX and with MT, though the latter was hardly the motivating factor. The variant text simply viewed the subject *λαός* as requiring a singular predicate.

27:17 The one accursed is the one who changes a neighbour's boundary markers. For the inviolability of a neighbour's property see comment at 19:14. גבול is rightly understood as a collective, hence the plural *ὅρια*. רעהו is always translated in the book without an *αυτου*.[19] Hex, however, does add *αυτου* to equal MT more precisely.

27:18 The accursed is the one who makes a blind man go astray on the road. What is probably meant is misdirection, rather than placing a *σκάνδαλον* before a blind person, as in Lev 19:14.

27:19 The one who subverts the cause of a proselyte and an orphan and a widow is accursed. This is a direct contravention of the command given at 24:17a; see comments ad loc. MT has no conjunction before "orphan," i.e. has the pattern ab+c rather than the LXX's a+b+c.

27:20 Vv.20—23 concern sexual mores. V.20 declares accursed the one who has sexual relations with his stepmother, for which see the discussion at 22:30(23:1). For the translation of כנף "wing" by *συγκάλυμμα* see comment at 22:30. There the root גלה is translated by *ἀνακαλύψει*, but that means the same as the *ἀποκαλύψει* here.[20]

27:21 For the law against bestiality see Exod 22:18, as well as Lev 18:23 20:15—16. The *n* text has added *πας* before the subject, but this hardly changes matters; "anyone who" and "the one who" amount to the same thing.

27:22 Also accursed is one who had sexual relations with a half sister; cf Lev 18:9 20:17. In MT the half sister is described as "his sister the daughter of his

19. See THGD 77—78.
20. See THGD 143.

father or the daughter of his mother," but LXX simplified this as ἀδελφῆς ἐκ πατρὸς ἢ ἐκ μητρὸς αὐτοῦ, "a sister from the father's side or from his mother's."[21] A B+ variant has omitted both cases of ἐκ, thereby changing the half sister to an aunt, forbidden at Lev 18:12—13 20:19. Hex has added αυτου after ἀδελφῆς to represent the suffix of אחתו, as well as after πατρός to equal אביו of MT.

27:23 Also accursed is the one who had relations with his mother-in-law. The Hebrew word חתנתו means a female relative through marriage, not necessarily a mother-in-law, though that relationship first springs to mind.[22] In the tradition other violations of the laws of consanguinity are also accursed, either before or after v.23. The B *b f n* text adds that of the sister-in-law, i.e. the sister of the wife, but this is not forbidden anywhere else in MT.[23] Also added by the *n* text is the case of an aunt, either paternal or maternal, which is forbidden by Lev 18:12—13 20:19.

27:24 The accursed one is he who strikes the neighbour by means of a trick; what is meant is killing one's neighbour, not out in the open, but by some secret strategem. Murder was ordinarily dealt with by the judicial process, but this was the secret slaying of a fellow-Israelite. In fact, δόλῳ renders בסתר "in secret."[24] LXX never translates the suffix of רעהו in Deut,[25] but hex does add αυτου to make up for it.

27:25 The one accursed is one who takes bribes for slaying an innocent person, i.e. ψυχὴν αἵματος ἀθῴου. Innocence is described as being of innocent blood, i.e. innocent of bloodshed. δῶρα understands שחד rightly as a collective, hence the plural. The Byz text articulates the infinitive πατάξαι to emphasize its purposive character.

---

21. See SS 69.
22. Aq opted for νύμφης "daughter-in-law which is also possible. Tar[OJ] both have חמות "mother-in-law," and Tar[N] has חתנתיה "female in-law."
23. See THGD 123.
24. Aq renders by ἐν ἀποκρύφῳ.
25. See THGD 77—78.

27:26 The final curse pronounced is a more general one; it applies to "every person who does not persist in all the words of this law to do them." MT has אשר לא יקים את (דברי התורה) "who will not uphold the words ...." LXX defined the relative pronoun by *πᾶς ἄνθρωπος ὅστις*. In the tradition Syh has placed *πᾶς* under the asterisk, an obvious mistake in transmission for *πᾶς ἄνθρωπος*.[26] LXX also renders את דברי by *ἐν τοῖς λόγοις* wherein it follows Sam which adds כל before "words of."[27] The verb *ἐμμενεῖ* plus *ἐν* does not show the transitive nature of the Hebrew construction, although "to abide by, persist in" is not far removed from the sense of "cause to stand, establish, uphold" of the Hebrew.[28]

26. Although both Tar^J and Tar^N do witness to גברא as an antecedent to the relative pronoun.
27. As do Kenn 84,464^{mg},538,581,651.
28. Jerome in his Commentary ad Galatas (II 3) has transmitted the entire verse as found in The Three. Aq read *maledictus qui non statuerit verba legis huius ut faciat ea, et dicet omnis populus: vere.* Sym translated it: *maledictus qui non firmaverit sermones legis istius ut faciat eos, et dicet omnis populus: amen.* Theod has *maledictus qui non suscitaverit sermones legis huius facere eos, et dicet omnis populus: amen.*

Chapter 28

28:1 Vv.1—14 state what Israel may expect if they truly obey the Lord by living in accordance with the mandate given in the law code (*πάσας τὰς ἐντολὰς αὐτοῦ*). For *καὶ ἔσται ἐάν* see comment at 6:10—11. The emphatic use of the cognate free infinitive is rendered in LXX by a cognate dative of means; *ἀκοῇ ἀκούσῃς* means "you should really obey." For *φυλάσσεσθαι καὶ ποιεῖν* see comment at 5:1. LXX follows Sam in joining the two infinitives by a conjunction over against MT. In LXX both the collocation "careful to do" and "careful and do" occur in almost equal proportions in Deut.[1] For the *ἅς* clause see comment at 4:2.

In the tradition most witnesses have an adaptation of the 27:1, reading *ως αν διαβητε τον ιορδανην εις την γην ην κυριος ο θεος υμων διδωσιν υμιν* before *ἐάν*. This has no basis in MT, and the oldest witnesses, B 848, both support the shorter LXX text. Furthermore, the singular *ἀκούσῃς* and the *σου* of the protasis not only equal MT, but are supported by the singular for the rest of the verse by all Greek witnesses. The singulars singled out are, however, only supported by cod B, though 848, which has a broken text here, seems on the basis of line length to have had the singular as well.[2] The preponderance of the secondary (*εισ*)*ακουσητε* and *υμων* readings is probably due to the influence of the popular gloss from 27:1, which was consistently plural.

The witnesss of 848 supporting the middle form *φυλάσσεσθαι* was determinative for establishing the LXX text as well. The majority active inflection *φυλασσειν* represents the gradual replacement in Hellenistic Greek of the middle by active forms, but Deut still prefers the middle.[3] LXX also represents the minority text for the relative pronoun *ἅς* rather than *οσας*, but LXX is supported inter alia by the uncials A B F M, and is probably to be preferred.[4]

The apodosis is introduced by *καί* in imitation of MT, and is signaled by the future *δώσει*. Since *δώσει* represents נתן in its meaning "set, place" it takes

1. In List 25 in THGD 92—93 11 instances obtain with *καί*, and 13, without.
2. See discussion at THGD 110—111.
3. See the note in THGD 83.
4. See THGD 107.

an accusative σε, not the carelessly substituted σοι of 848+;[5] the Lord "will set you on high over all the nations τῆς γῆς." It is not certain whether τῆς γῆς means "the earth" or simply "the land," i.e. the land of Canaan, but this uncertainty is also the case with הארץ of MT; the former does seem likelier. The text of LXX has the accusative πάντα τὰ ἔθνη, which is supported only by B and 848, all others having the genitive. Both are possible after ἐπί, but the combination of B and 848 must be respected as LXX.[6]

28:2 The theme of this section is introduced by πᾶσαι αἱ εὐλογίαι αὗται which refers to vv.3—13a, with vv.13b—14 restating the condition of obedience. V.2b restates the condition as well. In the restatement most witnesses also add the ἀκοῇ of v.1 before the cognate ἀκούσῃς, but the earliest witnesses, 848 and 963, both lack it, and MT does not support it; it must be secondary. A popular variant substitutes the compound εισακουσης for the simplex; either is sensible, and LXX is based on the oldest witnesses, B and 963. Both occur in this chapter, the simplex at vv.1,2,13 and 49, and the complex at vv.9,15,45,58 and 62. The tradition throughout witnesses to the volatile nature of ἀκούω vs εἰσακούω, with variation attested for each of the nine instances.

28:3 The use of the participle as predicate in LXX translating the pattern of participial predicate is characteristic of the blessing formula; comp the curse formulae of 27:15—26 where the adjective ἐπικατάρατος is used.[7] Such nominal clauses also occur in vv.4—6, after which optatives occur consistently through v.36 wherever God is the subject of blessing or curse. That the desiderative changes to a factual later in the chapter is clear from the future verbs (with God as subject) in vv.49,59—61,63—65,68. I would understand the nominal structures of vv.3—6 also as potential rather than as factual; thus "blessed may you be in the city and blessed may you be in the field." It must be admitted, however, that this cannot be determined from the grammar of either the Greek or the Hebrew. In MT these could be promises: "blessed shall

5. For which see THGD 66.
6. The Three all support the genitive. It is clear that the genitive is an old variant based on understanding ὑπεράνω as a preposition governing the genitive; see THGD 83.
7. See SS 79.

you be ...," though see comment at v.8, but in LXX these pronouncements are probably to be taken as desiderative.

28:4 The blessing is called on the offspring, both of you and of your land as well as on the young of your cattle and of your sheep. MT has פרי "fruit" for offspring, which LXX neatly renders by *τὰ ἔκγονα* (of your belly) and *τὰ γενήματα* (of your land) resp.[8] The popular variant *εγγονα* is an error created by assimilation, and should not be taken seriously. MT has a third "fruit": ופרי בהמתך. Since the word before the phrase ended with the letters מתך its omission by LXX was due to homoioteleuton. Hex has supplied a translation: *και καρπος κτηνων σου*. For the translations *βουκόλια* and *ποίμνια* for שגר and עשתרות resp. see comment at 7:13.

28:5 MT declares blessed your טנא "basket" and your משארת "kneading pan." The two terms recur in a curse context at v.17. The former also occurs at 26:2,4 where it is rendered by *κάρταλλον* "basket." These are the only occurrences of these terms in the Hebrew Bible. LXX interprets these terms as *αἱ ἀποθῆκαι σου καὶ τὰ ἐγκαταλείμματά σου* "your storehouses and your reserves." Since טנא is some kind of container, LXX took the word to refer to a container for the products of the soil, hence, "storage houses, granaries." The second term was etymologized. Since the root שאר means "to be left over" the term "remnants, reserves" was a logical, even if incorrect, interpretation. The Greek is a good example of the ingenuity of the translator in making sense of a passage which he did not understand.

28:6 The final nominal clauses declare you blessed "when you come in" and "when you go out." The Hebrew pattern of ב plus bound infinitive plus pronominal suffix as subject is rendered literally by *ἐν* plus marked infinitive plus *σε* as subject.

An A+ variant text reads *ευλογητος* for both cases of *εὐλογημένος*, as does 848. The source for the variant is unknown, but it is hardly LXX in view of the participles used throughout vv.3—5. In fact, the text of 848 has other peculiarites at this point, which are clearly not LXX, but betray the possible

8. Aq substitutes *καρπός* for *τὰ ἔκγονα*.

influence of some kind of formulaic blessing.[9] εὐλογητός occurs only once in Deut, at 7:14; for its use see comment ad loc.

28:7 The use of the optative mood begins here with παραδῴη. In the tradition a popular A M variant text has added an ad sensum σοι which in turn led to a bewildering variety of variants such as παραδωσει in turn leading to παραδωσει σοι or παραδω σοι. But only the optative supported by 848 can be the original text.[10] The subject of the verb is יהוה in MT, but LXX expanded it as κύριος ὁ θεός σου;[11] hex placed ὁ θεός σου under the obelus to show its lack of an equivalent in MT. The enemies are described as τοὺς ἀνθεστηκότας σοι, which does translate what הקמים עליך intends idiomatically. The participle נגפים "smitten" is well rendered by a perfect passive participle of συντρίβω, viz. συντετριμμένους "having been crushed, beaten," which is an adverbial accusative stating how the Lord would deliver the enemies into the people's power. Thus "may the Lord your God deliver up your enemies who withstood you, beaten before you."

Since in the b part of the verse God is no longer subject, future tenses are used: "by one road they will go out to you, and on seven roads they will flee from you." The last verb is modified by an ἀπό phrase, though MT has לפני. A Byz variant text "corrects" the ἀπό to προ, a reading probably betraying recensional influence of some kind.

28:8 MT has the short form יצו which contrasts with יצוה of Sam. It is not impossible that the optatives of LXX in vv.7—36 may well show the original intent of the Hebrew text; see also the MT vocalization of ידבק at v.21 and of יולך at v.36 as short forms. In any event, LXX has interpreted the short form as precative, with its optative ἀποστεῖλαι modified by ἐπὶ σέ "may he send upon you." This is simpler than MT's verb יצו "command" modified by אתך, which the Masoretes vocalized as "ʾittəkā." The usage is, as far as I could discover, unique in the Hebrew Bible, and its precise nuance is difficult to discover; possibly "ordain (blessings) with you on ...." The rendering ἐπί with accusative may well represent the intent of MT; although the rendering of the

9. See the discussion of the 848 text in THGD 69.
10. See Walters 238—239 as well as THGD 83.
11. See Appositives 1.1.3.

verb by ἀποστεῖλαι is unusual, the verb was used at Lev 25:21 as well for צויתי with the modifier τὴν εὐλογίαν. The blessing is called for "in your storehouses and in all things where you put your hand" together with the locative, "on the land which the Lord your God is giving you." The term for storehouses, ταμιείους, is popularly contracted to ταμειους but the contracted form only became popular in later Hellenistic times. For the οὗ clause as translation of משלח ידך see comments at 12:7 and 23:20. For the relative clause see comment at 1:20.

28:9 The position of "a holy people" is an exalted one; it is a position to which the Lord may raise you up to be a holy people for himself. For λαὸν ἅγιον see comment at 7:6, and cf 14:2 26:19.[12] LXX renders MT's "as he swore to you" by ὃν τρόπον ὤμοσεν τοῖς πατράσιν σου. This is obviously ex par, since almost every time ὤμοσεν occurs in the book it is modified by τοῖς πατράσιν; exactly the same words occur at 19:8 29:13. Hex apparently changed τοῖς πατράσιν σου to σοι so as to equal MT.

V.9b states the conditions: "if you obey the voice of the Lord your God, and walk in his ways." The first clause does not equal MT, which has תשמר את מצות, but rather is the positive equivalent to the negative condition of v.15: לא תשמע בקול. The Byz text changes "obey the voice" to φυλαξῃς τας εντολας, which shows recensional influence. Also in the tradition is an A F M majority gloss ο θεος σου after κύριος 1°. MT has only יהוה, and the shorter text is supported by the oldest witnesses, B 848 and 963; the gloss is clearly secondary.[13] For "walk in his ways" see comment at 10:12. It should be noted that in all 11 cases of this formula in Deut the ἐν is always present,[14] and its omission by 848+ must be considered an error.[15]

28:10 LXX has changed the sense of MT, which says "all the nations of the earth shall see that the name of the Lord has been called over you"; by adding σε after "see" the sense becomes quite different; the ὅτι clause now becomes a causal clause, i.e. "all the nations ... shall see you, because the Lord's name

12. The αλὸν of the critical text is of course a misprint for λαὸν.
13. See THGD 76—77.
14. See List 26 in THGD 94.
15. See THGD 67.

has been called for you," i.e. you are called by the name of the Lord—you are known as his people. This then gives a rationale for the final clause *καὶ φοβηθήσονταί σε*; the nations will be afraid of you, because you are known by the name of the Lord; you are called by his own name; this automatically inspires fear. In the tradition the Byz text has added *επι* before *σοι*, which is probably recensional, since MT has עליך.

28:11 This verse continues the future of v.10 as a divine promise of much material prosperity ("will increase you as to goods"). The subject in MT is simply יהוה, but LXX has the fuller designation *κύριος ὁ θεός σου*, and hex has placed *ὁ θεός σου* under the obelus. This prosperity will obtain according to MT: בפרי of your belly and בפרי of your cattle and בפרי of your land, all of this being "on the land which Yahweh swore to your fathers to give to you." For the first two cases of בפרי the Greek has *ἐπὶ τοῖς ἐκγόνοις* and for the last one, *ἐπὶ τοῖς γενήμασιν*, as being more appropriate for land. *ἔκγονος* is a good translation for the fruit of sentient beings, i.e. "offspring," whereas *γενήματα* refers to the produce of the fields.[16] The popular variant *εγγονοις* "grandchildren" is an error created by palatal nasalization, and could hardly have been intended.

28:12 The text reverts to the optative with *ἀνοίξαι*: "May the Lord open his good treasury, the sky." For the notion of the divine treasuries of moisture, comp Job 38:22: *θησαυροὺς χιόνος, θησαυροὺς δὲ χαλάζης*, and at Gen 7:11: *οἱ καταρράκται τοῦ οὐρανοῦ*. The verb is modified by a purposive infinitival structure, *δοῦναι τὸν ὑετὸν τῇ γῇ σου ἐπὶ καιροῦ αὐτοῦ*. LXX has realized the bound structure מטר ארצך sensibly as an objective genitive, i.e. as rain for your land, for which see 11:14. The *αὐτοῦ* has its reference in *ὑετόν*; it is the rainy season.

In LXX this infinitival structure is modified by another infinitival construction, *εὐλογῆσαι πάντα τὰ ἔργα τῶν χειρῶν σου*. LXX says that the point of God's giving rain at the appropriate time is to bless all your agricultural efforts. MT has the singular מעשה ידך, but the plural is not necessarily textual; furthermore, מעשה and מעשי are homophonous.[17] For similar express-

16. For the parallels see List 40 in THGD 97.
17. And 29 Kenn mss do attest to the plural ידיך. The Tar vary: Tar^{O} has עובדי ידך; Tar^{J} reads עובדי ידיכון, and Tar^{N}, עבד ידיכון.

ions see 2:7 14:28. MT has a different text in that the second infinitive is coordinate with the first one, ולברך. It is then a second purpose for Yahweh's opening his good treasury, the sky, i.e. not only will rain be given for the land in the appropriate season, but by it the Lord will also bless all the labors of your hands.[18]

In the tradition, hex has reordered *σοι κύριος* so as to equal the יהוה לך of MT. An A M V Byz *z*+ variant has changed *οὐρανόν* to the adjective *ουρανιον*; since the nominal follows *τὸν θησαυρὸν αὐτοῦ τὸν ἀγαθόν*, the change to *τον ουρανιον* was almost automatic; it is, however, a mistake. The Byz text has also added the ad sensum gloss *σοι* after *δοῦναι* ex par; after all, *δίδωμι* is commonly modified by a dative showing the indirect object. Of more significance is the majority variant text reading *της γης* for *τῇ γῇ*, since the genitive equals MT more precisely. But all the uncials read the dative, and it is probably original.

The b part of the verse is an exact copy of 15:6b, rather than a translation of MT; in fact, only the first half equals MT, whereas the text *καὶ ἄρξεις* to the end has no counterpart in MT at all, and hex has placed it under the obelus. See comments at 15:6.

28:13 MT begins the verse with a conjunction, but LXX begins asyndetically, as do Pesh and Vulg. The verb *καταστῆσαι* also renders נתן at 1:15 16:18 17:15 in the sense of appoint leaders such as judges or rulers. Here it simply means "to set, place, ordain a position," so "set you at the head and not at the tail." The subject of the verb in MT is יהוה, to which LXX has added *ὁ θεός σου* ex par; hex has recognized this as an addition by placing the phrase under the obelus.

The Greek reinterprets רק, which here must mean "only," i.e. "and you will only be at the top, and not will you be at the bottom." LXX uses a temporal particle *τότε*, thus explicating what the Lord's setting you at the head rather than at the tail means; "and then (i.e. at that time) you will be at the top." What the Greek says is that when the Lord sets you at the head rather than at the tail, then you will be ....

The b part restates the condition which will achieve this exalted status; it is conditional on your obedience to the divine commandments. The *ὅσα*

18. Though Kenn 9 does read לברך.

(clause) is dependent on ἐντολῶν, and is an error for ὅσας, since ἐντολῶν is feminine. Throughout the book ὅσα is only used with neuter plural antecedents, and the critical text should be changed. *οσα* is the result of haplography, since in the uncial script E and Σ are easily confused; thus ΟΣΑΣΕΣΗ easily became ΟΣΑΕΣΗ. For the clause see comment at 4:2. For φυλάσσειν καὶ ποιεῖν see comment at 5:1.

28:14 This verse explicates the condition by means of a stern warning against violating "all the words which I am commanding you today." For the relative clause see comment at 4:2. MT has אתכם as modifier of "commanding," but LXX has σοι under pressure of the common form of the formula. The formula occurs 37 times in the book, and only nine times does ὑμῖν occur, whereas in 28 cases σοι does. For δεξιὰ οὐδὲ ἀριστερά see 2:27 5:32 17:11,20. The collocation modifies παραβήσῃ, and enjoins strict adherence: "deviate neither to the right nor to the left." Such deviation specifically refers to idolatry; it is defined by the infinitival structure "to walk after other gods to serve them." Most witnesses join A M in reading *η* rather than οὐδέ; the variant is probably based on 17:20. The second infinitive, λατρεύειν, refers to cultic service, and is more specific than לעבד, but here it is correctly understood as referring to idol worship.

28:15 With v.15 the long section on the curses following on disobedience begins, a section which continues through v.68. V.15 is the negative parallel to vv.1—2; cf comments ad loc. For καὶ ἔσται ἐάν see comment at 6:10—11. The protasis is much like v.1, even to the extent of lacking a translation of וחקתיו, which hex supplied under the asterisk as *και τα ηκριβασμενα αυτου*; cf comments ad loc. The *t* text has added *και τα κριματα αυτου*, which was probably mediated either by Theod or Sym. Differences between vv.1 and 15, beyond the addition of the negative particle μή, are ἀκοῇ ἀκούσῃς instead of εἰσακούσῃς, φυλάσσασθαι for φυλάσσειν, and ἅς instead of ὅσας. That v.1 has influenced the tradition is clear from the introduction of *ακοη* by an *s z*+ variant text; *φυλασσασθαι* occurs in B, and for ὅσας some *n*+ mss read *ας*, whereas *O* read *οσα*. For the ὅσας clause see comment at 4:2. Over against

MT's לעשות LXX follows v.1 in reading *καὶ ποιεῖν*, only cod F omitting the *καί* to equal MT.[19]

The apodosis is introduced by *καί* in imitation of MT, and parallels v.2 almost exactly in MT, but not in LXX. In v.2 באו was translated by *ἥξουσιν*, but here by *ἐλεύσονται*, and השיג(ו)ך was rendered by *εὑρήσουσίν σε* in v.2, but here by *καταλήμψονταί σε*. Either translation is adequate. V.2 has, however, influenced the tradition in that *O* Byz read *ευρησουσιν* "find" for *καταλήμψονται* "befall."

28:16—19 These verses are the exact counterpart to vv.3—6, except that vv.4 and 5 are transposed. The only difference between the two sets of verses is the substitution of "cursed" for "blessed." For the interpretation of vv.16—19 see comments at vv.3—6.

28:20 Vv.20—36 use optatives whenever God is the subject. The first curse is "may the Lord send you *τὴν ἔνδειαν καὶ τὴν ἐκλιμίαν καὶ τὴν ἀνάλωσιν* on everything that you undertake (lit. where you put your hand), whatever you do." The three nouns may be translated as "poverty and famine and destruction." The first noun has מארה "curse" as its counterpart in MT; presumably the curse is understood in terms of the result of the curse, viz. "scarcity, poverty."[20] The second noun means "famine," but MT has מהומה "panic." The Greek concretizes the Hebrew noun, describing what creates the מהומה.[21] The third noun in MT, מגערת, is a hapax legomenon, though its root גער is well-known in the sense of "to rebuke." To the Greek apparently the divine rebuke meant *ἀνάλωσιν* "destruction."[22] For *πάντα οὗ ἂν ἐπιβάλῃς τὴν χεῖρά σου* see comment at 12:7. *ὅσα ἂν ποιήσῃς* is somewhat of a doublet on the *οὗ* clause, but it equals MT.

V.20b describes the extent of the curse. It is "until he should exterminate you, and until he should destroy you quickly." The first verb, *ἐξολεθρεύσῃ* (*σε*), represents השמידך of Sam rather than the Ni bound infini-

19. Kenn 18,67,107*,109*,150,168*,227 and 239 do read ולעשות.
20. So too Theod and Aq with *σπάνιν*; Sym has *ἀχορτασίαν* "hunger, starvation."
21. Aq has *φαγέδαιναν* "a cancerous sore"; Sym has *ἐμβρίμησιν* "indignation," and Theod reads *ἐκλιμίαν*.
22. Aq has *ἐπιτίμησιν* "censure, criticism" which is probably what מגערת means.

tive of MT. In LXX both verbs have God as actor, whereas in MT the first is a passive structure. In LXX the two ἕως clauses are fully parallel.

The verse ends with a διά phrase, followed by a διότι clause. מעלליך occurs only here in the Pentateuch, and its translation by ἐπιτηδεύματά σου was to become common later in the prophetic books. The plural term means "way of life, manner of living," and is an excellent choice in this context. In MT it is part of the bound phrase רע מעלליך, which LXX renders by an adjectival phrase τὰ πονηρὰ ἐπιτηδεύματά σου. In MT this is succeeded by a relative clause אשר עזבתני "by which you forsook me." The Greek made this a διότι clause. The phrase is rhetorically tied rather loosely to the foregoing: "because you abandoned me." It gives the reason for your evil way of life, whereas MT states that the evil deeds consist of abandoning me. The Byz text changed με to κυριον, by which the entire verse becomes consistent in referring to God in the third person.

28:21 The curse reads: "May the Lord make τὸν θάνατον cling to you." The term θάνατος is often used to render דבר "a fatal pestilence," for which see Note at Exod 5:3.[23] The curse is intended to be fatal: ἕως ἂν ἐξαναλώσῃ σε; the subject is θάνατον. For the εἰς ἥν clause see comment at 1:8.

28:22 The curse calls down seven afflictions. These are given as instrumental datives which render ב phrases of MT; these are the ones with which the Lord may smite you.[24] The first is ἀπορίᾳ "distress," a general word chosen to render שחפת, the meaning of which is uncertain; the word occurs only once elsewhere, Lev 26:16, where it is also rendered by the same word as here. The second one is πυρετῷ "fever" for קדחת, followed by ῥίγει "shivering, cold" for which MT has דלקת, a hapax legomenon derived from a well-known root meaning "to burn," hence usually rendered "inflammation." Presumably the translator thought of the ague, in which fever brings on a bout of shivering. The fourth affliction is ἐρεθισμῷ "irritation" for חרחר, another rare word usually connected with חרר "to glow, burn, scorch.[25] The Greek word also

---

23. Aq translates by λοιμόν, but The Others retain θάνατον.
24. See SS 124.
25. Aq translates by περιφλευσμῷ, and Theod and Sym, by περιφλογισμῷ, both words meaning "a scorching."

occurs at 31:27, where it renders מרי "rebelliousness"; comp also ἐρεθιστής at 21:18, characterizing a rebellious son, מורה. It is difficult to reconstruct what the translator had in mind; was it the restlessness engendered by a fevered state, or possibly an itchy heat rash? This is followed by φόνῳ "slaughter, murder" for חרב "sword," for which see Note at Exod 5:3. The last two, ἀνεμοφθορίᾳ and ὤχρᾳ, are crop diseases usually translated resp. by "blight," i.e. destroyed by the wind, and "mildew."[26]

V.22b promises that these afflictions "will pursue you until they should destroy you." The ἕως clause represents MT's עד אבדך "until you perish," but LXX insists on the divine afflictions being the agents of your destruction. The only significant changes found in the tradition were made by hex, which at least in some places placed εν before the datives to represent the preposition ב in MT.

28:23 This verse is coordinate with v.22b, i.e. constitutes a further result of God's smiting you. MT states that שמיך, which is over your head, shall be copper, but LXX has σοι ὁ οὐρανός. The שמיך is unusual, and LXX tried to make sense out of it by rendering the suffix by a preposed σοι, which then modifies ἔσται, i.e. "and there shall be to you the sky which ...." The A F M *O*′⁾ *y*+ text has omitted σοι, which makes for smoother Greek.[27] Another attempt at simplifying the text represented by a popular F V variant text kept σοι but omitted ὁ 2° and ἡ 2°, i.e. the articles used as relative pronominal particles are removed. But both attempts are secondary; the less elegant text of LXX is original. Lev 26:19 uses the same figure but reverses the metals. The point is, however, the same; a metalic sky and earth means total drought, and hence no crops.

28:24 The Greek has a different interpretion of the verse from that of the Masoretes, who made the first cut after the pair אבק ועפר; this created a difficulty in that it is then unclear what the subject of ירד must be. LXX solves this by cutting between the two, with the second noun, χοῦς, serving as subject of

---

26. For τῇ ὤχρᾳ Aq has ἐν ἰκτέρῳ "with jaundice," but Sym has ἐν ἐρυσίβῃ "with rust."
27. Both Tar[JN] read שמיא, which would show the same attempt at smoothing the text as that of the A text.

καταβήσεται. This then also affects the rendering of השמדך which the Masoretes vocalized as a Ni bound infinitive, "(until) you are annihilated." LXX translates by a doublet in which the verbs are both singular subjunctive transitive verbs, i.e. "until it (i.e. *χοῦς*) eradicate you and until it destroy you." The second of these has been put under the obelus by hex to show its absence in MT.

This then leaves only the rendering for אבק as part of the opening curse: "may the Lord give dust as the rain for your land." *τὸν ὑετὸν τῇ γῇ σου* is a fitting translation for the bound phrase את מטר ארצך. This in LXX is explicated by the future tense, showing what this will entail, viz. "that dust will come down on you out of the sky until ...." The Greek does distinguish between the two words for dust, but they are synonyms, and can hardly be distinguished in translation.

28:25 The curse will involve defeat by your enemies. "May the Lord give you *ἐπικοπήν* before your enemies." The noun translates נגף vocalized as a Ni participle, i.e. "stricken, smitten"; the Greek word means "a cutting down, a slaughter," and is a sensible rendering.[28] In the tradition *ἐπικοπήν* becomes *επισκοπην* in A B+, an old copyist error, which produces nonsense in this context. The error is probably Christian in origin, since the notion of *επισκοπη* was particularly prevalent among Christians.

In the following explication, which is the obverse of the blessing in v.7, the Greek levels the number to agree with *τῶν ἐχθρῶν*, whereas MT has singular pronominal references: אליו and לפניו over against the plural antecedent איביך (presumably because one does not make a foray against more than one enemy at a time).

In the last clause MT reads והיית לזעוה "and you will become a trembling, fright, terror (to all the kingdoms of the earth)." This is probably intended as a reference to the exile of the Judean kingdom in 586 BCE. At least, that is how LXX understood it; it has its *καὶ ἔσῃ ἐν διασπορᾷ*, using a prepositional phrase with the verb "to be" in the Hebraic sense of "become,"

28. Aq has a passive participle like MT in *θραυόμενον* "broken in pieces, shattered." The tradition records two readings for Sym, but only *τροπούμενον* "put to flight" can be correct; the other one, *προσκόπτοντα*, "smitten" is a revision of LXX, and must be Theod.

so "and you will become a dispersion among the kingdoms of the earth." So "a terror to all the kingdoms" is made into "a diaspora among all the kingdoms." What makes this interesting is that the Alexandrian interprets the diaspora as a divine punishment. In Jer 41(34):17, where God says ונתתי אתכם לזועה לכל ממלכות הארץ, LXX in obvious dependence on this verse translates *καὶ δώσω ὑμᾶς εἰς διασπορὰν πάσαις ταῖς βασιλείαις τῆς γῆς*.

28:26 V.26 is still part of the curse of v.25, and details another result of the anticipated defeat at the hands of your enemies. The Greek follows Sam in omitting "all" from לכל עוף. Hex, however, has added *πασιν* under the asterisk before "the birds" to equal MT. "Your corpses will become food for the birds of the sky, and for the wild beasts of the earth." MT has לבהמת which LXX has specified more particularly as *θηρίοις* which makes good sense. Here בהמה must refer to carnivores as at 32:24, a rare usage found more often in the prophets, especially in Jer.[29] The term *ἀποσοβῶν* is contextually apt for מחריד, since what must be intended is not simply "one who frightens, scares," but one who chases away the birds and animals from the unburied carcasses.

28:27 The curse pronounced has the Lord smiting you *ἐν ἕλκει* Αἰγυπτίῳ *ἐν ταῖς ἕδραις* "with an Egyptian boil in the seats," probably a reference to hemorrhoids. MT makes these two coordinate afflictions בשחין מצרים ובעפלים. The last word always has a Qere reading ובטחרים when it refers to hemorrhoids. The word means bumps, and טחרים explains that mounds or bumps on the human body are specifically hemorrhoids; cf *ταῖς ἕδραις* of LXX.[30] In the tradition Αἰγυπτίῳ becomes *αιγυπτιων* in a V *b f*+ variant text; this error is rooted in an auditory confusion; the word is followed by *ἐν* and the addition of *nu* to the dative singular is an obvious mistake.

The second bodily affliction is גרב "mange, scab," which LXX translates by *ψώρᾳ ἀγρίᾳ* "severe itch," probably in the sense of an uncontrollable itch, the word *ἀγρίᾳ* meaning "wild." Since *ἀγρίᾳ* has no isolate basis in MT hex has placed it under the obelus.

---

29. See BDB s.v.
30. Aq has *εἰς τὰς ἕδρας*, whereas Sym more delicately has *εἰς τὰ κρυπτά*.

The third affliction wished on the disobedient is *κνήφη*, a hapax legomenon but a noun related to *κνίζω* "scratch, tickle," so it must mean an itch, something to scratch. The Hebrew word חרס is also a hapax legomenon, and is usually also translated by itch or scabies.[31] Hex has added *εν* before *κνήφη* to show the ב of MT.

Presumably the *ὥστε* clause applies only to *κνήφῳ*. The divine affliction is in any event one that cannot be healed. The clause renders an אשר clause of MT.[32]

28:28 The three afflictions are *παραπληξίᾳ* "madness," *ἀορασίᾳ* "blindness"[33] and *ἐκστάσει διανοίας*. The last term literally means displacement of the mind, and intends extreme horror, terror. The Hebrew term is תמהון לבב "bewilderment, confusion of mind".[34]

28:29 *μεσημβρίας* is a genitive showing time within which "you will be groping about"; this is expressed in MT by a prepositional phrase בצהרים. The *ὡσεί* clause with its optative verb: "as the blind might grope in the dark," is a fine rendering for the כאשר clause, in insisting on the potential nature of the "as" clause. The translator found the clause תצליח את דרכיך peculiar with "you" being responsible for prospering "your" ways. As part of the curse it would make more sense if God, (as a consequence of the divinely inflicted curse introducing this section in v.28), were to be held responsible for your ways not succeeding. So the translator uses the third person *εὐοδώσει*.

The following clause then once again makes a contrast by using the second person: "and then you will be wronged and plundered all the time, and there will be no one coming to help you." As at v.13, which see, LXX uses *τότε* "then, at that time," whereas MT has אך, which can either be taken in an asseverative sense, or in a restrictive, contrastive sense. I suspect that the latter may well have been intended; i.e. in contrast to prospering your ways you will be wronged, etc. LXX, however, makes it temporal, as though "he will not

31. Theod read בחרש, and so has *ἐν ὀστράκῳ*. Aq corrects to *ἐν κνησμῷ*, while Sym has *ἐλεφαντιάσει* "elephantiasis," for which see the statement in Salvesen 160.
32. See SS Inf 133.
33. Aq rendered עורון either by *πηρώσει* or *πωρώσει*; both mean "blindness."
34. Sym translates תמהון by *θάμβῳ* "amazement"; see Salvesen 160.

only not prosper your ways, but at that time you will be wronged,[35] etc. The translator apparently had the restrictive sense of אך in mind.

In the concluding clause MT has no equivalent for σοι, and hex, accordingly, put it under the obelus. It is, of course, an ad sensum interpretation, a way of avoiding the use of βοηθῶν absolutely.

28:30 Vv.30—34 describe the evil deprivations which you will suffer. V.30 begins in MT with "a woman you will betroth, and another man shall ravish her." LXX tones down the language somewhat with "a wife you will take, and another man will possess[36] her." The other clauses stress the same theme: "a house you will build, and you will not inhabit it; a vineyard you will plant, and not will you harvest it." MT has תחללנו which literally means "you shall render it common," i.e. adapted to common or profane use; comp comment at 20:6.[37] The *b* text has carried through the notion of the first clause that another will enjoy the fruits of your efforts, and substitutes ετερος οικησει for "you will not inhabit," and ετερος τρυγησει for "not will you harvest." These are of course secondary.

28:31 You will not enjoy the use of your animals. In each of three devastations the nominal clauses of MT have a passive participle as predicate, and the Greek translates each one literally without a linking verb. This creates a kind of staccato effect in Greek: "your ox butchered before you, and you may not eat of it, etc." In the second one ישוב "shall return" is translated by a passive ἀποδοθήσεταί (σοι). In the last clause, which is exactly the same as v.29, the σοι has a Hebrew counterpart in לך, in contrast to v.29; cf comment ad loc.

28:32 LXX does not repeat the unnecessary σου for θυγατέρες, as MT necessarily does in בנתיך, and most Greek witnesses do as well. But the original text is assured by the support of 848 and 957.[38] The compound subject has δεδομένοι as participial predicate, but in the masculine. Most witnesses change to the feminine by attraction to θυγατέρες immediately preceding it, but LXX

35. Instead of ἀδικούμενος The Others have συκοφαντούμενος (retroverted from Syh).
36. Instead of ἕξει Aq renders literally by συγκοιτασθήσεται.
37. Aq rendered the verb literally by λαϊκώσεις.
38. See THGD 78.

follows the masculine נתנים of MT; the text is also assured by the support of 848.[39] To be given "to another nation" means to be captured as slaves. Most witnesses substitute οψονται for βλέψονται, but B 848 support LXX which assures the originality of LXX;[40] the two are synonyms. The verb is coordinated in MT with וכלות, the free infinitive of כלה "be exhausted, fade, waste away." This is rendered by a medical term, σφακελίζοντες which is used to indicate subjection to a gangrenous condition, to caries or decay. Applied to eyes, as here and at Lev 26:16, it indicates failing or dimming of sight. So "your eyes shall look with dimming vision for them."[41] The translator used the neuter plural, αὐτά, to indicate "your sons and daughters," possibly having παιδία in mind. In MT this is followed by כל היום "constantly," which LXX omits, and hex has added ολην την ημεραν under the asterisk to make up for the omission.

The last clause in MT is somewhat unusual: ואין לאל ידך. NJPS translates this as "but you shall be helpless"; NRSV reads "but be powerless to do anything," and RSV has "and it shall not be in the power of your hand to prevent it." These undoubtedly get the sense of the Hebrew, as does LXX with its καὶ οὐκ ἰσχύσει ἡ χείρ σου "and your hand shall be powerless," a free but adequate interpretation. An *f n+* text reads the present tense, ισχυει, but this is palaeographically inspired by the similarity of Σ and E.

28:33 The plural ἐκφόρια is used of the produce of the land, and correctly interprets פרי.[42] As in MT LXX preposes the compound modifier, whereas the subject modified by a relative clause, "a people whom you do not know," follows the verb. The term πόνους is used metonymically for the products of your toil to equal יגיע.

The last clause contains the particle רק "altogether, constantly" modifying the passive participles עשוק ורצוץ "constantly oppressed and crushed." LXX omits the particle completely and simply has ἀδικούμενος (for which see v.29) καὶ τεθραυσμένος "shattered, broken up." Hex rectified the omission by

39. See THGD 83.
40. See THGD 74.
41. Aq makes it τελούμενοι, which renders כלות literally, but not sensibly; Sym and Theod have ἐκλείποντες.
42. Aq of course renders it by καρπόν.

adding *τοτε* after *ἔσῃ* under the asterisk. For *τοτε* rendering רק see comment at v.13.

28:34 LXX translates משגע by *παράπληκτος* "maddened";[43] comp v.28. The instrumental מן of MT is neatly translated by *διά* plus the accusative "because of, on account of" with the plural *ὁράματα* correctly interpreting מראה as a collective. Byz has exchanged a synonym *οψη* for *βλέψῃ*, which is an old reading already supported by 963.

28:35 The curse consists of the Lord smiting you *ἐν ἕλκει πονηρῷ*; this must be taken as a collective in view of the *ὥστε* clause ending the verse, which specifies no healing "from the sole of your feet to your head." So one might render the phrase by "with bad sores or boils." These are to be "on the knees and on the legs"; *κνήμας* means the lower legs, i.e. below the knees, whereas MT has שקים, which more commonly refers to the upper legs or thighs. In any event, the locations are only illustrative, metonymic for the whole body.

The last clause is a *ὥστε* clause, correctly understanding the relative clause of MT as probable result, in which תוכל becomes an infinitive plus *σε*,[44] thus "so that you cannot be healed."[45] The extent of the affliction is from *ἴχνους τῶν ποδῶν σου*, (which MT has in the singular מכף רגלך), to your head, in other words, from tip to toe, or if one must, from toe to tip!

28:36 The final curse in the optative is *ἀπαγάγοι*: "may the Lord bring you and your leaders away." MT has מלכך "your king,"[46] and the change to *τοὺς ἄρχοντάς σου* is theologically motivated; see discussion at 17:14. *ἄρχοντας* is modified by a relative clause. Quite unusual is the translator's choice of the compound *καταστήσῃς* to render יקים. The more usual rendering of the Hi of קום is either *ἀνίστημι* or the simplex *ἵστημι*; in fact, *καθίστημι* for הקים is unique in the Pentateuch, and it only occurs five times elsewhere (3 times in Jer, and once each in Job Isa). But in the sense of "appoint, ordain" it is appropriate with *ἄρχοντας*.

---

43. Sym preferred *παράφορος* "frenzied, mad."
44. See SS Inf 133.
45. Instead of *ἰαθῆναι* Aq has *ὑγιαθῆναι*, which is a synonym.
46. The Three do have *βασιλέα σου* (retroverted from Syh[m].)

The translator makes no distinction between גוי here and the עם in v.33; both are rendered by ἔθνος. Not only will you be led away to an unknown nation, but you will become idol worshippers, i.e. "you will serve other gods,[47] even wooden and stone ones." The Greek has ξύλοις καὶ λίθοις in apposition to θεοῖς, whereas MT uses singulars, עץ ואבן in the sense of made of wood and stone.

28:37 The idiom היית ל is expressed in LXX by ἔσῃ ἐν, and it inserts ἐκεῖ between the two, thereby tying this verse to the preceding. Since this has no equivalent in MT, hex has placed the word under the obelus. In MT what "you will become" is given as לשמה למשל ולשנינה "an appalment, a proverb and a taunt." Presumably the first word is also intended as something verbal, i.e. an expression of horror. LXX has interpreted the three somewhat freely by αἰνίγματι "enigma, puzzle,"[48] παραβολῇ "comparison, analogy," and διηγήματι "tale, story,"[49] The three terms are all intended in a pejorative sense, i.e. Israel will become in the speech of peoples a puzzle—how could so great a nation have fallen so low, a proverbial example of a fall from grace, and a tale told concerning a people enslaved among all the nations. In other words, people will talk in disparaging terms of a once-great Israel. Only the first of the three is governed by ἐν representing the preposition of לשמה in MT. Since all three are governed by a ל in MT, hex has added εν before παραβολῇ and διηγήματι as well.

28:38 Your fields will produce little for you, i.e. "you will bring out much seed into the field, and you will bring in (but) little." The Byz text has a more literal rendering for תאסף with its συναξεις but it thereby destroys the fine balance between ἐξοίσεις and εἰσοίσεις.

The reason for this crop failure is ἡ ἀκρίς "the locust," which will devour αὐτά. The plural is ad sensum for the ἐκφορία; see v.33; the singular suffix of יחסלנו should not be pressed.

47. Using λατρεύσεις, not δουλευσεις as in v.64; see Daniel 68,101.
48. Aq rendered לשמה by εἰς ἀφανισμόν, but Sym has εἰς ἀπορίαν (retroverted from Syh^{m}); see Salvesen 161.
49. Aq thought of the wrong root שנה and translated by δευτερώσει.

28:39 Your vineyard will be unproductive as well. MT uses the plural כרמים, but then later makes reference to it by a singular pronoun in תאכלנו. The translator has done the opposite, using ἀμπελῶνα, but translating the suffix of תאכלנו by αὐτά. These are both ad sensum adjustments in LXX. One normally only plants one vineyard, but the grapes constituting its fruit would be referred to by a plural.

Though you may plant and work up a vineyard, you will not drink its wine, οὐδὲ εὐφρανθήσῃ ἐξ αὐτοῦ. This is hardly a translation of the Hebrew ולא תאגר, which means "and not will you gather in, store (i.e. the fruit)," but rather a further reflection on drinking wine, which makes the heart merry. Not having wine available means that you will not make merry because of it.[50] And all this because the worm will devour them. Since MT lacks a prepositional phrase modifying the verb, hex has placed ἐξ αὐτοῦ under the obelus.

28:40 Your olive orchards will fail. In a similar vein to the preceding two verses: "You will have olive trees in all your borders, and (i.e. but) you will not anoint with oil." The reason given is that ἐκρυήσεται ἡ ἐλαία σου "your olive tree will let drop (i.e. the still unripe olives)." MT has זיתך as subject, i.e. "your olives will fall off." זית is here a collective.[51]

28:41 What is meant by "and they will not be yours" is that your children will not remain with you. Children were generated inter alia to take care of one in old age, but they "will go away into captivity." Note that ἐν can be used with verbs of movement in the sense of εἰς "into."[52]

28:42 MT says "all your trees and the produce of your land the cricket will take over." LXX translates עצך by τὰ ξύλινά σου, which is unexpected since this noun usually means "things made of wood,"[53] though I suspect that here it means various kinds of wood (trees). In any event, these, along with the produce of your land, will be destroyed by the rust fungus, ἐρυσίβῃ.

---

50. Sym has οὐδὲ συνάξεις (retroverted from Syh^{m}).
51. As is obvious in Tar^{OJ} with ‘י(ן)תרון’, whereas Tar^{N} has ‘ייתתר נצייה (דזייתיכון)’, i.e. "the blossoms of your olive trees will remain (i.e. won't ripen)."
52. See SS 190—200.
53. Sym has the more usual τὰ ξύλα (retroverted from Syh^{m}).

28:43—44 The fortunes of proselyte and Israelite will be reversed. The proselyte's fortune "shall rise over against you *ἄνω ἄνω*, but you will go down *κάτω κάτω*." The repetition of the adverbs shows gradualness, thus "higher and higher" versus "lower and lower." In the tradition the 963 *d*+ text has these only once each, probably by haplography, though intentional shortening of the text, particularly in the *d* text which tends to abbreviate, should not be ruled out.

The new status is reflected at the economic level, a reversal of the blessings anticipated in vv.12b—13a, i.e. the role of creditor and debtor will be reversed; *οὗτος* (referring to the proselyte) will become the creditor. In the tradition *οὗτος* appears as *αυτος* in *C'*ʾ s+, which is indeed a more literal rendering of הוא,[54] though LXX usually renders the pronoun by the demonstrative.

Also changed is the verbal root of *δανιεῖ* (and of *δανιεῖς*) in *oI z*+ to *δανεισει(ς)*, thereby reflecting *δανείζω*, rather than *δανίζω* with its Attic future. The variant text was created by confusion between the two roots, which not only mean the same, but in Hellenistic times were also pronounced alike in the present stem. The Attic future is clearly original. LXX preposed the dative modifier of *δανιεῖς* representing תלונו. Hex corrected the word order by its *ουκ εκδανιεις τουτω*. Note also the change of the simplex verb to the compound, with no significant change in meaning, i.e. "lend" vs "lend out"; both expect payment of interest charges. The compound is also supported by 963 Byz+, but the change is merely a stylistic one.

In v.44b the promise of v.13a becomes a curse: the proselyte will become (*εἰς*) *κεφαλήν, σὺ δὲ εἰς οὐράν*. In the tradition a B popular reading changes the *εἰς* phrases into a predicate nominative, i.e. *κεφαλη* and *ουρα* resp. This is also sensible, but it is not what MT says, nor is it original;[55] comp v.13.

28:45 This verse serves as a general summarizing conclusion to vv.15—44, as the reference to *πᾶσαι αἱ κατάραι αὗται* shows. "All these curses" are personified, not only as coming upon you, but also as chasing you, and catching you. These in turn are modified in עד השמדך "until you are annihilated."

54. The Others also all have *αὐτός*.
55. See THGD 61—62.

But the translator substituted for this "ἕως ἂν ἐξολεθρεύσῃ σε καὶ ἕως ἂν ἀπολέσῃ σε, which is not a translation of MT at all, but an importation from v.20, where this occurs (though also modified by ἐν τάχει at the end). Since quantitatively there are two ἕως clauses, but only one עד clause in MT, hex has marked the second one as an extra by placing it under the obelus.

The reason for the threatened annihilation of Israel is expressed in the ὅτι clause—it was Israel's disobedience: "you did not obey the voice of the Lord your God φυλάξαι his commandments and τὰ δικαιώματα αὐτοῦ, which he commanded you."[56] The A+ text has the simplex rather than εἰσήκουσας, but the translator preferred to use the compound so as to stress the notion of obedience. Another A+ text added σε after the infinitive to indicate its subject, but this would be otiose, since the verb it complements is already inflected in the second person singular. For "his commandments and his ordinances," see comment at 4:1.[57] In the tradition the infinitive appears popularly as a marked present middle infinitive του φυλασσεσθαι, but the unmarked aorist is supported by B 963, and must be original. The middle is, however, common in LXX in the sense of "keep a law, observe, follow."[58]

28:46 Over against MT's והיו referring to "all these curses" of v.45, LXX has the singular καὶ ἔσται, because the compound subject is σημεῖα καὶ τέρατα, and as neuter plurals takes a singular predicate. For "signs and wonders" see comment at 4:54. Usually the collocation reflects what God has done for Israel, but here these are signs of divine displeasure with his people. LXX also changes the intent of MT considerably. In MT לאות ולמופת modify היו, thus "they shall become signs and wonders," along with two ב phrases also modifying the verb, בך "against you," and בזרעך "against your seed." LXX has changed this around so that the ל phrases become the subject, and the verse may be rendered "And there shall be signs and wonders among you and among your seed forever." What the translator has done is to disregard the ל prepositions altogether. What is odd about this interpretation is that the signs and wonders do not necessarily refer to the curses of v.45 at all, but seem to

56. Aq articulated the infinitive as τοῦ φυλάξαι to show the marker of לשמר; Sym had τοῦ φυλάσσειν.
57. Instead of τὰ δικαιώματα αὐτοῦ Aq has his usual τὰ ἀκριβάσματα αὐτοῦ for חקתיו (retroverted from Syh^{m}).
58. See Bauer s.v. 2b.

introduce an entirely new sentence. In MT this verse is part of the conclusion, but in LXX it is tied to the following verse, which the editorial punctuation of the critical text also indicates.

28:47 The reason for the signs and wonders of v.46 happening to you: "because you did not serve the Lord your God with gladness and with a good heart, because of the abundance of all things." In MT this is to be taken with the following verse, i.e. as the reason for v.48, but not so in LXX. The translator intentionally chose *ἐλάτρευσας* rather than *εδουλευσας* to render **עבדת** to show that Israel had failed to serve cultically, to worship, with *εὐφροσύνῃ καὶ ἐν ἀγαθῇ καρδίᾳ*.[59] There had been no evidence of gratitude in Israel's actions. The adjectival phrase *ἀγαθῇ καρδίᾳ* is a rare one. It does occur in sapiential literature (Prov 14:33 Eccl 9:7 Sir 26:4 33:13b[30:27]), but rarely elsewhere. (I found only 2Chr 7:10 and Judith 8:28). What the phrase probably means is integrity, sincerity of intention. The worship of God must be wholehearted, without reserve.

28:48 This verse, though it contrasts with v.47 in using *λατρεύσεις* in a positive sense,[60] actually serves as a bridge to the remainder of the chapter, and more particularly to vv.49—57. What is envisioned is that "you will serve your enemies." Here *λατρεύω* is used not in a cultic sense, but simply in the sense of service as a slave.[61] The translator would naturally choose the same verb to emphasize the contrast between serving the Lord your God in v.47 and serving your enemies here. Obviously the service of God is not the same as the service of one's enemies. *ἐχθροῖς* is modified by a relative clause, *οὓς ἐπαποστελεῖ κύριος ἐπὶ σέ*, for the Hebrew אשר ישלחנו יהוה בך. One notes that LXX in the interests of good Greek did not translate the pronominal suffix of the verb. This did not deter Origen, however, from adding *αυτους* after the verb under the asterisk in hex to represent it. Most witnesses follow the F M

59. See Daniel 68—69.
60. See Daniel 68—69.
61. Theod accepted LXX's verb, but Aq, followed by Sym, translated **עבדת** more appropriately by *δουλεύσεις*. All Three render איביך, however, by the singular *τῷ ἐχθρῷ σου* presupposing איבך as in Kenn 14. On Theod's reading see f.n.59 in Daniel 114.

reading adding *ο θεος σου* after *κύριος*, but this has no support in MT, and must be ex par.

V.48b states the matter graphically: "he (i.e. the Lord) will place an iron *κλοιόν* on your neck until he would annihilate you." The adjectival phrase translates the Hebrew bound structure על ברזל "yoke of iron."[62] *κλοιόν* means "a collar," and as a rendering for על occurs only here in the Pentateuch (*ζυγόν* is more common); it also occurs throughout the story of Rehoboam's reply to the request of "all Israel" for relief in 3Reg 12, but nowhere else in the OT.

28:49 *ἐπάξει* "shall bring" is a most unusual rendering for ישא "shall raise, lift up." In fact, the active verb only occurs for נשא once elsewhere in OT; at Isa 10:24 LXX reads *πληγὴν γὰρ ἐπάγω ἐπὶ σέ*.[63] Here, however, it is contextually driven, probably influenced by the relative clause of v.48, where the Lord also would be sending enemies against you. Here it is "a nation from far off," in fact, "from the end of the earth," whom the Lord will send against you. This nation is described in MT as כאשר ידאה הנשר "as the eagle pounces (or swoops)." LXX interprets the verb as a nominal: *ὡσεὶ ὅρμημα ἀετοῦ* "like the swooping of an eagle." In MT this is probably meant to describe the suddenness of an attack. The text then goes on with no further reference to the כאשר clause with "a nation אשר לא תשמע לשנו" usually understood as a nation whose language you would not understand. But LXX did not understand it in this way. The translator took the image of the swooping of the eagle to refer to the silence of the attack, and so translates the continuation as "a nation whose voice (or better 'the sound of which') they did not hear"; it would be a surprise attack.[64] In the tradition the relative *οὗ* becomes *ο* in a popular B variant text, probably by attraction to its antecedent *ἔθνος*, but it should be genitive to agree with *αὐτοῦ*.[65] Here the oldest witness, 963, witnesses to the original text.

28:50 The phrase עז פנים probably means "stern, unyielding in appearance," and is interpreted by LXX as *ἀναιδὲς προσώπῳ* "ruthless in appearance,"

---

62. Aq renders על by *ζυγόν*. For the adjectival phrase see SS 63.
63. Which The Three correct: Aq to *ἀρεῖ*, and Theod and Sym to *ἐπαρεῖ*.
64. Aq rendered לשן by *γλώσσης*.
65. See THGD 58.

which is not a bad rendering. This is explicated by the ὅστις clause. The odd periphrastic structure פנים לזקן is properly understood as πρόσωπον πρεσβυτέρου. The Greek says ὅστις οὐ θαυμάσει which is then modified by "face of the elder"; the idiom θαυμάσει πρόσωπον "honor the face" here means "which will not respect (the elder)."[66] In the tradition the B Byz+ text reads πρεσβυτου instead of πρεσβυτέρου, but זקן is never rendered by πρεσβύτης in Deut, only by πρεσβύτερος or γερουσία.[67]

This ruthless nation is also one which does not pity a youth. The verb יחן really means "to be gracious," and so to be merciful,[68] which throughout the OT is usually translated by ἐλεέω "take pity, be merciful."

28:51 That distant nation will devour the offspring of your cattle and the produce of your ground, for which see v.11. MT continues with עד השמדך as it did in vv.20,24,45,61, but LXX disregards this, continuing with a ὥστε clause. Hex has added εως αν εχτριψη σε under the asterisk to fill the lacuna. The omission may well have been a considered one, however, in view of the עד clause at the end of the verse, which is similar to the one omitted. Instead of the ὥστε clause MT has a relative clause which makes the collocation, אשר to the end of the verse, parallel with the first part of the verse. LXX preferred to make the verse a unity, and so changed the relative clause so as to make it integral to it. The ὥστε clause with infinitive now shows the (probable) result of κατέδεται; it is "so as not to leave for you grain, wine, oil ... until it should destroy you."[69] The subject of ἀπολέσῃ must still be the ἔθνος of v.50. The list of "grain, wine, oil" has the nouns unconnected, whereas in MT "oil" is joined by a conjunction. An A+ variant does add και before ἔλαιον, but this is stylistic, rather than recensional. Elsewhere in the book this list is joined by καιs throughout.[70] For βουκόλια τῶν βοῶν σου καὶ τὰ ποίμνια τῶν προβάτων σου see comment at v.18.

---

66. Aq renders the idiom by ὃς οὐ λήψεται, which simply renders ישא literally; Theod translates as ὃς ου θαυμάζει, whereas Sym is more idiomatic with ὃς οὐ τιμήσει.
67. See THGD 59.
68. Aq translates לא יחן by οὐ δωρήσεται "he will not bestow grace, gifts."
69. See SS Inf 133.
70. See list 41 in THGD 97.

28:52 MT threatens siege on the part of the enemy; והצר לך בכל שעריך occurs twice in the verse introducing both parts of the verse, but LXX avoids the notion of siege altogether. In fact, LXX changes the first instance to *καὶ ἐκτρίβῃ σε ἐν πάσαις ταῖς πόλεσίν σου*. The subjunctive verb indicates that this continues the *ἕως ἄν* construction ending v.51, thus "(until it destroy you), and wipe you out in all your cities." For *πόλεσίν σου* for שעריך see comment at 12:15.[71] This destruction will continue until *καθαιρεθῶσιν τὰ τείχη σου τὰ ὑψηλὰ καὶ τὰ ὀχυρά*. Unusual is the plural verb, since neuter plural subjects usually take a singular verbal predicate.[72] The reference to walls must be to walls of all the cities of the land; note *ἐν πάσῃ τῇ γῇ σου*.[73] *τείχη* is modified by *ἐφ' οἷς σὺ πέποιθας ἐπ' αὐτοῖς*, which is purely in imitation of MT. The use of the perfect verb is unusual as a rendering of the participle בטח; one might have expected a present tense, but the perfect is contextually driven.

The second part of the verse has *καὶ θλίψει σε* for והצר לך, again avoiding the notion of siege, but insisting that the distant nation "will afflict you in all your cities." This is in turn followed in MT by בכל ארצך, which LXX omits, probably because of homoioteleuton, and it is restored under the asterisk by hex as *εν παση τη γη σου*. That the omission was original LXX is clear from the fact that the relative clause which follows was introduced by *αἷς*, i.e. *πόλεσίν* is its antecedent, whereas it should have been *η*, as in hex.[74] Hex has also reordered the *αἷς* clause by transposing *σοι* to the end to equal the נתן יהוה אלהיך לך of MT.

28:53 The enemy's attack will result in terrible shortage of food; comp v.51. This will result in cannibalism; for *ἔκγονα τῆς κοιλίας σου* see comment at v.4 and at 7:13. This collocation is particularized as "*κρέα* of your sons and of your daughters," since it is the object of *φάγῃ*. These were those *ὅσα ἔδωκέν σοι κύριος*. MT makes the subject "Yahweh your God," and most witnesses

71. Instead of *καὶ ἐκτρίψῃ σε* Aq Sym have *πολιορκῆσαί σε* (retroverted from Syh[m]); comp Jer 39:2.
72. SS 198 explains this as "dass nicht von den Mauern einer Stadt die Rede ist, sondern von denen aller befestigten Städte des Landes," which may well have been in the mind of the translator.
73. See SS 198.
74. The Three indeed all have *ᾗ*, presupposing *γῇ*.

add *ο θεος σου*. It is, however, likely secondary; 963 supports LXX and Sam lacks an expressed subject entirely.[75] In fact, throughout the curse materials of this chapter normally only Lord occurs, i.e. without an appositive, when he is the actor, whereas when the people's actions are referred to, "Lord your God" is used. In other words, LXX is here more consistent than MT.[76]

The reason for this fearful state is expressed by two *ἐν* phrases: "in your *στενοχωρίᾳ* and in your *θλίψει*, with which your enemy afflicted you." Both nouns are modified by *σου*, which has no basis in MT, and hex has placed both under the obelus. The two nouns in Hebrew are resp. מצור and מצוק.[77] A gloss after *ὁ ἐχθρός σου*, either as (*ο*) *εν ταις πολεσιν σου* or as *εν πασαις ταις πολεσιν σου*, is a popular one taken over ex par; see vv.55 and 57.

28:54 The nominal האיש הרך "the tender person" becomes simply *ὁ ἅπαλος* in LXX, and so hex has prefixed *ο ανηρ* under the asterisk. It is unnecessary to the sense, and was simply abbreviated in Greek. The other element in the compound is *τρυφερὸς σφόδρα* "very delicate."[78] In MT this coordinate structure is a pendant construction according to Masoretic accentuation; thus it means "As for the tender and very delicate person, (his eye shall be evil against)." The translator interpreted this somewhat differently by making the verb transitive, viz. *βασκανεῖ* plus a dative of means *τῷ ὀφθαλμῷ*.[79] For this practice being declared evil, see Sir 14:6,8. What LXX makes of it is "the tender and very delicate shall bewitch with the (evil) eye." In MT תרע עינו means "he will begrudge." LXX does not render the suffix of עינו, though a popular (hex?) addition of *αυτου* does obtain.[80]

The accusative modifiers of *βασκανεῖ* are *τὸν ἀδελφὸν καὶ τὴν γυναῖκα ... καὶ τὰ καταλειμμένα τέκνα*. In MT both "brother" and "children" have third masculine singular suffixes. In the tradition an *αυτου* has been added by most witnesses after *ἀδελφόν*, and by hex after *τέκνα*. *γυναῖκα* is modified by *τὴν ἐν κόλπῳ αὐτοῦ*. Most witnesses articulate *κόλπῳ*, but B 963 as the oldest

75. See THGD 55.
76. Cf Appositives 2.1.
77. Aq renders these etymologically by *περιοχῇ* "enclosing, containment" and by *ἐπιχύσει* "a pouring upon," presupposing the root יצק, rather than the צוק of MT.
78. Aq has *τρυφητής*, whereas Sym has *σπάταλος* "lascivious."
79. Aq translates the verb literally by *πονηρεύσεται*.
80. See SS 101.

witnesses do not; the articulation is probably a stylistic improvement.[81] The relative clause modifying *τέκνα* contains the verb *καταλειφθῇ*. The majority text witnesses to an *αυτω* gloss, but both B and 848 support LXX, as does MT.[82]

28:55 MT continues with מתת which LXX renders by *ὥστε δοῦναι* and in view of *βασκανεῖ τῷ ὀφθαλμῷ* of v.54 this is not an incorrect rendering;[83] it still means that the tender and very delicate will by casting an evil eye negate giving anything. One can then render the structure by "so as not to give."[84] The phrase *ἀπὸ τῶν σαρκῶν* is, like its parent מבשר, partitive: "any of the flesh." The relative pronoun *ὧν* modifies *σαρκῶν*, not the nearer *τέκνων*.

The reason for his stinginess is given in the *διά* structure; it is "because of nothing having been left to him ...." This represents a מבלי structure in MT.[85] For the two *ἐν* phrases see comments at v.53. The *σου* modifying *θλίψει* has no basis in MT, and hex has put it under the obelus. Most witnesses omit the *σου*, but it is present in the oldest mss, and was present in hex; it is likely original. The final relative clause is singular in MT: "which your enemy will afflict," but LXX makes this plural; this is an improvement, since the reference has consistently been to the distant enemy who invades. LXX here follows Sam, which reads יציקו לך איביך. The relative pronoun *ᾗ* is inflected by attraction to its antecedent *θλίψει*. For the final *ἐν* phrase see v.52.

28:56 This verse is the feminine counterpart to v.54. Over against v.54 the *ἁπαλή* is *ἐν ὑμῖν*, rather than *ἐν σοί*, but MT has the singular, and the change to the plural is unexpected, and inexplicable in view of v.54. The relative clause in MT has נסתה כף רגלה, which LXX has interpreted by *πεῖραν ἔλαβεν ὁ πούς αὐτῆς*, omitting the כף and rendering the verb by "taken on to attempt," i.e. made an attempt. The infinitive is in turn modified by *βαίνειν* representing the free infinitive הצג. This tender and delicate woman does not even try to walk on the ground, because of *τὴν τρυφερότητα καὶ διά τὴν*

81. See THGD 106.
82. See THGD 74.
83. It is, however, a rare equivalence; see SS Inf 104.
84. The marginal reading *μὴ δοῦναι* of ms 321 confirms this understanding.
85. See SS Inf 132.

ἁπαλότητα "because of delicacy and tenderness." The abstracts represent the Hebrew abstracts התענג and רך correctly.[86]

For βασκανεῖ τῷ ὀφθαλμῷ αὐτῆς see comment at v.54. The accusative modifiers are "her husband who is in her bosom, and τὸν υἱόν and her daughter." LXX has disregarded the suffix of בבנה, and hex has accordingly added αυτης to make up for it.[87]

In the tradition σφοδρα has been added by most witnesses after τρυφερά, but this is imported from v.54. A popular 963 variant text has transposed τρυφερότητα and ἁπαλότητα, but the order of LXX equals MT, and is original. The αὐτῆς modifying ἄνδρα has no equivalent in MT, and hex has placed it under the obelus.

28:57 Syntactically the first part of the verse (through τέκῃ) is coordinate with the accusatives modifying βασκανεῖ of v.56, viz. τὸ χόριον ... καὶ τὸ τέκνον. So great will be her need that she will secretly eat "her afterbirth, which goes out between her thighs,[88] and the child which she might bear." MT has בבניה, but LXX has the singular as more appropriate, and does not translate the suffix, which is otiose; it is of course her baby, not someone else's ὃ ἂν τέκῃ. But the majority of witnesses do add αυτης. B 963+, however, do not, and clearly represent the original text.

The γάρ clause speaks of the ἔνδειαν πάντων, which stresses the lack of everything, i.e. utter want. For στενοχωρίᾳ and θλίψει see comment at v.53. For the dative singular relative pronoun, see comment at v.55. For "in your cities" see comment at 12:15. The majority text has added πασαις before "the cities," which is taken from v.55. Note that the oldest witnesses, B 848 and 963, all lack πασαις, and the shorter text is also found in MT.[89]

28:58 This begins the last major section of the chapter, warning against failure to obey the demands of the Law Code. V.58 constitutes the protasis, with the next two verses as the apodosis. The condition is your not being obedient in doing all the words of this law. Unexpected is εἰσακούσῃς for תשמר. The verb

86. Aq translates the relative clause by <ἣ> οὐκ ἐπείρασεν ταρσὸς ποδὸς αὐτῆς ὑφίστασθαι ἐπὶ τῆς γῆς ἀπὸ τῆς τρυφῆς καὶ <ἀπὸ> ἁπαλότητος.
87. As at v.54 Aq translates the verb by πονηρεύσεται.
88. Aq translates בשליתה by ἐν δευτερίῳ αὐτῆς.
89. See THGD 83—84.

normally renders שמע (197 times),[90] but only at v.9 Exod 16:28 and 2Chr 34:21 does it equate with שמר. The translator must have misread the word as תשמע. In fact, "be careful to do" makes a much better idiom. Oddly the original singular verb is only sparsely supported (only four witnesses), all others reading the plural; the singular also represents MT, and must be original. The phrase "words of this law" is described as *τὰ γεγραμμένα ἐν τῷ βιβλίῳ τούτῳ*; this law that Moses has been proclaiming to Israel is a written document, presumably comprising chh.12—26, and the designation "Law Code" is not inappropriate.

The heart of being obedient in practicing all the words of this law is summarized by an infinitival structure as "to fear this glorious and marvelous name, the Lord your God." For the rare rendering of נורא by *θαυμαστόν* see Note at Exod 15:11. As descriptive of the divine name, it is not inappropriate. The use of *θαυμαστόν* here, rather than the more common *φοβερός* rendering, may have been influenced by the coordinate *ἔντιμον*.

28:59 The use of *παραδοξάσει* "render extraordinary, exceptional" to describe the Lord's sending plagues stresses the extraordinary nature of the divine imposed plagues—they will be exceptional plagues indeed.[91] Both the plagues and the חלים "diseases" are characterized as נאמנים/נאמנות "certain," hence constant, persistent. The translator translated the first one describing plagues as *θαυμαστάς* "amazing," but the *νόσους* as *πιστάς* "constant, persistent," so chronic. The first rendering is unique in the OT; the translator may have been influenced by the verb *παραδοξάσει*, and used an adjective which would coordinate with *μεγάλας*. It certainly does not translate נאמנות. The Byz text has an odd variant which is palaeographically inspired, *πλειστας* for *πιστάς*.[92]

28:60 MT says "and he will bring back on you every sickness of Egypt." LXX makes the object *πᾶσαν τὴν ὀδύνην Αἰγύπτου τὴν πονηράν*. The term *ὀδύνην* is an unexpected rendering for מדוה which means "illness, disease"; it only occurs once elsewhere, at 7:15 where it is correctly translated by *νόσους*. The word is a general term meaning "pain," hence distress, so "every evil afflic-

90. According to Dos Santos.
91. Aq translated הפלא by *θαυμαστώσει*.
92. Sym understood the intent of נאמנים, as his *ἐπιμόνους* shows.

tion of Egypt."[93] Since MT has no equivalent for τὴν πονηράν, it is put under the obelus in hex. ὀδύνην is described by a relative clause, ἣν διευλαβοῦ ἀπὸ προσώπου αὐτῶν "of which you were in dread, were fearful." The plural is odd, but it follows the Hebrew. Possibly it presupposes the Hebrew מדוי, which Sam also read,[94] but this still does not explain the change in number in LXX which has ὀδύνην but αὐτῶν; presumably the translator took ὀδύνην as a collective. This is also the case with the last clause, καὶ κολληθήσονται ἐν σοί, where the plural verb again presupposes ὀδύνην as a plural concept.

28:61 חלי is here translated by μαλακίαν, rather than by the νόσους of v.59.[95] LXX follows MT in preposing the long modifier to the verb: "and every sickness and every plague τὴν μὴ γεγραμμένην in the book of this law"; the attributive participial construction correctly renders a relative clause in MT. Only the afflictions not mentioned in the book are referred to, since those mentioned need not be brought up. This was, however, too limited for the tradition, and the majority A variant text added και πασαν την γεγραμμενην, which has no support in MT, nor is it in the oldest witnesses, B 848 and 963.[96] The reference to "book of this law" must be to the Deut Code of chh.12—26. As in v.20, which see, LXX does not follow the עד השמדך of MT but rather the active form (Hi) of Sam; thus "until he (or it) annihilate you"; comp also vv.24,45,51.

28:62 This verse changes to the plural second person, which is continued through v.63, after which the singular returns with v.64. MT interrupts the plural with singulars in v.62b, and in the אשר clause of v.63. Sam is consistently plural, except for the אשר clause of v.63. Only LXX has a consistent plural text for these two verses.[97]

LXX translates נשארתם quite properly by καταλειφθήσεσθε.[98] ἀνθ' ὧν ὅτι "instead of" occurs only here in the book as a translation of תחת אשר,

93. Aq translates מדוה by ταλαιπωρίαν.
94. Kenn 14,84,101,107,167,605 read מדוי. The Tar all read the plural as well.
95. Aq has ἀρρωστίαν.
96. See THGD 74.
97. See THGD 110.
98. Theod followed LXX in the κατα- compound. Aq used ὑπο-, and Sym the περι- compound.

which only obtains four times in Deut. Twice, vv.47 and 22:29, it is rendered by ἀνθ' ὧν, i.e. without ὅτι, and once at 21:14, by διότι.

εἰς πλῆθος renders לרב literally, but the majority B 963 has τω πληθει. The Hebrew phrase only occurs twice elsewhere in the book, at 1:10 and 10:22. In both cases LXX reads τῷ πλήθει. The fact that 848 reads εἰς πλῆθος does not necessarily mean that it is original.[99] The bilingual scribe of 848 may well have been unconsciously influenced by his knowledge of the Hebrew. I would now read τῷ πλήθει as original LXX.[100] 848 does not support the dative, however, and the variant is probably a stylistic change. The ὅτι clause is in the plural, and only cod B changes to the singular, thereby agreeing with MT, but it is doubtful that this is recensional. Cod B has some odd readings in v.63 as well, and its character is somewhat unsteady here.[101]

28:63 For καὶ ἔσται plus ὃν τρόπον see comment at 6:10—11. The Lord once "rejoiced over you to prosper you and to increase you, so (now) the Lord will rejoice over you to annihilate you." That the Lord should delight in destroying Israel is a strong and unusual statement, but it shows the uncompromising nature of God's demand for obedience to the divinely given laws.[102]

That the infinitival marker was thought by Origen to be properly rendered by the articulation of the infinitive is well-known, so it is not surprising that hex should add του under the asterisk before ἐξολεθρεῦσαι. It might have been expected for ποιῆσαι and πληθῦναι as well, since both are marked by ל in the Hebrew, but the articulation of the infinitive was apparently a hit-and-miss affair for Origen, and only occasionally was a του prefixed to an unmarked infinitive of LXX by hex. MT, however, has another infinitive after ἐξολεθρεῦσαι, viz. ולהשמיד אתכם, and hex has added και του εκτριψει υμας under the asterisk as its equivalent.

MT makes the first cut in the verse at this point, placing the אתכם under the *ethnach*. LXX honors this tradition by changing to the finite verb in imita-

---

99. Over against THGD 84.
100. The Three all read τῷ πλήθει as well.
101. See THGD ch.4 in which the carelessness of the B scribe is amply illustrated, so that "Readings solely supported by B are seldom to be taken seriously" (p.48).
102. Tar do not avoid or change the statement, although Tar^J does use מימרא דײ׳ for יהוה in both parts of the verse. Rashi sidesteps the issue by having God cause the enemies to rejoice, i.e. making שיש causative: כן ישיש ה׳ את אויביכם עליכם.

tion of MT, *καὶ ἐξαρθήσεσθε ἀπὸ τῆς γῆς*. This clause is then coordinate with the *καὶ ἔσται* at the beginning of the verse. In the relative clause modifying *γῆς*, for which see comment at 1:8, the infinitive of LXX is inflected in the present *κληρονομεῖν*. All but four witnesses support the variant aorist *κληρονομησαι*, which is much more frequent in Deut. The present is, however, supported by B and 848, and the majority aorist is ex par.[103] Usually in this pattern Deut does use the aorist infinitive, but comp 4:5,14, where the present infinitive also occurs. MT inconsistently changes to the singular in the relative clause, for which see comment at v.62.

28:64 This verse is coordinate with v.63b, i.e. it is in the future, though reverting to the singular again. "The Lord your God will scatter you among all the nations hither and yon (literally "from the end of the earth to the end of the earth).[104] MT simply has יהוה as the subject, and *ὁ θεός σου* is an ex par addition, which hex duly placed under the obelus.

And in that homeless state you will serve other gods, wooden and stone ones. LXX did not render עבדת by λατρευσεις as one might expect, but rather by *δουλεύσεις*, thus the service is not simply a cultic service, but one of full servitude; you will become a *δοῦλος* of idols. Contrast this with v.36, where *λατρεύσεις* is used.[105] These other gods are described by a relative clause, *οὓς οὐκ ἠπίστω σὺ καὶ οἱ πατέρες σου* "whom you and your fathers did not know." Over against the present tense of v.36, LXX has the imperfect here. In the tradition *οὓς* became *οις* in the majority text by attraction to its antecedent *θεοῖς*, but the grammatically correct accusative is supported inter alia by B 848 963, and must be original text.[106] Also to be noted is the transposition of *ξύλοις καὶ λίθοις* to the end of the verse by hex so as to correspond to the Hebrew word order; for the LXX order comp v.36.

28:65 MT begins with "and among those nations לא תרגיע," i.e. you will find no repose. LXX, however, changes this so as to involve the Lord your God as the actor. This is already apparent at the beginning, where LXX has *ἀλλὰ καί*

103. See THGD 84.
104. Instead of *διασπερεῖ*, Aq has *διασκορπίσει*, which is a synonym.
105. See Daniel 68 over against 101.
106. See THGD 74.

"but even", whereas MT simply has a *waw*; then instead of the second person verb, the Greek has a third person transitive verb with pronominal modifier, thus "not will he grant you repose." MT has a parallel construction to this, in "and there will be no מנוח for the sole of your foot." LXX translates the noun by *στάσις* "stance, position, place to stand." The negative is *οὐδὲ μή*, and most witnesses have *ουδ ου μη*, but Deut avoids *ουδ ου* almost entirely.[107]

In the second part of the verse the divine involvement is one of giving you three things: *καρδίαν ἀθυμοῦσαν καὶ ἐκλείποντας ὀφθαλμοὺς καὶ τηκομένην ψυχήν* "a discouraged heart and failing eyes and a life wasting away." The participles translate nouns in MT. The first nominal is לב רגז "an excited, agitated heart."[108] The second participle represents כליון an abstract noun based on כלה "to come to an end, to fail."[109] The final participle modifies *ψυχήν* "person, the self." It means "melted," so wasted away. The Hebrew has דאבון, a hapax legomenon based on the root דאב meaning "to languish, faint."[110]

28:66 Your chances for survival are slim indeed. The first clause says "and your life shall be *κρεμαμένη* before your eyes." The notion is one of extreme precariousness, your life is suspended לך מנגד "to you in front." LXX has neatly rendered this by *ἀπέναντι τῶν ὀφθαλμῶν σου*. Hex, however, has a *σοι* under the asterisk after the participle,[111] which shows an unreflecting reaction on Origen's part. The notion of "being hung" might be understood as "hung like a thread." The next clause states "and you shall be fearful *ἡμέρας καὶ νυκτός*." The time represents a common idiom, but MT has the two reversed, and hex has transposed them to equal MT. The third clause states *καὶ οὐ πιστεύσεις τῇ ζωῇ σου*.[112] What it means is "you will have no confidence as to your life," i.e. your survival.

---

107. See THGD 114—115.
108. Aq translates רגז by *κλονουμένην* "driven into confusion, agitation."
109. Aq translates etymologically by *τελουμένους*.
110. Aq renders by *ἐκλιμώσσουσαν*, a hapax legomenon in its compound form; the simplex λιμώσσω means "to starve," so the compound probably means "to be gaunt from hunger."
111. Which The Three also had, but how they rendered מנגד is unknown.
112. Sym has *περὶ τῆς ζωῆς σου* instead of the dative. How he rendered תאמין is unknown.

28:67 LXX expresses time when by adverbial accusatives, *τὸ πρωί* and *τὸ ἑσπέρας*, whereas in MT these are ב phrases, "in the morning," and "in the evening." You will long for time to pass: in the morning you will say *πῶς ἂν γένοιτο ἑσπέρα* "How (soon?) might it become evening," i.e. if only it were evening. The translator is trying to render the idiom מי יתן "would that."[113]

The reason for this longing for time to pass is given by the two *ἀπό* structures in the second part of the verse: "from (i.e. by reason of) the fear of your heart, which you fear, and the sights of your eyes, which you see." In both phrases the relative clause uses cognate verbs as in MT: "fear which you fear ... sights ... which you see." The first relative pronoun *ἅ* has no expressed antecedent; one would expect the referent to be *φόβου*, but the pronoun is an indefinite neuter plural, which enhances the fearfulness; it refers to all the things you fear; after all, one does not fear fear. The Byz text tried to correct this by changing *ἅ* to *ου*, but that cannot be correct; in fact, this is probably palaeographically inspired as a partial dittograph of the *σου* which precedes it. The second relative pronoun is *ὧν*, which is grammatically wrong and was corrected to *α* by *b*+, but, as often, the pronoun of LXX was attracted to its antecedent *ὁραμάτων*.

28:68 The ultimate indignation. Again the Lord is the actor; he "will return you to Egypt in ships," i.e. as galley slaves. And this will be "by a route of which I had said: You will not again see it any more." This is a reference to 17:16, where the Lord makes the promise "you will not again return by this route." Almost all witnesses connect the two *ἐν* clauses by a *και*. Here B's shorter text, which equals MT, was taken as original, since it would be much more difficult to omit an original *και* than to add it.[114]

The object clause of *εἶπα* appears consistently in the plural, as does Sam, which is much more sensible than MT, which has תסיף for *προσθήσεσθε*, but התמכרתם for *πραθήσεσθε*, and then לאיביך instead of *τοῖς ἐχθροῖς ὑμῶν*.[115] MT also has לך to modify "I said," and hex has added *σοι* to equal it.[116]

113. Aq, followed by Sym, has the literalism *τίς δώσει*.
114. See THGD 131.
115. See THGD 110.
116. Sam has לכם, consistent with his plural text in the object clause which follows.

The future passive πραθήσεσθε translates a Hithpael, and is in my opinion intended here in the sense of "you will be offered for sale as slaves, male and female, and (i.e. but) there will be no buyer."

Chapter 29

29:1(28:69) This can best be viewed as a subscription to the conclusion of the Law Code, which is described as *οἱ λόγοι τῆς διαθήκης*. As a covenant the Code (chh.12—26) had attached a series of blessings for obedience and of curses for disobedience, and v.1 concludes this. Appropriately MT has this verse at the end of ch.28. This covenant is, however, not to be confused with the Sinai (Horeb) covenant. This one is the one which *ἐνετείλατο κύριος Μωυσῇ στῆσαι τοῖς υἱοῖς Ἰσραὴλ ἐν γῇ Μωάβ*.[1] The infinitive correctly renders לכרת which, when it refers to ברית, means "to set up, establish."

πλήν is used as a preposition with the genitive in the sense of "besides," and renders מלבד "except, besides." What is meant is that the covenant which he כרת with them at Horeb is not the same as the covenant established here in the land of Moab. Note that כרת is now rendered by a cognate verb *διέθετο*, thus "covenant which he covenanted."

In the tradition the relative *οὕς* appears as *οσα* in *O* Byz, obviously taken from Theod, and by the A F M majority text as *ης*. The latter is a rationalization which takes *διαθήκης* as the antecedent of the pronoun, but the translator intended it to be *λόγοι*. MT has את משה as modifier of קרא. Accordingly hex has added *τω* under the asterisk to equal the את, a variant which gained majority acceptance in the tradition.

29:2(1) Vv.2—9 recall to the Israelites how the Lord had led them since their exodus from Egypt. The section is given in second person plural throughout, which distinguishes it from what preceded it. The verse begins in MT with the same introduction as at 5:1, but ms 426 levels the LXX text with that of 5:1; all others read *πάντας υἱοὺς Ἰσραήλ* as modifier of *ἐκάλεσεν*, whereas ms 426 reads *παντα ισραηλ*. The subject of the relative clause is *κύριος*, which equals MT, but the majority of witnesses add *ο θεος υμων*, which is ex par, e.g. v.6. Its verb is modified by two locative structures: *ἐν γῇ Αἰγύπτῳ ἐνώπιον ὑμῶν*. The two are reversed in MT, and hex has also done so in order

1. Theod has *ὅσα* instead of *οὕς*, but the reference must still be to "words." Possibly he had *ῥήματα* instead of *οἱ λόγοι* as antecedent.

to correspond to the Hebrew.[2] The verb is also modified by three datives showing indirect objects: Pharoah, his servants, and all his land. Most witnesses also have the second one modified by *πασιν*, agreeing with MT's ולכל עבדיו, but B 848 and 963 all lack it, and clearly represent the original shorter text. The noun is translated by *θεράπουσιν*, which word also occurs in the same context at 34:11; the other two cases in Deut are at 3:24, where Moses calls himself God's servant, and at 9:27, where it is used of the patriarchs. Elsewhere it occurs in the Pentateuch only once in Gen, four times in Num, but 24 times in Exod (of which 21 render עבד). Elsewhere in the OT it only occurs three times in Jos, and 11 times in Job. It was obviously a favorite term of the Exod translator. Incidentally other renderings for עבד in Deut are *οἰκέτης* (8 times), *παῖς* (8 times) and *δοῦλος* (once).

29:3(2) This verse explicates *πάντα* of v.1. "All the things which the Lord did" were "the great *πειρασμούς* which your eyes saw, those great *τὰ σημεῖα καὶ τὰ τέρατα*." For these nouns see the discussion at 4:34 and 7:19. Odd in the context is the singular *σου* modifying "eyes," but this is based on MT. Only the *t* group levels the text to *υμων* (as did Pesh).

In the tradition, most witnesses support the A M text in reading the aorist *ειδον*, instead of the LXX's perfect *ἑωράκασιν*, but the latter is supported inter alia by B 848 and 963, and is exegetically to be preferred as well. The majority A M text also added *και την χειρα την κραταιαν και τον βραχιονα τον υψηλον* at the end; this has no support in MT, and is clearly ex par.[3]

29:4(3) This verse is best understood as a parenthetical remark. The terms, *καρδίαν*, *ὀφθαλμούς*, and *ὦτα*, are to be taken in a moral or spiritual sense. Israel had remained stubborn over against the Lord God, resisting his demands. What is unusual is the notion that the Lord God did not give you these, but LXX simply reproduces MT. MT only has יהוה for "Lord God," and so hex has placed *ὁ θεός* under the obelus. The use of the double name is highly unusual, and seems to reflect the use of the double name in Gen 2 and 3 (and see also Exod 9:30). Elsewhere I have suggested[4] that this might well be

2. Instead of *ἐνώπιον* Aq translated literally by *εἰς ὀφθαλμούς*.
3. See THGD 74 and 75.
4. Appositives 1.2. (p.261).

a reflection of Gen 3:22 over against 2:16—17, i.e. "of the temptation by which humanity, *ὁ* 'Ἀδάμ, yielded to the desire to know good and evil, and thereby lost the ability to understand the divine actions on his own." Since *ὑμῖν* immediately follows *θεός*, it is not surprising that a popular text has *υμων* instead of *ὑμῖν*; after all, *κύριος ὁ θεός* is almost always followed by a genitive pronoun, but here *ὑμῖν* represents לכם, and is original.

The exact intent of the *ἕως* phrase is not clear. It obviously modifies *ἔδωκεν*, but does this mean that Israel has always been recalcitrant even to the present time, or that this recalcitrance has lasted throughout the wilderness journey, and that only now is Israel ready to enter into the covenant referred to in v.1, i.e. the one in the land of Moab? Neither MT not LXX is clear on this point.

29:5(4) MT begins with ואולך "and I brought," which LXX changed to third person, making it refer clearly to the Lord, rather than possibly to Moses. Since the context has been *κύριος*, this leveling makes good sense. It was the Lord who really led Israel through the wilderness by pillars of cloud and of fire; Moses was simply his surrogate. It should be noted, however, that MT's intent with אולך was to indicate Yahweh as speaker, as the last clause in the next verse shows. The way in which LXX dealt with this assured this understanding. Had LXX not changed to the third singular, readers would automatically suppose that the first person verb referred to Moses. It should be noted that ms 426, a good witness for the hex text, reads *ηγαγον*, which equals MT.

The two clauses in the second part of the verse of MT both have a מן phrase modifying the verb, and both use the same verb for the predicate. The second clause, however, is in the second singular. LXX levels the two, making a consistent second plural reference throughout,[5] but translates the verb by different lexemes: *ἐπαλαιώθη* and *κατετρίβη*, i.e. clothes did not grow old, and sandals did not wear out. A marginal *s*+ reading, undoubtedly reflecting a reading from The Three, corrects the second verb to *επαλαιωθη*. Furthermore, LXX also omitted the מן phrase of the first clause, and hex added *επανωθεν υμων* under the asterisk to equal the missing מעליכם. For the clothes wearing out see 8:4.

5. See THGD 110.

29:6(5) The reference to "bread you did not eat" is to the provision of manna, for which see 8:3. Nor did Israel drink wine and *σίκερα*,[6] but rather water divinely provided from the rock, Exod 17:1—6 Num 20:2—13.

The purpose of God's providing food and drink in such marvelous ways is expressed in MT by the prophetic formula: למען תדעו כי אני יהוה אלהיכם. But in the preceding verse the first person verb אולך had been changed to third person, so as to make clear that it was Yahweh, not Moses, who had led the people in the wilderness. To be consistent, LXX also changed אני to *οὗτος*, to which the Byz text added *εστιν*. Once again ms 426 has corrected *οὗτος* to agree with MT, by its *εγω*.

29:7(6) The use of *ἕως* to render אל stresses the fact that the Israelites are now precisely at the place where Seon and Og came out to engage Israel in battle; they are still in the land of Moab. For the spelling of Ἐσεβών see comment at 1:4. For the account alluded to in vv.7—8, see 2:31—3:13. These came out to meet *ἡμῖν ἐν πολέμῳ*. The prepositional phrase means "in a state of warfare."[7] In MT this appears as למלחמה "for war." The Greek shows the condition in which they came out, whereas MT stresses the reason they came out. LXX answers How, and MT, Why. Instead of the dative a popular variant has the genitive *ημων*, which is also possible, though the dative is far more common throughout the OT.[8] The two accounts in chh.2—3 are laconically summarized as *καὶ ἐπατάξαμεν αὐτούς*.

29:8(7) The conquered land was now in Israel's possession. MT has ונתנה "and we gave it," but LXX corrects this to the singular in accordance with 3:12—13; it was Moses who distributed the land *ἐν κλήρῳ* to Rouben, Gaddi, and the half tribe of Manasse,[9] not the Israelites. As at 3:12,16, LXX renders

6. A word borrowed into Greek from the Aramaic שכרא. Aq translates by *μέθυσμα*.
7. See LS sub *ἐν* A.II.1.
8. The change to second person is simply an itacistic spelling. The support for the genitive by Sym and Theod is of course for *ἡμῶν*, not the *υμων* given in 344[mg]. This would have been clearer if the reading had been given as "*σ´ θ´ ἡμῶν* (cod *υμων*) 344."
9. Sym has *τοῖς Ῥουβιλαίοις καὶ τοῖς Γαδαίοις καὶ τῷ ἡμίσει τῆς φυλῆς τῶν Μανασσαίων* (retroverted from Syh). It is unlikely that Sym had a *lambda* instead of *nu* for the Roubenites, but Syh always spelled Ῥουβήν as *roubil*.

the Hebrew gentilic ראובני by Ῥουβήν; see comment at 3:12. In the tradition Γαδδί is changed to γαδ by *O* Byz, over against the לגדי of MT. For לגדי rendered by τῷ Γάδ, see 3:12,16; this may have been the source of the variant reading here.

29:9(8) Israel is exhorted to obedience, but LXX differs somewhat from MT. MT simply has שמרתם את דברי of this covenant, i.e. "you must observe the words of this covenant," which is followed by ועשיתם אותם "and do them." LXX changes this to "φυλάξεσθε ποιεῖν πάντος the words of this covenant." Hex placed πάντος under the obelus, it having no equivalent in MT, and then revised the text by omitting ποιεῖν but adding ποιειν αυτους at the end, to approximate MT. The main verb was changed to the present tense, φυλασσεσθε, by Byz, and to the aorist imperative, φυλαξασθε, by *C*''+, but the future is clearly original. Deut almost always translates the contextual, suffixal inflected verbs by the future. As in v.1 "the words of this covenant" refers to the Law Code of chh.12—26.

Rather unusual is the purpose given for being careful to effect the words of this covenant: ἵνα συνῆτε all the things you must do. The verb occurs for the Hi of שכל elsewhere in the Pentateuch only at Exod 36:1 of Beseleel and Eliab, to whom wisdom and understanding had been given συνιέναι ποιεῖν all the work concerning the tabernacle, i.e. "to understand how to do"; comp also the preceding verse, 35:35, where the infinitive has no MT counterpart; cf Notes ad loc. Here, however, the Hebrew probably means "to be successful, succeed" in all that you do, or as the note in NRSV has it "deal wisely."

29:10(9) With v.10 begins the conclusion concerning the covenant to be effected between the Lord and Israel along with its sanctions. The address begins with a nominal clause in MT: pronoun plus participle, which is rendered in LXX by ὑμεῖς ἑστήκατε "you are standing." The intransitive perfect of ἵστημι acts as a present tense and fits the normal translation pattern of Deut. The *C*'' *s* text has added an adverb of place, ωδε, but this is an epexegetical gloss unsupported by MT. The ὑμεῖς is modified by πάντες which in LXX follows σήμερον as in MT. B *n*+ transposed the two; so did Byz but it also inserted ωδε; 963+ omitted πάντες, but only LXX can be original.[10] The *πάντες* is particularly relevant and necessary, since it is in turn explicated in the remainder of the verse and in v.11. Those of v.10 comprise your *οἱ ἀρχίφυλοι, ἡ γερουσία, οἱ κρίται, οἱ γραμματοεισαγωγεῖς*, in short *πᾶς ἀνὴρ Ἰσραήλ*. Then v.11 goes on to list those included who do not comprise "every man of Israel." Those who do so are in each case united by *καί*, i.e. the pattern followed is that of a+b+c+d, whereas MT followed the abc+d pattern.

The first term represents ראשיכם "your heads," i.e. your chieftains, which LXX renders by "your tribal chieftains."[11] MT then has שבטיכם זקניכם "your tribes, your elders," which LXX transposes, reading שפטיכם "your judges" instead of שבטיכם; hex reorders these to equal the order of MT. Whether the translator actually had שפטיכם as his parent text or simply rationalized the text to make better sense cannot be determined. For *γερουσία* see comment at 19:12. For *γραμματοεισαγωγεῖς* see comment at 1:15.

29:11(10) The list explicating *πάντες* continues with three more: *αἱ γυναῖκες ὑμῶν καὶ τὰ ἔκγονα ὑμῶν καὶ ὁ προσήλυτος* "your wives and your offspring and the proselyte." As in v.10, MT joined only the last two items with a conjunction. The tradition added *και* to the beginning of the list as well in an A *oI' f y+* text in the fully correct notion that these were also part of the *πάντες* of v.10. MT has טפכם first with נשיכם second; LXX has reversed these, but hex has reordered them to equal MT. The term *τὰ ἔκγονα* had up to this point been used to render פרי (7:13 28:4,11,18,51,53), but here it is used to render טף (also at 31:12).[12] Hex preferred *τεκνα* here, probably taken from Theod; this reading became the A M majority text as well.

With the proselyte MT begins a second singular tradition, which continues through the next two verses as well, before reverting to the plural again. LXX continues with the plural to the end of this verse, before changing to the singular. Accordingly גרך promoted the hex addition under the asterisk of *υμων* after "proselyte" rather than *σου*.[13] The setting of Israel in a military camp is carried forward; the proselyte is identified as the one who was *ἐν*

10. See THGD 130.
11. Aq has *ἡ κεφαλή* <*ὑμῶν*>. The singular is surprising.
12. Aq and Sym render it by *τὰ νήπια* (retroverted from Syh^{m}).
13. For the omission of a genitive pronoun in LXX see SS 102.

μέσῳ τῆς παρεμβολῆς ὑμῶν, and includes the range *ἀπὸ ξυλοκόπου ὑμῶν καὶ ἕως ὑδροφόρου ὑμῶν* "from your woodcutter up to your water carrier." The last nominal translates שאב מימיך "your drawer of water."[14] The noun recurs only in Jos 9 (four times). In Deut eyes proselytes apparently were menial workers. MT has עד, but LXX follows the ועד of Sam with *καὶ ἕως*. The majority A M text has omitted the *καί*, but this is unlikely to be a recensional change.

29:12(11) The initial infinitive is complementary to *ἑστήκατα* of v.10: "(you are standing ...) *παρελθεῖν σε* into the Lord your God's covenant and into his curses (sanctions)," a literal rendering of MT's לעברך. The notion of passing over into a covenant is unique, and is probably merely a colorful way of saying "enter into." I would render "to enter his covenant." But entering the covenant also means accepting the sanctions-*ἀραῖς* means "curses" attendant on that covenant relationship, a fact which is expanded on later in the chapter; see vv.18—28.

That this understanding of *παρελθεῖν* is correct seems substantiated by the *ὅσα* clause modifying *διαθήκῃ ... ἀραῖς*. The covenant and the sanctions are those "which the Lord your God is covenanting with you today." The present tense translates the participle כרת of MT in predictable fashion. Incidentally, most witnesses omit *σε*, but the infinitive needs this as a singular subject to agree with the singulars which follow.[15]

29:13(12) The essence of the covenantal relation is expressed by a *ἵνα* clause; there are two necessary elements: you as his people, and he as your God; but the *ἵνα* clause governs only the first element: *ἵνα στήσῃ σε ἑαυτῷ εἰς λαόν*, whereas the second element is a promise. That Israel should become his people is, however, itself a divine action; it is God who establishes you as a people for himself. In the tradition the reflexive pronoun appears as *αυτω* in a B *C'*' s y+ variant text, but the contracted reflexive pronoun is rarely, if ever, used in Deut, and the reading is a careless error. Of more importance is LXX's omis-

14. Aq followed MT closely with *ἀπὸ ἐκκόποντος ξύλα σου ἕως ἀντλοῦντος ὕδατά σου* (retroverted from Syh^{m}).
15. See THGD 127—128.

sion of היום. In the LXX the immediacy of MT is lacking. Hex has, however, added *σημερον* under the asterisk after *σε*.

The second element is a promise with a future verb: *καὶ αὐτὸς ἔσται σου θεός*, rendering והוא יהיה לך לאלהים. This promise is not a sudden whim on God's part, but is in accordance both with what he had said to you, and with his oath "sworn to your fathers, Abraam and Isaak and Jacob"; for the latter see comment at 1:8, though there the oath refers to the promise of land. For the covenantal elements see Note at Exod 6:7, and comp Lev 26:12. For the Lord's choice of Israel as his people, see 7:6—8 26:18—19. In the tradition Byz and *C* read *και αυτος σοι εις θεον*, which is a more literal rendering of MT, and I suspect based on Theod.

29:14(13)—15(14) The two verses must be read together, since v.15 is the adversative to v.14. V.14 insists that the Lord (as speaker) is covenanting this covenant and *τὴν ἀρὰν ταύτην*, which nominal must be understood as a collective (comp the plural in v.12), i.e. not with you alone. In the tradition *C'' z+* read the active *διατιθημι*, but throughout the OT the active voice is never used in describing the *διαθήκη*, and only the mediopassive can be original.

V.15 begins with כי, but this must be taken in the sense of *ἀλλά*, since it is contrastive after "not ... alone." The adversative particle is followed by a *καί* ... *καί* structure, thus "both ... and." MT has for the first unit את אשר ישנו פה עמנו עמד היום "with those who are here with us standing today (before Yahweh our God)." LXX reads *καὶ τοῖς ὧδε οὖσιν μεθ' ἡμῶν σήμερον*, thus omitting the participle עמד and transposing ישנו פה. Hex has, accordingly, transposed *ὧδε οὖσιν* and added *εστωσι* under the asterisk before *σήμερον*. In the tradition of v.15b the A M *y+* text has transposed *ὧδε* after *μεθ' ἡμῶν*, a stylistic change by which "here today" are joined, but the LXX text is almost certainly original.[16] It might also be noted that the majority A B F M text reads *υμων* instead of *ἡμῶν* 3°. Similarly a popular A 963 text changes *ἡμῶν* 1°, but this is purely an itacistic error in spite of its popularity, probably impelled by the second person context in which this verse is set, but only in Greek can one confuse the second and first person plural pronouns. The Hebrew has עמנו in both cases, not עמכם, and that must be determinative, as is the case for *ἡμῶν* 2°, which is assured by the suffix of the Hebrew אלהינו.

---

16. See THGD 130.

What is not clear is who are intended by the ὑμῖν of v.14 in contrast (ἀλλά) to τοις οὖσιν μεθ' ἡμῶν. Both are plural, and on the face of it those who are here with us would be the same as the "you" who are being addressed in v.14. The distinction then must be that of Israelites (ὑμῖν, ἡμῶν) and the aliens, "the proselyte" referred to in v.11.

Disconcerting is the change of speaker after ἀλλά. In v.14 it is clearly the Lord who speaks, but in v.14 it has shifted to Moses, as the עמנו/μεθ' ἡμῶν indicates. The change is, however, already in MT, and LXX is simply following MT.

The second unit with which the Lord is covenanting is *τοῖς μὴ οὖσιν ὧδε μεθ' ἡμῶν σήμερον*. The divine covenant is to continue with succeeding generations, another way of saying "I will set my covenant between me and you *καὶ ἀνὰ μέσον τοῦ σπέρματός σου μετὰ σὲ εἰς γενεὰς αὐτῶν*. (Gen 17:7).

29:16(15) The ὅτι clause gives the basis for the Lord's making the covenant with the coming generations as well; note that the covenant adds *τὴν ἀρὰν ταύτην* (v.14), i.e. past experience in vv.16—17 gives ample impetus towards straying into idolatry. What you know is given in two את אשר structures, simplified as ὡς structures: you know "how we dwelt in Egypt land, and how we passed through the midst of nations, whom you passed through." The use of the repetitious relative clause is intended as an indefinite reference to various unlisted nations. So what is meant is "whatever nations there may have been with whom we were in contact." For the same idiom see 1:46.

29:17(16) The verse is still governed by the ὅτι introducing v.16, and is coordinate with the *οἴδατε* clause. *αὐτῶν* has as antecedent the *ἐθνῶν* of v.16. The two Hebrew terms for idols are both pejorative in character. שקוצי occurs only here in the Pentateuch, but its rendering as *βδελύγματα* became a standard translation for the Greek OT,[17] and גללי is a particularly derisive term, since it is a pun on the word גללים "pellets of dung," so "dung-idols." LXX commonly uses the generic term *εἴδωλα* as here.[18] The remaining pairs, "wood

17. Aq uses *προσοχθίσματα* "offensive objects."
18. Aq translates by *καθάρματα*, a term applied to refuse, slag, in any event to that which is thrown away in the process of cleansing.

and stone, silver and gold," refer to the composition of idols, i.e. "of wood and stone, of silver and gold."

29:18(17) It is unlikely that the translator intended the two *μή* structures to be taken as questions, since they render פן. So the text should be repunctuated by replacing the period at the end of v.17 and the two question marks in v.18, all by colons. The verse is then dependent on what has gone before. God is making his covenant with the next generation as well, because you have seen idol worship at first hand, and if there would be no established covenant with you and your descendants, there might well be some who would be tempted to engage in the worship of other gods. That is what is feared, hence "lest there be among you some man or woman or clan or tribe, whose heart ...." In other words, this is forestalled by the establishment of the covenant.[19] The Masoretes vocalized פנה as a participle, but the translator understood it as a verb, hence *ἐξέκλινεν*. The structure אשר לבבו was well-rendered by LXX as *τίνος ἡ διάνοια*; of course the suffix is rendered by the genitive case, not by a separate pronoun, but hex has added an *αυτου* under the asterisk nonetheless. LXX disregarded the next word, היום, altogether, because the verb was understood as a past tense, and *σημερον* would be quite meaningless; nevertheless hex has added it under the asterisk as well. For the majority reading of *υμων* for *ἡμῶν*, the comment at v.15 is equally valid. It has no claim to originality whatsoever.

The second פן/*μή* clause introduces a rather forced metaphor, which is not immediately clear. MT has "lest there should be among you a root producing as fruit poison and wormwood." In other words, such an idolator would constitute a hidden source of poisonous and bitter fruit. This is then explained by vv.20—28. The translator had trouble with this figure, and understood the poison and wormwood as the environment in which the root was growing; in fact, the notion of the root producing fruit may well have troubled him as well, and so he has the root, not producing fruit, פרה, but *ἄνω φύουσα* "growing upward."[20] Hex has placed *ἄνω* under the obelus as having no equivalent in MT, even though *φύουσα* by itself was nowhere near the equivalent

19. Instead of *πατριά* for משפחה Aq has *συγγένεια*.
20. Aq also fudged a bit here with his *αὐξάνουσα* "increasing."

of פרה; rather the adverb plus participle was its rendering. Then the modifiers ראש ולענה were rendered by ἐν χολῇ καὶ πικρίᾳ "in gall and bitterness."[21]

In the tradition, A B+ read ενοχλη for ἐν χολῇ. This reading goes back to Hebr 12:15; its author rewrote this clause by omitting ἐστιν ἐν ὑμῖν, adding a genitive πικρίας after ῥίζα (and dropping καὶ πικρίᾳ) and scrambling ἐν χολῇ by transposing the letters χο into a present subjunctive ἐνοχλῇ, thus "lest some root of bitterness, having grown up, should create trouble"—a fine sentiment indeed, but it is not that of Deut. The A B variant is of course not to be taken seriously.

29:19(18) For καὶ ἔσται ἐάν see comment at 6:10—11. LXX has taken the והתברך clause as part of the protasis, i.e. as coordinate with ἀκούσῃ. "To bless oneself" probably here means "to congratulate oneself." LXX's aorist middle subjunctive form, ἐπιφημίσηται, occurs only here in OT, and probably can be understood in that same sense. In MT it is quite possible to understand this clause as the beginning of the apodosis; thus NJPS has "when such a one hears the words of these sanctions, he may fancy himself immune." Similarly, RSV, "one who, when he hears the words of this sworn covenant, blesses himself in his heart."[22]

What he says is "May it be allowed for me that I should walk in the dictates (literally, wandering) of my heart." Hebrew has שלום יהיה לי introducing the כי clause, and ὅσια occurs only here for שלום.[23]

What follows is an anacoluthon. Obviously this kind of arrogant, self-centered behaviour is not to be permitted. God would not permit it, as the next verse makes clear, and when the punishment comes, this self-centered sinner might well carry the innocent down to destruction as well. One might translate this construction by a dash, i.e. "-- lest the sinner should destroy the innocent."[24] The Hebrew is obscure here with למען ספות הרוה את הצמאה "so as to sweep away the well-watered with the dry"; what seems to be meant is that

21. The word ראש "poison" is more common as the word for "head," and Aq accordingly has κεφαλήν. What "increasing a head" was supposed to mean remains mysterious.
22. The Tar interpret variously: Tar^{O} by יחשב "consider," Tar^{J}, by יתייאש "be doubtful," and Tar^{N}, יתפייס "take comfort, satisfaction."
23. As expected Aq translates by εἰρήνη.
24. Dogniez-Harl actually add "en même temps" to make this clear.

everything will disappear.[25] The translator rendered the את by an accusative, presumably understanding the first noun as the subject of ספות. He realized that this was figurative language, but, not understanding it, he interpreted contextually; what he made it mean was that the one who walks in the dictates of his own heart (i.e. the sinner) might well, in doing so, endanger, in fact, destroy the other (i.e. the innocent).

29:20(19) This is to be taken as the apodosis of v.19, i.e. "should one hear ... and congratulate himself ... saying ... -- lest ..., (then) God will not be willing to show him mercy." This also makes sense out of the anacoluthon ending of v.19. The verb *εὐιλατεύω* only occurs twice in OT elsewhere, at Jud 16:15 as well as at Ps 102:3, where it also renders the root סלח. There God is described as *τὸν εὐιλατεύοντα πάσαις ταῖς ἀνομίαις σου*. In all three cases the verbal form is modified by a dative.

Over against this, ἀλλ' ἤ "then the anger of the Lord and his jealousy shall burn against the man." The verb *ἐκκαυθήσεται* translates Sam's יחר, rather than the יעשן "smoke" of MT.[26]

MT continues with a striking figure "and every curse of this covenant ... shall crouch down on him," i.e. shall rest on him. LXX realizes the figure by its *κολληθήσονται ἐν αὐτῷ*;[27] this is of course what the figure means—they will cling to him. LXX correctly understood האלה to be collective, and rendered it by the plural. LXX levels the text of v.20 to agree with v.21 by its "*πᾶσαι αἱ ἀραὶ τῆς διαθήκης ταύτης*, which are written *ἐν τῷ βιβλίῳ τοῦ νόμου τούτου*," but MT has no equivalent for *τῆς διαθήκης ταύτης*, and has "in this book." Hex has duly placed both "of this covenant" and *τοῦ νόμου* under the obelus, and changed *τούτου* to *τουτω* to equal MT. For *τοῦ νόμου* see comment at 28:61.

Furthermore, "the Lord will wipe out his name מתחת the sky"; LXX neatly shows the double preposition by *ἐκ τῆς ὑπό*. To wipe out one's name is

25. The Tar allegorize the two terms as referring to "inadvertent sins" and "sins of intention." The Others render by *ἡ μεθύουσα τὴν διψῶσαν*.
26. The Others read *καπνώσεται* (retroverted from Syh).
27. I am sceptical of A.Rofe's conclusion (Textus XIV[1988], 167—169) that this is textually promoted by a variant דבקו text as read in 1QS. All this proves is that the Qumranis understood the figure as did LXX.

to erase all memory of an individual, which is the worst fate that could be envisaged by an Israelite.

29:21(20) This person the Lord will set aside, i.e. designate εἰς κακά, a phrase which correctly understands לרעה as meaning "for bad ends." The abstract feminine singular can be rendered by a neuter plural. Instead of שבטי "tribes of," LXX has the more common υἱῶν to refer to Israelites; one suspects that the translator was careless at this point, since at 33:5 the same phrase occurs, but it is correctly rendered by φυλαῖς Ἰσραήλ.

The norm that the Lord will use to separate such a man will be "all the curses of the covenant τὰς γεγραμμένας." MT has the passive participle referring to ברית, which, as της γεγραμμενης, is also attested in a popular A F M variant reading. But the translator levelled with v.20, where "all the curses of this covenant" are αἱ γεγραμμέναι. The variant text is hardly to be taken as a recensional correction, but is rather the result of attraction to the inflection τῆς διαθήκης, which immediately preceded the participle.

29:22(21) The opening verb ἐροῦσιν is not realized until v.24, where the verb is repeated with πάντα τὰ ἔθνη as subject, i.e. what "the next generation ... and the stranger" will say is not said, but presumably incorporated in what all the nations will say in v.24. This next generation is identified as οἱ υἱοὶ ὑμῶν οἳ ἀναστήσονται μεθ' ὑμᾶς. Unclear is the syntax of the coordinate "and the stranger who would come from a land far off." Syntactically the καὶ ὄψονται could coordinate with the ἀναστήσονται of the οἵ clause, or it might have as its subject the coordinate οἱ υἱοί and ὁ ἀλλότριος; in other words, one might translate: "and shall say ... which shall arise after you, (along with the stranger who would come from a land far off), and shall see the plagues ..., even all the nations shall say ...." On the other hand, the parenthetical statement might be understood as coordinate, i.e. "and the stranger ... and they shall see ...." The text is rhetorically very loose in both MT and LXX, and it is not fully clear what was intended.

LXX differs from MT in the ἅς clause at the end of the verse, which modifies τὰς νόσους (αὐτῆς). In MT the verb is cognate to its antecedent: את תחלאיה אשר חלה (note that Sam spells the verb חלא) "sicknesses which he sickened." The translator did not use a cognate verb at all, but contextualized freely with his ἀπέστειλεν.[28]

29:23(22) What they shall see when they look at the promised land: "brimstone and burned salt, not shall all its land be sown nor sprout." This is not how the Masoretes interpreted it. The word ארצה is marked with a *segolta* and מלח is marked with a *zarqa*.[29] What MT means is "Brimstone and salt; all its ground is burned; not shall it be sown nor sprout." The opening nouns are probably intended to show the means of burning, so better: With brimstone and salt all its ground is burned. But LXX has the participle κατακεκαυμένον modifying ἅλα rather than γῆ, i.e. it is the salt that is burned, not the ground. But as for the γῆ, "not will it be sown or sprout, nor shall any greenery come up on it."[30]

This was analogous to the destruction of the cities of the plain described in Gen 19. The noun מהפכת is verbalized in the ὥσπερ clause in LXX as κατεστράφη. Though it has a compound subject, "Sodom and Gomorra, Adama and Seboim," it is in the singular by attraction to Σόδομα. The destruction account in Gen 19 only mentions Sodom and Gomorrah, but Gen 14:8 does mention all four as constituting the cities of the plain, and Hos 11:8 mentions both Adama and Seboim. These are further described by the ἅς clause as "which the Lord had overturned ἐν θυμῷ καὶ ὀργῇ." The verb καταστρέφω is regularly employed to render מהפכה in the prophets; see Am 4:11* Is 1:7 13:19* Jer 27:40* 29:19* (the starred references are all to Sodom and Gomorrah). The wrath and anger are of course the Lord's, and adding αυτου would be otiose, but, since MT does have באפו ובחמתו, hex added αυτου to both nouns,[31] as well as repeated the preposition εν before the second noun. Also in the tradition ἐπ' αὐτῆς is changed to the accusative επ αυτην in a B F *C*'+ text; either is possible, but the oldest witness, 963, also has majority support.[32]

28. Not so Aq with his ἐνόσασεν (retroverted from Syh).
29. For these accents see I.Yeiven, Introduction to the Tiberian Masorah, transl. and ed. by E.J.Revell (Masoretic Studies 5; Missoula MO, 1980), nos.227, 230.
30. Sym has "grass" instead of "greenery," possibly βοτάνη (retroverted from Syh).
31. See SS 102.
32. See THGD 58.

29:24(23) The neuter plural might have been expected to require a singular verb, but LXX uses *ἐροῦσιν*; actually *τὰ ἔθνη* takes a plural verb throughout Deut.[33] The 963 Byz *f* text has added *της γης*, a gloss based on the common phrase "all the nations of the earth," which is here secondary. For this verse and its relation to vv.22—23, see comment at v.22. All the nations shall express puzzlement: "Why did the Lord do thus to this land"? This is followed by a מה question in MT, which represents the מה of על מה in the parallel query. It also means "Why." But LXX, confronted with a simple מה, understandably rendered it by *τίς*. This does not pick up the *διά* of *διὰ τί*, and so must mean "what (is this great outburst of anger)"?

29:25(24) All the nations will then answer their own queries; for *ἐροῦσιν* see comment at v.24. The response put into their mouth comprises vv.25—28. על אשר is simply translated by a causal *ὅτι*. The people have abandoned the covenant ..., *ἃ διέθετο τοῖς πατράσιν αὐτῶν*. The neuter plural pronoun is unexpected; in fact, the Byz text has "corrected" it to *ην*, so as to agree with *διαθήκην*. But the translator has in mind not only the covenant, but also its sanctions (see v.12), in short "all the words of this covenant" (v.9); i.e. all the elements and conditions of the covenant are intended by *ἅ*.

In the tradition many mss follow A F M in reading the itacistic spelling *κατελειπον*, which is not to be taken, however, as a true imperfect, but rather as an itacistic spelling of the aorist. One might also note the Hellenistic form attested by cod B, *κατελιποσαν*, which is the product of a later copyist, dating from a time when such Hellenistic forms were more common than in the time of the translator, who on the whole preferred second aorist forms.[34] LXX also realizes עמם "with them" as *τοῖς πατράσιν αὐτῶν*, which pedantically makes clear that "them" refers to their fathers, not to the subject of *κατέλιπον*.

29:26(25) The opening clause, וילכו, is subordinated as a participle, *πορευθέντες*, a common practice for this translator, particularly when it contributes little to what is intended. The stress is hardly on "going" but on the "serving, worshipping." In MT the relative pronoun has אלהים repeated before it, i.e. "served other gods, and worshipped them, gods which they did

33. See SS 198.
34. See THGD 138.

not know." LXX omitted the repeated "gods," simply continuing with the *οὕς* clause. Hex has supplied *θεοις* under the asterisk to equal MT. The *οὕς* clause does create a problem, however. The accusative is grammatically correct, but LXX tends to take on the inflection of its antecedent in Deut, and the majority text does have *οις*. The choice of the accusative was based on the evidence of the oldest witness, but a good case for *οις* as original text can indeed be made.[35]

The last clause reads *οὐδὲ διένειμεν αὐτοῖς* "nor had he allotted to them." The subject is the *κυρίου* of v.25, and the verb is probably a reference to 4:19, where it is said that the Lord had assigned, *ἀνένειμεν*, the heavenly bodies to all the nations which are under the sky; see discussion ad loc.[36]

29:27(26) LXX changed ויחר אף יהוה "and the anger of Yahweh burned" to a construction in which *κύριος* is the subject, thus "And the Lord was angered with wrath—*ὠργίσθη θυμῷ*, i.e. "And the Lord became very angry." The infinitive shows the result or consequence of that anger: "so as to bring (upon it)." MT has the infinitive להביא modified by an את construction, which would normally be rendered by a simple accusative modifier. But the translator avoided having the Lord actually bring "all the curses written in this book" on it (i.e. on the land), and added a preposition *κατά*, thus "according to all the curses ...." In other words, the curses themselves are not brought on the land, but were the norm which God used to bring ruin and destruction on the land. The change is an attempt at greater preciseness on the translator's part.

In the tradition the word for "curses" is the compound *κατάρας*, which a popular A F M text has changed to the simplex *αρας*, probably due to the influence of the simplex earlier in the chapter. But the simplex reflected אלה, and the compound renders קללה, rightly taken as a collective. Almost all the same witnesses also add *της διαθηκης*.[37] MT characterizes the book simply by בספר הזה, which was well-rendered by *ἐν τῷ βιβλίῳ τούτῳ*. Before the discovery of 848 no one would have suspected that this was the original translation,

35. See THGD 107.
36. Sym has rendered the clause by *οὐδὲ προσῆκον αὐτοῖς* "nor belong to them." Aq renders the verb חלק literally by *ἐμέρισεν*. See also Salvesen 148—149.
37. See the discussion at THGD 75.

since only one ms, 58, supported τούτῳ, all others having του νομου τουτου, (with two mss omitting τουτου because of homoioteleuton). But it is now clear from this first century BCE witness that the original text was closer to MT than suspected.[38]

29:28(27) MT has a somewhat more graphic statement with its ויתשם "and he uprooted them," which LXX rendered by καὶ ἐξῆρεν αὐτούς "and he removed them." This the Lord did "in anger and ὀργῇ καὶ παροξυσμῷ." MT has the preposition repeated for the second and third nouns as well, and hex has added εν before ὀργῇ and παροξυσμῷ, so as to equal MT. Furthermore, the last noun is modified by μεγάλῳ σφόδρα, whereas MT has only גדול, so hex placed the σφόδρα under the obelus.

The second clause refers to exile; the Lord cast them out into another land ὡσεὶ νῦν. This betrays the actual situation of the people; the exile in a foreign land is "as at present." In MT this reads כיום הזה.[39]

29:29(28) LXX translates MT accurately. Note the use of δέ to contrast τὰ φανερά with τὰ κρυπτά. The contrast seems to refer to the present (the clear, evident matters), over against the future (the hidden matters which belong to the Lord our God). φανερά translates נגלת "revealed matters," and so clear, evident ones. These are ours and our children's, and consist of carrying out (ποιεῖν) all the words of this law, i.e. the Law Code.

It might be noted that itacistic spellings already occurred in BCE times. The spelling of ἡμῖν as υμιν is attested as early as 848, and note as well the B+ support for the misspelling of both cases of ἡμῶν. Only MT can inform whether the second or first personal pronoun was intended.

---

38. See THGD 84.
39. Theod and Aq translate more literally by ὡς ἡ ἡμέρα [αὕτη].

Chapter 30

30:1 For *καὶ ἔσται ὡς* see comment at 6:10—11. The verb *ἔλθωσιν* is plural in spite of the neuter plural subject *πάντα τὰ ῥήματα*. The plural verb may well be due to the explication of "all these words" by the coordinate *ἡ εὐλογία καὶ ἡ κατάρα*.[1] *ἔδωκα* is here a calque for נתתי in the sense of "put, place, set," thus "which I put before you." In the tradition the A F M majority text reads the perfect *δεδωκα*. The two are commonly confused, but the perfect was used only when the context demanded it (11 times in the book, all but three found in chh.1—3). Usually the aorist obtains (35 times), as a kind of default past tense.

The second clause has *δέξῃ* as rendering for the Hi of שוב; "you shall receive" does interpret השבת even though the Hebrew is normally transitive; here it has no accusative modifier and LXX correctly understood the idiom as "to reflect, consider." The point is that you have taken to heart, and thought about the blessing and the curse. The conditional, which is continued in the next verse, is localized "*ἐν πᾶσιν τοῖς ἔθνεσιν* whither the Lord your God has scattered you"; i.e. an exilic situation is presupposed. MT has הדיח as verb, which has more the notion of "banish" than scatter. For the majority *εαν* for *ἄν* see comment at 5:27.

In the tradition *σε διασκορπίσῃ* is transposed by the majority hex text, thereby equalling MT. MT also read יהוה אלהיך; in fact, it does so eight times in the first six verses, but in four cases LXX does not represent the אלהיך as here. It is likely that the parent text simply had יהוה in these cases; at least the trend in the tradition was clearly to add אלהיך ex par.[2]

30:2 V.2 is also part of the protasis. Just pondering on the blessing and cursing is not sufficient; you must also "return to the Lord your God, and obey his voice." This notion of conversion from an evil, disobedient way of life to an obedient one over against the divine commands is the underlying motif of this section (to v.10). The norm for judging this obedience is *κατὰ πάντα* which I am commanding you today. For the *ὅσα* clause see comment at 4:2. And for

1. See SS 198.
2. See Appositives Sect.2.1. for a fuller discussion.

"out of your whole heart and person" see comment at 4:29. The obedience must be unrestrained, one of complete devotion. Over against MT, which has אתה ובניך between the two structures, LXX simply continues with "out of his whole heart and person" immediately after the relative clause. Hex has of course added *συ και οι υιοι σου* under the asterisk after *σήμερον*, so as to equal MT. The shorter text of LXX is smoother than that of MT, and it may have been omitted by LXX as otiose.

In the tradition our oldest witnesses do not support the LXX compound *ὑπακούσῃ*. Here 848, along with *b n*+, has *επακουσῃ*, but Deut never uses this compound, and it probably originated in a copyist error, in which the initial *upsilon* was misread as *epsilon*. B has *εισακουσῃ*, which does occur elsewhere in the book, but it is further supported only on the margin of an *s* ms, and *ὑπακούσῃ* must be original.[3]

30:3 MT begins the apodosis with שב ... את שבותך, an idiom usually understood to mean "and he will restore your fortunes." Unusual is the use of the Qal rather than the Hi.[4] LXX has taken the modifier in the same sense as Tar^{JN} did with its *τὰς ἁμαρτίας σου*, and revised the verb contextually by its *ἰάσεται*, which is much like the ויקבל of the Palestinian Targums. So the Lord will heal your sins; what is meant is that the harm done by Israel's disobedience will be undone; they will return to their former healthy state. The subject is *κύριος*, but MT adds אלהיך, and hex has also added *ο θεος σου* to represent it; cf comment at v.1.[5]

That this was a legitimate understanding of the Hebrew שב את שבותך seems clear from the next clauses, "and he will have mercy on you, and *πάλιν συνάξει σε* out of all the nations." The adverb is a good rendering of the Hebrew idiom שבו plus verb. The divine restoration from exile will follow on Israel's repentance. MT has a relative clause modifying "nations," which differs from its parallel in v.1 only in its verb, הפיץ instead of הדיח; LXX uses

3. See THGD 68.
4. According to Syh^m The Three rendered the verb by *convertit* (presumably = *ἐπιστρέψει*), after which Sym added *tibi* (i.e. *σοι*). Aq translated את שבות by a cognate noun *conversionem tuam* (= *τὴν ἐπιστροφήν σου*), whereas Theod and Sym translated by *captivitatem tuam* (= *τὴν αἰχμαλωσίαν σου*), which Tar^O also represents by its גלתך, whereas Tar^{JN} speak of "your guilt, debt."
5. As did The Three.

the same verb for the two, *διασκορπίσῃ*, which is actually more accurate for הפיץ, and also changes the pronoun: *εἰς οὕς*, rather than *οὗ ἄν*. Both verbs have a second singular pronominal suffix rendered by *σε*, but in v.1 it precedes the verb, and in v.3 it follows it. As in the first clause, the subject in LXX is simply *κύριος*. Since MT here also had the modifier אלהיך, hex has added *ο θεος σου* to equal it.

In the tradition the Byz text has (*εξ*)*ιλασται* instead of *ἰάσεται*, which can only be explained as a palaeographically inspired error.[6]

30:4 This verse elaborates on the theme of restoration from exile. LXX has exaggerated the dispersion over against MT's בקצה השמים "at the edge of the sky" by including both limits, i.e. *ἀπ' ἄκρου τοῦ οὐρανοῦ ἕως ἄκρου τοῦ οὐρανοῦ*. The *O*+ text has omitted *ἕως*—fin, but this was due to homoioteleuton, and its similarity to MT is mere coincidence, i.e. it was not hex. LXX's text makes the diaspora from one end of the sky to the other. In any event, "the Lord your God will gather, and take you from there." In the tradition the majority B 963 text has repeated the subject *κυριος ο θεος σου* for the last clause as well, but this is obviously not original, but ex par.

30:5 In this verse the promise of return to the promised land is explicitly made. The land is described as that "which your fathers possessed," and "you will possess it." Twice hex corrects the word order of *σε ποιῆσαι* to equal the suffixal position of the pronoun in Hebrew. The second case is unusual, in that הרבך "will increase you" is translated by the verbal figure *πλεονασόν σε ποιῆσαι*. Thc adjective occurs only here and at 1Macc 4:35 in OT, but its meaning is fully clear. The verbal adjective means "numerous," and the collocation correctly translates the Hebrew.

30:6 MT has the notion of מל לבב "circumcize the heart," for which see מלתם את ערלת לבבכם at 10:16 and comment ad loc. That this means that the heart will be cleansed is clear, and LXX makes this explicit by its translation of the verb by *περικαθαριεῖ* "purify, cleanse, purge." The choice of the *περι-* compound is well-made, since the usual rendering for מול is *περιτέμνω*. The

6. Daniel 313, f.n.52 states that these are the habitual equivalents of כפר, but this is only true of the compound.

translation is unique, but comp Jos 5:4: *περιεκάθαρεν* also rendering the verb מול. The infinitive *ἀγαπᾶν* gives the purpose of the divine action of purification; it is to love the Lord your God. For "with your whole heart and with your whole person," see comment at 4:29.[7]

The verse ends with a *ἵνα* clause: *ἵνα ζῇς σύ*, translating למען חייך. Only here in Deut is חייך rendered by the inflected verb plus pronoun; at v.19 this collocation translates תחיה אתה (וזרעך). In the tradition the majority A text has amplified the pronoun by *και το σπερμα σου*, which, in spite of the hex placement of this under the obelus, is an early (prehexaplaric) ex par addition, almost certainly from v.19, and not original text.[8]

30:7 "These curses" must refer to the "curses" of 29:12,20,21, (and see also vv.14,19), which accompanied the covenant made with Israel in Moab; in this new state of restoration they will be put "on your enemies and on those who hate you, who have pursued you." MT designates "these curses" as "all these curses," and hex has added *πασας* under the asterisk to equal the כל of MT.

30:8 The preceding verse had centered on "your enemies," and here the change of focus is shown by using *σύ* before the second person singular verb, *ἐπιστραφήσῃ*, as in MT. MT uses תשוב ושמעת in the idiomatic sense of "you will again obey," but LXX, by using the middle form of *ἐπιστρέφω*, shows תשוב somewhat more literally, i.e. "you will turn yourself about," i.e. repeat, do again. The structure can then be rendered "and as for you, you will once again obey." LXX has "voice of the Lord *τοῦ θεοῦ σου*," which follows the text of Sam. MT has only יהוה.[9]

The translator again disregarded the כל before "his commandments," but hex has supplied *πασας* under the asterisk to represent it. For the *ὅσας* clause see comment at 4:2. In the tradition *ὅσας* is changed in F *C'' s*+ text as *ας*, but the A B majority text is certainly original.

30:9 For MT's תותיר "make to abound" LXX has *πολυωρήσει* which means "to treat carefully." The verb only occurs elsewhere twice in Pss (11:8 137:3)

7. For *ἐκ* rendering an instrumental ב see SS 127.
8. See THGD 75.
9. But Kenn 109,129 also add אלהיך.

but not for הותיר.[10] Since MT's verb is modified by לטובה, i.e. give you abundant prosperity, the translator may have intended the verb to cover the entire idiom in the sense of being careful in treating you well. In any event, LXX does not translate לטובה separately, and hex has added *εις αγαθον* after *κτηνῶν σου* to represent it. What LXX lacks, however, is the notion of wealth, prosperity, which MT clearly portrays, and the hex gloss at least in part restores this.

MT has "in all the work of ידך", but LXX follows Sam's ידיך.[11] The work of your hands is then to abound "in the offspring of your belly, and in the produce of your land, and in the offspring of your cattle," which corresponds to the order of Sam. MT has the last two prepositional phrases transposed, and hex has rearranged them to agree with the Hebrew.

The reason for this promise of abundance is given in the ὅτι clause: *ἐπιστρέψει κύριος ὁ θεός σου εὐφρανθῆναι ἐπὶ σὲ εἰς ἀγαθά*. MT has no equivalent for *ὁ θεός σου*, and hex has duly placed it under the obelus. The future verb renders ישוב used as in v.8 to show repetition. So with the marked infinitive לשוש it means "shall return to rejoice"; the translator has adopted the Hebrew idiom into Greek. The phrase לטוב is translated by *εἰς ἀγαθά*; the plural is used to indicate "for good ends." Divine rejoicing then does result in prosperity for the objects of his rejoicing. And the divine rejoicing will be as of old "concerning your fathers." For God's rejoicing see 28:63.

30:10 Here the requirements promoting this divine joy are given; such joy will only obtain when two conditions are met: a) "if you obey the voice of the Lord your God to observe his commandments and his ordinances (*δικαιώματα*) and his judgments, which are written in the book of this law." MT has only two nouns modifying לשמר, and so hex has placed *καὶ τὰ δικαιώματα αὐτοῦ* under the obelus. This is, however, incorrect; it is the third one, *καὶ τὰς κρίσεις αὐτοῦ*, which has no counterpart in MT. In Deut *δικαίωμα* is the regular rendering for חק(ה), whereas *κρίσις*, with almost complete consistency, renders משפט. The participle in LXX is sensibly in the feminine plural in agreement with the last noun in the list, *κρίσεις*, though MT has a feminine

10. The Three translate more literally: Aq by *περισσεύσει*, Sym by *αὐξήσει*, and Theod by *πληθυνεῖ*.
11. Also supported by 25 Kenn mss, as well as by Pesh Vulg.

singular הכתובה; this should probably be understood as a collective which can modify a plural.[12]

In the tradition most witnesses add *πασας* before *τὰς ἐντολάς*, but B 848+ do not, and neither does MT, and the shorter text must be original, though the fact that the *πασας* was placed under the obelus proves that it was a prehexaplaric plus. This is also true of the majority variant plus *και ποιειν* after *φυλάσσεσθαι*.[13] Again B 848 show that LXX was often closer to MT than was earlier realized.[14]

b) The second condition is a thoroughgoing repentance, i.e. *ἐπιστράφῃς ἐπὶ κύριον τὸν θεόν σου* "you turn yourself to the Lord your God (with your whole heart and with your whole person)." For the *ἐξ* phrases see comment at 4:29. The Byz text substitutes the future *επιστραφηση* for the aorist subjunctive, but the latter is expected after *ἐάν*, and must be original.

30:11 Vv.11—14 state that this *ἐντολή* is within your reach. V.11 begins with *ὅτι*, which relates this section to the preceding, giving an impulse for living up to the two conditions given in v.10. One might paraphrase its intent by "For after all." For the *ἥν* clause see comment at 4:2. This commandment *οὐκ ὑπέρογκός ἐστιν οὐδὲ μακρὰν ἀπὸ σοῦ ἐστιν* "is not excessive, nor distant (i.e. out of reach, unattainable) from you." MT has נפלאת "wonderful" for *ὑπέρογκος*, and has transposed *οὐδὲ πακράν* after *ἀπὸ σοῦ*. Hex has also transposed the structures to agree with MT's ממך ולא רחקה.[15] But LXX by its word order connects it with *μακράν*, giving it a local meaning.[16]

30:12 That it is not *μακρὰν ἀπὸ σοῦ* (v.11) is clear, both from the fact that it is not *ἐν τῷ οὐρανῷ* (v.12) nor *πέραν τῆς θαλάσσης* (v.13). A B *C'' s*+ gloss has added *ανω* after *οὐρανῷ*; this is simply a dittograph of the last three letters of *οὐρανῷ*, and should not be taken seriously.[17] The use of the direct speech marker is anacoluthic, since no verb of saying precedes it; one might interpret

12. See GK 122s and comp also 145k.
13. For the epexegetical infinitive see SS Inf 62.
14. See for both variant texts THGD 84.
15. Aq has translated לא נפלאת הוא ממך by *οὐκ τεθουμαστωμένη αὕτη ἀπὸ σοῦ* (retroverted from Syh).
16. See SS 151.
17. See THGD 123.

it by "(that you should think) saying," or "saying (to yourself)." The future verbs as predicate, *ἀναβήσεται* ... *λήμψεται* are deliberative in nature,[18] and the response means "Who might go up for us into the sky, and take (in the sense of bring) it for us." The *αὐτήν* refers to *ἐντολή* of v.11. In Hebrew this is a suffix to יקח, and therefore comes before לנו. Hex transposes *ἡμῖν αὐτήν* to correspond to the Hebrew order.

The final clause is presented paratactically, but in sense gives the point to the *τίς* structure. In MT this constitutes two paratactic clauses with verbs with prefixal inflections, a pattern which often intends result, thus "so that he may make us hear it, and we should observe it." LXX has changed the first verb to a participle, "and on hearing it we may perform." But the Greek thereby destroys the connection between מי and the subject of ישמענו, by transforming the *S*—P plus *Pronoun (modifier)* pattern to a participle in which the *S* is lost, and the pronominal modifier becomes the actor. Nor is the suffix of נעשנה rendered in LXX, it being unnecessary in Greek, though hex does add *αυτην* under the asterisk. I would translate "that on hearing it we might do (it)."[19]

30:13 This verse parallels v.12 in form, i.e. "nor is it beyond the sea *λέγων* Who might ..., and take it for us," along with an *ἀκουστήν* structure ending with *ποιήσομεν*. Parallel to "Who might ascend for us to the sky," v.13 has "Who might cross for us over the sea," but then follows exactly with *καὶ λήμψεται ἡμῖν αὐτήν* as in v.12. The rest of the verse is an exact copy of its parallel in MT: וישמענו אתה ונעשנה; LXX apparently renders the first clause in Aquilanic fashion (see f.n. at v.12). It seems strange that the translator would suddenly differentiate between the clause in v.12 and here, now discovering that the verb was Hi, and therefore transitive. I strongly suspect that the majority A F M text, which reads *ἀκούσαντες αὐτήν* instead of *ἀκουστὴν ἡμῖν ποιήσει αὐτήν*, *καί* is original text. The text printed as critical text is probably a correction, possibly originating in the Byz tradition. I would now correct the critical text so as to read *καὶ ἀκούσαντες αὐτήν*, as in v.12. As in v.12, hex

18. See Porter 424—425.
19. Aq has *καὶ ἀκουστὴν ἡμῖν αὐτὴν ποιήσει*, which is his way of rendering the Hi of שמע.

added an *αυτην* at the end of the verse under the asterisk to represent the suffix of נעשנה.

30:14 LXX omits the opening כי, making the nearness of the matter an independent statement, which carries on the notion that it is neither in the sky nor across the sea that *τὸ ῥῆμα* is to be found. Actually the omission of כי may have been intentional, since v.14 can hardly be understood as the reason for the previous statement. If the relationship were to be verbalized, an *ἀλλά* would have been more appropriate. The Byz text has added a *οτι* to represent the כי, which could be a recensional correction; in any event, it is secondary. The *ῥῆμα* must refer to the initial *ἐντολὴ αὕτη* with which the section began in v.10.

This nearness is so intimate (*σφόδρα*) that it is "in your mouth and in your heart." This is modified by a marked infinitive לעשתו "to do it," which is somewhat awkward. LXX has relieved this awkwardness by adding *καὶ ἐν ταῖς χερσίν σου* after "heart," which, because it has no Hebrew basis, was placed under the obelus in hex. It serves a useful purpose, however, to introduce *αὐτὸ ποιεῖν*. The picture might well be clarified by putting a comma after *καρδίᾳ σου*, thus "and (it is) in our power to effect it (i.e. *τὸ ῥῆμα*).[20] It might be noted that *αὐτὸ ποιεῖν* is transposed in most witnesses, which does equal MT. The choice of word order for LXX was based on two factors; it is supported by the oldest witness, cod B, and the word order of LXX, which disagrees with MT, is in fine Greek style.[21]

30:15 Vv.15—20 present the alternative to Israel: life or death. The use of the perfect, *δέδωκα*, is most appropriate; Moses had placed before Israel the alternative of good and evil, and it now remains for Israel to make its choice; comp 11:26. The verb represents נתתי in the sense of "put, place." LXX has a different way of presenting the alternatives from that of MT. In MT the one side is "life and good" and the alternative is "death and evil." LXX presents this in two sets of alternatives: "life and death," and "good and evil." Hex has transposed the "death" and "good," and has also added *και* between the two sets so as to equal MT exactly.

---

20. See SS 210.
21. Cf also SS Inf 155.

30:16 MT begins rather oddly with: "which (אשר) I am commanding you today," (for this see comment at 4:2), i.e. without an antecedent to the אשר, and LXX provides it with *ἐὰν δὲ εἰσακούσῃς τὰς ἐντολὰς κυρίου τοῦ θεοῦ σου*, possibly adapted from v.10. Hex has appropriately placed this text under the obelus, since it has no counterpart in MT. Most witnesses, including A F M, have the verb and *σου* in the plural. which can hardly be original in view of the context. The only second person plurals in the chapter occur in v.16b with *ζήσεσθε καὶ πολλοὶ ἔσεσθε*, in v.18 (except for *σοι*) and in v.19a, for which comp MT. Problematic is the use of *δέ* after *ἐάν*, which B Byz omit. But it is much more difficult to explain an addition of *δέ* than its deletion, and it is probably to be understood as original. The *ὅσας* for אשר appears as *ας* in B Byz, and either is possible.[22]

What Moses is commanding is given in three complementary infinitives, *ἀγαπᾶν*, *πορεύεσθαι* and *φυλάσσεσθαι*, all presented asyndetically. For the first one see comment at 6:5. For the second, MT has ללכת בדרכיו, which LXX renders literally, but almost all witnesses add *πασαις* before *ταῖς ὁδοῖς αὐτοῦ*, which hex has placed under the obelus. But here 848 witnesses to a text which equals MT exactly; it has no *πασαις*, and the word must be taken as an early prehexaplaric gloss, the source of which may well have been 19:9.[23] The third infinitive in the majority text has a *και* before it, which equals ולשמר, and appears in the active, *φυλασσειν*. The choice of LXX is, however, based on the combined witness of B and 848, which makes it likely to have been original.[24] The infinitive is triply modified by "his *τὰ δικαιώματα*, *τὰς ἐντολάς* and *τὰς κρίσεις*." The order of numbers one and two is that of Sam, and they are reversed in hex to equal the מצותיו וחקתיח of MT.

The apodosis is introduced by a conjunction in MT, and begins with two clauses in second singular, but which LXX changes to the plural, *καὶ ζήσεσθε καὶ πολλοὶ ἔσεσθε*, after which it becomes singular again with MT. Both clauses are unique to the book, and even the singular *ζῇς* only occurs three times in the book (vv.6,19 12:19). I can see no good reason for LXX's change to the plural, unless it be that it was influenced by the *ἵνα ζῆτε καὶ*

22. See THGD 106 for the choice of *ὅσας*.
23. See THGD 84.
24. See THGD 75.

πολυπλασιασθῆτε of 8:1, though this seems somewhat far-fetched. The tradition was not bothered by the inconsistency at all, and it remains puzzling. The text then goes on rendering MT in the singular. Note the relative clause εἰς ἣν εἰσπορεύῃ ἐκεῖ reproducing the Hebrew שמה with an otiose ἐκεῖ. LXX does add πάσῃ in rendering בארץ, and hex places it under the obelus.

30:17 Vv.17—18 constitute a final warning against idolatry. The condition is presented in v.17. LXX translates the verb יפנה by μεταστῇ, thus "should your heart turn aside."[25] This change of heart is explicated by a series of paratactic clauses: μὴ εἰσακούσῃς καὶ πλανηθεὶς προσκυνήσῃς θεοῖς ἑτέροις καὶ λατρεύσῃς αὐτοῖς. The middle clause represents two paratactic verbs in MT: ונדחת והשתחוית "and you are pulled away and you worshipped," for which see comment at 4:19.

30:18 The apodosis is a declaration: ἀναγγέλλω σοι σήμερον ὅτι. The present tense is exactly right for rendering the neutral הגדתי, and the majority M V variant future αναγγελω is obviously the result of haplography, and is not an intentional change. With σήμερον a future would presumably mean sometime later today, which no one could have intended. MT has the plural לכם as equivalent for σοι. Since the rest of the verse is in the plural the σοι is unusual, presumably singular under pressure of the singular which preceded the verse.[26]

The ὅτι clause gives the content of the declaration, and is put into the plural: ἀπολεῖσθε, πολυήμεροι γένεσθε, ὑμεῖς διαβαίνετε. MT has the last one in the singular אתה עבר, but LXX follows the consistently plural text of Sam, as does Pesh. The first verb is given special emphasis by a cognate dative noun before it, thereby rendering the cognate free infinitive of MT, thus "that you will most certainly be destroyed"; comp 25:15. For the second one see comment at 25:15. For the last one see comment at 4:22; it is modified in MT by לבא, which LXX omits; hex has added εισελθειν under the asterisk to represent it.[27] Most witnesses add another relative clause, ης κυριος ο θεος σου διδωσιν σοι, before the third construction, i.e. as a first modifier for γῆς. This

25. Sym uses a passive construction ἀποσταθῇς (retroverted from Syh).
26. The BHS note citing LXX and Vulg as supporting a second singular pronoun is misleading, since Vulg has the entire verse in the second singular.
27. See SS Inf 60.

has no basis in MT, but was an early ex par gloss added in prehexaplaric times, (since the clause is under the obelus in hex).[28]

30:19 V.19a calls heaven and earth as witnesses that Israel has been given the choice of life and death, with vv.19b—20 urging Israel to make the choice of life. V.19a continues with the second plural; i.e. the witness is individualized, and comes to each one of you, but with the imperative ἔκλεξαι the people are corporately addressed, i.e. the nation as a whole is involved in blessing and curse.

What heaven and earth are to witness to begins with the preposed modifiers τὴν ζωὴν καὶ τὸν θάνατον. For δέδωκα see comment at v.15. The verb is modified by the prepositional phrase πρὸ προσώπου ὑμῶν, though MT has פלניך. The translator continues with the plural, only turning to the singular with v.19b, which seems more logical than changing to the singular in the middle of the call to witness. "Life" and "death" are constituted by "blessing" and "curse" resp., a constitution not as obvious in MT with its singular (i.e. corporate) reference in the preceding prepositional phrase.

The imperative is introduced by καί, which imitates MT's ובחרת. The καί is omitted by B *n*+, thereby improving the style, but it is clearly part of LXX, as both 848 and 963, as well as most other witnesses, show.[29] The imperative is a final demand on Israel to make the proper choice of "life." For the ἵνα clause see discussion at v.6, as well as the comment at 11:8. καὶ τὸ σπέρμα σου occurs only here in the book, though comp the dative at 28:46.

30:20 V.20a defines how this life is obtained by means of three infinitival constructions: by loving the Lord your God, by obeying his voice, and ἔχεσθαι αὐτοῦ. The middle of ἔχω here means "to attach oneself to, to cling to," and is commonly modified by a genitive. It thus adequately renders לדבקה בו,[30] though it is unique in OT.

The ὅτι clause makes the choice of v.19 more immediate; life means your dwelling in the land of promise. הוא is translated by τοῦτο, which is neuter pointing to the infinitive, thus "this is your life and your length of days,

28. See List 10 in THGD 88—89.
29. See THGD 79.
30. Aq has a word for word rendering: κολλᾶσθαι ἐν αὐτῷ.

viz. your dwelling ...." LXX has added *σε* to designate the subject of the infinitive *κατοικεῖν*. For the relative clause modifying *γῆς* see discussion at 1:8.

Chapter 31

31:1 MT begins with וילך "and went (Moses, and spoke these words)," and continues in v.2 with ויאמר. LXX was faced with the problem of identifying what "these words" could refer to. If they referred to what Moses was about to say, the initial וילך was odd indeed. But if they meant what went before, as האלה would seem to imply, then the reading of a Qumran text ויכל, along with a כל modifying "these words," would be more appropriate. LXX clearly read such a text, and has *καὶ συνετέλεσεν* Μωυσῆς λαλῶν *πάντας τοὺς λόγους τούτους*.[1] What "all these words" refers to is all that has gone before. V.1 in LXX is thus a subscription to the end of chh.1—30, and v.2 is a new beginning for chh.31—33.[2]

31:2 Vv.2—6 narrate Moses' address to the people. LXX correctly interprets the Hebrew idiom for a person's age: בן מאה ועשרים שנה by *ἑκατὸν καὶ εἴκοσι ἐτῶν*, with "years" in the genitive (denoting measure of time). Hex has created a Hebraism by adding *υιος* before the number under the asterisk for the בן. אנכי is rendered by *ἐγώ εἰμι* quite sensibly. Because of his advanced age he is no longer able *εἰσπορεύεσθαι καὶ ἐκπορεύεσθαι*. In MT these infinitives are reversed, and hex has transposed them as well, to equal MT.

For the final clause LXX has translated the initial conjunction by *δέ*, which is rare in the book,[3] and may well have been chosen because of the unusual syntagm: ויהוה אמר. The choice of *δέ* in Deut is usually exegetically founded. Here it shows contrast between the two subjects: "I (will be unable)," and "the Lord (said)."

31:3 The nominal pattern, in which the predicate becomes a pronoun plus participle, occurs twice in the verse as הוא עבר, but is rendered by LXX as though the participle were articulated: *ὁ προπορευόμενος* (*πρὸ προσώπου σου*); this was probably done to distinguish these syntagms from the use of הוא as

1. See also Tov 104.
2. Sym has *καὶ πορευθεὶς* Μωυσῆς *ἐλάλησεν τοὺς λόγους τούτους* (retroverted from Syh^m), whereas Theod and Aq rendered וילך literally by *καὶ ἐπορεύθη* (from Syh).
3. Aejmelaeus (123) states that out of a total of 1282 cases of *waw* introducing a normal paratactic clause, only 34 are rendered by *δέ* in the book.

subject, with a verb as predicate, where the subject is rendered by the personal pronoun *αὐτός*. In other words, the articulated participle does not presuppose the text of Sam: הוא העבר,[4] but rather the articulation represents the pronoun. That this is actually the case is clear from the second *ὁ προπορευόμενος*, which also renders a הוא עבר. Note that עבר also occurred in v.2, but there transitively: תעבר את, and was sensibly translated by *διαβήσῃ* plus an accusative. The Lord your God is then "the one going before you; *αὐτός* will annihilate these nations from before you, and you shall dispossess them." This contrasts with what follows: "and Yesous is the one going before you, as the Lord has spoken." Yesous will then take Moses' place, but it is the Lord, not Yesous, who will effect victory over the Canaanite nations.

In MT the second part of the verse is asyndetic, but LXX renders smoothly by *καὶ Ἰησοῦς*, which follows Sam. In the tradition the *ἀπό* phrase modifying *ἐξολεθρεύσει* is changed to *προ* in a popular variant text, but this is due to *πρὸ προσώπου σου* occurring twice in the verse; these both represented לפניך, but the *ἀπό* phrase equals מלפניך.

31:4 For the destruction of Seon and Og see 3:1—7. These are called *τοῖς δυσίν* kings of the Amorrites. MT has no equivalent for *δυσίν*, and hex has correctly placed it under the obelus. The Amorrites are characterized as *οἳ ἦσαν πέραν τοῦ Ἰορδάνου*, as at 3:8 4:47; the clause also has no counterpart in MT, and is therefore put under the obelus in hex.

These are further identified by a relative clause in MT as those אשר השמיד אתם "whom he destroyed." LXX has a different understanding in that this clause becomes an analogy, a *καθότι* clause "even as he annihilated them." This hardly presupposes a different text with כאשר; it is rather exegetical in nature; it carries on the notion of *καθά* earlier in the verse; God will act as he did on that occasion; as he annihilated them, so will he do to the Canaanite enemy.

31:5 Vv.5—6a are in the second person plural in MT, though LXX returns to the singular in v.6a, but see comment at v.6b. The change to the plural seems quite arbitrary; nor is there an obvious reason for the return to the singular at the beginning of v.6 in LXX.

4. As BHS maintains.

MT begins with ונתנם, which is coordinate with ועשה of v.4, and meant "and he shall give them," i.e. deliver them up, but the translator took it as coordinate with השמיד, and translated it by an aorist καὶ παρέδωκεν. The antecedents of the pronouns must be kept straight in these verses. In v.4 αὐτοῖς refers to the Canaanites, but αὐτῶν and αὐτούς refer to the two kings. MT intended the suffix of the first word in v.5 to be a reference to the Canaanites, whereas LXX continued the reference to the kings, but the αὐτοῖς of v.5, together with להם, must be to the Canaanites. So LXX begins with "and the Lord delivered them up before you."

The remainder of the verse contrasts with this statement. The verb is in the future, and constitutes an order: "you shall do to them as I commanded you." Instead of the καθότι clause MT has a longer text: ככל המצוה אשר צויתי אתכם. LXX did not translate אשר כל המצוה at all. Instructive in the workings of hex is the attempt to "fix up" the LXX text. To Origen MT had no equivalent for καθότι so he placed it under the obelus, and then added καθα πασαν την εντολην ην under the asterisk. Readers of the *O* text must have been baffled by a text reading καθοτι κατα κ.τ.λ. In the tradition the *O* Byz text made a stylistic improvement by changing ἐνώπιον ὑμῶν into εις τας χειρας υμων, which fitted better after παρέδωκεν. A similar improvement is witnessed in the B *b n*+ text, which substituted υμιν. But the awkward παρέδωκεν ἐνώπιον ὑμῶν must be original.[5]

31:6 MT retains the plural for the imperatives, and switches back to the singular with the כי clause. LXX has all the imperatives in the singular. The first one, ἀνδρίζου "act like a man," occurs only here in the Pentateuch, but does occur more often in later books as a rendering of חזק. There are two positive words of encouragement, ἀνδρίζου καὶ ἴσχυε, both appropriately in the present tense, since a continuity of such a state is ordered. This is then followed by three negative commands, "do not fear, nor be frightened (or cowardly), nor be scared," but MT has only two, אל תיראו ואל תערצו. Obviously the first one is rendered by μὴ φοβοῦ, but which one renders ערצו "tremble" is not clear. At Jos 1:9 δειλιάσῃς translates תערץ, whereas πτοηθῇς does not occur for the root ערץ anywhere else in OT. So Origen may have been correct in placing μὴ πτοηθῇς under the obelus.

5. See THGD 127.

The ὅτι clause constitutes the basis for these encouraging words. The stress remains on the role of the Lord your God. LXX has ὁ προπορευόμενος as at v.3, μεθ' ὑμῶν ἐν ὑμῖν, not "before you," for עמך in MT. Why the translator should have changed to the plural only for these two prepositional phrases is puzzling, though comp 20:4 where μεθ' ὑμῶν also modifies this same participle; this could have been in the background, but then why the addition of a second (doublet?) phrase? It too must modify the participle, for it can hardly modify the verbal clause which follows, since not only does it begin with οὐ μή, but it is modified by σε.

Actually the solution lies in reviewing the participle used. MT does not read הוא עבר as at v.3, but הוא ההלך. But הלך is not normally rendered by προπορεύομαι, but rather by the simplex πορεύομαι.[6] Ms 848 actually reads the simplex form here, and it alone represents the original text form, whereas the majority text was created under the influence of v.3. An examination of the instances in OT in which the compound was used where MT had הלך, impels that conclusion. It shows that the compound was usually chosen because the verb was modified by a prepositional phrase representing the προ element such as πρὸ προσώπου plus pronoun (1:30,33 Exod 32:34), ἐναντίον αυτοῦ (Ps 84:13 96:3), or ἔμπροσθέν σου (Isa 58:8). In four cases the compound represents הלך לפני and not merely הלך (Gen 32:20 Exod 14:19 32:1,23). In two cases free renderings are involved (Exod 33:14 Prov 4:18), and only two cases do not follow the expected route: Gen 32:19 where the compound is modified by an ὀπίσω phrase, and Deut 20:4 where it is modified by μεθ' ὑμῶν, and for which see comment ad loc. In short, the critical text should read with 848 πορευόμενος. Possibly the ἐν ὑμῖν was added to show that, though the Lord was going with you, he was at the same time among you, in your midst. The majority A F M V text has omitted it, but in view of B 848 support this must be a secondary omission, probably precisely because of its difficult relation to the preceding μεθ' ὑμῶν.

The verse ends with the double assurance οὐ μή σε ἀνῇ οὔτε μή σε ἐγκαταλίπῃ "he will not let you go, nor abandon you," which is once again in the singular. σε ἀνῇ represents ירפך well, though it is used only here, and at its parallel in v.8 in the Pentateuch.[7] Instead of οὔτε μή the majority A text has

6. According to Dos Santos, 875 times.
7. Aq renders the verb by παρήσει.

ουδ ου μη, but Deut never uses this structure. Its popularity is assured by its NT occurrence in Hebr 13:5.[8] Also in the tradition is the transposition of *σε ἀνῇ* and of *σε ἐγκαταλίπῃ* by hex to agree with the ירפך and יעזבך resp. of MT. A popular spelling for *ἐγκαταλίπῃ*, shared inter alia by A F M V, is *εγκαταλειπῃ*, but the aorist must be original in view of *ἀνῇ* in the parallel clause. The popularity of the variant spelling is enhanced by the Hebr 13:5 text, which also spells it thus, but that is merely an itacistic spelling of the aorist.

31:7 In vv.7—8 Moses addresses Yesous. The opening imperatives of v.6 are repeated here. The *γάρ* clause explains the reason for urging Yesous to be manly and strong; it is because "you will go before this people into the land ..., and you will give it to them as a possession." MT reads "you will go with this people," and LXX's "before this people" continues the notion of v.3, where the status of Yesous is defined as "one going before." For both verbs an emphatic *σύ* precedes, (representing an אתה in MT), which stresses that it is not me (Moses), but you (Yesous), who is to lead the people in their conquest of the land of promise.[9] For the relative clause modifying *γῆν* see comment at 1:8.

31:8 LXX has simplified the rather verbose opening part of the verse by summarizing the two nominal clauses יהוה הוא ההלך לפניך הוא יהיה עמך as an attributive phrase modifying *κύριος*: *κύριος ὁ συμπορευόμενος μετὰ σοῦ*; this then serves as the subject of the two verbal clauses *οὐκ ἀνήσεί σε οὐδὲ μὴ ἐγκαταλίπῃ σε*. The notion ההלך is neatly combined with יהיה עמך in a compound expressing "going with." This gave Origen a hard time. He added *αυτος* under the asterisk after *κύριος* for the first הוא; the *σοι* after the participle he probably inherited as an old gloss, supported by the majority A F M V text, and which he allowed to stand to represent לפניך, and then before *μετά* he added *αυτος εσται* under the asterisk. In this way he could approximate MT somewhat more closely.

8. See THGD 114—115.
9. See Prijs 18.

The verse ends with the first two negative commands of v.6, but here δειλία clearly represents תחת "be frightened." For ουδ ου μη instead of οὐδὲ μή see comment and the last footnote at v.6.

31:9 Vv.9—13 constitute instructions to read the book of the law publicly every seven years. MT states that Moses wrote את התורה הזאת, but LXX levels with v.24, where Moses finished writing πάντας τοὺς λόγους τοῦ νόμου τούτου εἰς βιβλίον, though substituting τὰ ῥήματα for "all the words." Actually the Hebrew of v.24 lacks "all," reading את דברי התורה הזאת על ספר, a text which LXX translates more exactly here than at v.24 itself. In the tradition a popular A F M V text adds παντα before τὰ ῥήματα, which is clearly secondary. Since εἰς βιβλίον has no basis in MT, hex placed it under the obelus.

The second clause begins with καὶ ἔδωκεν for MT's ויתנה. The translator found a rendering of the suffix otiose for Greek, but hex added αυτο under the asterisk to represent it. For the Levites as τοῖς αἴρουσιν τὴν κιβωτὸν τῆς διαθήκης κυρίου see comment at 10:8. Not only were the Levites the recipients, and thus the guardians of this book of the law, but also τοῖς πρεσβυτέροις τῶν υἱῶν Ἰσραήλ; thus both religious and civil leaders became responsible for the Law book. In MT the second recipients are designated as אל כל זקני ישראל. Hex has added πασιν before ταῖς to equal the כל; note also that LXX has τῶν υἱῶν Ἰσραήλ as the more usual reference to Israel.

31:10 The verse begins with καὶ ἐνετείλατο αὐτοῖς Μωυσῆς ἐν τῇ ἡμέρᾳ. This differs from MT in that אותם follows משה, but LXX usually places a pronominal modifier immediately after the verb. The majority text has transposed αὐτοῖς Μωυσῆς to equal MT. The Hebrew also has no counterpart for the ἐν phrase, and so hex placed it under the obelus. The actual orders which Moses communicated follow the direct speech marker λέγων, and comprise vv.10b—13.

V.10b specifies the time and occasion; the time is "after seven years," and the occasion is given in general terms as ἐν καιρῷ ἐνιαυτοῦ ἀφέσεως. καιρῷ translates מועד, and refers to a set time; what is meant is "in the year set for release." For the "year of release" see comment at 15:1. The second phrase ἐν ἑορτῇ σκηνοπηγίας is more specific; the particular καιρός is the feast of tabernacles.[10] For the term *σκηνοπηγίας* see comment at 16:16.

31:11 LXX renders בבוא appropriately by a *συν-* compound with *ἐν τῷ συμπορεύεσθαι* "when (all Israel) comes together"; the Hebrew simply has "when ... enters." For *ὀφθῆναι ἐνώπιον κυρίου τοῦ θεοῦ σου* see discussion at 16:16. For "the place which the Lord would choose" see comment at 12:5. LXX has added the subject *κύριος* over against MT, and hex placed it quite correctly under the obelus. Actually most witnesses have also added *ο θεος σου* ex par.

The command to read is in the plural: *ἀναγνώσεσθε*, which is strange in a singular context. The *O* mss have this in the singular, which may well be a hex correction. The last phrase, *εἰς τὰ ὦτα αὐτῶν*, is a literalism which is, however, easily understood as "in their hearing." The *αὐτῶν* refers to Ἰσραήλ.

31:12 MT begins with הקהל, a free infinitive, which, when used as an isolate syntagm, is imperatival in nature, but LXX renders it by *ἐκκλησιάσας*, which is contextually difficult. One would at least expect the plural, and Byz has precisely that with *εκκλησιασεντες*, whereas the majority A F M V text read an imperative *εκκλησιασατε*, but both of these variant texts are attempts at simplifying the text. I suspect that the translator was inattentive to the fact of his plural imperative in v.11, and mistakenly took הקהל as a singular participle; after all, the plural imperative of v.11 would make much better sense as a singular. I would understand the construction as a circumstantial participle showing the condition for reading the law, thus "having assembled."[11] The people are then listed by classes: "men and women, *καὶ τὰ ἔκγονα* and the proselyte who is in your cities." The Hebrew has והטף which LXX correctly understood as a collective; its translation by *ἔκγονα* occurs elsewhere in the OT only at 29:11, but it is adequate. MT has גרך but LXX does not translate the suffix, considering it otiose in view of its limiting structure *τὸν ἐν ταῖς πόλεσίν σου*. For *πόλεσίν* see comment at 12:15. Hex has added *σου* so as to represent the suffix.

---

10. Aq translates הסכות by *τῶν συσκιασμῶν* "of the overshadowings," and Theod and Sym have *τῶν σκηνῶν*.
11. Theod and Aq follow LXX, but Sym has *συναθροιζόντων*.

This is followed by two *ἵνα* clauses, (each representing למען), indicating the purpose of the reading of the law to the people. The first one is literal: "in order that they may hear." The second one, "in order that they may learn," naturally has a complementary infinitive modifying it: "to fear the Lord your God." The "your" is *ὑμῶν*, i.e. plural, imitating MT's אלהיכם, signaling the change to the plural, which then continues to the end of the section (v.13). MT does not have an infinitive, but continues with two paratactic clauses: ויראו "and they shall fear," and וישמרו "and they shall be careful."[12] That LXX would use an infinitive to complement *μάθωσιν* is fine, but then it makes a break, continuing with a future *καὶ ἀκούσονται* (apparently reading וישמעו, but see comment at v.13) followed by an infinitive *ποιεῖν* (for לעשות). This must then be understood as "and (so) they will be obedient in effecting all the words of this law." The translator not only misread the more sensible ישמרו as ישמעו, but also failed to recognize the coordinate nature of the two paratactic clauses.

In the tradition B Byz+ have levelled the number problem by changing *σου* to *υμων*. This would make the verse consistent, but the inconsistent text of LXX equals MT at this juncture, and is original.[13]

31:13 A further result of the seven year cycle of reading the law: "their sons, who did not know, will (also) hear and learn to fear the Lord their God." The verbs *ἀκούσονται καὶ μαθήσονται* may well have been the stimulus for the misreading of ישמרו as ישמעו in v.12. Or was that an intentional leveling of the text? The *ὅσας* clause modifying *ἡμέρας* has the pattern: pronoun plus present tense, *αὐτοὶ ζῶσιν*, but MT has אתם חיים; LXX follows Sam, however, which has הם as subject of the relative clause. For the *εἰς ἥν* clause see comment at 4:22.

31:14 Vv.14—15 require Moses and Yesous to come to the tent of witness, and state that the Lord came down. What the Lord said to Moses was "behold the days of your death are near at hand." In MT the subject is ימיך למות "your days (i.e. time) to die." Hex tried to fix this up by a simple transposition of

12. See SS Inf 124.
13. See THGD 57—58.

τοῦ θανάτου and *σου*, but this mechanical correction does not really equal MT; in the resultant text *σου* would still be understood as modifying *θανάτου*.

Moses is told to summon Yesous, and they are to stand *παρὰ τὰς θύρας τῆς σκηνῆς τοῦ μαρτυρίου*. MT has the imperative התיצבו "station yourselves," which is not incorrectly rendered by *στῆτε*, but the prepositional phrase in MT has no reference to "doors," neither here, nor in the clause which describes their carrying out the divine orders in v.14b. It does, however, occur in v.15 with reference to the pillar of cloud על פתח האהל. The translator has been engaging in a certain amount of leveling in these two verses, i.e. in all three cases he levelled to על פתח אהל rather than the באהל of v.14. For the term "tent of testimony" as a translation for אהל מועד see Note at Exod 27:21.

In v.14b Moses and Yesous do as they were ordered. LXX, however, has again amplified the text. MT has "Moses and Joshua went (and they stationed themselves ...)," but the Greek has added *εἰς τὴν σκηνὴν τοῦ μαρτυρίου* to modify *ἐπορεύθη*. Hex has signalled this by placing the phrase under the obelus.

31:15 V.15a of MT has been considerably amplified in the Greek. The initial word in MT is וירא vocalized by the Masoretes as a Ni, hence "and (Yahweh) appeared." But LXX begins with *καὶ κατέβη* "and (the Lord) came down," a unique equation; in fact, the verb *καταβαίνω* is normally the rendering for ירד.[14] MT continues with יהוה באהל בעמוד ענן, thus "and Yahweh appeared in the tent in a pillar of cloud." For this LXX has "and the Lord came down in a cloud and stood at the doors of the tent of witness." As usual hex witnesses in a purely quantitative fashion to the Hebrew parent text by adding *εν τη σκηνη* under the asterisk after the first verb, and then placing "and stood—witness" under the obelus. It should be added that the majority A F M V text has *εν στυλω νεφελης* instead of *ἐν νεφέλῃ* as well. The source of the LXX text must have been Num 12:5, which does, however, have *ἐν στύλῳ νεφέλης* instead of *ἐν νεφέλῃ*, and has *τῆς* (*θύρας*) rather than the *τάς* of our verse, but for the rest is exactly the same text. Whether the accusative plural or the genitive singular is original in our verse is clear from the support pattern. Only seven

14. Theod and Sym have *καὶ ὤφθη* (retroverted from Syh).

mss read the singular in v.15a, whereas in v.15b only five witnesses read a singular. For Deut the tent of witness had doors. The "door(s) of the tent" in the rest of the Greek Pentateuch is inconsistent in number. By my count Exod has the singular six times and the plural 12; Lev has 15 cases of the singular over against eight plurals, and Num has eight vs four, thus totals of 29 vs 24. In the tradition the *τῆς σκηνῆς* at the end of the verse is amplified by *του μαρτυριου* by 963 *oI s t+*, whereas B 848 support LXX, which in turn equals MT. The gloss is taken from the end of v.15a.[15] It should also be noted that the leveling referred to with respect to "doors of the tent" did not extend to the prepositions. In v.15 the prepositions are *ἐπί*, but in v.14 they are *παρά*. In this way the translator differentiates between the "standing" of Moses and Aaron (as *παρά*), and that of the Lord (as *ἐπί*).

31:16 Vv.16—22 interrupt the flow of vv.14—15 and v.23 which deal with Yesous as successor to Moses, whereas vv.16—22 are a prose introduction to the Song of Moses in ch.32. The section begins with a dire prediction that after Moses' death the people will apostasize, for which they will be divinely punished.

The use of the Hebrew predicative participle is, as usual, rendered by a present tense of imminent action; *κοιμᾷ* as a middle form is idiomatic for "(you) are about to go to sleep."[16] To sleep with one's fathers means "to die." This introductory statement sets the stage for the people's abandonment of the faith: "This people arising will apostasize after strange gods," i.e. will proceed to apostasize (literally fornicate). Note the use of antonyms; Moses will *κοιμᾷ*/שכב, and the people *ἀναστάς*/קם.

LXX follows Sam in retaining the singular *οὗτος εἰσπορεύεται* (referring to Israel), but then changing to the future plural with *ἐγκαταλείψουσιν*; MT retains the singular עזבני, and does not change to the plural until ועזבתים of v.17. LXX (and Sam) look on the entrance into the promised land as a corporate act of the people, and so the singular is appropriate. The apostasy is the act of Israelites, of individuals, and hence the plural. The logic of MT on number seems to be more arbitrary.

15. See THGD 75.
16. Also adopted by Theod and Sym, but Aq has the uncontracted form *κοιμᾶσαι*.

In any event, this eventual idolatry means *ἐγκαταλείψουσίν με καὶ διασκεδάσουσιν τὴν διαθήκην μου*. The verb *διασκεδάζω* is regularly employed for the Hi of פרר, and means "to break up. shatter," hence violate (my covenant).

In the tradition Byz has levelled the text by making both *ἐκπορνεύσει* and *οὗτος εἰσπορεύεται* plural, i.e. λαός is understood as a collective, and its predicate is made plural. Also the verbosity of *ἐκεῖ εἰς αὐτήν* is alleviated, either by omitting *ἐκεῖ* by *C*'' *s*+, or by changing *εἰς αὐτήν* to *κληρονομησαι αυτην* by Byz, which is ex par; see v.13.

31:17 LXX translates וחרה אפי "and my anger will burn" idiomatically by *καὶ ὀργισθήσομαι θυμῷ* "and I will be angry with wrath," i.e. I will be very angry. For הסתרתי "I will hide (my face)" LXX has *ἀποστρέψω*. Onc might have expected *κρύψω*, *ἀποκρύψω* or *κατακρύψω*, but the verb *ἀποστρέφω* is more common (30 times vs 12), though the distribution is distinctive. Of the 30 cases all but two (Ps 118:19 with *τὰς ἐντολάς σου*, and Prov 4:27 with *σὸν πόδα*) have *τὸ πρόσωπον* as modifier, whereas only one case of *κρύπτω* with *πρόσωπον* as modifier (Job θ´ 34:29) and none with its compounds, occurs. It occurs three times in Deut (also in v.18 32:20), 13 times in Pss, seven in Isa, three in Ezek, and once each in Exod, Prov, Jer and Mic.[17]

With *καὶ ἔσται κατάβρωμα* the text changes to the singular again. The singular individualizes, as does *αὐτόν*, and cf *ἐρεῖ* in the remainder of the verse. By *κατάβρωμα*, for which see 28:26, "prey" is intended. The Lord's anger will be expressed by his abandoning the covenant breaker to his fate, i.e. becoming prey to *κακὰ πολλὰ καὶ θλίψεις*. A V *b*+ text does change *ἔσται* to *εσονται*, which only by coincidence agrees with Sam. The next verb *εὑρήσουσιν* is plural with the compound subject *κακὰ πολλὰ καὶ θλίψεις*, not singular, as might be expected, by attraction to the nearer neuter plural subject *κακά*.[18] A singular would be confusing in view of the preceding singular clause.

The reason for all these calamities will be recognized by the idolatrous Israelite. He will attribute it as being *διότι οὐκ ἔστιν κύριος ὁ θεός μου ἐν ἐμοί*. MT begins this with הלא "is it not?" This would expect an affirmative ans-

17. Based on HR.
18. See SS 198.

wer.[19] The idolator recognizes that all these calamities have found me "because the Lord my God is not (i.e. no longer) with me." LXX has added *κύριος* over against MT.[20]

31:18 For *ἀποστρέψω* see comment at v.17.[21] The verb is emphasized by a cognate dative noun, which translates a cognate free infinitive, thus "but I will certainly turn my face away from them." Hebrew has no equivalent for *ἀπ' αὐτῶν*, which follows Sam's מהם, as well as the MT of v.17, while *O*, (possibly representing hex), has omitted it, and so equals MT. Note that the text has again reverted to the plural. The *αὐτῶν* makes it necessary to continue with plural verbs *ἐποίησαν* ... *ἐπέστρεψαν*, though MT retains singular ones. LXX also distinguishes between *τὰ κακά* "calamities" for רעות in v.17, and *τὰς κακίας* "evil deeds" for הרעה.

31:19 MT has three imperatives addressed by the Lord to Moses, the first of which is in the plural: כתבו, and the other two more logically in the singular, למדה and שימה. LXX has levelled these to the plural *γράψατε* ... *διδάξατε* ... *ἐμβαλεῖτε*. LXX considered the addressees to be Moses and Yesous in line with v.14, and comp 32:44: *αὐτὸς καὶ Ἰησοῦς*.

The translator dealt somewhat freely with the first clause; MT has כתבו לכם את השירה הזאת, for which LXX has *γράψατε τὰ ῥήματα τῆς ᾠδῆς ταύτης*. LXX did not render לכם, either considering it otiose (see comment on "ethical dative" at 1:7), or as contradicted by the next two clauses, i.e. it was to be written not for yourselves, but for the instruction and direction of the people. Hex of course had no such fine insights, and so added *εαυτοις* under the asterisk. On the other hand, MT had no counterpart to *τὰ ῥήματα*; here the translator was pedantically correct; after all, one does not write songs; one sings them, hence "the words of this song." Cf also v.30.

The purpose underlying teaching the words of this song is "in order that this song may serve as a witness for me among the Israelites."[22]

---

19. Sym more freely has ἦ or ἦ ἄρα "indeed" (retroverted from Syh).
20. Sym omits it, reading "ὁ θεός μου ἐν μέσῳ μου (retroverted from Syh).
21. Aq and Sym translate by *ἀποκρύψω*. Aq also added the participle *ἀποκρύβων* to represent the free infinitive.
22. Theod and Sym retain *εἰς μαρτύριον* of LXX, but Aq translates as *εἰς μάρτυρα* "for a witness," rather than "for a testimony."

In the tradition *διδάξατε* appears as a future *διδαξετε* in B F+, but this can hardly be original in view of the Hebrew למדה and of the coordinate *γράψατε*.[23]

31:20 The *γάρ* clause explains how this song will effect the Israelites when they become idolatrous. V.20 sets out the scenario under which the words of this song will become a witness against them. God is going to bring them into *τὴν γῆν τὴν ἀγαθήν*. MT has only האדמה here, and hex has placed *τὴν ἀγαθήν* under the obelus. The phrase "the good land" often occurs in the book (1:35 3:25 4:22 6:18 9:4,6, and see 31:21 as well). Note that LXX promises that "I will bring *αὐτούς*; in fact, the Greek is consistently plural throughout the verse, whereas MT has the singular, except for two clauses ועבדום ונאצוני, and then goes back to the singular in the last clause, a bewildering mixup in number that defies analysis. LXX levels the text by keeping to the plural throughout. In the tradition, B Byz add *δουναι αυτοις* after "which I swore to their fathers"; this does equal Sam, but this is irrelevant; the phrase is ex par.[24] For *γῆν ῥέουσαν γάλα καὶ μέλι* see comment at 6:3. This is followed by three paratactic verbal clauses in MT: ואכל ושבע ודשן, which the Greek turns into two by reducing the middle one to a participle as *ἐμπλησθέντες*, subordinated to *κορήσουσιν*; this apparently derives from *κορέω*, a hapax legomenon, equalling *κορέννυμι* "be sated."[25] The combination "being filled they will be sated," is somewhat more tautologous than MT's "they will be sated and grow fat," but it does get the point across that the people will lack nothing in the promised land.

In spite of this "they will turn to strange gods, and serve them, *καὶ παροξυνοῦσίν με*, and shatter my covenant." *παροξύνω* "provoke to anger, irritate" is commonly used for the Pi of נאץ "to scorn, be contempuous of," e.g. Num 14:11,23 16:30.[26] For *διασκεδάσουσιν* for הפר see comment at v.16.[27]

23. See THGD 140.
24. See THGD 122 as well as List 1, *ibid* 86.
25. Aq rendered דשן by *πιανθήσονται*. Sym subordinated it to *ἐπιστραφήσεται* (*ἐπὶ θεοὺς ψευδεῖς*) as *παχυνθείς* (retroverted from Syh).
26. Aq has *διασυροῦσιν* "disparage, ridicule."
27. Theod retains LXX, but Aq has *ἀκυρώσει* "cancel, void," and Sym has *ἀθετήσουσιν*.

31:21 LXX has omitted the first part of MT: והיה כי תמצאן אתו רעות רבות וצרות, and hex has added a translation from Aquila under the asterisk: *και εσται οταν ευρωσιν αυτον κακα πολλα και θλιψεις*, which then serves as the condition for the opening clause of LXX. In LXX the opening clause is paratactically presented "and this song shall be set up as a witness in opposition." The omission of the condition given in MT does not jeopardize the understanding that this verse shows the reaction (*ἀντικαταστήσεται*) or response as a witness to the possible scenario envisioned in v.21. *κατὰ πρόσωπον* is used absolutely without a genitive pronoun in spite of MT's לפניו. Together with the verb *ἀντικαθίστημι* it has the legal sense of being set up over against a defendant, i.e. as a witness—*μαρτυροῦσα* (for לעד) for the prosecution.[28] Hex has added *αυτου* to render the suffix of לפניו, which most witnesses have contextualized by changing it to the plural *αυτων*.

The reason for this testimony of the song is given in a *γάρ* clause: "it will not be forgotten from the mouth of their seed," i.e. succeeding generations will still sing this song. LXX continues the plural of v.20 with *αὐτῶν*; in fact, does so for the rest of the verse, whereas MT uses the singular. In the tradition (*οὐ γὰρ*) *μὴ ἐπιλησθῇ* becomes *επιλησθησεται* in a popular 963 variant text. But 848 supports the *μή* text, as do all the uncials, and is almost certainly original.[29] The majority A F M V tradition has also added *απο στοματος αυτων και* before *ἀπό*, i.e. "from their mouth and from the mouth of their seed," but B 848 963 all support the shorter text of LXX.[30]

A second *γάρ* clause is added, which affirms divine knowledge of *τὴν πονηρίαν αὐτῶν*. This is a free paraphrase of יצרו "his form," hence his inclination. LXX has a contextual interpretation. *πονηρίαν* characterizes *ὅσα ποιοῦσιν ὧδε σήμερον*, whereas MT refers to what they are now inclined to do. According to LXX their disposition was evil, which fits nicely into the context.[31] I would translate the *οἶδα* clause as "for I know their evil disposition which they are putting into effect here today, (even) before I bring them in."

28. Aq translates it by *εἰς μαρτύριον*.
29. See THGD 75.
30. See THGD 80—81.
31. Aq translates יצר literally by *τὰ πλάσμα*. Syh^{m} attributes *σπέρματος αὐτῶν* (retroverted) to Theod, but this cannot be correct, since the reading must refer to *σπέρματος αὐτῶν* in the preceding clause.

It should be noted that MT also has no counterpart to ὧδε.[32] For the ἥν clause see comment at 1:8. MT has no equivalent for *τοῖς πατράσιν αὐτῶν*, but in the many cases of this pattern in the book the verb "he swore" always has a dative modifier; the gloss is original, though it is ex par.[33]

31:22 LXX has Moses writing the song *ἐν ἐκείνῃ τῇ ἡμέρᾳ*. Since MT has ביום ההוא, which is normal Hebrew word order, hex has transposed *ἐκείνῃ* after the noun to equal the Hebrew word order. The verb *ἐδίδαξεν* has a double accusative, which is good Greek. The *C'' b d+* variant *τοις υιοις* is, I suspect, the result of palaeographic confusion.

31:23 This verse logically concludes the vv.14—15 account concerning Yesous. If it were placed there, the subject of *ἐνετείλατο*, which is not expressed in MT, would naturally be *κύριος*. In the present context, however, it would be more fitting to have Moses as subject, and LXX has taken it in this way. In fact, most witnesses actually add *μωυσης* after the verb. But B 963+ lack it, and there is no need for it, nor for an *αυτω* after *εἶπεν*, which is also attested by a majority text, but again not by B 963+.[34] Yesous is encouraged by the same imperatives as in v.7, *ἀνδρίζου καὶ ἴσχυε*; see comment ad loc. In fact, the following *γάρ* clause is similar to that of v.7 as well, except that "you will enter before the face of the people" becomes *εἰσάξεις τοὺς υἱοὺς Ἰσραήλ*, which equals the parent text.[35] With the *ἥν* clause MT and LXX part company. For MT Yahweh is speaking, and so it reads אשר נשבעתי להם ואנכי אהיה עמך. But to LXX the speaker is Moses and the third person is used: *ἥν ὤμοσεν κύριος*[36] *αὐτοῖς καὶ αὐτὸς ἔσται μετὰ σοῦ*.[37]

In the tradition Ἰησοῦ has been articulated in most cursive mss. This was probably added by hex to represent את. The majority of witnesses have added *υιω ναυη* which is probably hex in origin; also cf 1:38 32:44 and 34:9.

---

32. See THGD 71.
33. But Kenn 75 also adds לאבתם, and Sam added לאבתיו.
34. See THGD 123.
35. For a defence of MT and LXX see Prijs 98.
36. Instead of *ὤμοσεν κύριος* The Others read *ὤμοσα* (retroverted from Syh).
37. For the second clause Theod read {*εγω*} *ἐγώ εἰμι ἔσομαι μετὰ σοῦ* (retroverted from Syh which mistakenly copied *ἐγώ* twice).

31:24 For ויהי plus timer see comment at 1:3; here the temporal condition is introduced by *ἡνίκα*, with the apodosis obtaining in v.25. The *δέ* shows change of subject to Μωυσῆς. LXX has added *πάντα* over against MT, but this has no real textual significance. What is significant is that he wrote the entire law code in a book, i.e. *ἕως εἰς τέλος*. This represents עד תמם.[38] Hex added *αυτων* to show the suffix of the Hebrew, but this makes little difference; with or without an *αυτων* it would still mean the same: right up to the end, i.e. without leaving anything out.[39] In the tradition the Byz text has λαλων rather than *γράφων*; this is of course secondary, created under the influence of the oft-recurring notion of Moses' speaking (the law).

31:25 MT identifies the subject of "gave orders" as משה. LXX omitted it as unnecessary in view of the identification in the protasis, but hex added it to equal MT more exactly. The Levites are identified as *τοῖς αἴρουσιν τὴν κιβωτὸν τῆς διαθήκης κυρίου*, for which see comment at 1:8. "Those carrying the ark" represents a bound phrase in MT: נשאי ארון, which the Greek renders idiomatically by an accusative modifying a participle.[40]

31:26 The direct speech marker λέγων at the end of v.25 introduces what Moses "commanded" in vv.26—29, though only v.26a and v.28a are actually orders, the remainder of the speech giving reasons for the commands. MT begins with the free infinitive, which, as an isolate structure, is imperatival, and so can continue with a contextualized ושמתם "take and place." LXX subordinates the former as a participle, and places the stress where it belongs, on *θήσετε*, thus "having taken the book of this law, you must put it." At 10:2 the Lord had ordered Moses to put the two tablets which the Lord had inscribed *εἰς τὴν κιβωτόν*, which, according to v.5, was duly done. By contrast the Levites are to put the book of the law *ἐκ πλαγίων* of the ark, i.e. "next to the ark," מצד ארון. The distinction betwen the two involves the two tablets of the Decalogue which remained inside the ark, and the Deut law book which was to be left next to or at the side of the ark. MT has the singular noun, but LXX normally has the plural *πλάγιοι* throughout the OT.

38. See SS Inf 114.
39. Aq translates by *τελειωσώσεως αὐτῶν*.
40. See SS 69.

With v.26b, and continuing through v.27a, the singular is used, after which the plural second person continues to the end of the section (v.29). This is simply in imitation of MT which it follows exactly. The *καὶ ἔσται* represents והיה, which often represents a result clause in MT, and LXX should be understood in the same way: "that it (i.e. the presence of the book next to the ark) would serve as a witness among (or possibly against) you." That book will always be there in place to serve as a constant reminder of what the demands of the Lord are upon his people.

31:27 Moses explains why it is important that this book of the law should be a constant witness against Israel; it is because (*ὅτι*) I am fully aware of your *ἐρεθισμόν* and your hard neck (i.e. stiffneckedness). The term *ἐρεθισμόν* "rebelliousness" is well-chosen to translate מריך.

A *γάρ* clause follows, and with it the text reverts to the second plural. MT has הן בעודני חי, which LXX renders by a genitive absolute, disregarding the הן, *ἔτι (γὰρ) ἐμοῦ ζῶντος* "for while I was still alive."[41] The Byz text has *ει* before *ἔτι*, which is obviously recensionally inspired (by Aq?). The genitive construction is modified by *μεθ' ὑμῶν σήμερον*, i.e. "with you now," and the main clause follows as *παραπικραίνοντες ἦτε τὰ πρὸς τὸν θεόν*. The verb occurs here for the first and only time in the Pentateuch, and renders the verbal figure ממרים הייתם. Though on the surface it would seem to be closer to the root מרר "to be bitter" than to מרה "to be contentious, fractious," it occurs nine times for מרה Hi, and eight times for the Qal. Obviously translators did not distinguish carefully between the two roots.[42] The modifier is *τὰ πρὸς τὸν θεόν* "the things that pertain to God," for which comp *τὰ πρὸς κύριον* at 1:36. In MT this is a prepositional phrase עם יהוה,[43] but LXX substitutes *τὸν θεόν* for יהוה. Why the translator should have substituted *τὸν θεόν* for the divine name is puzzling, particularly in view of 9:7,24. It does "place Israel's mutinous nature even more strictly in perspective—not just as rebellious against their own God, but against deity; it was humanity pitted against

41. See SS 179.
42. Aq was more careful, and translates the participle by *προσερίζοντες*.
43. Aq also uses a preposition *μετά* instead of *τὰ πρός*.

God."[44] It should be noted that 848 has יהוה as well as *τον θεον*, but this is probably due to the common collocation *κυριον τον θεον* in the book.[45]

The verse ends in MT with ואף כי אחרי מותי "how much the more after my death." LXX weakens this by its *πῶς οὐχὶ καὶ ἔσχατον τοῦ θανάτου μου* "how then not also after my death." The use of *ἔσχατον* is most peculiar, since it seems to be used as a preposition governing the genitive in the sense of "beyond, after," but it is only recognized as a noun, i.e. "the beyond time of my death," i.e. after my death, and so rendering אחרי; comp also v.29.

31:28 The imperative is still directed to the Levites; they are to assemble "your tribal chiefs and your elders and your judges and your *γραμματοεισαγωγεῖς*." This amplifies MT, which completely lacks an equivalent for *καὶ τοὺς κριτὰς ὑμῶν*, and has for the first two "all the elders of your tribes." LXX not only omits כל, but has also made two clauses out of "tribal elders, viz. "tribal chiefs and elders." The Greek term is clearly for שטרים, for which see comment at 1:15, (see also 16:18 29:10). It is clear that the translator more or less susbstituted 29:10: *οἱ ἀρχίφυλοι ὑμῶν καὶ ἡ γερουσία ὑμῶν καὶ οἱ κριταὶ ὑμῶν καὶ οἱ γραμματοεισαγωγεῖς ὑμῶν*, though substituting the synonym *τοὺς πρεσβυτέρους* for *ἡ γερουσία*, and disregarding MT; cf comments ad loc. Oddly enough, there is no evidence that hex tried to correct the text. Of course, the general effect is clear; the leaders are to be assembled to hear Moses.

The second part of the verse gives the reason for the assemblage; it is "in order that I may speak in their *ὦτα*, (for which see comment at v.11), and call as witnesses heaven and earth *αὐτοῖς*." The dative pronoun represents בם in the sense of "against," for which see comment at 4:26. The translator correctly interprets the long forms of the verbs by using *ἵνα* plus subjunctive verbs, showing purpose. What Moses would speak are "*πάντες* these words." MT lacks an equivalent for "all," and hex has placed it under the obelus.[46]

31:29 As in v.27b Moses gives a reason for his warnings by means of a *γάρ* clause, viz. the people will wilfully abandon the instructions given. This will happen *ἔσχατον τῆς τελευτῆς μου*, for which see comment at v.27.[47] MT des-

---

44. Appositives 264; see the discussion at 263—264.
45. See THGD 71.
46. But Kenn 5,9*,129,136,181,260 do have כל.
47. Aq renders literally: *μετὰ θάνατόν μου*.

cribes what this willful abandonment is as: השחת תשחתון וסרתם from the way which I commanded you. The Hebrew stresses ruination, destruction (and a turning away), but LXX emphasizes rather a lawless behaviour: *ἀνομίᾳ ἀνομήσετε* (*καὶ ἐκκλινεῖτε*).[48] In both MT and LXX a cognate expression places stress on the verbal idea: "act completely corruptly."

Of course a judgment will follow: "*τὰ κακά* will overtake you *ἔσχατον τῶν ἡμερῶν*." For *τὰ κακά* "calamities" as a rendering for הרעה see comment at 29:21. The *ἔσχατον* structure is an adverbial accusative "at the end of days," a translation of באחרית הימים, a term designating that indefinite future time when God will straighten everything out, when justice will prevail, and rewards and punishments will be meted out. A popular variant on *ἔσχατον* is *επ εσχατου/-των*, i.e. either singular or plural, probably under the influence of the oft-recurring *επ* phrase in the book (4:30 8:16 13:9 17:7 32:20).

A *ὅτι* clause gives the reason for all this in typical Deut terms: "because you will do evil before the Lord, so as to anger him by the works of your hands." The term *τὸ πονηρόν* denotes evil in general, for which see 4:25.

A popular variant text has added *του θεου υμων* after *κυρίου*, but there is no support for the gloss in MT, nor in the oldest texts (including 848), and it is simply ex par.[49] The final prepositional phrase is a clear example of *ἐν* being used in an instrumental sense. You have angered the Lord "by the words of your hands." MT has "works" in the singular מעשה, but it must be taken as a collective; only "works" fits the intent here.

31:30 This constitutes a superscription for the Song of Moses in ch.32. For *εἰς τὰ ὦτα* see comment at v.11. The term *ἐκκλησίας Ἰσραήλ* occurs here for the first time in OT. The term *ἐκκλησία* was to become the most common rendering for קהל (75 times over against 38 for *συναγωγή*).[50] *συναγωγή* was the more usual term for קהל in the Pentateuch (Gen, 3 cases; Exod, 1; Lev, 4; Num, 11, but in Deut, only at 5:22).[51] For *ἕως εἰς τέλος* see comment at v.24. Hex has also added *αυτων* after *τέλος* to represent the suffix of תמם.

48. Aq remains closer to MT with *διαφθορᾷ διαφθερεῖτε καὶ ἀποστήσεσθε*.
49. See THGD 75.
50. According to the count of Dos Santos.
51. According to HR.

Chapter 32

32:1 Vv.1—3 constitute a call to attention, an exordium. The first line calls upon heaven to pay attention *καὶ λαλήσω*.[1] The λαλήσω represents the long form in Hebrew: אדברה; in other words, λαλήσω is intended as a hortatory subjunctive: "and let me speak." The opening imperative, *πρόσεχε*, is an idiomatic translation of האזינו "give ear."[2]

The subject of the second line is *ἡ γῆ*, an exact translation of הארץ. Only B 848 (and Chr) support the articulated noun, all other witnesses omitting the *ἡ* under the influence of the unarticulated *οὐρανέ* of line 1.[3] The phrase modifying the verb is *ῥήματα ἐκ στόματός μου*, which is LXX's translation of the bound phrase אמרי פי.[4]

32:2 Line one has *τὸ ἀπόφθεγμά μου* as subject. The term usually means a short, pithy, proverbial saying, and occurs elsewhere in OT only at Ezek 13:19, where *μάταια ἀποφθέγματα* renders כזב, thus "false utterances." Here it translates לקחי "my instruction," i.e. what I took in, what I learned. Since it is parallel to *τὰ ῥήματά μου* one might best translate it here by the neutral "my utterances." The verb in MT is יערף "may it drip," which LXX renders by a more abstract notion, *προσδοκάσθω* "be expected, awaited."[5]

Line two reads "and let my words come down like dew." Lines three and four present two more similes modifying "come down": "like *ὄμβρος* (a shower) on the wild grass, like *νιφετός* (snow, rain)[6] on the sown grass." *ὄμβρος* is LXX's rendering of שעירים, a hapax legomenon, which is contextually generally understood as some kind of moisture which falls on the earth.[7] *ἄγρωστον* refers to herbage which grows in the wild, and *χόρτον* contrasts with it, as grass or greenery which has been cultivated.

---

1. Sym translates *ἄκουε οὐρανὲ ἐν τῷ λαλεῖν με* (retroverted from Syh[b]).
2. Theod and Aq presumably read *ἐνωτίζου* (retroverted from Syh[b]).
3. See THGD 84.
4. See SS 69,
5. Aq translated the verb by *γνοφωθῇ* (retroverted from Syh[b]), for which see Ps 64:13, where Aq translates רעפו by *γνοφωθήσεται*.
6. Aq read *ψεκάδες* "raindrops," hence "showers."
7. Aq translates the word by *τριχιῶντα* "a hairy creature" referring to a demon; apparently he thought of שעיר "satyr, demon."

32:3 MT reads: (for the name of Yahweh) אקרא "I would call," but LXX has understood this as a preterite: *ἐκάλεσα*. In the Greek the fact that "the name of the Lord I have invoked" is taken as the basis for the order: "ascribe (*δότε*) majesty to our God." The term *μεγαλωσύνην* "greatness, majesty" occurs only here in the Pentateuch and renders גדל. To ascribe majesty to God means to say "God is great"; compare the Arabic *Allahu-l-akbar* as intoned from the minarets in Islam.

32:4 The term צור applying to God occurs not only in this verse, but also at vv.15,18,30,31 and 37. The word means "rock," but it is never translated thus in LXX, which substitutes *θεός* throughout, except for v.37 which see. Presumably the term was used as a poetic name for God to designate the deity as the one who was solid, firm, unmoveable, but the translator consistently avoided a direct translation, thereby precluding any possible misunderstanding of the metaphor.[8] *θεός* represents a nominative pendens: "As for God his works are genuine." The adjective *ἀληθίνα* is LXX's rendering for תמים "perfect, whole," an equation occurring only here in OT. The adjective more commonly renders אמונה, and תמים is usually rendered by *ἄμωμος*, which admittedly would hardly seem appropriate as applied to God's works. The Hebrew word rendered by *τὰ ἔργα* is in the singular, but its collective nature represents a good interpretation.

In line two משפט is literally rendered by *κρίσις*, and the homophonous plural *κρισεις* of the A B F majority text is secondary. The plural spelling was facilitated by the plural subject *ὁδοί*, but the more difficult singular, supported by 848, is original.[9] What is meant is "and all his ways constitute judgment." In MT this line is a כי clause, but LXX renders this by *καί*, which is much simpler, an interpretation also followed by NRSV. Another possibility is to take the כי as an asseverative particle, as NJPS does: "Yea, all his ways are just."

The last line in MT reads צדיק וישר הוא "righteous and upright is He." The Greek identifies הוא as *κύριος*, though most mss articulate it. This is certainly not automatically to be rejected, since *κύριος* does not here represent

8. Aq has *ὁ στερέος*, while Theod has *ὁ πλάστης* (retroverted from Syh^{b}).
9. See THGD 84—85.

the tetragrammaton; nonetheless all but M of the old uncial texts support the unarticulated noun, and it is probably to be taken as original. Unique is the rendering of ישר by *ὅσιος*. The Hebrew adjective is almost always translated by *εὐθύς* (or *εὐθής*), and *ὅσιος* is the usual rendering for חסד. But to say that God is *εὐθύς* might have been thought inappropriate; he may command men to be *εὐθύς*, but he himself is pure, sinless, holy, *ὅσιος*.

In the tradition of line three most witnesses have added *εν αυτω* as an explanatory gloss. To say "a faithful God and there is no injustice" seems incomplete. That it must mean "there is no injustice with God" is clear, and the gloss makes the implicit explicit.

32:5 The Hebrew is uncertain in the first line, and the translator did his best to make some sense. The Greek line reads *ἡμάρτοσαν οὐκ αὐτῷ τέκνα μωμητά*. I would interpret *οὐκ αὐτῷ* as modifying *τέκνα*, which in turn must be the subject of the verb. If the line was intended as a single syntagm I would translate it as "disgraceful children who are not his have sinned."[10] The verb is not the usual rendering for the Hebrew שחת.[11]

The last line is quite straightforward: "a generation crooked and perverse," a line which provoked similar sentiments in the NT; see Matt 17:17 Lk 9:41 and Phil 2:14.

32:6 Line one in MT reads: Will you repay Yahweh thus? LXX rendered it by the verb *ἀνταποδίδοτε* "repay, requite," then added an accusative modifier *ταῦτα*, and interpreted זאת adverbially as *οὕτως*, thus "are you paying these things back to the Lord thus, (you foolish and unwise people)"? Actually by having both *ταῦτα* and *οὕτως* as modifiers it is not fully clear how the translator understood זאת. One could also understand זאת as represented by *ταῦτα* and the *οὕτως* as an addition ad sensum.

The second line is also a question in MT, and LXX can also be understood in that way. In MT the two hemistichs are both introduced by הוא,

10. Dogniez-Harl have broken it up into three syntagms which is admittedly not impossible: "ils ont commis des fautes, ils ne sont plus ses enfants, ils sont blâmables."

11. Interesting are the later attempts to render the line. Sym has *διέφθειραν πρὸς αὐτὸν οὐχ υἱοὶ αὐτοῦ τὸ σύνολον*, possibly reading מאומה for מומם. Aq translates the verb in the same way but renders לו by *αὐτῷ*; see the discussion in Salvesen 162—163.

probably to indicate that both are governed by הלוא, i.e. each is a לא type question. LXX did not understand it in this way, but removed the הוא from the second half, and substituted *καί*, thereby making it coordinate with the first hemistich. On the other hand, in good conscience the translator did not neglect the second הוא, but added it to the first one by his (*οὐκ*) *αὐτὸς οὗτος*, which created an odd line: "did not he, this your father, acquire you," and then continued with "and make you and create you," as part of a single question.[12] The rendering of ויכננך by *καὶ ἔκτισέν σε* is an interesting reinterpretation. The Hebrew verb means "to establish, make firm," but LXX was influenced by the coordinate *ἐποίησεν*, and understood it as "he created you." This may have been intended by the translator as a play on words, since in the first hemistich he used *ἐκτήσατό σε*, and here *ἔκτισέν σε*.[13]

32:7 MT has the first and last imperatives, זכר and שאל, in the singular, and the second one, בינו, in the plural. LXX has levelled the first two as plural, as did Sam, but then put the third one perforce (in the light of a singular verb and three singular suffixes) in the singular. By *ἡμέρας αἰῶνος*[14] and *ἔτη γενεᾶς γενεῶν* are meant the distant past, when the Lord had rescued his people (acquired, made and created them (v.6) from the house of bondage, from Egypt.

32:8 *ὅτε* plus finite verb is used to render ב plus bound infinitive.[15] Unique in OT is the equation *διεμέριζεν* and הנחל. In fact, this verb usually renders the root חלק. Furthermore, as Dogniez-Harl astutely point out,[16] the usual rendering of the Hi of נחל, *κατακληρονομέω*, is reserved for the land promised to Israel.[17] The apportioning was a process, and the translator showed this by his use of the imperfect.

The two parts of the first stich are in perfect parallelism: ב, plus bound infinitive, plus subject (עליון/pronominal suffix), plus modifier. LXX changed

---

12. Aq translated the last verb יכנן by *ἑτοίμασεν*.
13. The fanciful rewriting of the text by Walters (220—225) should be rejected; it is pure fancy and an example of the kind of textual hocus-pocus popular a century ago, but now hopefully abandoned by responsible textual scholars.
14. See SS 64.
15. See SS Inf 86.
16. P.325.
17. Aq used *ἐκληροδότει*.

the construction by using ὡς instead of ὅτε for the second line, but the intent was the same. The parallel verb is διέσπειρεν "he was scattering," and as parallel to ἔθνη LXX has υἱοὺς Ἀδάμ, both referring to mankind in general. The translator may well have had the tower of Babel story of Gen 11:1—9 (see especially v.8) in mind, i.e. the scattering of peoples by the Lord.

The second stich adds a new feature in its second part. He (i.e. ὁ ὕψσιτος) set the boundaries of the nations, "according to the number of the sons of God." What is meant is that the Most High divided up the nations in such a way that each one had a divine protector. Presumably these "sons of God" were the same as the συναγωγῇ θεῶν in whose midst God makes judgment, Ps 81:1. It is not surprising that the tradition almost unanimously changed υἱῶν to αγγελων, but 848 does read υἱῶν, and the reading is assured.[18] The change to "angels" was clearly a later attempt to avoid any notion of lesser deities in favor of God's messengers. Admittedly the notion of guardian angels, even of peoples, did become widespread. MT, however, has בני ישראל, though a Qumran text[19] does witness to "sons of God."[20] MT then has a different notion. The Most High has fixed the boundaries of peoples in accordance with the number of Israelites. It is unlikely, however, that this was the parent text of the translator; in fact, it would be much easier to understand an original בני אל being changed to בני ישראל for theological reasons.

32:9 MT presents this verse as a כי clause, but this can hardly be a causal כי, if the ישראל of v.8 is not original text. So if the כי is original text, it was probably an asseverative כי, and the verse should be rendered: "Indeed Yahweh's portion is his people; Jacob is the lot of his inheritance." In Sam יעקב is in apposition to עמו, and ישראל is parallel to Jacob, occurring at the end of the verse, i.e. "the lot of his inheritance is Israel." LXX follows Sam in having Ἰσραήλ at the end.

But LXX also does not recognize an initial כי, but instead introduces the verse by καὶ ἐγενήθη. I suspect that with a parent text reading "sons of God" rather than "Israelites" in v.8, the כי made little sense to the translator, and a

18. See THGD 85.
19. See P.W.Skehan, A Fragment of the "Song of Moses" (Deut 32) from Qumran, BASOR 136 (1954), 12—15.
20. See the discussion in Tov 290.

simple "and became" was a neutral replacement, which made better sense. So what LXX came up with was "And his people Jacob became the Lord's portion, Israel, the lot of his inheritance." The term *σχοίνισμα* from *σχοινίς* "rope, cord" represents well the חבל of MT, i.e. the measuring cord used to determine an inheritance.

32:10 MT begins with ימצאהו "he found him (in a desert land)," but LXX avoids the notion that God found Israel, as though she had been lost; rather by taking direction from verbs in the second stich, *ἐκύκλωσεν*, *ἐπαίδευσεν*, *διεφύλαξεν*, which all speak of divine solicitude for his people and of active care, the translator found a new word, *αὐτάρκησεν*, a denominative creation from the adjective *αὐταρκής* "sufficient," thus "he made self-sufficient." In a desert land God enabled his people to survive.[21] Note that the translator correctly renders the old preterite prefix inflection of Hebrew by aorist verbs.

The second line in MT is parallel to בארץ מדבר. It reads ובתהו ילל ישמן "and in a waste, a howling wilderness." The translator seemed, quite understandably, at a loss to make sense out of this. Instead of בתהו LXX has *καὶ ἐν δίψει*, which has nothing to do with תהו, but does it possibly reflect the translator looking at ימצאהו, which he had after all discarded, and seeing a צמא in it? But then came ילל "howling," which also made no sense, and he simply contextualized. A vigorous thirst could be called *καύματος*, "a burning thirst"; this is no longer a translation, but rather product of someone trying to make some kind of sense. The last word, ישמן, "a wasteland, wilderness" is colorfully paraphrased by *ἐν ἀνύδρῳ* "in a waterless (place?), sensibly locating the area producing the burning thirst.[22]

The last two lines make sense as a particularization on God's part of the opening *αὐτάρκησεν αὐτόν*: he encircled him (i.e. gave him protection), and taught him, and guarded him as *κόρην ὀφθαλμοῦ*. LXX connects the verbs by *καί* throughout, whereas MT has its verbs asyndetic. Since the verbs end with הו– suffixes, dittography/haplography may well have created the differences. LXX does not translate the suffix of עינו, which is quite unnecessary in Greek;

---

21. Theod and Aq translated the verb by *εὗρεν*, but Sym has *ἠπόρησεν* "was at a loss"; unfortunately the context is not extant, which makes the Sym reading impossible to interpret; see Salvesen 164.
22. Aq renders literally by *ἐν κενώματι ὀλολυγμοῦ ἠφανισμένης*, whereas Sym has *καὶ ἐν ἀτάκτῳ ἀοικήτῳ ἠφανισμένῃ*. See the fuller discussion in Salvesen 164—165.

God would hardly guard Israel as the apple of someone else's eye. Hex, however, added *αυτου* under the asterisk to show the suffix.[23]

32:11 MT has the prefix inflection throughout the verse: יעיר, יפרש, יקח, and ישא; LXX's translation begins with an aorist optative in line one: "as an eagle would watch over its nest," and then continues with an aorist indicative for the rest, except for a subordinating participle, *διείς*, in line three. After line one the verse narrates in past tense, taking the prefixal Hebrew inflection rightly as an old preterite, which has survived particularly in poetry. So the comparison clause is line one, and the remaining lines realize the comparison as applying to what God has done. I would translate the verse: "As an eagle would watch over its nest, so (*καί*) has he (i.e. the Lord) yearned over his young; opening up his wings he received them and bore them on his shoulders." In other words, LXX takes only line one as the "as" clause, and takes the rest of the verse as the "so" part. MT, on the other hand, is ambiguous. It presents every clause asyndetically, and it is unclear how far the "as" part extends, though from the content it must extend at least through line two. NJPS and ZürB extend it through line two, thereby at least avoiding the notion of God's גזלים. But RSV, with equal reason, makes all of v.11 governed by "as," and then takes v.12 as the "so" realization.

LXX also presents a somewhat different picture from that of MT. Instead of an eagle יעיר "arouses, awakes," LXX has *σκεπάσαι*. To the translator it was God's constant watch over his people that was intended, and the change is obviously an attemept to make the figure fit the notion of divine providence.[24]

The second line is quite different as well. MT has על גווליו ירחף "he broods over his nestlings," but this is overly graphic when applied to deity (see above re NJPS and ZürB), and the translator introduced a new verbal notion with *ἐπεπόθησαν* "desired, yearned for."

Lines three and four are much closer to the Hebrew. The participial realization of יפרש "spread out" as *διείς* from *διΐημι* is good Greek and, though a unique equation in OT, does make good sense with *πτέρυγας*.[25] The

23. As one might expect The Three all added *αὐτοῦ*.
24. Aq translated by *ἐξεγείρων* (retroverted from Syh[b]).
25. Aq has *ἐκπετάσας* (adapting to the participial construction of LXX?); Sym has *ἥπλωσεν* (retroverted from Syh[b]).

Hebrew does have a problematic singular pronominal suffix on יקחהו, as well as with ישאהו, which sensibly should refer to גוזליו, rather than to קנו. LXX solves this by its *αὐτούς* in both cases, thus with *νεοσσοῖς* as referent, not *νοσσιάν*. For the Hebrew it could be argued that קנו involves the contents of the nest, and that "nest" is used metonymically for the nestlings.

32:12 MT has יהוה בדד ינחנו, i.e. has a singular suffix; the singular is continued in the next hemistich as well in עמו. These must have the עמו of v.9 as antecedent. LXX realizes these sensibly by plurals: *αὐτούς*, *μετ' αὐτῶν*. The verb ינחנו is understood as a preterite, hence *ἦγεν*. The insistence of this verse is on the fact that *κύριος μόνος*, not any *θεὸς ἀλλότριος*, led them.[26]

32:13 Line one reads "He made them go up on the *ἰσχὺν τῆς γῆς*"; what is probably meant is the fertility of the land as at Gen 4:12. This is LXX's rendering of במותי ארץ "high places of the land,"[27] taking the phrase as meaning the high spots, i.e. the best parts of the land.[28] This is obviously what is meant at Isa 58:14 *ἀναβιβάσει σε ἐπὶ τὰ ἀγαθὰ τῆς γῆς*.[29]

For the second line LXX follows Sam's יאכלהו "and he made him eat," rather than the ויאכל of MT, which is highly peculiar with its change of subject to the people, but then reverting thereafter to a divine subject. LXX has "he nourished *αὐτούς* (for which see comment at v.12) with the produce of the fields."

Instead of a transitive ינקהו "he made him suck," LXX interprets by an intransitive *ἐθήλασαν* "they sucked." This is almost certainly a textual matter. The translator would hardly have taken God as actor out of the picture on his own, and his text was probably read without a *he*, i.e. as ינקו. Only the last phrase needs comment. MT has מחלמיש צור "from a flint rock." LXX has "from solid (*στερεοῦ*) rock."[30] The figure of "oil from solid rock" is, I believe, unique; oil, like honey, was fine food, and the Israelites were not

---

26. Aq renders בדד by *ἐξαιρέτως* "only, solely."
27. Aq translates literally by *ὑψώματα*. On Aq's rendering of במות and במה see Daniel 51—52.
28. See Dogniez-Harl for this line.
29. See Daniel 36.
30. Aq read *ἐκ ἀκροτέρου στερεοῦ* (retroverted from Syh[b]).

only fed the products of the field, they were by divine favor also given oil and honey from the most unlikely source.

32:14 The syntax of the verse is uncertain in MT; a list of agricultural products is given, but only for the last structure is there a verb, which can only apply to the last line. The translator was aware of the problem, and tied the first four lines to v.13 as modifiers of a verb; the nearer one is *ἐθήλασαν*, but sensibly these should be taken as additions to the products of the fields; accusative modifiers are *βούτυρον* and *γάλα* "butter (of cattle) and milk (of sheep)." In other words, the translator took lines three and four of v.13 as interruptive; thus butter and milk also constitute modifiers of *ἐψώμισεν*. Two *μετά* phrases add to the list; the first is *μετὰ στέατος ἀρνῶν καὶ κριῶν υἱῶν ταύρων καὶ τράγων* "with the fat of lambs and of rams, of the offspring of bulls and of goats," and the second one, *μετὰ στέατος νεφρῶν πυροῦ*. For *υἱῶν ταύρων καὶ τράγων* MT has בני בשן ועתודים "sons of Bashan and goats." The translator interpreted Bashan in the light of אבירי בשן of Ps 22:13 (translated as *ταῦροι πίονες*) or of the פרות הבשן of Am 4:1; he realized that animals were intended, and hence substituted *ταύρων*.[31] The second *μετά* phrase translates MT's עם חלב כליות חטה literally; fat of kidneys or kidney fat (of wheat) is a metaphor for the best or finest, so "of the very best wheat."

The last line reads "and (of) the blood of grapes they drank wine." But MT has תשתה, a second person singular verb,[32] and "wine" represents חמר, an infinitival noun from a verb meaning "to ferment, foam up," thus "and you drank fermented grape juice."[33]

32:15 MT has a difficult and at times quite uncertain text. The first strophe seems to mean: "And Jeshurun became fat and kicked. You became fat, gross, coarse." The last word is completely unknown and the translation is contextual. Jeshurun is a poetic word for Israel.

---

31. This could hardly satisfy Aq who has *υἱῶν* Βασὰν *καὶ καιρίμων*. Aq was obviously more interested in reflecting the Hebrew than in making sense; he reflects the root עתד "be ready," and must have read עתידים instead of עתודים. That this made little or no sense did not seem to trouble Aq.
32. Theod has *ἔπιεν*; Aq,*πίεσαι*, and Sym, *ἔπιες*.
33. For חמר Aq has *αὐστηρόν* "harsh, rough." Sym read *ἀμιγές* (retroverted from Syh).

LXX made two lines out of the first hemistich, with ’Ιακώβ as subject of line one, and ὁ ἠγαπημένος “the beloved” freely translating ישרון on the basis of its root ישר, for the second line.[34] The first line presumably revolves about וישמן, though “and Jacob ate and was filled,” is admittedly barely a paraphrase, and just how it was intended to interpret וישמן baffles me.[35] The second line revolves about ויבעט “and he kicked.” The line reads “and the beloved kicked,” and apparently reflects ישרון ויבעט.

Line three has three verbs in third person rather than the second person of MT: “he (presumably the beloved) became fat, heavy, broadened,” all terms showing that Israel prospered. Whether the verb כשית meant “be widened, broadened” as LXX has it, or not is not known, but is probably as good a guess as any.[36]

For v.15b MT again reverts to third person. Only the last line needs comment. The Hebrew has ישעתו וינבל צור “and he treated with contempt the Rock of his salvation.” The Greek has *καὶ ἀπέστη ἀπὸ θεοῦ σωτῆρος αὐτοῦ* “And he abandoned God his saviour.” Only here is God spoken of as *σωτήρ* in the Pentateuch.[37] For the term צור translated by *θεοῦ* see comment at v.4.[38]

32:16 Instead of יקנאהו LXX has *παρώξυνάν με* “they excited, irritated me.”[39] MT speaks about God, but LXX makes God the speaker. The change must have been intentional, since it also applied to יכעיסהו, which became *ἐξεπίκρανάν με*; it could hardly be textual, since the suffixes are quite different: *-hu* vs *-ni*. But the first person is peculiar, since the context is third person throughout. Again in this verse the old preterite Hebrew inflection obtains, rightly understood by the translator, who used the aorist. Over against MT the Greek uses different prepositions in the two lines. *ἐπ’ ἀλλοτρίοις* is here probably causal in its intent: they irritated me by reason of strange (gods); in the next line *ἐν* is used instrumentally, i.e. by their abominations

34. Aq translates by the elative *εὐθύτατος*, and Theod and Sym by *εὐθύς*, all reflecting the root ישר.
35. The Three all render the word by *ἐλιπάνθη*.
36. Theod with little inventiveness has *ἐλιπάνθη* (retroverted from Syh[b]).
37. See Daniel 277.
38. Aq translates by *στερεόν* (retroverted from Syh[b]), and Theod, by *πλαστήν* (from Syh[m]).
39. Aq renders the verb literally by *ἐζήλωσαν*.

they embittered me.[40] In MT the preposition ב is used for both. The verb *ἐξεπίκρανάν* (*με*) is a hapax legomenon in OT, and is unexpected for יכעים "provoke to anger."[41] Incidentally cod B was influenced by the parallel compound *παρώξυνάν* (*με*) to change the compound to *παρεπικραναν*, but this is further supported by only one rather aberrent ms, 799. The rarer *ἐκ*- compound is to be preferred. It might also be noted that בתועבת is given a pronominal modifier in Greek; LXX adds an ad sensum *αὐτῶν*.

32:17 MT begins with יזבחו לשדים "they sacrificed to demons (and not God)." The term שדים occurs only here and at Ps 106:37; in both places LXX renders by *δαιμονίοις*. Classically the term is the adjective corresponding to *δαίμων*, a god or goddess, or more commonly semi-divine beings. Here the adjective is nominalized, and so equals *δαίμων*. The line might well be translated: "they sacrificed to deities, but not to God"; the *δαιμονίοις* clearly belong to the *ἀλλοτρίοις* of v.16. In fact, they are called "gods whom they did not know."

They are further described as *καινοὶ πρόσφατοι ἥκασιν* "new, recent ones (i.e. deities) appeared," ones "which their fathers did not know." Most witnesses separate the two adjectives by *και*, but B 848 both show this stylistic simplification to be secondary.[42] MT has "your fathers," but, in line with the *αὐτῶν* of v.16, LXX uses a third person pronoun. The verb in MT is שערום. The verb occurs only here, but it is almost certain that the translator understood the word correctly in view of the well-known cognate verb "šaʿara" in Arabic, meaning "to know."[43] The translator, out of respect for good Greek style, did not retranslate the suffix, it having been translated by the inflection of the relative pronoun *οὕς*.

32:18 For *θεόν* as translation of צור see comment at v.4. Uncertain is the Hebrew תשי which LXX rendered by *ἐγκατέλιπες*. Tar^{N} also understood it in this way.[44] The other two targums understood the verb as an old spelling for

40. See SS 126.
41. Aq "corrects" to *παρώργισαν*.
42. See THGD 75.
43. But Aq had a homophonous root in mind meaning "to be hairy," and rendered it by *ἐτριχίων αὐτούς*. What that should mean in this context is baffling.
44. As its שבקתון indicates. This targum uses the second plural throughout the book, and the plural has no textual significance.

תשה which is fully possible, since *tinšay* in due course became *tiššeh* in MT. This would be a good parallel to the second hemistich, which has תשכח "forget." *θεόν* is described as *τὸν γεννήσαντά σε* "the one who begot you."[45]

In line two *θεοῦ* translates אל,[46] who is described as "the one nourishing you." That is not what MT says; it has an exact parallel to the first hemistich with מחללך "the one bringing you forth."[47]

32:19 LXX renders וינאץ "and he rejected, spurned" by a doublet. The problem was occasioned by the second part of the verse מכעס בניו ובנתיו. What does the "anger, or vexation, of his sons and his daughters" mean? How does this fit in with "he rejected, spurned"? By understanding וינאץ as *καὶ ἐζήλωσεν καὶ παρωξύνθη*, i.e. the two aspects of נאץ, one of divine jealousy and one of provocation or irritation, the translator could separate the two notions by taking *ἐζήλωσεν* in an absolute sense, and using *παρωξύνθη* with line two. By understanding *υἱῶν* and *θυγατέρων* as objective genitives, the second line can be translated as "and he was stirred up by anger against his sons and daughters."[48] LXX does not repeat *αὐτοῦ* for the second noun over against MT, which of course does repeat the suffix.

32:20 The form *ἀποστρέψω* is best understood as an aorist subjunctive in view of the long form אסתירה of MT, i.e. as a hortatory subjunctive. The rendering "let me turn my face from them" is not a literal rendering of MT "let me hide ...," but it is the usual one; see comment at 31:17. The second line differs from the intent of the Masoretes, who vocalized אראה as a Qal. By its preposed *καί* it follows Sam's ואראה. LXX interpreted the verb as a Hi: "I will show, make to see," thus *δείξω*; thereby LXX avoided any notion that God had not known (see) what was to take place *ἐπ' ἐσχάτων*, an apparent attack on divine omniscience.[49] The object of *δείξω* differs from MT as well. In MT God says "I will see what their latter end will be," but LXX is slightly different. *δείξω* is modified by *τί ἔσται αὐτοῖς ἐπ' ἐσχάτων* "what will hap-

45. Theod and Aq adopted LXX, but Sym translated by *γεννήσεώς σου*.
46. Which Aq as always renders by *ἰσχυροῦ*.
47. Aq renders the participle literally by *ὠδίνοντος* "the one suffering birthpangs."
48. The translation by Dogniez-Harl is apt: "et il fut exaspéré de colère contre ses fils et ses filles."
49. See Prijs 45.

pen to them in the latter days," i.e. in the end time, or possibly in the time after Moses' death, 31:29.[50] The subject of מה has become in Greek a prepositional phrase signifying time when.[51]

The reason is given in a *ὅτι* clause. Its first line is similar to v.5b, which see. Here a different compound is used, *ἐξεστραμμένη*, rather than *διεστρ.*, but the meaning is the same: "it is a perverse generation," for MT's "a generation of perversions."

In the parallel line they are called "children (literally sons) in whom there is no *πίστις*." The noun translates אמן, which means "trust, fidelity," and *πίστις* is best understood in this same way. It is not to be confused with the later NT use of the term.

32:21 The verse is introduced by *αὐτοί*/הם to indicate the change in subject. This is also intended to contrast with the אני of the second stich. God had been speaking; now it is "they" who constitute the theme. The two stichs are in complete parallelism. "As for them, they have made me jealous with a no-god" is parallel to "as for me, I shall make them jealous with a no-people"; similarly, the second hemistichs are also parallel. By a לא אל "no-god" MT refers to the recognition of an idol as god.[52]

The parallelism in the second hemistichs (lines two and four) is not as clear as in the first ones. The verb is the same: *παρώργισαν*/*παροργιῶ*, but the prepositional phrases are not as neatly parallel as in the first ones. In MT these are both ב phrases: בהבליהם vs בגוי נבל, but in LXX they become *ἐν τοῖς εἰδώλοις αὐτῶν* and *ἐπ' ἔθνει ἀσυνέτῳ*.[53] Thc first of these is not a literal rendering. The term הבל means "a puff of breath," hence something ephemeral, unsubstantial, worthless.[54] And so they are false gods, meaningless idols. Oddly enough, the translator also used a different preposition, *ἐν*, for this phrase, over against the *ἐπ'* of the other three phrases. In line four God says I will anger them *ἐπ' ἔθνει ἀσυνέτῳ* "with a people lacking understanding;[55] a "foolish people" is indeed one without understanding.

50. So Prijs 98.
51. SS 102 calls it a free translation.
52. Theod and Aq read *ἐν οὐκ ἰσχυρῷ*.
53. For the difference in prepositions see SS 126, where the *ἐπ'* is taken as causal.
54. The Others translate the term by *ἐν ματαίοις* (retroverted from Syh^b).
55. Aq preferred *ἀπορρέοντι* for rendering נבל.

32:22 The basis for the judgment of v.21 is given in a *ὅτι* collocation; it is based on the Lord's consuming anger against idolatry. The anger is called a *πῦρ*, which *ἐκκέκαυται ἐκ τοῦ θυμοῦ μου*. The prepositional phrase translates באפי "in my nostril," a term commonly used for "wrath, anger." Note that the verb is in the perfect; the kindled fire remains burning.

The next three verbs are vocalized by MT as narrative past tenses: "burned ... consumed ... enflamed," but the translator took these all as future, as a coming judgment, a rendering which the consonantal text allows; thus "it shall burn to Hades below, consume the ground and its produce, enflame the foundations of mountains." For "Hades below" MT has שאול תחתית "Sheol at its lowest level."[56]

In the tradition the second line is introduced by a conjunction in MT, but only a few scattered witnesses read *και* before *καυθήσεται*. In fact, lines three and four are also joined by conjunctions in MT, but are asyndetic in LXX. Only the uncials and a few scattered cursives read *κάτω*; most have the reading of Sym, *κατωτατου*, though only *κάτω* can be original. *κατά* would be difficult to explain as an early error from an original *κατωτατου*.

32:23 The Masoretes have vocalized אספה to mean "I will sweep away," which is not overly meaningful in the context. The consonants could also be vocalized to mean "I will gather, collect," which is how the translator understood it with his *συνάξω*, hence "I will gather calamities on them." Both Pesh and Vulg confirm LXX's rendering.

The second line renders MT well: (And) my arrows I will expend against them, though adding a conjunction at the beginning. In both lines the translator used *εἰς αὐτούς*, though MT has עלימו and בם resp.

32:24 The opening word, *τηκόμενοι*, "melted, thawed," is used metaphorically in the sense of "wasted away"; MT has מזי possibly "sucked out"; in any event, LXX presupposes a devoiced sibilant, i.e. as מסה.[57] In LXX the participle is modified by *λιμῷ καὶ βρώσει ὀρνέων* "by famine and by the

56. Which The Three insisted on as well: Aq, by *κατωτάτω*; Sym, *κατωτάτου*, and Theod, *ὑποκατωτάτου*.

57. Aq rendered by *καθαιρεθέντες λιμῷ* (retroverted from Syh[m]).

eating of birds." MT has רעב ולחמי רשף (מזי). Apparently the translator intended *βρώσει* to equal ולחמי (or ולחם). And *ὀρνέων* stands for רשף which apparently does mean "birds"; at least, the word is also rendered by *πετεινός* in Sir 43:14,17b. The word was also known to Aquila in this sense.[58]

Line two is difficult, since it consists of two adjectives in the nominative singular. The first one, *ὀπισθότονος*, refers to tetanic convulsions, here probably nominalized to equal *ὀπισθοτονία*, and the second, *ἀνίατος*, means "incurable." But their position in the verse must make them coordinate to *τηκόμενοι*. It seems to stand as an ejaculation by itself "and convulsions (are) incurable," i.e. taking the nominalized adjective as a collective.[59] MT is no help; it has וקטב מרירי probably "and a bitter pestilence," but the meaning is quite uncertain.[60]

Lines three and four read "the teeth of wild animals I will send against them, even those (i.e. of animals) which crawl angrily on the ground." The word *θηρίων* represents בהמות, probably correctly. The word usually refers to domesticated cattle, but in this context the translation is sensible. The Hebrew חמת can mean "poison" or "wrath." In the present context, i.e. characterizing wild animals, it is usually understood to mean poison, but the translator rendered it by *θυμοῦ*. The final phrase is *ἐπὶ γῆς* "on the ground," modifying *συρόντων* "those crawling." MT has זחלי עפר "crawling things of the dust," i.e. creepers in dust.[61]

32:25 The first two lines contrast *ἔξωθεν* "outside" with *ἐκ τῶν ταμιείων* "out of the inner chambers," i.e. inside. The two lines are connected by *καί*, following Sam rather than MT. In line one LXX has added a pronominal modifier *αὐτούς* for good sense, though this is absent from MT, and hex has accordingly put the pronoun under the obelus. Line two has no verb, but the meaning is clear. Just as the sword shall bereave them outside, so fear shall destroy from within.

---

58. Aq renders ולחמי רשף by *καὶ βεβρωμένοι πτηνῷ* (retroverted from Syh).
59. Dogniez-Harl obviously share the problem, and render the line by "pris de convulsions incurables."
60. Aq makes it *καὶ δηγμοῖς παραπικρασμοῦ* "and with the stings of bitterness" (retroverted from Syh).
61. Instead of *ἐπὶ γῆς* Theod and Aq have *χοῦν*.

Lines three and four also have no predicate. All that is said is "a youngster along with a virgin, a suckling (babe) with one who has become old," but the meaning is equally clear: all shall perish indiscriminately.[62]

32:26 The Hebrew אפאיהם is a hapax legomenon, and its meaning is unknown. LXX has in its place *διασπερῶ αὐτούς* which may reflect LXX's attempt at reading a corrected text, possibly reflecting a root such as פוץ.[63] LXX did make sense, probably based on the context of line two.

Line two reads "Pray let me stop (i.e. put an end to) their memory from mankind."[64] The presence of *δή* is to ensure the reading of *παύσω* as a hortatory subjunctive, reflecting the long form אשביתה "let me put to rest." The translation of מאנוש recognizes אנוש as a collective, which it must be in the context.

In the tradition a popular A F M text reads *καταπαυσω* for *παύσω*, but both B and 848 support the simplex form. On the other hand, B 848+ are secondary in their change of *δή* to *δε*. A *δέ* is quite inappropriate here, and is simply a copyist error.

32:27 Neither the LXX nor MT is particularly transparent. MT begins with a לולי clause, which seems to say "unless I should fear the provocation of the enemy." In its place LXX has a line which is also difficult: *εἰ μὴ δι' ὀργὴν ἐχθρῶν ἵνα μὴ μακροχρονίσωσιν*. I have no idea how LXX got to the *ἵνα* clause while MT simply has אגור "I should fear." I would understand *ἐχθρῶν* as an objective genitive, i.e. what is referred to is divine anger against enemies. So I would take the line to mean "Were it not because of (my) anger at the enemies."[65] I would then take the two *ἵνα μή* clauses and the *μή* clause as interpreting the purpose of that divine anger: "in order that they might not live long, and in order that the adversaries might not increase, lest they should

62. Instead of *καθεστηκότος πρεσβύτου* Aq has *ἀνδρὸς πολιάς*; Theod also has *πολιάς*, but Sym reads *πολιοῦ* for *πρευβύτου*.
63. Aq also had trouble with it as his *καὶ ποῦ εἰσιν* (retroverted from Syh^m^) shows. This reflects a redivision of MT as אף איהם.
64. For *μνημόσυνον* in LXX see Daniel 229—231.
65. Aq translated *εἰ μὴ ἐν παροργισμῷ ὑποστελλομένου*; Sym had *εἰ μὴ δι' ὀργὴν ἐχθροῦ πάντοτε*, and Theod, *εἰ μὴ δἰ' ὀργὴν ἐχθροῦ κωλύσω* (all retroverted from Syh^b^).

say ...." The second ἵνα μή clause has as counterpart in MT: פן ינכר צרימו "lest their adversaries should misconstrue (or make strange statements)." Over against LXX, this is asyndetic.[66]

Only the final פן/μή statement is fully clear: "lest they should say Our hand is high; and it was not the Lord who did all these things."[67] This then explicates the συνεπιθῶνται of the previous line. MT has "our hands," but numerous mss read ידנו, as LXX apparently did.

In the tradition hex has added ημων under the asterisk afer ὑπεναντίοι, but this equals Sam; MT has a third personal pronominal suffix. Most mss, including B, wrongly articulate ὑψηλή. Since this is a predicate adjective, it cannot be correct; it is an auditory dittograph, /hi hipsili/.[68]

32:28 With v.28 God is no longer the speaker; in fact, only with v.34 does he return as such. Here MT reads "For they are a people lacking counsel, and there is no understanding in them." In both parts "people" is referred to in the plural: המה and בהם. LXX disregards המה entirely, translating "For it is (ἐστιν) a nation lacking counsel." And for תבונה LXX has ἐπιστήμη "knowledge."[69] The reference is here to the ἐχθρῶν of v.27; they are the people, the nation, referred to in αὐτοῖς.

32:29 By reading the opening לו particle as לא, LXX has changed the sense of MT considerably.[70] MT in v.29 has a conditional sentence: "Had they been wise, they would have considered this," followed by "they would have understood their latter end." But LXX has οὐκ ἐφρόνησαν συνίεναι ταῦτα "they were not understanding (enough) to comprehend these things." The second line then reads "let them be concerned for the coming time."[71]

32:30 The syntactic pattern of the verse is How ... unless, with the "how" clause in the conditional future, (i.e. "how can one chase a thousand, and two

66. Aq has μήποτε ἀποξενώσωσιν θλίβοντας αὐτούς (retroverted from Syh[b]).
67. For a full analysis of the difficulties of this verse see Dogniez-Harl ad loc.
68. See THGD 103—104.
69. Aq translated more accurately by φρόνησις.
70. As obtains in Kenn 325 633*.
71. Aq translated the verse by ὄφελον ἐσοφίσθησαν ἐπίσταθαι αὐτήν. συνετισθήτωσαν εἰς ἐσχάτην αὐτῶν.

remove myriads,") and the "unless" clause in the aorist. Whether this refers to Israel or to Israel's foes is not certain in view of the ὅτι clause of v.31, which seems to suggest that the reference is still to the enemy.[72] On the other hand, clearly with vv.34—42 the Lord is executing vengeance on Israel's enemies, and one can understand vv.32—33 more easily as referring to enemies as well. On balance, I would suggest that the poet, as well as the translator, had Israel in mind. Then the "thousands ... myriads" are Israel's foes.

The verb in line two, *μετακινήσουσιν* "alter, remove" is not an exact rendering of יניסו "put to flight," though removing the enemy would, one supposes, indeed get rid of them; the verbs in MT for the "how" lines are in strict parallelism: "pursue ... put to flight."[73]

The *εἰ μή* part also consists of two lines. The subject of line three is צורם "their Rock" in MT. LXX as usual renders צור by *ὁ θεός* but neglects the suffix reading "unless God had sold them, and the Lord had delivered them up." The emphasis is on the *εἰ μή* clauses; it is Israel's God who is the central figure. The omission of the suffix of צורם makes the reference to "God" an absolute one. The antecedent of the *αὐτούς* pronouns must be the thousands/myriads referring to the *ἐχθρῶν/ὑπεναντίοι* of v.27.

In line four *παρέδωκεν* is at best but a free rendering of MT, which has הסגיר. Admittedly "caused to shut (them) up" is not a clear parallel to מכר "sold," whereas the LXX's "delivered them up" is a fine parallel.[74]

32:31 LXX's "not are their gods like our God" represents לא כצורנו צורם "Not like our Rock is their Rock." For צור as a term for God see comment at v.4. But to the translator the enemies were polytheistic, and so LXX has the subject in the plural *οἱ θεοί*.[75]

The second line is not clear in MT: "and our enemies פלילים." The term is uncertain. It also occurs at Exod 21:22 where it seems to mean "arbiters,"

---

72. Rashi apparently also put this in the mouth of the enemy: איכה ירדף אחד ממנו אלף מישראל.

73. Aq is more exact with his *φυγαδεύσουσιν*.

74. Theod and Aq render the verb literally with *συνέκλεισεν*.

75. Aq translates line one literally by *οὐχ γὰρ ὡς ὁ στερεὸς ἡμῶν στερεὸς αὐτῶν*. Sym translates interpretatively as *οὐ γὰρ ὡς ὁ φύλαξ ἡμῶν ὁ φύλαξ αὐτῶν*. Theod, however, made the subject plural: *ὅτι οὐχ ὡς φύλαξ ἡμῶν φύλακες αὐτῶν*. Salvesen 167 suggests that Sym Theod may have thought of נצר.

but LXX translates בפלילים there by *μετὰ ἀξιώματος* "with a judicial decision," which is of no help here. LXX has made the line contrastive with a *δέ*, and taken פלילים as a pejorative term by using *ἀνόητοι* "lacking understanding."[76] LXX probably did not understand the term, and made a contextual judgment. In the light of "their gods" the statement "but our enemies are without sense" is sensible, even though it is probably not what MT meant.

32:32 Vv.32—33 constitute a *γάρ* clause, a second causal clause for v.31. The metaphors in v.32 are connected with the vineyard. That their vine should be from the vine of Sodom and their branch from Gomorrah is intended to brand the enemy with the symbols of wickedness described in Gen 19. Line two does not translate MT's text, which simply reads "and from the fields (i.e. the vineyards) of Gomorrah." LXX created a parallel to "their vine" of line one, whereas MT's parallel is to "from the vine of."

Lines three and four continue the figure of grapes. For רוש "bitter venom" LXX has *χολῆς* "bile," as at 29:18. The last line is plural in MT: "(their) clusters are bitter to them," but LXX makes it singular: *βότρυς πικρίας αὐτοῖς* "(it is) a cluster of bitterness to them."

32:33 LXX created a mixed figure with its "the wrath of dragons is their wine," a play on the notion of the outpouring of wrath.[77] For the second line MT has "and the cruel poison of vipers." LXX again uses *θυμός* "wrath," this time for ראש "poison," and for אזכר "cruel" it has *ἀνίατος* "incurable." Incurable wrath is an odd figure; presumably what the translator intended was to stress the fact that the vipers' wrath was permanent, not to be assuaged,[78] and that wrath translated into a bite is indeed incurable.

32:34 MT opens with הלא הוא כמס עמדי. What הוא refers to must be either the general evil referred to in the preceding verses, or the dire fate awaiting

76. Sym has *βιαῖοι* (retroverted from Syh^{m}), whereas Theod simply transliterated the Hebrew פלילים. Obviously neither translator had a clear idea what the term meant.
77. Aq preferred *κητῶν* to *δρακόντων* as a translation of תנינם (retroverted from Syh).
78. Aq understood ראש as "head"; he translated the line *καὶ κεφαλὴ βασιλίσκων ἄσπλαγχνος* "and the head of cobras is without pity," presumably because it is the snakes' head that strikes without warning.

the enemies in the following verses. Similarly uncertain is the plural ταῦτα of LXX; here too either reference is possible. The passive participle כמס is completely unknown. Sam has כנוס "gathered, collected," which LXX's συνῆκται seems to support. LXX also has added an ἰδού which has no support in MT.[79]

Line two with its ἐσφράγισται "sealed up" in the divine treasuries would support the understanding of ταῦτα as referring to the coming judgments of vv.35ff., i.e. the lots, fates, destinies of the wicked are sealed up; this seems more plausible than a reference to the evils perpetrated by the enemies being sealed.

In the tradition most witnesses add παντα after ταῦτα, but this is an ex par gloss with no claim to being original text.

32:35 LXX follows Sam's ליום in ἐν ἡμέρᾳ. This fits in with ἐσφράγισται of v.34, i.e. "sealed up in my treasures" is inter alia my recompense in the day of vengeance. MT has לי "mine is (vengeance)," which is also sensible, though the parallel of ליום and לעת is more striking. The subject of the opening nominal clause in MT is נקם ושלם usually understood as "vengeance and recompense." LXX not only read ליום for לי; it also took ושלם as a separate clause, i.e. "and there is repayment." But that recompense is God's, hence ἀνταποδώσω; it is sealed up in "my" treasuries. This would then have understood שלם as a Piel free infinitive, which the consonantal text allows. This accords with the later tradition found in NT (Rom 12:19 Heb 10:30) of ἐμοὶ ἐκδίκησις, ἐγὼ ἀνταποδώσω,[80] and the Tar follow a similar interpretation.[81]

Line two is a graphic description of that day of vengeance as the occasion "when their foot trips up." The ὅτι construction consists of two coordinate nominal clauses, "for the day of their destruction is near, and the things readied for them (i.e. their lot) is at hand." πάρεστιν translates the participle

79. Sym translated the hemistich by μὴ οὐχὶ τοῦτο ἀπόκειται παρ' ἐμοί.
80. Sym translated similarly: ἐμοὶ ἐκδικήσεις, καὶ ἀνταποδώσω (retroverted from Syh[b]). Silvesen 168 suggests that the plural noun may well be due to corruption of the Syh text; presumably what she meant was the presence of the *seyame* signifying a plural.
81. Though Tar[N] has a circumlocution: ואנא הוא דמשלם, whereas Tar[JO] have אנא אשלם.

חש "rushes, hastens," but LXX hints at its arrival; their destiny is here; its time has arrived.[82]

32:36 The first part of the verse is a *ὅτι* clause, consisting of two verbal structures. It is quoted word for word in Ps 134:14. Here that the Lord *κρινεῖ* his people does not mean "execute judgment against," but rather "on behalf of" his people.[83] After all, line two reads "for his servants *παρακληθήσεται*," i.e. will be persuaded. This translates יתנחם "be sorry, take comfort," even at times "repent oneself."

MT of the second half is difficult. It is a כי clause, probably intended to show the state under which the first stich is invoked, thus "when he will see כי אזלת יד ואפס עצור ועזוב." Presumably this כי introduces the object clause, i.e. "(see) that." What אזלת יד means is not certain. The verb is feminine of אזל, so "power has gone"(?). LXX has in its place *παραλελυμένους αὐτούς* "(for he saw) them undone," which seems to me a free paraphrase, i.e. the disappearance of power as applied to the Israelites could be understood in this way. The last three words of MT mean "both bound and freed do not (i.e. no longer) exist." LXX has made of this a further reference to *αὐτούς* of line three, *καὶ ἐκλελοιπότες ἐν ἐπαγωγῇ καὶ παρειμένους* "and deserted in captivity, and passed by (i.e. forsaken),"[84] which is also a free rendition in which the first participle interprets אפס, and עצור becomes *ἐπαγωγῇ*; i.e. "in captivity," in the sense of being tied up, bound. Then עזוב was understood as coordinate, not to עצור, but to אפס עצור.[85] I would translate: "For he saw them undone, even deserted in captivity and forsaken."

In the tradition most witnesses transpose *παραλελυμένους αὐτούς*. Either order is possible, though the popular order is the more usual, but the oldest witnessses A B F all support the order of the critical text, which must be original.

82. Instead of *ἕτοιμα* Aq has *καιρίως*.
83. See Driver ad loc.
84. In spite of Walters 130 who says that here "*παρειμμένους* can only mean *released*." This seems to me to be a case of special pleading.
85. Sym translated the line by *εἶδεν γὰρ ὅτι ἠτόνησα χεὶρ καὶ ἐξέλιπεν οἱ συνεχόμενος καὶ ὁ ἐγκαταλελειμμένος* (retroverted from Syh^m). At least his translation shows that MT was his parent text. See the discussion of the line in Salvenen 168—169.

32:37 MT begins with ואמר, and the intended tense is uncertain. It could be contextually taken as a future as most moderns do, but LXX makes it aorist, and adds *κύριος* as subject: "and the Lord said." What he said was "Where are their gods, in whom they trusted (in them)"?[86]

The second line renders צור חסיו בה "the Rock in whom they trust." LXX has *ἐφ' οἷς ἐπεποίθεισαν ἐπ' αὐτοῖς*, omitting a translation of צור, probably because the usual rendering, for which see comments at v.4, would have been repetitious; it would have been odd to have read "where are their gods, the god in whom they trust."[87] Because of this adaptation by LXX, בה had perforce to be put into the plural as well. The prepositional phrase is of course otiose, and a better translation would have omitted this Hebraism.

32:38 The verse is dependent on v.37, since it begins with a relative clause with the same referents as the plural pronouns of v.37, i.e. the enemies. LXX, however, has changed the person of the verbs in lines one and two from third to second person. In MT the אשר is subject of the verbs "who ate ... drank," but the Greek changed this to "whose ... you ate ... you drank." Dogniez-Harl shrewdly remark that in this way the LXX disassociates the Hebrews from idolatrous nations, i.e. they only took part in the cult, they had not instituted it themselves.[88]

Lines three and four are correctly understood as representing short forms of MT, i.e. "let them arise ..., help, ... be." In MT the subject of the last verb is סתרה, a hapax legomenon in MT; the root סתר is well-known as meaning "to hide." It is a feminine singular noun, i.e. an abstract noun paralleling the concrete noun סתר "a covering, hiding place," and so its usual translation as "protection" is probably correct. LXX, however, translates it by *σκεπασταί*, a word attested only in OT.[89] The root means "to shelter, protect," hence "protectors." LXX thereby levels with the plural of line three.

86. Both Tar^{JN} attribute אלהימו to Israel: the former as דחלתהון דישראל and Neoph. as אלהי דישראל. The question is then not God's, but of the אומיה "the nations," in Neoph, and of סנאה "a hater," in Jon.
87. Aq translated צור by *στερεός*, and Theod by *φύλακες* (retroverted from Syh^m).
88. P.338 on 32:38.
89. *Ibid* at 32:38.

32:39 MT begins with ראו עתה כי אני אני הוא "See now that as for me I am He." LXX does not translate word for word; instead of עתה it repeats ἴδετε.[90] Since this is a central affirmation of faith in the reality of God, over against the query of the Lord in vv.37—38, the repetition of ἴδετε serves to place extra stress on the importance of what is to be noted, viz. ὅτι ἐγώ εἰμι. LXX also shortens אני אני הוא, probably by disregarding one אני. The shorter text does change the sense of MT, since it serves, not as identification, but as existence or reality. MT states who he is; LXX affirms that he, in contrast to "their gods," exists; he is real. Implied is the irreality of the gods of the nations.

This is what line two also affirms: "and there is no god besides me." The prepositional phrase adequately translates the עמדי "along with me" of MT. The line has God saying: I alone am God.

The next two lines characterize God's activity: "I may kill, and I may keep alive; I may strike, and I can heal."[91] In MT only the third verb מחצתי is not in the prefixal inflection, and the translator correctly understands the neutral character of the suffixal inflection, and makes it future, πατάξω.[92]

The final line translates MT adequately, differing only in that the Masoretes vocalized מידי as a singular noun; LXX takes it as a plural, ἐκ τῶν χειρῶν μου, which the consonantal text allows.

32:40 The verse does begin with ὅτι/כי, but I doubt that it is to be understood as causal; what is stated in v.40 is the avowed and sworn intention to put vv.41 and 42 into effect; in other words, the ὅτι beginning v.41 indicates an object clause. What the translator has done, however, is to add a new line, a parallel to line one. Hex recognized that καὶ ὀροῦμαι τὴν δεξιάν μου had no equivalent in MT, and placed it under the obelus. It does serve a useful purpose, however, in defining what raising one's hand to heaven means—it is not

90. The Others all read ἴδετε νῦν (retroverted from Syh[b]).
91. For the use of the future as omnitemporal see Porter 423—424; for the nature of the future in general see 403—439. For the use of ποιέω to represent the Hi see SS Inf 134—135.
92. Sym has lines three and four as θανατώσω καὶ ζωώσω παίσω καὶ ἐγὼ ἰάσομαι (retroverted from Syh[b]).

in prayer, but indicates an asseveration.[93] In the tradition τὴν δεξιάν is changed to the dative in the majority of witnesses. The accusative, supported by the oldest witnesses, A B F, is the Classical usage, whereas in later Hellenistic Greek the dative becomes more common in the oath formula.[94]

The last line continues with a common oath formula, ζῶ ἐγώ "As I live," but has the prepositional phrase εἰς τὸν αἰῶνα modifying it, which is unusual. Apparently what the formula means is "As surely as I live for ever." It correctly represents what MT says.

32:41 This, along with v.42, is what the Lord has sworn by himself to do. Line one reads: "I will whet my sword like lightning." The bound phrase ברק חרבי uses ברק as a metaphor for "flashing," i.e. my flashing sword, and the translator mistook the idiom; he understood "the lightning" literally, and made it a comparison. To whet the sword like lightning would mean to make it flash. MT also has a different syntactic pattern, in that the first stich is the protasis of a condition, and the second is the apodosis. LXX makes all four lines coordinate after ὅτι.

Line two reads "and my hand shall hold fast judgment." Presumably κρίματος will then constitute God's whetted sword.

The last two lines render MT adequately except for omitting the suffix of צרי. This is fully otiose in Greek. They are God's own ἐχθροῖς. Hex has, however, duly added μου. It might be noted that ἀνταποδώσω is used twice for two different verbs. But when it renders אשיב, it is modified, not only by the dative showing indirect object, but also by an accusative δίκην (for נקם), i.e. I will repay my enemies with a δίκην "judgment," whereas for אשלם, only an indirect object "those hating me" obtains. It should also be noted that it is not vengeance, as in MT, but δίκην that God effects to repay his enemies.

32:42 The opening μεθύσω is probably a future, rather than an aorist optative,[95] since the verb in line two is καταφάγεται. Since the second stich con-

93. J.Lust, Fst C.J.Labuschagne = Suppl VT LIII, 155—164 diasagrees, believing that the collocation "raise the hand" on God's part means to intervene, but the next two cola do not make this likely.
94. See THGD 137.
95. The question is not merely academic in view of a Qumran text which had the long form (אשכירה).

tains only מן phrases, they must somehow modify the verbs of the first stich—I suggest אשכיר and תאכל resp., i.e. line three relates to line one, and line four to line two. The sense of the first combination is then: "I will intoxicate my arrows with blood, with the blood of the slain and of captives."[96]

The parallel pair reads: "And my sword will devour flesh from the head of the rulers of the enemies."[97] The translation *ἀρχόντων ἐχθρῶν* does not equal MT, which has (ראש) פרעת אויב. The plural *ἐχθρῶν* is understandable in view of the plural noun preceding it, but פרעת presumably means "long hair, locks"; *ἀρχόντων* "rulers" may be based on another root פרע which is thought to occur at Jdg 5:2, where בפרע פרעות בישראל is rendered in the A text tradition by *ἐν τῷ ἄρξασθαι ἀρχηγοὺς ἐν Ἰσραήλ*. The translator must have been aware of some such meaning for פרעות.[98]

32:43 The LXX text represents a longer and different parent Hebrew from MT. A Qumran text containing this verse was discussed by P.W.Skehan,[99] a text which represents in part the parent text of LXX. I shall refer to this text simply as Q. The Greek text has eight lines, whereas MT has only four hemistichs. The hemistichs have some kind of counterpart in LXX in lines three, five, six and eight. Q has six hemistichs, which have counterparts in LXX for the following lines: one, two, five, six, seven and eight. Thus only line four has no extant counterpart in Hebrew.

Lines one and two read "rejoice, O heavens, with him, and let all the sons of God worship him." Over against this Q has הרנינו שמים עמו והשתחוו לו כל אלהים. The rendering of the Hi of רנן by *εὐφραίνω* is unique to this verse. In fact, the root, mainly in the Qal, is rendered elsewhere in OT by

96. See LS sub *αἰχμαλωσία* II.
97. Instead of the compound *καταφάγεται* The Three read the simplex. Either one is adequate.
98. Sym rendered line four as *ἀπὸ κεφαλῆς ἀνακεκαλυμμένης ἐχθροῦ* (retroverted from Syh^{m}), understanding פרעות in the sense of "uncover"; see Aramaic "entblössen," and also the rendering of פרע by the B text at Jdg 5:2 as *ἀπεκαλύφθη* (*ἀποκάλυμμα ἐν Ἰσραήλ*). Aq rendered פרעות by *ἀποπεπετασμένων*, for which see Exod 5:4 32:25.
99. In BASOR 136 (1954) 12—15. The significance of Q and its relation to LXX vs MT has been much discussed since the publication of Father Skehan's article. The latest is that of A.Van der Kooij, Fst C.J.Labuschagne = Suppl.VT LIII (1994), 93—100, who argues for the originality of a six cola text.

εὐφραίνω only in the prophets (nine times in Isa and once in Jer). For an exact copy of the second line of Q, (except for the initial conjunction), see Ps 97:7. LXX interprets אלהים as *υἱοὶ θεοῦ*, i.e. the lesser deities. It is not surprising that the majority F V text has substituted *αγγελοι* for *υἱοί*, as in line four.

Line three translates the opening hemistich of MT incorrectly. The Hi verb is addressed to the nations גוים/*ἔθνη*, but the Hebrew verb has עמו "his people" as a verbal modifier, thus "make his people ring out (for joy)." LXX plays on עמו in a double entendre, as עם "with" and עם "people," so *μετὰ τοῦ λαοῦ αὐτοῦ*.[100]

Line four reads "and let all the angels of God confirm for him." This must have had a Hebrew parent text. It not only serves as a parallel to line two, but it also serves to introduce the *ὅτι* of line five, i.e. "confirm for him that ...."

Line five represents Q, rather than MT, with its "blood *τῶν υἱῶν* (*αὐτοῦ*)."[101]

For line six the texts of Q and MT are the same, but LXX has a doublet rendering for the verb, with *καὶ ἐκδικήσει*, and *καὶ ἀνταποδώσει δίκην*. For the latter see v.41. In fact, except for the first rendering, the remainder of the line along with line seven has adapted the first person of lines three and four of v.41 to a third person version. One might have expected an *αυτου* after *μισοῦσιν*, as translation for the ולמשנאיו of Q; in fact, a popular variant has done precisely that ad sensum. Hex has placed all of line seven under the obelus, since it has no counterpart in MT.

Line eight reads "and the Lord shall purify the land of his people." Neither MT nor Q has a named subject, but LXX has added *κύριος*, though the subject has to be the same as for lines six and seven; it was quite unnecessary to add it, and a number of witnesses actually omit it, though the omission was probably not recensional. MT has אדמתו for *τὴν γῆν*, which is difficult

100. Aq translates literally by *αἰνοποιήσατε ἔθνη λαὸς αὐτοῦ*; Theod has *ἀγαλλιᾶσθε ἔθνη λαὸς αὐτοῦ*.

101. The Others read *τῶν δουλῶν*. I am sceptical about the *τῶν ἀγγέλων θεοῦ* attributed to Sym (retroverted from the Syriac Commentary of Ishodad); it rather reflects the LXX text of line four. Salvesen 170 maintains that I believe the Sym reading to be a revision of LXX's *τῶν υἱῶν αὐτοῦ*. I believe nothing of the kind. My placement of the reading in Apparatus II simply means that Ish 139 has it as equivalent. As editor I did not editorialize, but merely presented the facts.

indeed. The text of Q omits the suffix, as does LXX, which, if MT is original, is a simplification of the text.[102]

32:44 LXX begins by taking over an exact copy of 31:22 "and Moses wrote this song on that day, and taught it to the Israelites." This has no counterpart in MT here, and one *O* ms has omitted it.[103]

Then follows a translation of MT, except that instead of (words of) השירה הזאת LXX has *τοῦ νόμου τούτου*. The Greek thus combines both the writing of the Song of Moses with the proclamation of "this law," i.e. the Deut Law Code.

These differences between MT and LXX show LXX having two subscriptions. The first, which is without counterpart in MT, concludes the Song of vv.1—43 as a substitute for MT's subscription to the Song. LXX's change of MT's השירה constitutes an atttempt to bring the Song into the Law Code as its conclusion; it is then a subscription to the Law Code, as enlarged by the Song.

32:45 LXX has omitted את כל הדברים האלה entirely using *λαλῶν* in an absolute sense. The A F M V majority text does add (*παντας*) *τους λογους τουτους*, but support for the shorter text by B 848+ ensures its originality. In this way LXX has Moses ending all discourse, not just "all thse words," presumably the Law Code, with the people. This is, however, not factually correct, as the next verse makes clear. The omission is then an error on the part of the translator, probably occasioned by homoiarchon (את to אל).

32:46 LXX renders MT quite well, except that *τούτους* has no equivalent in MT, whereas LXX fails to translate the suffix of לבבכם. A genitive pronoun is quite unnecessary in Greek; *προσέχετε τῇ καρδίᾳ* can only refer to "your" heart. Actually almost all witnesses do add *υμων*, but B 848 by supporting the shorter text assure that it is LXX.[104]

---

102. Aq renders MT by *καὶ ἐξιλέεται γῆν αὐτοῦ λαὸς αὐτοῦ* (retroverted from Syh^{m}).
103. Ms 426 is often closer to MT in omitting Greek with no equivalents in MT. I suspect that its copyist was aware of what the obelus sign meant, and edited accordingly. Admittedly this cannot be proven.
104. See SS 101.

The text contains two relative clauses, both of which must refer to "all these words." The first relative pronoun is obvious; *οὕς* refers to *λόγους*, but the second one is *ἅ*. There is no neuter plural word anywhere in the context, so it can only refer to *λόγους*. The first clause refers to the words *οὕς* I am witnessing, and the more distant one, *ἅ*, reads "which you must command your sons to observe, and do all the words of this law." The indefinite neuter plural was probably used to allows for the "all the words of this law" within the clause. Did the translator unthinkly have *ρηματα* in mind? It should be noted that *n* has "corrected" *ἅ* to *ους*.

32:47 The opening *ὅτι* gives the basis for the *ἅ* clause of v.46. You must command ... to observe and do ..., "because this is not an empty word for you." The word *λόγος* refers to the *ἅ* clause in general, rather than to *νόμου*, which would be unlikely, since the context is "all the *λόγους* of this *νόμου*." It must be admitted that the translator could have been more exact in the use of pronouns; only common sense dictates what must have been intended.

The next *ὅτι* clause gives the proof that this is not an empty word for you: *αὕτη ἡ ζωὴ ὑμῶν*. Though *αὕτη* must refer to *λόγος*, it is feminine by attraction to *ζωή*. This tendency towards "attraction" is typical of this translator. That the Law Code constitutes life for the people is a basic notion for Deut.

This life is then concretized by "*μακροημερεύσετε* on the land." For the *εἰς ἥν* clause see comment at 4:22. LXX does not translate the suffix of **לרשתה**, though only B 848 plus one other ms represent LXX,[105] all other relevant witnesses adding *αυτην*, probably adding it ex par (see 11:8,29 30:18 31:13).

32:48 For **בעצם היום הזה** LXX has *ἐν τῇ ἡμέρᾳ ταύτῃ*. Hex tried to represent the **עצם** by adding *αυτη* after *ἐν*.

32:49 Moses is ordered to go up *τὸ ὄρος τὸ Ἀβαρὶμ τοῦτο*. The Hebrew has a bound structure, **הר העברים**, but no attempt to change the second *τό* to *του* is attested in the tradition.[106] The proper noun did suffer in the tradition,

105. See THGD 121.
106. Both Aq and Sym translated **העברים**, Aq, by *τῶν πέραν*, and Sym, by *τῶν διαβάσεων*.

however; aphaeresis resulted in βαριμ and βαρειν; apocopation, in αβαρει; confusion of μ/β, αβαρηβ, αβαριβ, as well as ααμαρειμ; assimilation, αραρειμ, and nasal confusion, αβαρειν.[107] The name Ναβαύ also resulted in no unanimity. The following variant spellings are attested: ναβαυτ, ναβαβ, ναυαυ. ναβαδ, ναβαρ, ναβαμ, ναβαν and ναβατ.

The relative clause, אשר על פני ירחו, is rendered by the prepositional phrase κατὰ πρόσωπον Ἰεριχώ; hex added το before the preposition, thereby equalling MT. The promised land is actually identified as "Canaan which I am giving the Israelites εἰς κατάσχεσιν." The noun occurs only here in the book, but is commonly used to render אחזה in Lev and Num.

32:50 Moses is ordered to die on the mountain ..., and be added to his people.[108] ὃν τρόπον governs two clauses which parallel for Aaron in past tense the imperatives directed to Moses. In both parts MT has the plural for τὸν λαόν, i.e. עמיך and עמיו resp., but LXX follows the singular of Sam for both.

32:51 The reason for Moses' dying in the land of Moab, and not being allowed to enter the promised land, is given here as ἠπειθήσατε my word, whereas MT makes this an act of rebellion מעלתם בי.[109] The Greek softens the direct rebellion against God by interpreting בי by τῷ ῥήματί μου, "you disobeyed my word." The verb is in the plural, because both Moses and Aaron were involved in the occasion described in Num 20:1—13, viz. the incident at ἀντιλογίας Καδῆς in the wilderness of Sin. At Kades Moses had not addressed the rock as ordered, but had struck it with his rod; for the divine judgment see v.12. The Hebrew speaks of the waters of מריבת קדש and both in the Num account, as well as here, the first word is translated as ἀντιλογίας "dispute, controversy."

This act of "rebellion" is then characterized by a second διότι/על אשר clause as οὐχ ἡγιάσατέ με among the Israelites. The exact meaning of "not sanctify me" is difficult to express. Holiness is divinity, and not sanctifying

107. See THGD 144.
108. Instead of προστέθητι Aq renders האסף literally by συλλέγητι "be gathered."
109. Aq more accurately has παράβητε for the verb.

God means failing to accord to God his status as God; it is a failure to recognize God as God, and as being central to the gift of water at Kades.

32:52 The opening ὅτι/כי can hardly be understood as a causal indicator, since what follows is a prediction which resulted from Moses' disobedience described in v.51. It seems to me that the כי must be asseverative, and the ὅτι is then to be taken as a Hebraism. If this be correct, one would have to understand the verse as "indeed you may see the land over against it (i.e. at a distance), but you may not go in there." MT has a longer text, adding אל הארץ אשר אני נתן לבני ישראל, for which comp v.49. Hex has added *προς την γην ην εγω διδωμι τοις υιοις ισραηλ* under the asterisk to equal it.

Chapter 33

33:1 The superscription describes Moses as ἄνθρωπος τοῦ θεοῦ, a term usually intended to describe prophets. Presumably as a man of God, blessings pronounced by him would be effective ones.

33:2 The name Σινά occurs only here in the book. The usual name for the mount of revelation in Deut is Χωρήβ. Not unexpectedly a number of mss read σιναι. The verse divides into two pairs of parallel lines. The first two read "The Lord came from Sina, and he appeared to us from Seir." What LXX seems to say is that Israel's God originally came from the Sina/Edomite region, and that he first made himself known in theophanic fashion in that desert area. This may then be a poetic reference to the burning bush episode described in Exod 3, where the Lord initially made himself known to Moses and through him to the Israelites. The verb ἐπέφανεν in particular was used in Hellenistic times for the appearance, the self-revelation of deity. Here it is used to render זרח, regularly used of the rising of the sun. MT also has למו in modification, "for them," thus "he arose, i.e. shone, upon them from Seir." The Hebrew reference probably refers to the Israelites, but what event the poet had in mind is not known, but comp Jdg 5:4, as well as Hab 3:3 where Teman, also in Edom, is mentioned as a place from which God appeared in a theophany.

Lines three and four read "And he hastened from Mount Pharan along with the myriads of Kades, (even his) angels with him on his right hand." I would understand line four to be parallel to "along with the myriads of Kades." What the line means is that the divine appearance was in the full company of his attendants. Precisely what is meant by "the myriads of Kades" is not known; that they are divine attendants seems clear.

The verb in the Hebrew of line three is הופיע "shine forth," a word used in theophanic settings for God's appearance. Why LXX should have used κατέσπευσεν "he hurried, hastened" is not immediately clear, though in the reflexive sense "to hurry oneself" it might be understood in the context to refer to hurrying to show oneself.[1]

1. Aq translates הופיע by ἀνεφάνη, and Sym, by ἐπεφάνη.

The Hebrew counterpart to *σὺν μυριάσιν* Καδής is אתה מרבבת קדש "he came from the myriads of Qadesh."[2] The Greek apparently thought of את "with" rather than אתה.[3] Καδής is simply a transliteration of קדש

The Hebrew counterpart to line four is uncertain. מימינו is translated by LXX adequately by *ἐκ δεξιῶν αὐτοῦ*,[4] but what אשדת למו means is completely opaque. The ancients divided the noun into אש "fire" and דת "law,"[5] but since דת is a Persian loanword found only in the latest books of OT that is not what אשדת ever meant. How LXX got to *ἄγγελοι μετ' αυτοῦ* from אשדת למו must remain a mystery. Could it be simply a wild guess based on the parllel *μυριάσιν* Καδής who accompanied him?

33:3—4 Line one reads "and he spared his people," but MT has "and (or indeed) he loves peoples," a peculiar statement which is at odds with the poem at large, e.g. v.11. "Peoples" are normally the enemies, not the beloved of God which term could only be applied to Israel. Could עמים possibly be a corruption of עמום, i.e., ʿmmo-ma "his people"(?).[6]

Line two reads "and all those sanctified (are) under your power (i.e. hands)." LXX has not rendered the suffix of קדשיו,[7] so hex has added *αυτου* to make up for it. Possibly the translator intentionally omitted the suffix in order to avoid the notion that God's sanctified ones should be under Israel's power.[8] Line three *καὶ οὗτοι ὑπὸ σέ εἰσιν* seems to have taken the enigmatic Hebrew והם תכו לרגלך as though it read והם תחת רגלך, though תכו ל could hardly be misread in this way—one suspects that the translator did not know

2. For a summary of old Jewish interpretations see Prijs 145—147.
3. Aq translated מרבבת קדש by *ἀπὸ μυριάδων ἁγιασμοῦ*, i.e. taking קדש not as a place name but as a noun meaning sanctification. Actually that impulse towards translating קדש would have served the LXX translator well; e.g. "myriads of holy ones (taken as a collective)" would have made a good parallel to the *ἄγγελοι* of line four. Note that Sym also translated the word but by *ἁγίαις*; cf Vulg *sanctorum*.
4. Aq has *ἀπὸ δεξιᾶς αὐτοῦ*.
5. E.g. Tar^{O} reads מגו אשתא אוריתא יהב לנא "from the midst of the fire he gave us the law." Aq has *πῦρ δόγμα αὐτοῖς*, and Sym rendered the noun by *πυρινὸς νόμος*.
6. The reading attributed to Aq *καὶ ἐπὶ ἔθνη* (retroverted from Syh^{m}) cannot possibly be correct; it must represent some error of transmission.
7. See SS 102.
8. Aq translates the line as *πάντες ἡγιασμένοι αὐτοῦ ἐν χειρί σου* (retroverted from Syh^{m}).

תכו at all and guessed from the context, i.e. "under your hands" could parallel "under your feet." What תכו means is completely unknown.[9]

The last line must be read together with line one of v.4. It reads "And he received from his words the law which Moses commanded us. MT's text is more or less reflected by this translation. It reads ישא מדברתיך תורה צוה לנו משה; LXX translated מדברתיך by ἀπὸ τῶν λόγων αὐτοῦ, with third masculine singular pronoun instead of a second singular. But the word occurs only here in OT and that it is the same as דבריך is not at all certain. Furthermore, MT makes a clear division between the two verses, and has no equivalent for *ον*, i.e. "Moses commanded the law to us (as an inheritance for the congregation of Jacob)."[10] LXX has taken קהלת not as a singular which is how the Masoretes vocalized it, but as a plural, *συναγωγαῖς*, in the dative showing advantage "for the congregations (of Jacob).

33:5 MT makes the verb ויהי past tense "and he became," but LXX has a future *καὶ ἔσται*. For the translator the verse is a prediction. It is not certain who is referred to in LXX. In MT it must refer to the Lord: "And he became king in Jeshurun (a poetic word for Israel)," but the translator seems to have an earthly ruler in mind. From the context it would seem to be a kind of *Moses redivivus* that is contemplated. This is also made likely by LXX's unwillingness to render מלך as "king" but merely by *ἄρχων* "ruler," with בישרון being rendered by *ἐν τῷ ἠγαπημένῳ*, a collective for the people of Israel;[11] for the rendering of ישרון see comment at 32:15.

This will take place *συναχθέντων ἀρχόντων λαῶν ἅμα φυλαῖς Ἰσραήλ*. This is not what MT has, since instead of *λαῶν* it has the singular עם, i.e. "heads of the people," a reference to Israel, not to "peoples." Here *ἀρχόντων* translates ראשי "heads." יחד is intended as an adverb, i.e. "the tribes of Israel together," but LXX has altered this to mean "together with," made necessary once עם is taken to represent "peoples" over against Israel.

9. Aq translates the line as *καὶ αὐτοὶ ἐπλήγησαν ἐν τοῖς ποσίν σου* (retroverted from Syh^{m}); Aq apparently read הכו as from נכה.

10. Aq has instead of LXX's text *αἴρουσιν ἀπὸ ῥημάτων σου· νόμον ἐνετείλατο ἡμῖν Μωυσῆς* (retroverted from Syh^{m}).

11. Theod and Sym translate בישרון מלך by *ἐν τῷ εὐθεῖ βασιλεύς*.

33:6 The blessing of Reuben. The first line renders MT exactly: "Let Reuben live and not die," but the second one does not. MT says: "And let his men be few (i.e. a number). MT recognized that Reuben was insignificant as a tribe, and the blessing is no more than one of preserving it from complete extinction. The translator changed the line into a real blessing "And may he be abundant in number," quite the opposite of MT.[12]

33:7 The blessing of Judah. LXX omits ויאמר after "and this to Judah," and hex has added *και ειπεν* to make up for it. Line one renders MT exactly: "Listen, o Lord, to the voice of Judah," but the second line reinterpreted the Hebrew. MT has a transitive verb with suffix תביאנו "may you (the Lord) bring him (i.e. Judah) back to his people." What is meant is that Judah should once again be joined to the people of Israel. But the translator had no historical separation of the tribe from the rest of Israel in mind; it is the Lord who is implored to come (literally enter in) to his people. Possibly what the Greek meant to say was to ask the Lord to dwell among his people; after all, the temple was in Jerusalem of Judea. Instead of *εἰσέλθοις ἄν* most witnesses read *εισελθοισαν*, a reading based on a wrong division of words in old uncial texts in which words were written together. The plural is barely sensible, and is an obvious mistake.[13]

Line three is difficult in MT since ידיו is plural but the verb רב is singular. LXX disregards the difficulty of the Hebrew and uses a plural verb, *διακρινοῦσιν* "decide"; that equation is also unique in OT, though the simplex is a common rendering for the verb ריב.[14] LXX is not satisfied with mere contention; his hands must decide, i.e. overcome.

The last line renders MT literally even to the extent of translating מן by *ἐκ*. A help "from" his enemies ("adversaries" in MT) must mean "against." The help derives from the inimical status of relations between Judah and her enemies.

---

12. Aq renders literally with *καὶ ἔστω ἀνδράσιν αὐτοῦ ἀριθμός*, and Sym has *ἔστωσαν ὀλιγοστοὶ αὐτοῦ ἀριθμός* (both retroverted from Syh^{m}).

13. Sym has *ἐπὶ τὸν λαὸν αὐτοῦ ἐξάξεις αὐτόν*.

14. Aq has his usual rendering for רב *δικάσεται* (*αὐτῷ*). Sym has translated the line by *αἱ χεῖρες αὐτοῦ ὑπερμαχήσουσιν αὐτοῦ*, which equals Vulg: *manus eius pugnabunt pro eo*; see Salvesen 173.

33:8 Vv.8—11 constitute the blessing of Levi. V.8 begins with *δότε Λευί* "give to Levi *δήλους αὐτοῦ καὶ ἀλήθειαν αὐτοῦ (τῷ ἀνδρὶ τῷ ὁσίῳ).*" The two terms in MT are תמיך ואוריך; instead of second singular suffixes, i.e. "your" referring to God, LXX has *αὐτοῦ*, i.e. belonging to Levi. For the Hebrew terms "Thummim and Urim" see Note at Exod 28:26, where, however, LXX has *τὴν δήλωσιν καὶ τὴν ἀλήθειαν*. The plurals are as far as I know limited to OT and are used in the context of means of ascertaining the will of deity. Just what "his Manifestations and his Truth" meant to the translator is not obvious, but for a suggested explanation of the Greek terms see Note at Exod 28:26.[15] Just who is intended by "the holy man" is not clear, though the next lines refer to the occasion described in Exod 17:1—7 and Num 20:2—13. On that occasion the Israelites lacked water to drink and quarreled with Moses and Aaron (only Moses is referred to in Exod 17) at Massah—*Πείρᾳ* and at Meribah—*'Αντιλογίας*, resp "Trial" and "Strife." Since Aaron was recognized as the father of the Levites what is probably intended here is the personified tribe of Levi. MT refers to the holy man as לאיש חסידך; LXX disregarded the suffix as inappropriate in view of the incident alluded to.

LXX avoids the direct accusation of MT's second singular verbs נסיתו and תריבהו, though unfortunately it does imitate MT by reproducing the suffixes by pronouns (*αὐτόν*) within the relative clause. The verbs are rendered in the indefinite third plural "they tempted ... they reviled." Since there are no plural antecedents these are simply indefinite as in "they say, on dit, Mann sagt."[16]

33:9 MT begins with "the one saying לאביו ולאמו," but LXX disregards the suffixes as being otiose;[17] the majority tradition has added *αυτου* in both cases, possibly, though not necessarily, hex in origin. What he (i.e. Levi) was saying is *οὐκ ἑώρακά σε* which makes the statement direct rather than reflecting the indirection of the third person suffix לא ראיתיו.

15. Sym renders the two lines as *τελειότης σου καὶ διδαχή σου τῷ ἀνδρὶ τῷ ὁσίῳ*, which represents an attempt to make some kind of sense. Vulg renders similarly: *perfectio tua et doctrina tua viro sancto tuo*; see Salvesen 174.
16. Sym has for lines three and four: *ὃν ἐπείρασας ἐν δοκιμασίᾳ, ἐδοκίμασας αὐτὸν ἐπὶ τοῦ ὕδατος τῆς ἀντιλογίας*.
17. See SS 101.

But not only did the Levite abandon parents, he also "did not recognize his brothers, and even his children he renounced." The verb *ἀπέγνω* is used to represent לא ידע. Though this is not incorrect, the tradition, possibly hex, (*O b f y*), changed the verb to *ουκ εγνω* as more suitable for rendering MT.

The rejection of family is, however, not viewed to the discredit of Levi, as the last two lines make clear: "he guarded your oracles and kept your covenant." In MT this is put into a כי clause, i.e. it gives the reason for the neglect of family on Levi's part. Accordingly hex has added *οτι* before line three. For the translator this appeared unnecessary; the contrast between the negatives of lines one through three with the positives of lines four and five was sufficient.

33:10 The verse describes the twofold duties of Levites: to explicate God's law and to perform cultic duties. The first is described in lines one and two "they must make manifest your judgments (*δικαιώματα*) to Jacob, and your law (*νόμον*) to Israel." The verb *δηλώσουσιν* recalls the *δήλους* of v.8 and was probably intentionally chosen for that reason. It is not incorrect for יורו,[18] but it is the only time that the equation appears in the Pentateuch.[19] One might render it by "they must explicate." The *δικαιώματα* are the various laws contained in the law codes,[20] whereas *νόμον* is the overall term used for law, though the Hebrew תורה has the wider connotation of (divine) instruction, and so could be, and eventually was, applied to the entire Pentateuch.

The second part was not fully understood by the translator. MT has "they shall place incense in your nostril (i.e. for you to smell), and whole offerings on your altar." Since אף "nostril" is often used metaphorically for "anger," LXX took it in this sense, and line three reads *ἐπιθήσουσιν θυμίαμα ἐν ὀργῇ σου* "they must lay incense when you are angry," and the term כליל "whole offerings" was understood as "wholly, entirely" of time as *διὰ παντός* "continually." So one might translate "they shall place incense continually on your altar when you are angry." But just possibly *διὰ παντός* was actually understood as the continual sacrifice?[21] Then line four would read "even a

18. Though Tov 244 points out a Qumran text reading ויאירו; see also P.W.Skehan, CBQ 19 (1957), 436.
19. Aq renders the verb by *φωτίσουσιν*.
20. Aq prefers to translate משפטיך by *κρίματα* <*σου*>.
21. As Daniels 265—268 maintains.

continual sacrifice on your altar.[22] This is, however, not likely to have been intended, since the translator omitted the conjunction of וכליל, thereby making *διὰ παντός* modify the verb *ἐπιθήσεται*.

Readers of the two lines found the notion of putting incense on God's altar when he was angry difficult, and an F *b*+ text read *εν εορτη* instead of *ἐν ὀργῇ*, an obvious palaeographically inspired correction. According to its text the Levites burned incense on the occasion of God's feast. Most witnesses read the genitive instead of (*ἐπὶ*) *τὸ θυσιαστήριον*, but the oldest witness, cod B, has the accusative. Either makes sense.

33:11 The first two lines are not at all problematic. They represent the Hebrew adequately, though *δέξαι* "receive" is not quite the same as תרצה. For the Ni of רצה Lev did favor the use of *δέχομαι* (five times). For the Qal v.11 is unique in OT in its use of this verb. The Hebrew adds the dimension of receiving favorably, viewing with approval.[23]

Line three reads "bring down (i.e. smite) the loins of his enemies who rise up against him." The term *ἐχθρῶν* has no equivalent in MT and its presence has created some difficulty in the tradition. A weakly supported B tradition has transposed *ἐπανεστηκότων ἐχθρῶν*. Since this was followed by *αὐτοῦ*, which in the variant tradition followed the participle rather than the noun, a change to the dative was a natural development. Both are, however, secondary. Ms 58 has omitted *ἐχθρῶν*, which then equals MT. This is probably not accidental, since this ms often omits passages under the obelus, and as in the case of ms 426 has apparently engaged in posthexaplaric activity.[24]

The last line in MT is somewhat cryptic. It reads ומשנאיו מן יקומון "and those who hate him from (that) they should arise." Actually the Masoretes were aware of this and took ומשנאיו with the preceding line.[25] The rendering of LXX undoubtedly states more clearly what MT must have intended, "And let those who hate him not (i.e. never) rise up." What MT actually says is best represented by in NRSV: "of those that hate him, so that they do not rise again."

22. Aq translated כליל by *τέλεον* and Sym, by *ὁλοκαυώματα* (retroverted from Syh^m^); see the remarks of Daniel 270—271.
23. Aq renders more literally by *εὐδοκήσης*.
24. See THGD 113 and 131.
25. See Prijs 104.

33:12 The blessing of Benjamin. LXX follows Sam in beginning with *καί*.[26] LXX interprets the bound phrase ידיד יהוה correctly by "beloved by the Lord." MT ends the first hemistich with עליו "besides him." Since עליו occurs both before and after חפף it may have been omitted as otiose already by Sam, which LXX then follows.

The next line begins with *καὶ ὁ θεός* as subject, for which there is no support in MT, though it has been suggested that the omitted עליו was read as עליון.[27] But LXX never translated עליון by *ὁ θεός* throughout the OT; in fact, it almost always becomes *ὕψιστος* (49 times).[28] The line reads "And God overshadows him continually (i.e. all the days)," with a present tense verb, *σκιάζει*, rendering the participle חפף.[29] It should be noted that not only did LXX add *ὁ θεός* as subject, but it joined this line to the preceding with a *καί* as well, for which there is also no basis in MT.

For the last line LXX translated שכן by *κατέπαυσεν* "rested," though earlier in the verse it had used *κατασκηνώσει* for ישכן. "To rest between his shoulders" is an idiom for nestling on the hillsides. The pronoun *αὐτοῦ* has no obvious antecedent, since Βενιαμίν is used in two senses. As antecedent for *αὐτοῦ* it must refer to the land assigned to the tribe, but *αὐτῷ* in the previous line refers to Benjamin as people.

33:13 The blessing of Joseph is given in vv.13—17. Characteristic of the poem is a series of six *ἀπό* phrases in vv.13—15, all of which are to be taken as predicates of *ἡ γῆ αὐτοῦ* in v.13. What is intended is "his land shall partake of the Lord's blessing," or "may his land partake ...." The Lord's blessing is then characterized by the various phrases that follow; in fact, no verb actually occurs until line three of v.16. The first line of the poem is then determinative with its "his land" in the nominative. MT is much clearer with its Pual participle מברכת "blessed," i.e. "blessed of Yahweh is his land." The trans-

26. So also in Kenn 152,196,206.
27. See note in BHS: l עליון.
28. According to Dos Santos.
29. Theod had *σκεπάσει*. Aq took חפף as a denominative of חפה "bridal chamber," and also created a neologism based on *παστός* "bridal chamber," viz. *παστώσει*.

lator, by misreading the word as a prepositional phrase, has set the pattern for the next lines as well.[30]

Line two begins with ἀπὸ ὡρῶν. The word ὡρῶν is here to be understood as "fruits, products"[31] as the Hebrew makes clear. MT has ממגד "from the fine products."[32] The same form occurs twice in v.14 (rendered by καθ' ὥραν and ἀπό), once in v.15 (as ἀπὸ κορυφῆς) and once in v.16 (as καθ' ὥραν). Obviously the translator had trouble with the word and contextualized it throughout. The line may be translated: "of the products of heaven, even of dew)."

The third line reads "and of the abysses of springs below," which is a free paraphrase of MT's ומתהום רבצת תחת "and of the abyss crouching below." LXX does not continue the personified figure of a crouching abyss, but interprets its intent as the depths producing the necessary waters to irrigate the land. The Hebrew figure also occurs in Gen 49:25, but its translation there is at best a free paraphrase; cf comment ad loc.

33:14 The first hemistich in MT is וממגד תבואת שמש "and of the choice fruits of the sun's products." This is paralleled by וממגד גרש ירחים. The word גרש is quite uncertain. It is usually rendered contextually as also meaning products, crop, but this is a mere guess. The translator understood תבואת as τροπῶν, i.e. turnings (of the sun), thus the solar cycle, and גרש by analogy as the conjunction (of the moon), i.e. its phases.[33] μήνη means "moon," but in the plural it can mean "months." The verse then may be rendered as "and in due season of the products of the solar cycle and of the conjunction of the months."

33:15 LXX translated the first hemistich correctly: "and of the top of the mountains of old," and then made the second line an exact parallel by substituting κορυφῆς of line one for מגד.[34] This is not a translation, but rather a

30. Dogniez-Harl also had trouble with the construction and rendered it freely by "que la bénédiction de Seigneur vienne sur la terre," followed by a series of "par" phrases.
31. See LS sub ὥρα B.III.
32. Aq translates מגד by τραγημάτων.
33. Aq translated ממגד גרש as <ἀπὸ> τραγημάτων ἐκβολῆς, understanding גרש as from the well-known root meaning "drive out, cast out."
34 . Aq of course read τραγημάτων. Sym made it ὀπώρας "autumn."

rewrite. Admittedly it makes a fine couplet: "both from the top of the ancient mountains, and from the top of the everlasting hills," but that is not what the Hebrew says. It should be noted that ἀρχῆς "beginning, source" is unusual for קדם (though see v.27); it is more common as ἀπ' ἀρχῆς (for מקדם) in the sense of "from of old" (i.e. from the beginning).

33:16 The first hemistich in MT is much clearer than its translation in Greek. It reads "from the choice fruits of the land and its fulness." LXX rendered ממגד as in line one of v.14 by καθ' ὥραν in due season,"[35] but then changed ארץ ומלאה to γῆς πληρώσεως. Hex has added under the asterisk an αυτης at the end, but one would also expect a και to separate the two words. I would take γῆς as an objective genitive, thus "of the land's fulness," i.e. that which fills the land, viz. its produce.

The parallel hemistich reads ורצון שכני סנה "and the favor of the one dwelling in the bush," obviously a reference to the burning bush episode of Exod 3. The translator rendered רצון by τὰ δεκτά which is quite possible. This is followed by a dative, thus "the things acceptable to." LXX was not satisfied with the notion that the Lord dwelt in a bush. God is omnipresent; he dwells in heaven. But what Exod 3 describes is the Lord who revealed himself. The episode was a moment of revelation, not a description of God's dwelling place, and LXX interpreted שכני as τῷ ὀφθέντι "to the one who appeared (in the bush)."[36]

Line two is apparently to be taken as the subject of ἔλθοισαν: "let them (i.e. τὰ δεκτά) come upon the head of Joseph."

The last line is syntactically in disarray. It reads "and on the top—he having been glorified among (his) brothers." δοξασθείς is in the nominative singular, and can only refer to 'Ιωσήφ of the preceding line. But this is in the genitive. Possibly what happened is that 'Ιωσήφ being indeclinable was thoughtlessly referred to as though it were nominative. Only a genitive really makes sense here, a correction that was made by four mss. But the ungrammatical nominative must be original, since no copyist, however careless, would change a genitive to the nominative. The only sense I can make of

35. Sym again has ὀπώρας.
36. Sym is said to have had δέκατα, though this looks to me like a copyist error for δεκτά.

it is as "And as for (the one) glorified among (his) brothers (may they be) on (his) head." The line must intend "and on the crown of the one glorified among (his) brothers," but it is most peculiar way of putting it in Greek. The Hebrew reads ולקדקד נזיר אחיו "and on the crown of the one consecrated among his brothers." The line is exactly the same in Gen 49:26, where LXX has *καὶ κορυφῆς ὧν ἡγήσατο ἀδελφῶν*. LXX did not translate the suffix of אחיו, and hex added *αυτου* after *ἀδελφοῖς* to represent it.[37]

33:17 LXX follows Sam in reading שור rather than שורו. MT states that to the firstborn of (his) bull הדר לו "is glory for him." LXX renders this by *τὸ κάλλος αὐτοῦ* "his beauty," which translation is unique in OT. The figure is certainly a vigorous one. So is that of the next line: "the horns of a unicorn are his horns." *μονοκέρωτος* is the usual rendering in OT for ראם, though the ראם "a wild ox" has two horns. The translation is particularly odd in speaking of the *κέρατα* of the unicorn. To the translator a *μονοκέρωτος* must have had two horns; Joseph consists of Ephraim and Manasseh, two tribes, not "one horn." and note also the plural pronoun in the next line as well: "with them he will gore nations together even to the end of the earth." MT has the last strucutre phrased in peculiar fashion. It reads יחדו אספי ארץ. The adverb "altogether" could refer to the "ends (note the plural) of the earth," or it modifies the verb, which is how the Masoretes accented it.[38] The Greek interpretation apparently supports the latter interpretation. That the translator was troubled by the structure is clear from his rendering of אספי ארץ by *ἕως ἐπ' ἄκρου γῆς* probably intending "as far as on the edge of the earth."

The last two lines refer to the actual tribes constituting Joseph. LXX follows Sam in reading הם rather than the והם in line three.[39]

33:18 Vv.18—19 constitute the blessing of Zabulon. V.18 calls on Zabulon to rejoice "in your going out" (i.e. to sea), but the second line refers to Issachar in third person, "and as for Issachar (may he rejoice) in his tents." MT has a second person suffix, באהליך, i.e. Zabulon is addressed in the first hemistich,

37. Aq translated נזיר אחיו by *ἀφωρισμένου ἀδελφῶν αὐτοῦ*, whereas Sym read *φυλάξαντος τοὺς ἀδελφοὺς αὐτοῦ*, possibly understanding נטר as Salvesen 175 suggests.
38. Sym has *ὁμοῦ πέρατα γῆς*.
39. Also in Kenn 18,674.

but Issachar in the second. Since the second line has no verb, the verbal notion of the first is carried over into the second. But the translator realized that *τῷ Ζαβουλὼν εἶπεν*, and an address to another tribe was out of order. This inconsistency was then rationally repaired by using *αὐτοῦ* instead of *σου*. In the tradition the V *b*+ text felt the oddity of *αὐτοῦ* and changed it to *σου*, which only by coincidence equals MT.

33:19 The first stich in MT reads: "the nations <to> a mountain they will summon; there they will sacrifice proper sacrifices." I take זבחי צדק to mean not sacrifices of righteousness which would seem to me a meaningless term, but sacrifices according to prescription, i.e. proper or correct sacrifices.[40] LXX must have had a different parent text for its line one. It begins with *ἔθνη ἐξολεθρεύσουσιν* "they shall annihilate nations," but this has no counterpart in MT except for the initial עמים. It then continues in second person with *καὶ ἐπικαλέσεσθε ἐκεῖ* for the third person יקראו שם. The rest of the stich is also put into second person *καὶ θύσετε θυσίαν δικαιοσύνης* with *θυσίαν* in the singular. The first two lines may be translated "nations they shall annihilate. And there you will invoke (i.e. the deity) and sacrifice a proper sacrifice." I take *δικαιοσύνης* as a calque for the Hebrew צדק.

The second stich in MT refers to the peoples. It is a כי clause and may be rendered: "For the abundance of the seas they suckle, even the hidden hoards of the sand." LXX has all this refer to the tribe. Rather than "they suckle" LXX has *θηλάσει σε*; "the wealth[41] of the sea shall suckle you, and the trade of those who inhabit the sea coast." The last line is only remotely a paraphrase of the Hebrew, probably taking its cue from חול "sand" as seashore.[42] But the Hebrew is itself peculiar in that the words which I rendered as "hidden hoards" are synonyms; both שפוני and טמוני mean "hidden things of," and LXX may have had a different parent text.

33:20 Vv.20—21 constitute the blessing of Gad. The opening line refers to *ἐμπλατύνων Γάδ* "one who enlarges Gad," a reference to God. What is

40. Though see SS 65.
41. Instead of *πλοῦτος* Aq read *πλήμυρα*.
42. Aq has *ἀποθέτους κεκρυμμένους ἄμμου*, whereas Sym reads *ἀποθήκας κεκρυμμένας ἄμμου*, both of which interpret the MT text.

enlarged is its borders; cf 12:20 19:8. The last line is presented paratactically in MT, but without a conjunction as in Sam, and by a subordinate participle.[43] The rendering of קדקד by *ἄρχοντα* is unique. The Hebrew word means "scalp, crown, head," which differs from *ἄρχων*, which normally can only mean "head" in the sense of chieftain, ruler; in v.16 the word was correctly rendered by *κορυφῆς*. But in coordination with *βραχίονα* "arm" it must have been intended to mean "head," though I can find no parallel for it; at least, "tearing arm and ruler" could hardly be meaningful. It might be noted that Byz made sense by changing *βραχίονα* to *βασιλεα*, thus making the phrase "king and ruler."

33:21 The text of MT is highly uncertain. The first clause seems to say "and he saw a first part for himself," usually understood by moderns as "he chose the best part for himself" as an allusion to the tribe being given the first choice of land before crossing the Jordan in Num 32. LXX translates by *καὶ εἶδεν ἀπαρχὴν αὐτοῦ*. The noun is regularly used in the sense of firstfruits, but normally in the plural, though the singular is also possible.

LXX continues with *ὅτι ἐκεῖ ἐμερίσθη γῆ* "for there land was apportioned." MT has no word for "land," but it does have כי שם חלקת which is somehow reflected by the Greek. This is followed by a genitive absolute construction,[44] which describes the conditions obtaining under which the land was divided: *ἀρχόντων συνηγμένων ἅμα ἀρχηγοῖς λαῶν* "when the chieftains were gathered together with the rulers of peoples." I can make little consistent sense out of MT's מחקק ספון ויתא ראשי עם which is MT's counterpart to the line. Presumably by *λαῶν* is meant the other tribes, probably those which settled in Canaan.

The last two lines are recognizable as renderings of MT. They do, however, reinterpret the Hebrew text which says "he performed the justice of Yahweh (צדקת יהוה), and his judgments with Israel." The subject is apparently Gad. This was theologically questionable to the translator who insisted that יהוה had to be the subject and so he rewrote the text to read

43. The line is translated by Aq as *καὶ θη<ρεύ>σει βραχίονα καὶ κορυφήν*. Cod reads *θησει ... κορυ{μ}φην*.
44. Obviously the comma in the critical text is in the wrong place, and must be placed before, not after, *ἀρχόντων*.

δικαιοσύνην κύριος ἐποίησεν καὶ κρίσιν αὐτοῦ μετὰ Ἰσραήλ. This is a clever translation; even the word order of MT is retained, but *κύριος* is in the nominative, i.e. is the subject, and משפטיו is rendered by a singular, thereby making a better parallel to *δικαιοσύνην*. So it is the Lord who "performed justice and his judgment with Israel." The Byz text has "corrected" *κρίσιν* to *κριματα* which equals the plural of MT. Apparently hex also corrected *κύριος* to *κυριου* to equal MT.

33:22 The blessing of Dan. Dan is called *σκύμνος λέοντος* "a lion's cub," for which see Gen 49:9 where it is applied to Judah. For line two LXX followed Sam's ויזנק. That Dan should leap from Basan shows that the Danites had already moved to the north; see Jdg 18.

33:23 The blessing of Nephthali. Line one translates MT correctly, except for the plural *δεκτῶν* for רצון, for which see v.16.[45] It reads "Nephthali is a satiety of favors." As is usual with the name Naphthali most witnesses close the final syllable with a *mu*, but the -λι ending equals the Hebrew and is original. Line two interprets מלא by *ἐμπλησθήτω* "let him be filled" plus an accusative modifier *εὐλογίαν παρὰ κυρίου*. This interprets the bound phrase ברכת יהוה correctly as a blessing the source of which is the Lord.

Line two interprets מלא by *ἐμπλησθήτω* "let him be filled" with the accusative modifier *εὐλογίαν παρὰ κυρίου*. It is line three, however, which shows how the translator has interpreted the verse as a whole. The verb in MT, ירשה, is an imperative "inherit, possess," which means that the *Νεφθαλί* of line one is a vocative; the tribe is being addressed. But LXX translates ירשה by a future verb *κληρονομήσει* "he (i.e. Nephthali) shall possess the sea and the south." Thus the blessing is all in third person.

33:24 Vv.24—25 are the blessing of Aser. The first line is not fully clear as to the intent of the *ἀπό* modifying *εὐλογημένος*. I would suggest that it is used in the same sense as *ἐπικατάρατος ἀπό* at Gen 3:14 "cursed beyond (all cattle, etc.)" said of the snake. So "blessed is Aser beyond sons." This is a good interpretation of ברוך מבנים אשר. In the tradition the B *O b n*+ text read

45. Aq and Sym render this literally by *εὐδοκίας*.

ευλογητος instead of the participle, but that is unusual for Deut occurring only at 7:14.[46]

Line two begins with *και ἔσται*, i.e. it, as well as line three, constitutes a prediction. But in MT there is no conjunction (though there is one in Sam), and the verb is the short form יהי. In MT it is a wish "May he be (agreeable to his brothers)." The *d* group has changed the verb to *εστω*, which equals MT. Line three is asyndetic in LXX and continues in the future. MT here has וטבל, which the Masoretes have vocalized as a participle, which presumably would be best understood to carry on the precative use of the verbal idea. LXX says "he shall dip his foot into oil."[47] The Byz text introduces the line with *και*, whcih is probably a recensional changed introduced from one of The Three.

33:25 Line one continues the third person of v.24, but then changes to second person with MT in line two. MT is unfortunately difficult in both parts. The subject of the first nominal clause is a hapax legomenon and its meaning is unknown. LXX apparently took מנעליך as without the מ prefix, and also made it singular, rendering it by *τὸ ὑπόδημα αὐτοῦ* and adding *ἔσται* as a linking verb. Thus "his sandal shall be of iron and brass."

Line two also has a hapax legomenon as subject. דבא is completely unknown, and *ἡ ἰσχύς* is as good a guess as any.[48] The line is without a verb, the *ἔσται* carrying over from line one.

33:26 With v.26 the concluding section begins. The first line has been vocalized by the Masoretes so as to put ישרון in the vocative: "There is no one like God, o Jeshurun," but LXX has *οὐκ ἔστιν ὥσπερ ὁ θεὸς τοῦ ἠγαπημένου*, which the consonantal text permits, and is also supported by Pesh.[49] For *τοῦ ἠγαπημένου* see comment at 32:15.

Lines two and three are best read together in the Greek: "the one riding upon the sky is your help, even the magnificent one of the firmament." The first line renders MT adequately, though בעזרך is a prepositional phrase, but the exact meaning of the preposition is not fully clear. Driver renders "as your

46. See THGD 134. The Three all read *εὐλογητός*.
47. For the use of *ἐν* in the sense of *εἰς* see SS 136.
48. Aq translates by *ἕξις* "bodily state" (retroverted from Syh[m]).
49. As well as by Vulg: *non est deus alius ut deus rectissimi.*

help"; NRSV has "to your help"; NJPS, "to help you," and ZürB, "zu Hilfe." LXX disregards the preposition as does Vulg.

The last line in MT reads ובגאותו שחקים "And the skies in his majesty," i.e. as parallel to שמים. Thus "A rider through the heavens ... and through the skies in his majesty." In form "in his majesty" would be parallel to בעזך, but not in sense.[50]

33:27 Line one reads *καὶ σκέπασις θεοῦ ἀρχῆς* which is syntactically a loose structure presupposing something like "is to you" as predicate, i.e. "And (you will have) the protection of the God of old." MT has a nominal clause "the God of old is מענה "a refuge."[51]

The second line reads "and under the support (*ἰσχύν*) of the everlasting arms"; again the understood context is "you will be" or "are." MT has no equivalent for *ἰσχύν* which the translator added ad sensum.[52]

Line three is understood as a future *καὶ ἐκβαλεῖ* "and he will cast out" for ויגרש, which the Masoretes vocalized as a preterite "and he drove out," but the consonantal text allows for an interpretation as a future.Similarly the Masoretes vocalized ויאמר to mean "and he said." The translator contextualized neatly by *λέγων*. The imperative השמד "destroy," i.e. the inhabitants of Canaan, is perforce reinterpreted by the translator who had taken ויגרש as a future as a second person future middle optative *ἀπόλοιο* "may you perish, be destroyed."

33:28 As in v.27, LXX read the Hebrew verb as a future, though the Masoretes vocalized וישכן as a past tense. So LXX constitutes a promise "And Israel shall dwell securely" rather than a statement of past security.

The second and third lines are problematic. MT reads בדד עין יעקב אל ארץ דגן ותירוש. LXX has *μόνος ἐπὶ γῆς Ἰακωβ ἐπὶ σίτου καὶ οἴνου*. The parent text must be that of Sam with על instead of אל. What may have happened is that LXX read על instead of עין as well. If that was the case the על and the על ארץ were transposed by LXX, which created an exact rendering of

50. Sym has translated line three by *καὶ ἐν εὐπρεπείᾳ αὐτοῦ ἐν ταῖς νεφέλαις* (retroverted from Syh^{m}).
51. Theod has *καὶ ἀπὸ ὕψους θεοῦ ἀρξῆς*, and Sym has *κατοικτηρίῳ θεοῦ ἀπὸ ἀρξῆς*.
52. Sym has *ὑποκάτωθεν βραχίονες τοῦ κόσμου (mundi)*.

its parent text. Admittedly this is a highly speculative reconstruction requiring a number of successive steps. It is more likely that the translator was completely puzzled by "Alone is the fountain of Jacob on (or to) a land of grain and wine," and simply put in something that fitted the context. In any event, hex added *γης* before *σίτου* to equal MT. One might note that in both cases *ἐπί* governs a genitive, which would argue against the variant B *C*'' + text reading a dative *σιτω και οινω*.[53] Note also that Compl has *πηγη* instead of *ἐπὶ γῆς* which would equal MT, but Compl probably changed the text to agree with its Hebrew text.[54]

The last line reads "and the sky is cloudy with dew for him (i.e. for Israel/Jacob)." The Hebrew has אף שמיו יערפו טל "And (or indeed) his skies shall drip with dew." *συννεφῆς* occurs only here in OT but its meaning is clear. The translator has paraphrased freely, — he has not even used a verb to render יערפו - but the rendering is not incorrect.

In the tradition *αὐτῷ* in a popular B variant text becomes *σοι*. This actually equals the text of Sam, and the correctness of the critical text is not certain. Either שמיו or שמיך makes sense.[55]

33:29 The first stich of MT: Blessed are you, O Israel; Who is like you, a people saved by Yahweh? is literally rendered by LXX. For the second stich LXX took the first word מגן "shield" as a verb, and line three thus reads "your help shall serve as a shield." The next line has simplified a difficult MT by "and the sword (shall be) your boast." MT reads ואשר חרב גאותך. I can make very little sense out of אשר unless it be understood as "as."[56] Most moderns bypass the relative pronoun and translate the rest as a bound phrase "and the sword of your majesty (or triumph)." The translation of גאותך by *καυχημά σου* is sensible; your triumph is that of which one can boast.

The last hemistich in MT reads "And your enemies shall feign obedience to you, and you will tread on their high places (i.e. on their backs)." LXX translates the verb of the first clause, יכחשו, by *ψεύσεται*, i.e. "shall deceive,"

53. See the discussion in THGD 137.
54. Dogniez-Harl raise the question whether *ἐπὶ γῆς* might not be a palaeographic error for *πηγη*, but this would leave *ἐπί* for אל ארץ unexplained.
55. Sym translated the line as *καὶ ὁ οὐρανὸς αὐτῷ γνοφωθήσεται δρόσῳ* (retroverted from Syh^{m}).
56. Aq makes the line read *καὶ ὡς μάχαιρα καύχησίς σου* (retroverted from Syh^{m}).

probably understanding the verb as a Qal rather than as Ni (as vocalized in MT). The second line, however, has rendered the prepositional phrase על במותימו by *ἐπὶ τὸν τράχηλον αὐτῶν*. This is an old Jewish tradition which is also reflected in all the Tar which read "on the nape of the necks of their kings."[57]

---

57. I.e. על פריקת צוארי מלכיהון (with some spelling variations in Tar[JN] on the middle two words); see also Daniel 33—34.

Chapter 34

34:1 LXX transliterates ערבת "plains, steppes" rather than translating the word, and then renders אל by ἐπί (plus accusative); this does make sense since Moses went up onto the mountain.[1] Specifically the spot is called ἐπὶ κορυφὴν Φασγά, but this is of no great help since the location is not known. It must have been a vantage point on the Abarim range from which wide stretches of Canaan could be seen.[2] In any event, it is described as being ἐπὶ προσώπου Ἰεριχώ "over against Jericho."

The Lord showed him all the land, which in MT is defined as את הגלעד עד דן. LXX disregards both preposition and article and simply has the ambiguous Γαλαὰδ ἕως Δάν. These are probably intended to designate the northern parts of the Promised Land. Galaad lay in Transjordan and Dan in the extreme north.

In the tradition, *C'' s z+* tried to clarify the position of Phasga as being κατα rather than ἐπί (the face of Jericho), but it was still over against Jericho. The various names in the verse suffered in the tradition. Ἀραβώθ became αραβωτ, αραβωβ, αρωθ and αραμωθ, whereas Ναβαύ was misspelled as ναβαν, ναβατ, νααν, βαν and it even became μωαβ. Φασγά was miscopied as βασγα, φασια, σφαγα, σφασγα, φαγαν and φας. Hex did correct Γαλαάδ by prefixing the article to represent the הגלעד of MT.

34:2 Also shown were "all the land of Nephthali and all the land of Ephraim and Manasseh and all the land of Judah up to the farthest sea (i.e. the Mediterranean Sea)." This equals MT except for "land of" before Nephthali which has no equivalent in MT. The omission of γῆς by the hex ms 58 is probably a posthexaplaric revision. As expected, Νεφθαλί is spelled with a final *mu* in most witnesses as is usual wherever this name occurs in LXX. Here along with vv.1 and 3 all the Promised Land is shown to Moses. The picture described is an ideal one; though on a clear day one can see a fair dis-

1. Aq renders the two prepositional phrases as ἀπὸ ὁμαλῶν Μωὰβ ἐπὶ ὄρος Νεβώ (retroverted in part from Syh^{m}).
2. According to Eusebius, Aq rendered הפסגה by ἡ λαξευτή, though this would hardly have been in the nominative.

tance it would not be possible to see all the area mentioned from anywhere on Mt. Nebo.

34:3 What remains is "the desert and the environs of Jericho, the city of palms, up to Segor." What is meant by *τὴν ἔρημον* is clear only from the Hebrew; it is the Negeb, the desert of south Judah. I have translated *τὰ περίχωρα* as "environs," a word used to render הככר for which see Note at Gen 13:10. As for Σήγωρ its location is unknown. It was the small city to which Lot escaped when Sodom and Gomorrah were destroyed. All that can be said is that it lay to the south, possibly near the southern end of the Dead Sea. But the location is not important; what is of consequence is that the Lord showed Moses from the site of Phasga all the Promised Land from the far north to the far south. MT identified הככר as the בקעת ירחו. LXX disregarded בקעת entirely, and so hex has supplied its equivalent as *πεδιου*.

34:4 In v.1 Moses is mentioned and then referrred to as *αὐτῷ* (the Lord showed "him"). Here MT also used a pronoun: "the Lord said to him," but LXX identifies "him" as Μωυσήν. In the relative clause modifying *γῆ*, God swore to Ἀβραὰμ *καὶ* Ἰσαὰκ *καὶ* Ἰακώβ, i.e. in a pattern of a+b+c shared by Pesh, but MT has an ab+c pattern, i.e. has no conjunction before ליצחק. That the triad is an indirect object of *ὤμοσα* is clear, but the Byz text makes this explicit by using *προς*. This is quite unnecesssary since no other interpretation is possible in the context. What the Lord said was לזרעך I will give it, but he was addressing the three patriarchs, so LXX "corrects" to *τῷ σπέρματι ὑμῶν*.

The second part of the verse in MT reads "I have made you see with your eyes, but (and) you will not cross over thither." Instead of הראיתיך LXX simply has *ἔδειξα* modified by the dative *τοῖς ὀφθαλμοῖς σου*, thus "I have shown to your eyes," i.e. I have made you see. The addition of *σοι* after *ἔδειξα* in the tradition must be hex. A majority text has added a *και* before the verb, for which there is no support in MT nor elsewhere in the old versions, and is ex par, and another such text has added *αυτην* after it, which represents a simplification of the text.[3] LXX translated the second clause by *καὶ ἐκεῖ οὐκ*

3. See THGD 123—124. Vulg also adds *eam*.

εἰσελεύσῃ. Of course, the "crossing over" of MT means entering, but LXX refers to the Jordan, whereas MT refers to the Promised Land.

34:5 It is stressed that "Moses died there" in the land of Moab. A B *b n*+ variant text omits ἐκεῖ, since this is quite unnecessary in view of ἐν γῇ Μωάβ, but the cruder Greek text is clearly original.[4] Moses is here called an οἰκέτης κυρίου. Throughout Deut the term οἰκέτης has been reserved for Israel's status of slavery in Egypt, except for 15:17 where the literal meaning of "household servant" is intended for the Hebrew servant who refuses to leave his master after his six year period of servitude. The translator, by this choice of the term, dubs Moses as the involuntary slave of the Lord, one chosen by him, even against his will, according to Exod 4. Moses' death is described as διὰ ῥήματος κυρίου, here used causally: "by the word of the Lord," LXX thereby reflecting the account to Num 27:12—14. MT has על פי יהוה.

34:6 According to MT it was Yahweh who buried Moses. That this was the original account is clear from the next clause: "no one knew his grave." This was too much for LXX, so it used a plural verb ἔθαψαν so as to avoid the direct statement that the Lord buried him by using an indefinite plural.[5] I would translate "And Moses was buried." The translator took בגי "in the valley" as a proper name, i.e. as ἐν Γαί. The name was variously spelled in the tradition: as γαιι (Byz), γαιη, γη, γαιθ and γεθ, each of which admits of a palaeographic explanation.[6] The place where Moses died is further described as being in the land of Moab near οἴκου Φογώρ. The Hebrew בית פעור only occurs three times in OT, always modifying מול, and only in Deut (also at 3:29 4:46). LXX always translates בית by οἴκου; see comment at 3:29. מול is rendered by ἐγγύς as at 4:46, whereas at 3:29 it became σύνεγγυς.

That "no one knew his grave (i.e. where he was buried) unto this day" accents the uniqueness of the Moses phenomenon, a uniqueness stressed even more by MT where it is said that the Lord buried him. An A *O f z*+ text has

4. See THGD 128.
5. As in Tar^{N} as well as in one Sam ms.
6. The Three omit ἐν Γαί entirely, which is puzzling, particularly since the note includes ο´ as also omitting the phrase. I strongly suspect the writer of the marginal note of ms 344 of making the same error as some Greek mss. Its omission in some Greek mss as well is a case of parablepsis due to homoioteleuton.

changed *ταφήν* to *τελευτην*, but this can only be the product of a careless copyist.

34:7 MT begins with a nominal clause: ומשה בן מאה ועשרים שנה במתו. The translator rendered the initial ***waw*** by a *δέ* construction, which is unusual for him. I would render the *δέ* by "Furthermore." He also translated the Hebrew idiom for one's age idiomatically by a genitive, (120) *ἐτῶν*, and using *ἦν* before it.[7] In spite of this age "his eyes had neither dimmed nor were they destroyed." MT has לא כהתה עינו ולא נס לחה "his eye had not dimmed nor had his vigor abated (literally his freshness fled)." The translator must have tried to make sense out of נסלחה, but it is not clear how he did it. He did try to make a verb out of it,[8] but how he arrived at *ἐφωάρησαν* remains a mystery. Hex added under the asterisk *τα χελυνια αυτου* "his jaws," probably taking the phrase from Theod.[9] The word לחה is from the root לחח not לחה.

34:8 The Israelites mourned for Moses בערבת מיאב according to MT. LXX took ערבת as a place name, hence *ἐν* Ἀραβὼθ Μωάβ,[10] but then adds without MT provocation *ἐπὶ τοῦ* Ἰορδάνου *κατὰ* Ἰεριχώ "at the Jordan over against Jericho." Hex has rightly placed this under the obelus signifying its omission in MT. Its source is unknown, though see v.1 and 32:49.

The traditional thirty day period of mourning for a leader is called *αἱ ἡμέραι πένθους κλαυθμοῦ* Μωυσῆ. The heaping up of synonyms is typically Hebraic: "the days of weeping, (i.e.) of mourning for Moses." The Hebrew equivalent for the synonyms is בכי אבל. Origen noted that the verb יבכו had been translated by *ἔκλαυσεν*, but the cognate noun *κλαυθμοῦ* followed *πένθους*; accordingly he transposed the two in hex.

34:9 For Ναυή see comment at 1:38. According to LXX Iesous was filled with *πνεύματος συνέσεως* "the spirit of understanding," using a passive construction to represent the stative מלא of MT. MT has רוח חכמה. *σύνεσις* only

7. Theod and Sym substituted the participle *ὤν*.
8. Aq took לחה as לחי plus suffix and translated it *σιαγὼν αὐτοῦ*; The Others also understood it in this way: *τὰ χελύνια αὐτοῦ*.
9. See THGD 119.
10. Aq translates this by *πρὸς ὁμαλὰ* Μωάβ, and Sym, by *ἐπὶ τὴν πεδιάδα τῆς* Μωάβ.

occurs six times for חכמה in OT; in the Pentateuch it also occurs at Exod 31:6 35:35 as applied to the two architects of the tent of testimony, though at 35:35 it is a gloss on *σοφίας*. On the other hand, חכמה is translated by *σοφία* 153 times (and by *φρόνησις* 12 times, and *ἐπιστημή* five times).[11] Obviously the translator has chosen this word intentionally. From its use in Exod it appears that being filled with *σύνεσις* is a special endowment, and so it must be understood there.[12] The *O+* text, obviously under the influence of The Three, reads *σοφιας*.

The nature of *σύνεσις* becomes particularly clear from the *γάρ* clause. The spirit of understanding was the result of his ordination to leadership by Moses, i.e. "Moses had placed his hands on him." As a result "the Israelites obeyed him (*εἰσήκουσαν αὐτοῦ*), and acted as the Lord had commanded Moses."

34:10 Vv.10—12 constitute an encomium or eulogy on Moses. Moses is called a prophet who was unique in Israel. As prophet he was mediator between God and Israel; for the definition of prophet see Exod 7:1—2. Only of him could it be said that the Lord knew him *πρόσωπον κατὰ πρόσωπον*. For *πρόσωπον κατὰ πρόσωπον* see 5:4, and comp Gen 32:30(31). The reference פנים אל פנים is to Exod 33:11 where the phrase is, however, rendered by *ἐνώπιος ἐνωπίῳ*, for which see see Note ad loc.

In the tradition *ἔτι προφήτης* was transposed by hex to equal the order of נביא עוד of MT, but LXX had followed the order of Sam. Note also the literalism of *ὃν κύριος ... αὐτόν*, and only one ms omitted *αυτόν* to produce a better Greek. Here too hex "corrected" the word order to *αυτον κυριος* to agree with that of MT.

34:11 This uniqueness of Moses' prophetic status was shown "by all the signs and wonders"; this is rather awkwardly followed by a *ὅν ...αὐτόν* clause, which must refer to Moses.[13] These signs and wonders are referred to within the relative clause by *αὐτά*. A translation would have to represent the

11. According to Dos Santos.
12. The Three all read *σοφίας* as might be expected.
13. The Three all render this by *ὅσα ἀπέστειλεν αὐτόν*, though Aq may have read *ἅ* rather than *ὅσα*. That *ο′ α′* read *αὐτά* is simply a mistake; the plural occurred after *ποιῆσαι*, not after *ἀπέστειλεν*.

anacoluthic structure by a dash. Thus "by all the signs and wonders—whom the Lord had sent to do these things in the land of Egypt to Pharaoh ... (12) and the great wonders ...."

34:12 The initial *καί* joins *τὰ θαυμάσια ... καὶ τὴν χεῖρα* to the *αὐτά* of v.11, i.e. these too are accusative modifiers of *ποιῆσαι*.[14] Hex has reversed these to equal MT, and has added *παντα* before *τὰ θαυμάσια* and *πασαν* before *τὴν χεῖρα* so as to represent MT exactly. *τὰ θαυμάσια* represents המורא correctly as a collective, and hence the plural. The omission of כל before היד החזקה is understandable. יד is a singular, and a כל is unexpected. So it was Moses who effected (*ἐποίησεν*) these things (i.e. signs and wonders in Egyptland) "and the great marvels and the strong hand before all Israel."

14. See also THGD 132.

APPENDIX A

Proposed changes in the critical text of Deut

1:4	For Ἐδράϊν read Ἐδράιν
1:42	For Εἰπὸν read Εἶπον
2:10	Omit (
2:12	Omit)
2:34	For ἑξῆς read ἑξῆς,
2:34	For αὐτῶν, read αὐτῶν
3:1	For Ἐδράϊν read Ἐδράιν
3:5	For σφόδρα. read σφόδρα,
3:10	For Ἐδράϊν read Ἐδράιν
3:16	For Ἀρνών· read Ἀρνὼν
3:16	For ὅριον· read ὅριον
4:3	For ἡμῶν read ὑμῶν
5:25	For τοῦτο, read τοῦτο·
5:30	For εἰπὸν read εἶπον
6:20	For ἡμῖν read ὑμῖν
7:2	For αὐτούς, read αὐτούς·
8:9	Om αὐτῆς 2°
9:22	For κύριον read κύριον τὸν θεὸν ὑμῶν
11:2	For εἴδοσαν read εἴδοσαν,
13:2	For οὓς read οἷς
13:6	For οὓς read οἷς
13:9	For ἐσχάτῳ read ἐσχάτων
13:13	For Ἐξήθοσαν read Ἐξῆλθον
13:13	For οὓς read οἷς
16:4	For πρώτῃ read πρώτῃ,
18:10	For φαρμακός read φάρμακος
19:12	For χεῖρας read χεῖρας,
20:14	For ἀποσκευῆς read ἀποσκευῆς,
22:3	For σου, read σου·

22:3	For *εὕρης˙* read *εὕρης,*
22:9	For *σπείρης* read *σπείρης,*
23:3	Om *καὶ* 3°
24:13	For *καὶ ἔσται σοι* read *καί σοι ἔσται*
28:9	For *αλὸν* read *λαὸν*
28:13	For *ὅσα* read *ὅσας*
28:62	For *εἰς πλῆθος* read *τῷ πλήθει*
29:17	For *αὐτοῖς.* read *αὐτοῖς˙*
29:18	For *ἐκείνων;* read *ἐκείνων˙*
29:18	For *πικρίᾳ;* read *πικρίᾳ˙*
30:13	For *ἀκουστὴν ἡμῖν ποιήσει αὐτήν, καί* read *ἀκούσαντες αὐτήν*
31:6	For *προπορευόμενος* read *πορευόμενος*
31:11	For *αὐτῶν˙* read *αὐτῶν,*
33:11	For *ὀσφὺν* read *ὀσφῦν*
33:21	For *γῆ ἀρχόντων,* read *γῆ, ἀρχόντων*

Appendix B: Cod A in Deut

In the text histories of the middle books of the Pentateuch[1] the A text was in each case compared with that of Codex B, but no particular study of its character was made. The point of view in each case was a comparison of the two texts in order to establish their relevance in establishing the critical text.

This essay is an attempt made to discover just what kind of text the A tradition represents. What is particularly examined is the question: Are there recensional elements in this tradition? Furthermore, could there be other recensional characteristics which are not based on fidelity to the Hebrew, but rather internal to the Greek text itself?

List 1: Unique Readings

1:1 init] pr *και*

1:19 Χωρήβ] *σοχωθ*

1:34 *καί* 1°] + *ως*

2:10 ᾿Ομμίν] *οομμειν* (*ομμειν* hab mlt): dittography

2:13 om *καὶ ἀπάρατε*: homoiot

2:15 *τοῦ θεοῦ*] *κυριου* = MT; comp *του κυριου* 426 Arm[ap]; pr *κυριου* 72

2:19 *ἐχθραίνετε*] *εκχθραινετε*

2:31 *πρὸ προσώπον σου*] *σοι*

3:19 *κτήνη* 2°] pr *τα*: *κτήνη* 1° is articulated

4:9 *συμβιβάσεις*] -*βαεις* A*(|)

4:40 *μακροήμεροι*] *μακροχρονιοι*

5:5 *τὰ ῥήματα* (*κυρίου*)] *ενωπιον*

7:13 om *καί* 5°

---

1. J.W.Wevers, Text History of the Greek Numbers, MSU XVI.Göttingen, 1982; ibid ... Greek Leviticus, MSU xix. Göttingen, 1986; ibid ... Greek Exodus, MSU XXI. Göttingen, 1992.

9:10 *γεγραμμένας*] pr *τας*

9:26 *ὑψηλῷ*] *μεγαλω*

10:18 *προσήλυτον*] *πλησιον*

11:5 *ἕως*] *ως*

11:29 Γαριζίν] *γαζιρειν*: ms 72 has *γαζιριν*

12:2 *πάντας τοὺς τόπους*] *παντα τα εθνη*

12:17 om *καί* 5°

12:19 *πάντα τὸν χρόνον ὅσον ἄν*] *οσον αν χρονον*

12:20 *ψυχῆς*] *καρδιας*

12:31 *γὰρ βδελύγματα*] tr

13:15 *μαχαίρας*] -*ρης*

13:17 *καὶ ἐλεήσει*] et *καὶ πληθύνει* tr

13:17 *σε* 2°] + *και πλησθηση*: a doublet; cf 13:17-1°

14:8 *οὐ μαρυκᾶται*] *ουκ αναμαρυκαται*

15:5 *ἀκοῇ*] *ακουη*

15:5 om *καὶ ποιεῖν* A(|): ex homoiot

15:7 *σοι*] + *εν κληρω*; ex par

16:6 *θύσεις*] -*σαι*

16:13 *ποιήσεις*] *ποιεις*

16:20 *διώξῃ*] *φυλαξη*

17:11 *ἀναγγείλωσίν*] -*λων*

17:14 *αὐτήν*] *αυτης*

18:10 *εὑρεθήσεται*] *ευρησεται*

18:11 *τερατοσκόπος*] *τερατοσκοτος*: Π-Τ

18:19 *ὁ προφήτης/ἐπὶ τῷ ὀνόματί μου*] tr

19:19 *ποιῆσαι τῷ ἀδελφῷ αὐτοῦ*] *τω πλησιον ποιησαι*

19:20 *προσθήσουσιν*] *προσθησιν* A*

20:5 *ἕτερος*] *εταιρος*: itacism

20:8 *καρδίαν*] + *αυτου και*

21:5 *στόματι*] *ονοματι*: see *ὀνόματι* in preceding phrase

22:5 om *ὅτι*

22:19 *δυνήσεται*] -*σει* A*

22:24 *τὴν πύλην*] *την πυλης*

24:1 om *καὶ δώσει*

25:9 *οἰκοδομήσει*] *οικοδομησουσιν*

25:16 om *πᾶς ποιῶν ἄδικον* A*

25:18 (*τὸν*) *θεόν*] *κυριον*

25:19 om *τῶν κύκλῳ σου* A*: homoiot

25:19 om *ἐν τῇ γῇ*

26:16 *πάντα*] pr *κατα*

26:19 *σε* 2°] *σοι* A*

28:12 *δανιεῖς*] *εκδανιεις*

28:65 *ἐκλείποντας*] -*ποντα*

28:66 *κρεμαμένη*] *κεκραμενη*; cf *κεκραμμενη* *oI*—$^{15c\ pr\ m}$

29:4 *ὦτα*] pr *τα*

29:24 *κύριος οὕτως*] tr

29:28 om *ἀπό τῆς γῆς αὐτῶν*

31:2 *καί* 3°] *η*

31:11 *ᾧ*] *ον*

32:49 *ἴδε*] *ιδετε* A*

33:9 om *καὶ τοὺς υἱοὺς αὐτοῦ* A*

33:12 om *καί* 3°

33:13 *ὡρῶν*] *ορεων*

33:28 *αὐτῷ συννεφής*] tr

From the 66 unique readings in the above list at least six are thoughtless mistakes which result in an unhellenic text (2:19 4:9 19:20 22:19,24 26:19 32:49). Similarly the omission of ἐν τῇ γῇ at 25:19 leaves a text in which ᾗ is left hanging without an antecedent. Two omissions are clearly due to homoiot (2:13 15:5), and may be discounted as textually meaningless. On the other hand, there are three instances in which the shorter text makes good sense: at 24:1 the omission of καὶ δώσει creates a zeugmatic construction which is easily understood; at 25:16 πᾶς ποιῶν ἄδικον is an explanatory phrase apposite to πᾶς ποιῶν ταῦτα, and its omission makes for a terser statement, and the deletion of "from their land" at 29:28 removes an unnecessary phrase: it is quite obvious that the Lord will drive them out (from their land).

A terser text also results from A's οσον αν χρονον at 12:19 which is a rewrite of Deut's πάντα τὸν χρόνον ὅσον ἄν; similarly a simple σοι to modify παραδοῦναι at 2:31 instead of πρὸ προσώπου σου is fully intelligible. Other omissions concern single words, three cases of καί, 7:13 12:17 33:12, and one of ὅτι, 22:5. The omission of καί at 7:13 is awkward, and those at 12:17 33:12 also result in an inferior text. The omission of ὅτι at 22:5 changes a causal clause into an independent statement which is fully meaningful.

By contrast A occasionally amplifies the text. Three times a nominal is articulated and is sensible (3:19 9:10 29:4); the reverse does not occur. At 1:34 the addition of ως changes two paratactic clauses into a temporal conditional structure. The prefixing of κατα to "all these judgments" at 26:16 changes a direct modifier of ποιῆσαι into a prepositional phrase, probably under the influence of the common collocation "to do according to." The prefixing of και at the beginning of the book is highly unusual; tying Deut to the end of Numbers could hardly have been intended. At 20:8 the addition of αυτου και after καρδίαν is a thoughtless mistake in view of the concluding ὡς ἡ αὐτοῦ; A's gloss is completely tautological. At 15:7 the addition of εν κληρω to the clause "which the Lord your God is giving to you" is textually of little consequence; it is taken ex par (cf e.g. 15:4).[2] And at 13:17 A has added και πλησθηση, which is a doublet. A had also transposed ἐλεήσει and πληθύνει, so that the resultant text reads πληθυνει σε και ελεησει σε και πλησθηση.

Nominal inflection is only seldom involved. Twice an accusative is thoughtlessly changed to a genitive (17:14 22:24), and once, 31:11, a dative

2. See list 10 in THGD 88—89.

pronoun (by case attraction to its antecedent) is "corrected" to an accusative (modifying *ἐκλέξηται*). The change in inflection at 13:15 is to an Attic form. The change in number of *ἐκλείποντας* at 28:65 may be palaeographically inspired since an omicron begins the next word, i.e. ΣΟ becomes Ο; in any event it results in a senseless text.

Verbal inflection is occasionally involved, but only seldom does it create a better reading. The change of the future *θύσεις* to the aorist infinitive at 16:6 is possible, but that of *ποιήσεις* to the present tense is not sensible at v.13, nor of a future becoming a participle at 17:11, nor change of number at 25:9. Change of voice at 18:10 and of a present participle to a perfect at 28:66, on the other hand, are fully credible.

Cod A uniquely transposes text five times (12:31 18:19 19:19 29:24 33:28), probably for stylistic reasons, though this is not always clear. Two cases of transcription of place names, 2:10 11:29, are palaeographic in origin.

Of special interest is the large number of lexical changes uniquely attested by A. A number of these is probably due to palaeographic or auditory confusion, though at times creating a fully intelligible text. Such would be *ως* for *ἕως* at 11:5, *ακουη* for *ἀκοῇ* 15:5, *τερατοσκοτος* for *τερατοσκόπος* 18:11, *εταιρος* for *ἕτερος* 20:5, *ονοματι* for *στόματι* 21:5, and *ορεων* for *ὡρῶν* at 33:13. Two instances, 14:8 28:12, involve change from a simplex to a compound verbal stem, but with no real change in meaning.

At 31:2 the change of the conjunction *και* to the correlative is stylistic: "to go in *or* to go out." At 5:5 the change of *τὰ ῥήματα* to *ενωπιον* involves substantial change: "to announce to you before (the words of) the Lord"; in the context the change is explicable.

Some changes are due to the context. This is obviously the case at 9:26 where *μεγάλῃ* occurs twice in the verse to describe *ἰσχύι*; it is of course quite wrong modifying *βραχίονί*. At 12:2 the substitution of *παντα τα εθνη* for "all the places" is conditioned by *τὰ ἔθνη* as subject of the relative clause which follows. The substitution of *πλησιον* for *προσήλυτον* at 10:18 is easily explicable as the result of the commandment "to love your neighbour"; in fact A also has the variant infinitive *αγαπαν*, reading "to love the neighbour so as to give him food and clothing." At 19:19 *πλησιον* also occurs uniquely in A as a synonym for *ἀδελφῷ*. Synonyms also occur at 4:40 with *μακροχρονιοι* for *μακροήμεροι*, and at 12:20 with *καρδιας* for *ψυχῆς* (probably for stylistic variation?). At 16:20 the vigorous figure "pursue rightly the right(*δίκαιον*)" is softened to the more common idiom "*φυλαξη* rightly ...." At 2:15 *κυριου* for (*ἡ χεὶρ*) *τοῦ θεοῦ* equals יהוה (יד) of the Hebrew. It should be mentioned that *του κυριου* is also attested in ms 426 and Arm[ap], whereas ms 72 has *κυριου του θεου*. A similar change obtains at 25:18 where A has *τον κυριον* for *τὸν θεόν*, which variant is supported by Tar.

A final change occurs at 1:19. Deut has "and departing from Χωρήβ we travelled all that great and terrible desert," but A reads the place name *σοχωθ*. Succoth was the first desert way-station (Exod 12:37 13:20 Num 33:5) for the Israelites on their way out of Egypt into the desert, and A has "corrected" the text accordingly. After all, Horeb was, as contemporaries knew only too well, a long ways into the desert from Egypt.

In the next list almost unique readings of Codex A are given, i.e. readings in which A is supported by no more than five other scattered witnesses.

List 2: Almost unique readings

2:5 *δῶ*] *δωσω* A 121

2:6 *παρ'* 1°] *απ* A 458

3:1 *τήν*] *της* A 739

3:3 *καὶ τὸν Ὤγ*] pr *αυτον* A V 121

3:10 Ἐδραΐν] -*ραειμ* A B 509

3:13 Μανασσή] *μανν*. A 121

3:14 Μανασσή] *μανν*. A 458 121

3:20 om *ὑμῶν* 1° A 82-618 767 121-527

3:21 *διαβαίνεις*] -*βεννεις*(-*ννις* A) A 509

3:28 *κατίσχυσον*] *ενισχ*. A 413

4:1 *κριμάτων*] *ρηματων* A 121: aphaereis of *kappa*

4:32 *ἄνθρωπον*] pr *τον* A 73'-414 19 Tht *Dt*

4:32 om *εἰ* 2° -- fin A 458 Tht *Dt*[ap]: homoiot

4:35 *ἔτι*] *αλος* A Marc 12 32 Bo

4:43 Ῥαμώθ] ραμμωθ A 58

4:43 Μανασσῆ] μανν. A 121

4:49 πέραν] pr ο εστιν A Eth Arm

5:3 om κύριος A ^{Lat}cod 100 Eth

5:4 om ἐν τῷ ὄρει A Arm^{ap}

5:15 φυλάσσεσθαι] φυλαξεσθαι (σε) A 963; (+ σε mlt)

6:9 οἰκιῶν] οικειων A 56 458-767* 120*-122*

6:23 ἡμᾶς ἐξήγαγεν] tr A V 29 509

7:8 om καί 1° A 19′

8:2 om ἄν A 761 121 Tht I 240

8:7 γῆν] την γ. την A 52′ W^{I}-54 59

8:11 om μή 2° A M^{txt} 29 108* Eth^{-M}

8:12 οἰκοδομήσας] ωκοδ. A 417

8:15 ἐξαγαγόντος] αγαγοντος A* 392

9:6 om σήμερον A Arab = MT

9:11 τεσσαράκοντα 1° 2°] τεσσερ. A B* F 129 W^{I} 55

9:14 καὶ ἰσχυρόν/καὶ πολύ] tr A 75

9:15 om δυσίν A F 77 ^{Lat}cod 104 Sa$^{1te\ 2\ 3\ 17}$

9:18 τεσσαράκοντα 1° 2°] τεσσερ. A B* F 129 W^{I} 55

9:28 ἐξήγαγες] -γεν A V

10:11 αὐτῶν] υμων A 121

10:12 φοβεῖσθαι] -σθε A 527 55 319*: itacism

10:20 φοβηθήσῃ] προσκυνησεις A Cyr I 413

11:5 ἤλθετε] εισηλθετε A 71′; cf εισηλθατε 417

11:10 ὑμεῖς εἰσπορεύεσθε] tr A 392 68′-83

11:10 om ἐστίν A V(|) 55 Bo

11:13 om σου 3° A 121

11:15 *τοῖς* 2°] pr *και εν* A 509

11:17 *κύριος* 2°] *ο θεος* A 616*(vid) 121 68′

11:26 *ἐνώπιον ὑμῶν σήμερον*] *σημ. εναντιον υμ.* A Arab Arm Sa

11:32 *ταῦτα*] *μου* A 767 121

12:2 om *τὰ ἔθνη* A B 630[c]

13:14 *ἐτάσεις*] *εξετ.* A G-58-376 121 55

14:5 *πύγαργον*] *πυδαργον* A 121 68′

14:7 *ἀνάγουσιν*] *αναγει* A 29: cf MT

14:23 *εὐλογήσει*] *-ση* A 426[c] Eus VI 13: itacism

15:5 *εἰσακούσητε*] *ακουσης* A 72 Bo

17:4 Ἰσραήλ] pr *τω* A 414

17:14 *ἄρχοντα*] *αρχοντας* A V 121

19:3 *φονευτῇ*] pr *τω* A 82 799 121

21:9 *κυρίου τοῦ θεοῦ σου*] *του θεου* A 121; om *σου* 528

21:9 om *σου* A 528 121

21:19 *τοῦ τόπου*] *της πολεως* A 376 19(1°) 75*(c pr m) 122*

21:22 *κρεμάσητε*] *-ση* A 44 = MT

22:2 *ἐπίστῃ*] *-στηση* A*(vid) 82-426 18 319 Cyr I 561

22:4 *ἀναστήσεις*] *ανιστησεις* A 82-376-618

22:14 *παρθένια*] pr *τα* A B

22:18 *παιδεύσουσιν*] *-σωσιν* A M 127

22:22 *ἀμφοτέρους*] pr *αμα* A 121

23:25 *ὅσον*] + *αν* A 121 68′

24:6 *ἐνεχυράσεις*] *-ρας* A F*(vid) 426 56-664* 509

24:17 *ἐνεχυράσεις*] *-ρας* A B(mg) F 707* 56 121

25:3 *τεσσαράκοντα*] *τεσσερ.* A B* F M 129 W[I]

25:19 om *σου* 2° A 799

26:3 *ἔσται*] *αν ην* A 58 509 (sed cf *αν η* pl)

26:4 *αὐτόν*] *αυτο* A 121 509

26:10 om *κύριε* A(|) 618 ^{Lat}cod 100

26:10 *ἀπέναντι*] *εναντι* A 426^{txt} 413* 120 319

27:12 *Λευί*] pr *και* A Eth = MT

28:1 om *σου* 2° A 71

28:4 *γενήματα*] *εκγονα* A 509

28:20 om *ἄν* 4° A 707 767

28:31 *ὄνος*] *οινος* A 707 343′

28:42 om *τῆς γῆς* A* 19 730*

28:44 *σύ* 1°] *σοι* A 528 30 121: itacism

28:45 *εἰσήκουσας*] *ηκουσας* A 509

28:45 *φυλάξαι*] + *σε* A 130-321

28:45 *τὰς ἐντολάς*] pr *πασας* A 318-392

28:46 om *τοῦ* A F 246 392 18 319

28:48 *ἐπαποστελεῖ*] -*στελλει* A 53

28:54 *γυναῖκα*] + *αυτου* A Eth Bo Sa^{3}

28:55 *ἂν θλίψωσίν σε οἱ ἐχθροί*] *αν* (> 29) *θλιψει σε ο εχθρος* A 29 ^{Lat}codd 100 103 = MT

29:5 *τεσσαράκοντα*] *τεσσερ*. A B* M 129 W^{I} 55

29:8 Μανασσῆ] *μαννασση* A 121

29:9 *ποιήσετε*] -*σητε* A 318 68′-120 59

30:7 om *ὁ θεός σου* A 407 Eth^{CG}

31:4 *κύριος αὐτοῖς*] tr A ^{Lat}cod 100 Bo Pal

31:14 *ἠγγίκασιν*] *εγγ*. A 343 83

31:20 om *καὶ φάγονται* A* F*(c pr m vid) 458: homoiot

32:11 *νεοσσοῖς*] *νοσσοις* A B F 56 127 55*

32:34 *οὐκ (ἰδού)*] *ουχ* A V 30 55* 509

32:38 *ἠσθίετε*] *εσθιετε* A 799 121-392*: *εσθηεται* 376

33:1 om *τῆς* A 417-529

33:29 *σοι*] *σου* A 58 509

34:1 om *ἕως Δάν* A Eth

34:2 Μανασσῆ] *μανν.* A 121 LatLib geneal 496te

Out of the 100 variants given in list 2 there are 24 which constitute omissions, of which only seven consist of more than a single lexeme. Two of these, 4:32 31:20, were probably occasioned by homoiot. The omission of *ὁ θεός σου* at 30:7 still leaves *κύριος* as subject, whereas the omissions at 5:4 28:42 compress the text sensibly. This is not the case at 12:2 where the loss of *τὰ ἔθνη* leaves the verb in the relative clause without a needed subject. The loss of *ἕως Δάν* at 34:1 describes "all the land of Nephthali" without a limit, thus an exact parallel to "and all the land of Ephraim and Manasseh" which follows.

Omission of single lexemes involves five cases of a second person genitive pronoun (3:20 11:13 21:9 25:19 28:1), probably all stylistic in nature. The addition of a genitive pronoun is attested only once, 28:54. The divine name is omitted three times: in the nominative 5:3, the genitive 21:9, and the vocative 26:10; in no case is any ambiguity created by the shorter text. In two cases, 28:46 33:1, an article is omitted, whereas articles are added five times (4:32 8:7 17:4 19:3 22:14), but this is hardly enough to constitute a tendency. The omission of *καί* at 7:8 is awkward, and could not have been intended. The *ἄν* particle is left out in a *ὅπως* clause at 8:2, and in a *ἕως* construction at 28:20, but the particle is added at 23:25 in an infinitival structure, and at 26:3 with *ην* in a relative clause. At 8:11 *μή* is omitted before *φυλάξαι*, but this does not really change the meaning, since the infinitive is dependent on a *μὴ ἐπιλάθῃ* construction. The loss of *ἐστιν* in 11:10 does not change the meaning, nor does that of an otiose *δυσίν* at 9:15. The omission of *σήμερον* at 9:6 is more significant, since it is also not represented in the Hebrew.

Occasionally the A text has a plus, but none is significant. At 3:3 *αὐτόν* is repeated before "and Og," presumably for clarity. So too the addition of ο εστιν before "beyond the Jordan" at 4:49 makes doubly clear what is already clear by itself. At 11:15 τοῖς κτήνεσίν σου is wrongly coordinated with ἐν τοῖς ἀγροῖς σου by an introductory και εν; this thoughtless error created a most peculiar text indeed. Related errors are an introductory και in 458 and an εν in 318. At 27:12 only the last of a list of six tribes has καί before it. An A variant also connects the first and second with a conjunction; MT has a conjunction before each name (except of course the first one). At 22:22 a prefixed αμα to ἀμφοτέρους is partially a dittograph, and creates a barely intelligible reading. The only other additions in the list are both in 28:45. The variants add σε as subject of the infinitive φυλάξαι and a πασας before "his commandments." Both glosses would make sense.

Nominal change is rare in the above list; only twice is a noun involved; at 17:14 ἄρχοντα appears in the plural, which is sensible, whereas at 28:55 a plural construction becomes singular in an A reading; this may be due to Hebrew influence, MT also being singular. At 3:1 an accusative τήν, referring to ὁδόν which immediately precedes it, appears as a genitive, which is not impossible but is odd.

Other nominal changes (three) all involve pronouns. A nominative σύ is put into the dative spelling at 28:44, but this is merely an itacism, and must be read as a nominative. At 26:4 the masculine αὐτόν correctly reflects its antecedent κάρταλλον; an A reading has αυτο as though the diminuitive neuter were involved (but A also reads κάρταλλον!). And at 33:29 the dative σοι modifies ὅμοιός but the variant has the genitive, which, though infrequent, is attested as early as Hippocrates.

Change in verbal inflection is much more frequent in the list. Sometimes tense is involved: at 2:5 3:21 a present tense appears as a future, but the reverse obtains at 28:48; a present infinitive is changed to the aorist at 5:15. Change in mood, i.e. from indicative to subjunctive, may simply be an itacistic spelling as at 14:23, but not so at 22:18 29:9. Augment may be involved, it being added at 8:12, but removed at 31:14 32:38. At 22:2 a second aorist becomes a first aorist (of ἐφίστημι) with change in meaning. In three cases a plural verb appears as a singular, 14:7 15:5 and 21:22. At 15:5 the change also involves the simplification of a compound. The variant at 21:22 could be due to Hebrew influence since MT also has the singular. The variant form φοβεισθε for φοβεῖσθαι at 10:12 happens to make good sense, but the infinitive is the first of four parallel infinitives, and the variant is simply due to itacism. And finally at 9:28 a third person variant for ἐξήγαγες is anticipatory of the latter part of the verse, where κύριον becomes subject and an ἐξήγαγεν actually does occur.

The list witnesses to an occasional transposition, 6:23 9:14 11:10,26 31:4, but none is due to Hebrew influence. Characteristic of Codex A throughout is the writing of the word for "forty" as τεσσερακοντα, a spelling it shares with other uncials. Its origin is uncertain, possibly an Ionic form or one created by vowel dissimilation.[3] Furthermore, A shares with 121 throughout the spelling of Manasseh as μαννασση. Other variant spellings of proper names in the list are εδραειμ at 3:10 and ραμμωθ 4:43. Occasional evidence of late development is witnessed by νοσσοις for the correct νεοσσοῖς at 32:11 (formed from νέος), the retention of the reduplicative prefix of the root ἵστημι in the future of the compound, ανιστησεις at 22:4, and the evidence of uncertainty as to the correct spiritus (lenis or asper) at 32:34, ουχ before ἰδού.

As in the case of list one, so too in this list, Codex A witnesses to a large number of lexical changes (19). One of these was probably itacistically inspired, 6:9, but the rest are not as easily explicable. At 3:28 the variant compound changes the κατ- element to εν- in κατίσχυσον, but the two seem to mean exactly the same in the context. In three cases Deut's compound is simplified: at 8:15 ἐξαγαγόντος appearing in the simplex is an error due to the occurrence of ἀγαγόντος earlier in the verse; at 26:10 εναντι for ἀπέναντι does not change the sense of the passage, and at 28:45 εἰσήκουσας in the sense of "listen to, obey (the voice of the Lord)" is much better than the simplex variant. The reverse phenomenon obtains twice: at 11:5 ἤλθετε becomes εισηλθετε to fit the modifying εἰς phrase which follows it, whereas at 13:14 εξετασεις (for ἐτάσεις) represents an attempt to intensify the verbal idea: "you shall examine carefully" for "you shall examine."

Change of pronoun is twice involved. At 10:11 for "I swore to their (αὐτῶν) fathers" the variant reads υμων, and at 11:32 "all these (ταῦτα) ordinances" becomes μου "my." Both variants are sensible in the context, though the second has a coordinate "and these judgments" which A+ change to "and its (αυτου) judgments." Two variants (or possibly three) are palaeo-

3. See Mayser I,1 § 5,1 a β as well as Thack 62f.

graphically determined. At 28:31 *οινος* for *ὄνος* is a scribal mistake; the context refers to *μόσχος* and *πρόβατα*. So too the misspelling of *πύγαργον* as *πυδαργον* at 14:5; in fact I can find no evidence for the spelling with *delta* elsewhere. Also clearly palaeographic is the substitution of *ρηματων* for *κριμάτων* at 4:1: "hear the statutes and *κριμάτων*, which I am teaching you," i.e. the initial *kappa* is elided, producing an itacistic *ρηματων*. The change of *ἐνώπιον* to the more common (in Deut) *εναντιον* at 11:26 is not surprising; the words are semantically almost perfect synonyms. The variant *ενεχυρασας* for *ἐνεχυράσεις* at 24:6,17 involves no semantic change; instead of the root *ἐνεχυράζω* that of *ἐνεχυράω* is presupposed.

The remaining variants involve completely different lexemes, though the change of *παρ'* to *απ* at 2:6 does not intend a different meaning. Interesting is the change of *ἔτι* to *αλλος* at 4:35 in the collocation *οὐκ ἔστιν ἔτι πλὴν αὐτοῦ*. The variant is stylistically clearer, and may well indicate an attempt to make this theological statement concerning Israel's God unambiguous, though the copyist was probably influenced by the NT passage. A similar urge might explain the change at 10:20 of *φοβηθήσῃ* to *προσκυνησεις* in the command "the Lord your God you shall fear and you shall serve him and cleave to him and swear by his name." Not at all clear is the impulse at 11:17 to change "Lord" to *ο θεος* in the clause "which the Lord gave to you"; the Hebrew has יהוה. The variant *της πολεως* for *τοῦ τόπου* at 21:19 is obviously due to *τῆς πόλεως* in the phrase immediately preceding it. The same kind of conditions obtains at 28:4 where *εκγονα* replaces *γενήματα*.

Most of the variants in list two are easily explicable as nonrecensional in character; many are stylistic in nature; some are simply errors, but a few remain which seem to show an intelligent change, either due to Hebrew influence, or to a desire to clarify the text.

In the next list possible Hebrew influence on the A tradition is examined. That the variant supported by Codex A equals MT is taken for granted; only if the support is in some way ambiguous is the Hebrew cited or the relevant equation stated at the end of the citation.

List 3: A variants reflecting the Hebrew

1:4 'Αμορραίων] pr *των* A F 72΄-426 *C΄΄* *b* 246 *n* *s* 370 121-392 68΄-83-120 28 55 59 319 646 Tht *Dt*

1:4 Ὤγ] pr *τον* A 426-*oI* 417 b^{-108} 246 121 18′-83-669 55 646 Tht *Dt*

1:12 *μόνος φέρειν*] tr A M 82-426-*oI* 73* 129 392 ^{Lat}cod 100 Syh

1:16 ἀδελφοῦ] + *αυτου* A F M *O''* *C''* *f* 85′-321′ 121-318-392 *z* 28 55 59 319 407 646 Arab Arm Bo Eth Syh

1:17 *ἐπιγνώσῃ*] -*σεσθε* A M 82-707 *b d* 129 *n* 85^{mg}-344^{mg} *t* 121-392 68′ 55 ^{Lat}codd 91 92 94 95 Syh

1:20 ὑμῖν] *ημιν* A 82*(vid)-426^{c}-618 551(1°) Arab Arm^{ap}

1:21 om *ὑμῖν* 1° A F M V *O''* *C''* 129-246 370 *y* z^{-630c} 55 59 319 407 646 ^{Lat}cod 100 Co Syh

1:27 ᾿Αμορραίων] pr *των* A F M 82-*oI'* 129-246 343 121-318-392 z^{-630} 55 59

1:39 init B 963(vid) 82-707-*oI f* n^{-127} y^{-121} 128-630′ 55 407′ ^{Lat}cod 100 $Sa^{2\ 17}$] pr (⋇ M 85-344; c var) *και τα παιδια υμων α ειπατε εν διαρπαγη εσεσθαι* rell

2:3 *ἐπὶ* (*βορρᾶν*)] *προς* A 72-82-*oI* *C''* *s* 71′ 18′-630′ 28 319 407 646 ^{Lat}cod 100 Syh: צפנה

2:22 *ἐποίησαν*] -*σεν* A F M 82-$oI^{x(-618txt)}$ $d^{(-44)}$ 129 $t^{(-602)}$ 121-318-392 18′-83-669 55 59 Arm Syh

2:22 *κατεκληρονόμησαν* $B^{(mg)}$963 $cI^{x(-52txt\ 414\ 422)}$ *b n s* 71' 630 28 319 407' ^{Lat}cod 100 Arm Bo] + *terram eorum* Sa; + *αυτης* $131^{(mg)}$; + *αυτους* rell

2:24 om *οὖν* A 72-426 C''^{-417} 85′-321′ 28 319 Arab

2:28 *ποσίν*] + *μου* A F M V *O''* *d* 129-246 *t* 121-318-392 z^{-630} 59 646 Arab Bo Eth Syh

2:34 *πόλεων* ^{Lat}cod 100] + *αυτων* 527 Bo; + (⋇ Syh) *αυτου* rell

3:24 om *ἐστιν* A F 963(vid) *O''* *f* 121-318-392 59 Bo Syh

3:27 Λελαξευμένου] pr *του* A F M V *O''* *b f y* z^{-120} 59 646

4:5 *κύριος*] + *ο θεος μου* A F M V *O''* *b d* f^{-246} 343-344^{c} *t y* 83 59 Arab Bo Syh

4:26 *κληρονομῆσαι* (c var) B 963 72 125 630^{c}] + *αυτην* (-*τον* 82) rell

4:35 *οὗτος*] *αυτος* A F M O''^{-29} *f* 30′-343′ *y* 55 59 407 Eth Bo

5:6 *ὁ ἐξαγαγών*] (c var) *οστις εξηγαγον* A F M $O''^{-82\ 707}$ 422 d^{-106} n^{-458} 321^{txt*}-343-344^{txt} *t* 121-318-392 55 59 407 ^{Lat}cod 100 Arab Arm Eth Sa Syh

5:21 *ὅσα* B* 376′ *b d n t* 318 ^{Lat}DidascApost V 10] > 963; pr *παντα* (*παν* 53′) rell

6:3 *σοι ᾖ*] tr A F V 58-72 *C''* *f* $s^{-30'}$ *y* 28 55 59 319 407 646 Arm

6:15 *θυμῷ*] *θυμωθη* A B* F M 82-$oI''^{-15\ 72}$ 56-129 $n^{(-767)}$ y^{-121} 319^{c} Syh = *ο′ θ′*

6:17 *τὰ* (*μαρτύρια*) B V 963 *b* 106 *n t* 407′ Arm] pr *και* rell

6:17 *μαρτύρια* B V 963 72 761 106 *n* 407′ ^{Lat}cod 100 Luc *Athan* I 6 Arm Bo] + *αυτου* rell

7:1 *κληρονομῆσαι* B 963(vid) *C''* *b n s* 28 319 407′ 646 Cyr III 77 Arm^{te}] + *αυτην* rell

8:16 *ἐκπειράσῃ*] pr *ινα* A F M V *oI'* f^{-129*} 121-318-392 *z* 59 646

8:16 (*ἐπ'*) *ἐσχάτων* (*σου*)] *εσχατω* A O^{-376}-707* 127 121: באחריתך

8:17 init] pr *και* A F M^{txt} *O''* f^{-246} 127 *t y z* 59 646 ^{Lat}cod 100 Eth Arab Co Syh

8:18 om *καί* 2° A O''^{-29} f^{-56*} *n* 121-318-392 z^{-83} 55 646 ^{Lat}PsAug *Praedest* VIII 9 Arm Co Syh

9:3 *σου* 3°] +(c var) *και εξολεθρευσει αυτους* A F M O'^{-376}-29 *f* 730 t^{-799} y^{-318} *z* 55 59 646 Arab Arm Bo Eth Sa$^{lte\ 2\ 17}$ Syh

9:5 *οὐδέ*] *και* A 71′ Procop 344 Tht *Dt*^{ap} ^{Lat}cod 104 Arab

9:16 *χωνευτόν*] pr *μοσχον* A F M V *O''* *b d f* 54´-75´-767 *t y z*$^{-630c}$ 55 59 Arab Bo Sa$^{1ap\ 13}$ Syh = *ο´ θ´ σ´*

9:16 *παρέβητε* B V 58 *n* 509 ^{Lat}codd 100 104 Arm Co Eth] + (※ G^{c}) *ταχυ* rell

9:28 *μή* 1°] + *ποτε* A F M V *O''* *d f t y z* 55 59

11:19 *διδάξετε*] + (※ G Syh) *αυτα* A B F M V *O'*-29-707 *C''*$^{-414\ 417txt}$ *b d f s t y z* 55 59 319 407 Arab Co Eth Syh

13:3 *θεός*] + (※ G 85 Syh) *υμων* A F M V *O*$^{-82}$-29-707 *C''*$^{-52'\ 417}$ *b d*$^{-106c\ 125}$ *f*$^{-129}$ 54 *s*$^{-30'}$ *t* 121-527 83 28 59* 319 ^{Lat}Aug et Cyp passim Arab Co Eth Syh

13:9 *ἁι* 1° — *ἔσονται*] *η χειρ σου εσται* A F M V *oI*$^{-58}$ *C''* *f s*$^{-85mg\ 321'mg}$ *y* 83 28 55 59 319 ^{Lat}Cyp *Fortun* 5 FirmMat *Err* XXIX 1 Arm^{ap} Sa^{1}

13:12 *πόλεων*] + (※ G) *σου* A B *O*$^{-707}$ *b d* 129 *t* 392 55 319 407 Arab Arm^{ap} Eth^{-M} Sa Syh

13:12 om *σε* A F M V *O''* *C*-761 *b f* 130-321´ 76´ *y* 128-669 55 59 319 ^{Lat}FirmMat *Err* XXIX 2 Arab Arm Bo Eth Pal Syh

14:2 om *σε* A *O'*-72 *C''*$^{-131c}$ 19 53´ 54-75´ *s* 76´ 28 319 ^{Lat}cod 100 Arm^{te} Syh

14:22 *τά* 2° B 426 *d n t* 630^{c} 55] pr *και* rell

15:7 *τῶν ἀδελφῶν* B 54´-75´ 509] > Arab; pr (※ G) *εκ* rell

16:16 om *αὐτόν* A M^{txt} *O'*$^{-(15)\ 82}$-707 *b* 129 75´ 799 *y* 18´-630´ 407 Cyr X 944 Eus VI 10 ^{Lat}cod 100 Arab Arm Eth Syh

17:10 om *σφόδρα* (sub ob G Syh) A B V 707 129 121-318 68´-630^{c}(vid) Cyr I 881 ^{Lat}cod 100 Arab Bo Eth

17:14 *ὁ θεός* 848 707 52 319] > Bo; + *σου* rell

17:15 *ὁ θεός* B 848] > Bo^{A}; + *σου* rell

17:16 *διότι*] *πλην* A F M $oI^{\prime\prime-58}$ *C''* f^{-246} 30′-85^{txt}-130-$321^{\prime txt}$-343 *y* 18-68′-83-120 59 319 646

17·17 *οὐδὲ μεταστήσεται* = MT] *ινα μη μεταστη* A F M V $oI^{\prime\prime-58}$ *C''* *f* 127 30′-85^{txt}-130-$321^{\prime txt}$-343 *y z* 59 319 646 ^{Lat}Aug *Deut* 27 Arab Arm = σ′

18:4 *τοῦ σίτου* 848 29-72 46-550′ 125 246*(vid)] + *σου* rell

18:4 *τοῦ οἴνου* 125] + *σου* rell

18:4 *ἐλαίου*] + *σου* omn

18:4 *τῶν προβάτων* 848 29 414 56*] > V; + *σου* rell

18:5 *κύριος* B 848 Cyr I 861 ^{Lat}cod 100 Arm] + *ο θεος σου* rell

18:5 *αὐτοῦ* 1° B V 848 O^{-426} 422 *b d n* 85^{mg}-321^{mg}-346^{mg} *t* 68′ 407′ ^{Lat}cod 100 Arm Co Eth] *κυριου* rell

18:7 init B 848 *C''* *b d n* 85 *t* 318 28 407′ 646 ^{Lat}cod 100 Arm Bo] pr *και* rell

18:18 *ἐκ* B V 131^{mg} *b d* 246 *n* 30′ *ῡ* 318 18′-120-630′ 407′ Cyr passim Eus VI 96 100 427 La Arab Arm Bo Eth] + *μεσου* rell

18:20 *προσέταξα* (-*ξε* 422*) B 72 $C^{\prime\prime-131c\ 551}$ *n* $s^{-30'}$ 28 407′ 646 ^{Lat}cod 100 Arm Bo] + *αυτω* (-*του* 30*) rell

18:22 om *ἐκεῖνος* (sub ob Syh^{mg}) A* F K M V $O^{\prime\prime-82}$ *d* f^{-246} 458 *t* y^{-121} 59 319 Cyr I 432 Arm Syh^{txt}

19:1 *κατακληρονομήσητε*] -*μησεις* (aut -*σης*) A F K M $O^{\prime\prime-72}$ *b d f* 54*(c pr m) 85^{mg} *t y* 68′-83-120 59 319 Arab Arm Syh

19:1 *κατοικήσητε*] -*κησης* (aut -*σεις*) A F K M *O''* *b d f* 85^{mg} *t y* 83 59 319 Arab Arm Syh

19:2 (*ὁ*) *θεός* 381-707 75 730 59] > 58; + (※ Syh) *σου* rell

19:4 *πλησίον*] + *αυτου* A B F M V *O''* *d f* W^{I} *t y z* 59 319 Arab Arm Co Eth Syh

19:5 *πλησίον*] + *αυτου* A F M V *O''* *d f t y* 83 59 319 Arm Co Eth Syh

19:6 *καρδίᾳ*] + *αυτου* A F M V *O''* *d f t y* 68′-83 59 319 Arab Arm Co Eth Syh

19:8 *ὁ θεός* 848(vid) *oI*$^{-64}$-58-72 552 *b* 799 319] > Eth; + *σου* rell

19:11 *πλησίον* B 848 *C''*$^{-131c}$ *b* *n*$^{-767}$ *s* *z*$^{-83}$ 28 407′ 646 ^{Lat}cod 100 Luc *Athan* I 7] + *αυτου* rell = *ο′ α′ θ′*

19:14 (*τοῦ*) *πλησίον*] > Arab; + *σου* A F M V *O''* *C''* *b d f n s t y z* 28 59 407′ ^{Lat}cod 100 Arm Co Eth Syh

19:14 *πατέρες*] *προτεροι* A M V 72′-82-426 129 321′^{mg}-344^{mg} 392 407′ Phil V 242 ^{Lat}cod 100 Sa Syh

19:14 *κληρονομίᾳ* B] + *σου* rell

21:2 *γερουσία* F 848(vid) 376 19′ 44-610 458 30′ 74-76′ 68] + *vestra* Eth; + *σου* rell

21:2 *κριταί* 848(vid) 30′ 407] + *vestri* Eth; + *σου* (*σοι* 68) rell

21:5 *ὁ θεός* B 848(vid) 246 71′-527 630^{c} 319 ^{Lat}cod 100] > Eth; + *σου* rell

21:13 *πατέρα*] + (※ Syh^{m}) *αυτης* A V *O*-15 19 106 *n t* 319 407 Eth Arab Co Syh Barh

21:13 *σου* 2°] *σοι* A* 46′-52′ *b* 767 343 318 319 646 Bo Eth Sa^{8} Sa^{10}(vid) Syh; cf MT לך

21:16 *τοῖς υἱοῖς* 848(vid) Phil II 220 ^{Lat}Ambr *Cain* I 13] > 343; + *αυτου* rell

21:18 *πατρός* B 381′ *C''* *b n* *s*$^{-30′}$ 28 407′ 424 Arm] + *αυτου* rell

21:18 *μητρός* B *C''* *b* *d*$^{-106}$ *n* *s*$^{-30′}$ 71′ 630^{c} 28 407′ Cyr I 509 ^{Lat}cod 100] + *αυτου* rell = *ο′ α′ θ′*

22:21 *θύρας* B 848(vid) *b* 610 *n* 68′-120 407′ ^{Lat}cod 100 Arm Bo] + (+ *του* F M 72-426-*oI* 44 53′ 18^{c}-83-630^{c} 319) *οικου* rell

22:24 *πλησίον* B *C''* *b n s* 83 28 407′ 424 ^{Lat}cod 100] + *αυτου* rell = *α′ σ′ θ′ ο′*

22:26 *πλησίον* B 848(vid) *C''* *n s* 128-630[c]-669 28 407´ [Lat]cod 100] + *αυτου* rell = α´ σ´ θ´ ο´

22:28 *βιασάμενος* B *C''* *b n s* 318 28 407´ [Lat]cod 104 Arm] *abduit* [Lat]cod 100; + *αυτην* rell

23:9 *φυλάξῃ* 848(vid) *O*-72 *f*−129 128-630´ 55 319 Arm Bo Eth Syh] pr *και* rell

23:10 *ἐξελεύσεται* V 848(vid) 72 *C''* *b n*−127 *s*−30´ 28 509 [Lat]cod 100 Hi *C Pel* I 36 Arm Bo Eth] pr *και* rell

23:15 *κυρίῳ* B 848(vid) Phil I 153] + *αυτου* rell

23:22 *σοι*] pr *εν* A B *O* 16 *b* W[I] 321´mg 18´-120-630´ 55 509 [Lat]Fulg *Ep* I 11 Spec 65 Syh = ο´ α´ θ´

24:9 *ὁ θεός* 848(vid) *C''*−52´ 53-56mg-129 458 30´-85txt-343´ 602 407] > Eth[M]; + *vester* Arab; + *σου* rell

24:19 *δέ* B 82 *C''*−73´ *b n s t* 71-527 18´-120-630´ 28 407´ Arab Arm Eth Sa] > rell

24:19 *ἀμητόν*] + *σου* A F M V *O''*−72 *b f y* 68´-83 59 319 Cyr I 565 Eus VIII 2.256 Syh

25:5 *αὐτῶν* B 848(vid) 29 [Lat]cod 100] pr *εξ* rell

25:9 *αὐτοῦ* 1° B 848 *C''* *b* W[I]-75-127-767 *s* 28 407´ [Lat]cod 100 Aug *Quaest* VT 7 Arm] *ad eum* Arab; *coram domino et* Eth−C; > Eth[C]; + *προς αυτον* rell

25:14 *ἤ* B 29-82-376-381´ *C''*−57 528 106*-107´-125 129 *n*(−75) 30'-85txt-344 *t* 28 407´ Phil III 37 290 Clem *Prot* 134 [Lat]cod 100 Arm] *και* rell

25:16 *κυρίῳ* 848 Phil III 37 [Lat]cod 100 Spec 64 Arab] + *τω θεω σου* rell

26:5 *ἀποκριθείς* B 848 630[c]] > 29-82 125 Eth; -*θησης* (-*θης* 414-528) *και* rell

26:18 *εἶπεν* B 957 *n* Eth Sa[16]] *προειπε σοι* 59; + *σοι* (*σε* 376) rell

27:3 εἰσέλθητε] -θης A M *oII*$^{(-72)}$ *C''* 56´-129 30´-85´-321^{c}-343-344^{txt} *y*$^{(-71)}$ *z* 28 55 59 319 Cyr II 665

28:7 ὁδῷ] pr *εν* A 73´ *b d n t* 71-318-527 319 646 Syh

28:32 θυγατέρες F^{b} 848(vid) 957] + *σου* rell

28:51 ἔλαιον] pr *και* A 46 53 85^{mg}-321^{c}-344^{mg}-730 ^{Lat}cod 100

28:53 κύριος 963 707 *b*$^{-19}$ ^{Lat}cod 100 Arab Arm Sa] > B 630^{c} Eth^{-C}; + *ο θεος σου* rell

28:54 ὀφθαλμῷ B 848(vid) 963^{c} 707 *C'' b n s* 71 28 509 ^{Lat}cod 100 Arm Sa] *αδελφω* 963*; + *αυτου* rell

28:54 ἀδελφόν B 848(vid) 963 707 125 *n* ^{Lat}cod 100] *οφθαλμον αυτου* 16; + *σου* 46´-52´; *αυτου* rell

28:57 καὶ τὸ τέκνον B 963 707 *C'' b n s* 28 407´ 646 ^{Lat}codd 100 103 Arm Sa] > 53´; + *αυτης* rell

29:2 τοῖς B F^{b} 848 963 707 *b n* ^{Lat}cod 100 Arm Co Eth] pr *πασιν* rell

29:9 ταύτης] + *ποιειν αυτους* A F^{b} M *O*-15´-29-58 56-129 343´ 121-318-392 *z* 59 319 Syh

29:11 καί ult B 707 *b d* 85^{mg}-344^{mg} *t* 121 *z*$^{-83\ 630}$ 407´ Bo] > rell

29:21 τὰς γεγραμμένας] *της γεγραμμενης* A F M 15´-29-58 *C'*$^{\prime(-414txt)}$ 56* *s*$^{-321mg}$ *y*$^{(-71)}$ *z* 28 59 319 646 Arm Syh

30:1 σε διασκορπίσῃ B 848 *C'' b s* 28 407´ 646] tr rell

30:1 κύριος B 848(vid) 707 129^{txt} *n* ^{Lat}cod 100 Arm Co Eth] + *ο θεος σου* rell

30:3 κύριος 2° B 848 707 *C'' n*$^{-458}$ *s* 630^{c} 28 407´ 646 ^{Lat}cod 100 Arab Sa] > *b* 458 55 Eth; + *ο θεος σου* rell

30:9 καί 2° — σου 4° B 848 707 *b n*$^{-458}$ *s*$^{-30´}$ 18´-120-630´ 28 407´ ^{Lat}cod 100 Arm Sa Eth] > 458; post *σου* 5° tr rell

30:14 αὐτὸ ποιεῖν B *C'' s*$^{-30´}$ 28 407´] tr rell

30:16 *τὰ δικαιώματα*] et *τὰς ἐντολάς* 2° tr A *O* 57*(vid) ^{Lat}cod 104 Arab Bo Syh

31:6 *ἐν ὑμῖν* B M^{mg} 848(vid) *C''*$^{-413}$ *b n* 30′-85^{mg}-343′ 407′ 646 Arm Bo] > rell

31:7 *ἡμῶν*] *αυτων* A *d n t*

31:10 *αὐτοῖς Μωυσῆς* B 58-72 125 *n*$^{-54}$ 59 ^{Lat}Luc *Athen* I 9 Arm Bo] om *αὐτοῖς* 68; tr rell

31:12 *προσήλυτον*] + *σου* A M^{mg} *O'*$^{-15}$ *d*$^{-125}$ 129-246 *t* 121-392 *z*$^{-120\ 630c}$ 319 Cyr II 673 Syh

31:21 init B M V *oI*-58-707 129 *n*$^{-127}$ 318-392 *z*$^{-18}$ 55 59 407′ ^{Lat}codd 100 103 104 Arm Eth Sa] pr (※ 56 344 Syh; c var) *και εσται οταν ευρωσιν αυτον κακα πολλα και θλιψεις* rell = α′

32:43 *ἐχθροῖς*] + *αυτου* A F M V 29-58-376′ 56 W^{I}-54′ 121 68′ Tht *Dt*^{te} Eth Sa^{4} Syh

32:47 *κληρονομῆσαι* B 848(vid) 72] *εν κληρω αυτην* 376*(c pr m); > 53′; + *αυτην* rell

33:9 *πατρί* B 707^{mg} 44-125 458 527 et mlt patr] + *αυτου* rell

33:9 *καὶ τῷ μητρί* B 72 120 et mlt patr] > 707^{txt}; + *αυτου* rell

34:7 *ἐφθάρησαν* (c var)] + (※ M 85-344-346) *τα χελυνια* (c var) *αυτου* A F M^{txt} V *O*$^{\text{⁾}-82\ 707}$ *C''* *b d f*$^{-56*}$ *s t* 71-121-527 *z* 28 59 319 407 646 Arm

A large number of instances in the above list involves plusses in which the pattern of support suggests hexaplaric origins; in fact for a few instances an asterisk is actually attested, 1:39 2:34 9:16(2°) 11:19 13:3,12(1°) 15:7 19:2 21:13(1°),16 31:21 34:7. One suspects that quite a few were the result of earlier revisions, however, especially those in which the support for the Deut text is light, such as 1:16 4:26 7:1 17:14,15 18:4(2° 3° 4°) 18:5 19:14(3°) 21:2(2°) 22:16 23:15 25:5,16 26:5,18 28:32 32:47 33:9(twice).

A large number of additions shared by A deal with a pronoun modifying a noun to represent the pronominal suffix of a noun in MT. In good

Greek style such are often omitted, since the context is fully clear without such a pronoun. Thus *πλησίον* is never accompanied by *αυτου* in Deut, but an *αυτου* is added at 19:4,5,11 22:26 as well as *σου* at 19:14(1°). Sometimes LXX simply had *κύριος* for יהוה אלהיך and the majority text including A added *ο θεος σου* at 28:53 30:1,3 or represented an omitted אלהי by adding a *ο θεος μου* at 4:5. A *μου* has been added to *ποσίν* at 2:28, and an *αυτου* to represent the third masculine suffix at 6:17(2°) 19:6 21:18(1° 2°) 28:54(1° 2°) and 32:43, or the feminine suffix *αυτης* at 28:57, or the second singular *σου* at 18:4(1°) 31:12, and after *θεός* at 19:8 21:5 24:9. An unrepresented verbal suffix is accounted for as *αυτην* at 22:28 32:47 and as *αυτω* at 18:20.

Other plusses which cod A shares and which are also supported by the usual representatives of the hex tradition are the addition of *μοσχον* before *χωνευτόν* at 9:16(1°), of *ποτε* after *μή* at 9:28 to represent פן, of *μεσου* after *ἐκ* at 18:18 for מקרב, of *οικου* after "door" at 22:21 for פתח בית, of *εν* before *σοι* at 23:22 and of *πασιν* before *τοῖς θεράπουσιν* at 29:2. Plusses longer than one word are also witnessed. At 9:3 *και εξολεθρευσει αυτους* has been added after "before your face" to equal MT, and *προς αυτον* after *ἀδελφοῦ αὐτοῦ* at 25:9. and *ποιειν αυτους* has been added after "this covenant" at 29:9. All of these additions are glosses which equal the longer text of MT; all of them are supported by the hex witnesses, and most of them may well be hex in origin.

Also listed are cases of articulation when MT has an articulated noun and LXX lacks an article; these are found at 1:4(1° 2°),27. Also found are the additions of *και* by A plus hex witnesses, thereby equalling MT's text. Instances obtain at 6:17(1°) 8:17 14:22 18:7 23:10 and 28:51. Whether these are actually hex in origin or simply stylistic improvements corrections (or ex par) cannot be determined.

There are a few instances, however, where the hex origin is not at all certain. At 8:16(1°) *ἵνα* governs both *κακώσῃ* and *ἐκπειράσῃ*, but the Hebrew repeats למען before the second verb as well. Origen would thus normally have added *ινα* from one of The Three, but the pattern of support gives no hint of such. No *O* ms nor Arm or Syh support a second particle, and the source is not fully certain. At 23:9 the protasis "should you go out of the camp against your enemies" is introduced by כי and *ἐάν* resp., but the apodosis is, as often in MT, introduced by a conjunction in the Hebrew, but not so in Greek. In fact, the introduction of a *και* at this juncture by A+ must be due to Hebrew influence. But it is precisely the major hex witnesses, *O* Arm and Syh, which witness to the original shorter text of LXX, and again the source of the revision is uncertain. At 28:7 the addition of *εν* to introduce ὁδῷ clearly reflects the בדרך of the Hebrew. Of the usual hex witnesses only Syh (perforce because it is Syriac!) testifies to a preposition, whereas it is the Byzantine tradition, *b d n t*, which supports the preposition in A. At 28:51 the situation is not clear. In the Hebrew list, דגן תירוש ויצהר, only the last noun has a conjunction before it, whereas Deut simply lists *σῖτον οἶνον ἔλαιον*. That A and a few other scattered witnesses should add *και* before the last noun is probably simply due to a copyist's sense of ordinary Greek and not due to Hebrew influence at all.

Some instances of transpositions also obtain in the above list, but none of these, 1:12 6:3 24:13 30:1(1°),9,14,16 31:10, is likely to be hex in origin, although a few cases, e.g. 30:1,14 31:10, are so strongly supported that they create the suspicion that an earlier revision may have been responsible.

But there are also a number of cases in which A+ omit text which has no counterpart in MT. Such instances can hardly be due to Origen himself, since on his own well-known testimony he marked such instances with an obelus; in fact, Deut, as well as the other books of the Pentateuch, has a large number of such obeli correctly placed to show precisely such a course of action. And yet most of the omissions in the above list are also supported by the principal hex witnesses; cf 1:21 3:24 8:18 13:12(2°) 14:2 16:16 24:19(1°) 29:11 31:6 as well as 2:24 where only 72-426 Arab of the hex group lend support to the omission. Elsewhere[4] I have suggested that such situations probably reflect earlier recensional activity which was already witnessed in the parent text which Origen reworked in his fifth column of the hexapla.

This can, however, hardly apply at 17:10 where *σφόδρα* is sub ob in G and Syh, nor is the omission attested in any *O* ms or in Arm Syh. More problematic is 18:22, where *ἐκεῖνος* is placed sub ob on the margin of Syh, but is omitted by most of the major hex witnesses.[5]

Some cases of number changes in verbs to equal MT could be evidence for recensional change. At 1:17 Moses addresses the *κριταί* of the people in

4. See especially "PreOrigen Recensional Activity in the Greek Exodus," in Festschrift Robert Hanhart, MSU XX (Göttingen 1990) 121—139.
5. That is, by all but 82 and Syh^{mg}.

the plural throughout (vv.16—18), but the Greek changes to the singular in v.17a, though reverting to the plural in 17b. The well-supported A reading has a plural for the first verb in 17a, but then changes to the singular of Deut for *κρινεῖς* and *ὑποστείλῃ*. Were the A variant actually rcensional, surely all three verbs would have been changed to the plural.

At 2:22 MT reads "as he did to the sons of Esau"; the subject is Yahweh. But Deut has *ἐποίησαν* with the Ammonites as subject (cf.20). The A correction to *εποιησεν* could be based on the Hebrew. So too at 13:9(10), where the Hebrew reads "your hand shall be (against him)," Deut has the plural *αἱ χεῖρές σου ἔσονται*. A substantially supported A reading (but without *O* or Syh support) has changed this into a singular construction. At 19:1(1° 2°) the situation is somewhat different. Moses is addressing Israel in the collective singular: "thy God, thy God, thou shalt inherit, thou shalt dwell," but Deut changes midway to the plural, i.e. the two verbs become "you shall inherit, you shall dwell." A has a popular variant for both verbs as singular; both readings are supported by all the major hex witnesses, and its origin may well be based, not on the Hebrew, but rather on a stylistic urge towards a consistent text. The reading is probably prehex. At 27:3 the Hebrew also has a text consistently singular over against Israel. In the Greek the plural obtains in two subordinate (*ὡς ἄν* and *ἡνίκα ἄν*) clauses in the middle of the verse. An A variant (well-supported, but not by any of the usual hex witnesses) changes the second one to the singular. The first also appears in the singular in 246 18′-120-630′, which alone render the verse in the singular consistently. The change could be recensional, or simply be an attempt at smoothing out the text.

Change in number for a participle is seen at 29:21. It concerns *τὰς γεγραμμένας* which modifies "the curses (of the covenant)." In MT the participle is הכתובה, i.e. feminine singular modifying "of the covenant." A popular A reading has the genitive singular in concert with the Hebrew. It could be due to Hebrew influence or simply be influenced by *τῆς διαθήκης* which immediately precedes it.

In four other cases in the above list pronouns are involved. At 1:20 Deut has "the Lord our God is giving *ὑμῖν*," for which MT has לנו. A, along with a few scattered witnesses, has *ημιν* which equals the Hebrew. But this is also a homophone of *ὑμῖν*, and need not be due to Hebrew influence at all. At

4:35 it is said of Yahweh: הוא is God; this Deut renders by οὗτος. The popular A reading αυτος is a more exact rendering of the Hebrew. At 21:13(2°) σου γυνή is an adequate translation of לך לאשה, but the A variant reading σοι γυνη is a more literal rendering. Its only group support is that of *b*, and no *O''* ms supports the variant text. And at 31:7 Deut has "sworn to our fathers to give to them." Hebrew has both pronouns in third person as does A, this time only supported by the three Byzantine families, *d n t*.

Whether the change of preposition from ἐπί to προς at 2:3 is due to the postposition *he* directive of צפנה is not certain; it is closer to the intent of the Hebrew. Also puzzling is 8:16(2°); επ εσχατω σου does reflect the singular באחריתך but Deut's plural genitive easily becomes dative singular by the loss of a final *nu*. The variant at 6:15 is somewhat complicated since the variant text θυμωθη was apparently the hex text, whereas α´ followed the θυμῷ of Deut. The Hebrew does have a noun here: אף, but the change to a verb may have occurred earlier as a stylistic change; after the participle ὀργισθείς a finite verb may well have been expected.

The change of an articulated participle to a relative clause with first person aorist verb at 5:6 equals the Hebrew, but this is not due to that fact, but rather to the parallel version of the Decalogue in Exod 20:2. At 9:5 οὐδέ joins two διά phrases, the first of which is introduced by οὐχί. A plus scattered support uses και, which literally equals the *waw* of the Hebrew, but its origins may well be stylistic. So too the change of ἤ to και at 25:14 does equal MT exactly, but the change is more likely to be merely a stylistic one. More significant are two A variants in ch.17. V.16 begins with רק; in the context of the choosing of a king who is a native son, the verse says "except that he shall not ...," but Deut has διότι which changes the sense considerably. The popular A reading has πλην which must originate with the Hebrew. The following verse continues with further instructions for the king: "Nor shall he have numerous wives, nor shall his heart turn aside"; Deut renders the second clause adequately by οὐδὲ μεταστήσεται (αὐτοῦ ἡ καρδία). A popular A tradition shows the semantic relationship between the two clauses much more clearly by ινα μη μεταστη, a tradition also reflected by σ´; the rendering probably reflects another translation of the Hebrew. And finally at 19:14(2°) the boundaries of a neighbour's property are characterized as those which גבלו ראשים "former (generations) have established." Deut interpreted the noun as *οἱ πατέρες σου* which the A variant text made into *οι προτεροι σου* (with group *b* reading *οι προτερον σου*). The variant was clearly influenced by the Hebrew. On the other hand, the identification of *αὐτοῦ* as *κυριου* at 18:5 is hardly a hex change since *O* supports the pronoun.

From this study it is clear that the A text has been influenced by the Hebrew. Much of that influence was probably based on hex, but even when that is set aside a few cases in list three, as well as in lists one and two, remain in which non-hex revision explicable as due to Hebrew influence do remain.

If the A text represents recensional activity which is somewhat colored by Hebrew influence it might not be amiss to investigate other tendencies characterizing the A text.

From the first two lists one such tendency which might be of interest was the expansionary trend which the A text seemed to show. In list 4 such plusses which are not based on the Hebrew are given.

List 4: Plusses in the A text

1:8 Ἰσαάκ B* 72-381′ *b* 44′-125 53′ 458 85 71′-527 28] pr *τω* rell

1:8 Ἰακώβ B* 72-381′ *b* 44-125 53′ 458 85 799 71′-527 630^{c} 28] pr *τω* rell

1:27 *χεῖρας*] pr *τας* A F M 29-82-707-*oI* 129-246 121-318-392 z^{-630} 55

2:5 *τῷ* (Ἠσαύ) 82 *b* 53′-56 *n* 71′-527 Arm Eth] *των υιων* 376; *τοις υιοις* rell

2:6 *βρώματα*] pr *αργυριου* A F V 29-72-707^{c} *C′′* *s* 121 68′-83-120 28 59 319 646; + *αργυριου* B *b* f^{-129} 630 407′

2:12 *πρότερον* B* 426 *b d t* 71′-527] pr *το* rell

2:14 *γενεά*] pr *η* A M V O'^{-426}-707 52′552 *b d f n t* 121-318-392 68′-83-120 55 509

2:15 *ἐξαναλῶσαι*] pr *του* A F M V 963(vid) O''^{-376} 129-246 121-318-392 z^{-630} 55 59 646

3:1 *αὐτοῦ*] + *μετ αυτου* A F M V 82-*oI′* C''^{-77} 417 422 761txt 129-246 30′ 121-318-392 83-128-669 55 59 319 424: ex par

3:6 *γυναῖκας*] + *αυτων* A F M 82-*oI′* *C′′* *f s* 121-318-392 z^{-630} 28 55 59 319 646 Arab Co Eth

3:12 *ὄρους* B* V 106-125 54′-75′-767 *t*] *του* 417^{txt}; pr *του* rell

3:17 *Μαχανάραθ*] pr *απο* A F M V 82-*oI*′$^{-58}$ *C*′ *b f*$^{-56*}$ *s t* 121-318-392 68′-83-120 28 55 59 319 646 ^{Lat}cod 100 Arab Arm Co Eth^{G} Syh

3:21 *κύριος* 2° 376′ *b*$^{-19}$ 44 *n* 71′-527 ^{Lat}cod 100 Arm Co Eth Syh] > 381′; + *ο θεος ημων* (*υμων* 29-82-707; > 72 *d*$^{-44}$ *t*; rell

4:5 *οὕτως*] + *υμας* A F M V 82-*oI*′$^{-29}$ *f* 30 *y z* 55 59 646 Arab

4:7 *αὐτῷ*] pr *εν* A 618 *b d*$^{-125}$ *t* Arm^{ap}

4:20 *ὁ θεός* B 963 *C*′′ *b n s* 28 319 407′ ^{Lat}cod 100 Spec 44 Arm Bo Sa^{1}] *dominus* Arab Eth Sa^{17}; pr *κυριος* rell

4:27 *τοῖς* 2°] pr *πασιν* A B^{c1} *C*-414-422 *b* 56^{c1} *s* 71′-527 28 509 Bo Eth^{C}

4:29 *καὶ εὑρήσετε* (c var) B 963 53′ *n* 343′ 407′ Arm^{te}] > 30′; + *αυτον* rell

4:45 *ἐξελθόντων* B 58-707 *C*′′ *s* 392 28 319 407′ Arab Arm] pr *εν τη ερημω* 963 rell

5:32 *ἐνετείλατο* 963 376′-707 321 799 527 509 Syh] + *mihi* Eth; + *σοι* rell

5:32 *ἀριστερά*] pr *εις* (+ *τα* 72) A B F M *oI*-58-72 55 59 319 mlt lat patr Arm Bo

6:12 *μή*] + (c var) *πλατυνθη η καρδια σου και* A F M V 82-*oI*′ 131^{mg} *f* 54-75′ *y z* 55 59 407 646 Pal: ex 11:16

6:13 *αὐτῷ*] + *μονω* A F^{a} V 963 376-*oI*$^{-15}$ *C*′′ *b d f*$^{-56*}$ *n s t* 71′-121-527 68′-83-120$_{c}$ 28 319 424 646 Matth 4$_{10}$ Luc 4$_{8}$ Chr II 738 XI 212 Cyr passim Eus VIII 2.216 Tht *Dt* La Arm^{te} Co Syh

6:13 *τῷ* B* 963 376 551* *b* 767 730 Phil I 159 Cyr II 1124 Tht *Dt*^{te} ^{Lat}cod 100 Aug *Deut* 12 Spec 44; pr *εν* Tht *Dt*^{ap} Eth = MT; pr *επι* rell

6:15 *ἐξολεθρεύσῃ*] pr *και* A F F^{b} M *O*′′ 52 *d f n t y*$^{-121}$ 83 59 ^{Lat}cod 100 Arab Co Eth Syh

6:17 *θεοῦ* 963 376] *αυτου* 72; + *vestri* ^{Lat}cod 100 Arab = MT; + *σου* rell

6:23 *ἐξήγαγεν*] + *κυριος ο θεος ημων* A F M V 82-*oI*′ 56′-129 *y z* 55 59 Pal

6:23 ὤμοσεν] + *κυριος ο θεος ημων* A F M 82-*oI*$^{\prime\text{-}72}$ *f y z* 55 59 Pal

6:24 *πάντα τὰ δικαιώματα ταῦτα*] (c var) *πασας τας εντολας και τα κριματα* A F M 82-*oII*$^{-707}$ *C''* 56´-129 30´-85^{txt}-130-321´^{txt}-343´ *y*$^{-318}$ 28 55 59 319 646: ex par

7:8 *ἐν* 1°] pr *εκειθεν* A F V 82-*oII*$^{-707}$ *f*$^{-129}$ 127 121 59 407

7:15 *κύριος* B^{txt} *O*$^{-82}$ *b d n t* 55 ^{Lat}codd 91 92 94—96 100 Arab Arm Eth Pal Sa Syh] + *ο θεος σου* (> B^{mg} M 72´-82-618 129 318 Bo) rell

8:1 *γῆν*] + *την* (> 527 83) *αγαθην* A F M V *oI*$^{\prime\text{-}72}$ *C'' f* 85´-321´ *y z* 28 55 59 319 646: ex par

8:19 *σήμερον* B^{txt} G-376 W^{I}-127-767 392 ^{Lat}cod 100 Arab Syh] + *τον τε*(> *C''* 85´-321´-343 28 319 509 646) *ουρανον και την γην* rell

9:1 *κληρονομῆσαι*] pr *και* A *O*-58 *b d* 129 *n t* 121 509 Syh

9:11 *τεσσαράκοντα νυκτῶν*] pr *δια* A F M V G-29-b58-426 *C''*$^{-552\ 739}$ *b f*$^{-129}$ *n*$^{-54\ 75}$ *s t* 121-392 *z* 28 319 509 646 Syh: cf *τεσσαράκοντα* 1°

9:11 *διαθήκης*] pr *της* A 552 71´-121 *z*$^{-83\ 630c}$ Arab Bo

9:12 *κατάβηθι* B M *O''*$^{-58\ 376}$ *f*$^{-246*}$ *n* 121-392 59 Cyr IV 93 Arm Bo Syh] > 85´-321´ 28 Eth^{M}; pr *και* rell

9:18 *παροξῦναι*] pr *του* A F M *O'*$^{(-72)}$ 56´-129 *y z* 55 59

9:19 *ἐξολεθρεῦσαι*] pr *του* A F M *O'*$^{(-72)}$ 56´-129 *y z* 55 59

9:21 *καταλέσας*] *και κατηλεσα* A F 129 *t*$^{-602}$ 120: sed mlt *και κατηλεσα* hab

9:22 *κύριον* B 58 ^{Lat}codd 100 104(vid) Arab] + (c var) *τον θεον υμων* rell

9:23 *δίδωμι*] pr *εγω* A M *oI C''*$^{-528}$ *d s t* 71´-527 *z* 28 55 319 407´ 646 Bo

9:28 *μισῆσαι*] + *κυριον* A F M V *O''*$^{-72}$ 108^{mg} *d f* 54-75´ 130^{mg}-321´^{mg} *t y z*$^{-630c}$ 55 59 Sa

10:20 *αὐτῷ*] + *μονω* A 707^{mg} *C'' d f*$^{-56*}$ W^{I}-127-767 *s t* 619 28 319 424 624 Phil II 294^{ap} Cyr I 413 PsClem 143 ^{Lat}cod 100 Aug passim Eth Sa

10:20 *τῷ*] pr *επι* A F M *oI' b f*$^{-56*}$ 30´ *ὑ* 68´-83 55 59 Pal

10:22 *ἑβδομήκοντα*] + (+ *και ol* 83) *πεντε* A F V 376-*ol'* 131c *f* 75´-127 *s* 121-392 18-68´-83-120-669c 28 55 59 407 646mg Latcod 100 Bo: ex Gen 46:27; = *ο´*

11:4 *κύριος*] + *ο θεος* A F M V *ol'*–72 *f y*–527 *z* 55 407

11:12 *συντελείας*] pr *της* A F M V *ol*-58-72 77-414-529-761 610 *f*–129 458 121 18´-120-630´ 59 407 646

11:32 *ποιεῖν* 963 *O*-72 *b* 56* *n* 602 318 18´-630´ 407´] pr *του* (*τουτο* 799) rell

12:1 *ποιεῖν* (aut *ποιησαι*] pr *του* A B F M V *ol' f s y z* 28 55 59 Cyr I 417

12:18 *καὶ ὁ προσήλυτος*] pr (c var) *και ο λευιτης* A F M V 82-*ol'*–72 *b f y z*-18 55 59 Cyr I 880: ex par; cf *και ο λευιτης d t* Arab = MT

12:25 *σέ* (*σου* 458 La) B G-426-707txt *b d* 129 *n t* 392 407´ verss] + *εις τον* (> *ol'*–15) *αιωνα* rell

13:4 *ἀκούσεσθε*] pr (c var) *και αυτω δουλευσετε* A F M V 29-58 *C''*(–422) *b f*129 *s* 121-527 *z* 28 55 59 319 Arab: ex par

13:17 *ὅν*] pr (c var) *καθως ελαλησεν σοι* A F M V 29-58-72-82-707txt-*ol f*56txt *y*–71´ 55 59

14:28 *ἔργοις* B 52 129 WI-127-458 318 Armap] +(※ G) *των χειρων σου O*-58 *b d t* Syh: cf MT; + *σου* rell

15:8 *καθ'*] pr *και* A F M *ol'*–15 707 *C'' f* 85´-321´-730 121 83 28 55 59 319 646 Cyr I 568

15:10 *ἐπιδέηται*] + *σου* A F M V *ol*(–58) 422 *f y z*–630c 55 59 Cyr I 568

15:11 *γῆς* 1° B *O n* 30´-343 18´-120-630´ 407´ Latcod 100 Arab Bo Syh] + *σου* rell

16:6 *ἐξ*] *εκ γης* A F M V *O'*–82-707 *C'' b f s* 799 *y* 83 28 319 646 Eus VI 14 Latcod 100 Co Syh

16:15 *ἐάν* B *O*–82 *b d n*–127 *t* 509 Latcod 100 Arab Arm Co Syh] pr (c var) *επικληθηναι το ονομα αυτου εκει* rell: ex par

17:5 *ἐκείνην*] + (c var) *οιτινες εποιησαν το πραγμα το πονηρον τουτο επι την πυλην* A F M V *oI*$^{\prime-58}$ ^{72} *C*'' *b f s y z* 55 59 319 646 Bo^{B}

17:16 *πληθύνῃ*] pr *μη* omn (ex *μή* 1°)

18:10 *κληδονιζόμενος* B 72 *C*'' W^{I} *s*$^{-343}$ 28 407′ 646 Cyr III 464 X 724 ^{Lat}cod 100 Bo] pr *και* rell

18:19 *ἄνθρωπος*] + *εκεινος* A F M V *oI*' *f* 30′ *y* 18-68′-83 59 319 Cyr VII 105 730 VIII 688

19:8 *πᾶσαν* 848 *oII*$^{-707}$ *n* ^{Lat}cod 100] *κυριος* 707; > Arab; pr *κυριος* (+ *ο θεος* V) rell

19:15 *κατὰ ἀνθρώπου* 848(vid) 58] + *μαρτυρησαι* 82; pr (÷ Syh) *μαρτυρησαι* rell

19:21 fin B^{txt} F V *O*-29-707^{txt} 129 *n*$^{-127}$ 318-392 630^{c}(vid) ^{Lat}cod 100 Arab Arm Eth Sa Syh] + (c var) *καθοτι αν δω μωμον τω πλησιον ουτως δωσετε αυτω* rell: ex Lev 24:20

20:4 *διασῶσαι* B 848(vid) *s*$^{-30'}$ 28 407′ Cyr I 369 ^{Lat}cod 100 Arm] pr *και* rell

20:20 *ξύλον* B 848(vid) *O n* 30′ 630^{c} 407′] *το εν τω αγρω* 44; pr *το* rell

21:8 *κύριε* B 848 58 ^{Lat}cod 100 Arab Arm] pr *εκ γης αιγυπτου* 121 68′-83; *εκ γης αιγυπτου* 29 W^{I}-127-767 Cyr II 349 645 Sa^{10}; + (÷ Syh) *εκ γης αιγυπτου* rell

22:2 *αὐτῷ* B 848(vid) *b d*$^{-106}$ W^{I}-127-767 30′-344* 630^{c} 509 La Arm Eth] *αυτα* 71′; *αυτα αυτο* 54*-75*; + *αυτα* 376^{c}-*oI* 75^{c} 799 318; pr *αυτα* rell

22:21 Ἰσραήλ 848(vid) 58-426 ^{Lat}cod 100] *υιοις* 129^{txt}; pr (sub ob Syh) *υιοις* rell

22:22 *ἄνδρα*] pr *τε* A M 707 129 W^{I}-127 *y*$^{-318}$ 68′

23:14 *παραδοῦναι*] + *σοι* A M *oI*-58-707 129 54-75′ *y*$^{-318}$ 55 319

23:17 *τελισκόμενος*] + (c var) *προς πασαν ευχην* A M 707^{mg} *C''* *b* 56 *s*$^{-130}$ 71-121^{mg} 18-68′-83 28 407′ 424: ex v.18

24:19 *τῷ* 3° B 848(vid) 426 630^{c} 407′ ^{Lat}cod 100 Eth] + *πτωχω και* 82; pr (+ *και* 527) *τω πτωχω* (+ *σου* 527) *και* (> 44-125) rell: ex par

25:11 *ἄνθρωποι*] + *δυο* A B^{mg} 707^{c} *C''* *d s t* 121 28 646 Arab Co Eth

26:2 *σοι*] + *εν κληρω* A F M V *oI*$^{'-707}$ 131^{c} *f*$^{-129}$ 121 *z*$^{-630c}$ 59 319 ^{Lat}cod 100 Co: ex par

26:8 *βραχίονι* B V 72 16-46′-52 *b d*$^{(-125)}$ 53′ *n t* 71-121-318 68′ 319 Arm Bo Sa^{3}] + *αυτου* (*αυτω* 376*) rell

26:8 *ὑψηλῷ* B V 72′ 16-46′-52-529* *b d*$^{(-125)}$ 53′ *n t* 71-121-318 *z*$^{-83}$ 319 Arm Bo Sa^{3}] pr *τω* rell

26:10 *προσκυνήσεις* B 58 ^{Lat}cod 100 Eth] + *εκει* rell

26:12 *τῶν γενημάτων* B 848 58-72 630^{c} ^{Lat}cod 100] *omnis terrae* Eth^{M}; *terrae* Arm; + (+ *σου και* 664* 18′-68′-120-630*-669) *της γης* rell: ex par

27:7 *καί* 2°] pr *κυριω τω θεω σου* A F^{a} 963 *C''* *b d*$^{-44}$ W^{I}-127-767 *s*$^{-30\ 321*}$ *t* 28 55 407′ Arab Arm Co

27:9 *οἱ* 2°] pr *και* A 414-528 *d n*$^{-54}$ *t*$^{-370}$ 83-120 Arm Sa

27:15 *θήσει* 848(vid) 58 ^{Lat}cod 100 Eth] + *αυτα* 72^{c1} 121 68′-83; *εν αυτω* 343*; + *αυτου* 319; + *αυτο* (aut *αυτω*) rell

27:26 *ποιῆσαι* (aut *ποιειν*) B V 848(vid) 29-58-707 *C'*$^{-16\ 73'}$-414′-422 106 54-75-767 *t*$^{-799*}$ 121 *z*$^{-83}$ 319 407] > 381′-44-107*-125-610; pr *του* Gal 3 10 rell

28:1 *καὶ ἔσται* B 848 426 *b* ^{Lat}cod 100 Arm] > 106^{c} Arab; om *ἔσται* Eth; + (c var) *ως αν διαβητε τον ιορδανην εις την γην ην κυριος ο θεος υμων διδωσιν υμιν* rell: ex par: cf 27:2

28:2 *ἐάν* 848(vid) 963 58-82 *n*$^{-127}$ ^{Lat}cod 104 Arm Eth Sa] (+ *δε* 376) *ακοη* rell: ex v.1

28:7 *παραδῴη* F^{b} 848] + *σοι* 77 343΄ 646; -*δω* (aut *δωσει* aut -*δῴη*) *σοι* A M 58-376-*oI* $C''^{-414\ 761*}$ 127 85^{txt}-130-321-343΄ 121-318 68΄-83 28 55 646 Sa

28:9 *κύριος* B 848(vid) 963 *O*-707 *n* y^{-121} Tht *Dt* ^{Lat}codd 100 104 Eth^{-CG} Sa Syh] *ο θεος σου* 53 319; > V; + *λαον* 458; + *ο θεος σου* (> 18) rell

28:54 *κόλπῳ* B 963 58-707 f^{-246} 318-392 59] > d^{-106} Arab; pr *τω* rell

28:56 *τρυφερά* B 963 O^{-82} *n* Chr II 892 ^{Lat}cod 103 Eth Sa Syh] + *σφοδρα* rell: ex v.54

28:57 *ᾗ*] + *αν* A *C''* 127*(vid) *s* 28 407 646

28:57 *ταῖς* B 848(vid) 963(vid) *O*-707 *b* 106 n^{-127*} *t* 630^{c} Co Eth Syh] pr *πασαις* rell: ex v.55

28:61 *γεγραμμένην* B^{txt} M^{txt} 848 963 *O''* 16-46΄-52΄ 314 610 53΄-129 *n* 318-392΄ 18-83 55 59 319 407 ^{Lat}cod 100 Arm Eth Sa Syh] + (c var) *και πασαν την γεγραμμενην* rell

28:63 *εἰσπορεύεσθε* 500 Arm Co Eth] -*ρευη* B; -*ρευει* 707 55; *πορ.* F^{b} 18-630^{c}; -*ησθε* 71; pr *υμεις* rell

28:68 *ἐν* 2° B Eth^{M}] *και* 426; pr *και* F^{b} rell

29:3 fin B^{txt} 848 963 O^{-82} 129 *n* 318-392 120-128-630΄ ^{Lat}cod 100 Arab Sa Syh] + (c var) *την χειρα την κραταιαν και τον βραχιονα τον υψηλον* rell: ex par

29:11 init] pr *και* A M $oI^{(-58)}$ *f* 799 *y* 68΄-83 59 Arm Bo Eth

29:23 *ὀργῇ*] + *αυτου* A F M O''^{-707} 131^{c} 129 343΄ *y* z^{-630c} 59 319 646 Syh

30:10 *φυλάσσεσθαι* B 848 58] *και ποιεις* 125; -*σσειν* Phil III 287; + (÷ G Syh) *και ποιειν* rell: ex par

30:10 *τάς* 1° 848(vid) 58 125 Sa^{3}] pr (÷ Syh) *πασας* rell: ex par

30:16 *ταῖς* 848(vid) 426 71 Arab Arm^{te}] pr (÷ G Syh^{m}) *πασαις* rell

30:16 *φυλάσσεσθαι* (aut *φυλασσειν*)] pr *και* A F M V $O'^{,-707}$ C'' 125-106 $f^{-56txt)}$ *s t* $y^{(-71)}$ 18-68´-83-122 28 55 59 646 Arab Co Eth Syh

30:18 *γῆς* B 426-oII^{-29} 129 *n* 392 ^{Lat}codd 100 104 Arab Arm Eth] + (c var; ÷ G Syh^{m}) *ης κυριος ο θεος σου διδωσιν σοι* rell: ex par

31:8 *συμπορευόμενος* B 963(vid) *oI*-72´ *b* f^{-129} n^{-767} 30´-85 83-630^{c} 55 59 407´ Cyr II 673 ^{Lat}cod 100 Arm Co] > 125; + *σου* 121 68´; + *σοι* rell

31:9 *τά*] pr *παντα* A F M V $oI^{,-707}$ C'' *f* 30´ y^{-318} z^{-630c} 319 509 646 Arm Bo

31:15 *νεφέλῃ* B$^{(c)}$ 848 *b* W^{I}-54´-75 630^{c} 407´ ^{Lat}codd 100 103 Sa] -*λης* 413*; *στυλω νεφελης* rell

31:20 fin B 376´-707 $d^{(-125)}$ 129 n^{-127} *t* 318-392 630^{c} 59 407´ ^{Lat}codd 100 103 Eth Sa Syh] + *την διεθεμην αυτοις* rell: ex v.16

31:21 *ἀπό* B 848 963 426 19 53´ n^{-127} 799 71 59 ^{Lat}codd 100 103 Sa Syh] *επι* 376; pr (c var) *απο στοματος αυτων και* rell: ex par

31:21 *ποιοῦσιν*] + *μοι* A *b* 121 68´

31:23 *ἐνετείλατο* B 963 *O b* ^{Lat}codd 100 103 Arab Sa Syh] + *μωυσης* rell

31:23 *καί* 2° B V 963 58-707 ^{Lat}codd 100 103 Eth] pr (c var) *υιω ναυη* rell

31:23 *εἶπεν* B V 963 58 *n* 71 59 508 ^{Lat}codd 100 103 104 111 Arm Sa] + *αυτω* (*αυτων* 246) rell

31:30 *ἐκκλησίας* B F V *oI*-29-707 $C'^{,-16\ 52'\ 414}$ *b* d^{-106} f^{-129} *n* s^{-344mg} *t* 318-392 128-630^{c}-669-669^{I} 55 59] pr *της* rell

32:17 *πρόσφατοι*] pr *και* A M V $O'^{,-426}$ $C'^{,-615}$ *b d* f^{-56} $n^{-54\ 75}$ *s t y z* 28 55 59 319 407´ 646 Arab Arm Eth Sa

32:30 *κύριος* B F 426 W^{I} 30´ 55* Sev 515] *ο θεος* 46´-52´ 314 ^{Lat}Cant^{Verec} Eth; > 125; pr *ο* F^{b} rell

32:44 Μωυσῆς 2°] + *προς τον λαον* A F M V 82-$oI^{,-707}$ *f y z* 55 319 646 ^{Lat}cod 100 Arm Bo

33:6 *καί* 2°] *συμεων* V; + *συμεων* A M 82 *b* f^{-129} 127 121 68-122$^{c\ pr\ m}$

33:7 φωνῆς] pr της A O'–376 W[L]-127 30′-130-343-344[mg]-346[mg] 83 59

33:17 γῆς] pr της A F 72-381′ 414 *b d* 53 767 392 83 55 319 Chr I 80 Iust *Dial* XCI 1s

33:19 θύσετε] + εκει A 246 *z* 646

34:12 τὴν χεῖρα B 963 72′ C'᾽–(16) 615 *b n s* 318 28 55 59 407′ [Lat]cod 100 Arab Arm Co Eth] πασαν 53′; pr πασαν rell

Many of the plusses in the above list are stylistic in nature. Thus there are 16 cases of articulation[6] of nominals: of Ἰσαάκ, Ἰακώβ, χεῖρας, πρότερον, γενεά, ὄρους, διαθήκης, συντελείας, ξύλον, ἄνδρα, ὑψηλῷ, κόλπῳ, ἐκκλησίας, κύριος, φωνῆς and γῆς. The only oddity is the articulation of κύριος at 32:30; it probably came in under the influence of ὁ θεός, the subject of the preceding stich. That these cases of articulation are insignificant is clear from the fact that an articulated nominal is left unarticulated in 18 other cases in the A+ tradition. Of more importance is the trend towards articulation of infinitives (six cases): ἐξαναλῶσαι, παροξῦναι, ἐξολεθρεῦσαι, ποιεῖν (bis) and ποιῆσαι, since an article is never omitted by A+ before an infinitive in Deut.

The conjunction καί[7] is added 11 times and results in coordinate adjectives, nouns, prepositional phrases, infinitives, participles, imperatives, and clauses. In one case, 15:8, και is added before καθ' ὅσον and is probably palaeographically inspired. By contrast και is omitted by A+ only four times, 9:23 15:17 19:9 21:19.

Prepositions[8] are occasionally added, απο 3:17, εν 4:7, εις 5:32, επι 6:13 10:20, and δια 9:11. Omissions are attested only for εν at 10:21 24:16 28:48 and for εις 11:29 29:13.

Pronouns[9] are sometimes added; most common are genitive pronouns: 3:6 6:17 14:28 15:10,11 26:8 29:23, whereas an omission (of σου) occurs three times, 9:6 18:9 23:14. The dative is occasionally added to make explicit what is already implicit, 5:32 23:14 28:7 31:8,21,23, whereas σοι is omitted

6. For problems on articulation in Deut cf THGD, Ch.7, Sect.C.
7. Cf *ibid*, Sect K.
8. Cf *ibid*, Sect G.
9. Cf *ibid*, Sect D and E.

at 21:10 28:23. Direct modifiers (accusatives) are added at 4:5,29 22:2 27:15, but omitted at 24:21, and nominative pronouns to emphasize a verbal inflection occur at 9:23 28:63, and a demonstrative is added at 18:19 (but omitted at 14:7). The only other omissions of pronouns by A+ are of *τις* at 1:31, of *σε* at 29:12 and of *αὐτήν* at 31:19.

An expansionist tendency[10] in A+ is particularly evident with respect to the divine name. Thus *κύριος* is expanded to include "our God" at 3:21, "thy God" 7:15 28:9, and "God" at 11:4; *κυριος* is added before *ὁ θεός* at 4:20, or is added as subject at 19:8, but as *κυριος ο θεος ημων* twice at 6:23, or as *κυριον* the accusative subject of an infinitive at 9:28. At 9:22 *κύριον* is expanded to include "our God" as well. At 27:7 *κυριω τω θεω σου* is added as a modifier to *θύσεις*, and one might well also compare 30:18 where *γῆς* is amplified by a relative clause *ην κυριος ο θεος σου διδωσιν σοι*.

Another favored form of expansion in A+ is the word for "all." It was added before *τοῖς ἔθνεσιν* at 4:27, *ταῖς πόλεσίν σου* 28:57, *τὰς ἐντολάς* 30:10, *ταῖς ὁδοῖς* 30:16, *τὰ ῥήματα* 31:9 and *τὴν χεῖρα* at 34:12. On two occasions a proper name is identified is being "(the) sons of," Esau at 2:5, and Israel at 22:21. Twice *αὐτῷ* is defined as *μονω*, at 6:13 and 10:20, both in "him (only) shall you serve," and twice the adverb *εκει* is added to a verb, to *προσκυνήσεις* 26:10 and to *θύσετε* 33:19; cf also *εκειθεν* which is added after *ἐξήγαγεν κύριος ὑμᾶς* at 7:8. Two cases involve the addition of a proper noun to specify the unnamed subject, of *μωυσης* at 31:23 and *συμεων* for the second stich of 33:6; the latter is interesting in that the Deut text has "Reuben" as subject of the two stichs.

Most of the remaining glosses of individual words make explicit what is already implicit, such as *αργυριου* at 2:6 in "(for money) you shall buy food," of *εκ γης* for *ἐξ* in "from (the land of) Egypt" 16:6, of *μη* before *πληθύνῃ* 17:16, of *μαρτυρησαι* at 19:15 to show what *μάρτυς εἷς* did against a person, of *δυο* to describe men (fighting together) at 25:11, of *σφοδρα* at 28:56, or of *στυλω νεφελης* at 31:15 for "(descending in) a cloud." At 28:2 A+ added *ακοη* before *ἀκούσῃς* to intensify the verbal action, and at v.57 the *ἣ* clause is amplified by the grammatical particle *αν* on the analogy of *ὃ ἂν τέκῃ* earlier in the verse.

10. For many of the plusses discussed below cf *ibid*, Sect.H.

Quite a number of larger plusses are clearly explicative and serve to expand on or to clarify the text. Such are *μετ αυτου* at 3:1, of *εν τη ερημω* at 4:45 defining where Moses addressed the Israelites, the description of the promised land as *την αγαθην* in 8:1, of *εις τον αιωνα* to modify "that it may be well to you and your sons after you" at 12:25, of *καθως ελαλησεν σοι* at 13:17, or of "whoever did this evil matter at the gate" to describe the man or woman who is to be stoned at 17:5. So too at 21:8 of "from the land of Egypt" to elucidate *ἐλυτρώσω*, of *προς πασαν ευχην* to define the *τελισκόμενος* at 23:17, and of *της γης* to specify the produce at 26:12. Greater exactness is promoted at 28:61 by adding *και πασαν την γεγραμμενον* to the plagues "not written" in the book of the law, or of *την χειρα την κραταιαν και τον βραχιονα τον υψηλον* after "signs and those great wonders" at 29:3. Details are added in the spirit of the text at 31:20 of *ην διεθεμην αυτοις* to define "my covenant," of *υιω ναυη* at 31:23 as patronymic for Ἰησοῦ, and at 32:44 of *προς τον λαον* after "Moses went in." Some plusses are obviously ex par in origin: cf the cases at 16:15, 19:21, 26:2 and 28:1. A number of expansions appear to be doublets as those at 6:24, 12:18, 13:4, 24:19, 30:10 and 31:21. Not exactly a doublet is 6:12 where *πλατυνθη η καρδια σου και* is inserted before "you forget the Lord your God"; this gloss is probably based on 11:16. At 10:22 the "seventy souls" who came down to Egypt is "corrected" to "seventy-five" as in Gen 46:27 Exod 1:5. And finally at 8:19 the statement "I witness to you today" is translated into an oath formula by adding "by heaven and earth."

That A+ represents an expansionist tendency is clear when its omissions are contrasted. The list below includes all cases in Deuteronomy except those involving loss of an article, of *και*, of prepositions or of pronouns which were already discussed above.

List 5: Omissions

14:8 om ὀπλήν A *n*

14:14 om init — αὐτῷ 1° A^{txt} B *oI* *C*$'^{\prime\prime}$$^{-131}$ *b* 125 75 130-321′ 121 55 319 Bo Sa^{1}: homoiot

15:11 om ποιεῖν A *oI*-707 *b* 129 121-318-392 *z* 55 ^{Lat}cod 100 Arab Arm Sa^{3} ^{17}

20:16 om *τῶν ἐθνῶν* A F M 29-82-707-*oI*–15 56txt 392 *z*–68′ 319 509 LatAug *Ios* XXI 2: homoiot

25:7 om *τοῦ ἀδελφοῦ* 2° A 58 75 *s* 71-527 28 407

26:4 om *τοῦ θυσιαστηρίου* A*(vid) *d* 54-75′ 730

28:48 om *ἐπὶ σέ* A 121-318-392

33:5 om *ἄρχων* A 58-82 528 129 121-318 68′

34:11 om *πάσῃ* A M *oI*–15-707 *b f* 121-318 68′-83 Latcod 100 Co Eth

Obviously the A text is an expansionist one. Only one instance of a shorter text of more than two words obtains in Deuteronomy, 14:14, one which is clearly due to homoiot. These nine case of shorter text are the only cases of omissions by an A text not involving an article, a *και*, a preposition or a pronoun.

In List 3 there were eight cases of transpositions which were probably due to hex; the A text tradition was, however, itself quite free in the matter of word order; in fact, there are 30 cases of changes in word order which do not equal MT, a fact which should be borne in mind in assessing hex influence on the A tradition with respect to word order. No useful purpose would be served in presenting the list of 30 changes with full evidence, since it is the number of changes in order alone that is of significance.

In the first two lists nominal change was comparatively rare, and this is also true of the A tradition with wider support. Change in case obtains in the following cases: of genitive to dative:[11] *τῆς ψυχῆς* 13:6; *τοῦ ἀδελφοῦ* 15:3; *κυρίου* 18:1, and *σου* 20:11, or of genitive changing to accusative: *ἧς* 26:2; *προσώπου* 34:1. The dative becomes a genitive in *βασιλεῖ* 11:3; *τῇ γῇ* 11:14, or changes to accusative in *ᾗ* 19:14 (1° 2°), and *τῷ υἱῷ* 21:16. The accusative of Deut appears as genitive in *πρόσωπον* 2° 11:25; *αὐτό* 27:6; *τὸ θυσιαστήριον* 33:10, but as dative for *ἅς* 10:2; *οὕς* 13:2,6; *δυσμάς* 16:6. The variant involves both case and number in *ἧς*] *ας* 9:9; *οὕς*] *ης* 29:1; *αὐτῷ* 3°] *αυτους* 32:43. Gender change occurs only three times: *πεπτωκότας*] *-κοτα* 22:4; *αὐτούς*] *αυτα* 22:4, and *αὐτοῦ*] *αυτης* 22:8.

11. I give only the form in Deut since the change is defined in the description.

Change in number occurs for the following inflections in Deut: *οὖς*, *τοῖς ὕδασιν*, *ἀσάλευτα* (2), *καρπώματα*, *ὑμῖν*, as well as for *σου* (5), *τὴν δικαιοσύνην*, *σοι* (2), *εὐλογίαν*, *κατάραν*, and *ἐμοί* (which appears as *υμιν* by itacism from *ημιν*) at 31:17.

An occasional variant involves a slightly greater change: at 19:19 *τῷ ἀδελφῷ* becomes *κατα του αδελφου*, and at 29:12 *ἐν τῇ διαθήκῃ* is changed to *την διαθηκην*.

It is clear that nominal change in the A tradition is relatively insignificant, being limited to the usual copyist changes which characterize all textual families.

Change in verbal inflection was much more common in lists one and two, and this is also the case in the more widely supported A readings. Many are rooted in homonymy such as *κατελίπομεν*] -*λειπομεν*; *προσκυνήσῃς*] -*σεις*; *ἐξαρεῖ*] -*ρη*; *οἰκοδομήσας*] *ωκοδ.*; *οἶσθε*] *ησθε*; *κατακαύσετε*] -*σεται*, or *φοθεῖσθαι*] -*σθε*, and may be disregarded; their origin is rooted in a spelling mistake.

The tradition tends to avoid the Hellenistic -*οσαν* ending for the aorist in favor of the classical one; thus *ειδον* 7:19 10:21 11:2, though A does not join 376′ *b n* 30′-343′ 392 120 509 in reading *ηλθον* at 1:24, and at 32:5 it retains *ἡμάρτοσαν* (only 54′-75 59 Phil II 217 reading *ημαρτον*).

Occasionally voice is involved, but contextually with no semantic change. The following are involved: 2:8 *ἐπιστρέψαντες*] -*στραφεντες*; 5:25 *προσθώμεθα*] -*μεν*; 16:12 *φυλάξῃ*] -*ξεις*; 17:16 *προσθήσετε*] -*σεσθε*; 21:5 *ἐπέλεξεν*] *εξελεξατο*; 5:29 28:1 *φυλάσσεσθαι*] -*σσειν*, and 30:10 *εἰσακούσῃς*] -*ση*.

As might be expected modal change shows the gradual loss of modal distinctions in later forms of Greek. Thus the aorist subjunctive and the future indicative are occasionally confused: 1:42 *πολεμησετε*;[12] 12:20 *ἐρεῖς*] *ειπης*. More common is the confusion between the indicative and the subjunctive as 4:23 *ποιησετε*; 17:3 *προσκυνησουσιν*; 17:4 *ανηγγελη*; 25:1 *δικαιωσουσιν*; 31:29 *ανομησητε*, and 32:47 *μακροημερευσητε*. At 8:5 the optative *παιδεύσαι* is changed to the more common subjunctive. The only other variants are an

12. It will be obvious whether the variant or the Deut text is cited; only the Deut citation is accented.

imperative becoming an indicative in *εστρατοπεδευσατε* at 1:40, and the future *ἐπικαλέσεσθε* of 33:19 apppearing as an aorist imperative.

By far the most common change in verbal inflection concerns tense. Some instances are purely aspectual in nature, i.e. outside the indicative mood. In eight cases an infinitive is involved; three times a present infinitive becomes aorist in A+: 4:14 and 28:63 with *κληρονομησαι* and 34:7 *τελευτησαι*, and the reverse also obtains twice: 19:20 *ποιειν*, 29:20 *ευιλατευειν*. At 28:55 *καταλειφθῆναι* becomes perfect in the variant text.

At 1:21 an aorist imperative is changed to a present tense with *κληρονομειτε*, but the reverse occurs at 31:16 with *κοιμασαι*, whereas aorist subjunctives at 21:18 23:16 appear in the present in the A+ text as *παιδευωσιν* and *αρεσκη* resp. And at 3:27 a participle *ἀναβλέψας* is changed to an imperative, a change due to the contextual pressure of imperatives before and after the phrase. Change in tense for the participle obtains at 13:15: *ανελων* for *ἀναιρῶν*.

The remaining variants all involve the indicative mood. Four are future substitutes for the present of Deut. At 10:9 *εσται* does make good sense in "therefore there will be no portion"; at 12:10 the variant future occurs in "which the Lord your God shall cause you to inherit," since it is in a future context. At 13:1 *δῷ* (*σοι*) becomes *δωσει* (*σοι*), an obvious dittograph, i.e. /do si/ producing the variant /dosi si/.

In three cases an aorist is changed to a perfect, i.e. a simple past becomes a past with lasting effect. This makes sense at 24:1 with *ευρηκεν* or at 30:1 with *δεδωκα*, but is semantically not overly convincing at 3:24 with the verb *ηρξαι* "begin." So too at 3:9 the change of an aorist to a present *επονομαζουσιν* is clearly an error, since the context is past. Nor is the change of the present *ἐντέλλεταί* in 26:16 to an aorist an improvement; the context emphasizes future action and present demands (imperatives). Nor is A's use of the imperfect *εγκατελειπας* at 28:20 instead of the aorist a better reading, since the context is throughout aorist. At 1:22 the loss of *sigma* in *εἰσπορευσόμεθα* creates a present inflection; this is palaeographically conditioned by the consecution *σο*. And finally at 22:27 *εστιν* (found only in A V 121 55) instead of *ἦν* is clearly wrong; the clause reads "and there was no one helping her," and the present tense is inappropriate.

In general it must be said that change in verbal inflection in the A text does not show any particular trend. Most of the changes do not appear to be exegetical in nature, and show no particular characteristic which might describe a particular text tradition.

This is not the case with lexemic change with which list six deals below.

List 6. Change of Lexemes

1:26 *καί* 2°] *αλλ* A F M *O*'' 131^{mg} 129-246 121-318-392 *z*$^{-630}$ 55 59 646 Bo Sa$^{1\ 17}$ Syh = σ´

1:33 *προπορεύεται* (aut -*σεται*) B V 963 426 *b* 53´-56 54'-75 83-120-122] *πορευεται* (aut -*σεται*) rell

1:38 *κατακληρονομήσει*] -*ροδοτησει* A F M^{txt} V *O*''$^{-72\ 82}$ *C*''$^{-422\ 739}$ *d* 85´^{txt}-321´^{txt}-343´-730 *t* 121-318-392 68´-83-120 28 59 319 646

1:41 *ἔναντι* B M 72´ 52 *b*$^{-19}$ 106-125´ 129 767 *t* 121-318 68´-83-120-630^{c} 55 509] *εναντιον* rell

2:10 *πρότεροι*] *το προτερον* A F M V *oI*' 129-246 121-318-392 *z*$^{-630}$ 55 59 646

2:20 *ὀνομάζουσιν* B* 963 376´ 57* *b* 53´-56 *n* *επονομ*. (c var) rell

2:36 *ἐγενήθη* B V 963 *b d f*$^{-129}$ *n t* 71´-527 630 407´] *εγενετο* 130^{mg}-321´^{mg}; *ην* rell

3:27 λίβα] *νοτον* A F M^{txt} V 82-*oII*$^{-58}$ *C*''$^{(-73')}$ 129 30´-85´^{txt}-321-343´-346^{txt} *y*$^{-318}$ 28 59 319 = *οἱ* λ´

4:23 *ἑαυτοῖς*] *αυτοις* A F M V *O*''$^{-58\ 72}$ *f y z* 55 59 Syh

4:49 *ὑπό*] *απο* A B* V 72-618 *C d* 53´ 130-321´ 59 407

5:14 *ἐντὸς τῶν πυλῶν σου*] *παροικων εν σοι* A B F M^{mg} 29-72 *C*' *b f*--*129 n* 30´-85´^{txt}-321´^{txt}-343´ 71´-121-527 *z*$^{-83}$ 28 55 59 319 Arab: ex Exod 20:11

6:2 *ὅσας* B* V 376 *d* 54´-458 *t*] *οσα b* 75-767; *α* 53´ 392; *ας* 963 rell

6:5 *διανοίας* B M^{mg} 963 108^{mg} *f*$^{-129}$ *n*$^{-458}$ 85^{mg}-321´^{mg}-344^{mg} *z*$^{-18\ 83}$ 509 Tht *Dt*^{ap} Bo] *ψυχης* Cyr X 716; *καρδιας* rell

6:7 *διανιστάμενος*] *ανιστ.* A V 58-381 46-529 53´ n^{-127} 619 *z* Nil 528

6:18 *ἔναντι*] *-ντιον* A F M V 29-82 C^{-16} 106 30´ *t* 71´-121-527 630 319 509

6:24 *εὖ ἡμῖν ᾖ*] *πολυημεροι ωμεν* A M^{mg} 58-82 129 321´^{mg}-344^{mg} 121-392 68´ 55

7:25 *καί* 1° B* 646 Arm] *η* 15-82 *C''* 55 319 Pal; *ουδε* rell

8:2 *ἐκπειράσῃ*] *πειρ.* A F M O'^{-376} 108$^{(mg)}$106 56-129-664 *n t y* z^{-128} 55 59

9:5 *ἀσέβειαν* B G^{c} 108^{mg} 246*(c pr m) 127* 407´ Procop 344 ^{Lat}cod 104] + *και ανομιαν z*; *ανομιαν* (*-μειαν* 127^{c}; *ανοιαν* 129) rell

9:16 *ἑαυτοῖς*] *αυτοις* A M *oI* 129 *y z* 55 407 509*

9:19 *τούτῳ* B F V *C''* *b* 56^{txt} *n* 85´^{txt}-321´^{txt}-343´ 28 55 59 319 646 Sa^{13}] *εκεινω* rell = *ο´*

9:21 *συνέκοψα*] *συνετριψα* A F V *d t* 407

9:23 *ἐξαπέστειλεν* B F M V oII^{-707} f^{-129} 130^{mg}-321´^{mg} *z* 55 59] *απεστειλεν* rell

11:20 *οἰκιῶν*] *οικων* A F M *oI*-29-58 46 71´-392´ 407 Cyr I 481

11:22 *ὅσας*] *ας* A F *oI'* *C''* *f* 30´-85´-321´^{txt}-343-344^{txt} *y* 83-128 59 319 424

11:28 *ἀκούσητε*] *εισακ.* A F M V O'^{-G}-29-58 *cI'* 125´ $f^{(-53)}$ $n^{-75'}$ $s^{(-85txt)}$ t^{-799} 71-318-527 z^{-128} 319

11:32 *ταύτας*] *αυτου* A F M V oI'^{-58} *C''* d^{-106} *f* 30´-85^{txt}-130-321´^{txt}-343´ *y z* 28 59 319 Eth

11:32 *ὅσας* B *b d* n^{-767} 85^{mg} *t* 407´ Eth^{-M}] *οσα* 58 767 321´^{mg}; *ας* rell

12:1 *αἱ κρίσεις ἅς*] *τα κριματα α* A F M V *oII* *C''* *f s* $y^{-71'}$ *z* 28 55 59 319 407´ Cyr I 417 IX 868 X 205 Eth

12:2 *κληρονομεῖτε* (c var) B 82-376 $C'^{-73'}$ 246 *s* 28 319 407´ Cyr X 205] *-μησαι* 73´; *κατακληρονομησετε* Cyr IX 868; *κατακλ.* (c var) rell

12:14 *φυλῶν* B *n* ^{Lat}cod 100 Eth] *πολεων* rell

13:6 *βαδίσωμεν* B M^{mg} *d n* 85^{mg}-321´^{mg} *t* 630^{c}] *πορευθωμεν* rell: ex v.2

13:18 *ἀκούσῃς*] *εισακουσητε* A F M *oI*-707 *C''*$^{-16\ 73'}$ *d f n*$^{-54}$ *s*$^{-30'}$ *t* 71′-121-527 68′-83 28 55 319 407′ ^{Lat}cod 100 Arab Bo

14:6 *διχηλοῦν*] *διχηλευον* A M *O*-707 *d* 129 *n* 30′-343 *t* 71′-121 *z*$^{-630c}$ 55 509

14:10 *καί* 2° B *oI* 46 53′-246 121 *z* 407 ^{Lat}cod 100 Arm Bo Eth] *ουδε* rell

14:12 *ἁλιάετον*] *αλιετον* A F G-376-618 76-370* 71′-121 55 59 319

14:15 *ἐρωδιόν*] *αρωδιον* A B* V 707 56^{c}-129 W^{I} 30 121-318-392 55* 407′

14:16 *ἔποπα*] *υποπα* A B* F 29-72 30′-85′-343-346* 71′-121*-392′ 120 28 407′

15:5 *ὅσας* B *b* 68′-83-120] *ας* rell

15:7 *ἀποστέρξεις* B *n* 85^{mg}-321′ ^{mg} 509 ^{Lat}cod 100 Barh] *αποστρεψει* 527; -*στρεφεις* 799; -*στρεψεις* (c var) rell

16:14 *ἐν τῇ ἑορτῇ σου*] *εναντι κυριου του θεου σου* A F M^{txt} 29-72 *C''* 56^{txt} 30′-85^{txt}-130-321′^{txt}-343 121-318 18 28 59 319 407 646:ex v.11

17:1 *θύσεις*] *προσοισεις* (-*σει* M) A F M^{txt} *oI' C'' f* 30′-85^{txt}-130-321′^{txt}-343 *y z* 59 319 646

17:12 *ᾖ*] *γενηται* A F M V *oI*$^{(-58)}$ *C'' f s*$^{-321'c}$ *y* 68′-83 59 319 646

19:9 *ἀκούσῃς*] *εισακ.* (c var) A F M V *O''*$^{-72}$ *d f n t*$^{-799}$ 121-318-392 *z*$^{-18}$ 59 319

19:14 *κληρονομῆσαι*] *εν κληρω* A* B F V 29-58 *d f n t y z*$^{-18\ 83}$ 59 509 Arab Arm Eth Sa

20:5 *ἀποστραφήτω* B *b d* 246 *n* 321′^{mg}-344^{mg} *t* 71′-527 *z*$^{-83}$ 55 509 Phil II 124 Cyr I 369] *επιστρεψατω* 29; *επιστραφεισθω* 319; *επιστρεφατω* 121*; *επιστρ.* (c var) rell

20:6 *ἀποστραφήτω* B *b n* 321′ ^{mg}-344^{mg} *t* 18′ 509 Phil II 124 Cyr I 369] *επιστραφεισθω* 319; *επιστρ.* (c var) rell

20:7 *ἀποστραφήτω* B *b* 106 *n* 344^{mg}-346^{mg} *t* 318 18´-68´-120-630 509 646 Phil II 124 Cyr I 369] *ουκ επιστρ.* 77; *-φεισθω* 319; *επιστρ.* (c var) rell

20:11 *αὐτῇ* B F M^{mg} V *oII*$^{-707}$ *C’’* *b* *f*$^{-129}$ 30´-85^{txt}-130-321´^{txt}-343-344^{txt} 28 59 646 ^{Lat}cod 100 Arm Co Eth] *τη πολει* rell

20:18 *ἔναντι*] *-ντιον* A B F M V 426-*oII* 129 W^{I}-127 121-392 68´-83-630^{c} 59

20:19 *ἀγρῷ* B 848 376´ *b* *d* *n* 85^{mg}-321´^{mg} *t* 407´ Syh] *δρυμω* rell

21:16 *κατακληρονομῇ* B 848 76*(vid) Phil I 209^{UF}] *-μει* 318; *κληροδοτη* (c var) *C’’* *s* 28 407 646 Phil I 209te II 220; *κατακληροδοτη* (c var) rell

22:11 *ἐν τῷ αὐτῷ*] *επι το αυτο* A *C’’*$^{(-551)}$ *b*$^{(-314)}$ *d* 53´-56^{txt}-246 *n* 85´-321´-343-730 *t* 318 *z*$^{-83}$ 28 407 Procop 932 ^{Lat}cod 104

22:26 *καὶ τῇ*] *τη δε* A F M V *oI’*$^{-72}$ *C’’* *d* *f* 30´-85´-321´^{txt}-343-344^{txt} *t* *y* 83 28 55 59 646

23:9 *ῥήματος πονηροῦ*] *πονηρου πραγματος* (+ *και ρηματος* *C*) A 29 *C* 318 55*

23:14 *πρὸ* (*απο* 848 125) *προσώπου σου* B 848 376´ *b* *d* *n* 85^{mg}-321´^{mg} *t* 407´ Tht *Dt* ^{Lat}cod 100 Arm Syh] pr *εις τας χειρας σου* 68´-120 Eth; > 18; *εις τας χειρας σου* rell: ex par

24:11 *ἐν αὐτῷ*] *επ αυτω* A M* V 129 *y*$^{-318}$

24:13 *ἐνέχυρον* B$^{(mg)}$ 58 *d* *n* 85^{mg}-321´^{mg}-344^{mg} *t* 407´] pr *ιματιον αυτου το* V; *ιματιον* rell

24:14 *ἀπαδικήσεις*] *αποστερησεις* (*-σει* 77* 527) A F M V 82-*oI’* *C’’* *b* *f* *s* *y*$^{-392}$ *z* 28 59 319 407 646

25:2 *ὁ ἀσεβής* 957 72 *d* 53´ *n* 30´ ῦ 407 392; *ο ασεβων* rell

25:8 *αὐτοῦ* B M^{mg} V 848 321´^{mg}-344^{mg} 630^{c} Gie ^{Lat}cod 100 Arm Eth] + *εκεινης* 343; *εκεινης* rell

26:5 *ἀπέβαλεν*] *απελαβεν* A F 29-72-82 53´-56^{c1} 121-392 68

26:11 *ἐν* 1°] *επι* A M *oI*-58-707 *b d* 129 321mg *t*–799 71-318-392 18´-83-630´ 407´ Bo

26:14 *καθότι* B 848] *καθο* 321mg-730 509; *καθως* 458 71; *οσα* 125; *καθα* rell

28:1 *ἀκούσῃς*] *εισακουσητε* A F V 29-58 56 *s* 28 59 319 407

28:2 *ἀκούσῃς*] *εισακ.* A 15-29-82-426mg-707 57´-550´-761-*cII*–417 129 127 85´-321-730 121-527 28 55 319

28:6 *εὐλογημένος* 1°] -*γητος* A 848 85mg-321mg 121-318 68´ 55

28:6 *εὐλογημένος* 2°] -*γητος* A Mtxt 848 85mg-321mg 121-318 68´ 55

28:12 *οὐρανόν*] *ουρανιον* A M V 376-707 *d* 246 767 *t* 121 18´-68´ 630*-669 Phil II 89 Epiph III 205 Syh

28:14 *οὐδέ* B F V 246 18´-120-630´ 407´ 646 Phil II 22 Latcod 100 Arm Bo Eth] *η* rell: ex par

28:25 *ἐπικοπήν*] *επισκοπην* A B* 72-618 52´-131-417-528´ *b* 610 129 WI-767 321*-343*-730c 527 128 59 646

28:32 *βλέψονται*] *εσονται* A 85mg2-344mg2 121 68´

29:11 *ἔκγονα* B *b* 85mg-321mgc-344mg 602 18´-630 407´] *εγκονα* 321mg* 669; *εγγονα* 963 707 *d t*–602 120; *τεκνα* rell

29:18 *ἐν χολῇ*] *ενοχλη* A B* F*(c pr m) 29-72-82 54-75´ 121-318 68´-120* 59 319 Chr XVII 213: ex Hebr 12 15

29:27 *κατάρας*] *αρας* A F M *oI*´–58 *C*´´ *f* WI*(c pr m) *s*–321mg *y*(–71) 68'-83 28 55 59 646

31:4 *καθά* B V 82-707 414* *b* 129 *n*–458 18´-630´ 407´] *καθ* 458; *καθως* rell

32:8 *ὡς*] *ους* A V 72´ 19´ *d* 56´-129 WI-75´ 30´-85-343-344txt *t* 71 28 319 509 Cyr III 380 Tht I 81ap IV 472

32:8 *υἱῶν* 848 106c Iust *Dial* CXXXI 1(1°) Or VI 60 Arm Barh] *αγγελων* rell

32:24 *ἀποστελῶ* B F 963(vid) 426-707 56 121 Tht II 765] *εξαποστελω* Mtxt; *επαποστελλω* 53 509; *επαποστελω* rell

32:25 *πρεσβύτου*] *-τερου* A F M 64-376′-*oII*$^{-58}$ 56 54 344-730 121 68′-83 55 509 Tht II 781

32:26 *παύσω*] *καταπ.* A F M *O*'$^{-15}$ ^{82}-29-58 *C*''$^{-16\ 413\ 414\ 417\ 528\ 761txt}$ 56 *s y* 68′-83-120 28 55 424 Syh(vid)

32:42 *ἐχθρῶν* B F M 29-426 56 W^{Ic}-127 85′^{mg}-344^{mg}-346^{mg} 55 ^{Lat}codd 100 419 Cant$^{Gall\ Mil\ R\ Rom\ Sin\ Verec}$ Arm^{te} Co Eth^{-M} Syh$^{b\ vtxt}$] *θεων* 72; > Eth^{M}; + *domini* Arm^{ap}; *εθνων* rell

32:44 *εἰσῆλθεν*] *προσηλθεν* A F M^{txt} V 29-72-82 *C*'' *f* 85′-343-344^{txt}-346^{txt} *y* 28 55 319

33:17 *ἐπ'* B V 847 707 W^{I}-127-767 318 407′ ^{Lat}Tert passim] > 376′ 54-75′ 18-68′-120 59 646 ^{Lat}cod 100 Ambr passim Arm Bo Eth; *απ* rell

34:6 *ταφήν*] *τελευτην* A F$^{c\ pr\ m}$ M^{mg} 15-82-426 *f* 346^{mg} 121-318-392 *z*$^{-83}$ 646 Syh^{m} Barh(graece)

In lists one and two it was seen that the A tradition witnessed to a substantial number of lexemic changes; list six examined this trend in the context of wider support in the tradition.

A substantial number of these involve change of pronoun: thus the reflexive *ἑαυτοῖς* becomes *αυτοις* 4:23 9:16, the demonstrative *τούτῳ* changes to *εκεινω* 9:19, *ταύτας* becomes *αυτου* 11:32, *αὐτοῦ* appears as *εκεινης* 25:8, or *ὅσας* as *ας* at 6:2 11:22,32 15:5, and cf also *ὡς* as *ους* at 32:8. Once a pronoun is realized as its modifier: at 20:11 *αὐτῇ* becomes *τη πολει*.

Also fairly common is a change in conjunction; at 1:26 *καί* becomes *αλλ*, but *ουδε* at 7:25 14:10, and at 22:26 a *καί* construction changes to *δε*, and the A tradition prefers *και* to *ἤ* at 25:14, but *η* to *οὐδέ* at 28:14, and *και* to *οὐδέ* at 7:25.

Change in preposition is also well-attested in A+; it prefers *εναντιον* over against *ἔναντι*, 1:41 6:18 20:18, but never the reverse; so too *επι* instead of *ἐν* occurs at 22:11 (with change in case to the accusative as well), 24:11 26:11, and once *επ'* becomes *απ* 33:17. The only other change of preposition is *ὑπό* to *απο* 4:49, which is probably palaeographically inspired.

Fairly common is a change in simplex/compositum mainly in verbs. Simplification occurs at 1:33 (*προ*)*πορεύεται*, 6:7 (*δι*)*ανιστάμενος*, 9:23

(ἐξ)απέστειλεν, and 29:27 (κατ)άρας. Change of simplex to a composite form is much more frequent especially with the root ἀκούω. It changes to an εἰσακούω inflection at 11:28 13:18 19:9 28:1,2; this change is probably intended to intensify the meaning from a simple "hear" to the stronger — "obey." Other changes to compounds occur at 2:20 (επ)ονομαζουσιν, 12:2 (κατα)κληρονομειτε, 32:24 (επ)αποστελω and 32:26 (κατα)παυσω. Change of prepositional element obtains in ἀποστραφήτω (20:5,6,7) becoming επιστραφητω as well as in εἰσῆλθεν changing to προσηλθεν 32:44.

Uncertainty in the καθ stem is widespread in the Pentateuchal tradition, and the A tradition shares in this: at 26:14 καθότι appears as καθα, and at 31:4 καθά shows up as καθως.

The origin of some changes is fairly obvious. The A+ reading at 5:14 clearly comes from the well-known parallel passage in Exod 20:11. At 16:14 the variant tradition comes directly from v.11, whereas the εις τας χειρας σου tradition at 23:14 modifying the verb παραδίδωμι is very common in Deut; cf e.g. 20:13 21:10.

A substantial number of variants may well be rooted in palaeographic confusion: in most of these cases their secondary nature is immediately apparent; such is the case for οἰκιῶν (οικων) 11:20; διχηλοῦν (διχηλευον) 14:6; ἀποστέρξεις (αποστρεψεις) 15:7; ἀπέβαλεν (απελαβεν) 26:5; οὐρανόν (ουρανιον) 28:12; ἐπικοπήν (επισκοπην) 28:25, and at 29:18 ἐν χολῇ (ενοχλη). Some synonyms involve the same root: πρότεροι (το προτερον) 2:10; ἀσεβής (ασεβων) 25:2; εὐλογημένος (ευλογητος) 28:6 (1° 2°), and πρεσβύτου (πρεσβυτερου) 32:25.

There remains, however, a large number of readings not so easily explicable. Thus twice 1:38 21:16 the A tradition substitutes the root κατακληροδοτέω "take and distribute" for κατακληρονομέω "inherit," though the latter is common in Deut, and is usually left unchanged by A+. At 19:14 "(the land which the Lord thy God is giving to you) to inherit" becomes εν κληρω, which is a very common idiom modifying δίδωσιν throughout the book. Changes at times seem quite arbitrary: at 2:36 ἐγενήθη appears as ην, but at 17:12 ᾖ becomes γενηται — for no discernible reason.

A few words for birds in ch.14 seem to be dialectically different in the A+ tradition; these are ἁλιάετον - αλιετον; ἐρωδιόν - αρωδιον, and ἔποπα - υποπα.

Most changes concern synonyms, and one suspects stylistic reasons for many of the changes. A simple list of such is quite convincing. In each case the accented word is Deut: *λίβα* - *νοτον*; *διανοίας* - *καρδιας*; *κρίσεις* - *κριματα*; *βαδίσωμεν* - *πορευθωμεν*; *θύσεις* - *προσοισεις*; *ἀγρῷ* - *δρυμω*; *ἐνέχυρον* - *ιματιον*; *ἀπαδικήσεις* - *αποστερησεις*; *ἔκγονα* - *τεκνα*. Sometimes the variant is more specific as *εὖ ἡμῖν ᾖ*] *πολυημεροι ωμεν* at 6:24, i.e. "we may be longlived" rather than "it may be well with us." But the opposite seems to be the case with respect to Moses; at 34:6 "(no one knows his) grave," becomes *τελευτην* in A+, which is a bit pointless in the context. At 9:5 the change from *ἀσέβειαν* "impiety" to *ανομιαν* was probably made for variety's sake, since the word occurs in the same context in v.4. Later in the same chapter (v.21) A+ substitutes *συνετριψα* "shatter, crush" for *συνέκοψα* "beat, thrash," possibly stylistic, since beating the golden calf is not as effective as shattering it! At 28:32 the curse states inter alia "your eyes *βλέψονται* (*σφακελίζοντες εἰς αὐτά*)," i.e. "shall look towards them, being convulsed." A+ simplifies this by changing the verb to *εσονται*, "your eyes shall be convulsed towards them." At 12:14 A changes *φυλῶν* to *πολεων* as making better sense in "the place which the Lord thy God has chosen (as) one of thy *φυλῶν*" for A+ Jerusalem as "one of thy cities." Similarly at 32:42 the divine curse ends with *ἀπὸ κεφαλῆς ἀρχόντων ἐχθρῶν*; A makes the phrase read from "the head of the rulers of the nations" - *εθνων*, a more universal judgment. And finally at 32:8 reference is made to the Most-High having set the boundaries of nations according to the number of *υἱῶν θεοῦ*. An early reviser was unhappy with the phrase and changed it to *αγγελων θεου*, which reading dominated the tradition including that of A. It is, however, secondary as the text of the first century B.C. 848 demonstrates with its *υιων*.

It now seems possible to make some general statements about the nature of the A tradition. That the tradition has been somewhat influenced by hex seems clear, but it is also clear that Hebrew influence seems to be present beyond or outside the sphere of Origen's massive work.[13] Further identification of this recensional trend does not seem possible, though its Alexandrian origin does make one think of the elusive Hesychian recension.

13. Cf also U.Quast, Der rezensionelle Charakter einiger Wortvarianten im Buch Numeri, in Festsschrift Hanhart, MSU XX (Göttingen, 1990) 230—252. Quast has convincingly shown that the *ἀριθμέω* (vs *ἐπισκοπέω*/*ἐπισκέπτομαι*) tradition, which A partially shares, is recensional in character in Numbers.

The A tradition is basically an expansionist one. It only seldom contracts the text of Deut, and when it does the omission usually consists of only one or at most two words. On the other hand, the tradition has numerous glosses, many of which seem to be epexegetical in character. Others are likely due to contextual pressures.

The most interesting characteristic of the tradition is that of stylistic revision in which lexical equivalents or related semantemes are substituted for Deut lexemes. Many of these changes have become popular, as the last list shows; in fact, at times these have dominated the tradition. The variant tradition in the main does not seem rooted in a different exegetical tradition, however, though at times the variant reading may well be somewhat more specific. The tradition seems rather to show a tendency towards greater variety, though it must be admitted that at times this variety appears to represent change purely for change's sake.

Index of Greek words and phrases

A

B

Γ

Δ

E

Z

Η

Θ

Ι

O

Π

P

C

Φ

X

Ψ

Ω

Index of Hebrew words and phrases

ב

ד

ג

ה

ז

ח

י

ט

כ

ל

מ

נ

ס

ע

פ

צ

ש

ת

Topical Index

A

B

C

D

E

F

G

H

I

J

K

L

M

N

Q

R

S

T

U

V

W

Y

Z

Reviews

John A. L. Lee, JSS 45/1 (2000) 177-79.